QUEEN & COUNTRY™

GREG RUCKA

oni
PRESS

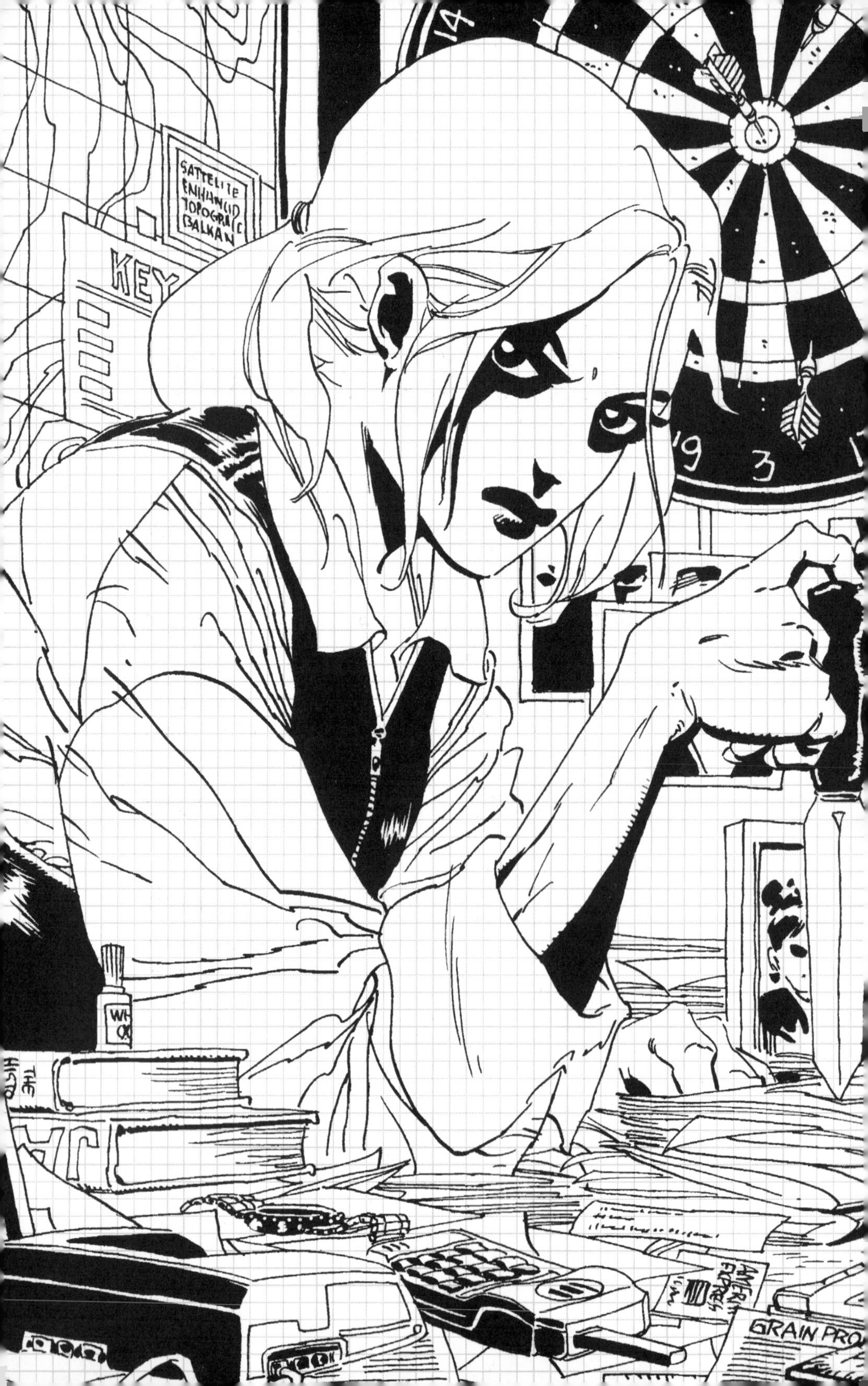
SATTELITE
ENHANCED
TOPOGRAPHIC
BALKAN
KEY
GRAIN PRO

QUEEN & COUNTRY™

WRITTEN BY
GREG RUCKA

ILLUSTRATED BY
STEVE ROLSTON, MIKE NORTON, & CHRIS SAMNEE

LETTERING BY
JOHN DRANSKI & DOUGLAS SHERWOOD

COVER BY
TIM SALE

BOOK DESIGN BY
KEITH WOOD

COLLECTION EDITED BY
JILL BEATON

ORIGINAL SERIES EDITED BY
JAMES LUCAS JONES

Published by Oni Press, Inc.
Joe Nozemack, publisher
James Lucas Jones, editor in chief
Randal C. Jarrell, managing editor
Cory Casoni, marketing director
Jill Beaton, assistant editor
Douglas E. Sherwood, editorial assistant

This collects issues 25-32 of the Oni Press comics
series *Queen & Country*.

ONI PRESS, INC.
1305 SE Martin Luther King Jr. Blvd.
Suite A
Portland, OR 97214
USA

www.onipress.com | www.gregrucka.com

First edition: August 2008
ISBN-13: 978-1-932664-96-6
ISBN-10: 1-932664-96-3

10 9 8 7 6 5 4 3 2 1

PRINTED IN CANADA.

TABLE OF CONTENTS

OPERATION: SADDLEBAG

WRITTEN BY
GREG RUCKA

ILLUSTRATED BY
MIKE NORTON & **STEVE ROLSTON**

LETTERED BY
JOHN DRANSKI

ORIGINALLY EDITED BY
JAMES LUCAS JONES

ROSTER

TARA CHACE—Special Operations Officer, designated Minder Two. Entering her third year as Minder.

FRANCES BARCLAY—Chief of Service, also known as "C." Distinguished service as CIA-Liaison, Chairman of the Joint Intelligence Committee, and as Head of Station Prague (85-88), Saigon (89-91), and Paris (91-94).

TOM WALLACE—Head of the Special Section, a Special Operations Officer with the designation Minder One. Responsible for the training and continued well-being of his unit, both at home and in the field. Six year veteran of the Minders.

PAUL CROCKER—Director of Operations, encompassing all field work in all theaters of operations. In addition to commanding individual stations, he has direct command of the Special Section—sometimes referred to as Minders—used for special operations.

NICK POOLE—Former Sergeant in the S.A.S. and the third man to occupy the position of Minder Three in less than a year.

DONALD WELDON—Deputy Chief of Service, has oversight of all aspects of Intelligence gathering and operations. Immediate superior to Crocker.

OPS ROOM STAFF   OTHERS

ALEXIS—Mission Control Officer (also called Main Communications Officer)– responsible for maintaining communications between the Operations Room and the agents in the field.

RON—Duty Operations Officer, responsible for monitoring the status and importance of all incoming intelligence, both from foreign stations and other sources.

KATE—Personal Assistant to Paul Crocker, termed PA to D.Ops. Possibly the hardest and most important job in the Service.

WALTER SECCOMBE —Permanent Under Secretary to the Foreign Office, a career civil servant with intimate knowledge of the inner workings of all levels of Government, and with the savvy to negotiate the corridors of power to achieve his own ends.

EDWARD KITTERING—Special Operations Officer, designated Minder Three. Has been with the Special Section for less than a year.

BRIAN BUTLER—A former sergeant in one of the British Army's oldest and most respected regiments. A unique individual who actually requested assignment with special section.

PROLOGUE

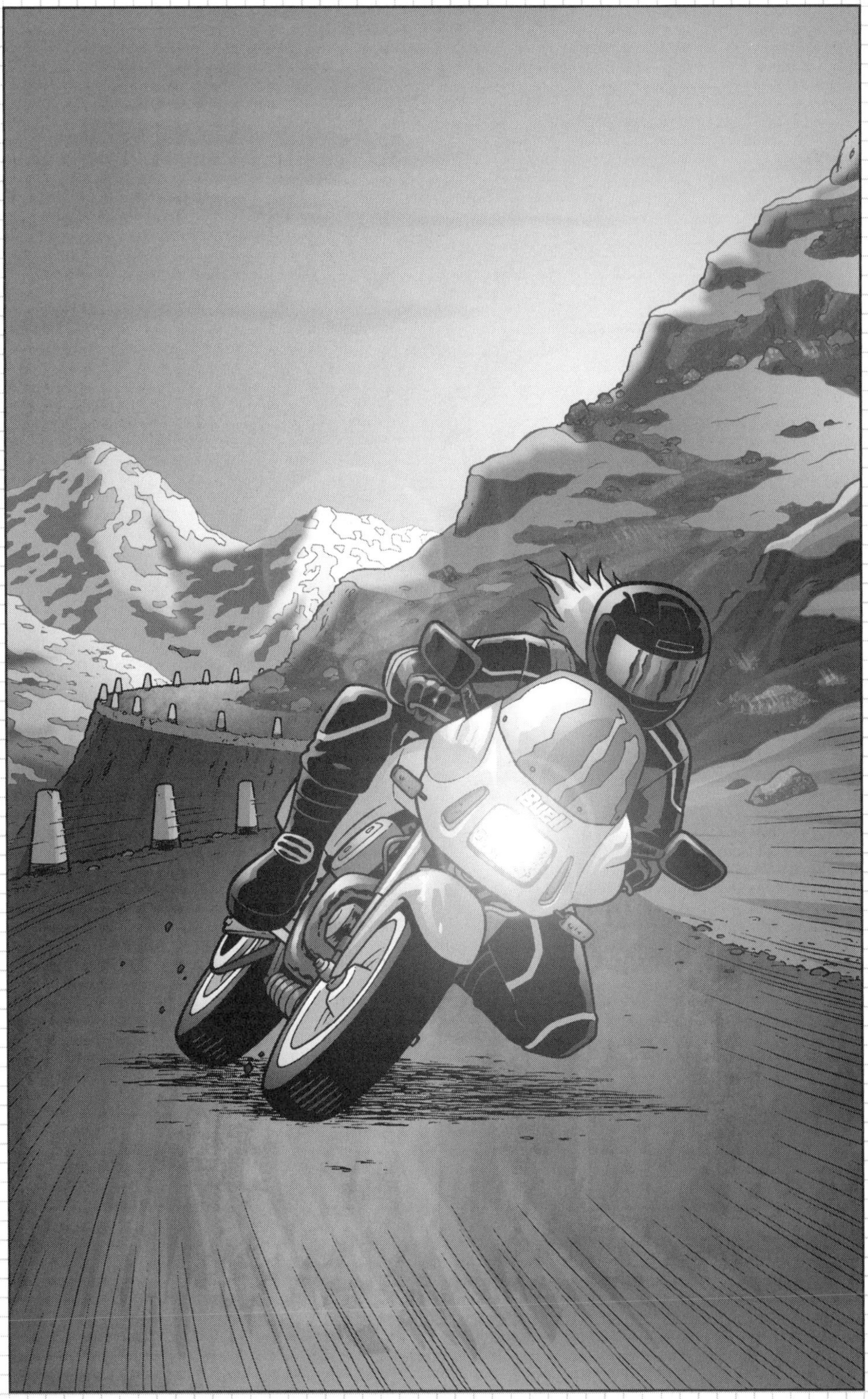

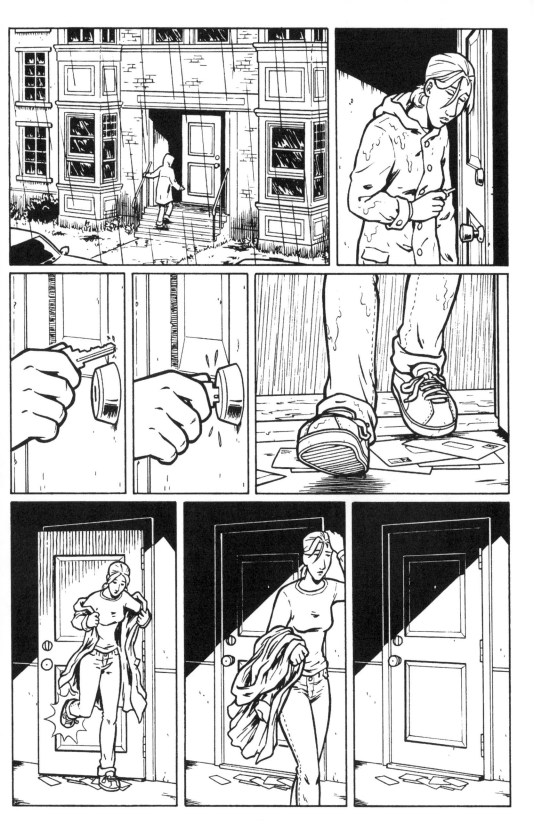

1

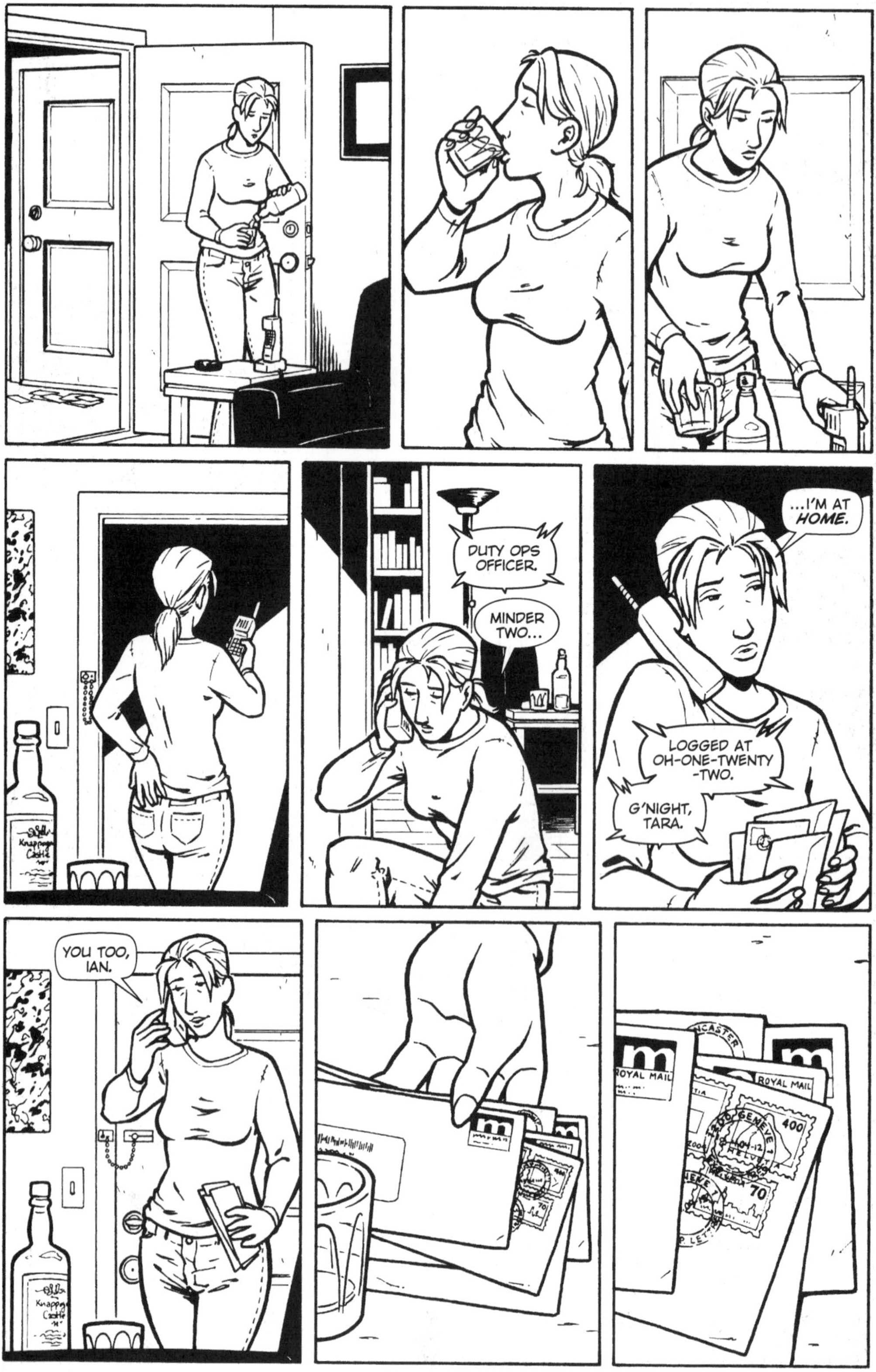
DUTY OPS OFFICER.
MINDER TWO...
...I'M AT *HOME.*
LOGGED AT OH-ONE-TWENTY -TWO.
G'NIGHT, TARA.
YOU TOO, IAN.
ROYAL MAIL
ROYAL MAIL

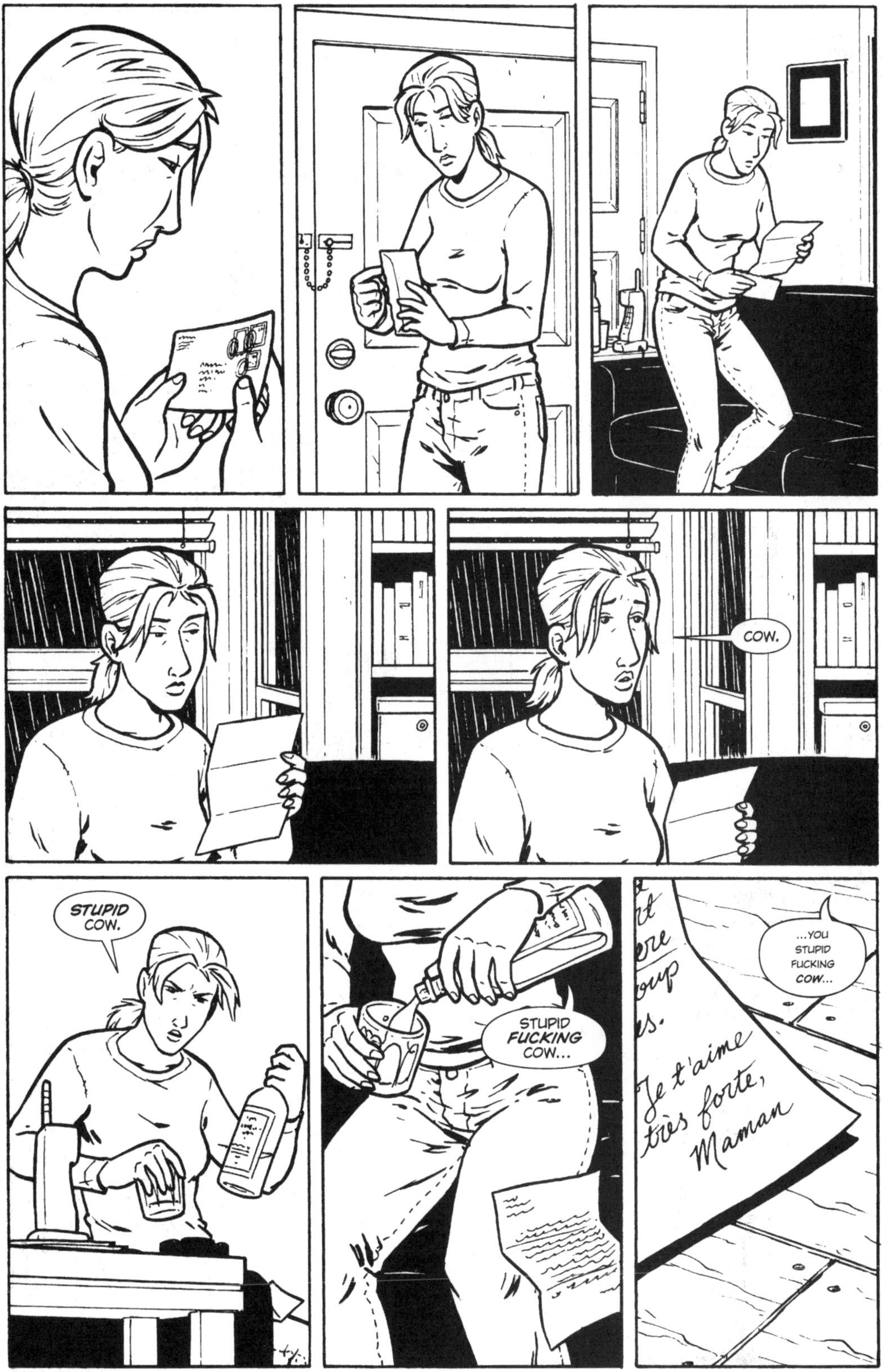
COW.
STUPID COW.
STUPID FUCKING COW...
...YOU STUPID FUCKING COW...
Je t'aime très forte, Maman

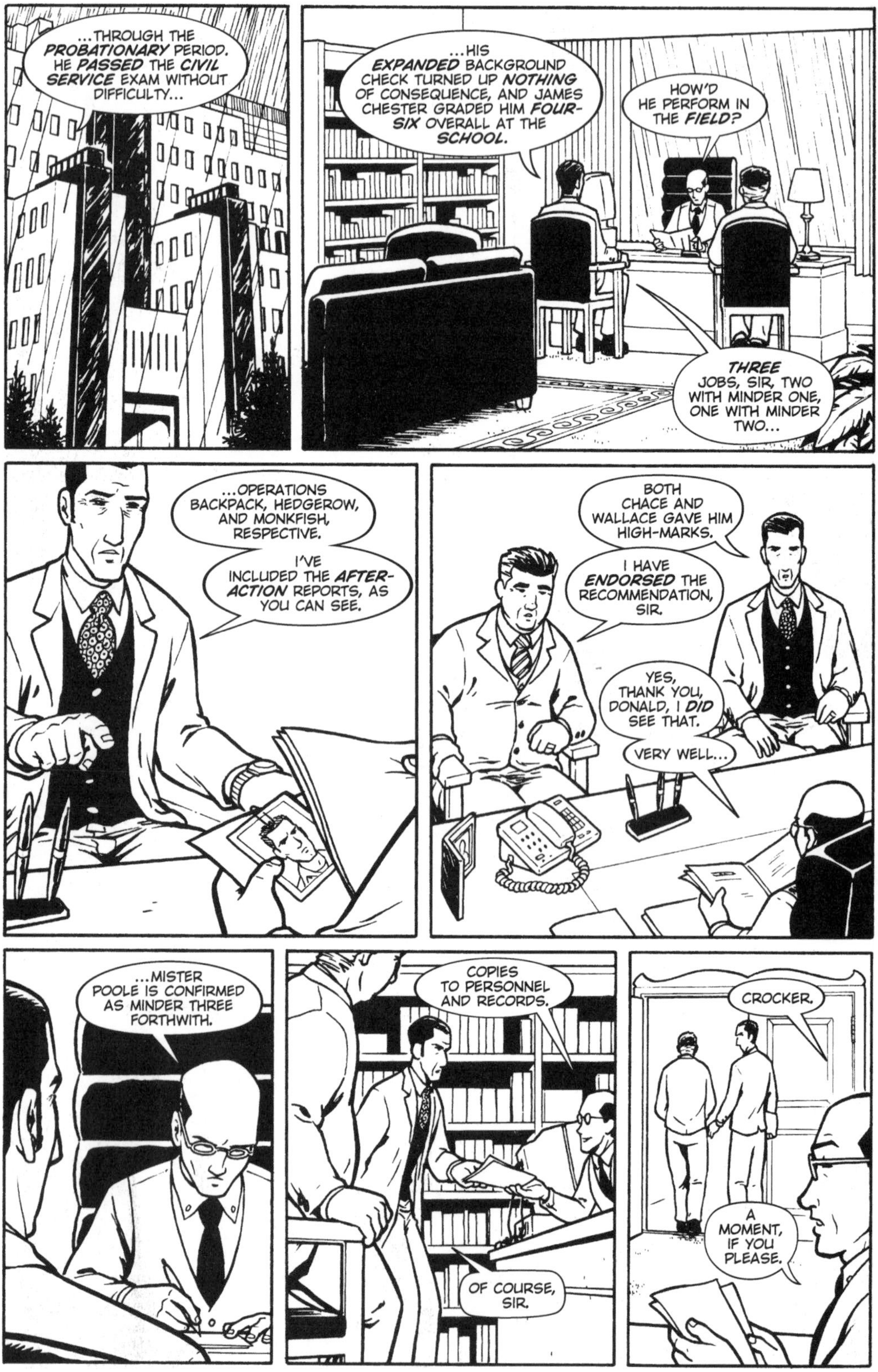
...THROUGH THE *PROBATIONARY* PERIOD. HE *PASSED* THE *CIVIL SERVICE* EXAM WITHOUT DIFFICULTY...
...HIS *EXPANDED* BACKGROUND CHECK TURNED UP *NOTHING* OF CONSEQUENCE, AND JAMES CHESTER GRADED HIM *FOUR-SIX* OVERALL AT THE *SCHOOL*.
HOW'D HE PERFORM IN THE *FIELD?*
THREE JOBS, SIR, TWO WITH MINDER ONE, ONE WITH MINDER TWO...
...OPERATIONS BACKPACK, HEDGEROW, AND MONKFISH, RESPECTIVE.
I'VE INCLUDED THE *AFTER-ACTION* REPORTS, AS YOU CAN SEE.
BOTH CHACE AND WALLACE GAVE HIM HIGH-MARKS.
I HAVE *ENDORSED* THE RECOMMENDATION, SIR.
YES, THANK YOU, DONALD, I *DID* SEE THAT.
VERY WELL...
...MISTER POOLE IS CONFIRMED AS MINDER THREE FORTHWITH.
COPIES TO PERSONNEL AND RECORDS.
OF COURSE, SIR.
CROCKER.
A MOMENT, IF YOU PLEASE.

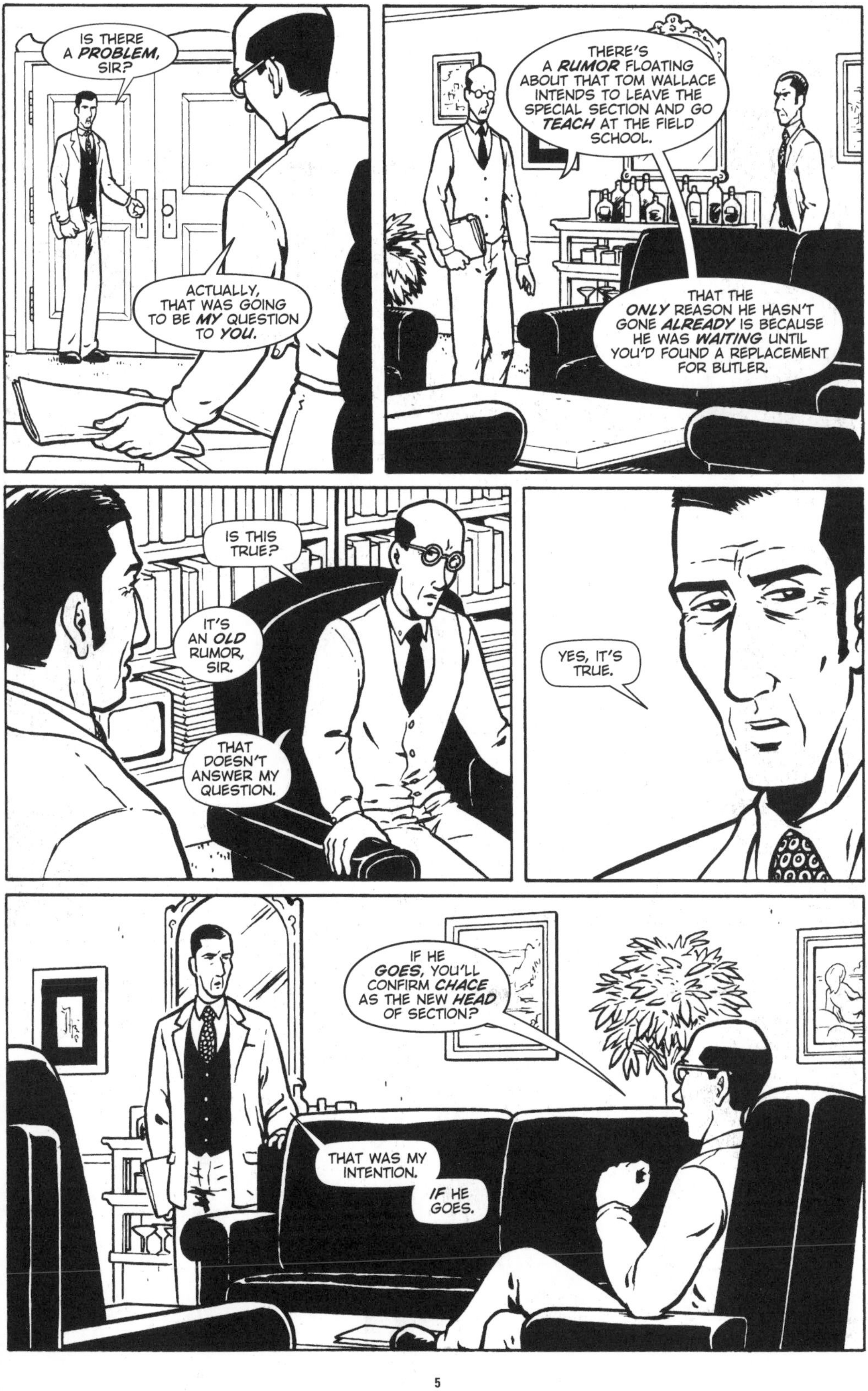
IS THERE A PROBLEM, SIR?
ACTUALLY, THAT WAS GOING TO BE MY QUESTION TO YOU.
THERE'S A RUMOR FLOATING ABOUT THAT TOM WALLACE INTENDS TO LEAVE THE SPECIAL SECTION AND GO TEACH AT THE FIELD SCHOOL.
THAT THE ONLY REASON HE HASN'T GONE ALREADY IS BECAUSE HE WAS WAITING UNTIL YOU'D FOUND A REPLACEMENT FOR BUTLER.
IS THIS TRUE?
IT'S AN OLD RUMOR, SIR.
THAT DOESN'T ANSWER MY QUESTION.
YES, IT'S TRUE.
IF HE GOES, YOU'LL CONFIRM CHACE AS THE NEW HEAD OF SECTION?
THAT WAS MY INTENTION.
IF HE GOES.

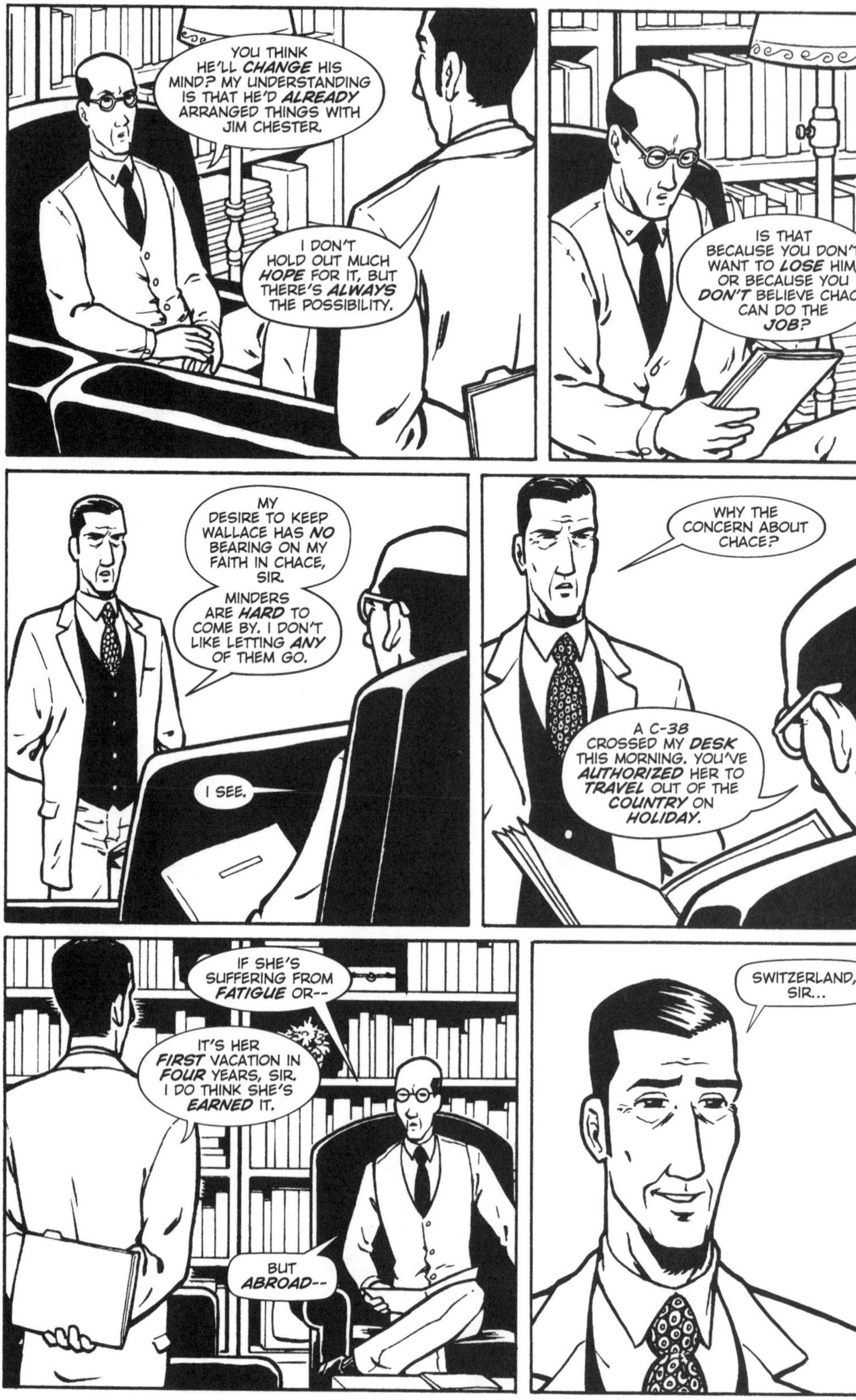
YOU THINK HE'LL CHANGE HIS MIND? MY UNDERSTANDING IS THAT HE'D ALREADY ARRANGED THINGS WITH JIM CHESTER.
I DON'T HOLD OUT MUCH HOPE FOR IT, BUT THERE'S ALWAYS THE POSSIBILITY.
IS THAT BECAUSE YOU DON'T WANT TO LOSE HIM, OR BECAUSE YOU DON'T BELIEVE CHACE CAN DO THE JOB?
MY DESIRE TO KEEP WALLACE HAS NO BEARING ON MY FAITH IN CHACE, SIR.
MINDERS ARE HARD TO COME BY. I DON'T LIKE LETTING ANY OF THEM GO.
I SEE.
WHY THE CONCERN ABOUT CHACE?
A C-38 CROSSED MY DESK THIS MORNING. YOU'VE AUTHORIZED HER TO TRAVEL OUT OF THE COUNTRY ON HOLIDAY.
IF SHE'S SUFFERING FROM FATIGUE OR--
IT'S HER FIRST VACATION IN FOUR YEARS, SIR. I DO THINK SHE'S EARNED IT.
BUT ABROAD--
SWITZERLAND, SIR...

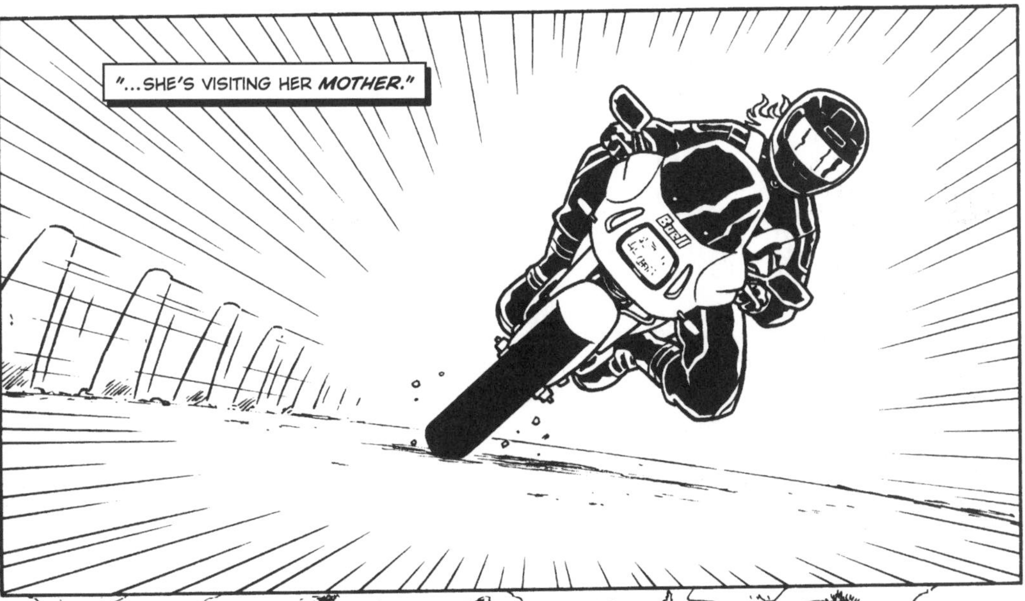
"...SHE'S VISITING HER *MOTHER.*"
Buell

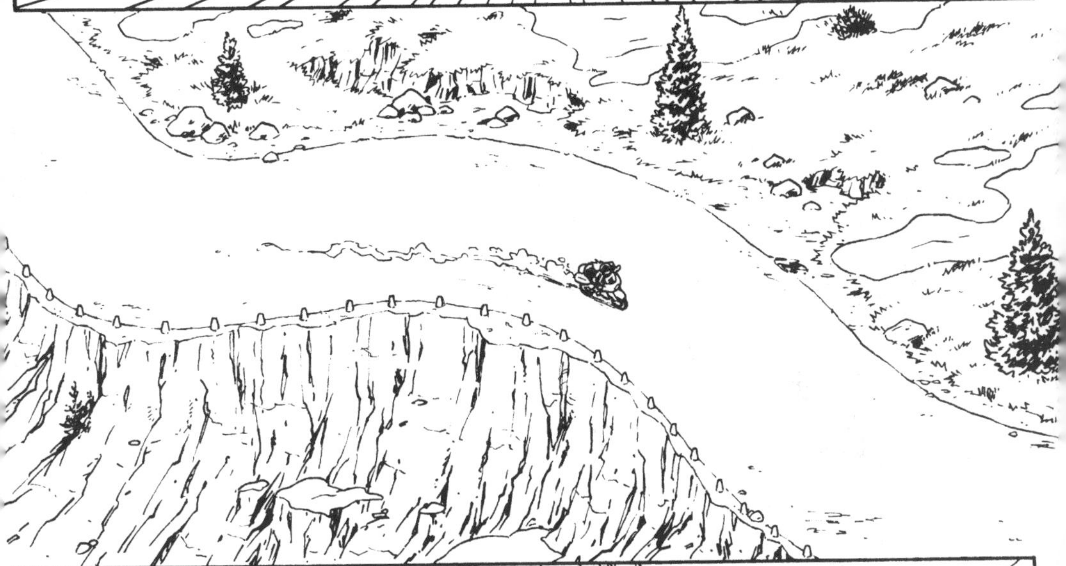

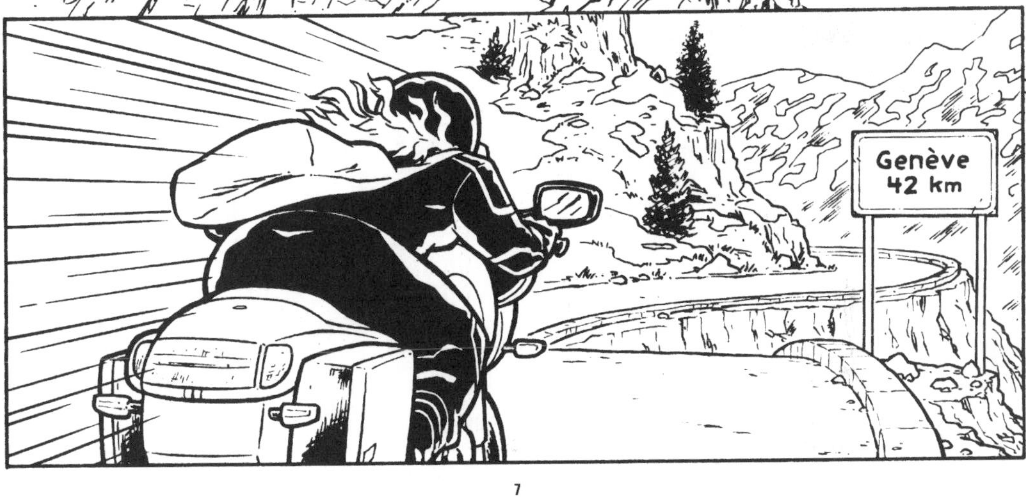
Genève
42 km

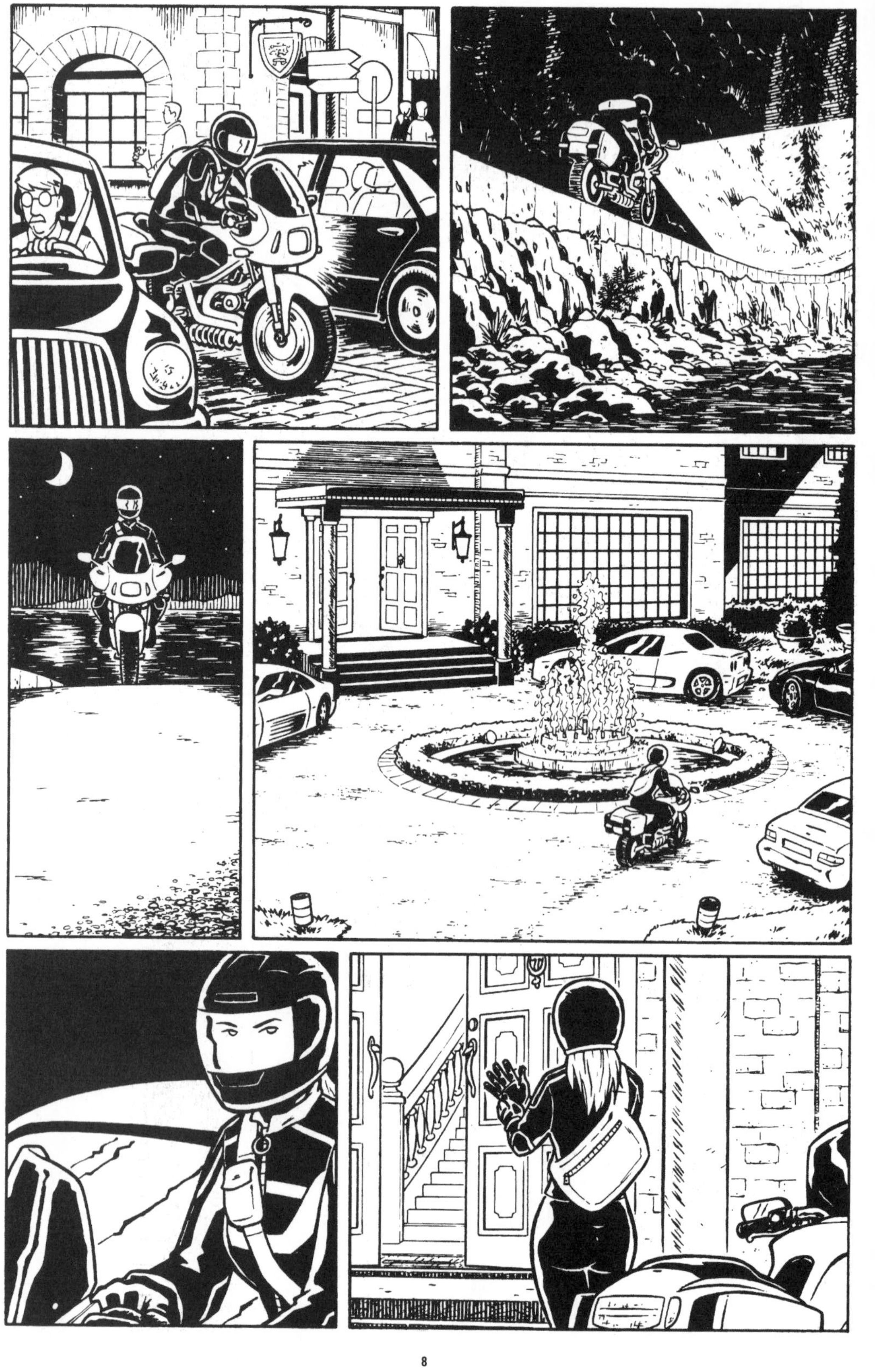

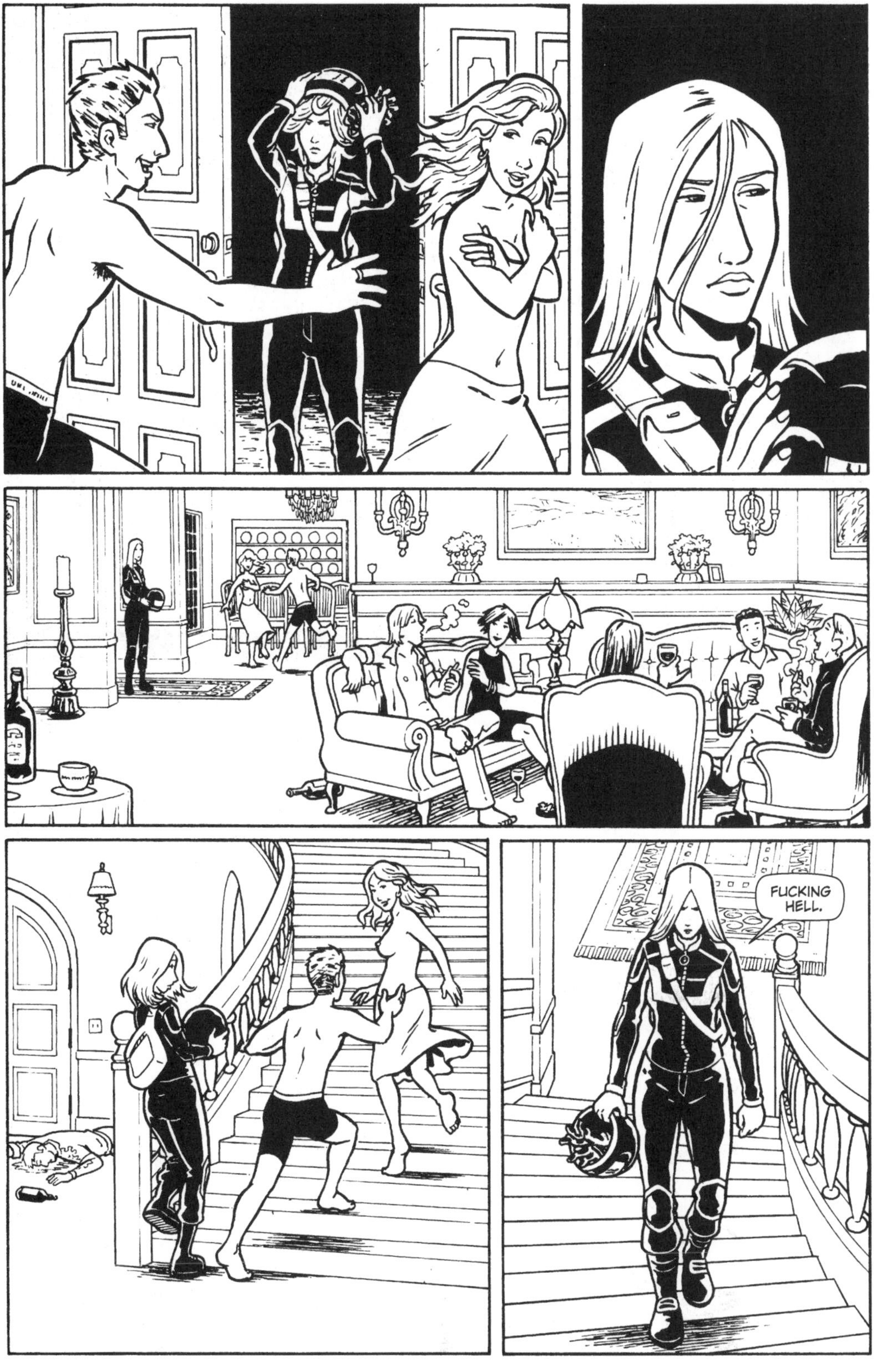
FUCKING HELL.

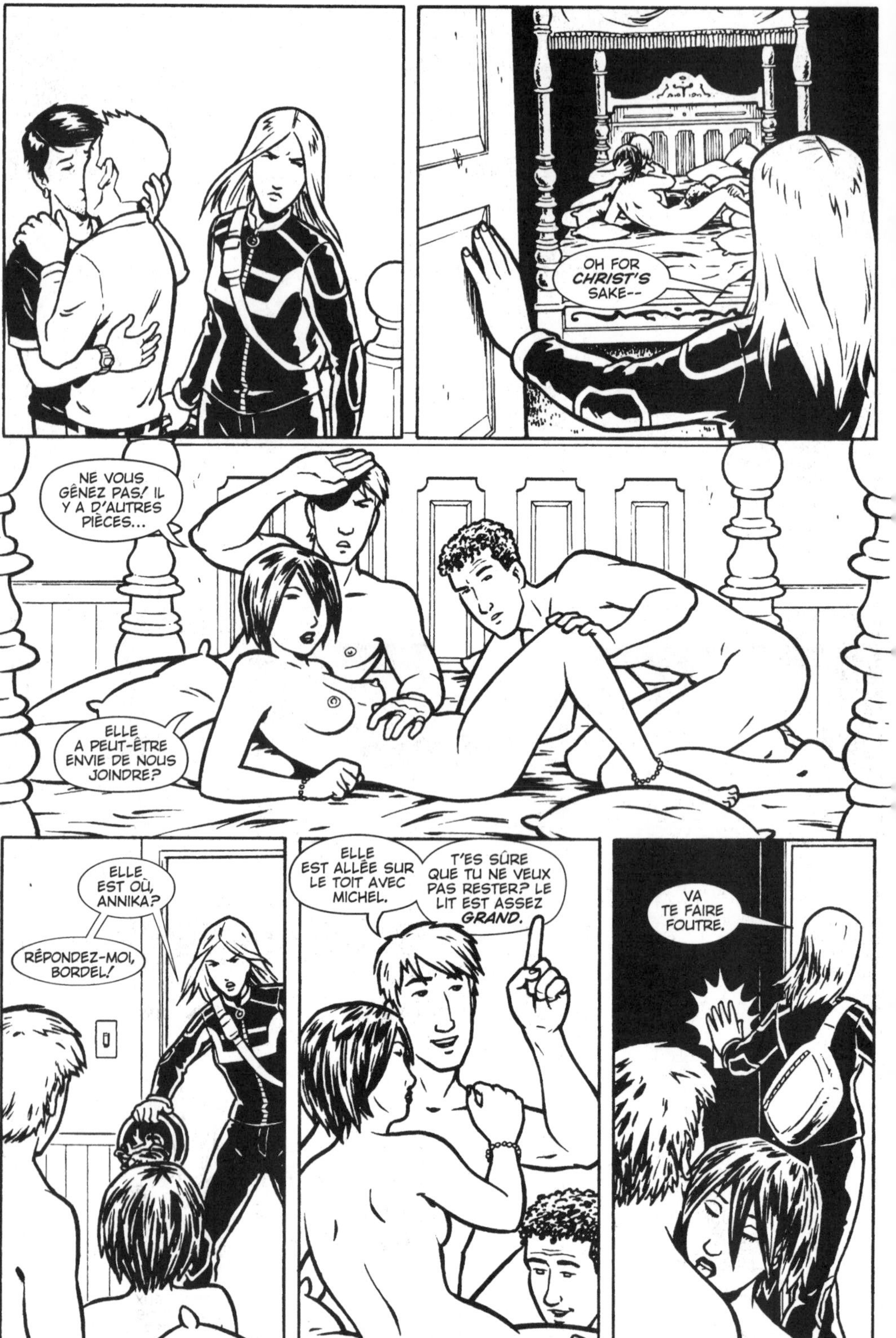
OH FOR CHRIST'S SAKE--
NE VOUS GÊNEZ PAS! IL Y A D'AUTRES PIÈCES...
ELLE A PEUT-ÊTRE ENVIE DE NOUS JOINDRE?
ELLE EST OÙ, ANNIKA?
RÉPONDEZ-MOI, BORDEL!
ELLE EST ALLÉE SUR LE TOIT AVEC MICHEL.
T'ES SÛRE QUE TU NE VEUX PAS RESTER? LE LIT EST ASSEZ GRAND.
VA TE FAIRE FOUTRE.

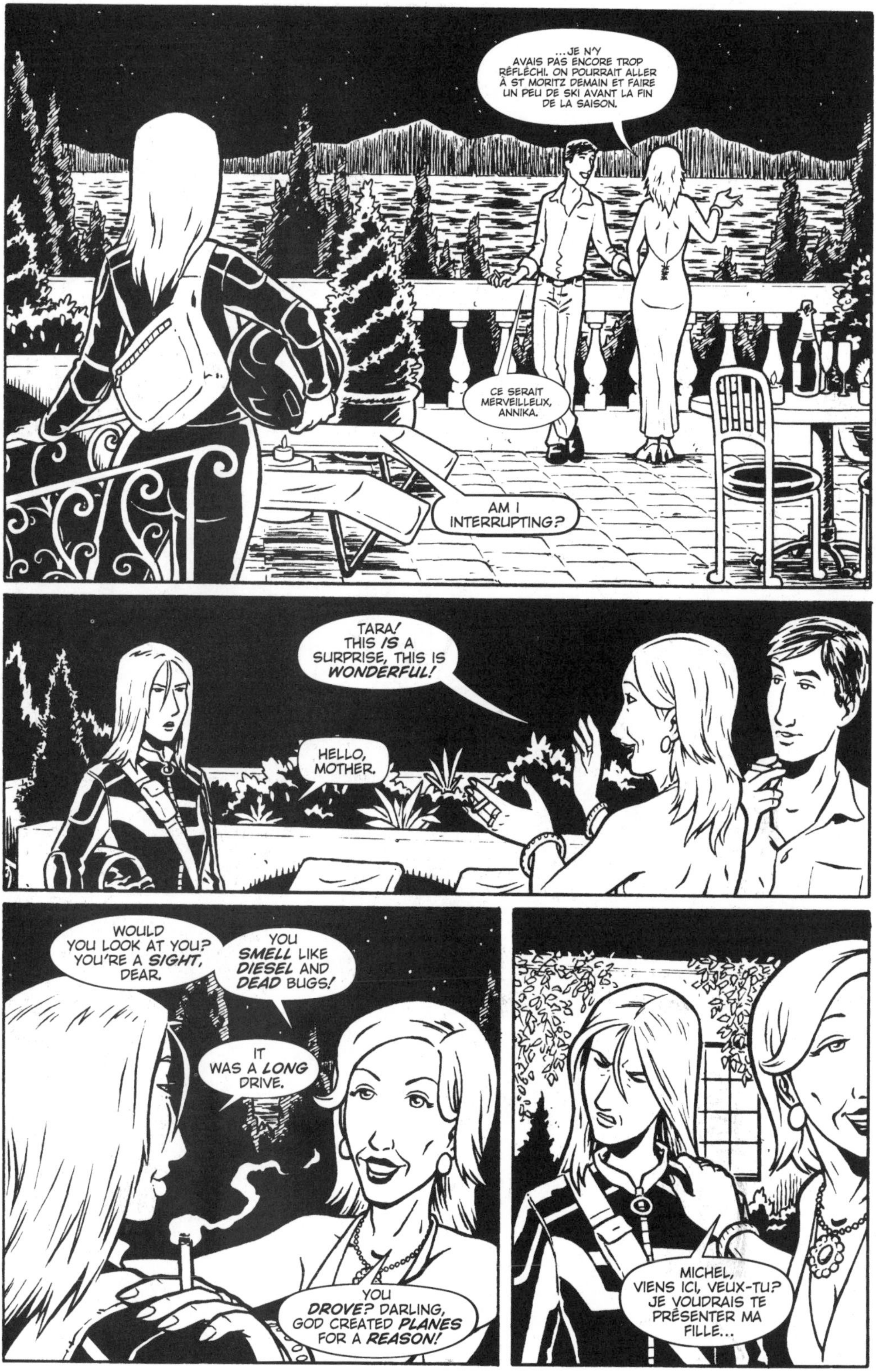
...JE N'Y AVAIS PAS ENCORE TROP RÉFLÉCHI. ON POURRAIT ALLER À ST MORITZ DEMAIN ET FAIRE UN PEU DE SKI AVANT LA FIN DE LA SAISON.
CE SERAIT MERVEILLEUX, ANNIKA.
AM I INTERRUPTING?
TARA! THIS *IS* A SURPRISE, THIS IS ***WONDERFUL!***
HELLO, MOTHER.
WOULD YOU LOOK AT YOU? YOU'RE A ***SIGHT,*** DEAR.
YOU ***SMELL*** LIKE ***DIESEL*** AND ***DEAD*** BUGS!
IT WAS A ***LONG*** DRIVE.
YOU ***DROVE?*** DARLING, GOD CREATED ***PLANES*** FOR A ***REASON!***
MICHEL, VIENS ICI, VEUX-TU? JE VOUDRAIS TE PRÉSENTER MA FILLE...

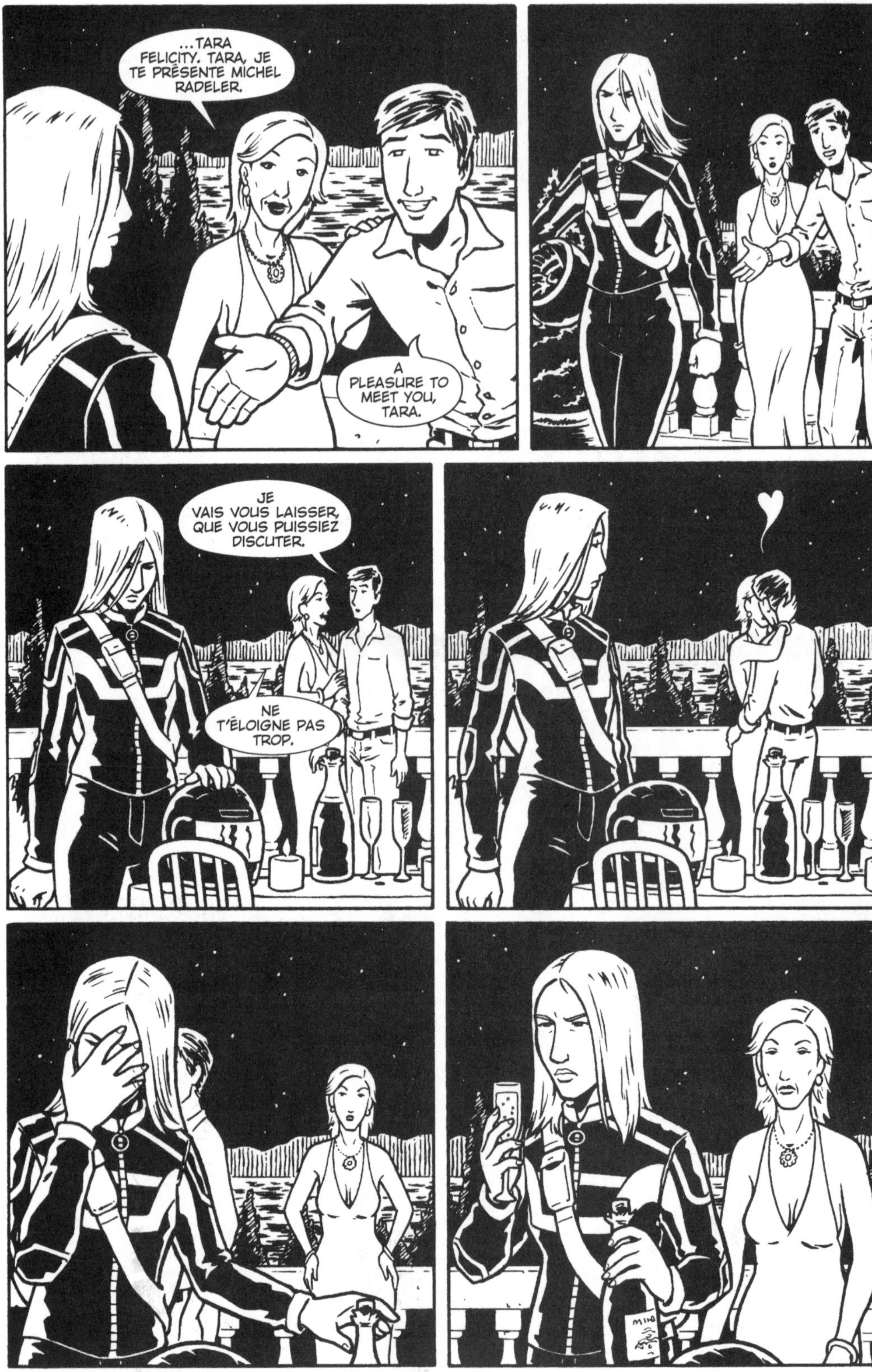
...TARA FELICITY. TARA, JE TE PRÉSENTE MICHEL RADELER.
A PLEASURE TO MEET YOU, TARA.
JE VAIS VOUS LAISSER, QUE VOUS PUISSIEZ DISCUTER.
NE T'ÉLOIGNE PAS TROP.

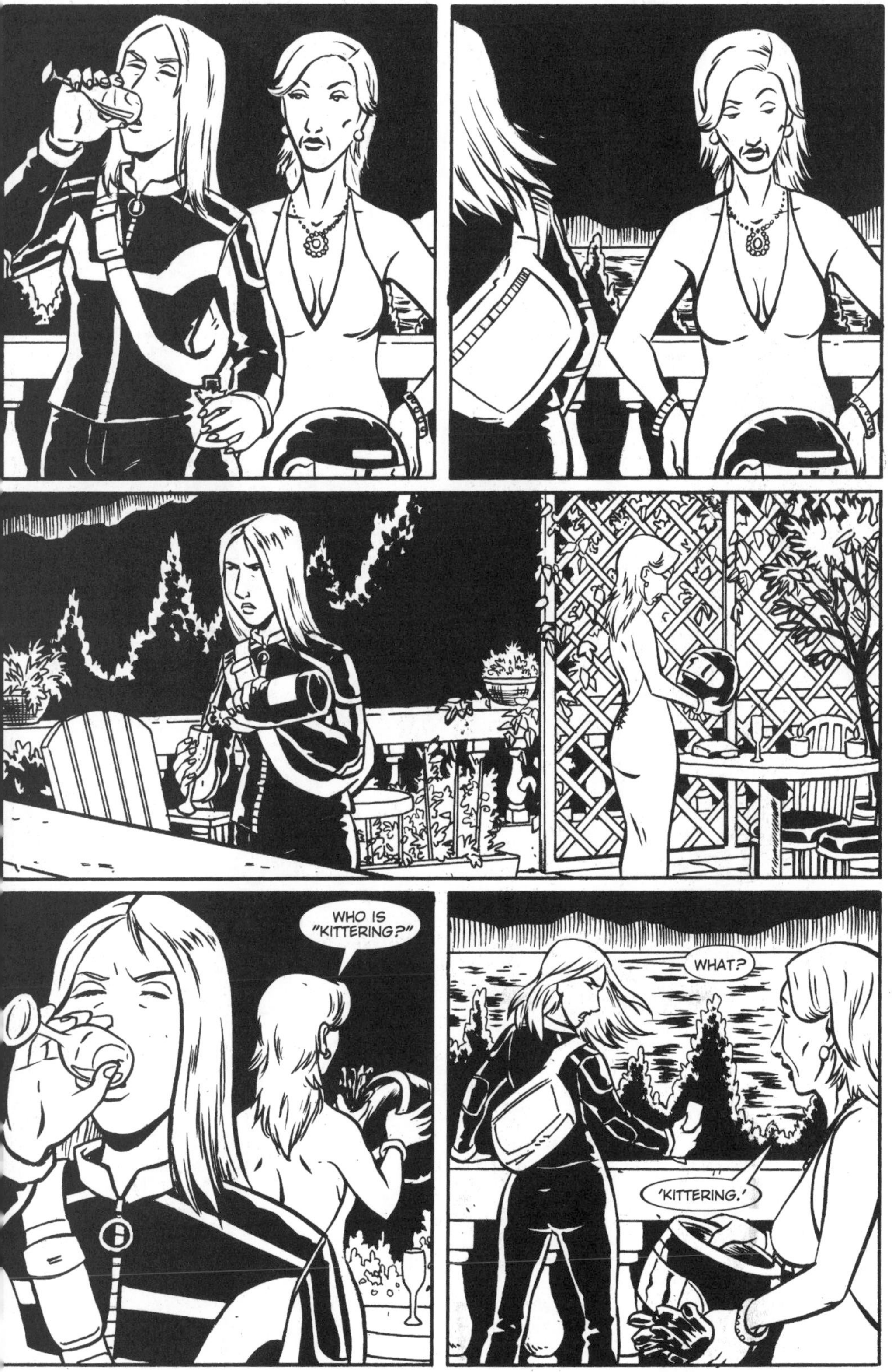
WHO IS "KITTERING?"
WHAT?
'KITTERING.'

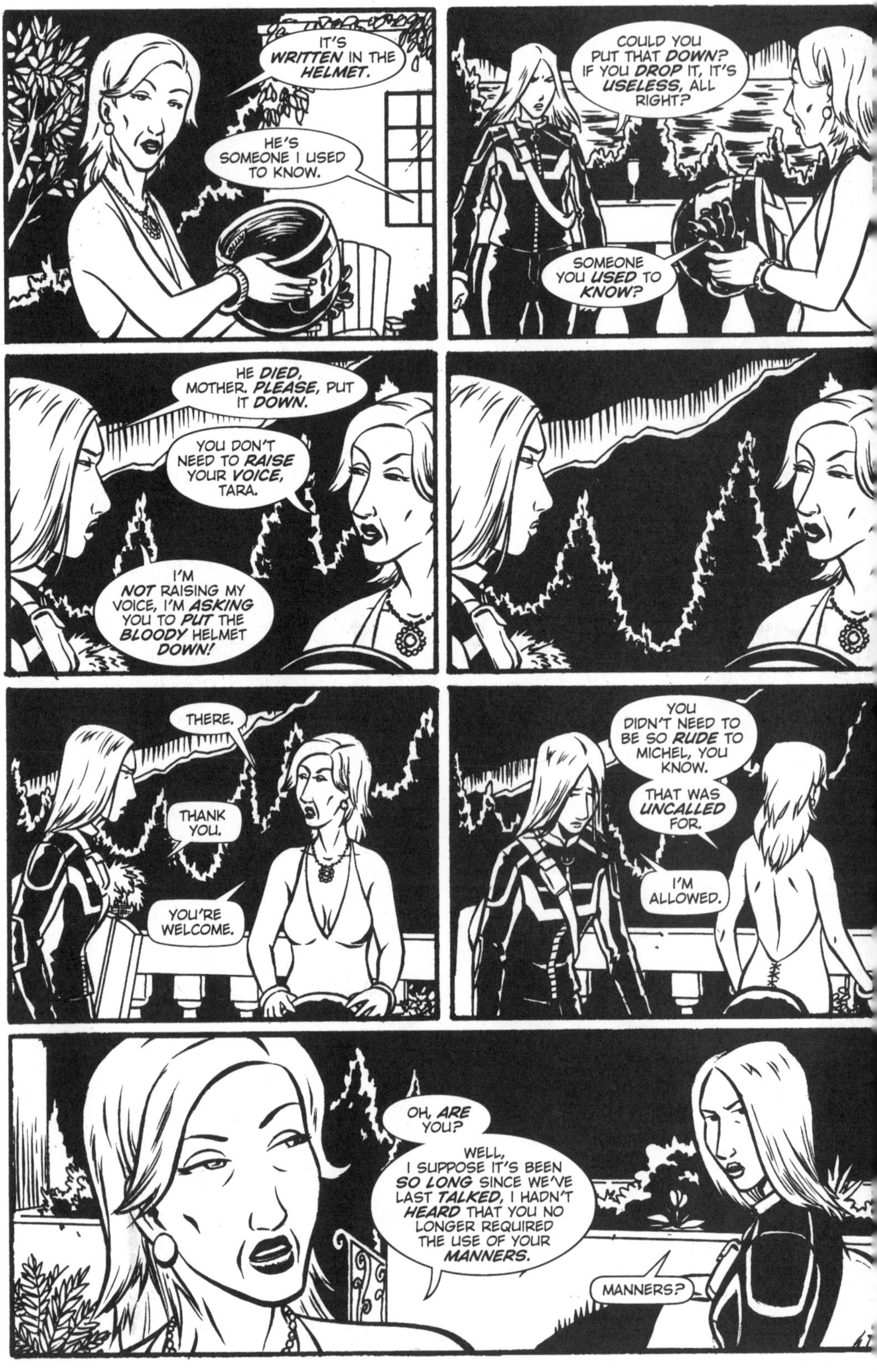
IT'S WRITTEN IN THE HELMET.
HE'S SOMEONE I USED TO KNOW.
COULD YOU PUT THAT DOWN? IF YOU DROP IT, IT'S USELESS, ALL RIGHT?
SOMEONE YOU USED TO KNOW?
HE DIED, MOTHER. PLEASE, PUT IT DOWN.
YOU DON'T NEED TO RAISE YOUR VOICE, TARA.
I'M NOT RAISING MY VOICE, I'M ASKING YOU TO PUT THE BLOODY HELMET DOWN!
THERE.
THANK YOU.
YOU'RE WELCOME.
YOU DIDN'T NEED TO BE SO RUDE TO MICHEL, YOU KNOW.
THAT WAS UNCALLED FOR.
I'M ALLOWED.
OH, ARE YOU?
WELL, I SUPPOSE IT'S BEEN SO LONG SINCE WE'VE LAST TALKED, I HADN'T HEARD THAT YOU NO LONGER REQUIRED THE USE OF YOUR MANNERS.
MANNERS?

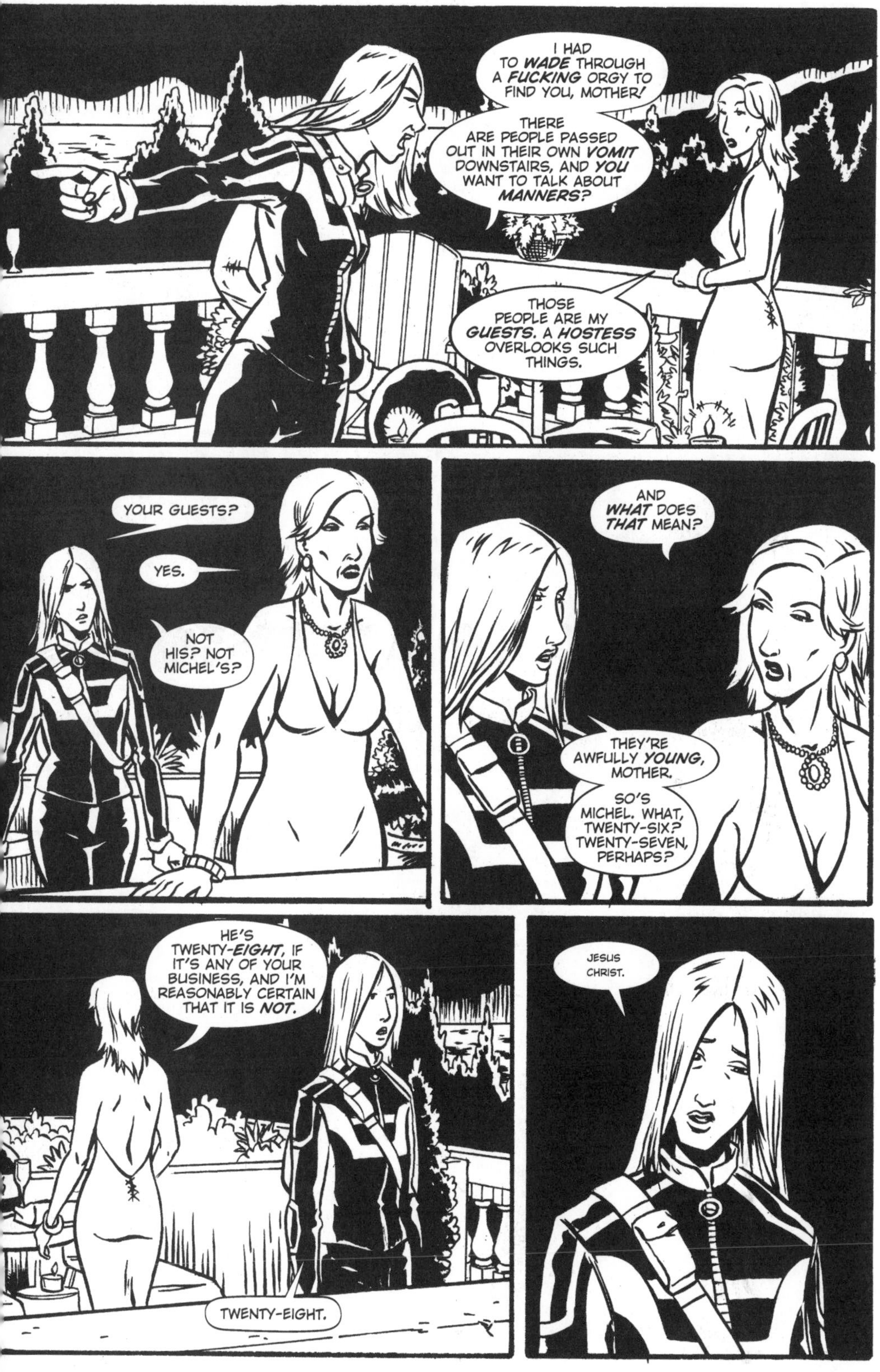
I HAD TO WADE THROUGH A FUCKING ORGY TO FIND YOU, MOTHER!
THERE ARE PEOPLE PASSED OUT IN THEIR OWN VOMIT DOWNSTAIRS, AND YOU WANT TO TALK ABOUT MANNERS?
THOSE PEOPLE ARE MY GUESTS. A HOSTESS OVERLOOKS SUCH THINGS.
YOUR GUESTS?
YES.
NOT HIS? NOT MICHEL'S?
AND WHAT DOES THAT MEAN?
THEY'RE AWFULLY YOUNG, MOTHER.
SO'S MICHEL. WHAT, TWENTY-SIX? TWENTY-SEVEN, PERHAPS?
HE'S TWENTY-EIGHT, IF IT'S ANY OF YOUR BUSINESS, AND I'M REASONABLY CERTAIN THAT IT IS NOT.
TWENTY-EIGHT.
JESUS CHRIST.

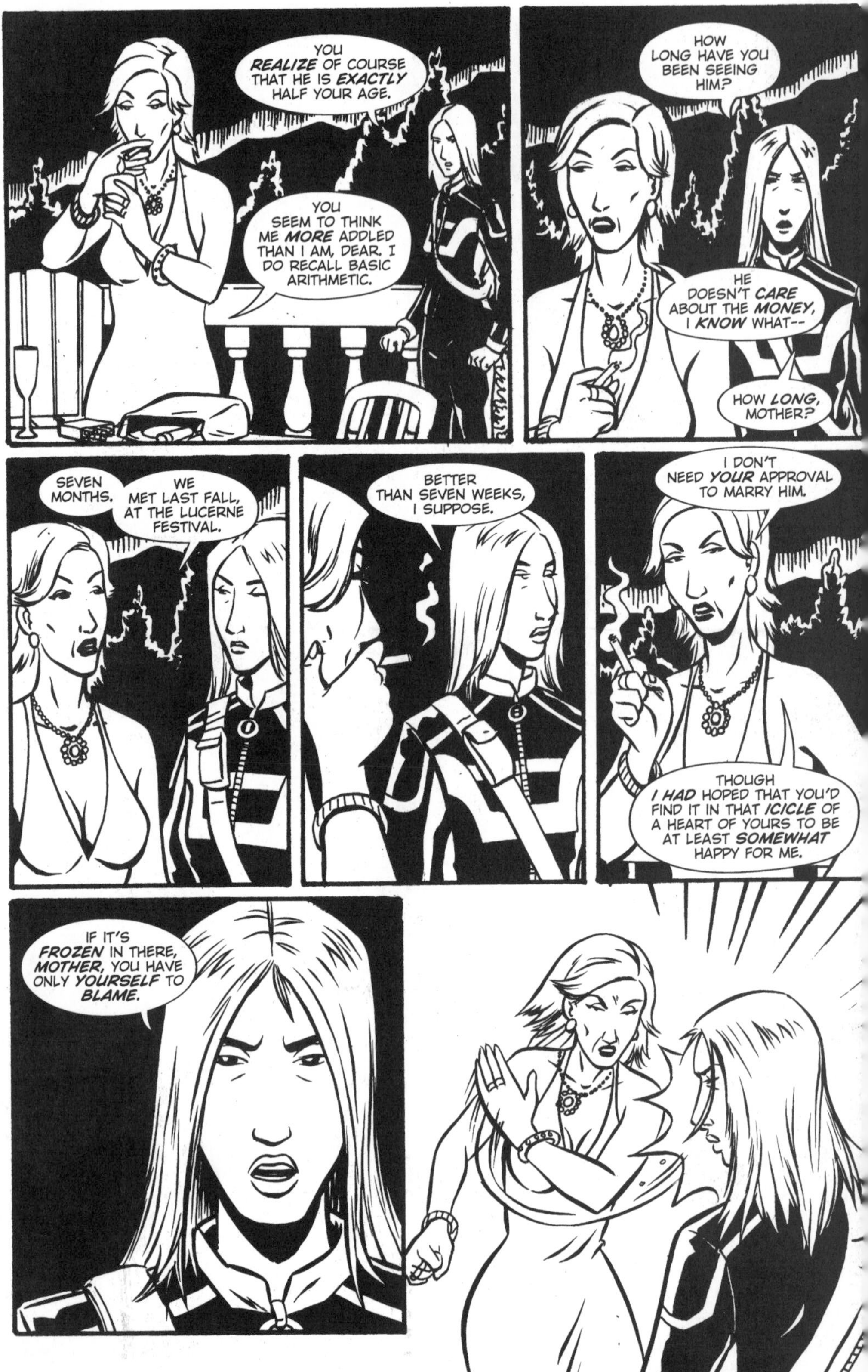
YOU REALIZE OF COURSE THAT HE IS EXACTLY HALF YOUR AGE.
YOU SEEM TO THINK ME MORE ADDLED THAN I AM, DEAR. I DO RECALL BASIC ARITHMETIC.
HOW LONG HAVE YOU BEEN SEEING HIM?
HE DOESN'T CARE ABOUT THE MONEY, I KNOW WHAT--
HOW LONG, MOTHER?
SEVEN MONTHS.
WE MET LAST FALL, AT THE LUCERNE FESTIVAL.
BETTER THAN SEVEN WEEKS, I SUPPOSE.
I DON'T NEED YOUR APPROVAL TO MARRY HIM.
THOUGH I HAD HOPED THAT YOU'D FIND IT IN THAT ICICLE OF A HEART OF YOURS TO BE AT LEAST SOMEWHAT HAPPY FOR ME.
IF IT'S FROZEN IN THERE, MOTHER, YOU HAVE ONLY YOURSELF TO BLAME.

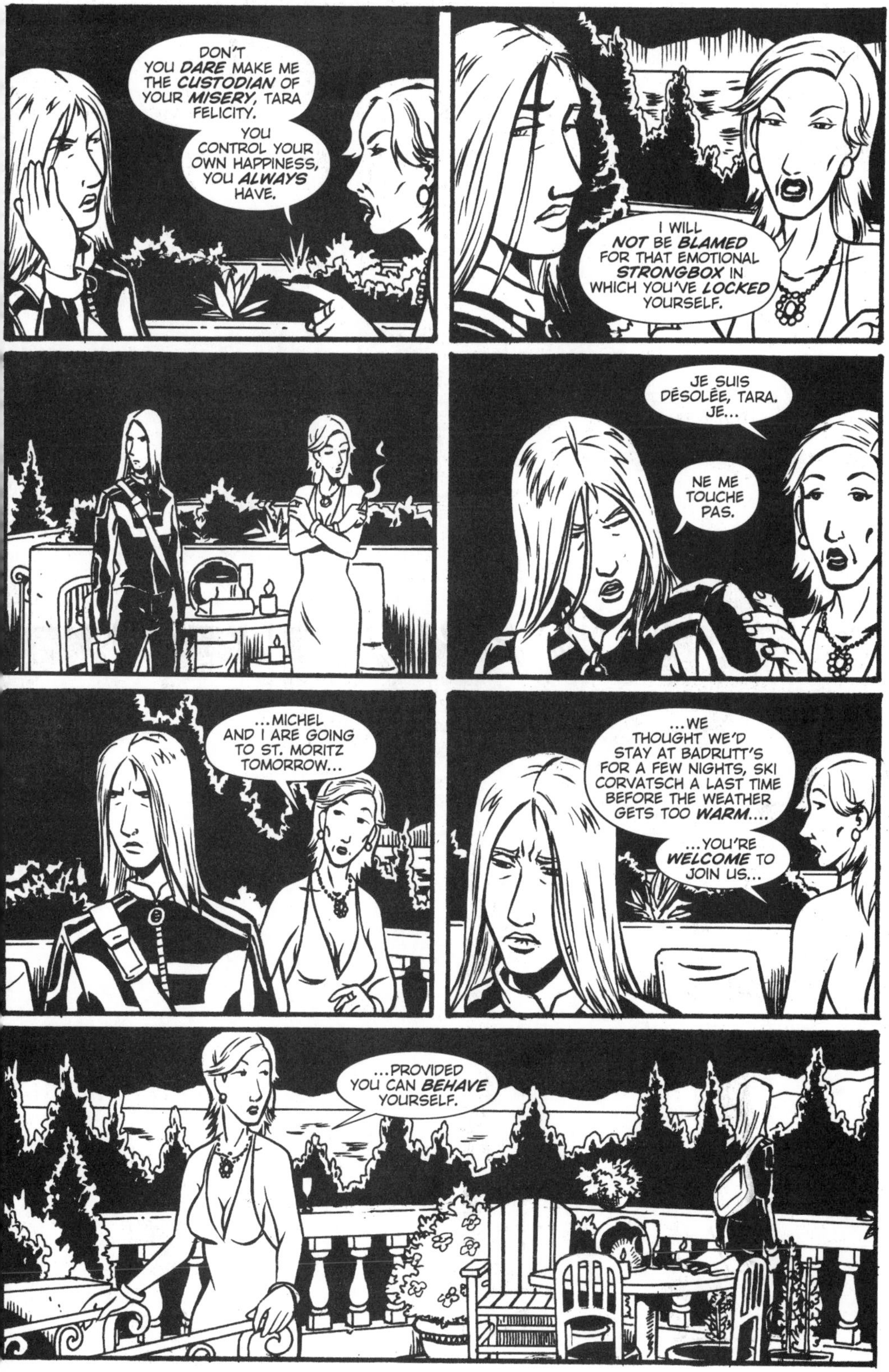
DON'T YOU DARE MAKE ME THE CUSTODIAN OF YOUR MISERY, TARA FELICITY.
YOU CONTROL YOUR OWN HAPPINESS, YOU ALWAYS HAVE.
I WILL NOT BE BLAMED FOR THAT EMOTIONAL STRONGBOX IN WHICH YOU'VE LOCKED YOURSELF.
JE SUIS DÉSOLÉE, TARA. JE...
NE ME TOUCHE PAS.
...MICHEL AND I ARE GOING TO ST. MORITZ TOMORROW...
...WE THOUGHT WE'D STAY AT BADRUTT'S FOR A FEW NIGHTS, SKI CORVATSCH A LAST TIME BEFORE THE WEATHER GETS TOO WARM....
...YOU'RE WELCOME TO JOIN US...
...PROVIDED YOU CAN BEHAVE YOURSELF.

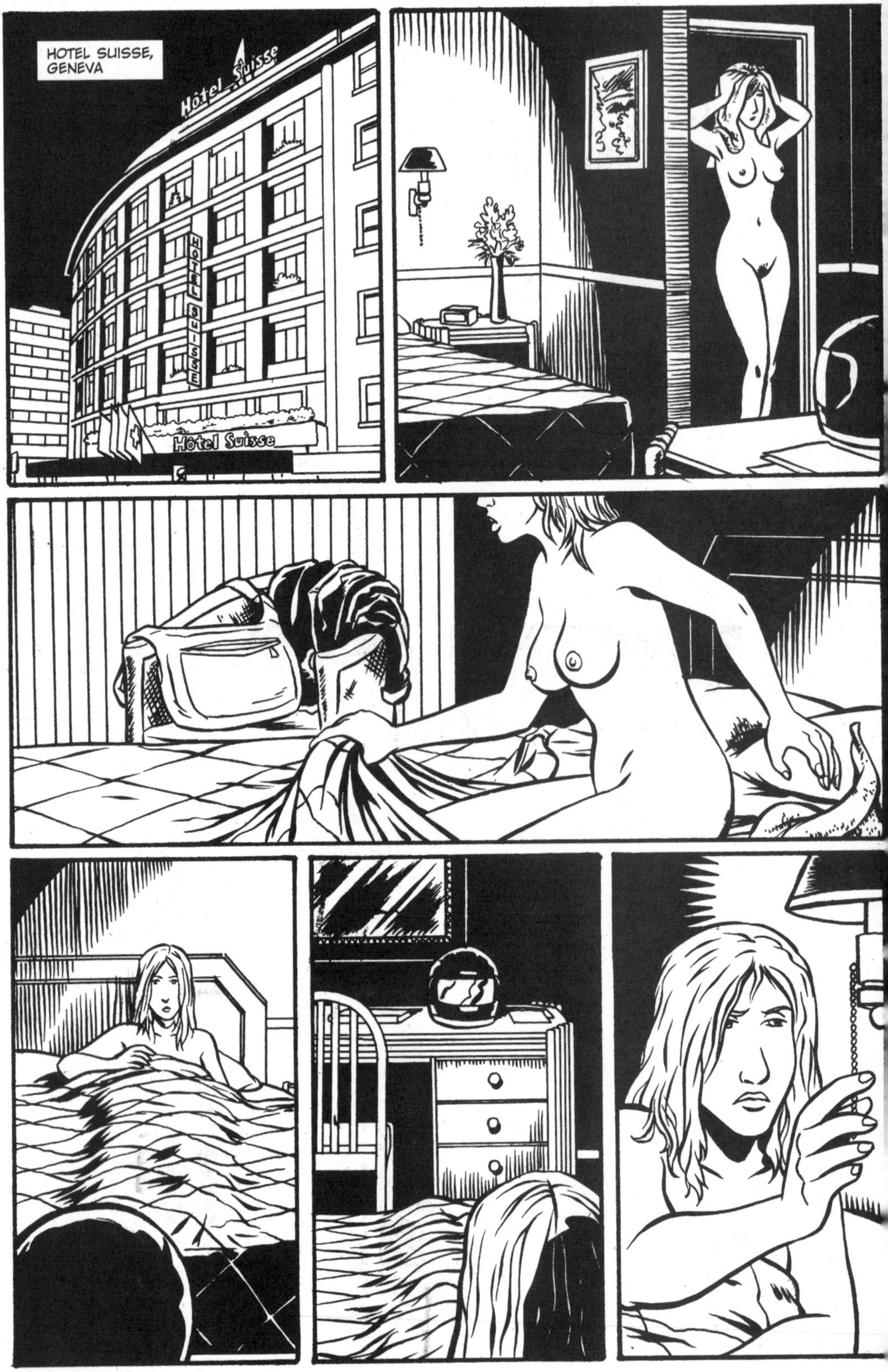
HOTEL SUISSE, GENEVA
Hôtel Suisse
HÔTEL SUISSE
Hôtel Suisse

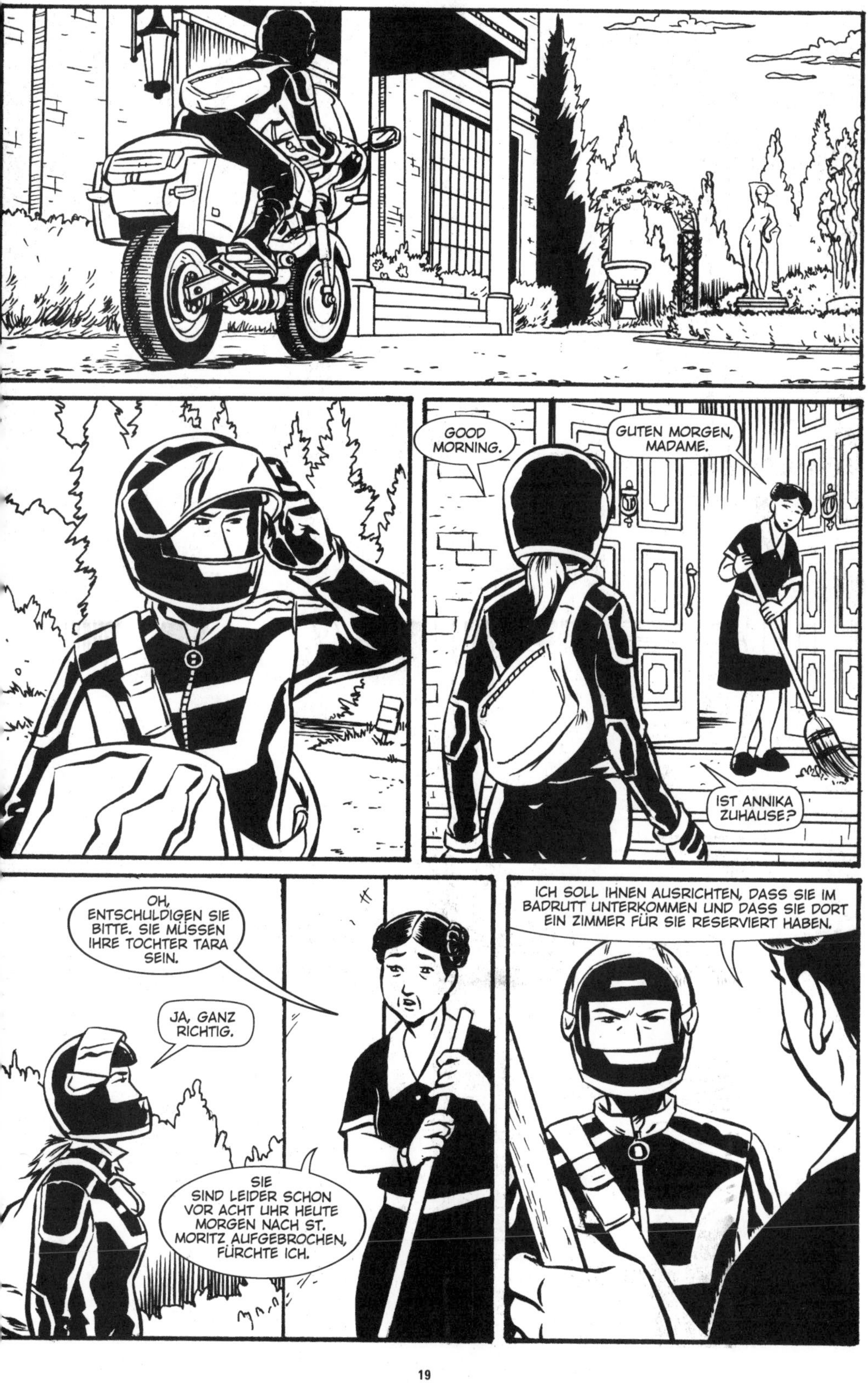
GOOD MORNING.
GUTEN MORGEN, MADAME.
IST ANNIKA ZUHAUSE?
OH, ENTSCHULDIGEN SIE BITTE. SIE MÜSSEN IHRE TOCHTER TARA SEIN.
JA, GANZ RICHTIG.
SIE SIND LEIDER SCHON VOR ACHT UHR HEUTE MORGEN NACH ST. MORITZ AUFGEBROCHEN, FÜRCHTE ICH.
ICH SOLL IHNEN AUSRICHTEN, DASS SIE IM BADRUTT UNTERKOMMEN UND DASS SIE DORT EIN ZIMMER FÜR SIE RESERVIERT HABEN.

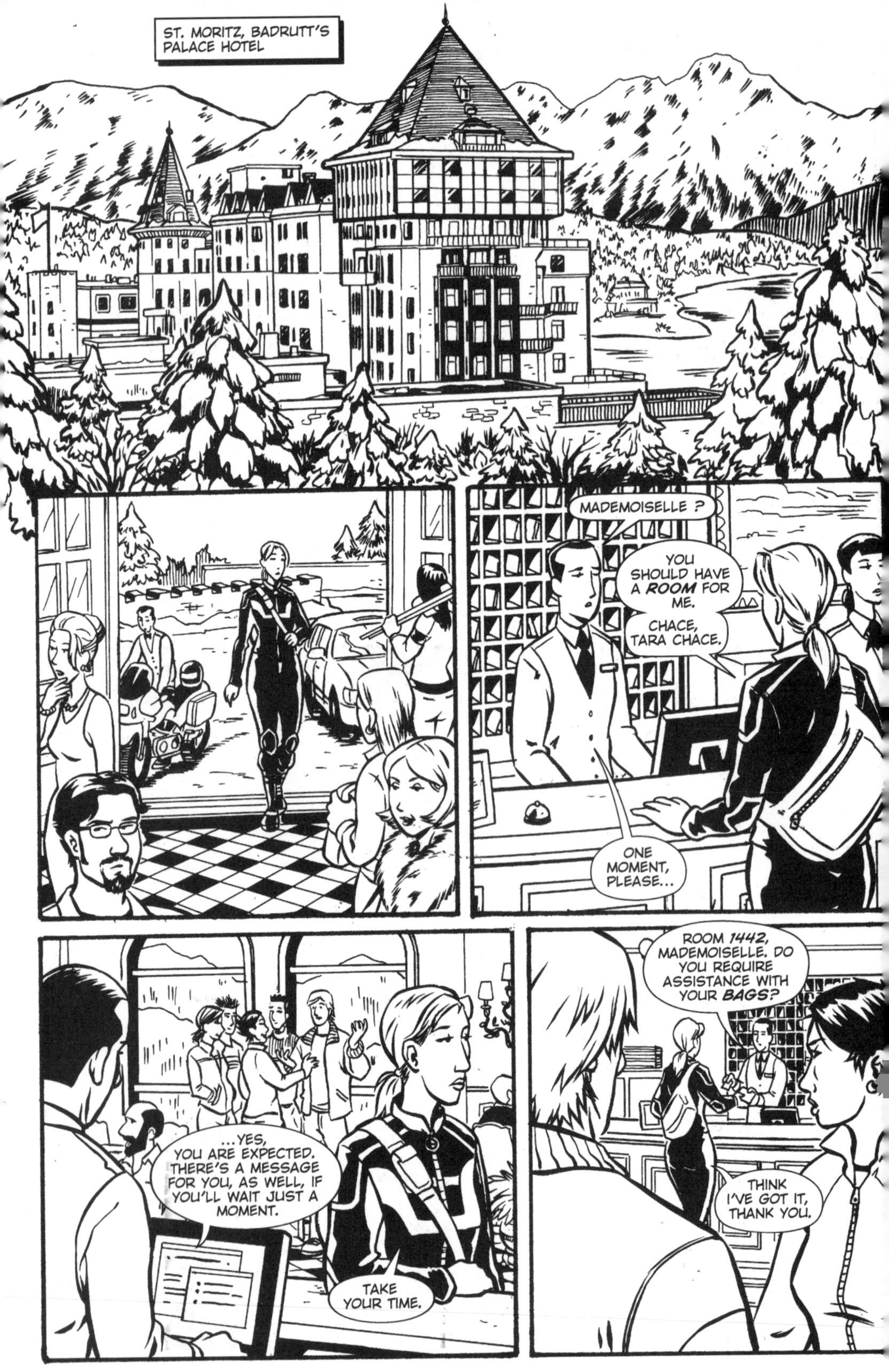

ST. MORITZ, BADRUTT'S PALACE HOTEL
MADEMOISELLE ?
YOU SHOULD HAVE A ***ROOM*** FOR ME.
CHACE, TARA CHACE.
ONE MOMENT, PLEASE...
...YES, YOU ARE EXPECTED. THERE'S A MESSAGE FOR YOU, AS WELL, IF YOU'LL WAIT JUST A MOMENT.
TAKE YOUR TIME.
ROOM *1442*, MADEMOISELLE. DO YOU REQUIRE ASSISTANCE WITH YOUR ***BAGS?***
THINK I'VE GOT IT, THANK YOU.

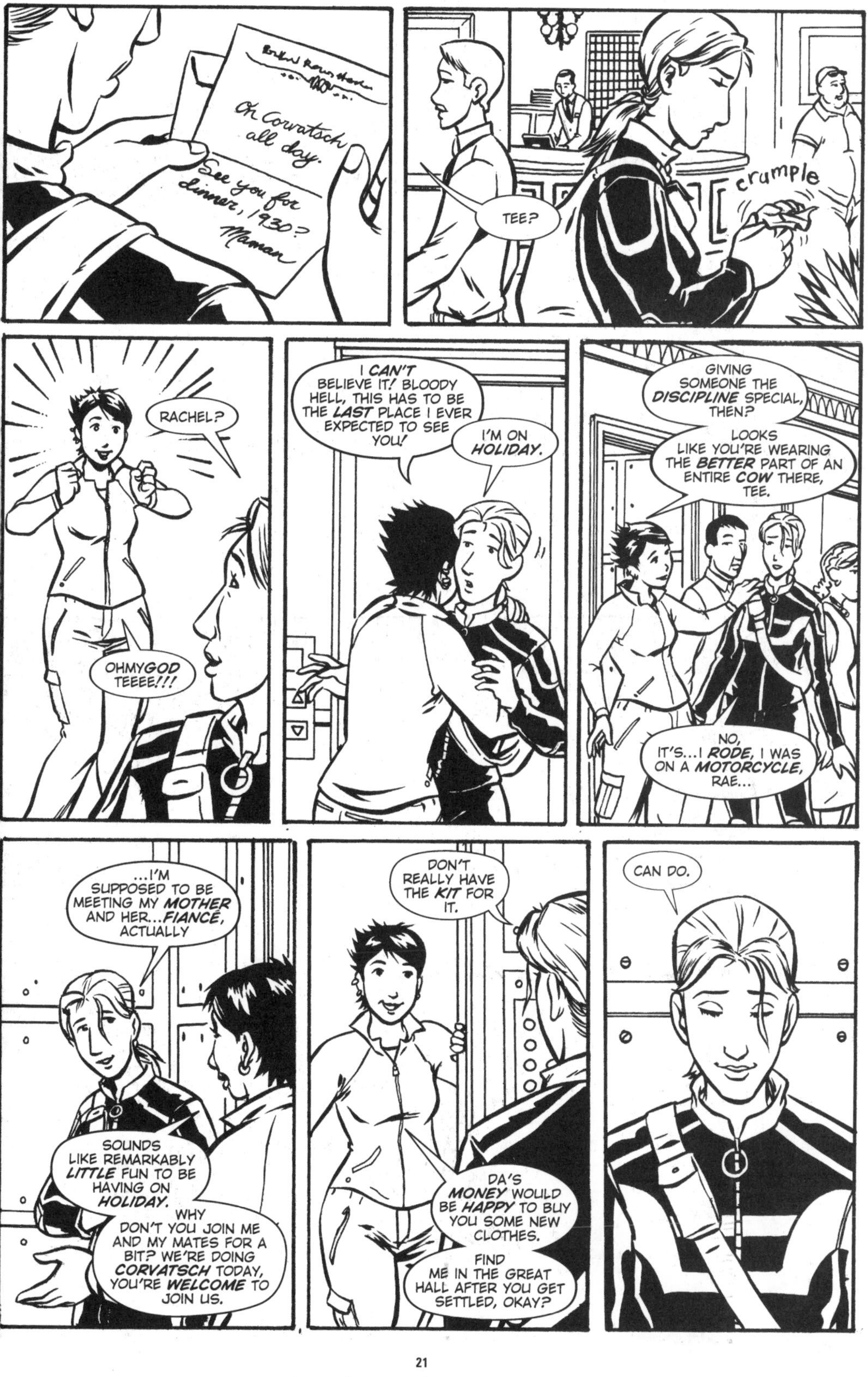
On Corvatsch all day.
See you for dinner, 1930?
Maman
TEE?
crumple
RACHEL?
OHMYGOD TEEEE!!!
I CAN'T BELIEVE IT! BLOODY HELL, THIS HAS TO BE THE LAST PLACE I EVER EXPECTED TO SEE YOU!
I'M ON HOLIDAY.
GIVING SOMEONE THE DISCIPLINE SPECIAL, THEN?
LOOKS LIKE YOU'RE WEARING THE BETTER PART OF AN ENTIRE COW THERE, TEE.
NO, IT'S...I RODE, I WAS ON A MOTORCYCLE, RAE...
...I'M SUPPOSED TO BE MEETING MY MOTHER AND HER...FIANCÉ, ACTUALLY
SOUNDS LIKE REMARKABLY LITTLE FUN TO BE HAVING ON HOLIDAY.
WHY DON'T YOU JOIN ME AND MY MATES FOR A BIT? WE'RE DOING CORVATSCH TODAY, YOU'RE WELCOME TO JOIN US.
DON'T REALLY HAVE THE KIT FOR IT.
DA'S MONEY WOULD BE HAPPY TO BUY YOU SOME NEW CLOTHES.
FIND ME IN THE GREAT HALL AFTER YOU GET SETTLED, OKAY?
CAN DO.

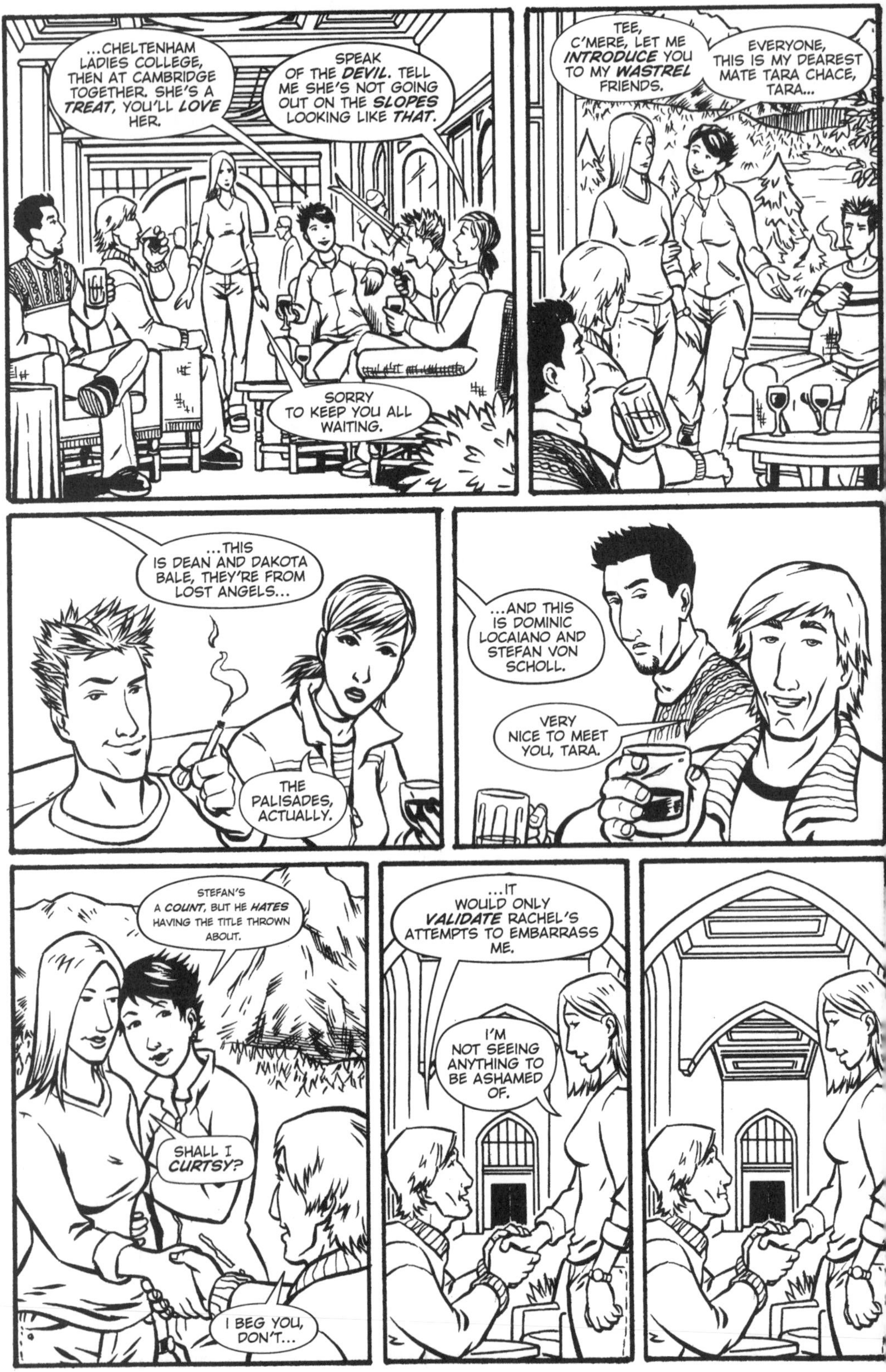

...CHELTENHAM LADIES COLLEGE, THEN AT CAMBRIDGE TOGETHER. SHE'S A *TREAT*, YOU'LL *LOVE* HER.
SPEAK OF THE *DEVIL*. TELL ME SHE'S NOT GOING OUT ON THE *SLOPES* LOOKING LIKE *THAT*.
SORRY TO KEEP YOU ALL WAITING.
TEE, C'MERE, LET ME *INTRODUCE* YOU TO MY *WASTREL* FRIENDS.
EVERYONE, THIS IS MY DEAREST MATE TARA CHACE, TARA...
...THIS IS DEAN AND DAKOTA BALE, THEY'RE FROM LOST ANGELS...
THE PALISADES, ACTUALLY.
...AND THIS IS DOMINIC LOCAIANO AND STEFAN VON SCHOLL.
VERY NICE TO MEET YOU, TARA.
STEFAN'S A *COUNT*, BUT HE *HATES* HAVING THE TITLE THROWN ABOUT.
SHALL I *CURTSY*?
I BEG YOU, DON'T...
...IT WOULD ONLY *VALIDATE* RACHEL'S ATTEMPTS TO EMBARRASS ME.
I'M NOT SEEING ANYTHING TO BE ASHAMED OF.

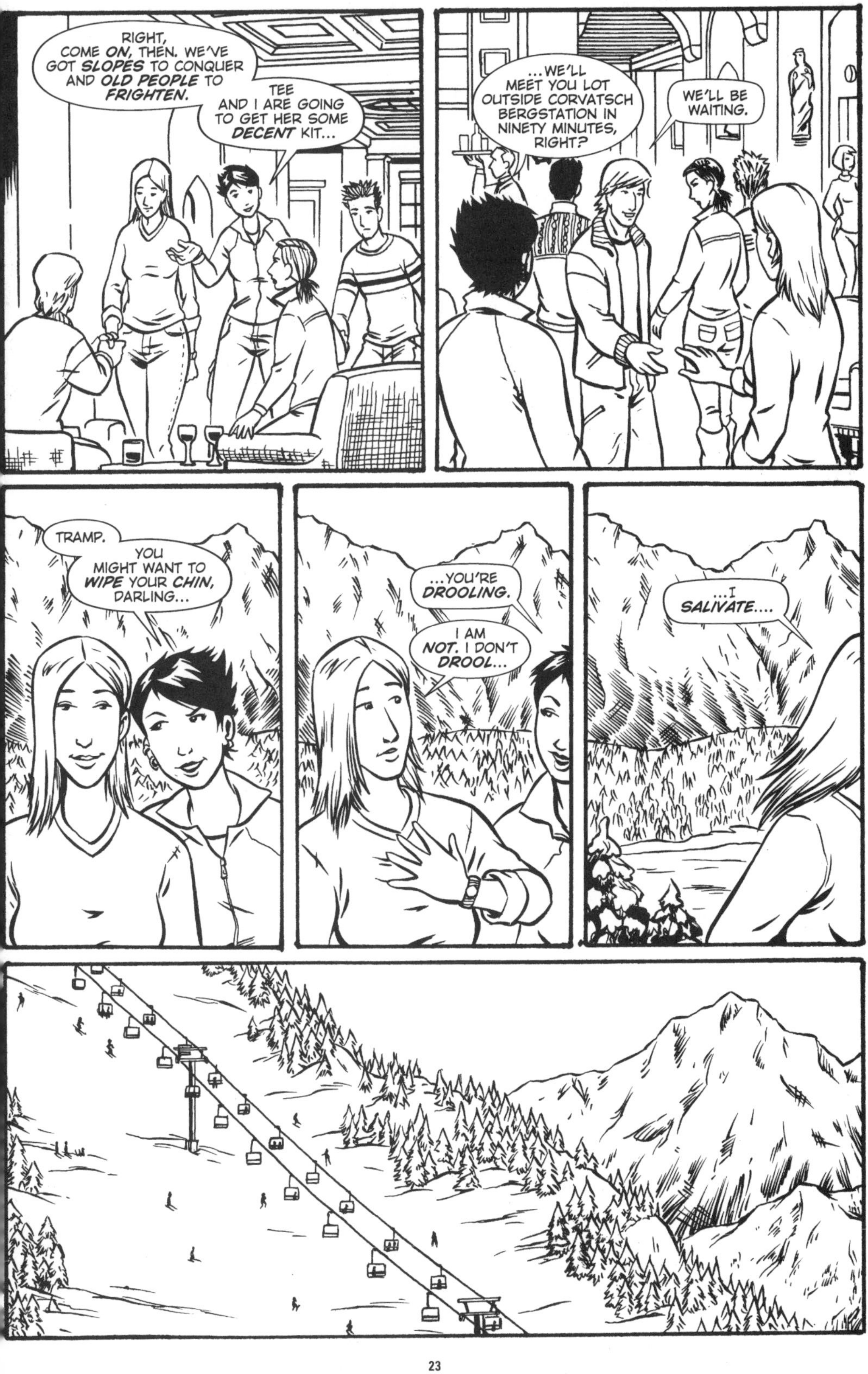
RIGHT, COME ON, THEN. WE'VE GOT SLOPES TO CONQUER AND OLD PEOPLE TO FRIGHTEN.
TEE AND I ARE GOING TO GET HER SOME DECENT KIT...
...WE'LL MEET YOU LOT OUTSIDE CORVATSCH BERGSTATION IN NINETY MINUTES, RIGHT?
WE'LL BE WAITING.
TRAMP.
YOU MIGHT WANT TO WIPE YOUR CHIN, DARLING...
...YOU'RE DROOLING.
I AM NOT. I DON'T DROOL...
...I SALIVATE....

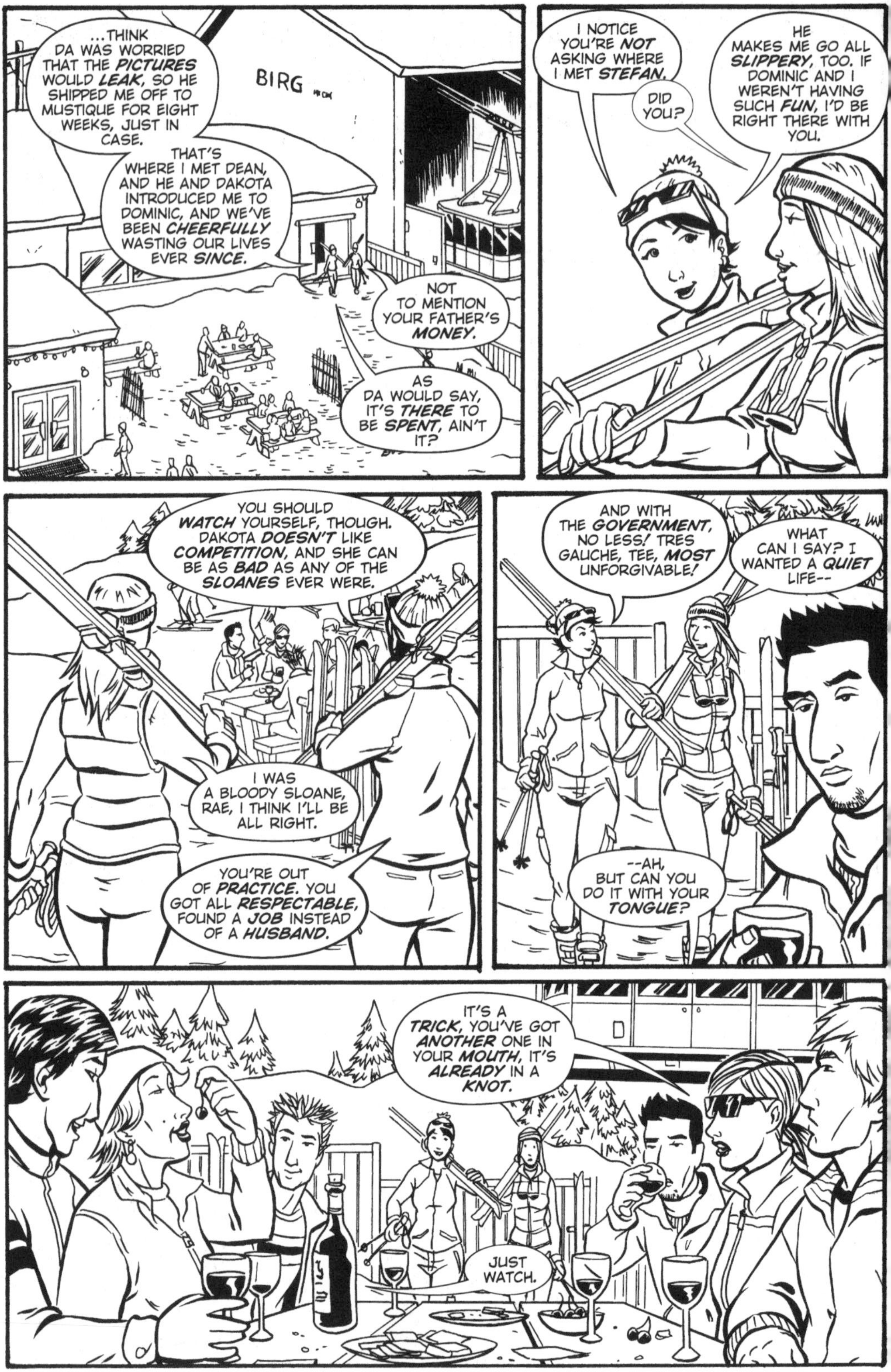
...THINK DA WAS WORRIED THAT THE **PICTURES** WOULD **LEAK**, SO HE SHIPPED ME OFF TO MUSTIQUE FOR EIGHT WEEKS, JUST IN CASE.
BIRG
THAT'S WHERE I MET DEAN, AND HE AND DAKOTA INTRODUCED ME TO DOMINIC, AND WE'VE BEEN **CHEERFULLY** WASTING OUR LIVES EVER **SINCE**.
NOT TO MENTION YOUR FATHER'S **MONEY**.
AS DA WOULD SAY, IT'S **THERE** TO BE **SPENT**, AIN'T IT?
I NOTICE YOU'RE **NOT** ASKING WHERE I MET **STEFAN**.
DID YOU?
HE MAKES ME GO ALL **SLIPPERY**, TOO. IF DOMINIC AND I WEREN'T HAVING SUCH **FUN**, I'D BE RIGHT THERE WITH YOU.
YOU SHOULD **WATCH** YOURSELF, THOUGH. DAKOTA **DOESN'T** LIKE **COMPETITION**, AND SHE CAN BE AS **BAD** AS ANY OF THE **SLOANES** EVER WERE.
I WAS A BLOODY SLOANE, RAE, I THINK I'LL BE ALL RIGHT.
YOU'RE OUT OF **PRACTICE**. YOU GOT ALL **RESPECTABLE**, FOUND A **JOB** INSTEAD OF A **HUSBAND**.
AND WITH THE **GOVERNMENT**, NO LESS! TRES GAUCHE, TEE, **MOST** UNFORGIVABLE!
WHAT CAN I SAY? I WANTED A **QUIET** LIFE--
--AH, BUT CAN YOU DO IT WITH YOUR **TONGUE?**
IT'S A **TRICK**, YOU'VE GOT **ANOTHER** ONE IN YOUR **MOUTH**, IT'S **ALREADY** IN A **KNOT**.
JUST WATCH.

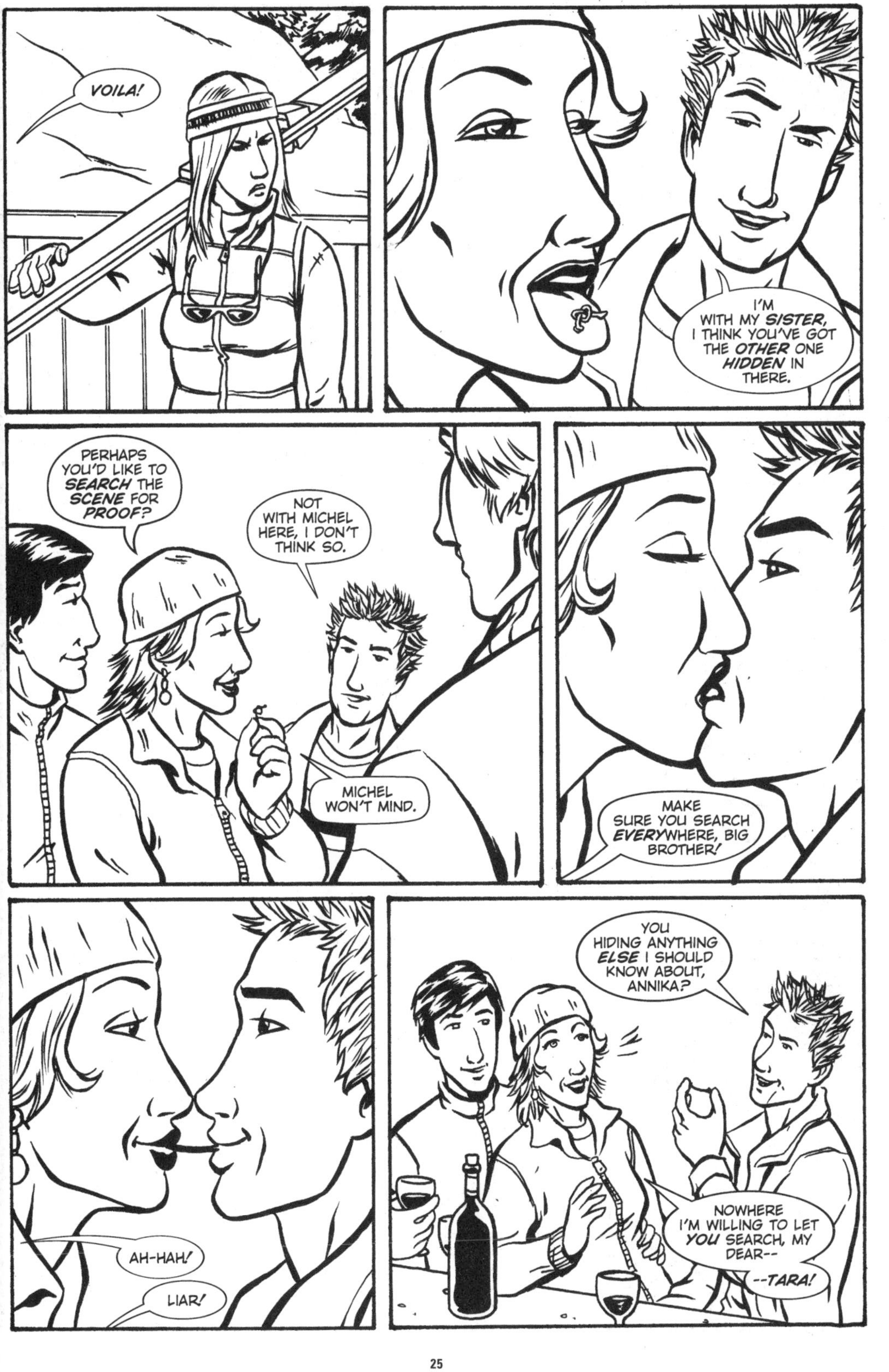
VOILA!
I'M WITH MY SISTER, I THINK YOU'VE GOT THE OTHER ONE HIDDEN IN THERE.
PERHAPS YOU'D LIKE TO SEARCH THE SCENE FOR PROOF?
NOT WITH MICHEL HERE, I DON'T THINK SO.
MICHEL WON'T MIND.
MAKE SURE YOU SEARCH EVERYWHERE, BIG BROTHER!
AH-HAH!
LIAR!
YOU HIDING ANYTHING ELSE I SHOULD KNOW ABOUT, ANNIKA?
NOWHERE I'M WILLING TO LET YOU SEARCH, MY DEAR--
--TARA!

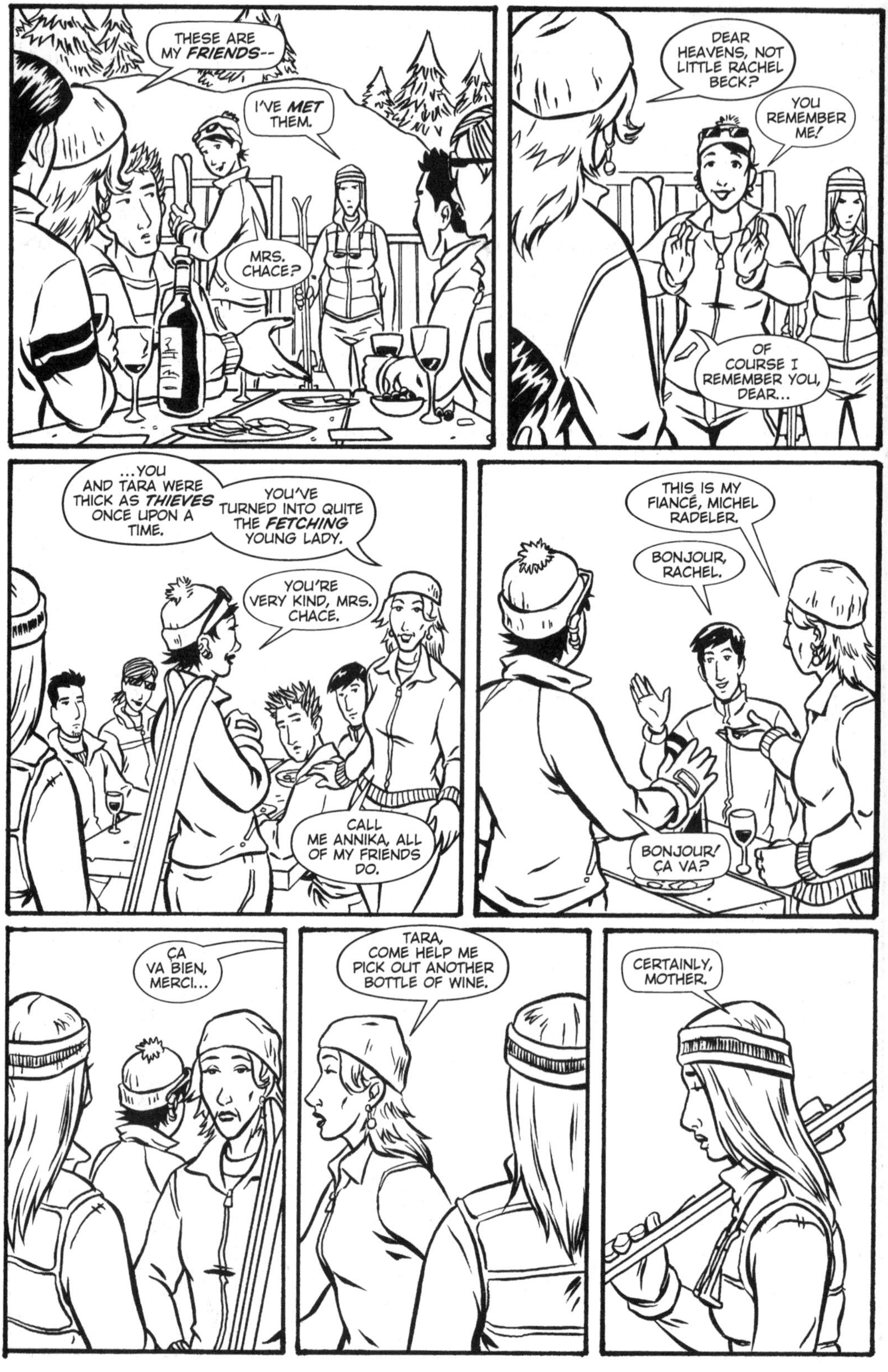
THESE ARE MY FRIENDS--
I'VE MET THEM.
MRS. CHACE?
DEAR HEAVENS, NOT LITTLE RACHEL BECK?
YOU REMEMBER ME!
OF COURSE I REMEMBER YOU, DEAR...
...YOU AND TARA WERE THICK AS THIEVES ONCE UPON A TIME.
YOU'VE TURNED INTO QUITE THE FETCHING YOUNG LADY.
YOU'RE VERY KIND, MRS. CHACE.
CALL ME ANNIKA, ALL OF MY FRIENDS DO.
THIS IS MY FIANCÉ, MICHEL RADELER.
BONJOUR, RACHEL.
BONJOUR! ÇA VA?
ÇA VA BIEN, MERCI...
TARA, COME HELP ME PICK OUT ANOTHER BOTTLE OF WINE.
CERTAINLY, MOTHER.

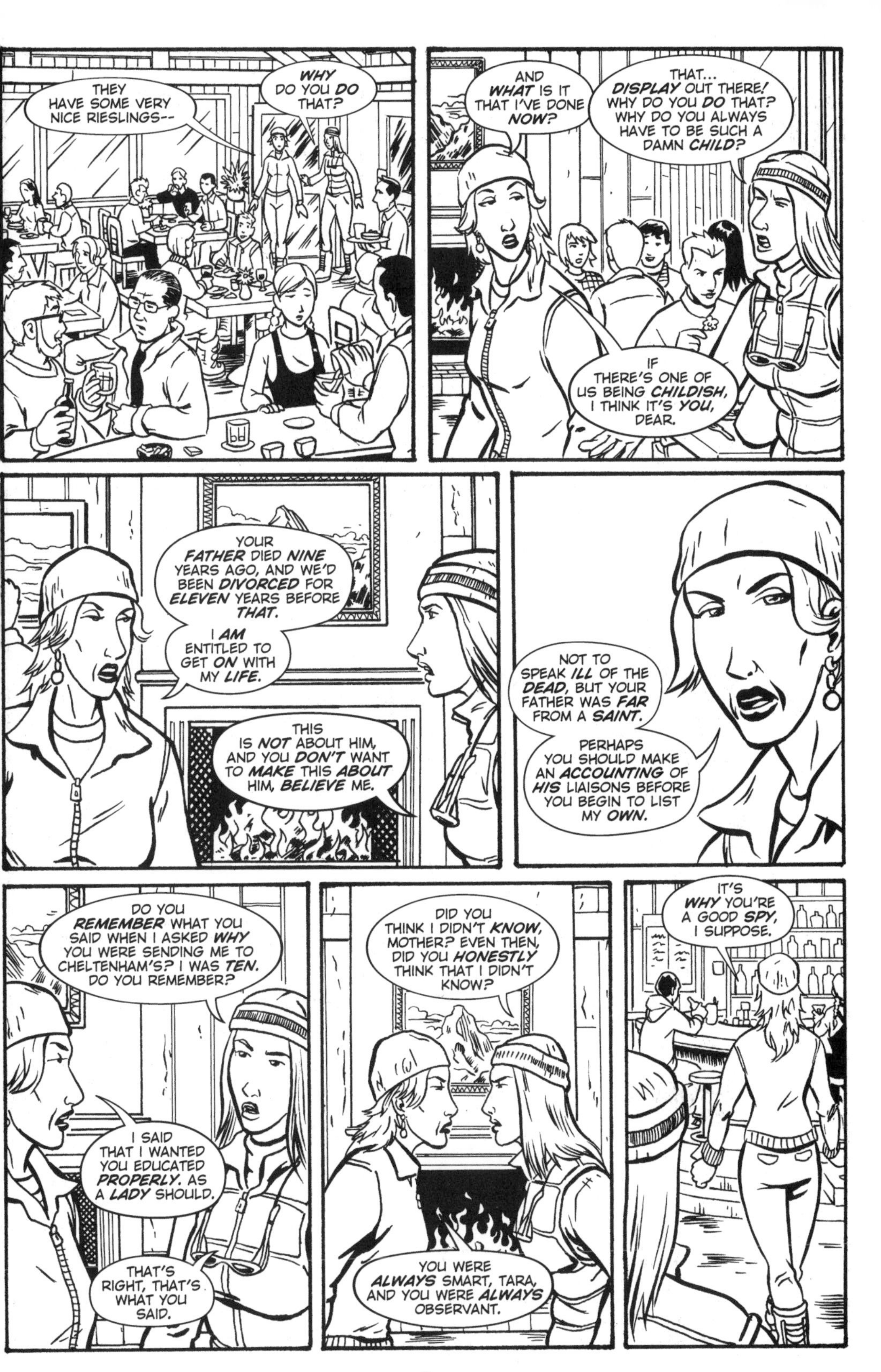
THEY HAVE SOME VERY NICE RIESLINGS--
WHY DO YOU DO THAT?
AND WHAT IS IT THAT I'VE DONE NOW?
THAT... DISPLAY OUT THERE! WHY DO YOU DO THAT? WHY DO YOU ALWAYS HAVE TO BE SUCH A DAMN CHILD?
IF THERE'S ONE OF US BEING CHILDISH, I THINK IT'S YOU, DEAR.
YOUR FATHER DIED NINE YEARS AGO, AND WE'D BEEN DIVORCED FOR ELEVEN YEARS BEFORE THAT.
I AM ENTITLED TO GET ON WITH MY LIFE.
THIS IS NOT ABOUT HIM, AND YOU DON'T WANT TO MAKE THIS ABOUT HIM, BELIEVE ME.
NOT TO SPEAK ILL OF THE DEAD, BUT YOUR FATHER WAS FAR FROM A SAINT.
PERHAPS YOU SHOULD MAKE AN ACCOUNTING OF HIS LIAISONS BEFORE YOU BEGIN TO LIST MY OWN.
DO YOU REMEMBER WHAT YOU SAID WHEN I ASKED WHY YOU WERE SENDING ME TO CHELTENHAM'S? I WAS TEN. DO YOU REMEMBER?
I SAID THAT I WANTED YOU EDUCATED PROPERLY. AS A LADY SHOULD.
THAT'S RIGHT, THAT'S WHAT YOU SAID.
DID YOU THINK I DIDN'T KNOW, MOTHER? EVEN THEN, DID YOU HONESTLY THINK THAT I DIDN'T KNOW?
YOU WERE ALWAYS SMART, TARA, AND YOU WERE ALWAYS OBSERVANT.
IT'S WHY YOU'RE A GOOD SPY, I SUPPOSE.

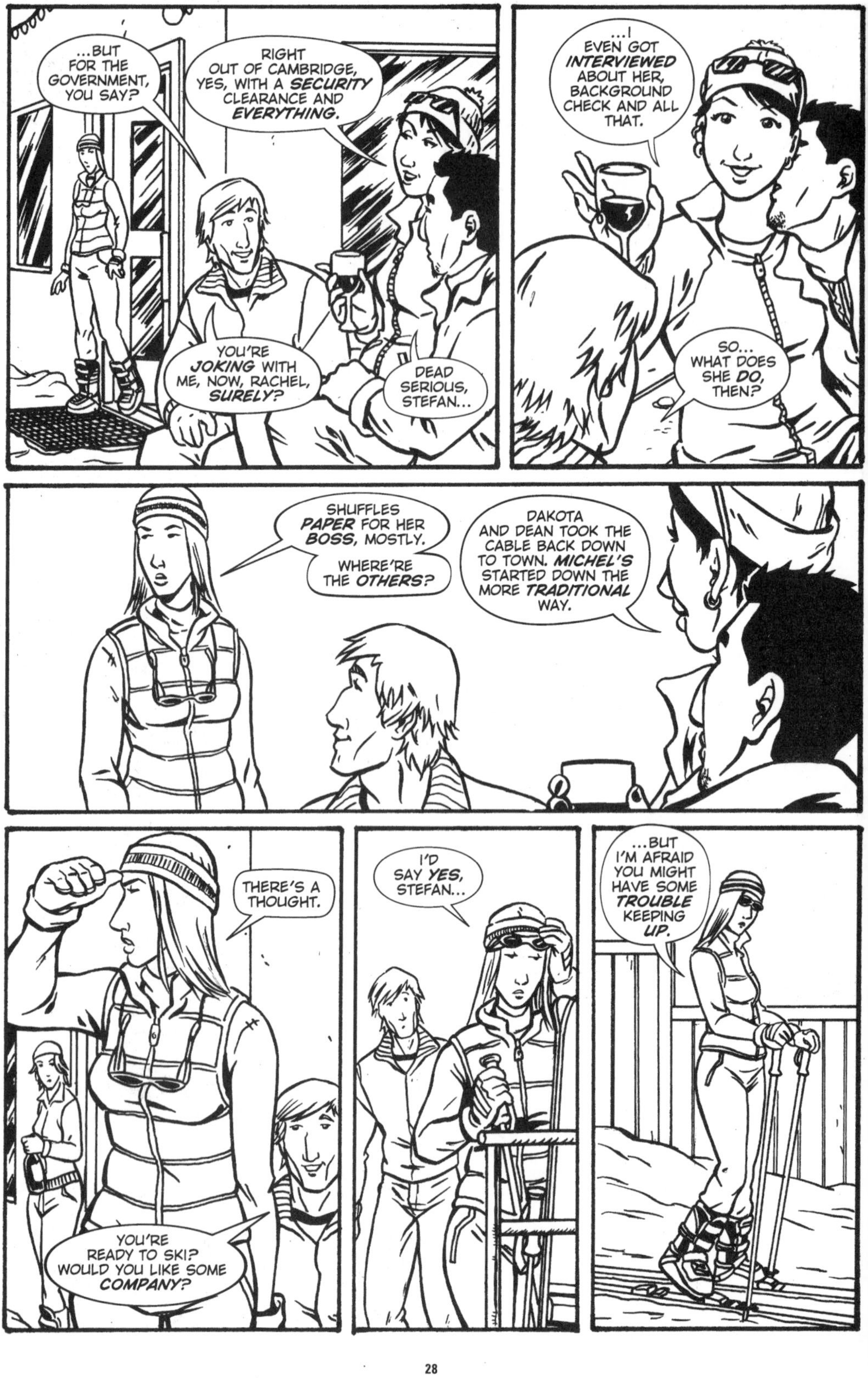
...BUT FOR THE GOVERNMENT, YOU SAY?
RIGHT OUT OF CAMBRIDGE, YES, WITH A ***SECURITY*** CLEARANCE AND ***EVERYTHING.***
YOU'RE ***JOKING*** WITH ME, NOW, RACHEL, ***SURELY?***
DEAD SERIOUS, STEFAN...
...I EVEN GOT ***INTERVIEWED*** ABOUT HER, BACKGROUND CHECK AND ALL THAT.
SO... WHAT DOES SHE ***DO,*** THEN?
SHUFFLES ***PAPER*** FOR HER ***BOSS,*** MOSTLY.
WHERE'RE THE ***OTHERS?***
DAKOTA AND DEAN TOOK THE CABLE BACK DOWN TO TOWN. ***MICHEL'S*** STARTED DOWN THE MORE ***TRADITIONAL*** WAY.
THERE'S A THOUGHT.
YOU'RE READY TO SKI? WOULD YOU LIKE SOME ***COMPANY?***
I'D SAY ***YES,*** STEFAN...
...BUT I'M AFRAID YOU MIGHT HAVE SOME ***TROUBLE*** KEEPING ***UP.***

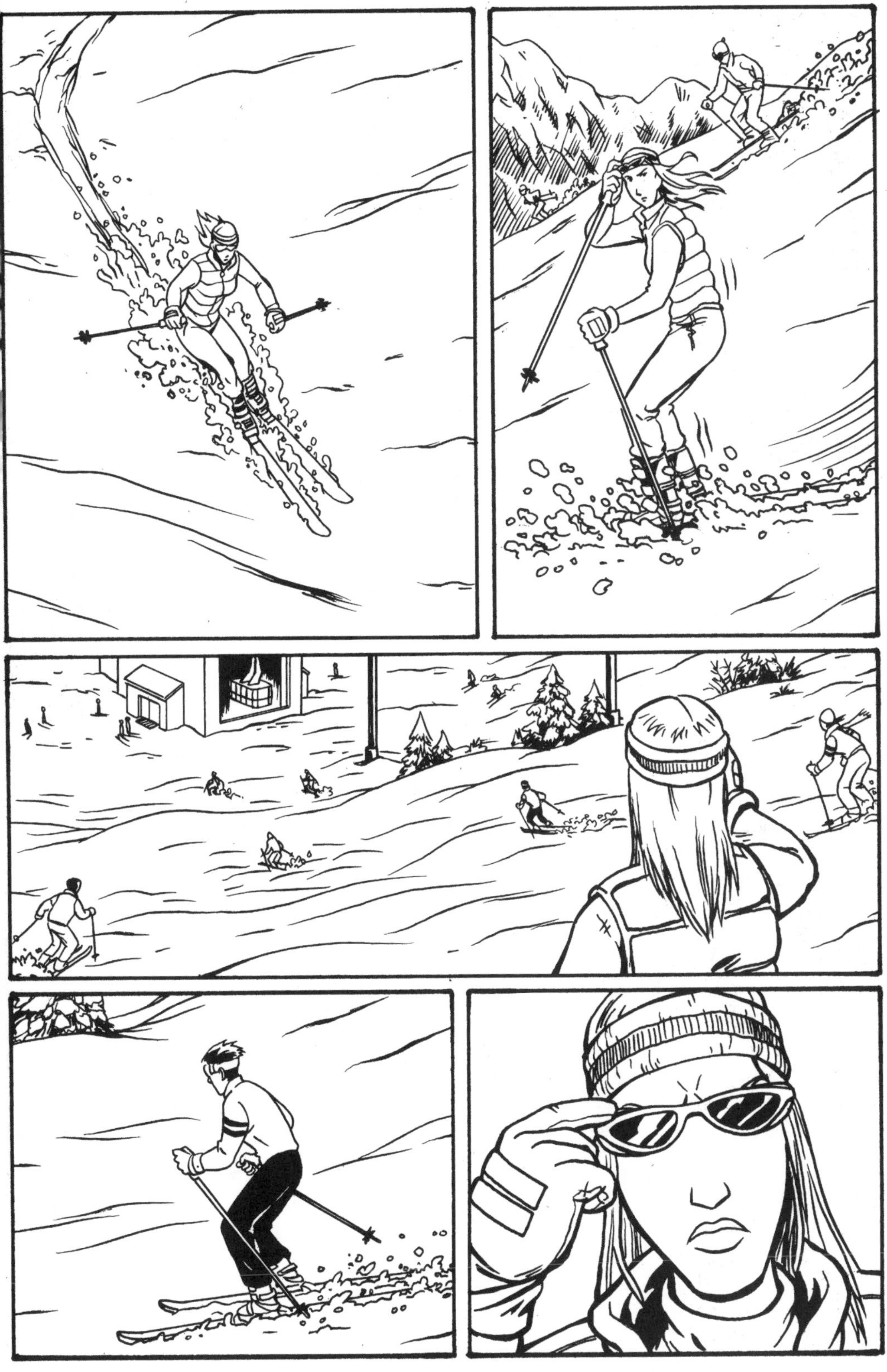

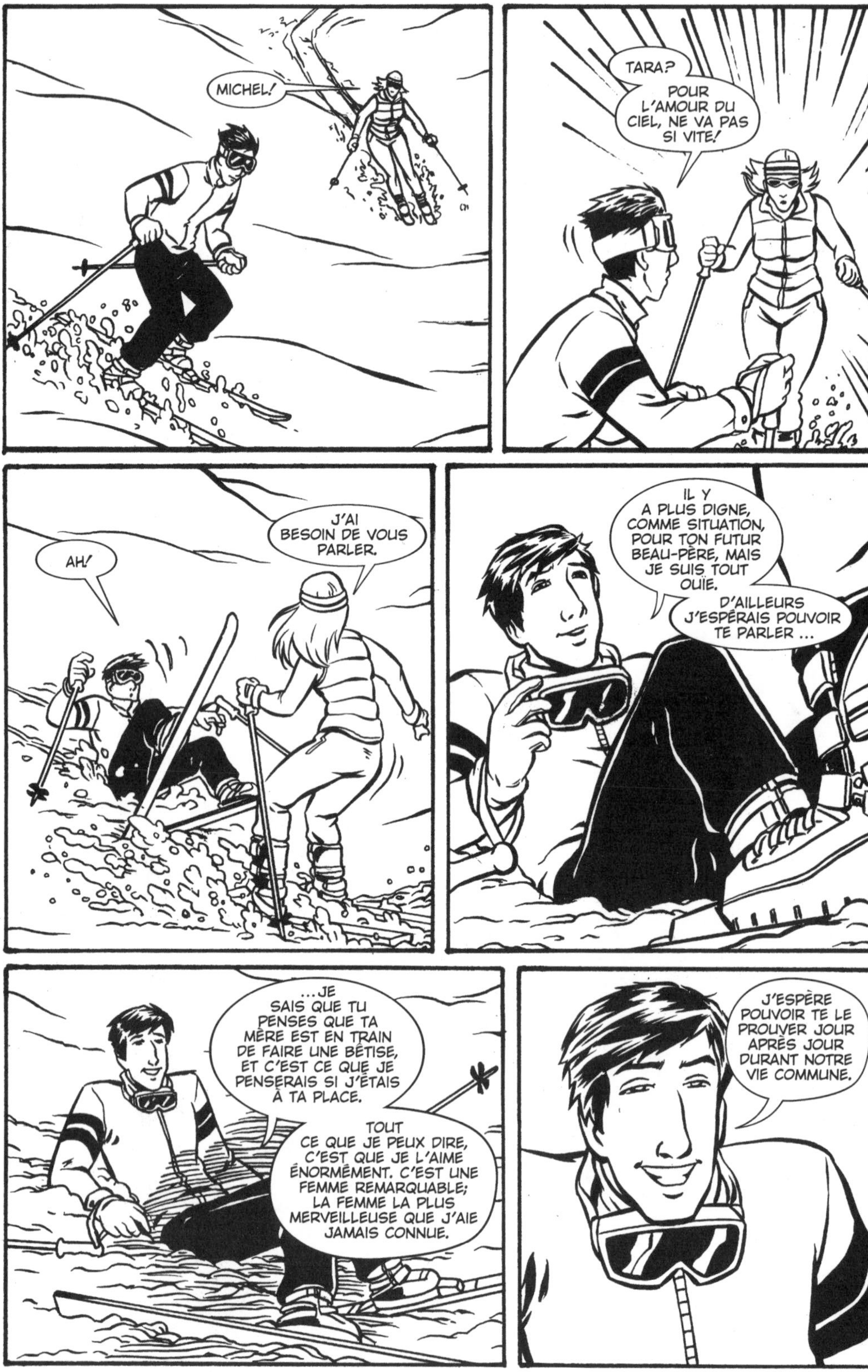
MICHEL!
TARA?
POUR L'AMOUR DU CIEL, NE VA PAS SI VITE!
AH!
J'AI BESOIN DE VOUS PARLER.
IL Y A PLUS DIGNE, COMME SITUATION, POUR TON FUTUR BEAU-PÈRE, MAIS JE SUIS TOUT OUÏE.
D'AILLEURS J'ESPÉRAIS POUVOIR TE PARLER ...
...JE SAIS QUE TU PENSES QUE TA MÈRE EST EN TRAIN DE FAIRE UNE BÊTISE, ET C'EST CE QUE JE PENSERAIS SI J'ÉTAIS À TA PLACE.
TOUT CE QUE JE PEUX DIRE, C'EST QUE JE L'AIME ÉNORMÉMENT. C'EST UNE FEMME REMARQUABLE; LA FEMME LA PLUS MERVEILLEUSE QUE J'AIE JAMAIS CONNUE.
J'ESPÈRE POUVOIR TE LE PROUVER JOUR APRÈS JOUR DURANT NOTRE VIE COMMUNE.

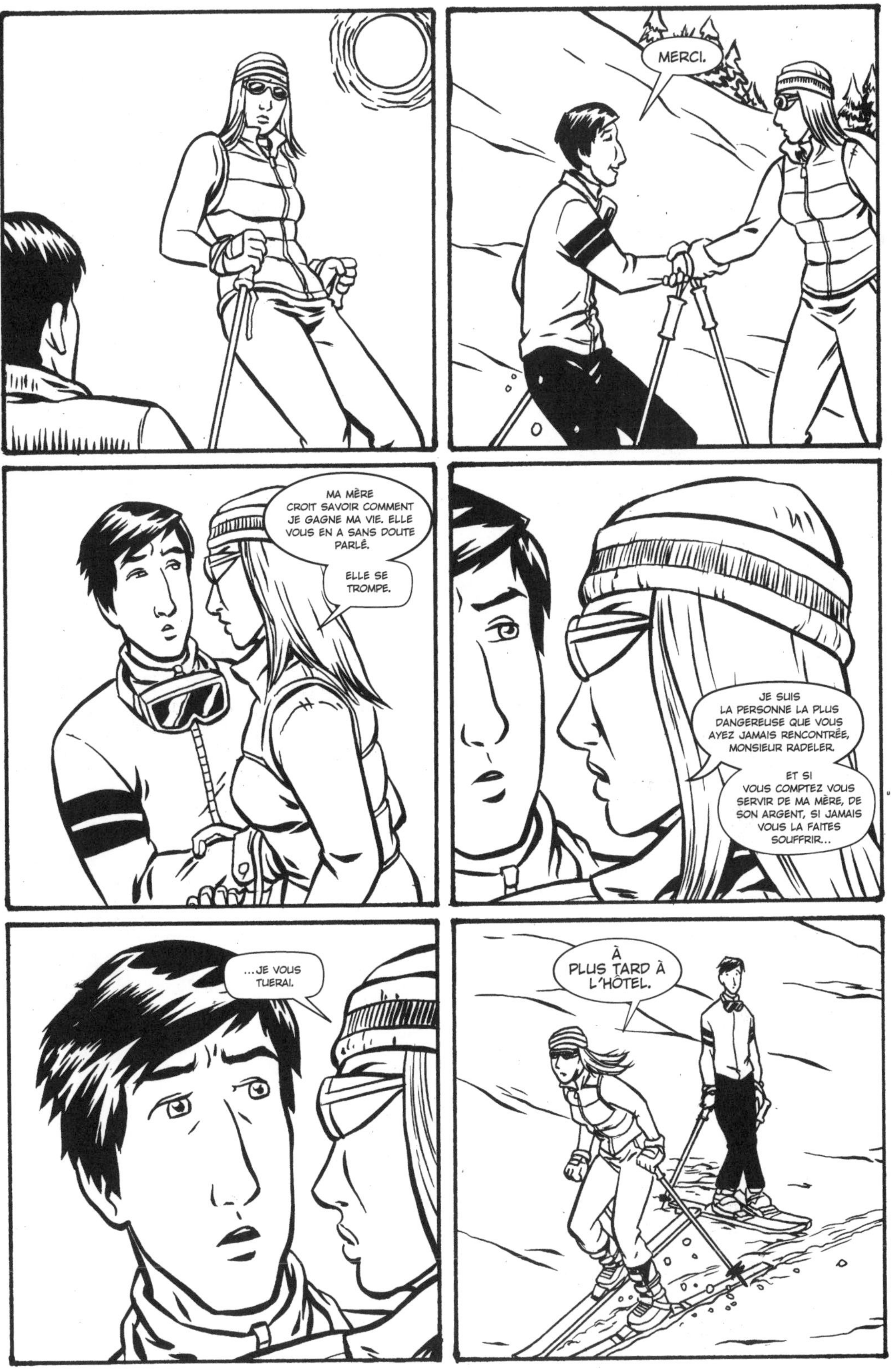
MERCI.
MA MÈRE CROIT SAVOIR COMMENT JE GAGNE MA VIE. ELLE VOUS EN A SANS DOUTE PARLÉ.
ELLE SE TROMPE.
JE SUIS LA PERSONNE LA PLUS DANGEREUSE QUE VOUS AYEZ JAMAIS RENCONTRÉE, MONSIEUR RADELER.
ET SI VOUS COMPTEZ VOUS SERVIR DE MA MÈRE, DE SON ARGENT, SI JAMAIS VOUS LA FAITES SOUFFRIR...
...JE VOUS TUERAI.
À PLUS TARD À L'HÔTEL.

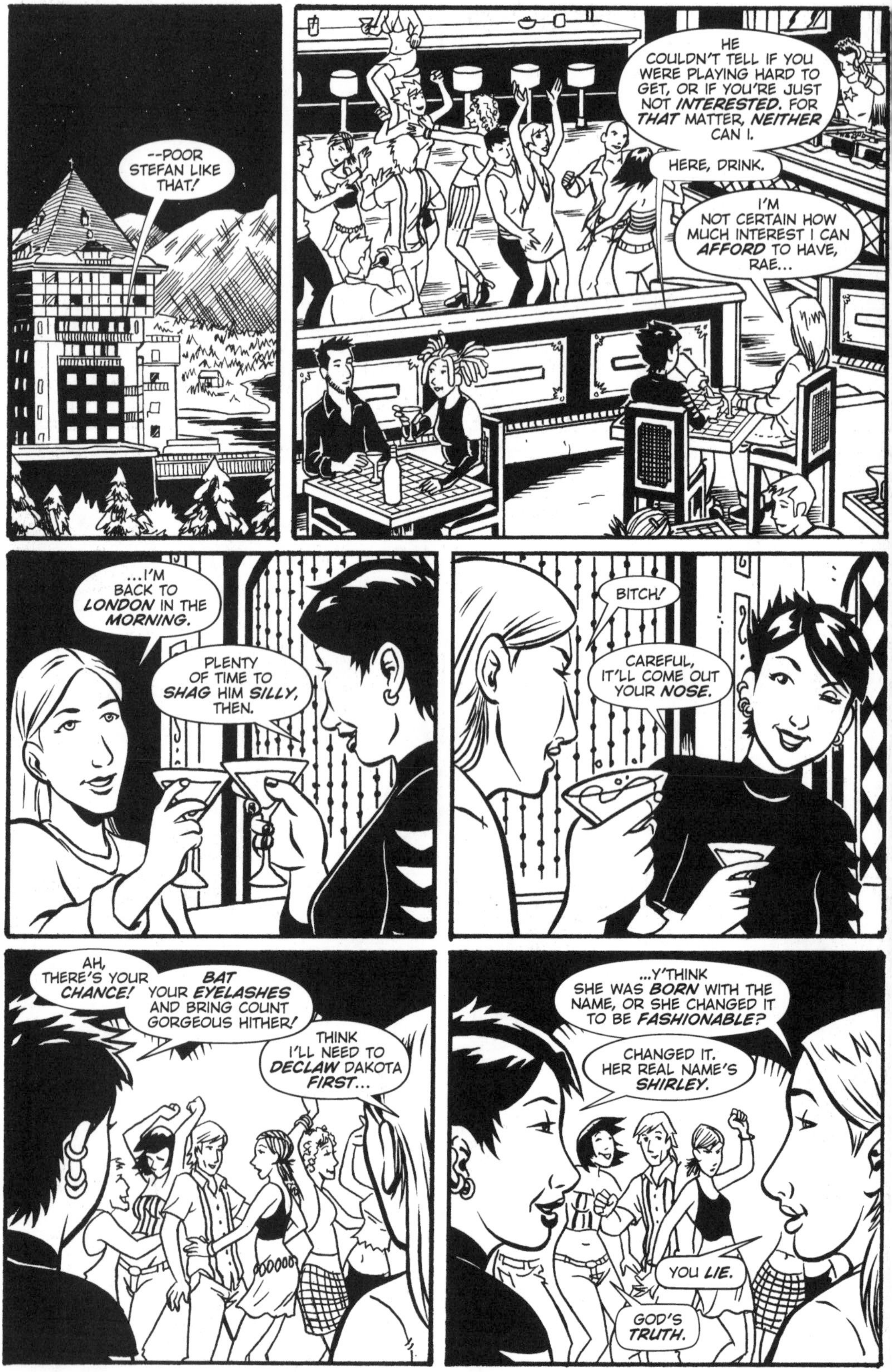
--POOR STEFAN LIKE THAT!
HE COULDN'T TELL IF YOU WERE PLAYING HARD TO GET, OR IF YOU'RE JUST NOT *INTERESTED*. FOR *THAT* MATTER, *NEITHER* CAN I.
HERE, DRINK.
I'M NOT CERTAIN HOW MUCH INTEREST I CAN *AFFORD* TO HAVE, RAE...
...I'M BACK TO *LONDON* IN THE *MORNING*.
PLENTY OF TIME TO *SHAG* HIM *SILLY*, THEN.
BITCH!
CAREFUL, IT'LL COME OUT YOUR *NOSE*.
AH, THERE'S YOUR *CHANCE!*
BAT YOUR *EYELASHES* AND BRING COUNT GORGEOUS HITHER!
THINK I'LL NEED TO *DECLAW* DAKOTA *FIRST*...
...Y'THINK SHE WAS *BORN* WITH THE NAME, OR SHE CHANGED IT TO BE *FASHIONABLE?*
CHANGED IT. HER REAL NAME'S *SHIRLEY*.
YOU *LIE*.
GOD'S *TRUTH*.

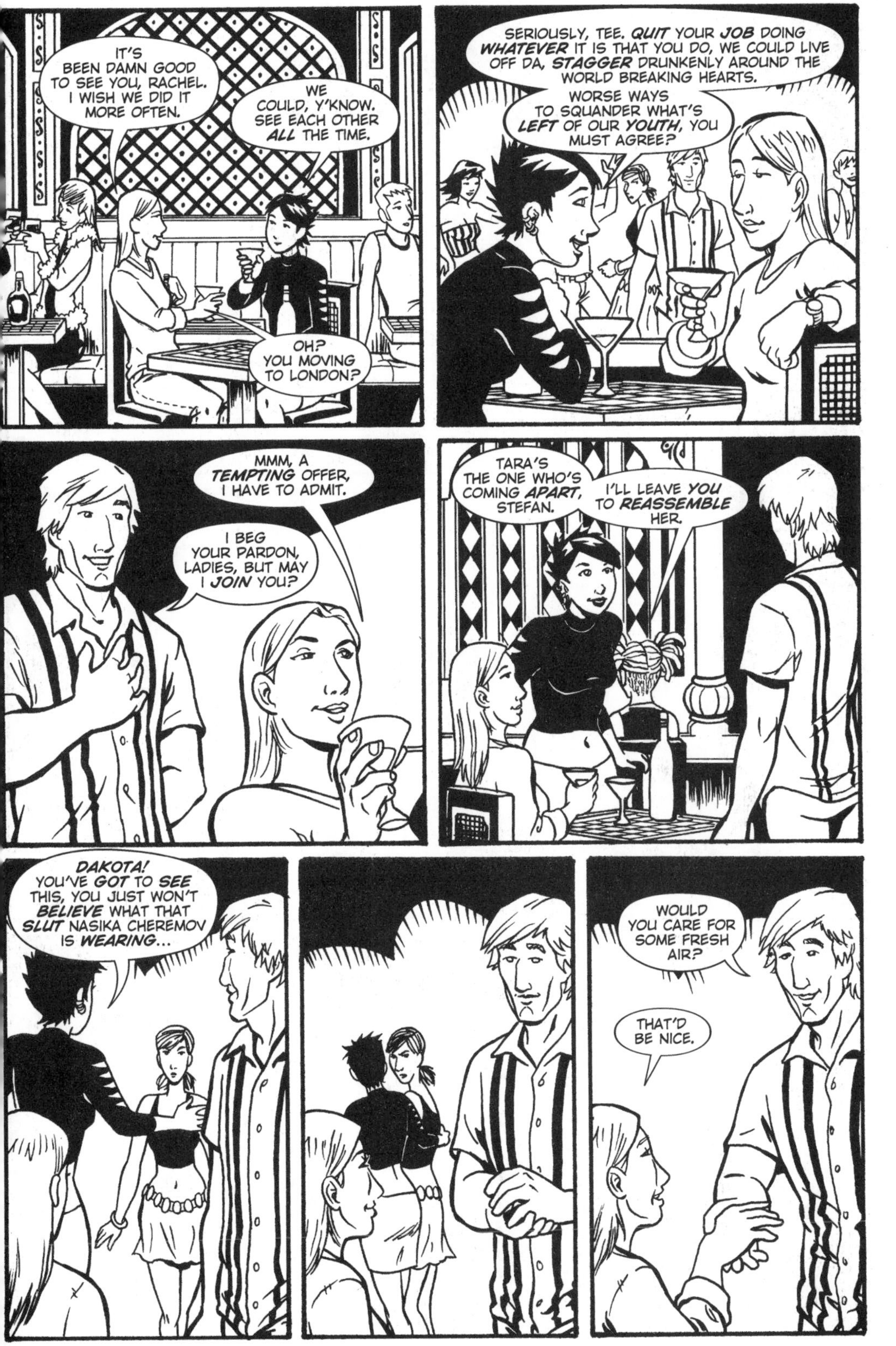
IT'S BEEN DAMN GOOD TO SEE YOU, RACHEL. I WISH WE DID IT MORE OFTEN.
WE COULD, Y'KNOW. SEE EACH OTHER ALL THE TIME.
OH? YOU MOVING TO LONDON?
SERIOUSLY, TEE. QUIT YOUR JOB DOING WHATEVER IT IS THAT YOU DO, WE COULD LIVE OFF DA, STAGGER DRUNKENLY AROUND THE WORLD BREAKING HEARTS.
WORSE WAYS TO SQUANDER WHAT'S LEFT OF OUR YOUTH, YOU MUST AGREE?
MMM, A TEMPTING OFFER, I HAVE TO ADMIT.
I BEG YOUR PARDON, LADIES, BUT MAY I JOIN YOU?
TARA'S THE ONE WHO'S COMING APART, STEFAN.
I'LL LEAVE YOU TO REASSEMBLE HER.
DAKOTA! YOU'VE GOT TO SEE THIS, YOU JUST WON'T BELIEVE WHAT THAT SLUT NASIKA CHEREMOV IS WEARING...
WOULD YOU CARE FOR SOME FRESH AIR?
THAT'D BE NICE.

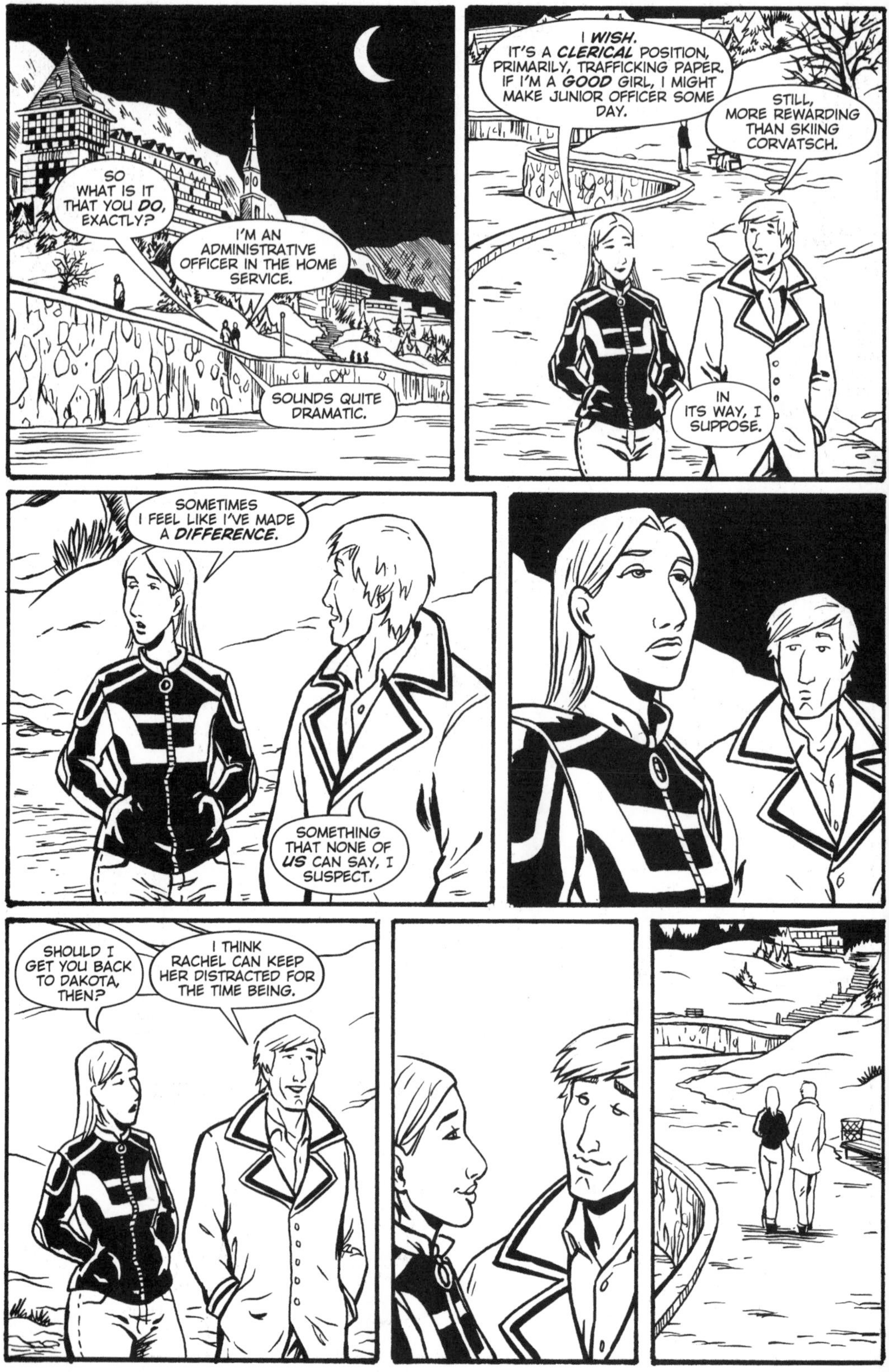
SO WHAT IS IT THAT YOU *DO*, EXACTLY?
I'M AN ADMINISTRATIVE OFFICER IN THE HOME SERVICE.
SOUNDS QUITE DRAMATIC.
I *WISH*. IT'S A *CLERICAL* POSITION, PRIMARILY, TRAFFICKING PAPER. IF I'M A *GOOD* GIRL, I MIGHT MAKE JUNIOR OFFICER SOME DAY.
STILL, MORE REWARDING THAN SKIING CORVATSCH.
IN ITS WAY, I SUPPOSE.
SOMETIMES I FEEL LIKE I'VE MADE A *DIFFERENCE*.
SOMETHING THAT NONE OF *US* CAN SAY, I SUSPECT.
SHOULD I GET YOU BACK TO DAKOTA, THEN?
I THINK RACHEL CAN KEEP HER DISTRACTED FOR THE TIME BEING.

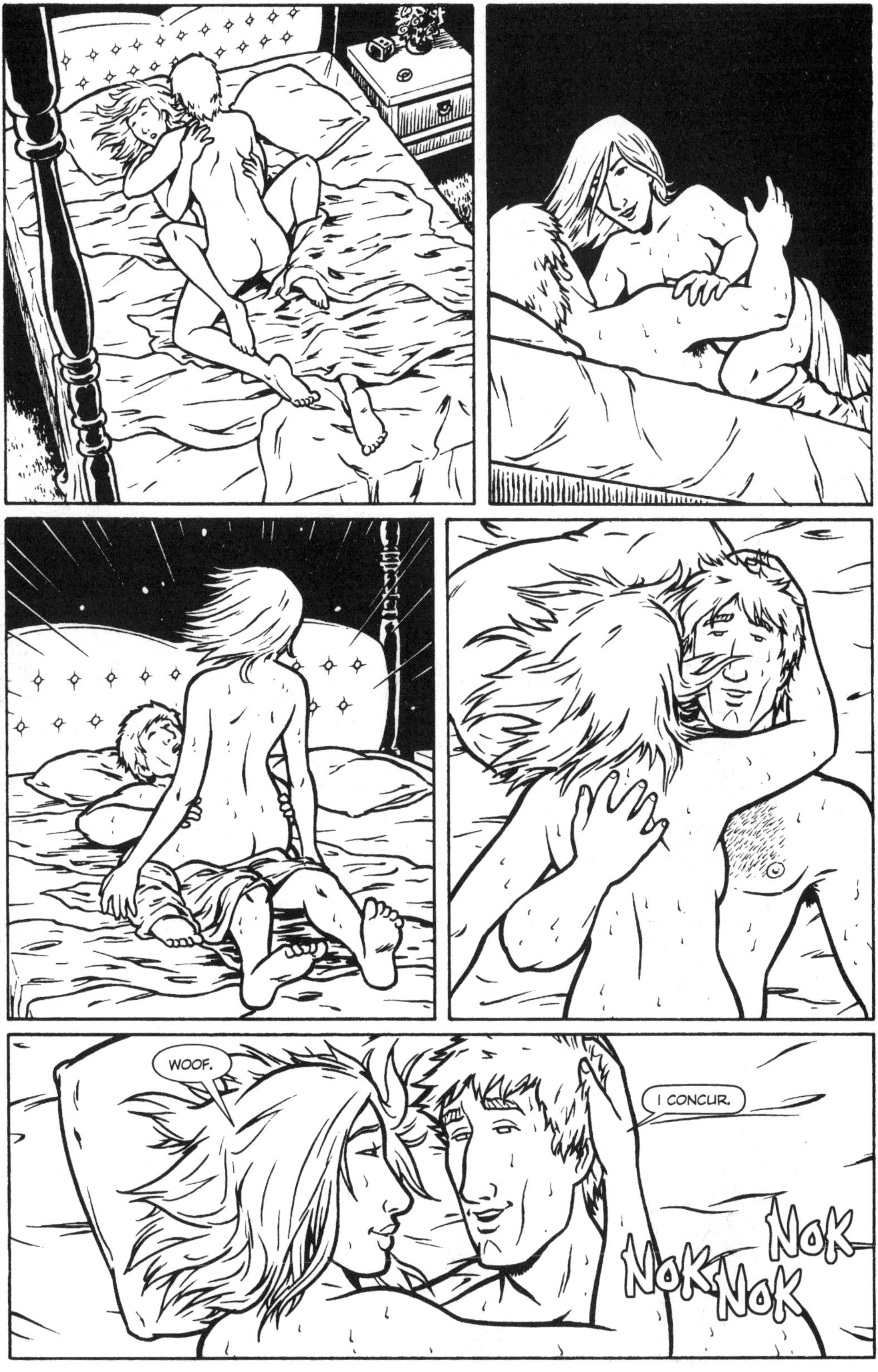
WOOF.
I CONCUR.
NOK
NOK NOK

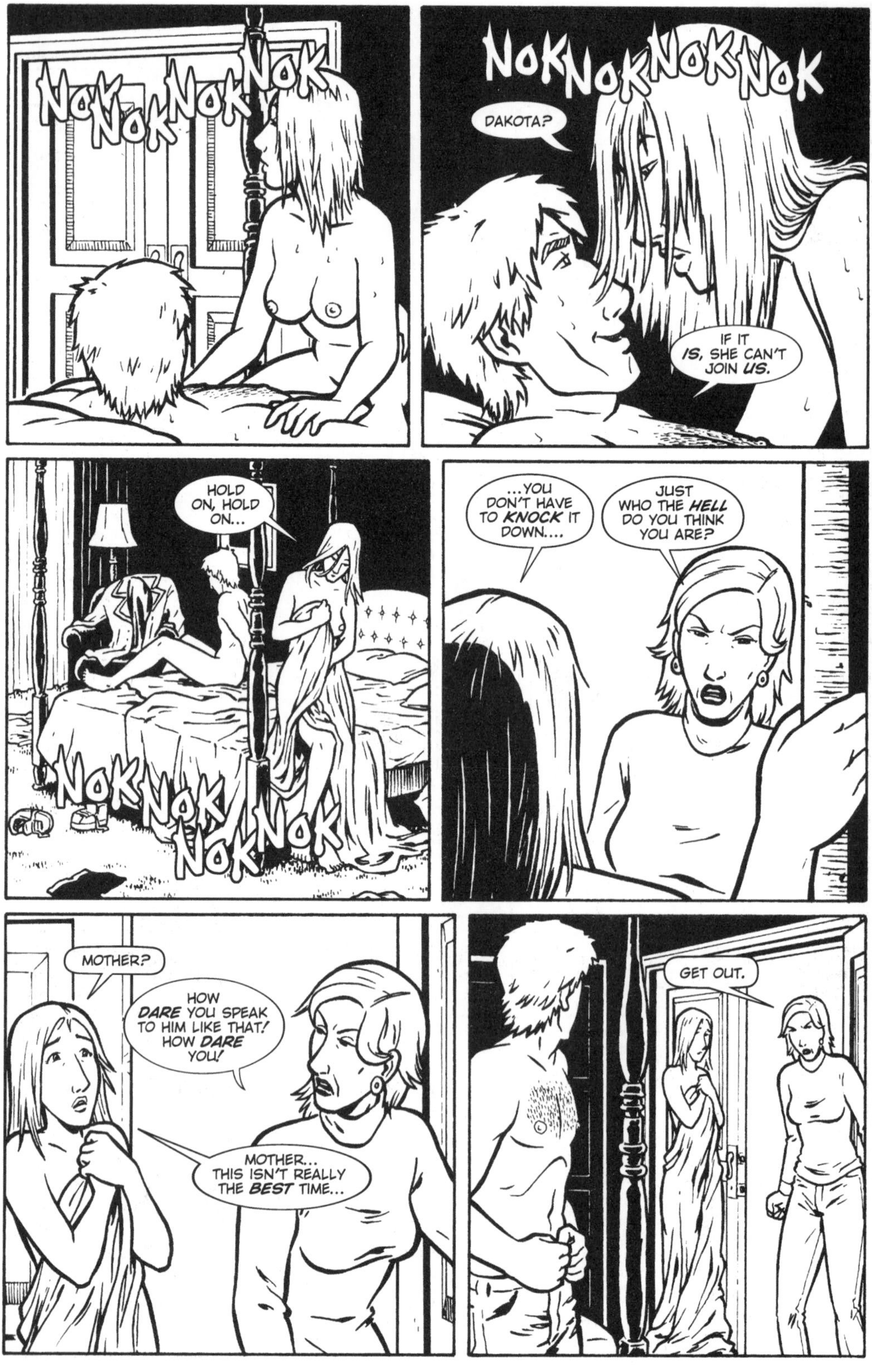
NOK NOK NOK NOK
NOK NOK NOK NOK
DAKOTA?
IF IT IS, SHE CAN'T JOIN US.
HOLD ON, HOLD ON...
NOK NOK NOK NOK
...YOU DON'T HAVE TO KNOCK IT DOWN....
JUST WHO THE HELL DO YOU THINK YOU ARE?
MOTHER?
HOW DARE YOU SPEAK TO HIM LIKE THAT! HOW DARE YOU!
MOTHER... THIS ISN'T REALLY THE BEST TIME...
GET OUT.

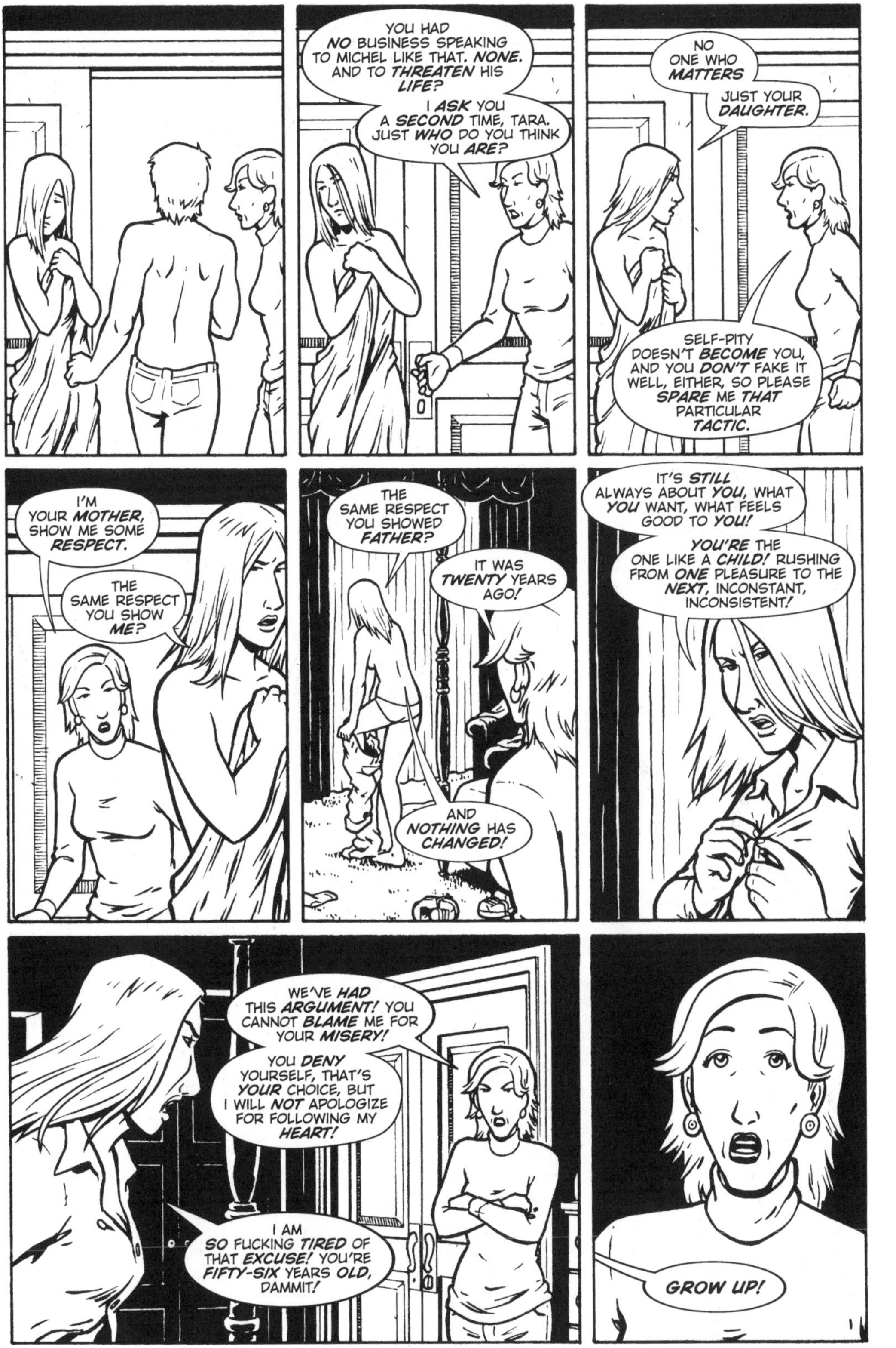
YOU HAD NO BUSINESS SPEAKING TO MICHEL LIKE THAT. NONE. AND TO THREATEN HIS LIFE?
I ASK YOU A SECOND TIME, TARA. JUST WHO DO YOU THINK YOU ARE?
NO ONE WHO MATTERS
JUST YOUR DAUGHTER.
SELF-PITY DOESN'T BECOME YOU, AND YOU DON'T FAKE IT WELL, EITHER, SO PLEASE SPARE ME THAT PARTICULAR TACTIC.
I'M YOUR MOTHER, SHOW ME SOME RESPECT.
THE SAME RESPECT YOU SHOW ME?
THE SAME RESPECT YOU SHOWED FATHER?
IT WAS TWENTY YEARS AGO!
AND NOTHING HAS CHANGED!
IT'S STILL ALWAYS ABOUT YOU, WHAT YOU WANT, WHAT FEELS GOOD TO YOU!
YOU'RE THE ONE LIKE A CHILD! RUSHING FROM ONE PLEASURE TO THE NEXT, INCONSTANT, INCONSISTENT!
WE'VE HAD THIS ARGUMENT! YOU CANNOT BLAME ME FOR YOUR MISERY!
YOU DENY YOURSELF, THAT'S YOUR CHOICE, BUT I WILL NOT APOLOGIZE FOR FOLLOWING MY HEART!
I AM SO FUCKING TIRED OF THAT EXCUSE! YOU'RE FIFTY-SIX YEARS OLD, DAMMIT!
GROW UP!

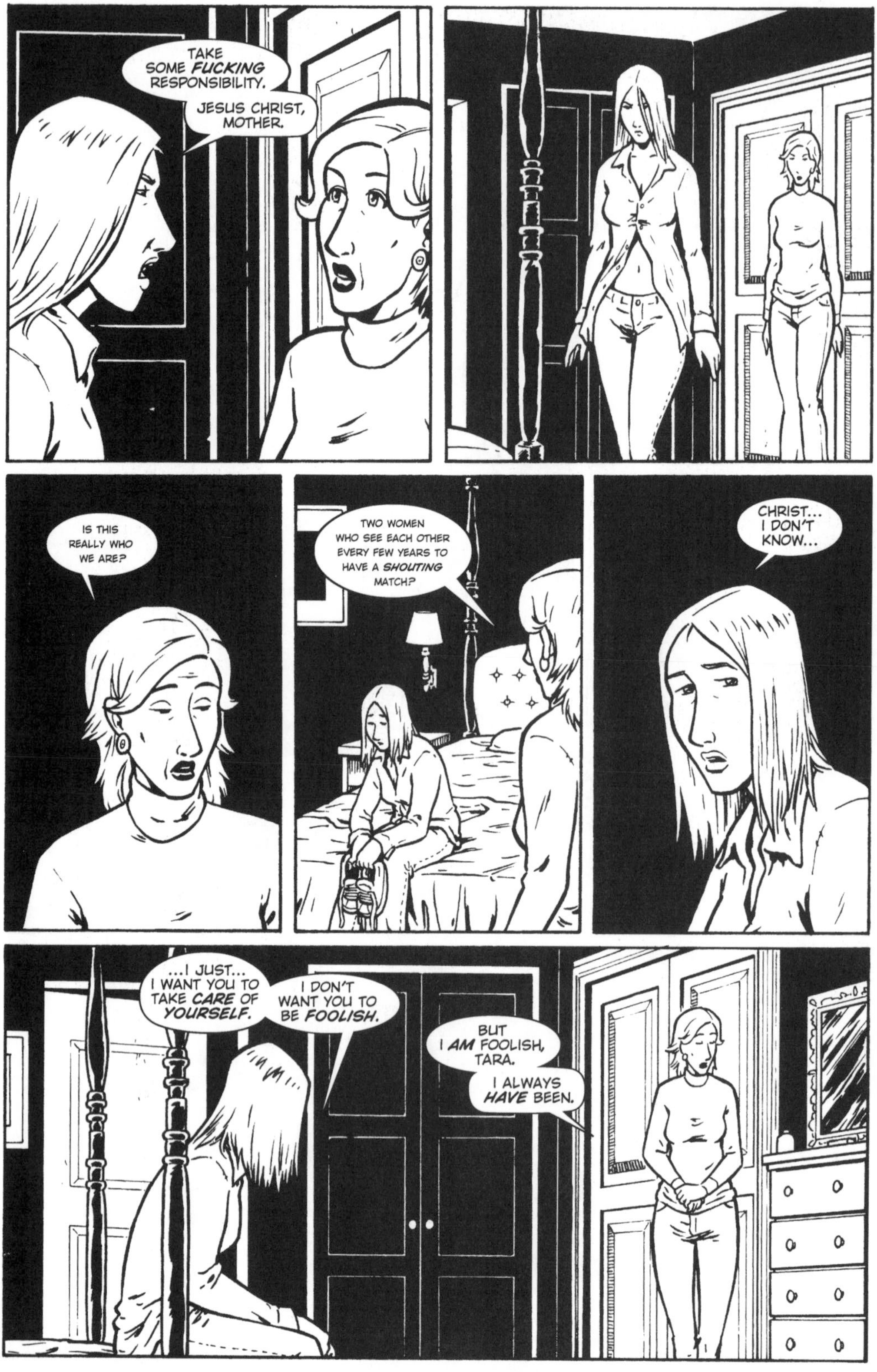
TAKE SOME FUCKING RESPONSIBILITY.
JESUS CHRIST, MOTHER.
IS THIS REALLY WHO WE ARE?
TWO WOMEN WHO SEE EACH OTHER EVERY FEW YEARS TO HAVE A SHOUTING MATCH?
CHRIST... I DON'T KNOW...
...I JUST... I WANT YOU TO TAKE CARE OF YOURSELF.
I DON'T WANT YOU TO BE FOOLISH.
BUT I AM FOOLISH, TARA.
I ALWAYS HAVE BEEN.

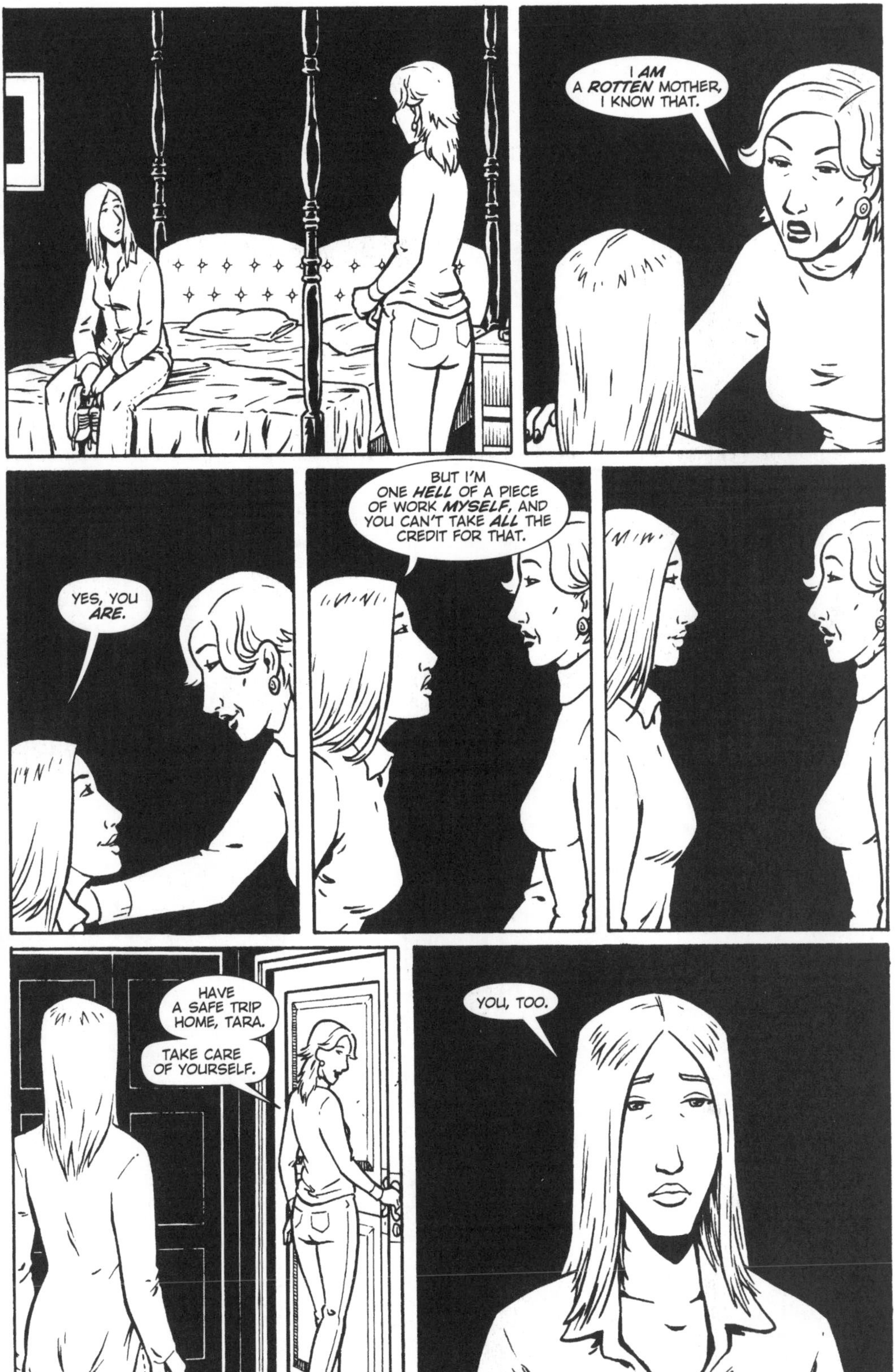
I AM A ROTTEN MOTHER, I KNOW THAT.
YES, YOU ARE.
BUT I'M ONE HELL OF A PIECE OF WORK MYSELF, AND YOU CAN'T TAKE ALL THE CREDIT FOR THAT.
HAVE A SAFE TRIP HOME, TARA.
TAKE CARE OF YOURSELF.
YOU, TOO.

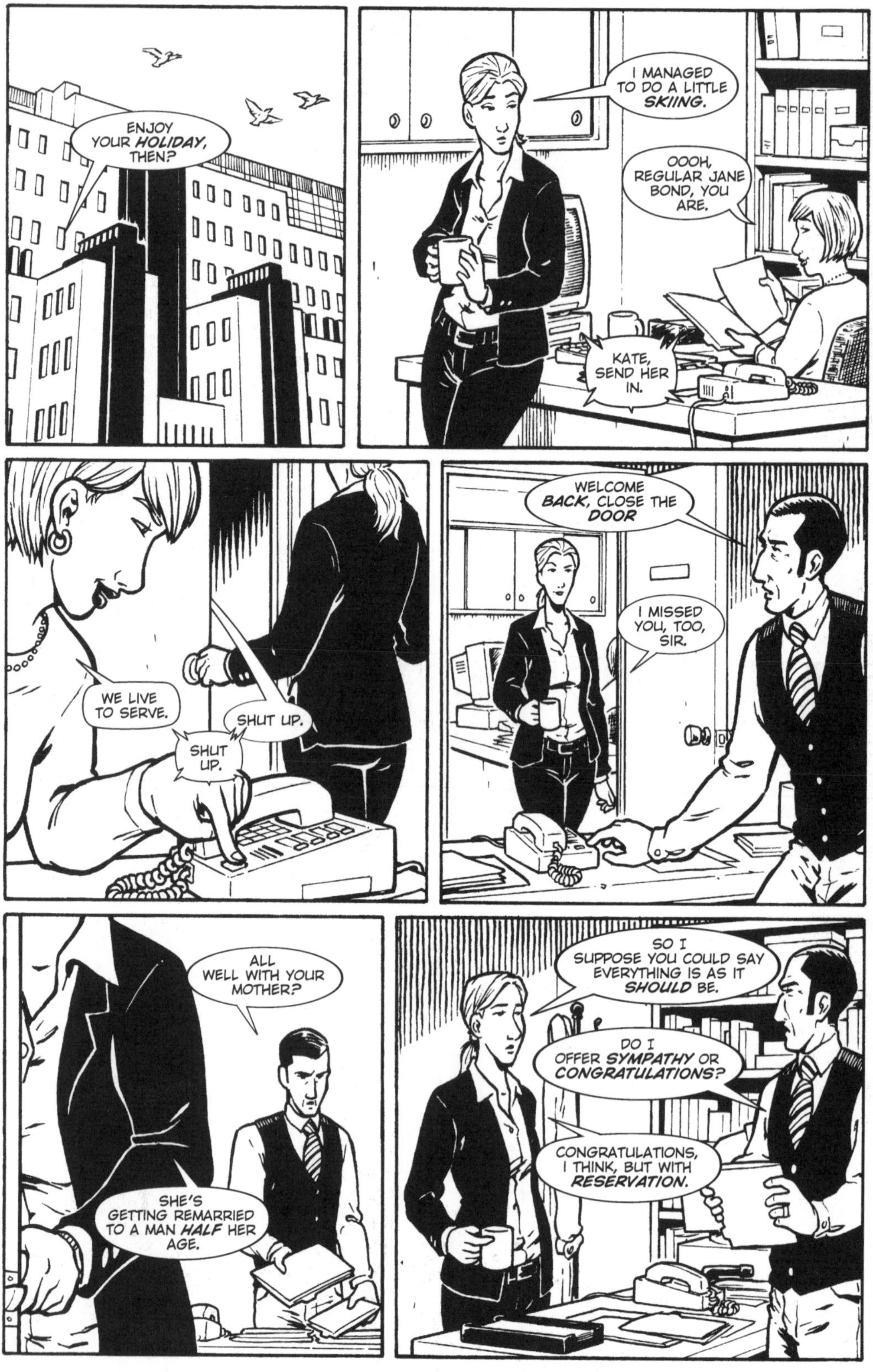
ENJOY YOUR HOLIDAY, THEN?
I MANAGED TO DO A LITTLE SKIING.
OOOH, REGULAR JANE BOND, YOU ARE.
KATE, SEND HER IN.
WE LIVE TO SERVE.
SHUT UP.
SHUT UP.
WELCOME BACK, CLOSE THE DOOR
I MISSED YOU, TOO, SIR.
ALL WELL WITH YOUR MOTHER?
SHE'S GETTING REMARRIED TO A MAN HALF HER AGE.
SO I SUPPOSE YOU COULD SAY EVERYTHING IS AS IT SHOULD BE.
DO I OFFER SYMPATHY OR CONGRATULATIONS?
CONGRATULATIONS, I THINK, BUT WITH RESERVATION.

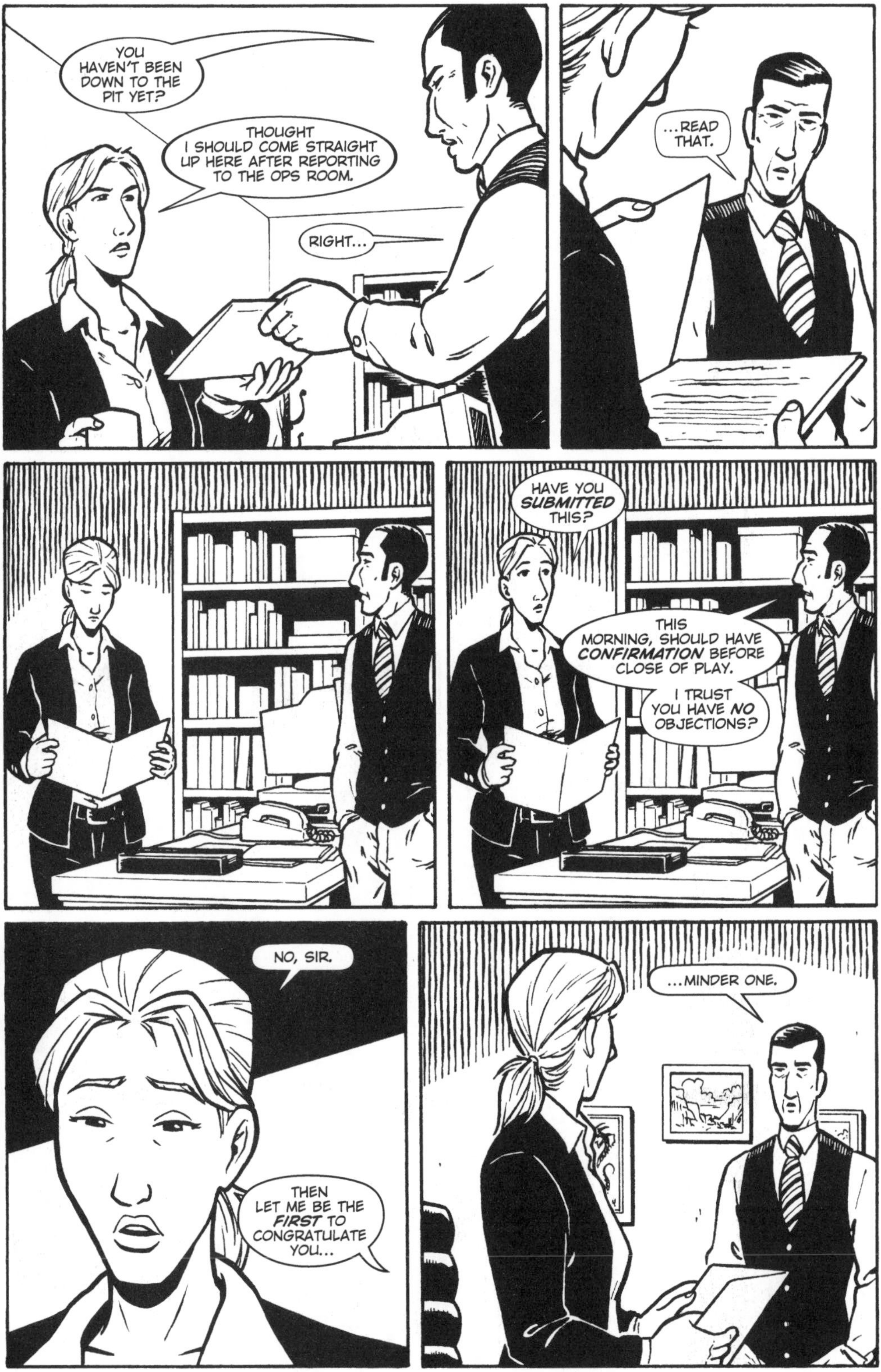
YOU HAVEN'T BEEN DOWN TO THE PIT YET?
THOUGHT I SHOULD COME STRAIGHT UP HERE AFTER REPORTING TO THE OPS ROOM.
RIGHT...
...READ THAT.
HAVE YOU *SUBMITTED* THIS?
THIS MORNING, SHOULD HAVE *CONFIRMATION* BEFORE CLOSE OF PLAY.
I TRUST YOU HAVE *NO* OBJECTIONS?
NO, SIR.
THEN LET ME BE THE *FIRST* TO CONGRATULATE YOU...
...MINDER ONE.

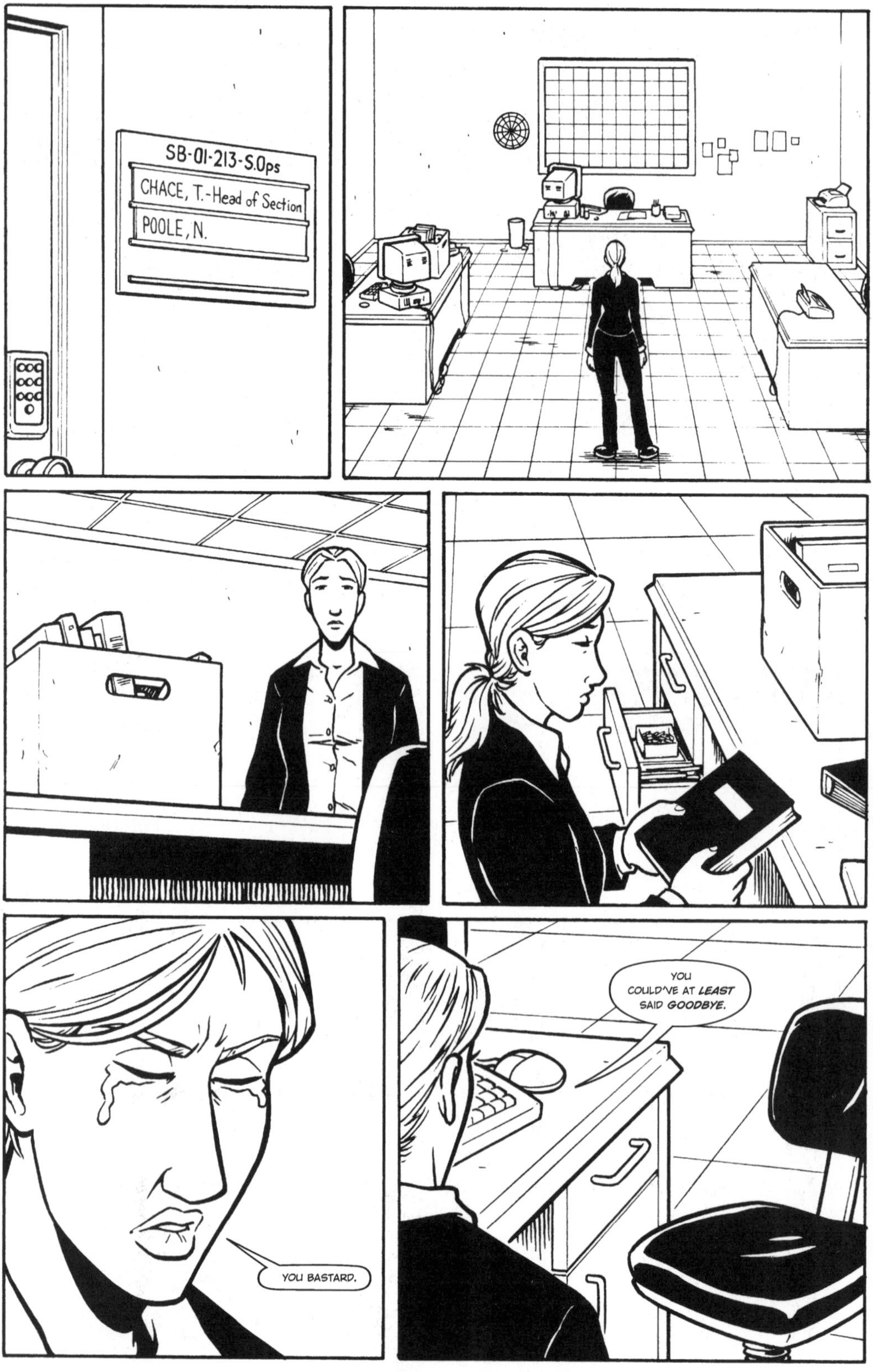
SB-01-213-S.Ops
CHACE, T.-Head of Section
POOLE, N.
YOU BASTARD.
YOU COULD'VE AT *LEAST* SAID *GOODBYE*.

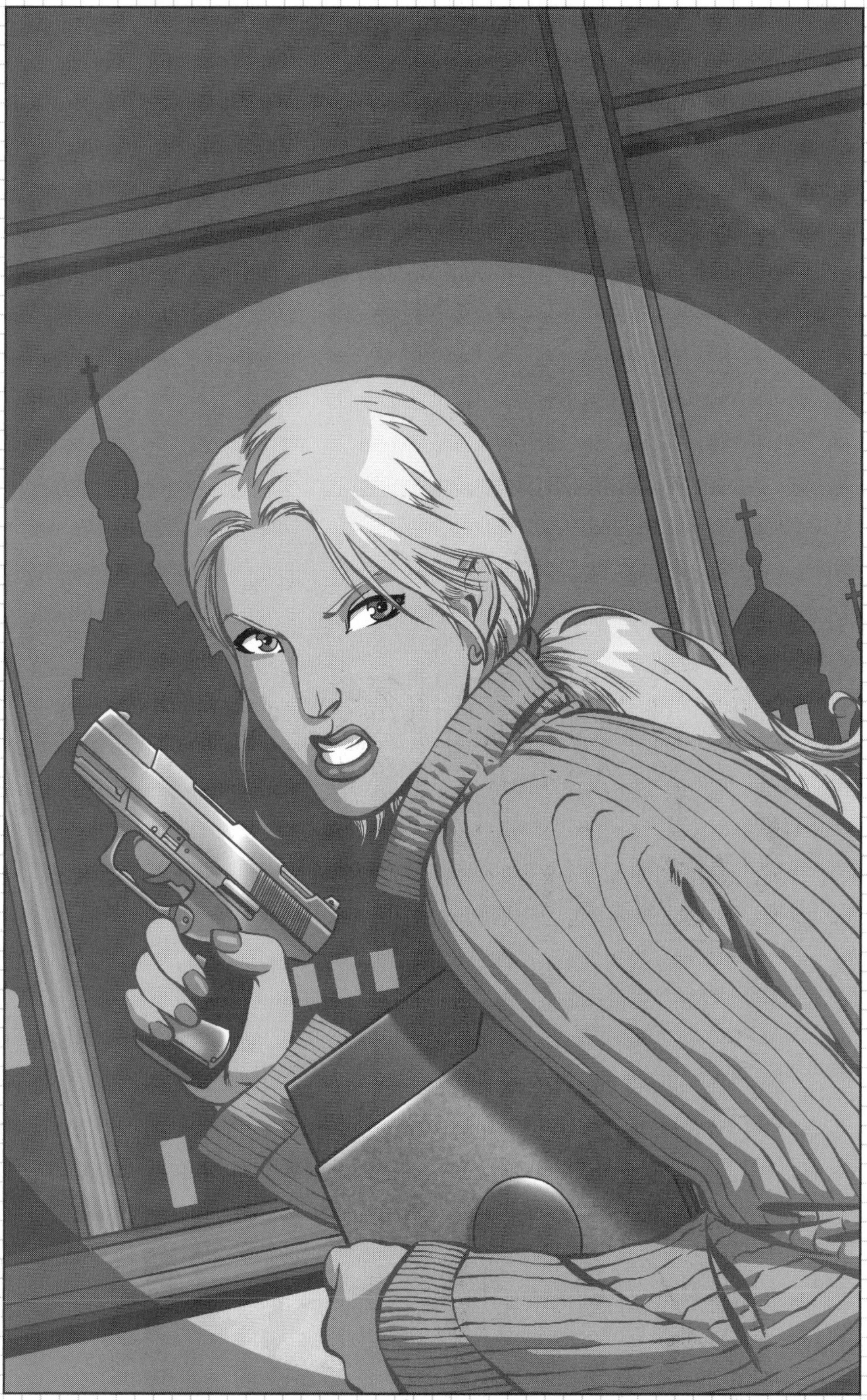

CHAPTER 1

ROSTER

TARA CHACE—Head of Special Section, designated Minder One.

FRANCES BARCLAY—Chief of Service, also known as "C." Distinguished service as CIA-Liaison, Chairman of the Joint Intelligence Committee, and as Head of Station Prague (85-88), Saigon (89-91), and Paris (91-94).

CHRIS LANKFORD—The fourth man to hold the title of Minder Three in less than 18 months. Untested, Lankford's yet to spend significant time in the field.

PAUL CROCKER—Director of Operations, encompassing all field work in all theaters of operations. In addition to commanding individual stations, he has direct command of the Special Section–sometimes referred to as Minders–used for special operations.

NICK POOLE—Former S.A.S. and recently christened Minder Two.

DONALD WELDON—Deputy Chief of Service, has oversight of all aspects of Intelligence gathering and operations. Immediate superior to Crocker.

OPS ROOM STAFF   OTHERS

ALEXIS—Mission Control Officer (also called Main Communications Officer)– responsible for maintaining communications between the Operations Room and the agents in the field.

RON—Duty Operations Officer, responsible for monitoring the status and importance of all incoming intelligence, both from foreign stations and other sources.

KATE—Personal Assistant to Paul Crocker, termed PA to D.Ops. Possibly the hardest and most important job in the Service.

TOM WALLACE—Former Head of Special Section and mentor of Tara Chace. Recently opted out of the Section in favor of a new career with a higher life expectancy.

EDWARD KITTERING—Special Operations Officer, designated Minder Three. Has been with the Special Section for less than a year.

BRIAN BUTLER—A former sergeant in one of the British Army's oldest and most respected regiments. A unique individual who actually requested assignment with special section.

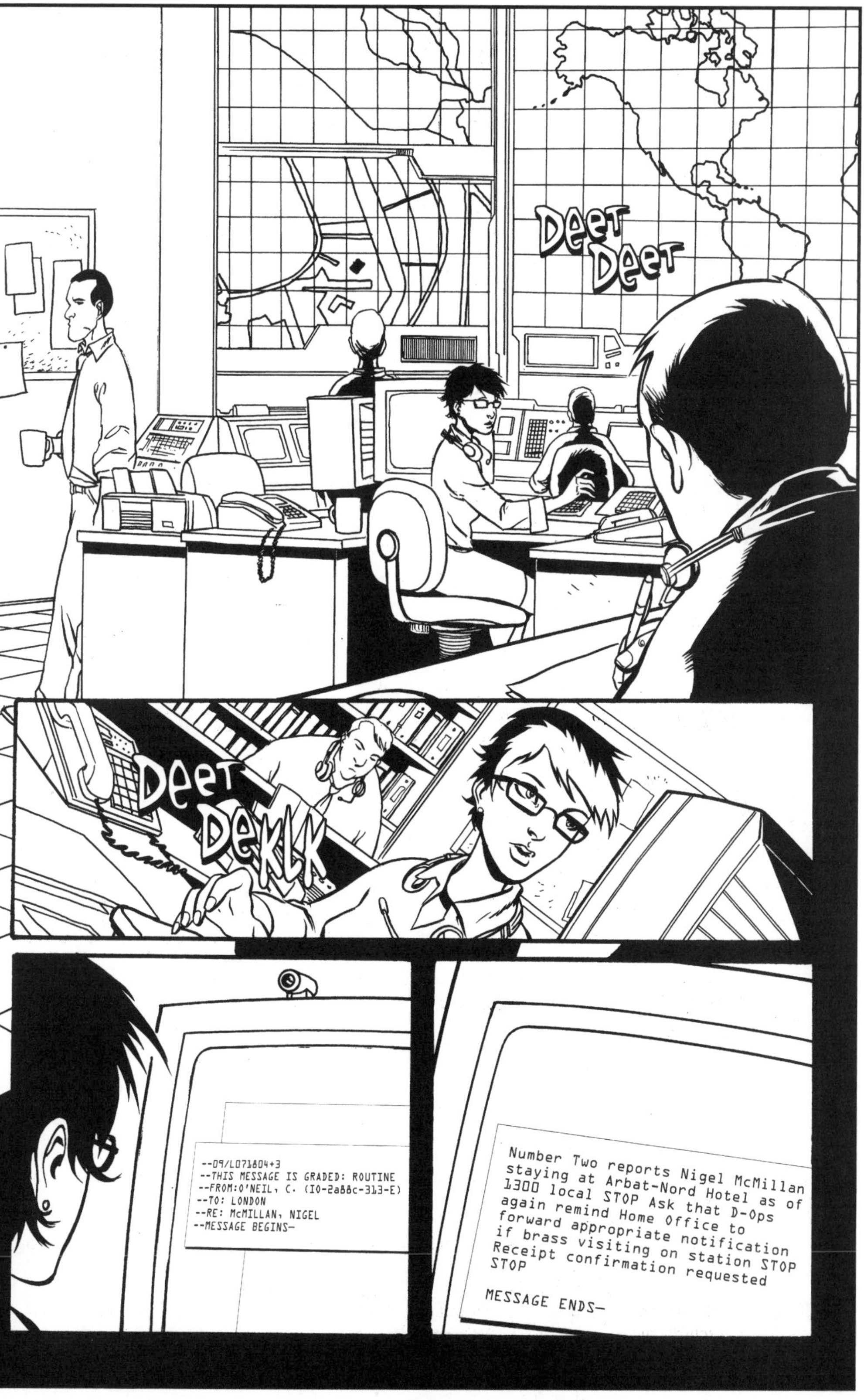
DEET DEET
DEET DEKLK
--09/L071804+3
--THIS MESSAGE IS GRADED: ROUTINE
--FROM:O'NEIL, C. (IO-2a88c-313-E)
--TO: LONDON
--RE: McMILLAN, NIGEL
--MESSAGE BEGINS—
Number Two reports Nigel McMillan staying at Arbat-Nord Hotel as of 1300 local STOP Ask that D-Ops again remind Home Office to forward appropriate notification if brass visiting on station STOP Receipt confirmation requested STOP
MESSAGE ENDS—

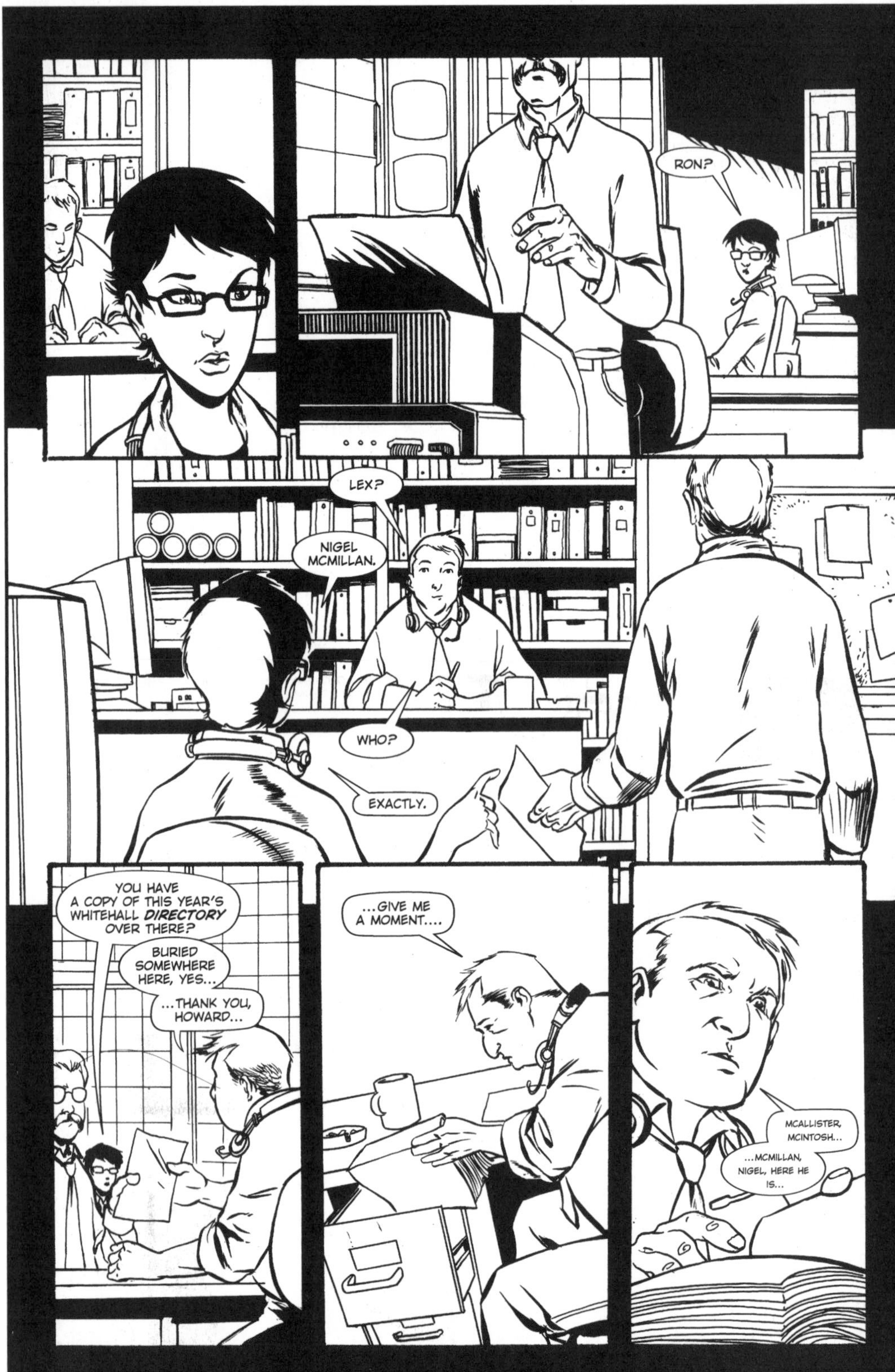

RON?
LEX?
NIGEL MCMILLAN.
WHO?
EXACTLY.
YOU HAVE A COPY OF THIS YEAR'S WHITEHALL *DIRECTORY* OVER THERE?
BURIED SOMEWHERE HERE, YES...
...THANK YOU, HOWARD...
...GIVE ME A MOMENT....
MCALLISTER, MCINTOSH...
...MCMILLAN, NIGEL, HERE HE IS...

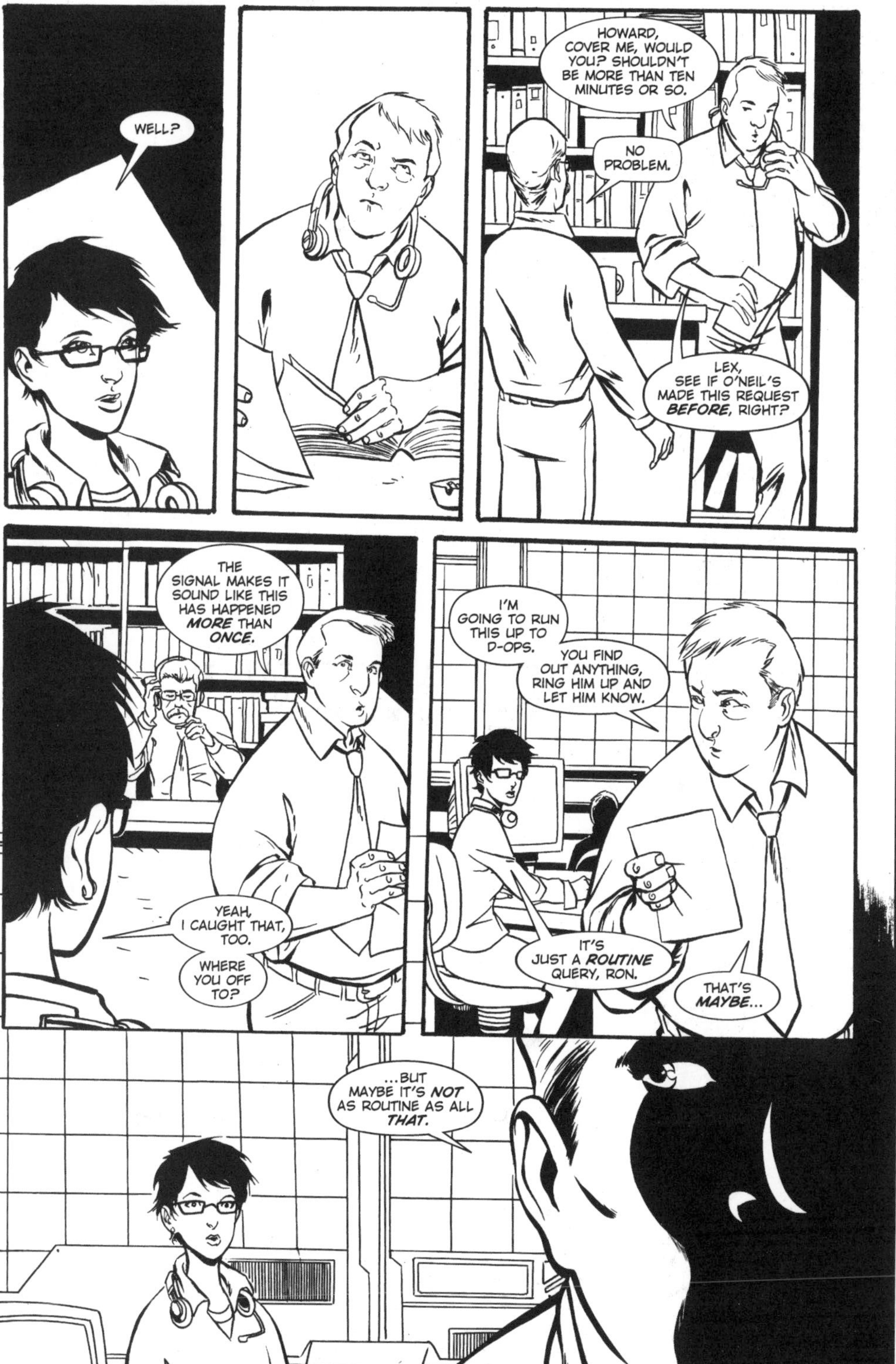
WELL?
HOWARD, COVER ME, WOULD YOU? SHOULDN'T BE MORE THAN TEN MINUTES OR SO.
NO PROBLEM.
LEX, SEE IF O'NEIL'S MADE THIS REQUEST BEFORE, RIGHT?
THE SIGNAL MAKES IT SOUND LIKE THIS HAS HAPPENED MORE THAN ONCE.
YEAH, I CAUGHT THAT, TOO.
WHERE YOU OFF TO?
I'M GOING TO RUN THIS UP TO D-OPS.
YOU FIND OUT ANYTHING, RING HIM UP AND LET HIM KNOW.
IT'S JUST A ROUTINE QUERY, RON.
THAT'S MAYBE...
...BUT MAYBE IT'S NOT AS ROUTINE AS ALL THAT.

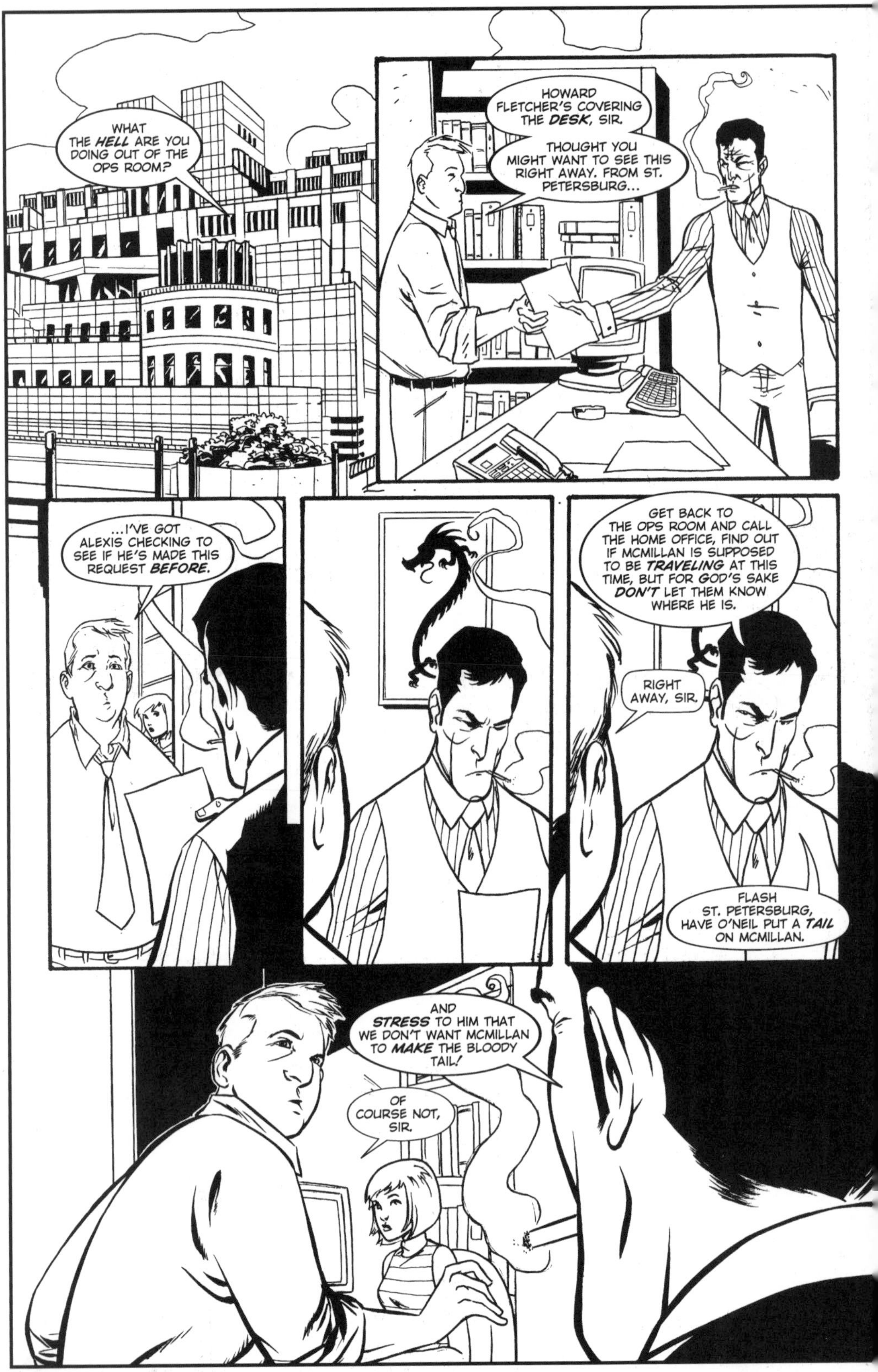
WHAT THE HELL ARE YOU DOING OUT OF THE OPS ROOM?
HOWARD FLETCHER'S COVERING THE DESK, SIR.
THOUGHT YOU MIGHT WANT TO SEE THIS RIGHT AWAY. FROM ST. PETERSBURG...
...I'VE GOT ALEXIS CHECKING TO SEE IF HE'S MADE THIS REQUEST BEFORE.
GET BACK TO THE OPS ROOM AND CALL THE HOME OFFICE, FIND OUT IF MCMILLAN IS SUPPOSED TO BE TRAVELING AT THIS TIME, BUT FOR GOD'S SAKE DON'T LET THEM KNOW WHERE HE IS.
RIGHT AWAY, SIR.
FLASH ST. PETERSBURG, HAVE O'NEIL PUT A TAIL ON MCMILLAN.
AND STRESS TO HIM THAT WE DON'T WANT MCMILLAN TO MAKE THE BLOODY TAIL!
OF COURSE NOT, SIR.

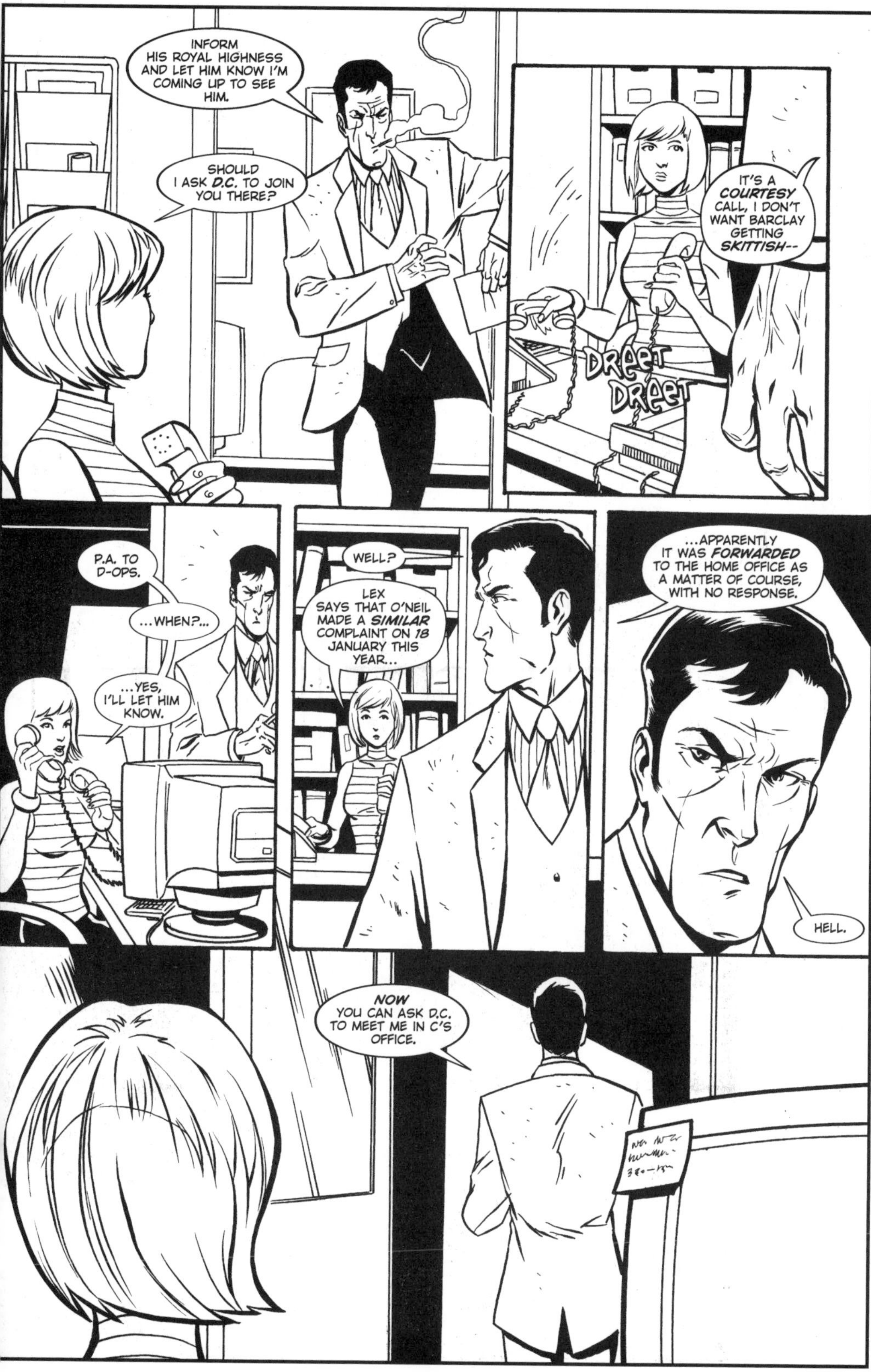
INFORM HIS ROYAL HIGHNESS AND LET HIM KNOW I'M COMING UP TO SEE HIM.
SHOULD I ASK D.C. TO JOIN YOU THERE?
IT'S A COURTESY CALL, I DON'T WANT BARCLAY GETTING SKITTISH--
DREET DREET
P.A. TO D-OPS.
...WHEN?...
...YES, I'LL LET HIM KNOW.
WELL?
LEX SAYS THAT O'NEIL MADE A SIMILAR COMPLAINT ON 18 JANUARY THIS YEAR...
...APPARENTLY IT WAS FORWARDED TO THE HOME OFFICE AS A MATTER OF COURSE, WITH NO RESPONSE.
HELL.
NOW YOU CAN ASK D.C. TO MEET ME IN C'S OFFICE.

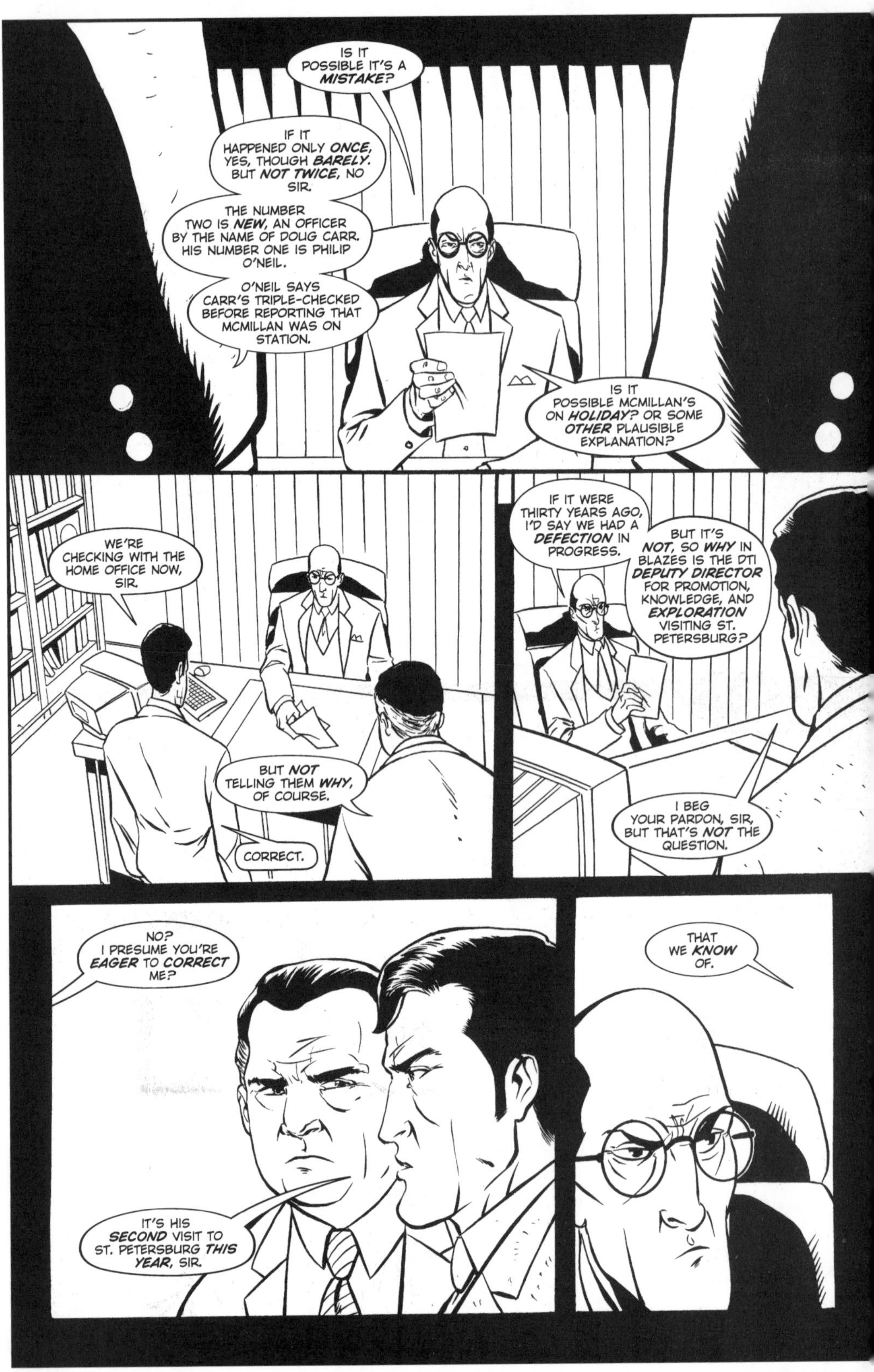
IS IT POSSIBLE IT'S A MISTAKE?
IF IT HAPPENED ONLY ONCE, YES, THOUGH BARELY. BUT NOT TWICE, NO SIR.
THE NUMBER TWO IS NEW, AN OFFICER BY THE NAME OF DOUG CARR. HIS NUMBER ONE IS PHILIP O'NEIL.
O'NEIL SAYS CARR'S TRIPLE-CHECKED BEFORE REPORTING THAT MCMILLAN WAS ON STATION.
IS IT POSSIBLE MCMILLAN'S ON HOLIDAY? OR SOME OTHER PLAUSIBLE EXPLANATION?
WE'RE CHECKING WITH THE HOME OFFICE NOW, SIR.
BUT NOT TELLING THEM WHY, OF COURSE.
CORRECT.
IF IT WERE THIRTY YEARS AGO, I'D SAY WE HAD A DEFECTION IN PROGRESS.
BUT IT'S NOT, SO WHY IN BLAZES IS THE DTI DEPUTY DIRECTOR FOR PROMOTION, KNOWLEDGE, AND EXPLORATION VISITING ST. PETERSBURG?
I BEG YOUR PARDON, SIR, BUT THAT'S NOT THE QUESTION.
NO? I PRESUME YOU'RE EAGER TO CORRECT ME?
IT'S HIS SECOND VISIT TO ST. PETERSBURG THIS YEAR, SIR.
THAT WE KNOW OF.

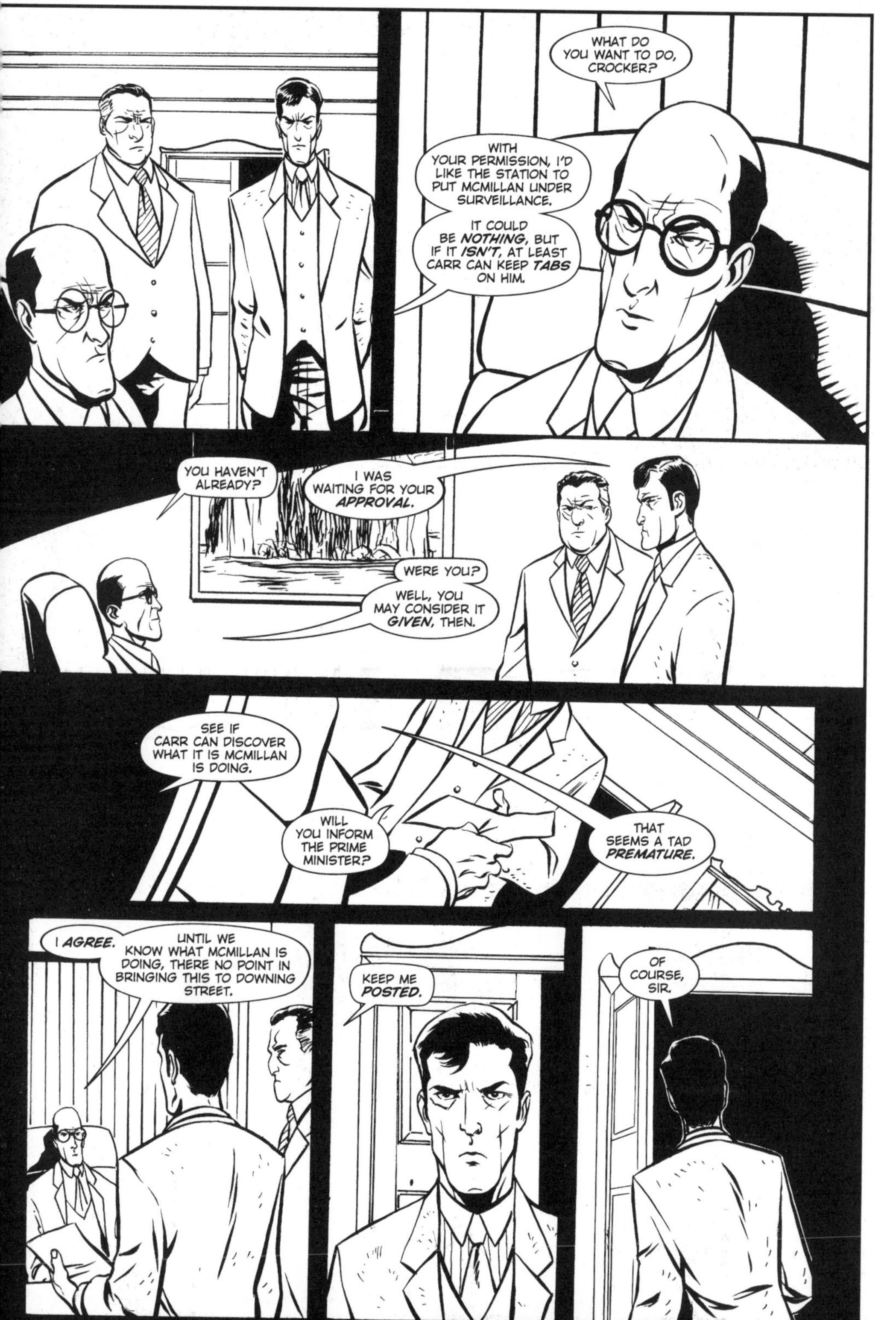
WHAT DO YOU WANT TO DO, CROCKER?
WITH YOUR PERMISSION, I'D LIKE THE STATION TO PUT MCMILLAN UNDER SURVEILLANCE.
IT COULD BE NOTHING, BUT IF IT ISN'T, AT LEAST CARR CAN KEEP TABS ON HIM.
YOU HAVEN'T ALREADY?
I WAS WAITING FOR YOUR APPROVAL.
WERE YOU?
WELL, YOU MAY CONSIDER IT GIVEN, THEN.
SEE IF CARR CAN DISCOVER WHAT IT IS MCMILLAN IS DOING.
WILL YOU INFORM THE PRIME MINISTER?
THAT SEEMS A TAD PREMATURE.
I AGREE.
UNTIL WE KNOW WHAT MCMILLAN IS DOING, THERE NO POINT IN BRINGING THIS TO DOWNING STREET.
KEEP ME POSTED.
OF COURSE, SIR.

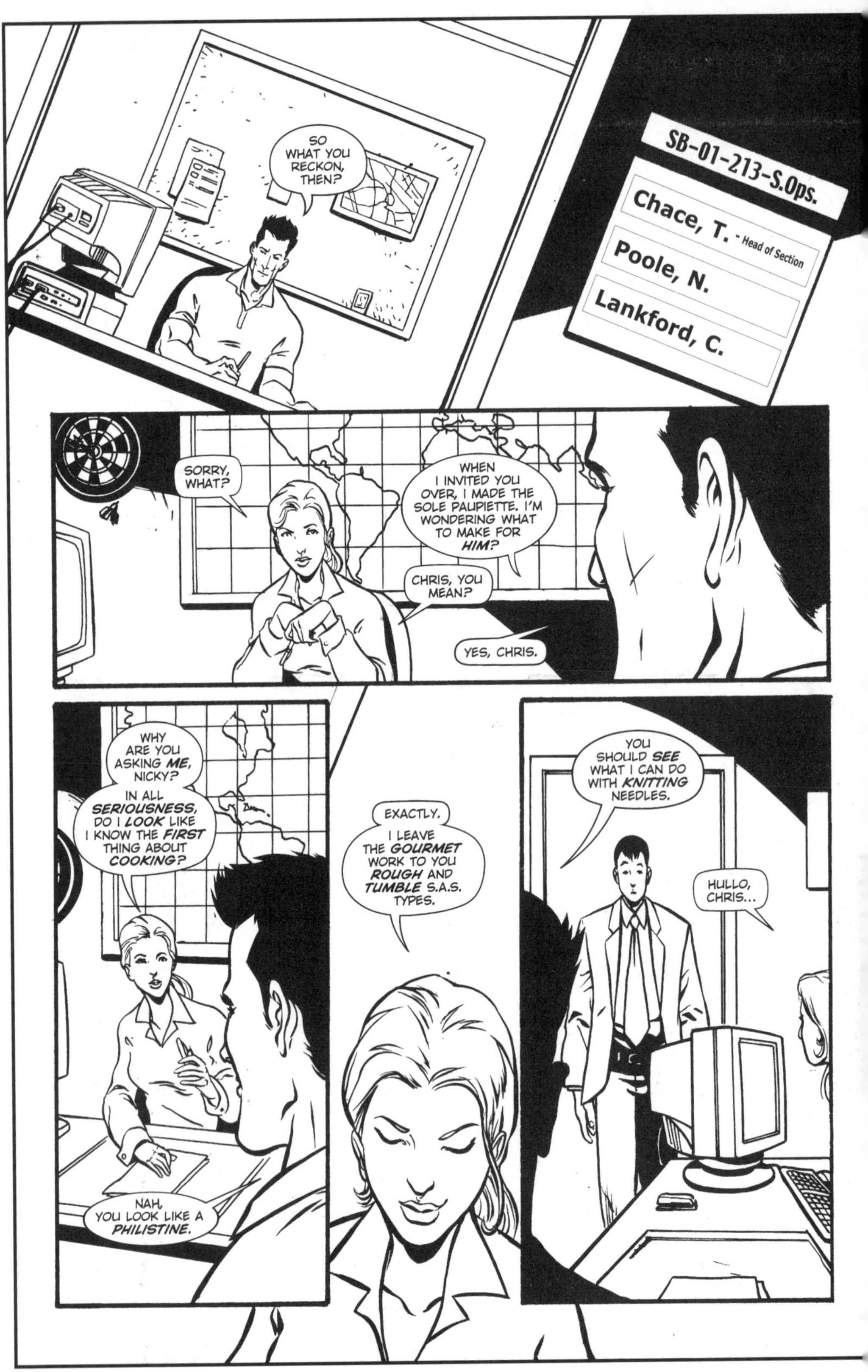
SO WHAT YOU RECKON, THEN?
SB-01-213-S.Ops.
Chace, T. - Head of Section
Poole, N.
Lankford, C.
SORRY, WHAT?
WHEN I INVITED YOU OVER, I MADE THE SOLE PAUPIETTE. I'M WONDERING WHAT TO MAKE FOR HIM?
CHRIS, YOU MEAN?
YES, CHRIS.
WHY ARE YOU ASKING ME, NICKY?
IN ALL SERIOUSNESS, DO I LOOK LIKE I KNOW THE FIRST THING ABOUT COOKING?
NAH, YOU LOOK LIKE A PHILISTINE.
EXACTLY.
I LEAVE THE GOURMET WORK TO YOU ROUGH AND TUMBLE S.A.S. TYPES.
YOU SHOULD SEE WHAT I CAN DO WITH KNITTING NEEDLES.
HULLO, CHRIS...

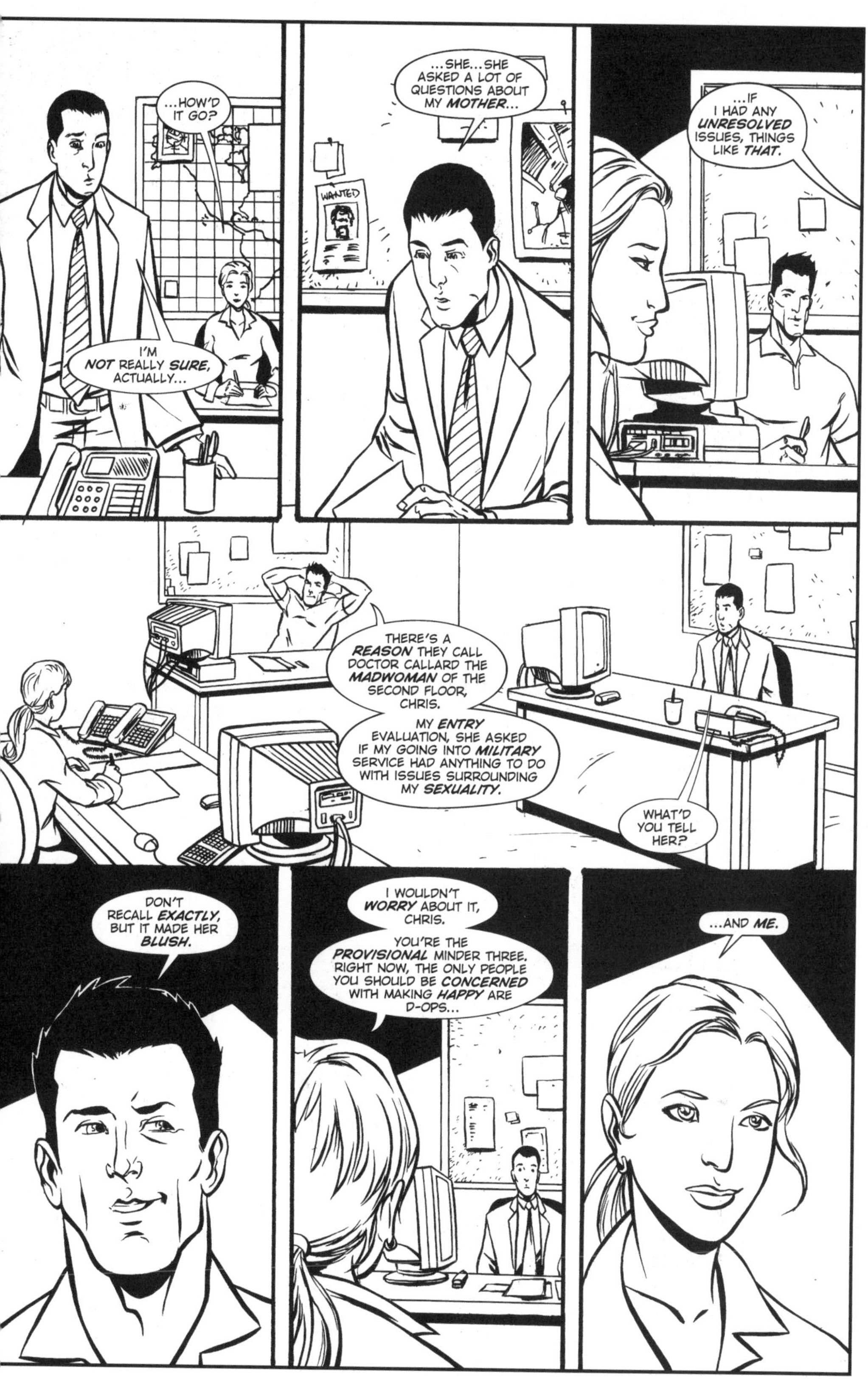
...HOW'D IT GO?
I'M NOT REALLY SURE, ACTUALLY...
...SHE...SHE ASKED A LOT OF QUESTIONS ABOUT MY MOTHER...
WANTED
...IF I HAD ANY UNRESOLVED ISSUES, THINGS LIKE THAT.
THERE'S A REASON THEY CALL DOCTOR CALLARD THE MADWOMAN OF THE SECOND FLOOR, CHRIS.
MY ENTRY EVALUATION, SHE ASKED IF MY GOING INTO MILITARY SERVICE HAD ANYTHING TO DO WITH ISSUES SURROUNDING MY SEXUALITY.
WHAT'D YOU TELL HER?
DON'T RECALL EXACTLY, BUT IT MADE HER BLUSH.
I WOULDN'T WORRY ABOUT IT, CHRIS.
YOU'RE THE PROVISIONAL MINDER THREE. RIGHT NOW, THE ONLY PEOPLE YOU SHOULD BE CONCERNED WITH MAKING HAPPY ARE D-OPS...
...AND ME.

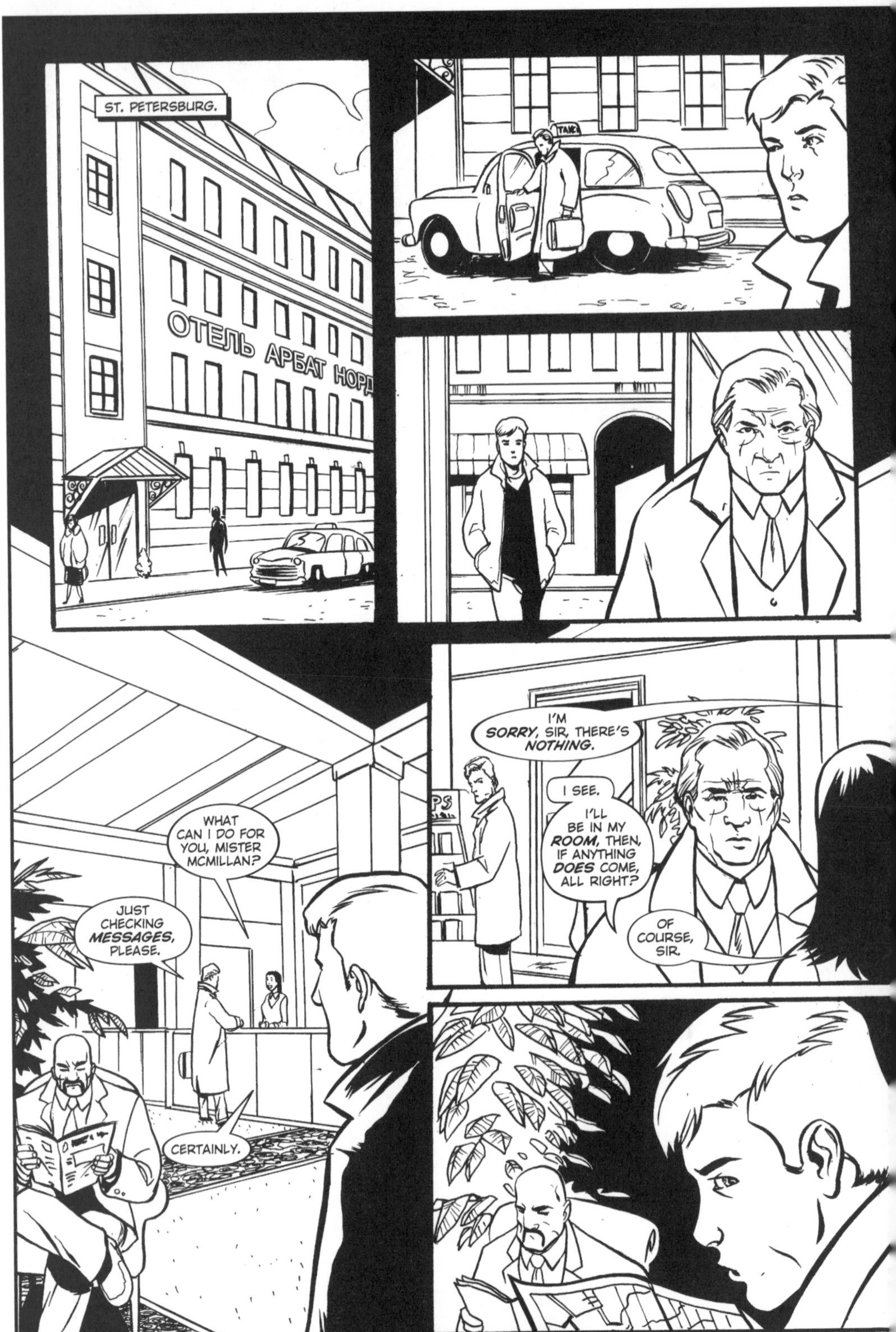

ST. PETERSBURG.
ОТЕЛЬ АРБАТ НОРД
TAXI
WHAT CAN I DO FOR YOU, MISTER MCMILLAN?
JUST CHECKING *MESSAGES,* PLEASE.
CERTAINLY.
I'M *SORRY,* SIR, THERE'S *NOTHING.*
I SEE.
I'LL BE IN MY *ROOM,* THEN, IF ANYTHING *DOES* COME, ALL RIGHT?
OF COURSE, SIR.

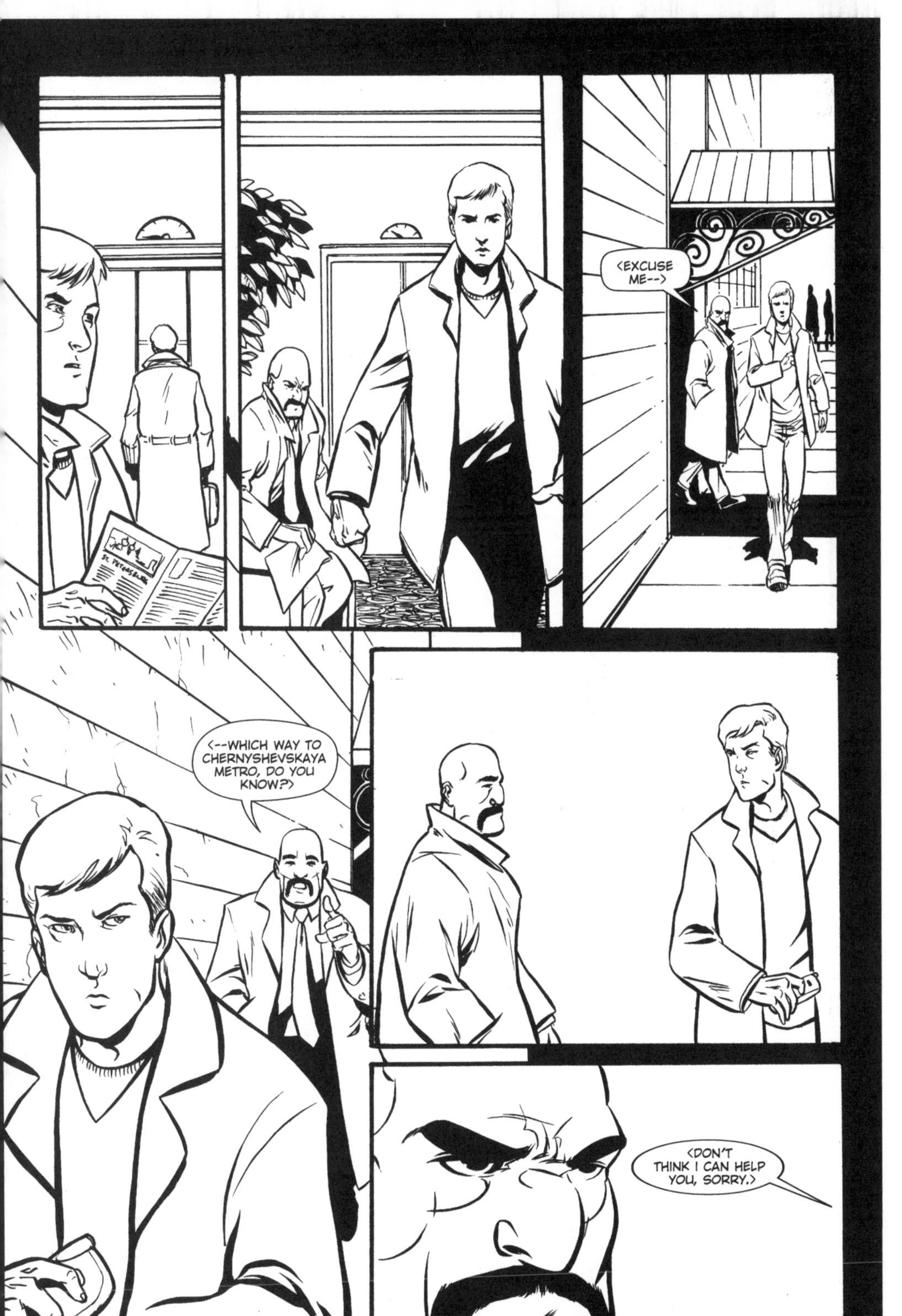
<EXCUSE ME-->
<--WHICH WAY TO CHERNYSHEVSKAYA METRO, DO YOU KNOW?>
<DON'T THINK I CAN HELP YOU, SORRY.>

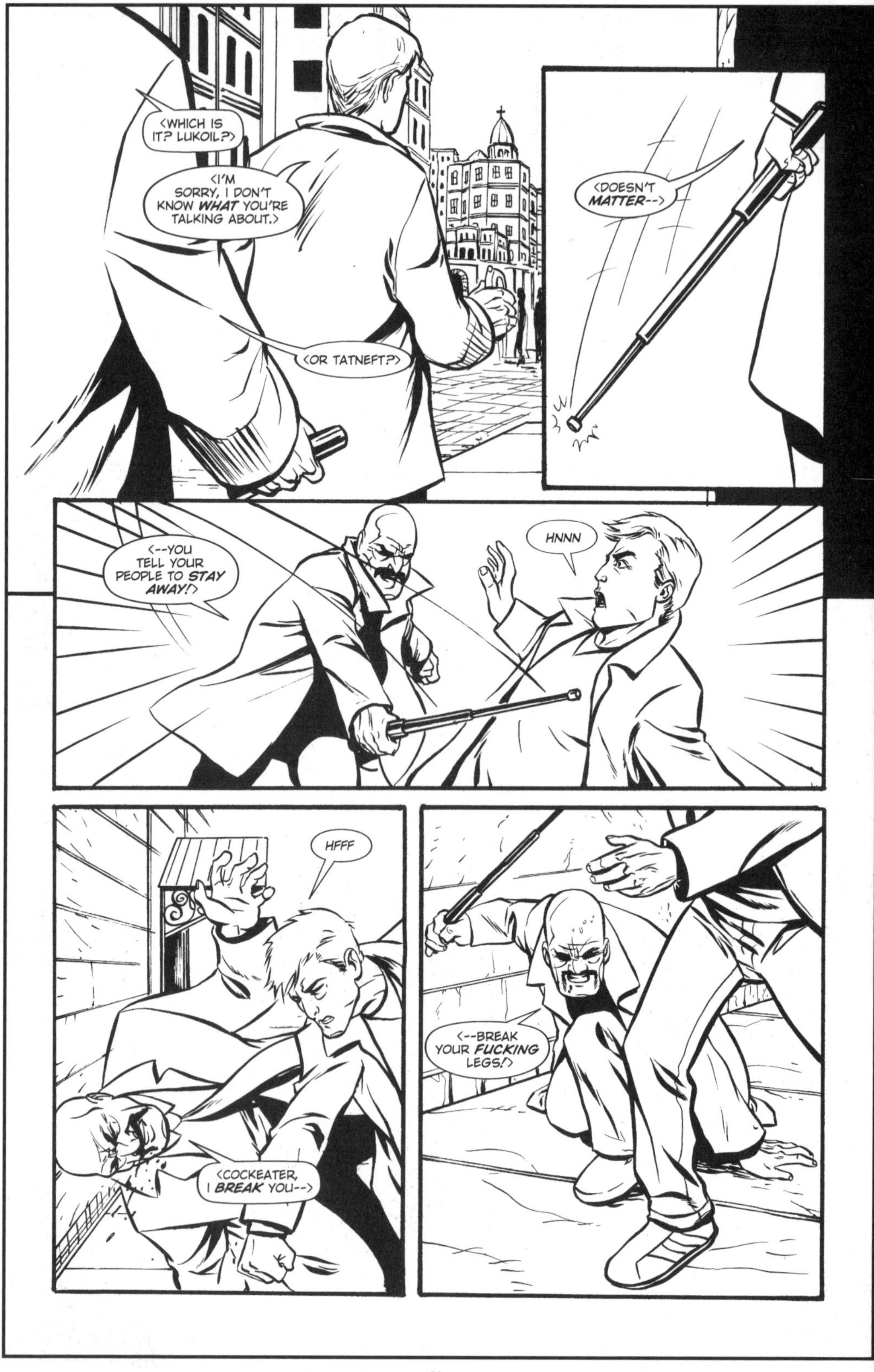

<WHICH IS IT? LUKOIL?>
<I'M SORRY, I DON'T KNOW *WHAT* YOU'RE TALKING ABOUT.>
<OR TATNEFT?>
<DOESN'T *MATTER*-->
<--YOU TELL YOUR PEOPLE TO *STAY AWAY!*>
HNNN
HFFF
<COCKEATER, I *BREAK* YOU-->
<--BREAK YOUR *FUCKING* LEGS!>

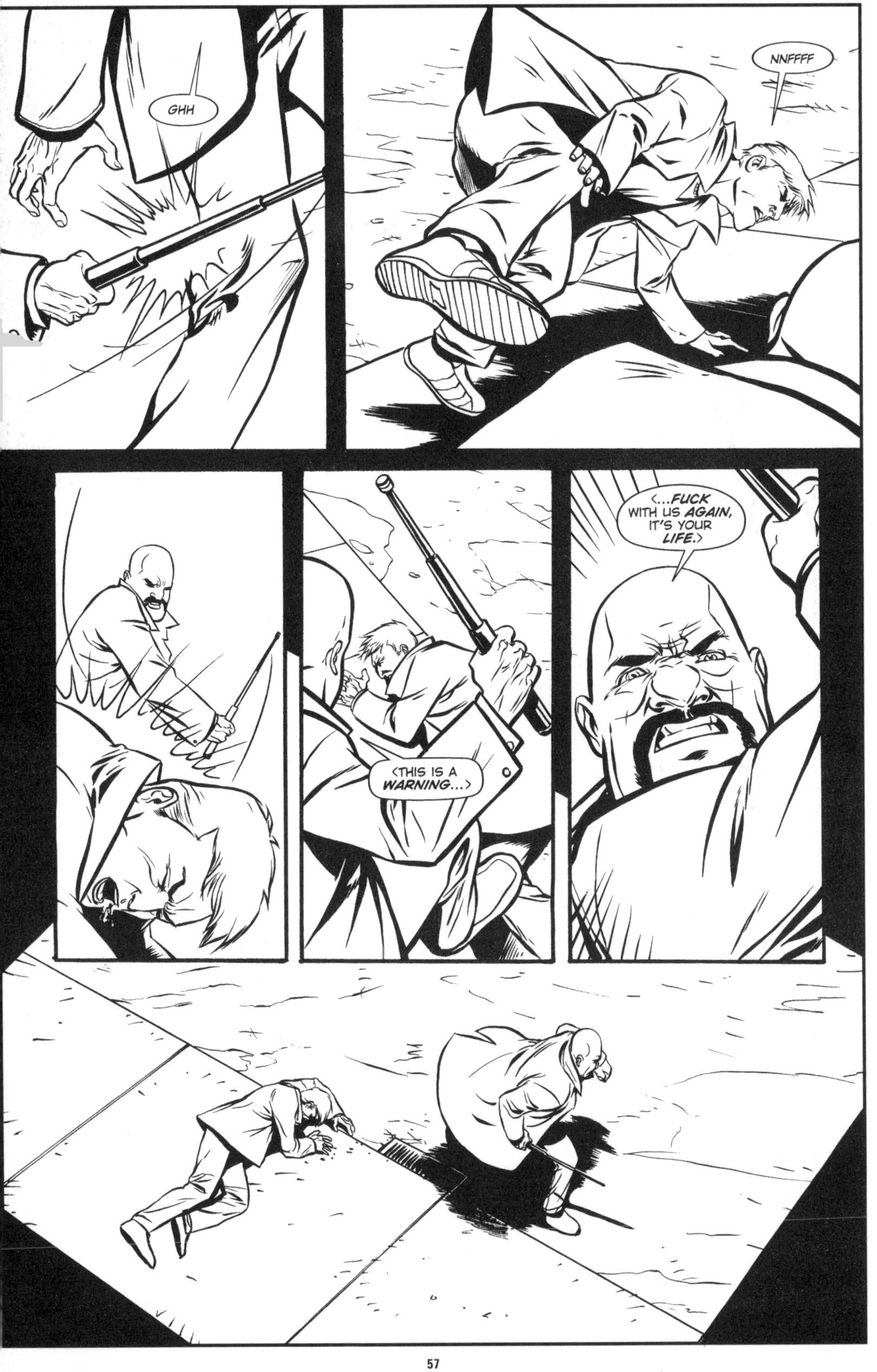
GHH
NNFFFF
<THIS IS A WARNING...>
<...FUCK WITH US AGAIN, IT'S YOUR LIFE.>

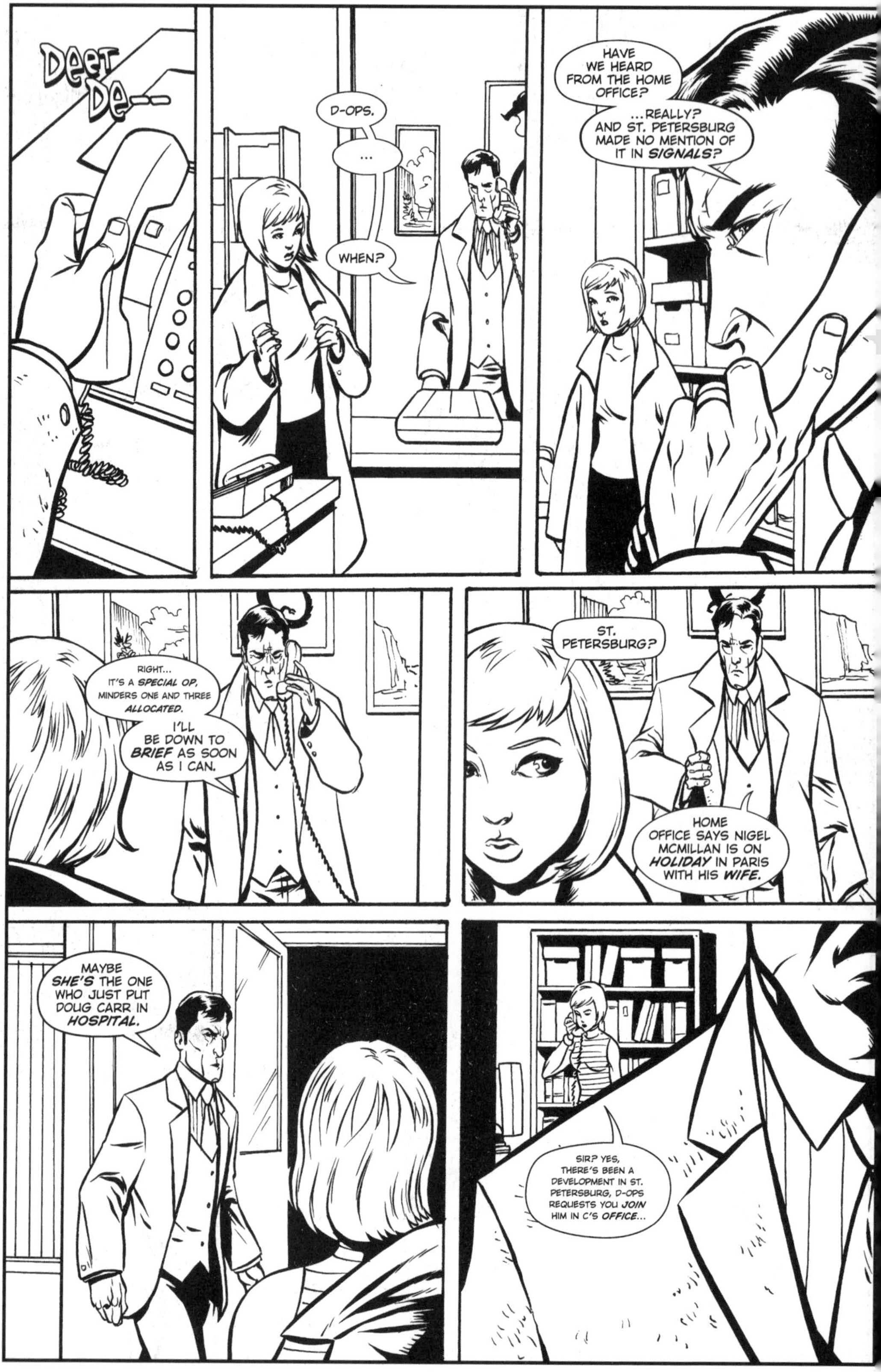
DEET DE--
D-OPS.
...
WHEN?
HAVE WE HEARD FROM THE HOME OFFICE?
...REALLY? AND ST. PETERSBURG MADE NO MENTION OF IT IN SIGNALS?
RIGHT... IT'S A SPECIAL OP, MINDERS ONE AND THREE ALLOCATED.
I'LL BE DOWN TO BRIEF AS SOON AS I CAN.
ST. PETERSBURG?
HOME OFFICE SAYS NIGEL MCMILLAN IS ON HOLIDAY IN PARIS WITH HIS WIFE.
MAYBE SHE'S THE ONE WHO JUST PUT DOUG CARR IN HOSPITAL.
SIR? YES, THERE'S BEEN A DEVELOPMENT IN ST. PETERSBURG, D-OPS REQUESTS YOU JOIN HIM IN C'S OFFICE...

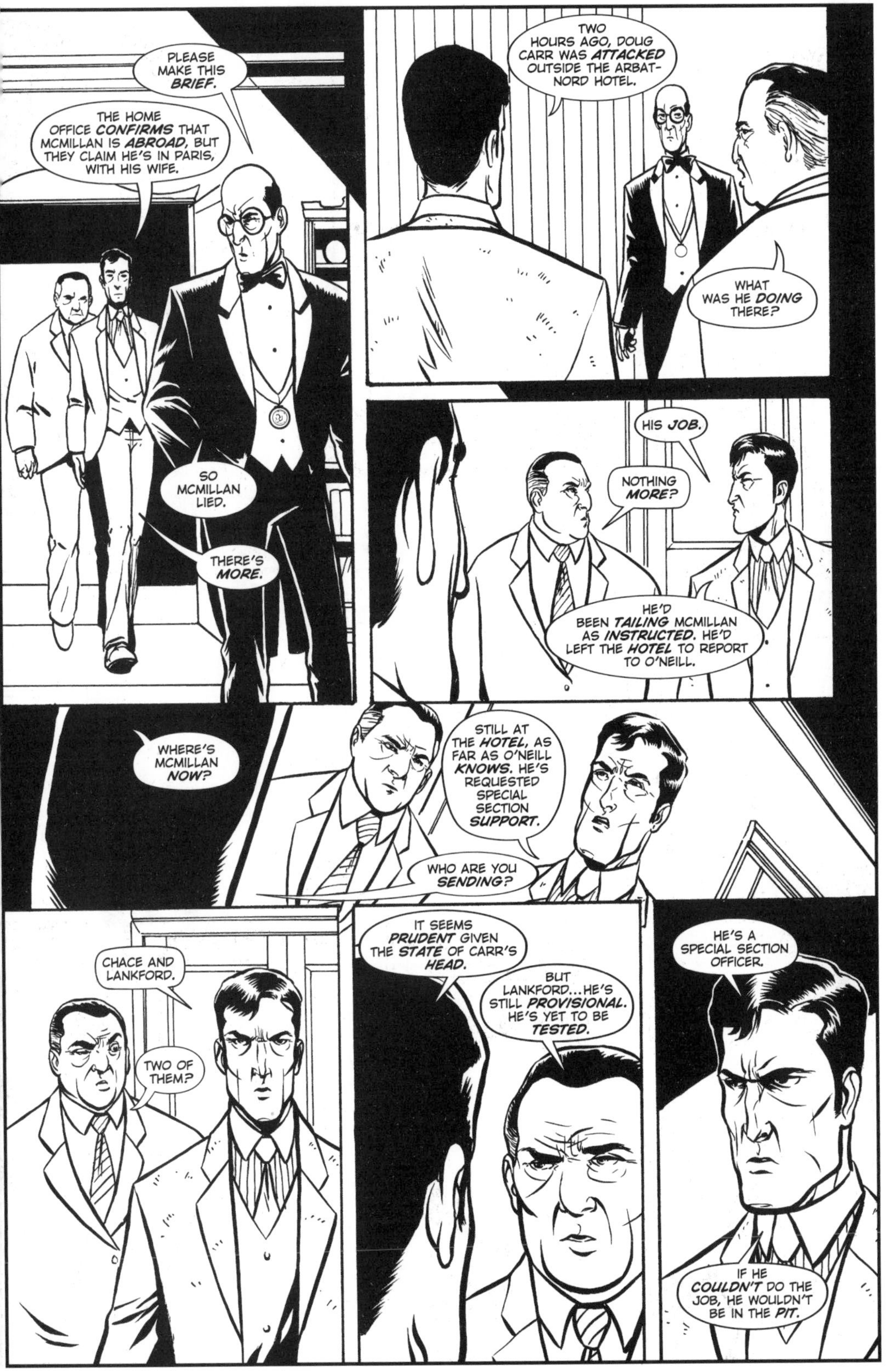
PLEASE MAKE THIS *BRIEF*.
THE HOME OFFICE *CONFIRMS* THAT MCMILLAN IS *ABROAD*, BUT THEY CLAIM HE'S IN PARIS, WITH HIS WIFE.
SO MCMILLAN LIED.
THERE'S *MORE*.
TWO HOURS AGO, DOUG CARR WAS *ATTACKED* OUTSIDE THE ARBAT-NORD HOTEL.
WHAT WAS HE *DOING* THERE?
HIS *JOB*.
NOTHING *MORE*?
HE'D BEEN *TAILING* MCMILLAN AS *INSTRUCTED*. HE'D LEFT THE *HOTEL* TO REPORT TO O'NEILL.
WHERE'S MCMILLAN *NOW*?
STILL AT THE *HOTEL*, AS FAR AS O'NEILL *KNOWS*. HE'S REQUESTED SPECIAL SECTION *SUPPORT*.
WHO ARE YOU *SENDING*?
CHACE AND LANKFORD.
TWO OF THEM?
IT SEEMS *PRUDENT* GIVEN THE *STATE* OF CARR'S *HEAD*.
BUT LANKFORD... HE'S STILL *PROVISIONAL*. HE'S YET TO BE *TESTED*.
HE'S A SPECIAL SECTION OFFICER.
IF HE *COULDN'T* DO THE JOB, HE WOULDN'T BE IN THE *PIT*.

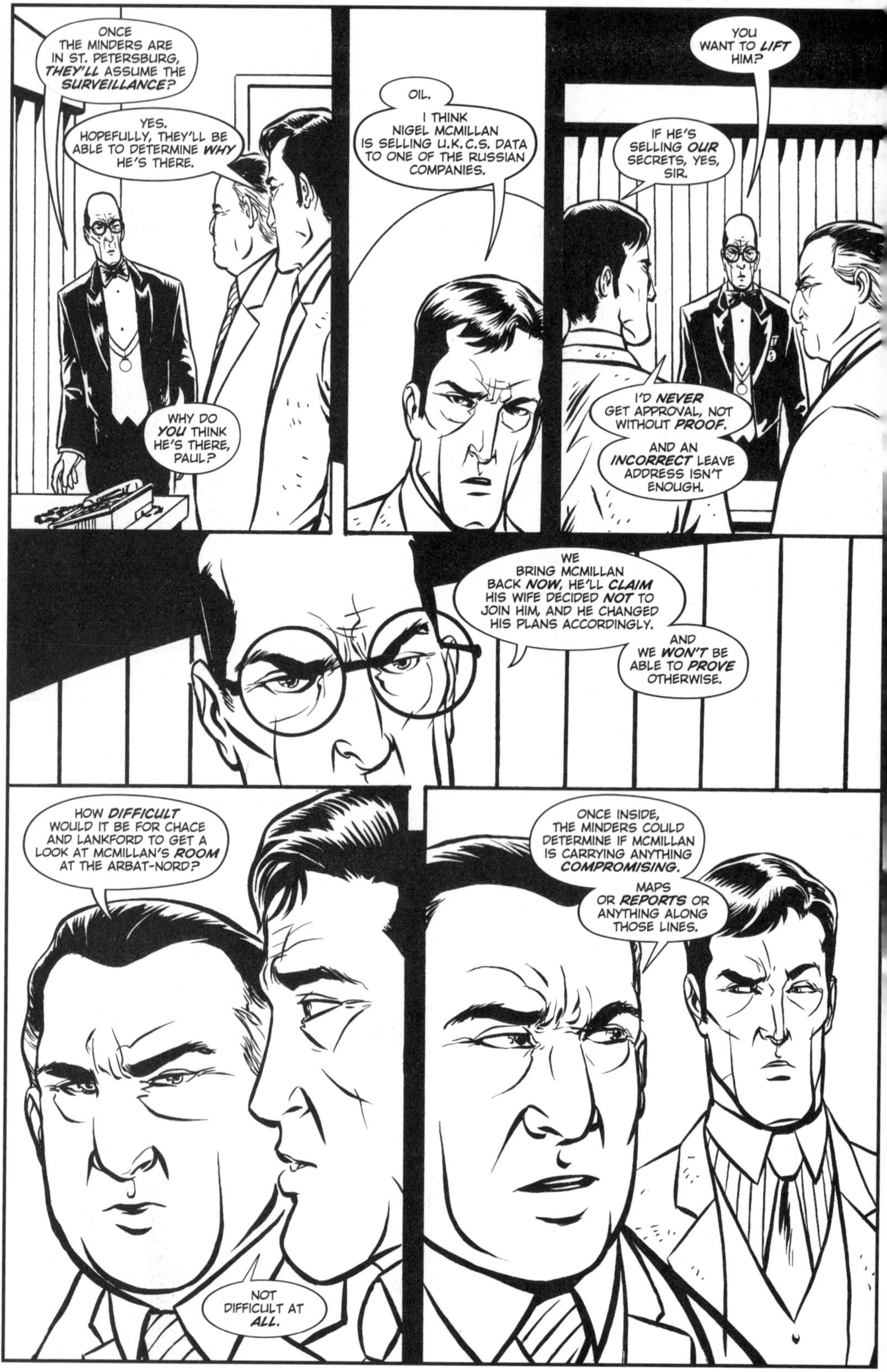
ONCE THE MINDERS ARE IN ST. PETERSBURG, **THEY'LL** ASSUME THE **SURVEILLANCE?**
YES. HOPEFULLY, THEY'LL BE ABLE TO DETERMINE **WHY** HE'S THERE.
WHY DO **YOU** THINK HE'S THERE, PAUL?
OIL.
I THINK NIGEL MCMILLAN IS SELLING U.K.C.S. DATA TO ONE OF THE RUSSIAN COMPANIES.
YOU WANT TO **LIFT** HIM?
IF HE'S SELLING **OUR** SECRETS, YES, SIR.
I'D **NEVER** GET APPROVAL, NOT WITHOUT **PROOF.**
AND AN **INCORRECT** LEAVE ADDRESS ISN'T ENOUGH.
WE BRING MCMILLAN BACK **NOW,** HE'LL **CLAIM** HIS WIFE DECIDED **NOT** TO JOIN HIM, AND HE CHANGED HIS PLANS ACCORDINGLY.
AND WE **WON'T** BE ABLE TO **PROVE** OTHERWISE.
HOW **DIFFICULT** WOULD IT BE FOR CHACE AND LANKFORD TO GET A LOOK AT MCMILLAN'S **ROOM** AT THE ARBAT-NORD?
NOT DIFFICULT AT **ALL.**
ONCE INSIDE, THE MINDERS COULD DETERMINE IF MCMILLAN IS CARRYING ANYTHING **COMPROMISING.**
MAPS OR **REPORTS** OR ANYTHING ALONG THOSE LINES.

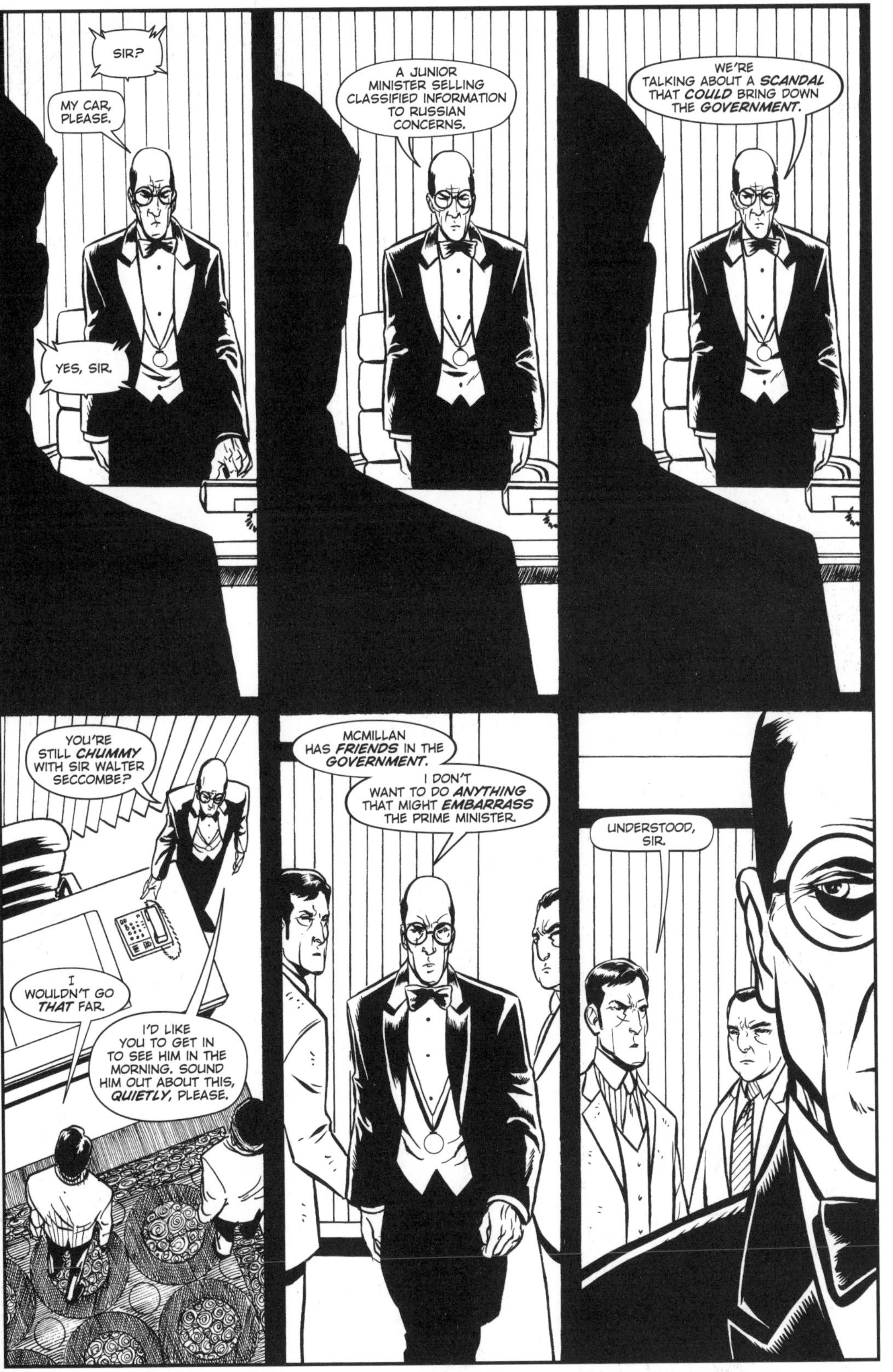
SIR?
MY CAR, PLEASE.
YES, SIR.
A JUNIOR MINISTER SELLING CLASSIFIED INFORMATION TO RUSSIAN CONCERNS.
WE'RE TALKING ABOUT A **SCANDAL** THAT **COULD** BRING DOWN THE **GOVERNMENT**.
YOU'RE STILL **CHUMMY** WITH SIR WALTER SECCOMBE?
I WOULDN'T GO **THAT** FAR.
I'D LIKE YOU TO GET IN TO SEE HIM IN THE MORNING. SOUND HIM OUT ABOUT THIS, **QUIETLY**, PLEASE.
MCMILLAN HAS **FRIENDS** IN THE **GOVERNMENT**.
I DON'T WANT TO DO **ANYTHING** THAT MIGHT **EMBARRASS** THE PRIME MINISTER.
UNDERSTOOD, SIR.

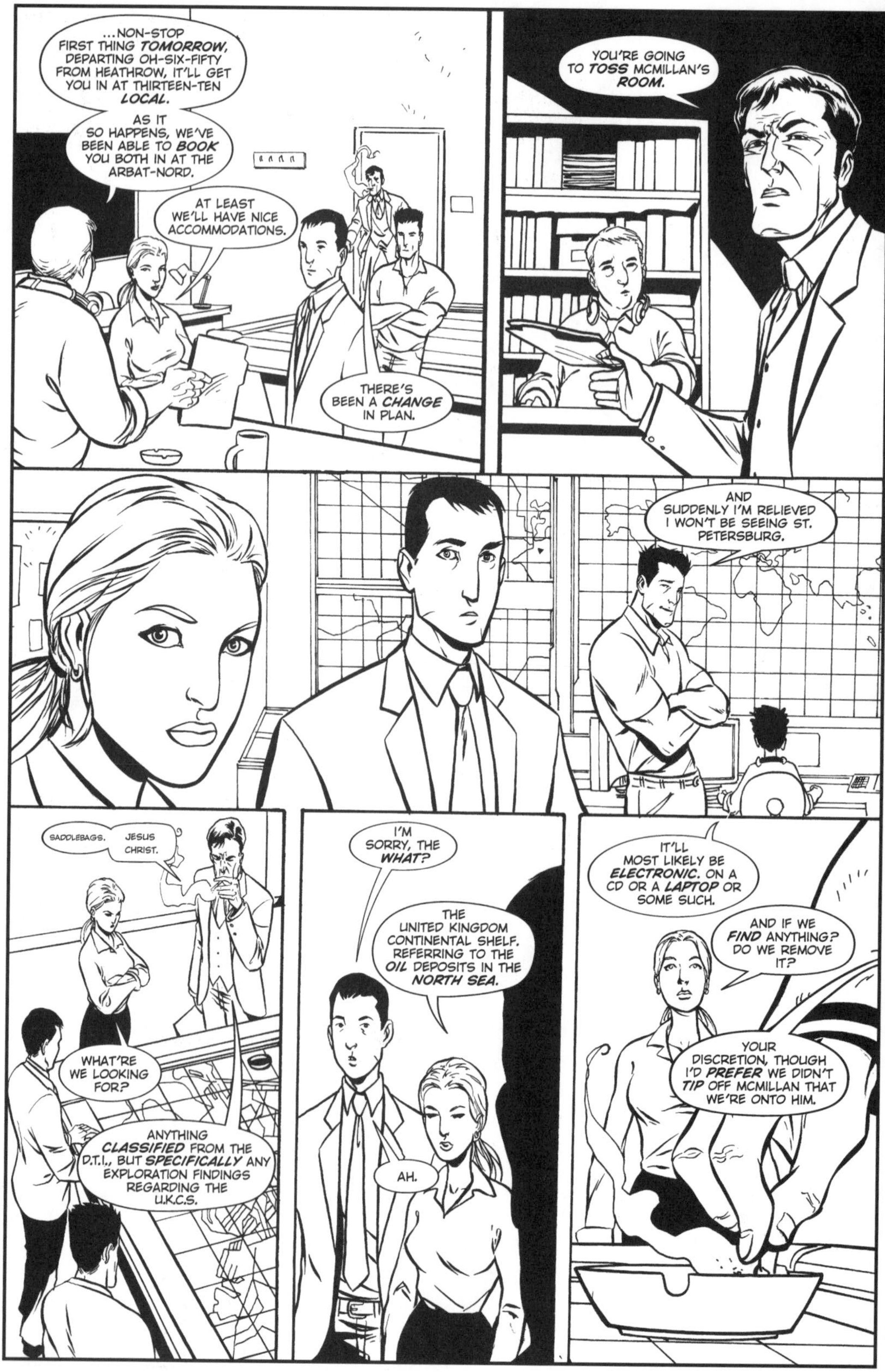
...NON-STOP FIRST THING TOMORROW, DEPARTING OH-SIX-FIFTY FROM HEATHROW, IT'LL GET YOU IN AT THIRTEEN-TEN LOCAL.
AS IT SO HAPPENS, WE'VE BEEN ABLE TO BOOK YOU BOTH IN AT THE ARBAT-NORD.
AT LEAST WE'LL HAVE NICE ACCOMMODATIONS.
THERE'S BEEN A CHANGE IN PLAN.
YOU'RE GOING TO TOSS MCMILLAN'S ROOM.
AND SUDDENLY I'M RELIEVED I WON'T BE SEEING ST. PETERSBURG.
SADDLEBAGS.
JESUS CHRIST.
WHAT'RE WE LOOKING FOR?
ANYTHING CLASSIFIED FROM THE D.T.I., BUT SPECIFICALLY ANY EXPLORATION FINDINGS REGARDING THE U.K.C.S.
I'M SORRY, THE WHAT?
THE UNITED KINGDOM CONTINENTAL SHELF. REFERRING TO THE OIL DEPOSITS IN THE NORTH SEA.
AH.
IT'LL MOST LIKELY BE ELECTRONIC. ON A CD OR A LAPTOP OR SOME SUCH.
AND IF WE FIND ANYTHING? DO WE REMOVE IT?
YOUR DISCRETION, THOUGH I'D PREFER WE DIDN'T TIP OFF MCMILLAN THAT WE'RE ONTO HIM.

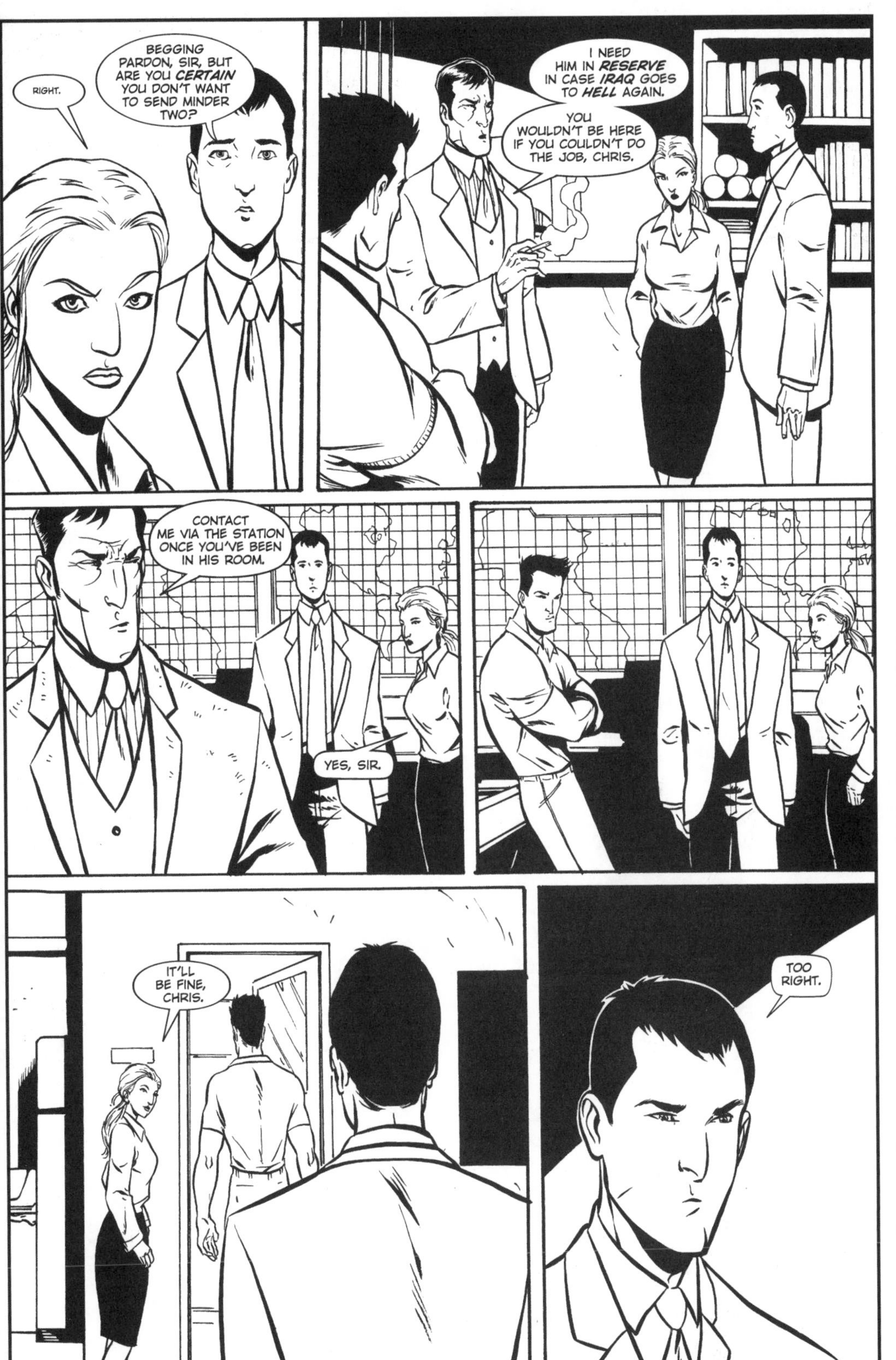
BEGGING PARDON, SIR, BUT ARE YOU CERTAIN YOU DON'T WANT TO SEND MINDER TWO?
RIGHT.
I NEED HIM IN RESERVE IN CASE IRAQ GOES TO HELL AGAIN.
YOU WOULDN'T BE HERE IF YOU COULDN'T DO THE JOB, CHRIS.
CONTACT ME VIA THE STATION ONCE YOU'VE BEEN IN HIS ROOM.
YES, SIR.
IT'LL BE FINE, CHRIS.
TOO RIGHT.

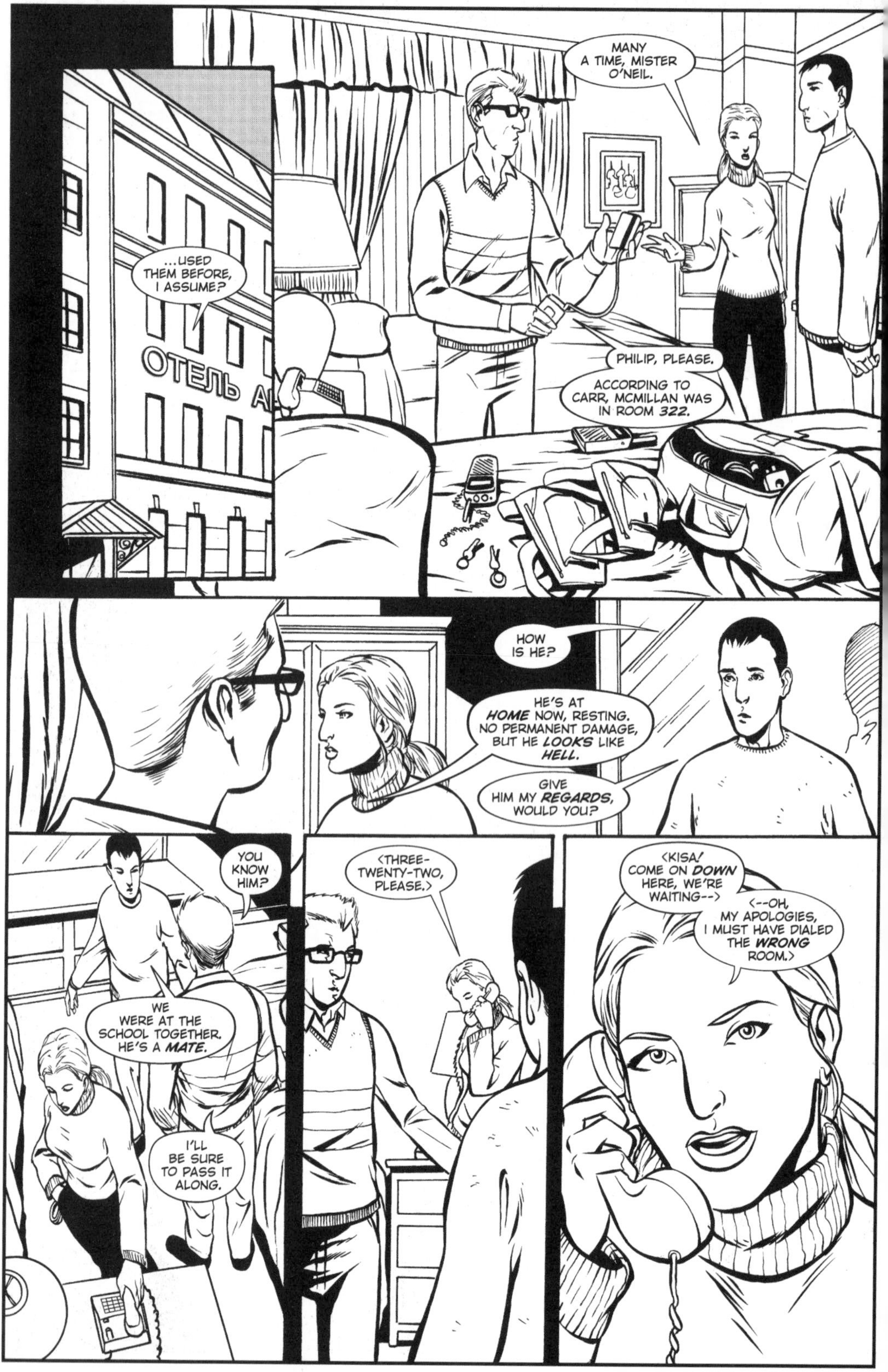
...USED THEM BEFORE, I ASSUME?
ОТЕЛЬ А
MANY A TIME, MISTER O'NEIL.
PHILIP, PLEASE.
ACCORDING TO CARR, MCMILLAN WAS IN ROOM **322.**
HOW IS HE?
HE'S AT **HOME** NOW, RESTING. NO PERMANENT DAMAGE, BUT HE **LOOKS** LIKE **HELL.**
GIVE HIM MY **REGARDS,** WOULD YOU?
YOU KNOW HIM?
WE WERE AT THE SCHOOL TOGETHER. HE'S A **MATE.**
I'LL BE SURE TO PASS IT ALONG.
<THREE-TWENTY-TWO, PLEASE.>
<KISA! COME ON **DOWN** HERE, WE'RE WAITING-->
<--OH, MY APOLOGIES, I MUST HAVE DIALED THE **WRONG** ROOM.>

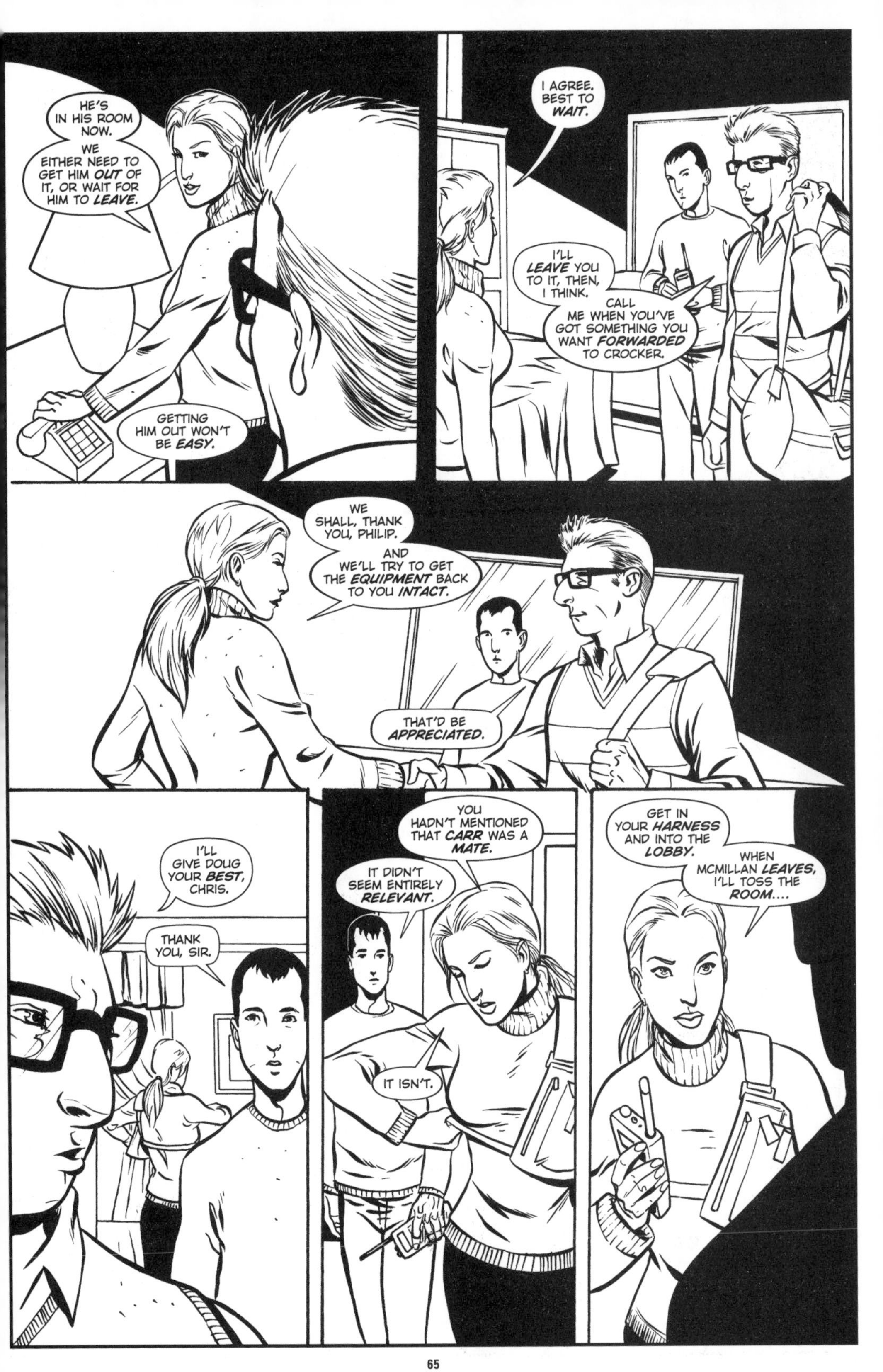
HE'S IN HIS ROOM NOW. WE EITHER NEED TO GET HIM *OUT* OF IT, OR WAIT FOR HIM TO *LEAVE.*
GETTING HIM OUT WON'T BE *EASY.*
I AGREE. BEST TO *WAIT.*
I'LL *LEAVE* YOU TO IT, THEN, I THINK.
CALL ME WHEN YOU'VE GOT SOMETHING YOU WANT *FORWARDED* TO CROCKER.
WE SHALL, THANK YOU, PHILIP.
AND WE'LL TRY TO GET THE *EQUIPMENT* BACK TO YOU *INTACT.*
THAT'D BE *APPRECIATED.*
I'LL GIVE DOUG YOUR *BEST,* CHRIS.
THANK YOU, SIR.
YOU HADN'T MENTIONED THAT *CARR* WAS A *MATE.*
IT DIDN'T SEEM ENTIRELY *RELEVANT.*
IT ISN'T.
GET IN YOUR *HARNESS* AND INTO THE *LOBBY.*
WHEN MCMILLAN *LEAVES,* I'LL TOSS THE *ROOM....*

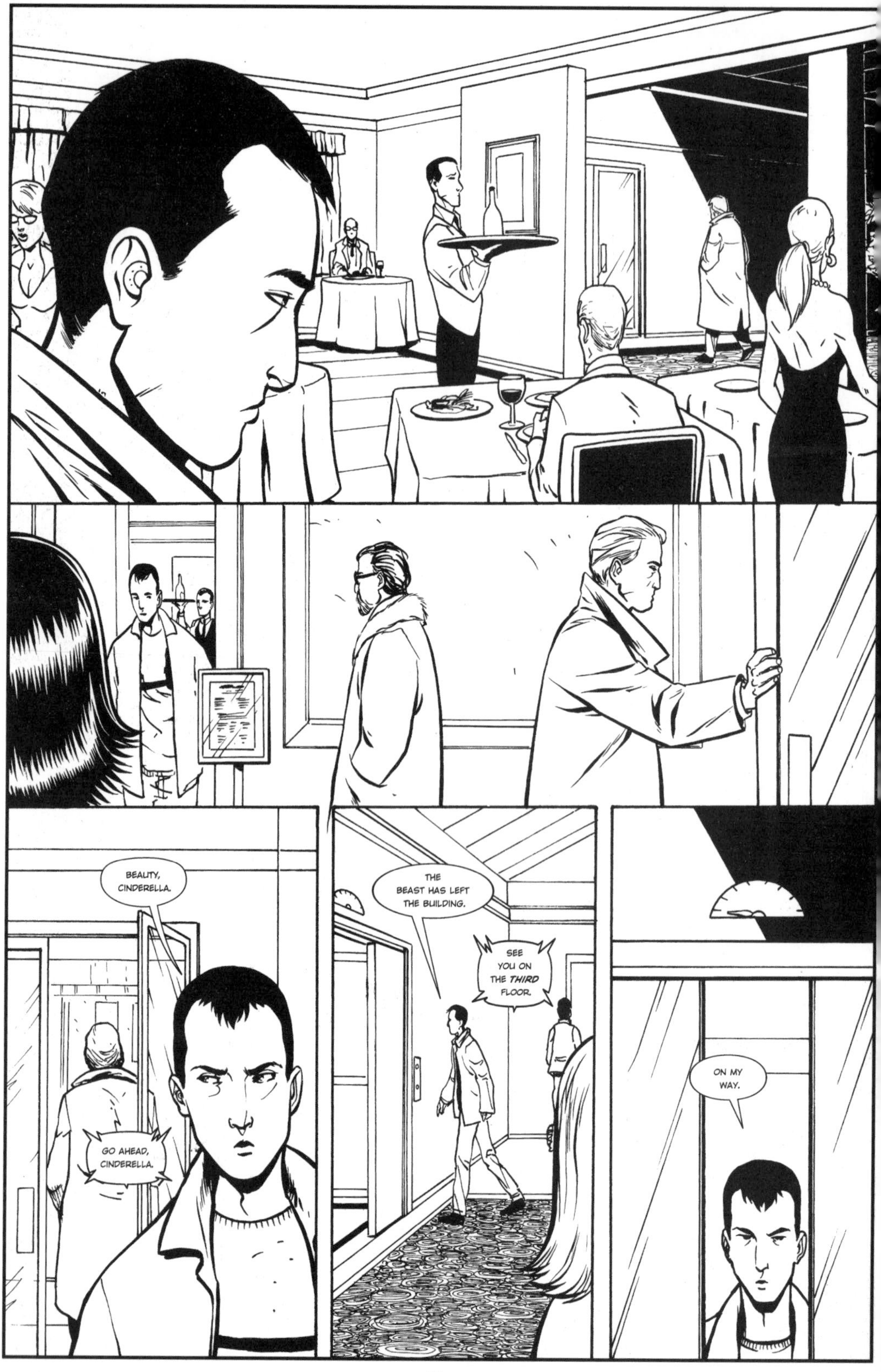
BEAUTY, CINDERELLA.
GO AHEAD, CINDERELLA.
THE BEAST HAS LEFT THE BUILDING.
SEE YOU ON THE *THIRD* FLOOR.
ON MY WAY.

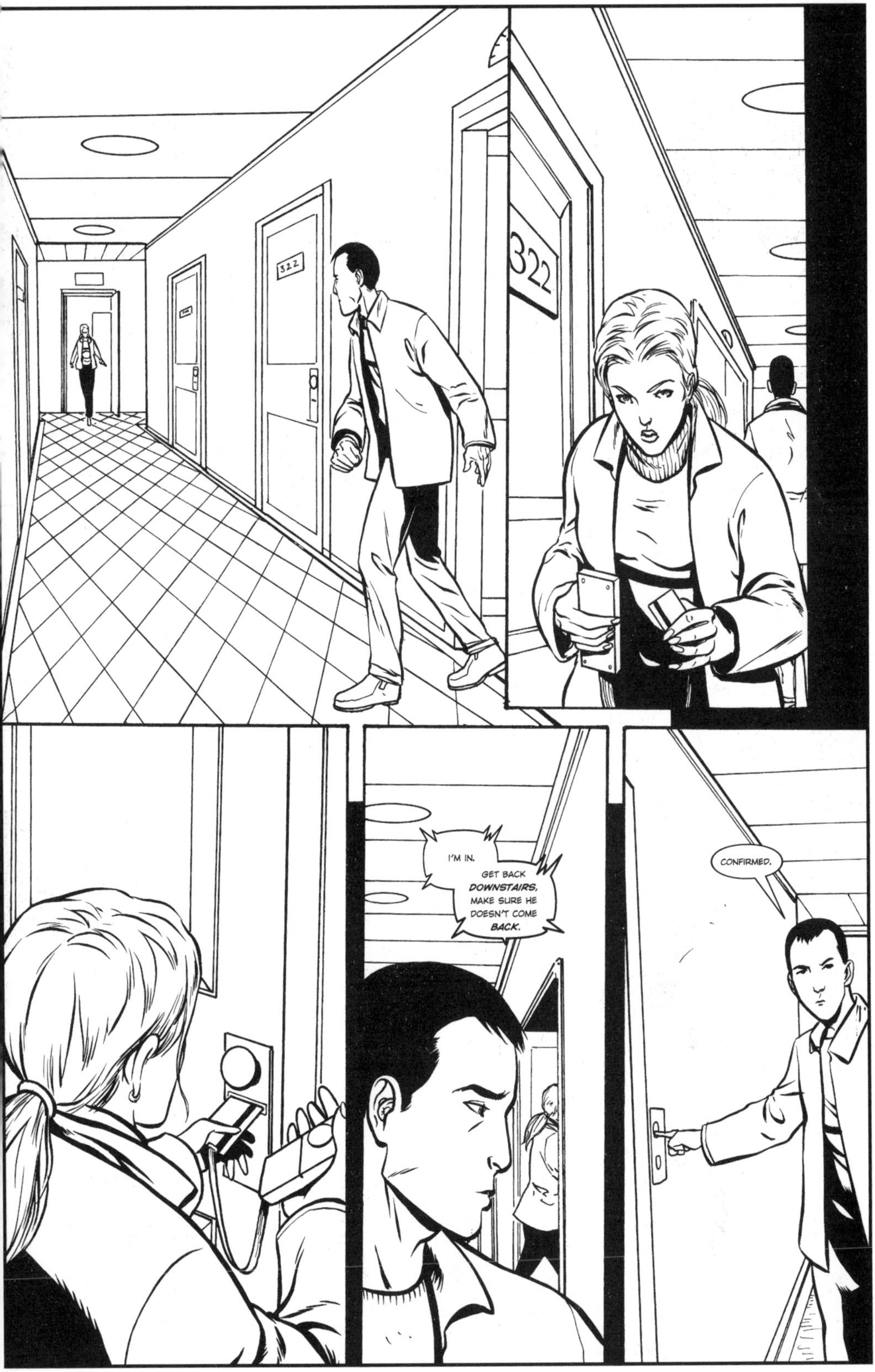
322
322
I'M IN.
GET BACK *DOWNSTAIRS*, MAKE SURE HE DOESN'T COME *BACK*.
CONFIRMED.

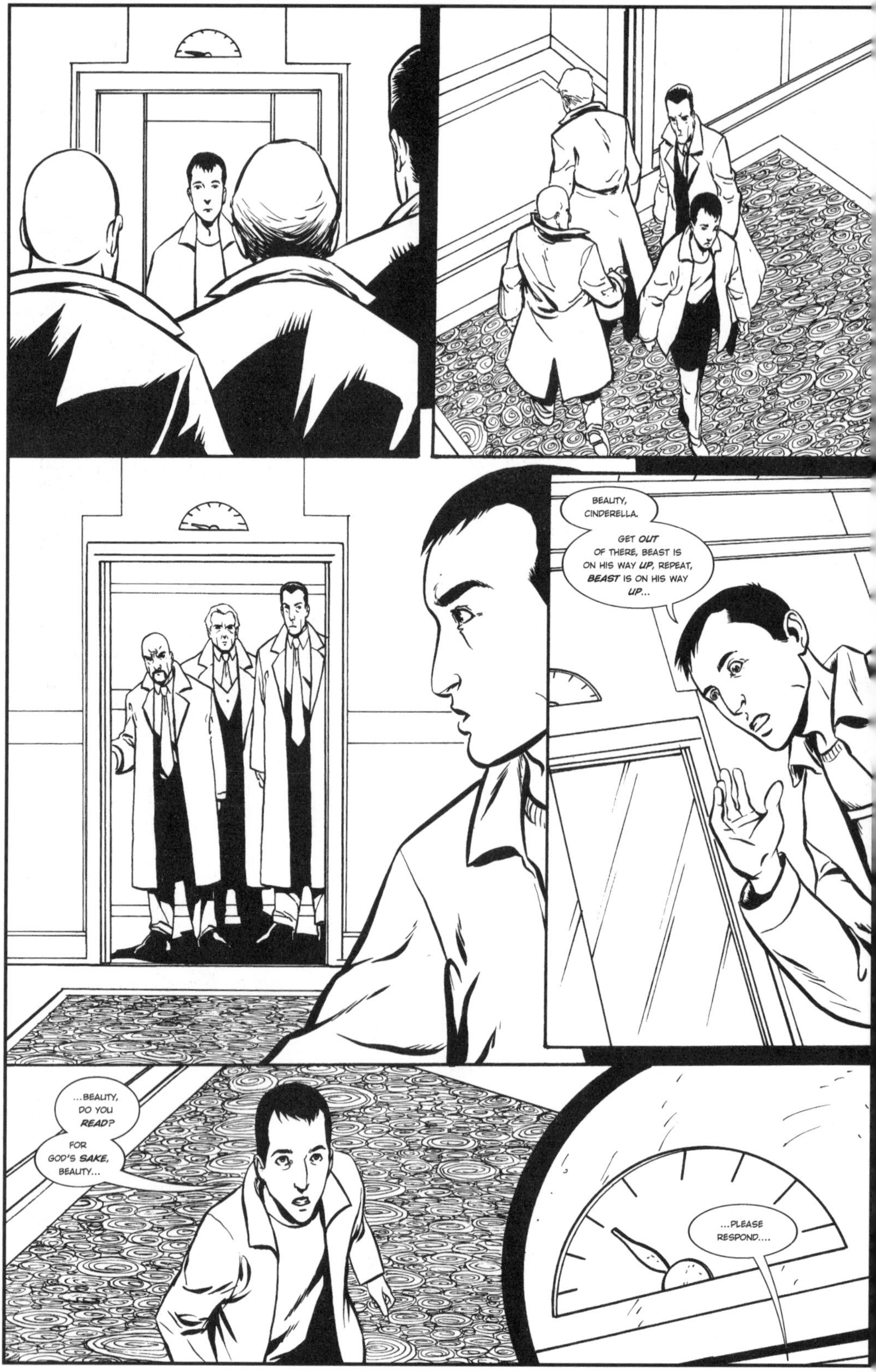
BEAUTY, CINDERELLA.
GET *OUT* OF THERE, BEAST IS ON HIS WAY *UP*, REPEAT, *BEAST* IS ON HIS WAY *UP*...
...BEAUTY, DO YOU *READ*?
FOR GOD'S *SAKE*, BEAUTY...
...PLEASE RESPOND....

CHAPTER 2

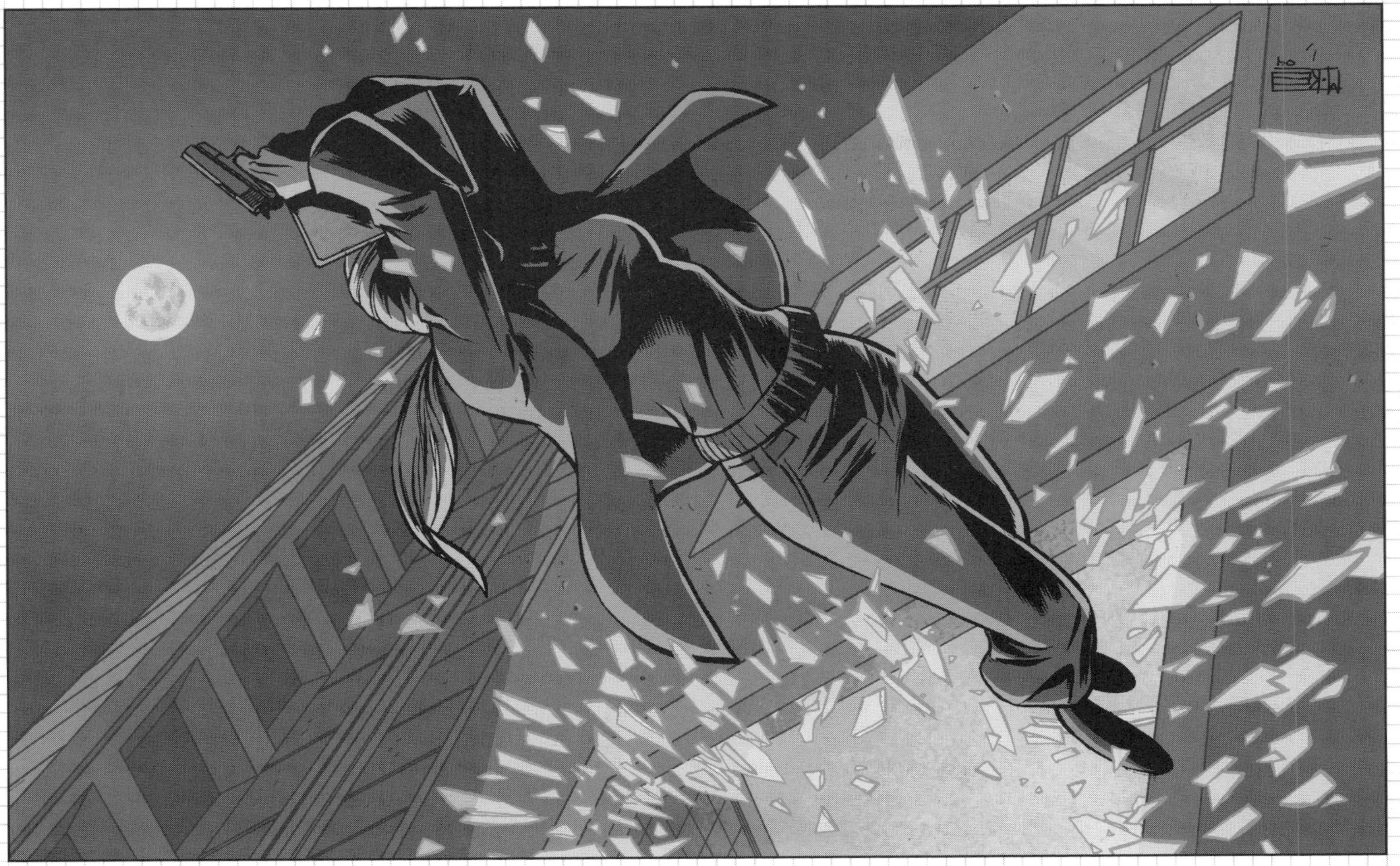

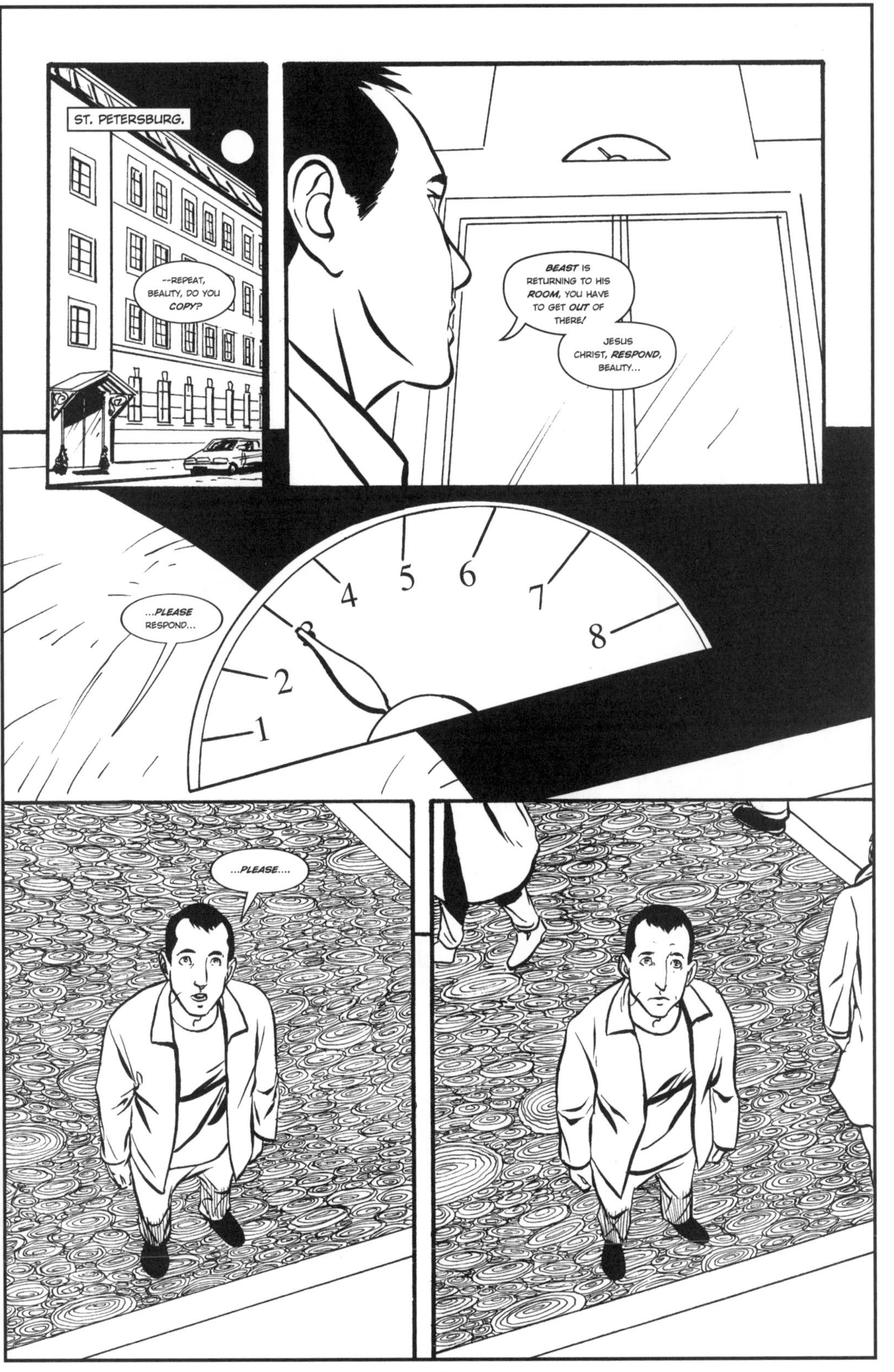

ST. PETERSBURG.
--REPEAT, BEAUTY, DO YOU COPY?
BEAST IS RETURNING TO HIS ROOM, YOU HAVE TO GET OUT OF THERE!
JESUS CHRIST, RESPOND, BEAUTY...
...PLEASE RESPOND...
1
2
3
4
5
6
7
8
...PLEASE....

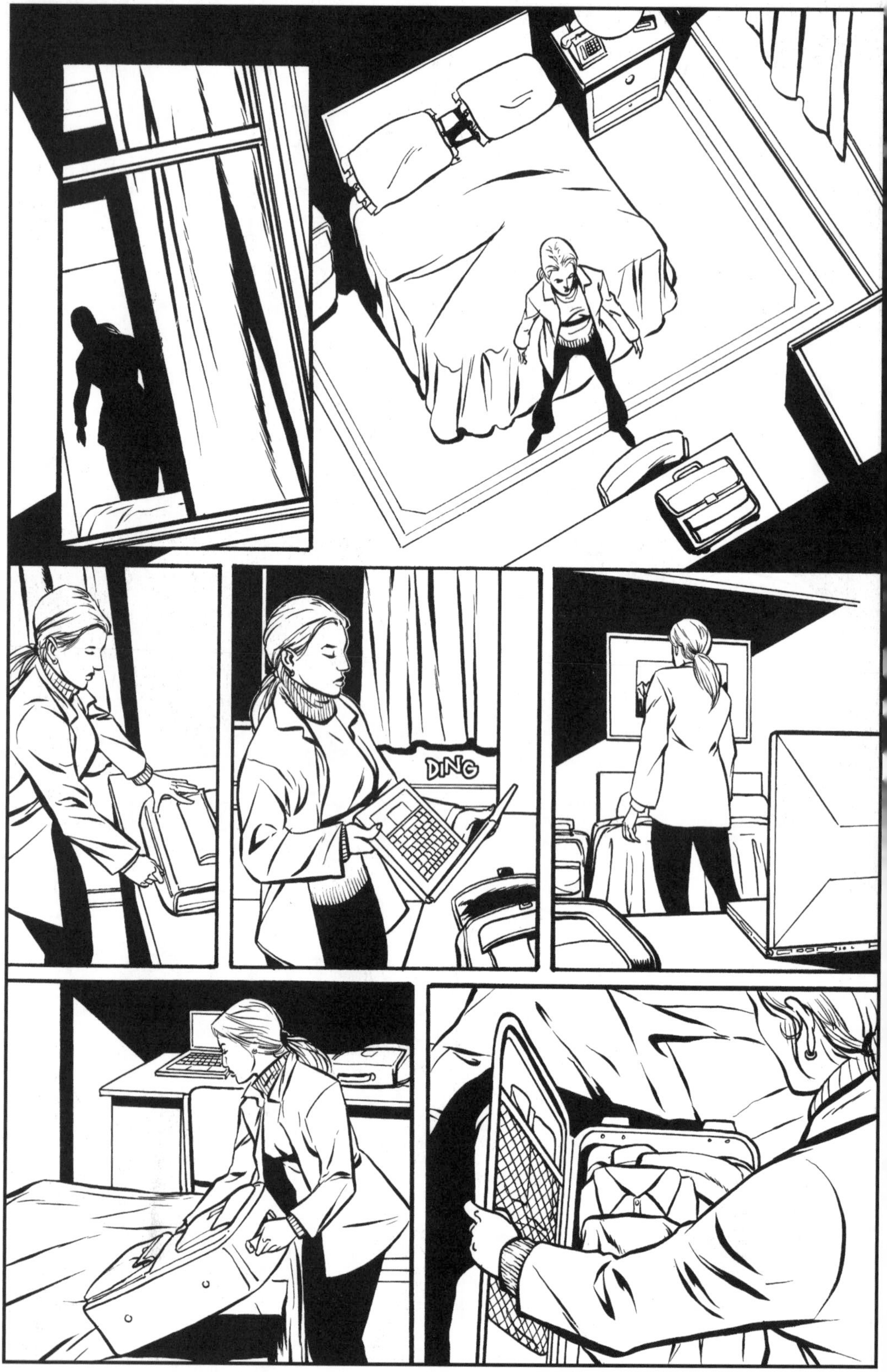
DING

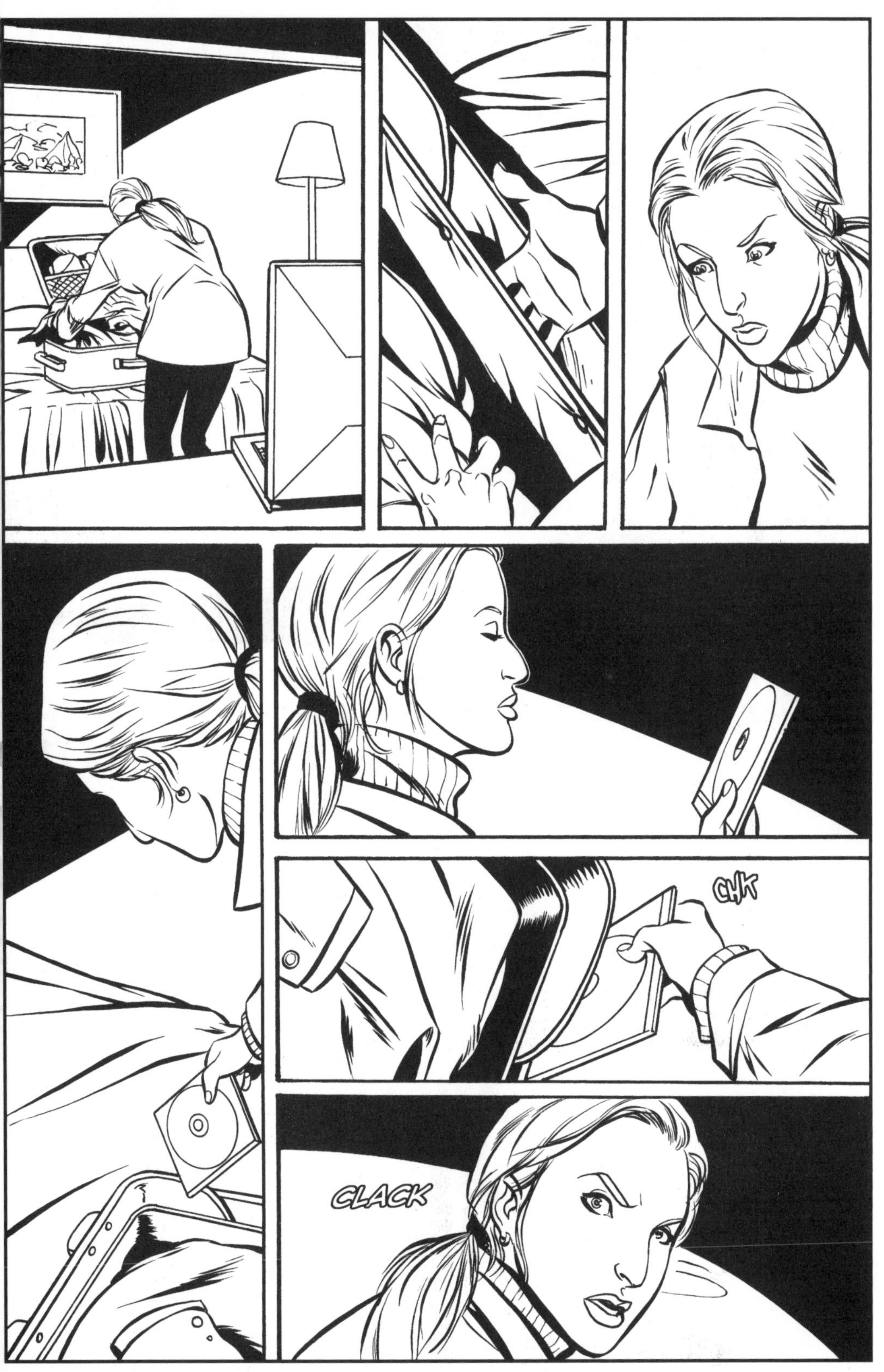
CHK
CLACK

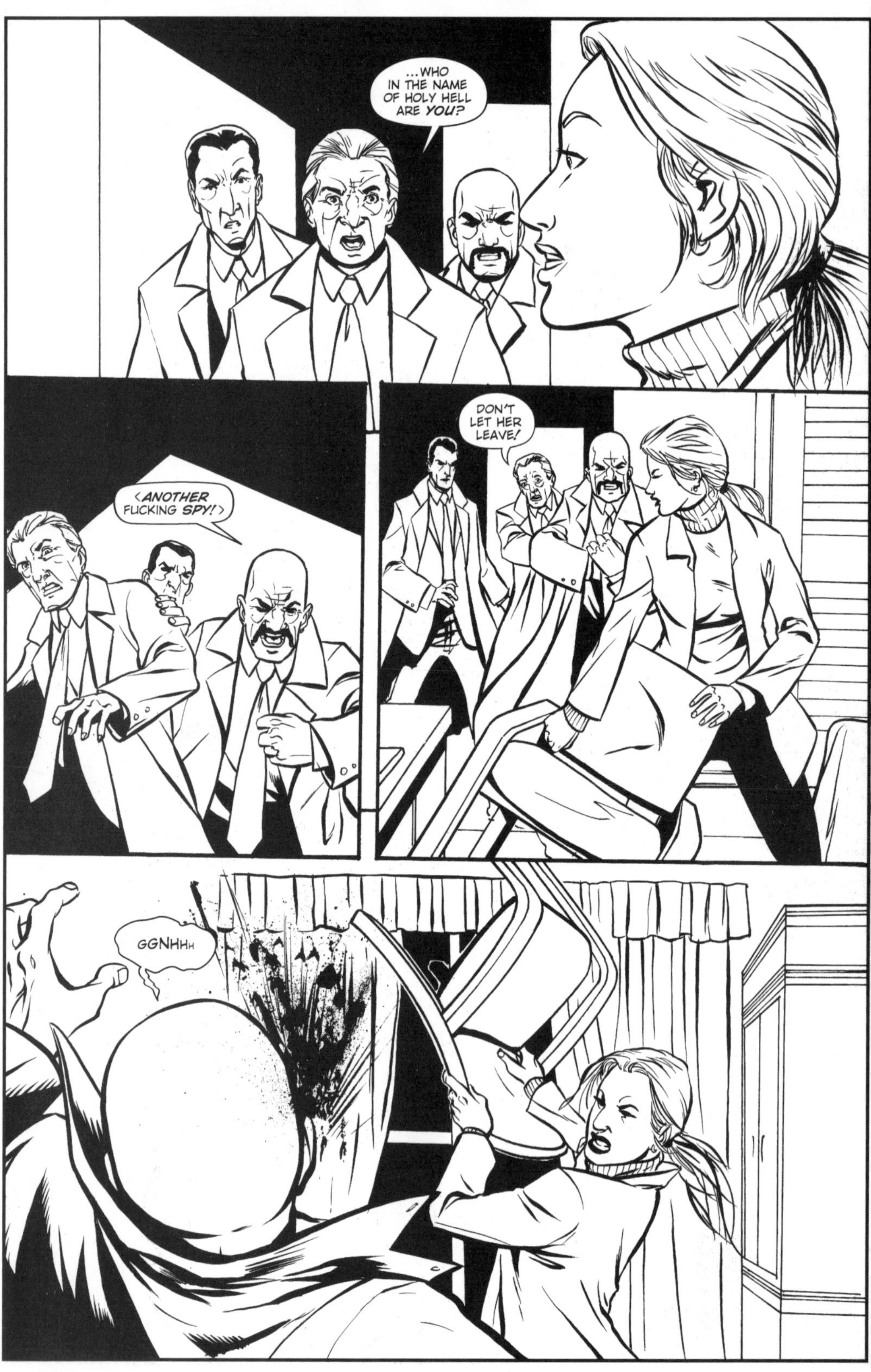
...WHO IN THE NAME OF HOLY HELL ARE YOU?
<ANOTHER FUCKING SPY!>
DON'T LET HER LEAVE!
GGNHHH

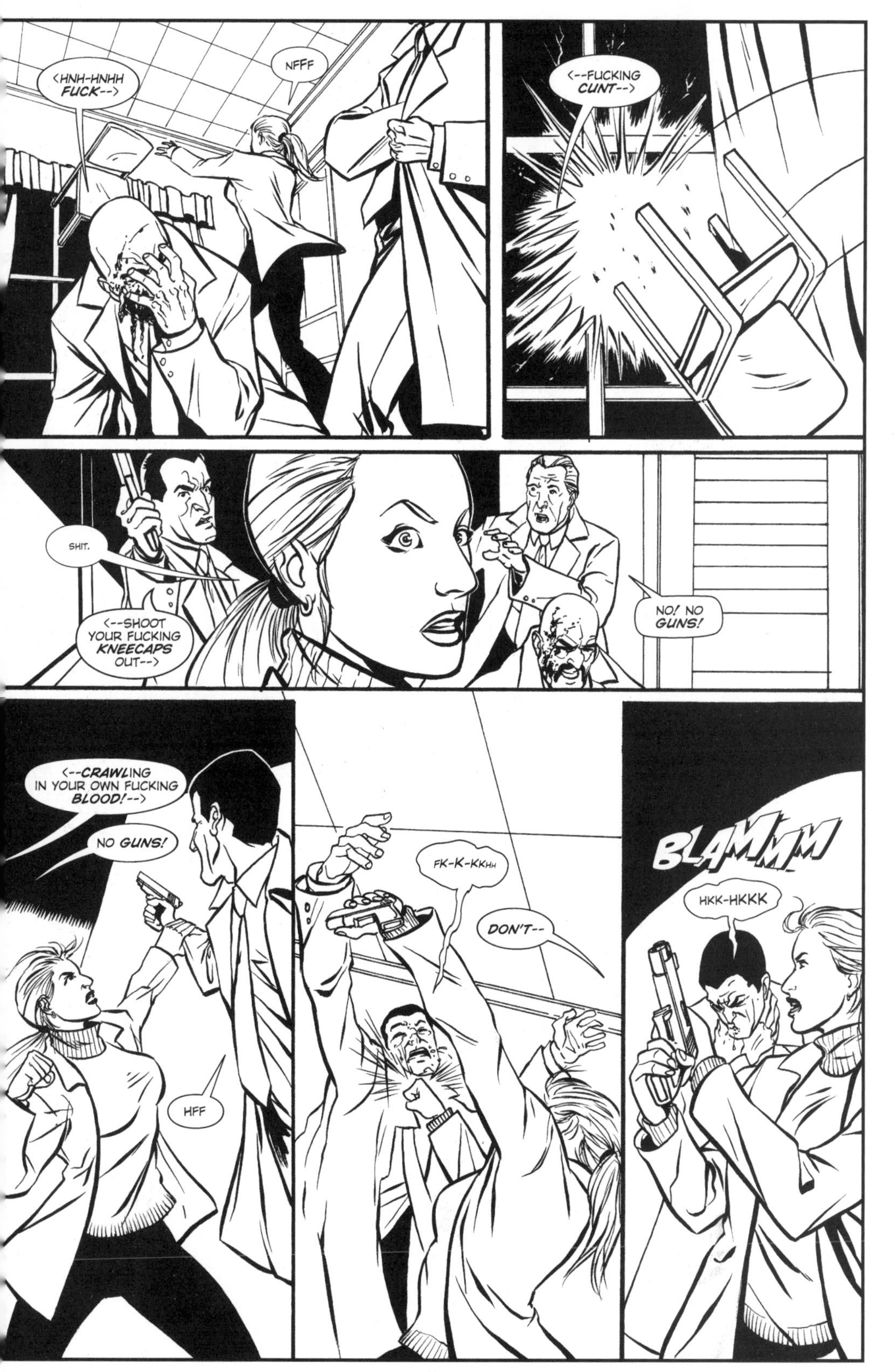

<HNH-HNHH FUCK-->
NFFF
<--FUCKING CUNT-->
SHIT.
<--SHOOT YOUR FUCKING KNEECAPS OUT-->
NO! NO GUNS!
<--CRAWLING IN YOUR OWN FUCKING BLOOD!-->
NO GUNS!
HFF
FK-K-KKHH
DON'T--
BLAMMM
HKK-HKKK

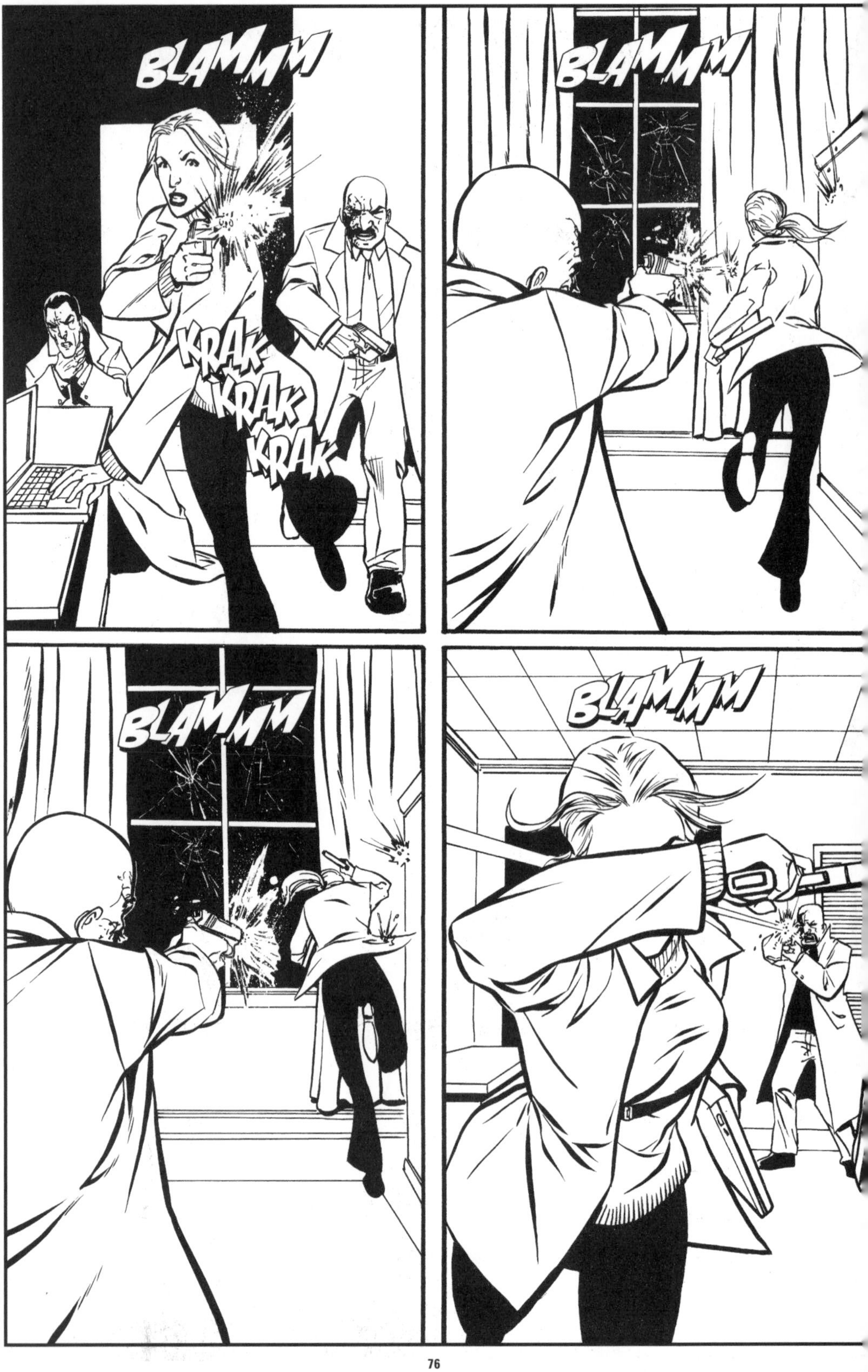

BLAMMM
KRAK
KRAK
KRAK
BLAMMM
BLAMMM
BLAMMM

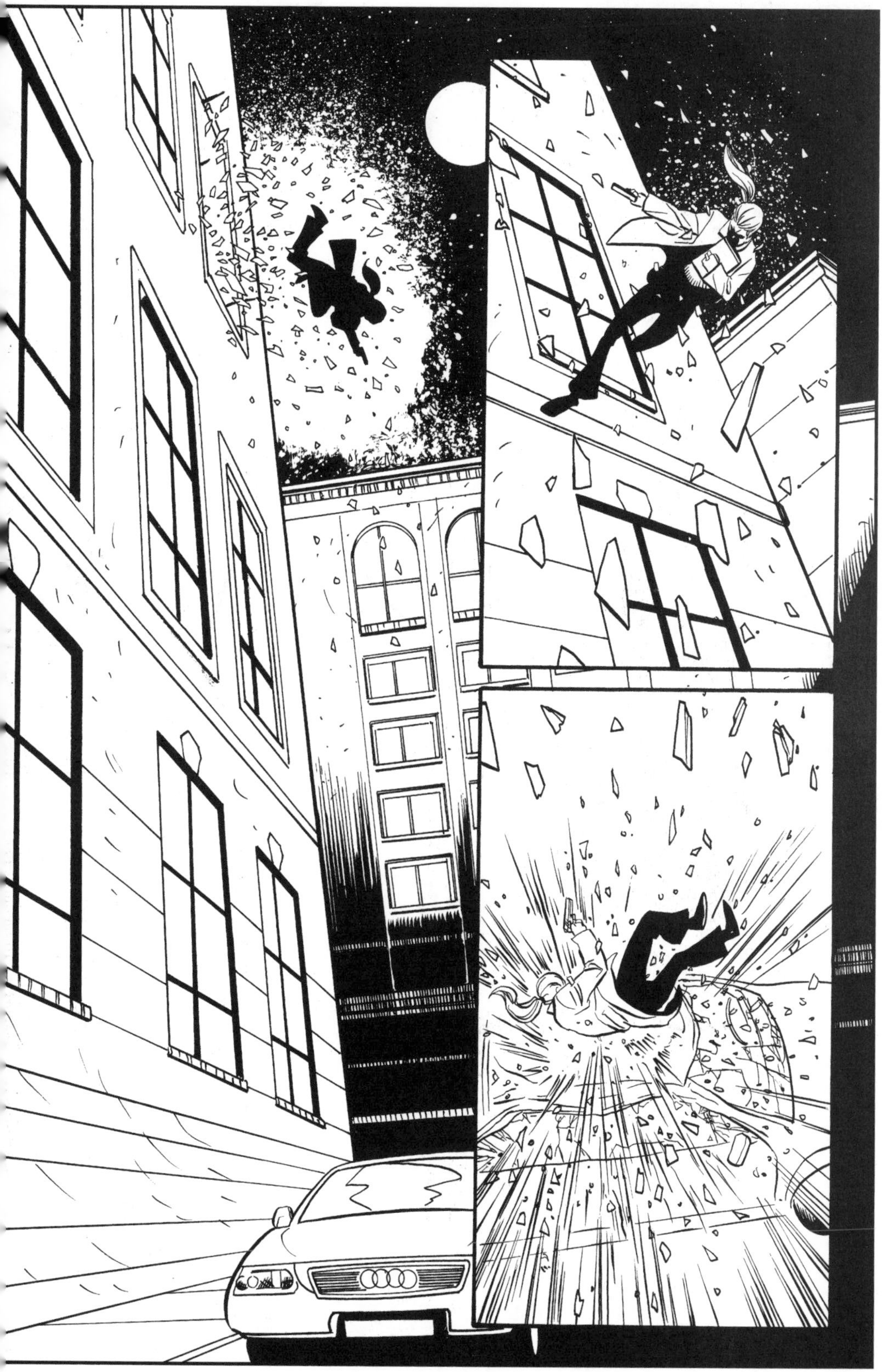

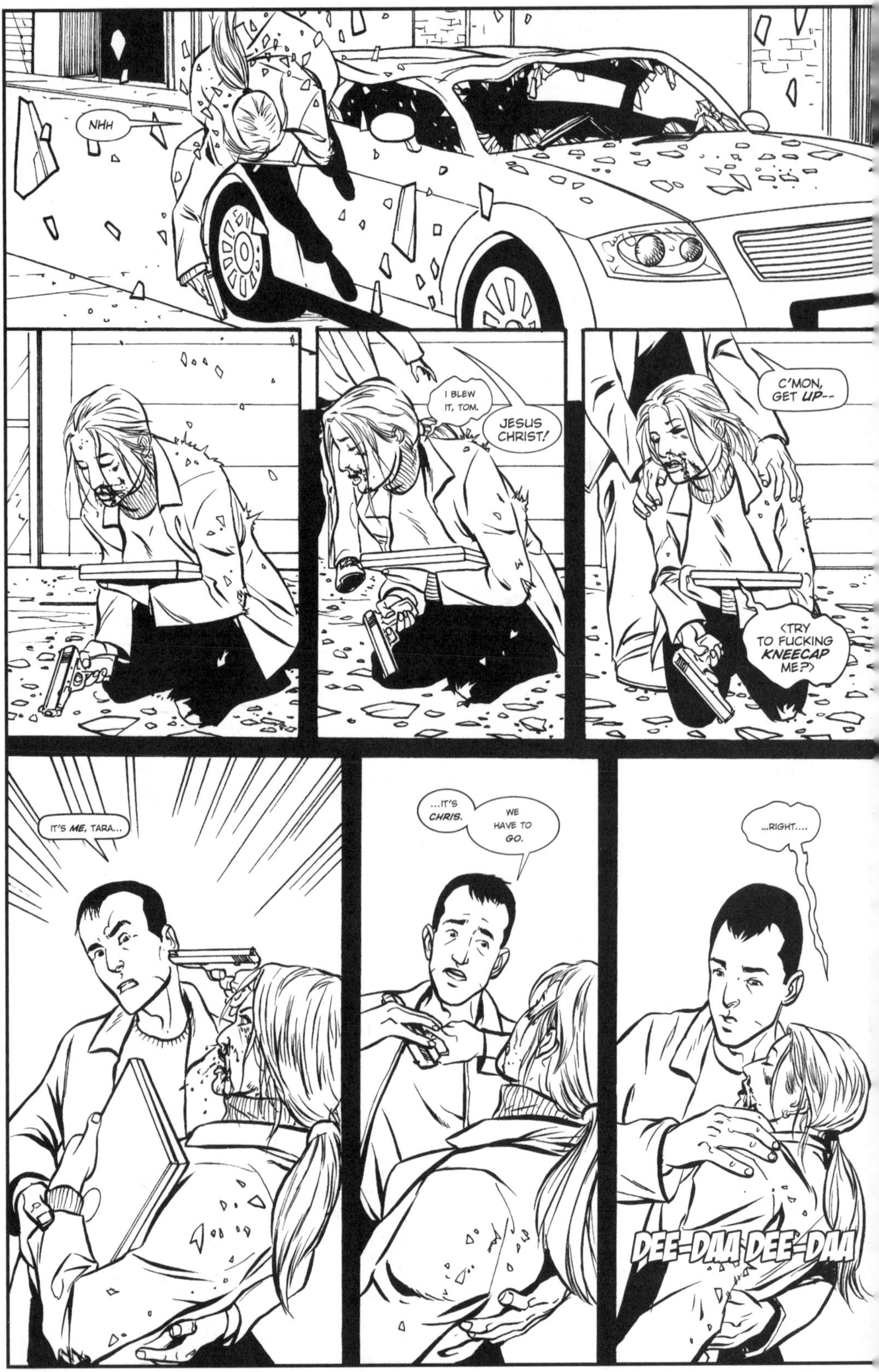
NHH
I BLEW IT, TOM.
JESUS CHRIST!
C'MON, GET UP--
<TRY TO FUCKING KNEECAP ME?>
IT'S ME, TARA...
...IT'S CHRIS.
WE HAVE TO GO.
...RIGHT....
DEE-DAA DEE-DAA

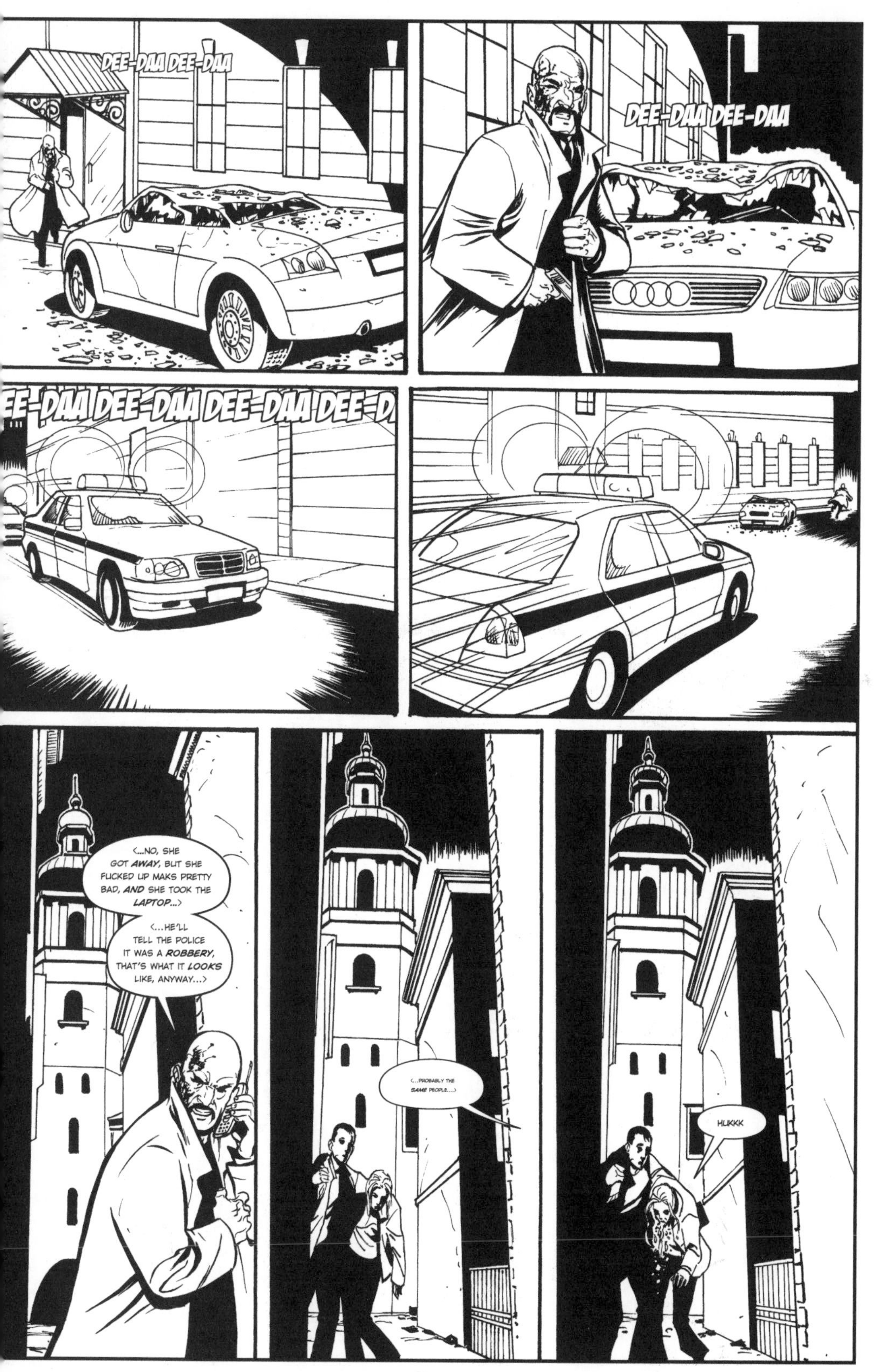
DEE-DAA DEE-DAA
DEE-DAA DEE-DAA
EE-DAA DEE-DAA DEE-DAA DEE-D
<...NO, SHE GOT **AWAY**, BUT SHE FUCKED UP MAKS PRETTY BAD, **AND** SHE TOOK THE **LAPTOP**...>
<...HE'LL TELL THE POLICE IT WAS A **ROBBERY**, THAT'S WHAT IT **LOOKS** LIKE, ANYWAY...>
<...PROBABLY THE **SAME** PEOPLE....>
HUKKK

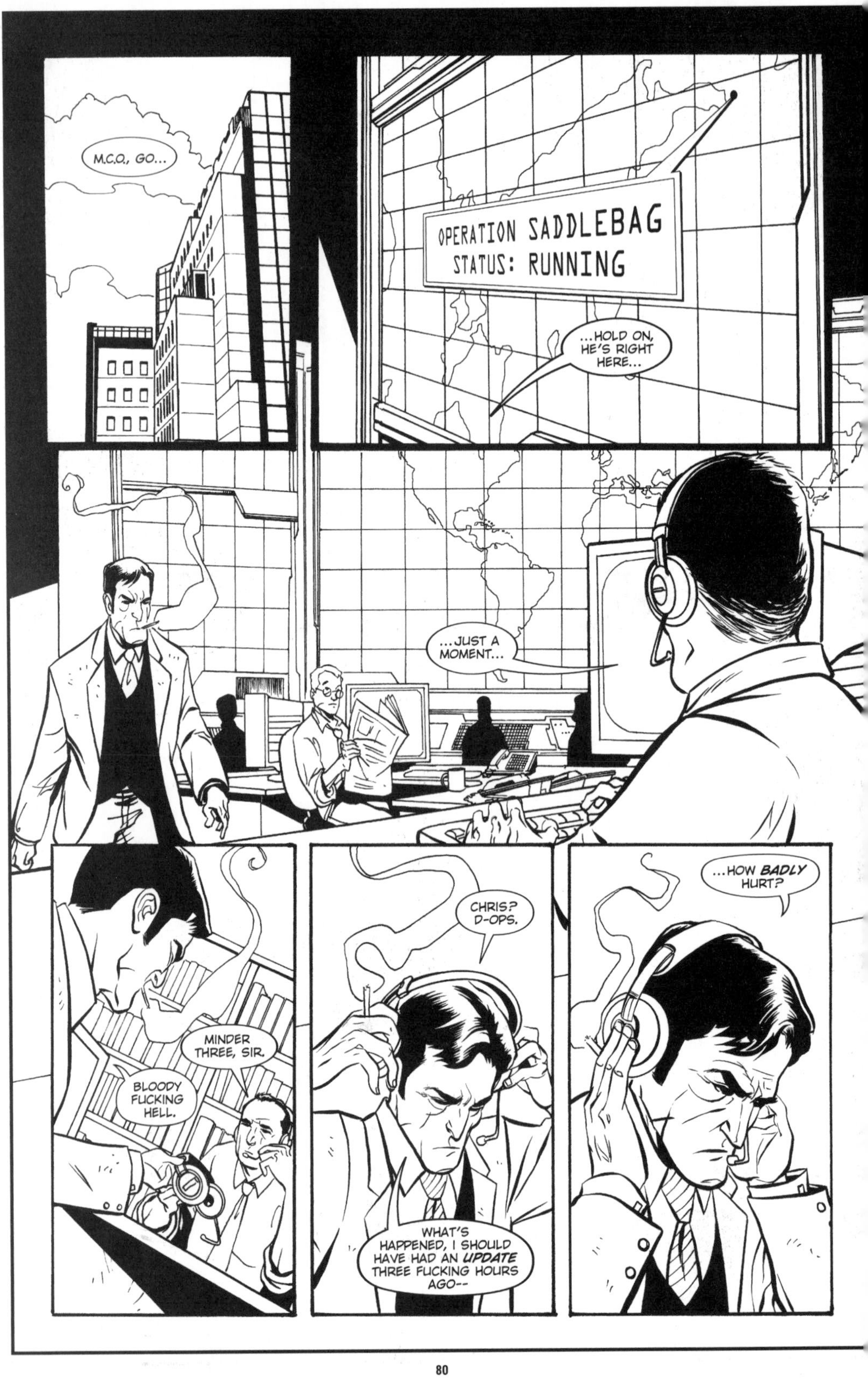

M.C.O., GO...
OPERATION SADDLEBAG
STATUS: RUNNING
...HOLD ON, HE'S RIGHT HERE...
...JUST A MOMENT...
MINDER THREE, SIR.
BLOODY FUCKING HELL.
CHRIS? D-OPS.
WHAT'S HAPPENED, I SHOULD HAVE HAD AN *UPDATE* THREE FUCKING HOURS AGO--
...HOW *BADLY* HURT?

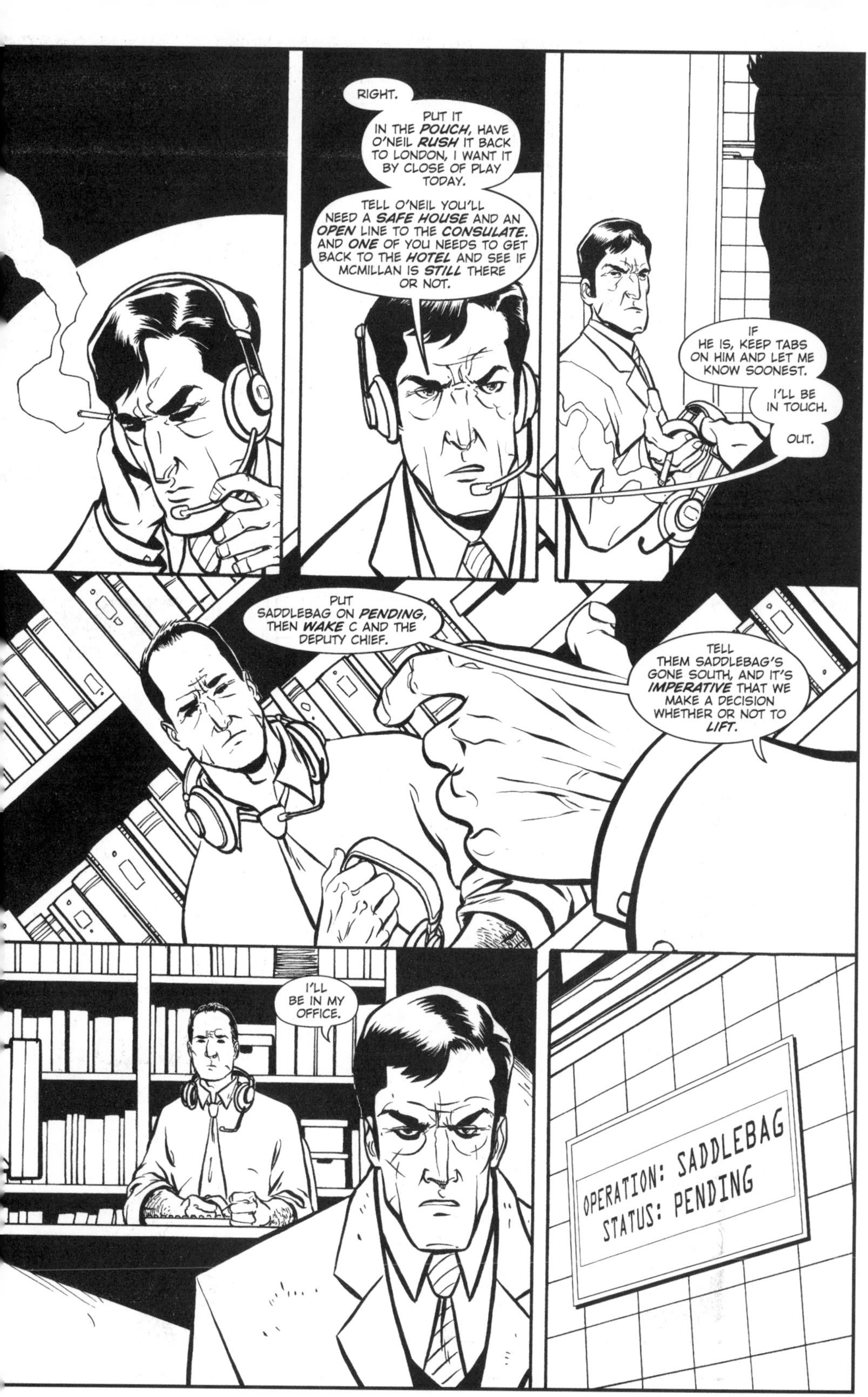
RIGHT.
PUT IT IN THE POUCH, HAVE O'NEIL RUSH IT BACK TO LONDON, I WANT IT BY CLOSE OF PLAY TODAY.
TELL O'NEIL YOU'LL NEED A SAFE HOUSE AND AN OPEN LINE TO THE CONSULATE. AND ONE OF YOU NEEDS TO GET BACK TO THE HOTEL AND SEE IF MCMILLAN IS STILL THERE OR NOT.
IF HE IS, KEEP TABS ON HIM AND LET ME KNOW SOONEST.
I'LL BE IN TOUCH.
OUT.
PUT SADDLEBAG ON PENDING, THEN WAKE C AND THE DEPUTY CHIEF.
TELL THEM SADDLEBAG'S GONE SOUTH, AND IT'S IMPERATIVE THAT WE MAKE A DECISION WHETHER OR NOT TO LIFT.
I'LL BE IN MY OFFICE.
OPERATION: SADDLEBAG
STATUS: PENDING

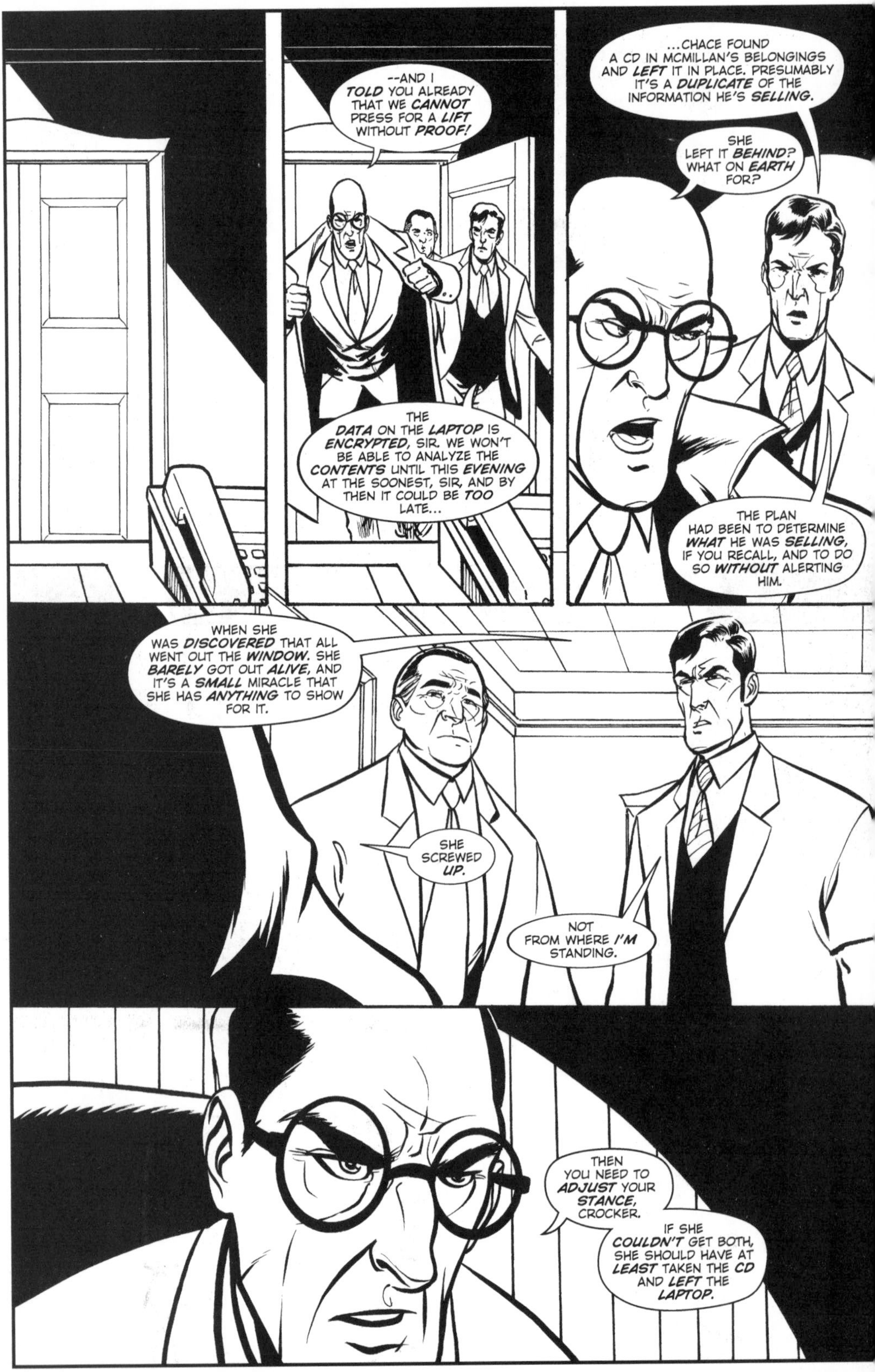
--AND I TOLD YOU ALREADY THAT WE CANNOT PRESS FOR A LIFT WITHOUT PROOF!
THE DATA ON THE LAPTOP IS ENCRYPTED, SIR. WE WON'T BE ABLE TO ANALYZE THE CONTENTS UNTIL THIS EVENING AT THE SOONEST, SIR, AND BY THEN IT COULD BE TOO LATE...
...CHACE FOUND A CD IN MCMILLAN'S BELONGINGS AND LEFT IT IN PLACE. PRESUMABLY IT'S A DUPLICATE OF THE INFORMATION HE'S SELLING.
SHE LEFT IT BEHIND? WHAT ON EARTH FOR?
THE PLAN HAD BEEN TO DETERMINE WHAT HE WAS SELLING, IF YOU RECALL, AND TO DO SO WITHOUT ALERTING HIM.
WHEN SHE WAS DISCOVERED THAT ALL WENT OUT THE WINDOW. SHE BARELY GOT OUT ALIVE, AND IT'S A SMALL MIRACLE THAT SHE HAS ANYTHING TO SHOW FOR IT.
SHE SCREWED UP.
NOT FROM WHERE I'M STANDING.
THEN YOU NEED TO ADJUST YOUR STANCE, CROCKER.
IF SHE COULDN'T GET BOTH, SHE SHOULD HAVE AT LEAST TAKEN THE CD AND LEFT THE LAPTOP.

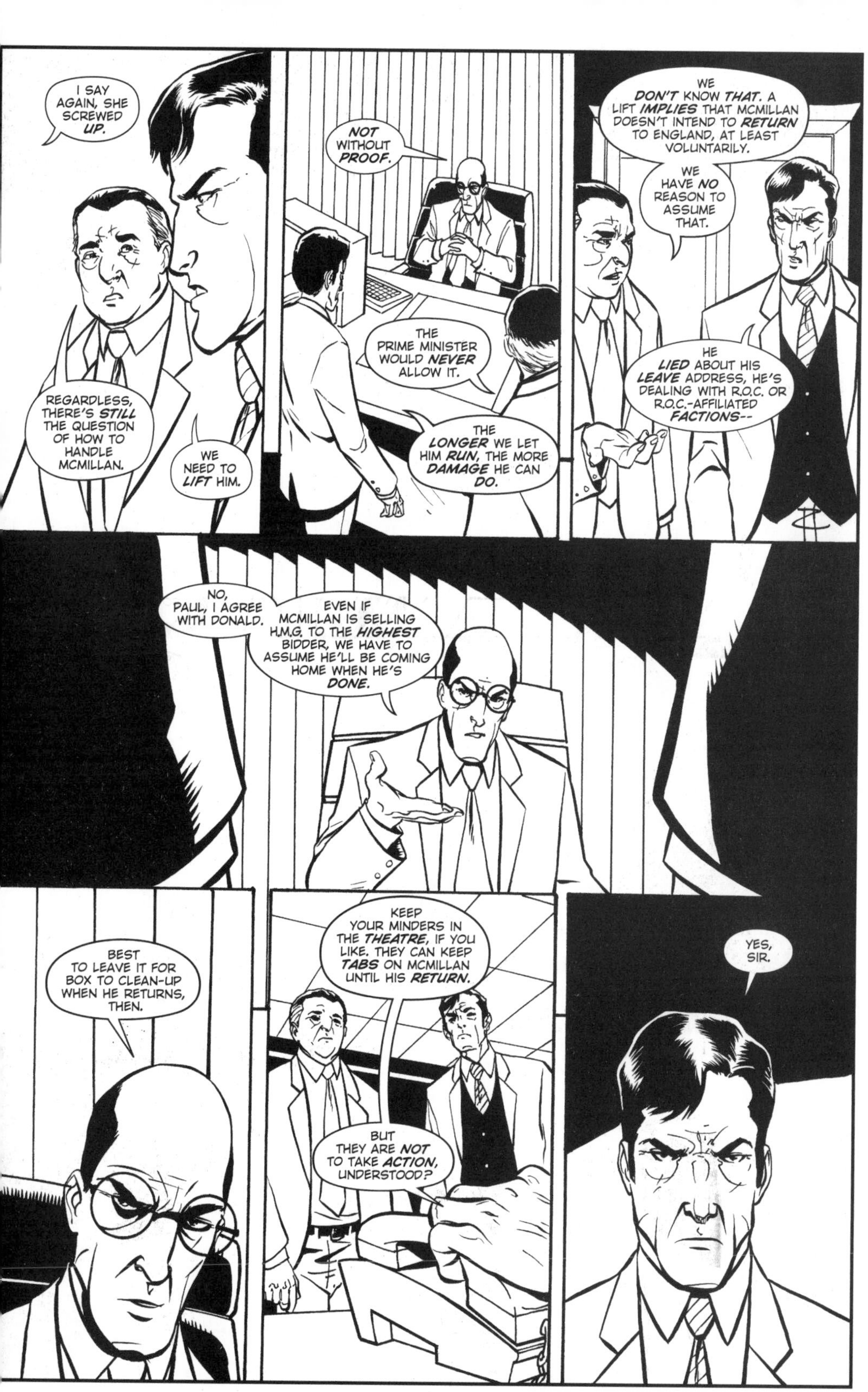
I SAY AGAIN, SHE SCREWED *UP.*
REGARDLESS, THERE'S *STILL* THE QUESTION OF HOW TO HANDLE MCMILLAN.
WE NEED TO *LIFT* HIM.
NOT WITHOUT *PROOF.*
THE PRIME MINISTER WOULD *NEVER* ALLOW IT.
THE *LONGER* WE LET HIM *RUN*, THE MORE *DAMAGE* HE CAN *DO.*
WE *DON'T* KNOW *THAT.* A LIFT *IMPLIES* THAT MCMILLAN DOESN'T INTEND TO *RETURN* TO ENGLAND, AT LEAST VOLUNTARILY.
WE HAVE *NO* REASON TO ASSUME THAT.
HE *LIED* ABOUT HIS *LEAVE* ADDRESS, HE'S DEALING WITH R.O.C. OR R.O.C.-AFFILIATED *FACTIONS--*
NO, PAUL, I AGREE WITH DONALD.
EVEN IF MCMILLAN IS SELLING H.M.G. TO THE *HIGHEST* BIDDER, WE HAVE TO ASSUME HE'LL BE COMING HOME WHEN HE'S *DONE.*
BEST TO LEAVE IT FOR BOX TO CLEAN-UP WHEN HE RETURNS, THEN.
KEEP YOUR MINDERS IN THE *THEATRE*, IF YOU LIKE. THEY CAN KEEP *TABS* ON MCMILLAN UNTIL HIS *RETURN.*
BUT THEY ARE *NOT* TO TAKE *ACTION*, UNDERSTOOD?
YES, SIR.

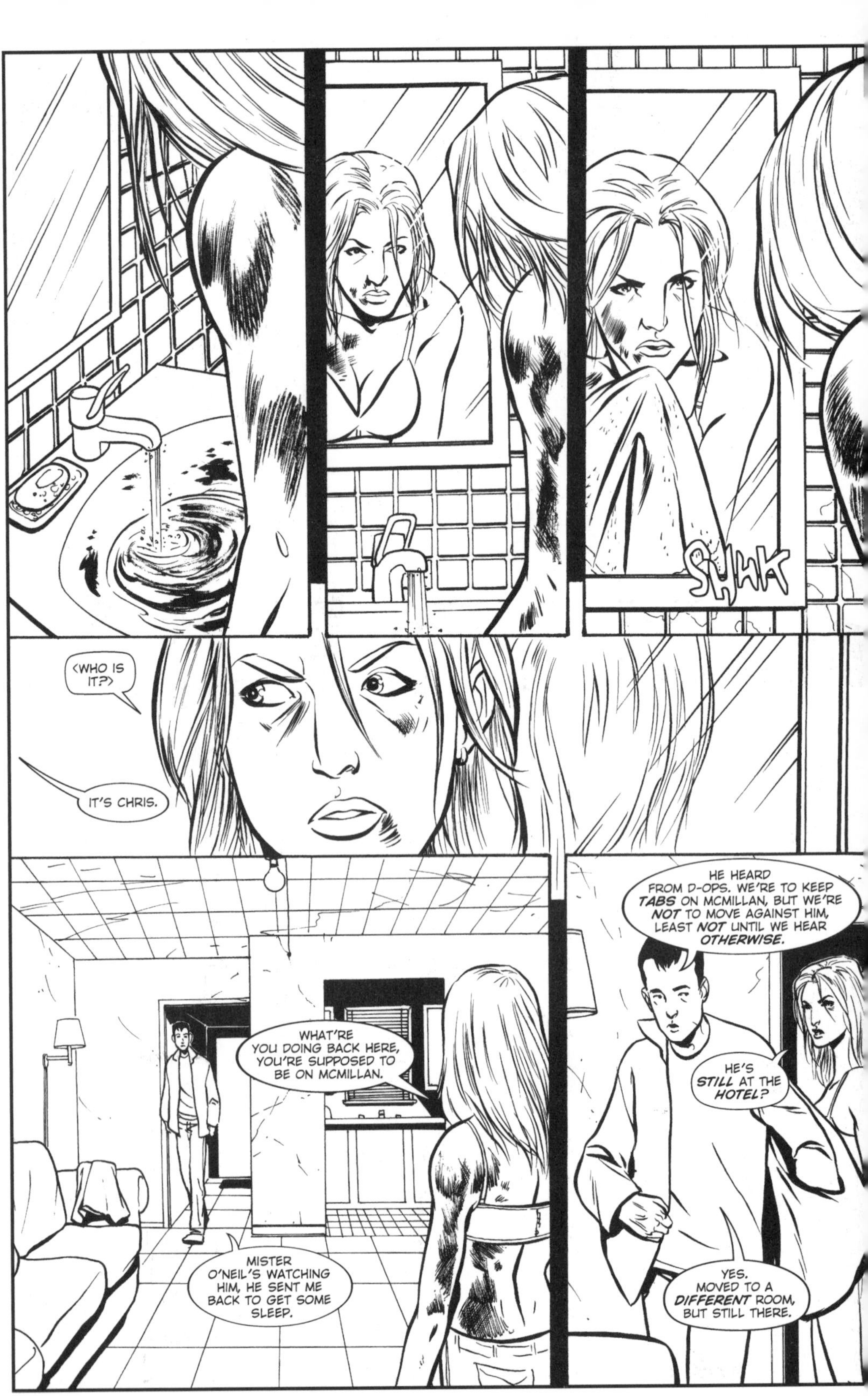
SHHK
<WHO IS IT?>
IT'S CHRIS.
WHAT'RE YOU DOING BACK HERE, YOU'RE SUPPOSED TO BE ON MCMILLAN.
MISTER O'NEIL'S WATCHING HIM, HE SENT ME BACK TO GET SOME SLEEP.
HE HEARD FROM D-OPS. WE'RE TO KEEP TABS ON MCMILLAN, BUT WE'RE NOT TO MOVE AGAINST HIM, LEAST NOT UNTIL WE HEAR OTHERWISE.
HE'S STILL AT THE HOTEL?
YES. MOVED TO A DIFFERENT ROOM, BUT STILL THERE.

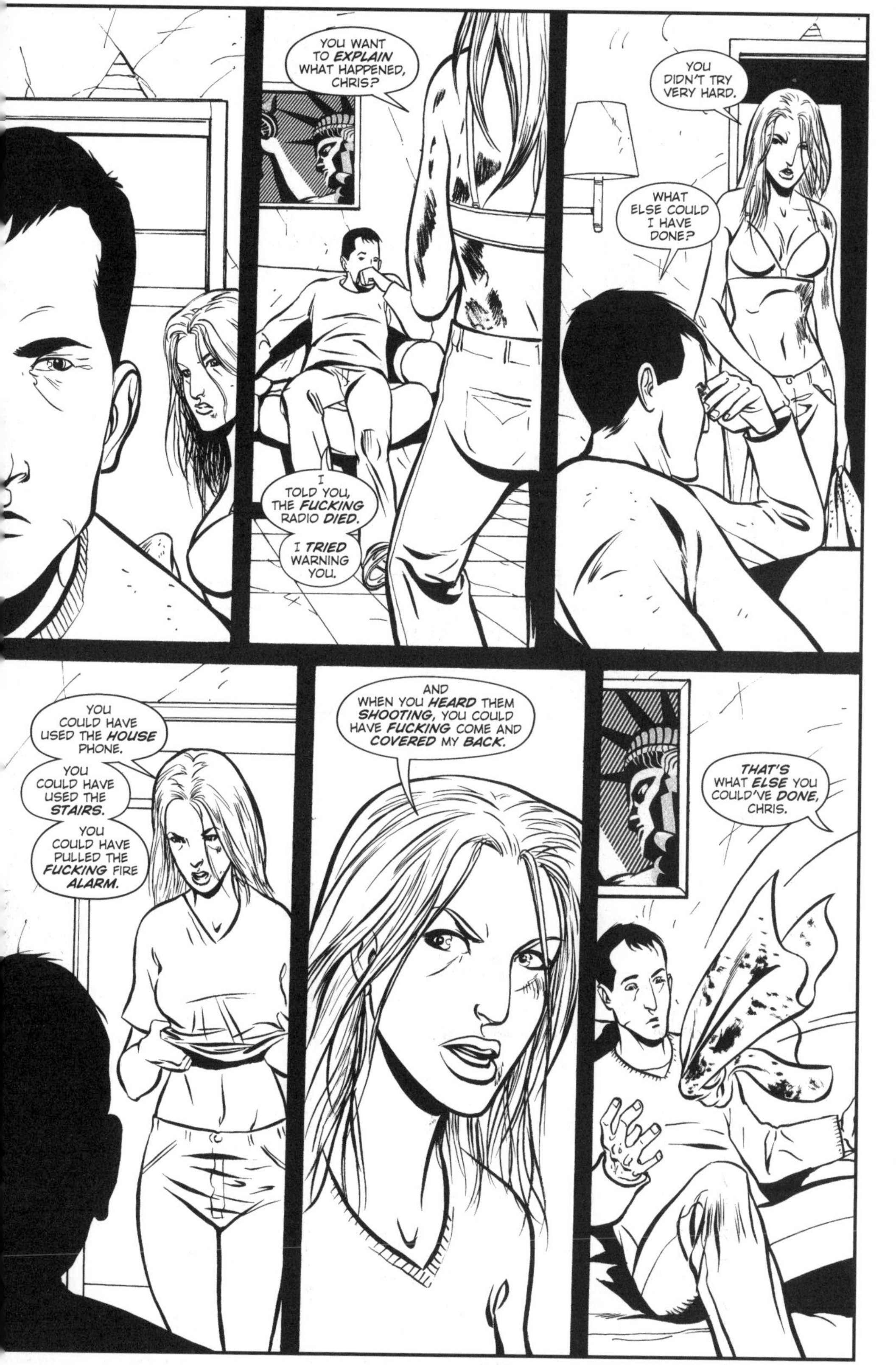

YOU WANT TO *EXPLAIN* WHAT HAPPENED, CHRIS?
I TOLD YOU, THE *FUCKING* RADIO *DIED*.
I *TRIED* WARNING YOU.
YOU DIDN'T TRY VERY HARD.
WHAT ELSE COULD I HAVE DONE?
YOU COULD HAVE USED THE *HOUSE* PHONE.
YOU COULD HAVE USED THE *STAIRS*.
YOU COULD HAVE PULLED THE *FUCKING* FIRE *ALARM*.
AND WHEN YOU *HEARD* THEM *SHOOTING*, YOU COULD HAVE *FUCKING* COME AND *COVERED* MY *BACK*.
THAT'S WHAT *ELSE* YOU COULD'VE *DONE*, CHRIS.

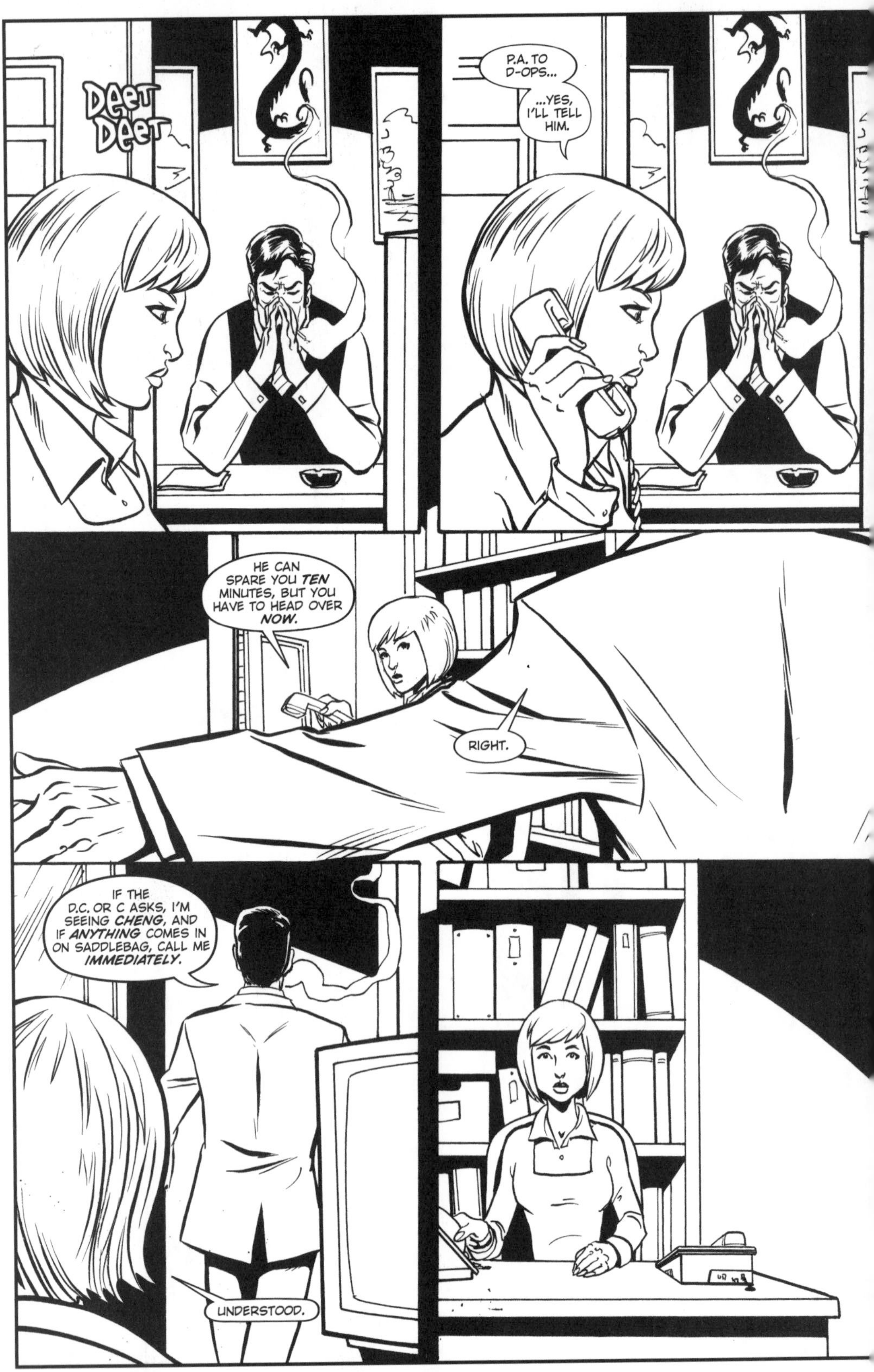
DEET DEET
P.A. TO D-OPS...
...YES, I'LL TELL HIM.
HE CAN SPARE YOU *TEN* MINUTES, BUT YOU HAVE TO HEAD OVER *NOW*.
RIGHT.
IF THE D.C. OR C ASKS, I'M SEEING *CHENG*, AND IF *ANYTHING* COMES IN ON SADDLEBAG, CALL ME *IMMEDIATELY*.
UNDERSTOOD.

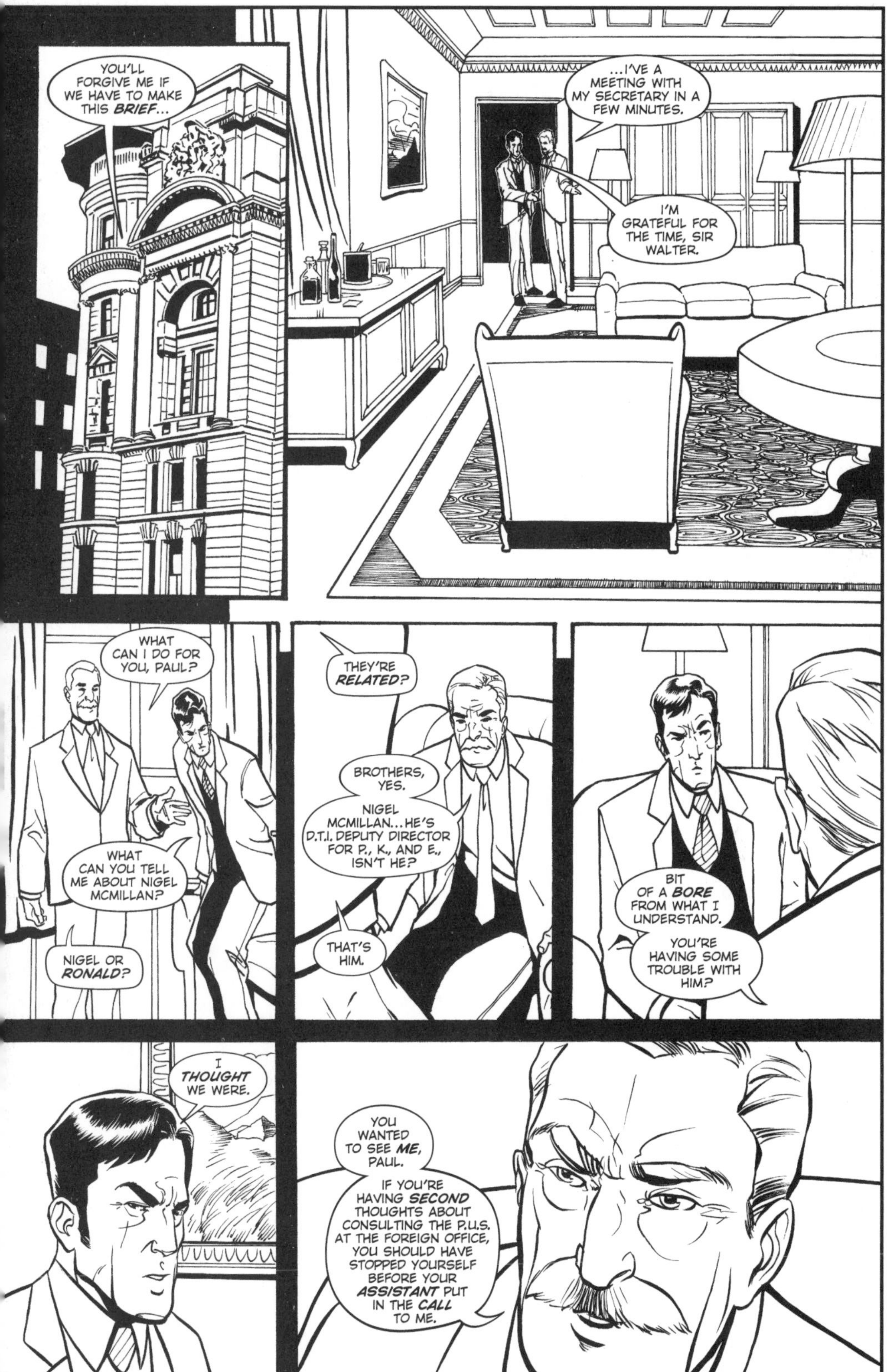
YOU'LL FORGIVE ME IF WE HAVE TO MAKE THIS *BRIEF*...
...I'VE A MEETING WITH MY SECRETARY IN A FEW MINUTES.
I'M GRATEFUL FOR THE TIME, SIR WALTER.
WHAT CAN I DO FOR YOU, PAUL?
WHAT CAN YOU TELL ME ABOUT NIGEL MCMILLAN?
NIGEL OR *RONALD?*
THEY'RE *RELATED?*
BROTHERS, YES.
NIGEL MCMILLAN... HE'S D.T.I. DEPUTY DIRECTOR FOR P., K., AND E., ISN'T HE?
THAT'S HIM.
BIT OF A *BORE* FROM WHAT I UNDERSTAND.
YOU'RE HAVING SOME TROUBLE WITH HIM?
I *THOUGHT* WE WERE.
YOU WANTED TO SEE *ME,* PAUL.
IF YOU'RE HAVING *SECOND* THOUGHTS ABOUT CONSULTING THE P.U.S. AT THE FOREIGN OFFICE, YOU SHOULD HAVE STOPPED YOURSELF BEFORE YOUR *ASSISTANT* PUT IN THE *CALL* TO ME.

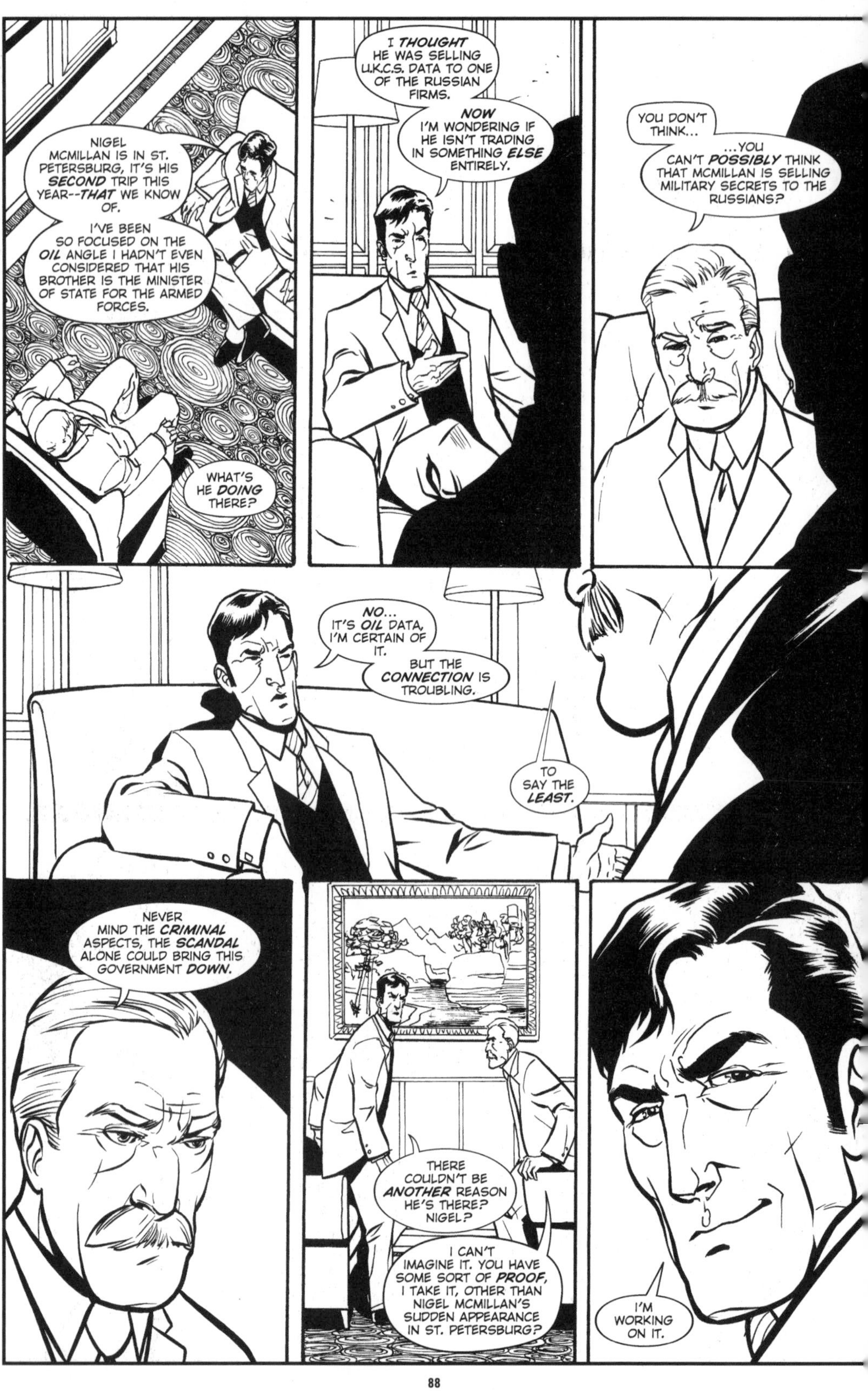
NIGEL MCMILLAN IS IN ST. PETERSBURG, IT'S HIS SECOND TRIP THIS YEAR--THAT WE KNOW OF.
I'VE BEEN SO FOCUSED ON THE OIL ANGLE I HADN'T EVEN CONSIDERED THAT HIS BROTHER IS THE MINISTER OF STATE FOR THE ARMED FORCES.
WHAT'S HE DOING THERE?
I THOUGHT HE WAS SELLING U.K.C.S. DATA TO ONE OF THE RUSSIAN FIRMS.
NOW I'M WONDERING IF HE ISN'T TRADING IN SOMETHING ELSE ENTIRELY.
YOU DON'T THINK...
...YOU CAN'T POSSIBLY THINK THAT MCMILLAN IS SELLING MILITARY SECRETS TO THE RUSSIANS?
NO... IT'S OIL DATA, I'M CERTAIN OF IT.
BUT THE CONNECTION IS TROUBLING.
TO SAY THE LEAST.
NEVER MIND THE CRIMINAL ASPECTS, THE SCANDAL ALONE COULD BRING THIS GOVERNMENT DOWN.
THERE COULDN'T BE ANOTHER REASON HE'S THERE? NIGEL?
I CAN'T IMAGINE IT. YOU HAVE SOME SORT OF PROOF, I TAKE IT, OTHER THAN NIGEL MCMILLAN'S SUDDEN APPEARANCE IN ST. PETERSBURG?
I'M WORKING ON IT.

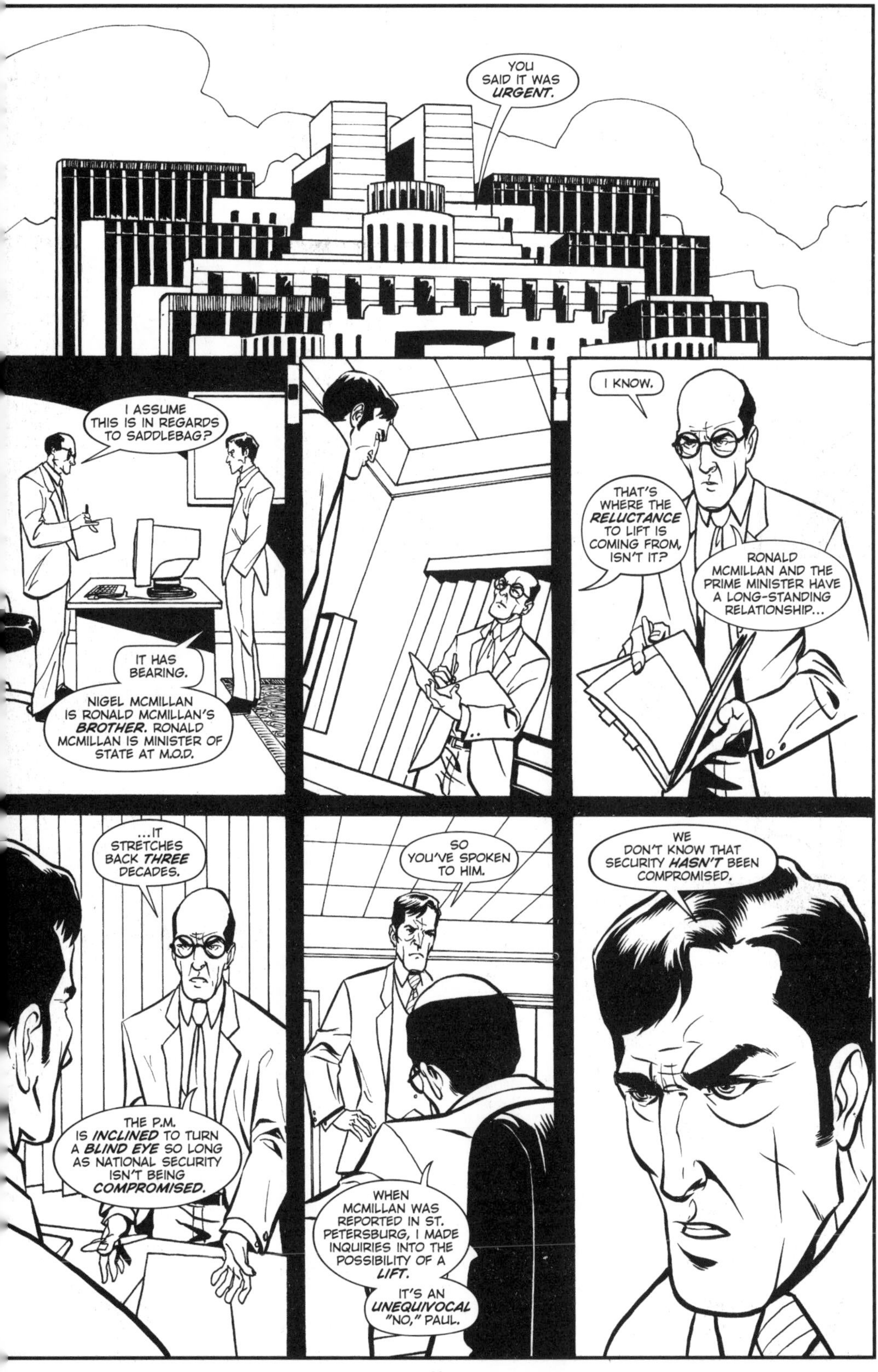
YOU SAID IT WAS URGENT.
I ASSUME THIS IS IN REGARDS TO SADDLEBAG?
IT HAS BEARING.
NIGEL MCMILLAN IS RONALD MCMILLAN'S BROTHER. RONALD MCMILLAN IS MINISTER OF STATE AT M.O.D.
I KNOW.
THAT'S WHERE THE RELUCTANCE TO LIFT IS COMING FROM, ISN'T IT?
RONALD MCMILLAN AND THE PRIME MINISTER HAVE A LONG-STANDING RELATIONSHIP...
...IT STRETCHES BACK THREE DECADES.
THE P.M. IS INCLINED TO TURN A BLIND EYE SO LONG AS NATIONAL SECURITY ISN'T BEING COMPROMISED.
SO YOU'VE SPOKEN TO HIM.
WHEN MCMILLAN WAS REPORTED IN ST. PETERSBURG, I MADE INQUIRIES INTO THE POSSIBILITY OF A LIFT.
IT'S AN UNEQUIVOCAL "NO," PAUL.
WE DON'T KNOW THAT SECURITY HASN'T BEEN COMPROMISED.

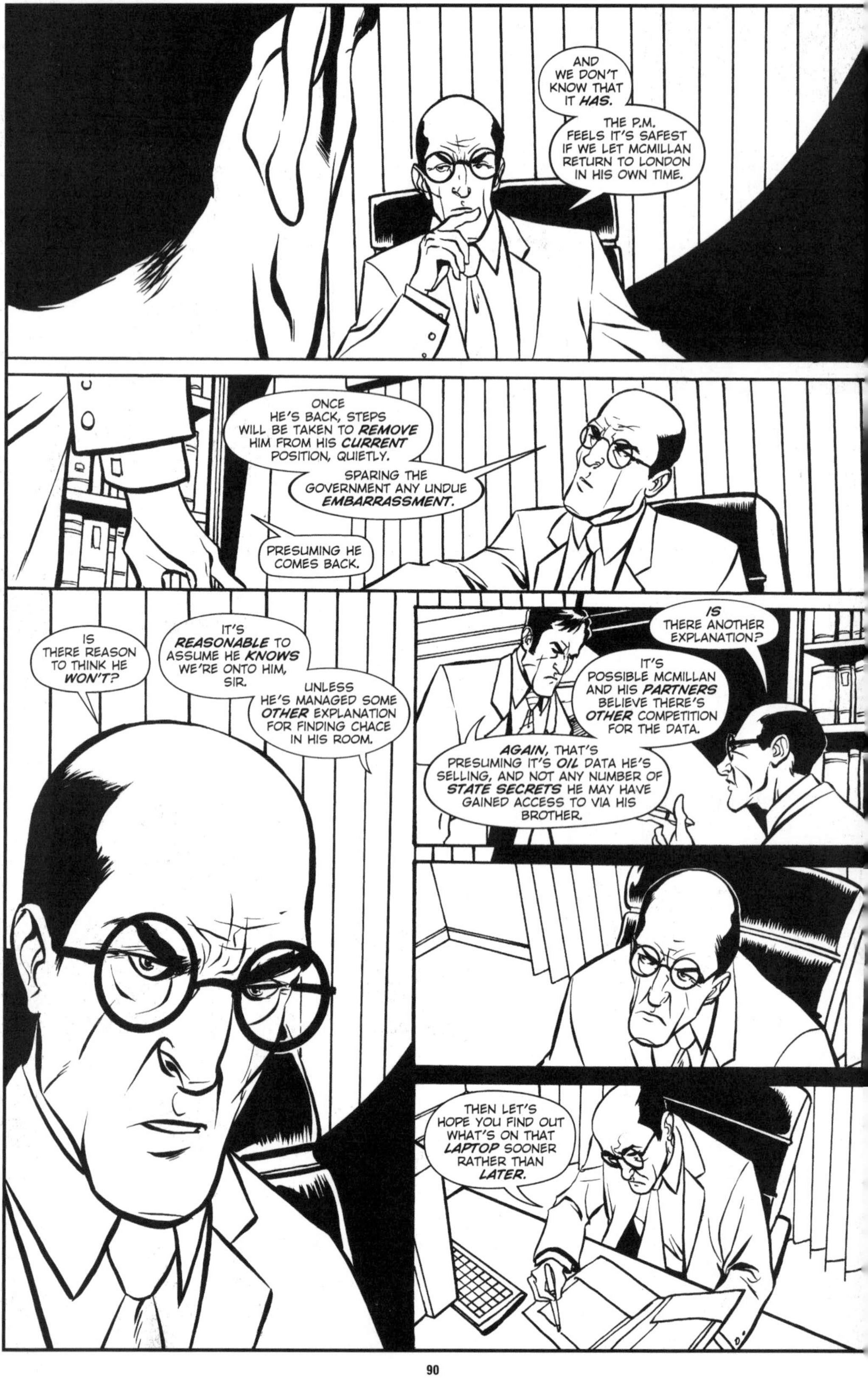
AND WE DON'T KNOW THAT IT HAS.
THE P.M. FEELS IT'S SAFEST IF WE LET MCMILLAN RETURN TO LONDON IN HIS OWN TIME.
ONCE HE'S BACK, STEPS WILL BE TAKEN TO REMOVE HIM FROM HIS CURRENT POSITION, QUIETLY.
SPARING THE GOVERNMENT ANY UNDUE EMBARRASSMENT.
PRESUMING HE COMES BACK.
IS THERE REASON TO THINK HE WON'T?
IT'S REASONABLE TO ASSUME HE KNOWS WE'RE ONTO HIM, SIR.
UNLESS HE'S MANAGED SOME OTHER EXPLANATION FOR FINDING CHACE IN HIS ROOM.
IS THERE ANOTHER EXPLANATION?
IT'S POSSIBLE MCMILLAN AND HIS PARTNERS BELIEVE THERE'S OTHER COMPETITION FOR THE DATA.
AGAIN, THAT'S PRESUMING IT'S OIL DATA HE'S SELLING, AND NOT ANY NUMBER OF STATE SECRETS HE MAY HAVE GAINED ACCESS TO VIA HIS BROTHER.
THEN LET'S HOPE YOU FIND OUT WHAT'S ON THAT LAPTOP SOONER RATHER THAN LATER.

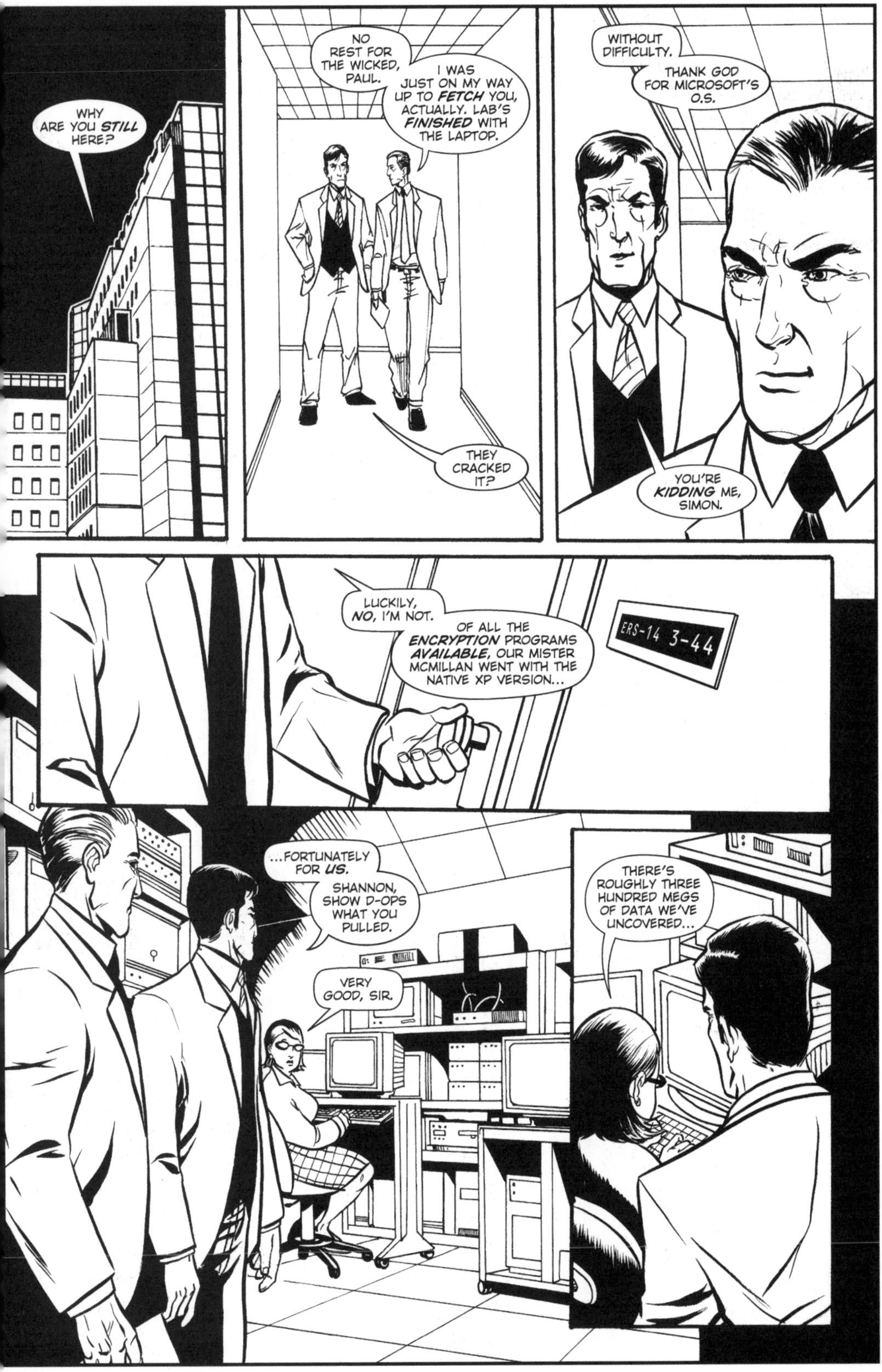
WHY ARE YOU STILL HERE?
NO REST FOR THE WICKED, PAUL.
I WAS JUST ON MY WAY UP TO FETCH YOU, ACTUALLY. LAB'S FINISHED WITH THE LAPTOP.
THEY CRACKED IT?
WITHOUT DIFFICULTY.
THANK GOD FOR MICROSOFT'S O.S.
YOU'RE KIDDING ME, SIMON.
LUCKILY, NO, I'M NOT.
OF ALL THE ENCRYPTION PROGRAMS AVAILABLE, OUR MISTER MCMILLAN WENT WITH THE NATIVE XP VERSION...
ERS-14 3-44
...FORTUNATELY FOR US.
SHANNON, SHOW D-OPS WHAT YOU PULLED.
VERY GOOD, SIR.
THERE'S ROUGHLY THREE HUNDRED MEGS OF DATA WE'VE UNCOVERED...

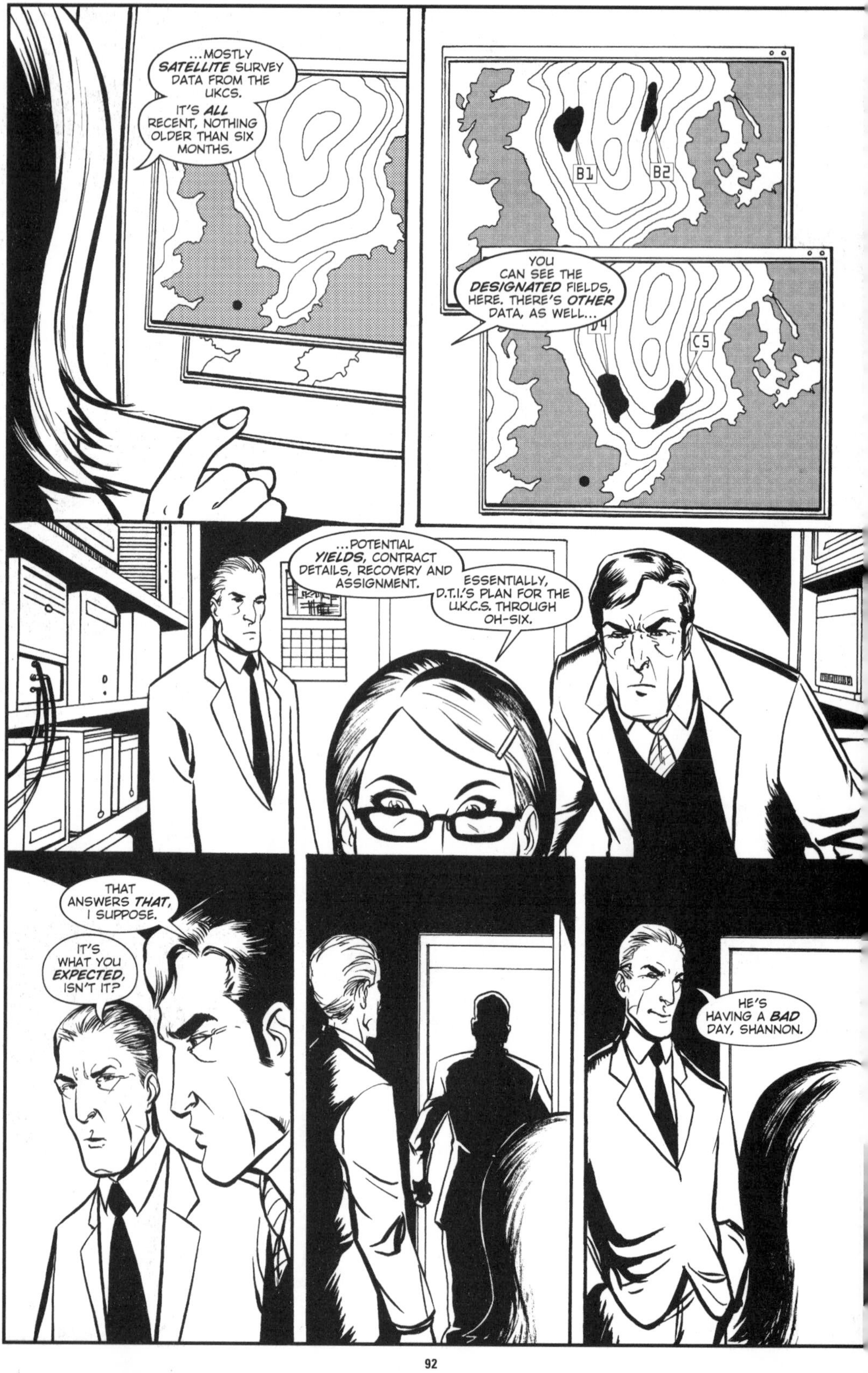
...MOSTLY SATELLITE SURVEY DATA FROM THE UKCS.
IT'S ALL RECENT, NOTHING OLDER THAN SIX MONTHS.
B1
B2
YOU CAN SEE THE DESIGNATED FIELDS, HERE. THERE'S OTHER DATA, AS WELL...
D4
C5
...POTENTIAL YIELDS, CONTRACT DETAILS, RECOVERY AND ASSIGNMENT.
ESSENTIALLY, D.T.I.'S PLAN FOR THE U.K.C.S. THROUGH OH-SIX.
THAT ANSWERS THAT, I SUPPOSE.
IT'S WHAT YOU EXPECTED, ISN'T IT?
HE'S HAVING A BAD DAY, SHANNON.

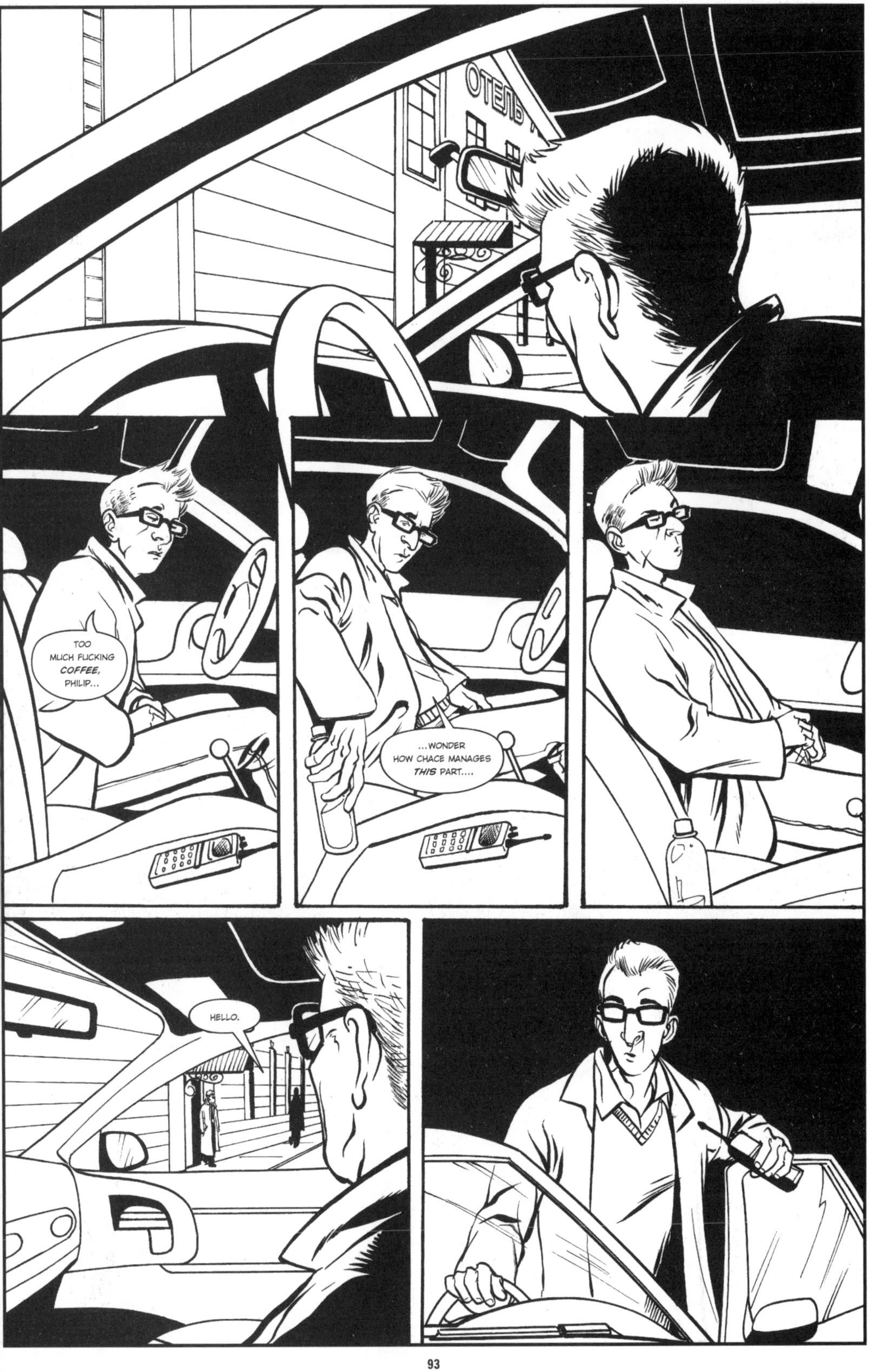
ОТЕЛЬ
TOO MUCH FUCKING *COFFEE,* PHILIP...
...WONDER HOW CHACE MANAGES *THIS* PART....
HELLO.

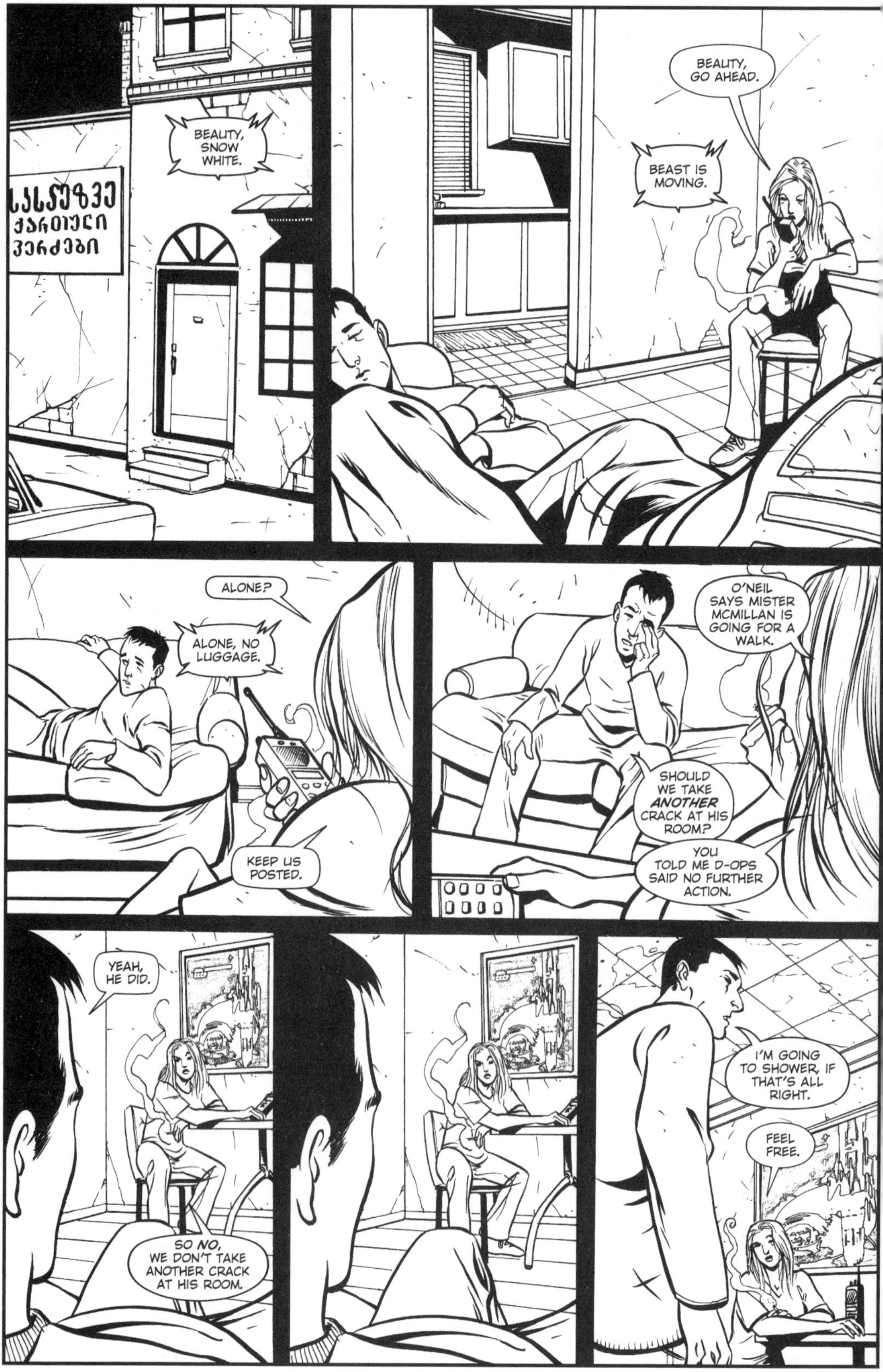
BEAUTY, SNOW WHITE.
BEAUTY, GO AHEAD.
BEAST IS MOVING.
ALONE?
ALONE, NO LUGGAGE.
KEEP US POSTED.
O'NEIL SAYS MISTER MCMILLAN IS GOING FOR A WALK.
SHOULD WE TAKE **ANOTHER** CRACK AT HIS ROOM?
YOU TOLD ME D-OPS SAID NO FURTHER ACTION.
YEAH, HE DID.
SO **NO**, WE DON'T TAKE ANOTHER CRACK AT HIS ROOM.
I'M GOING TO SHOWER, IF THAT'S ALL RIGHT.
FEEL FREE.

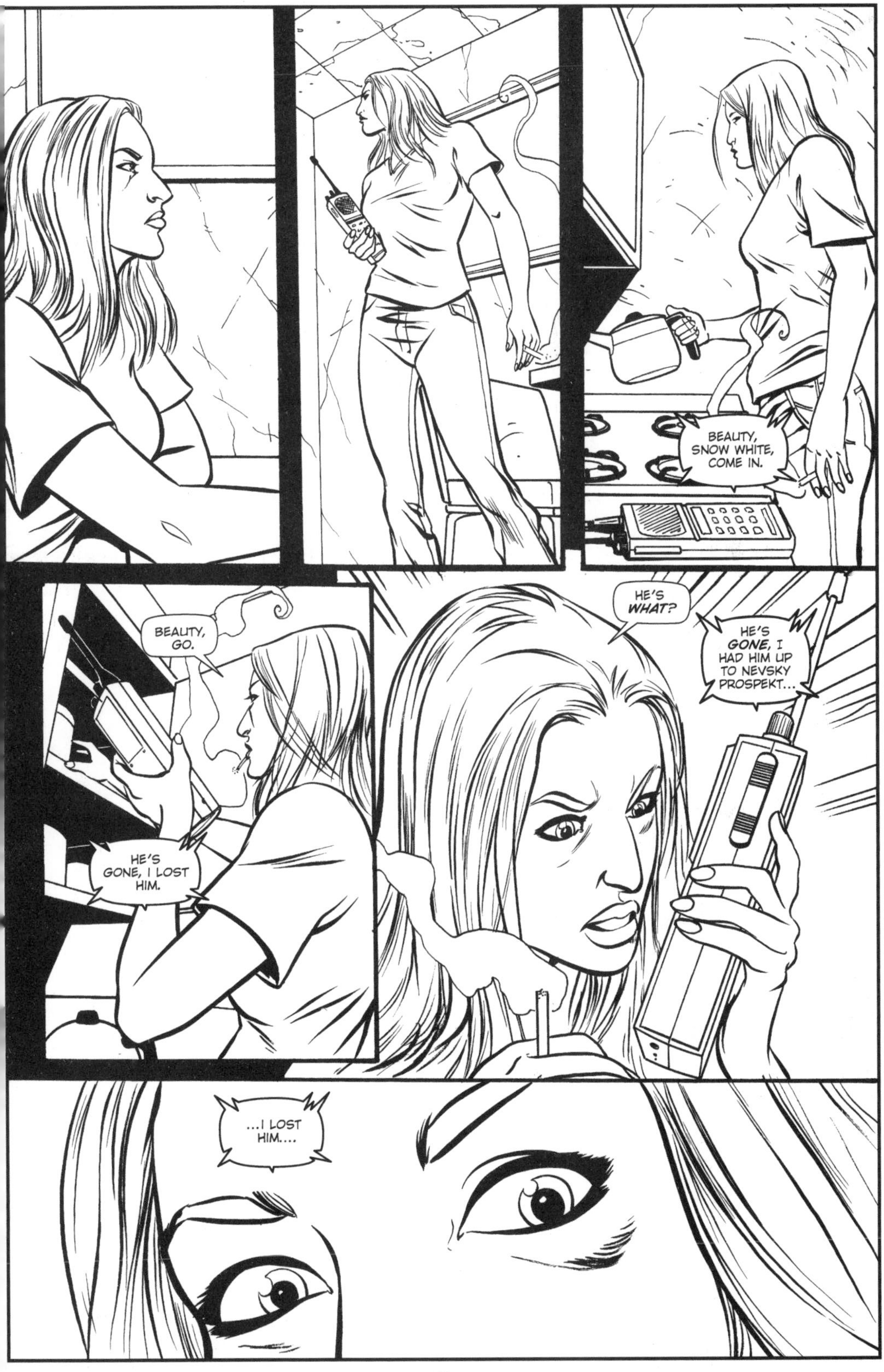
BEAUTY, SNOW WHITE, COME IN.
BEAUTY, GO.
HE'S GONE, I LOST HIM.
HE'S *WHAT?*
HE'S *GONE*, I HAD HIM UP TO NEVSKY PROSPEKT...
...I LOST HIM....

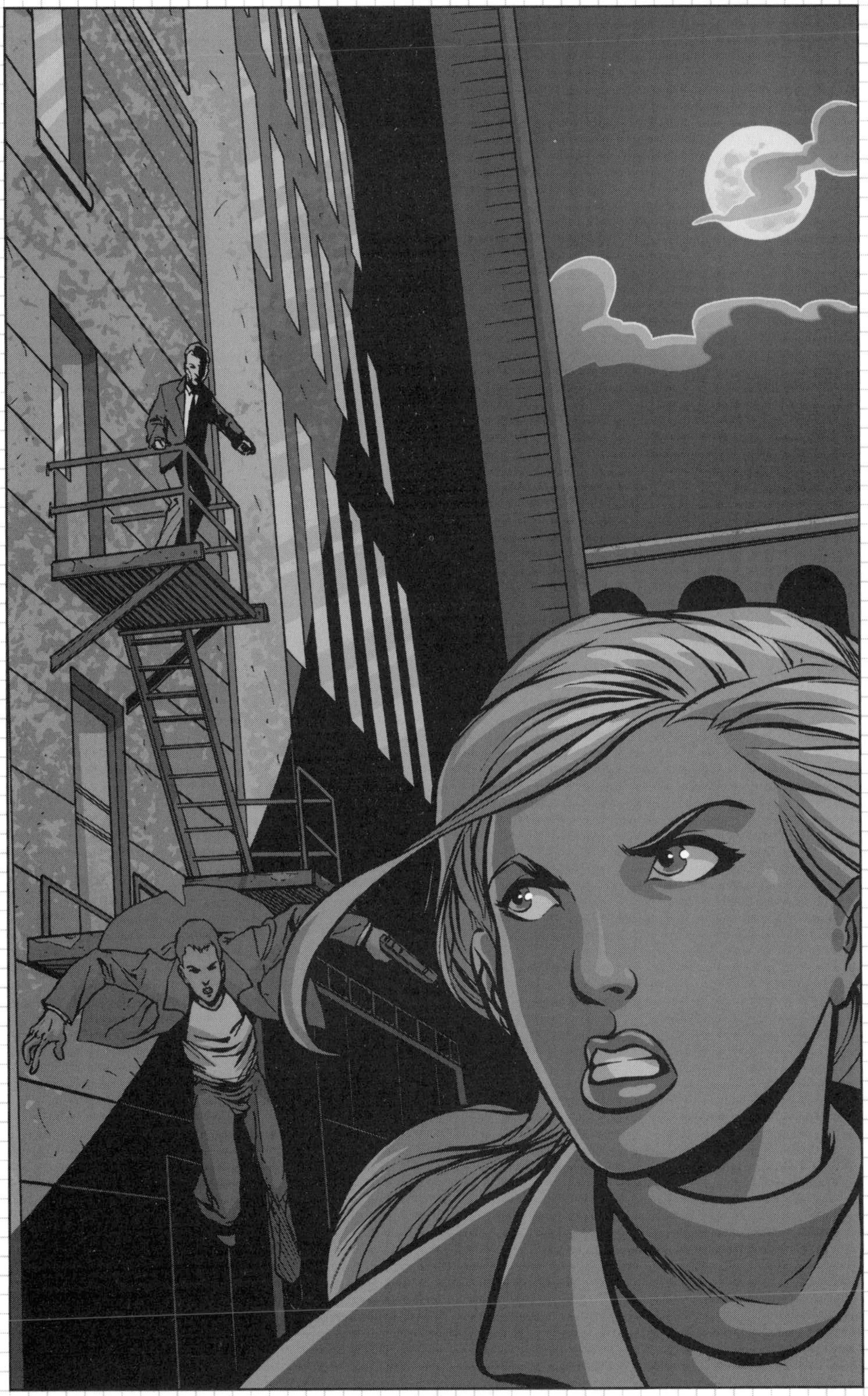

CHAPTER 3

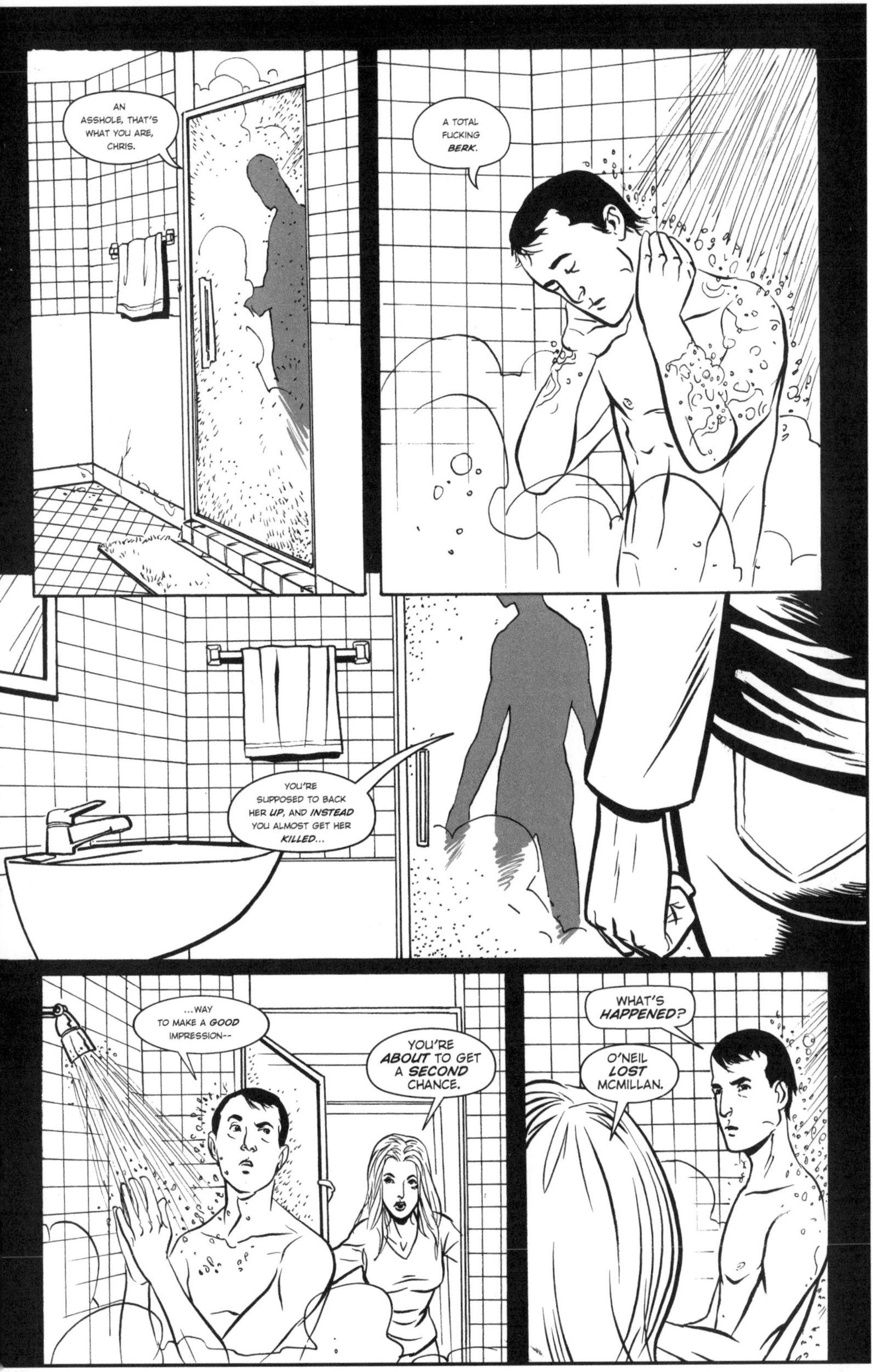
AN ASSHOLE, THAT'S WHAT YOU ARE, CHRIS.
A TOTAL FUCKING BERK.
YOU'RE SUPPOSED TO BACK HER UP, AND INSTEAD YOU ALMOST GET HER KILLED...
...WAY TO MAKE A GOOD IMPRESSION--
YOU'RE ABOUT TO GET A SECOND CHANCE.
WHAT'S HAPPENED?
O'NEIL LOST MCMILLAN.

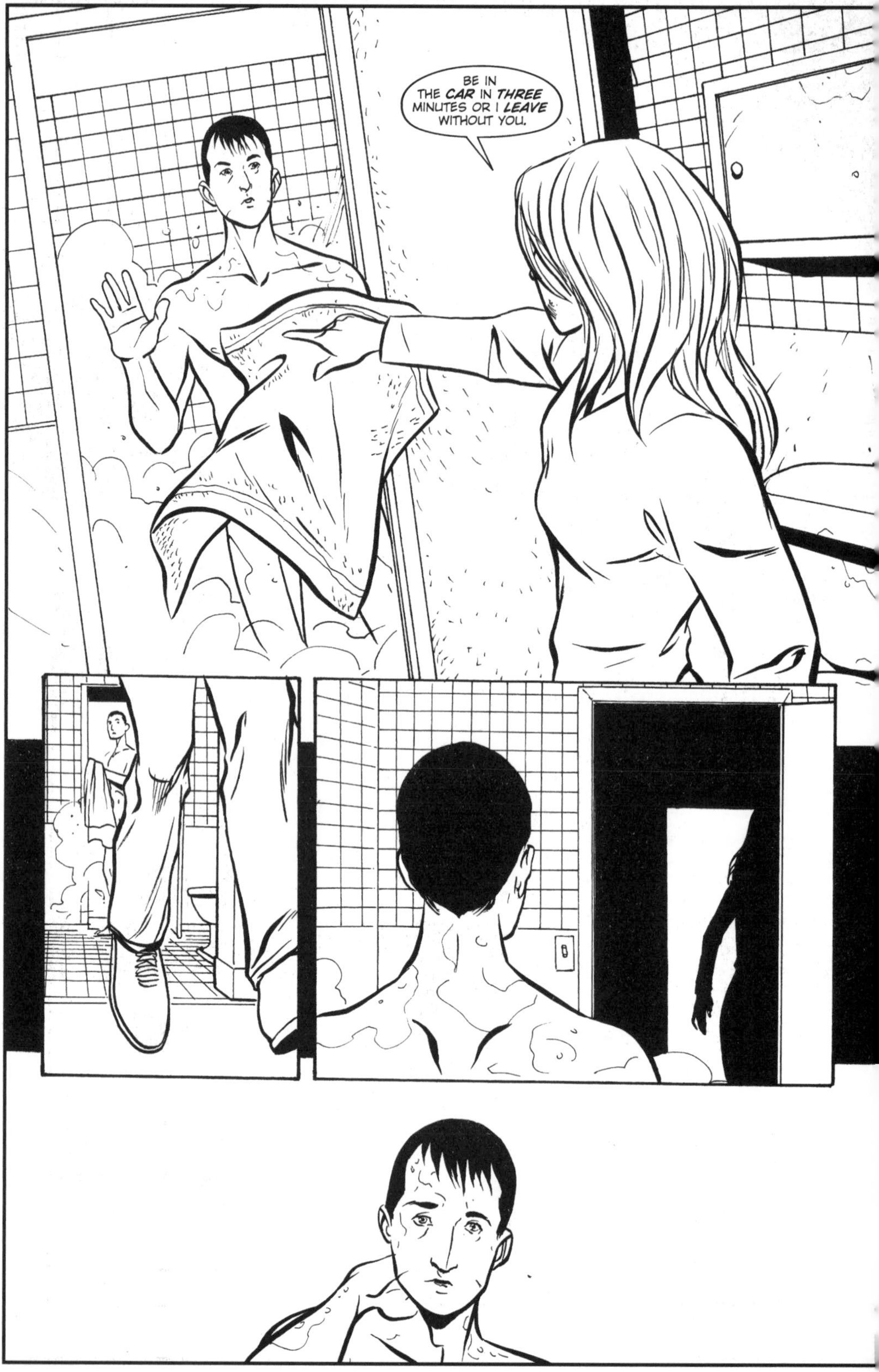
BE IN THE CAR IN THREE MINUTES OR I LEAVE WITHOUT YOU.

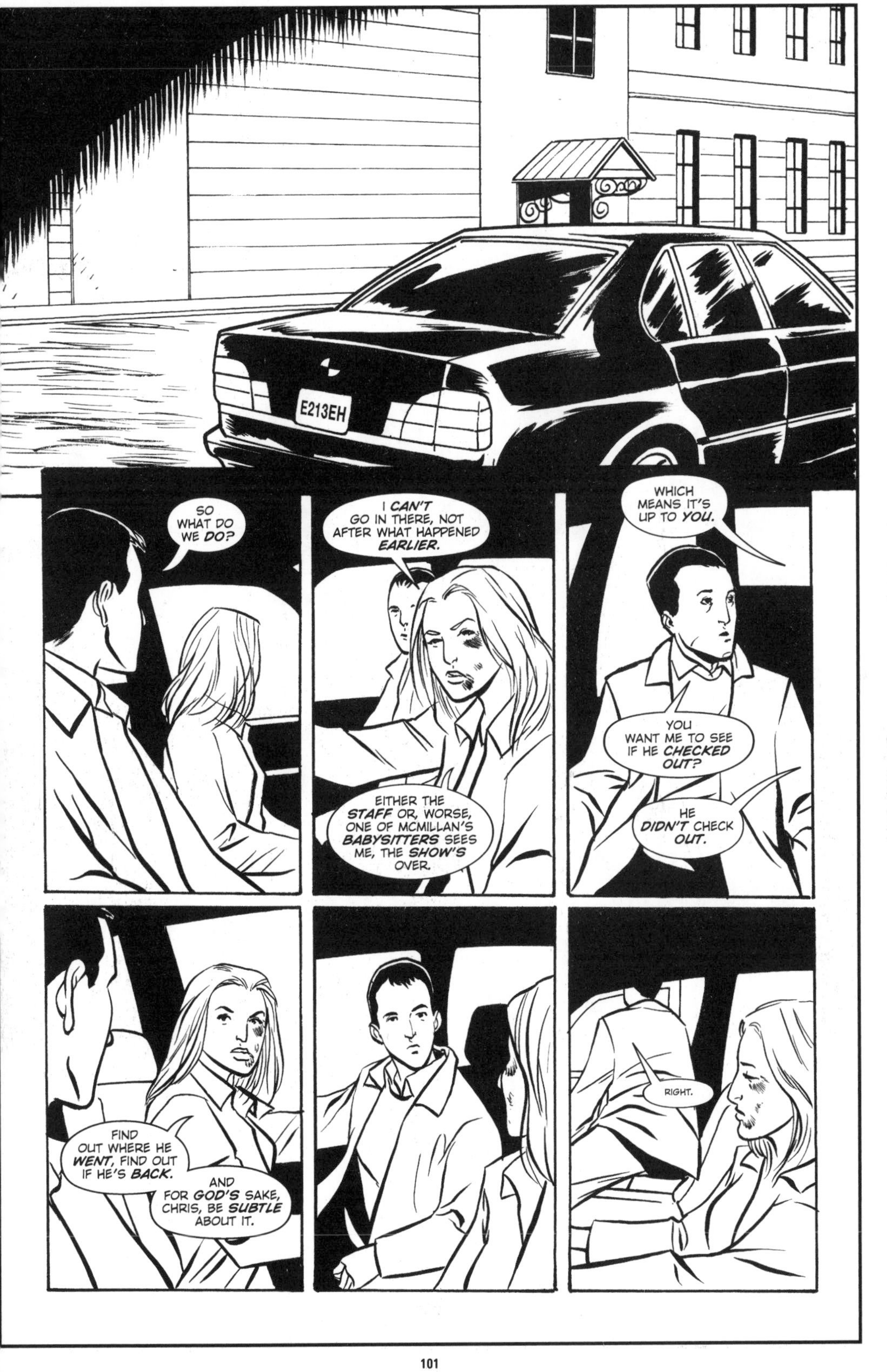
E213EH
SO WHAT DO WE DO?
I CAN'T GO IN THERE, NOT AFTER WHAT HAPPENED EARLIER.
EITHER THE STAFF OR, WORSE, ONE OF MCMILLAN'S BABYSITTERS SEES ME, THE SHOW'S OVER.
WHICH MEANS IT'S UP TO YOU.
YOU WANT ME TO SEE IF HE CHECKED OUT?
HE DIDN'T CHECK OUT.
FIND OUT WHERE HE WENT, FIND OUT IF HE'S BACK.
AND FOR GOD'S SAKE, CHRIS, BE SUBTLE ABOUT IT.
RIGHT.

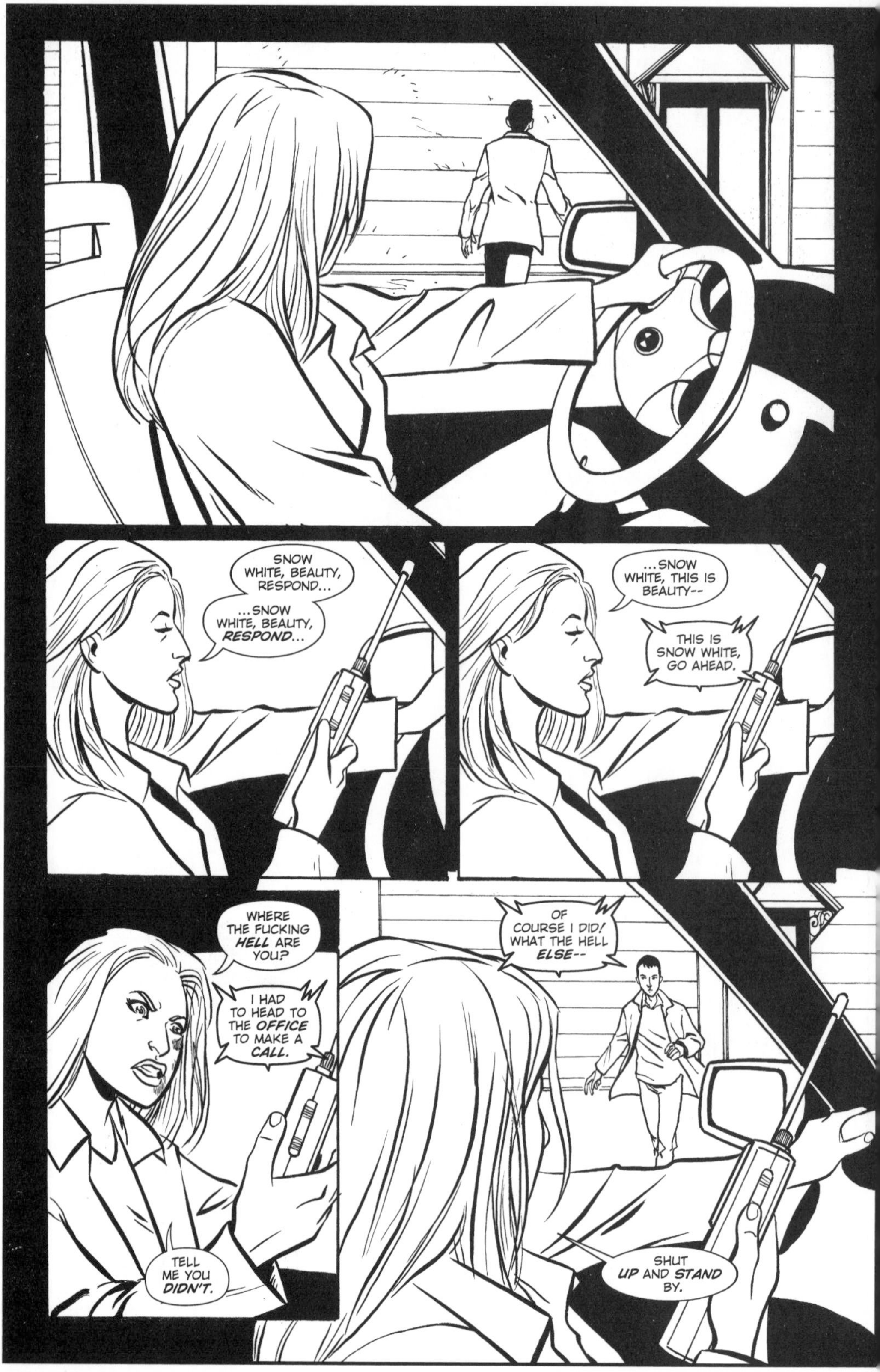
SNOW WHITE, BEAUTY, RESPOND...
...SNOW WHITE, BEAUTY, *RESPOND*...
...SNOW WHITE, THIS IS BEAUTY--
THIS IS SNOW WHITE, GO AHEAD.
WHERE THE FUCKING *HELL* ARE YOU?
I HAD TO HEAD TO THE *OFFICE* TO MAKE A *CALL*.
TELL ME YOU *DIDN'T*.
OF COURSE I DID! WHAT THE HELL *ELSE*--
SHUT *UP* AND *STAND* BY.

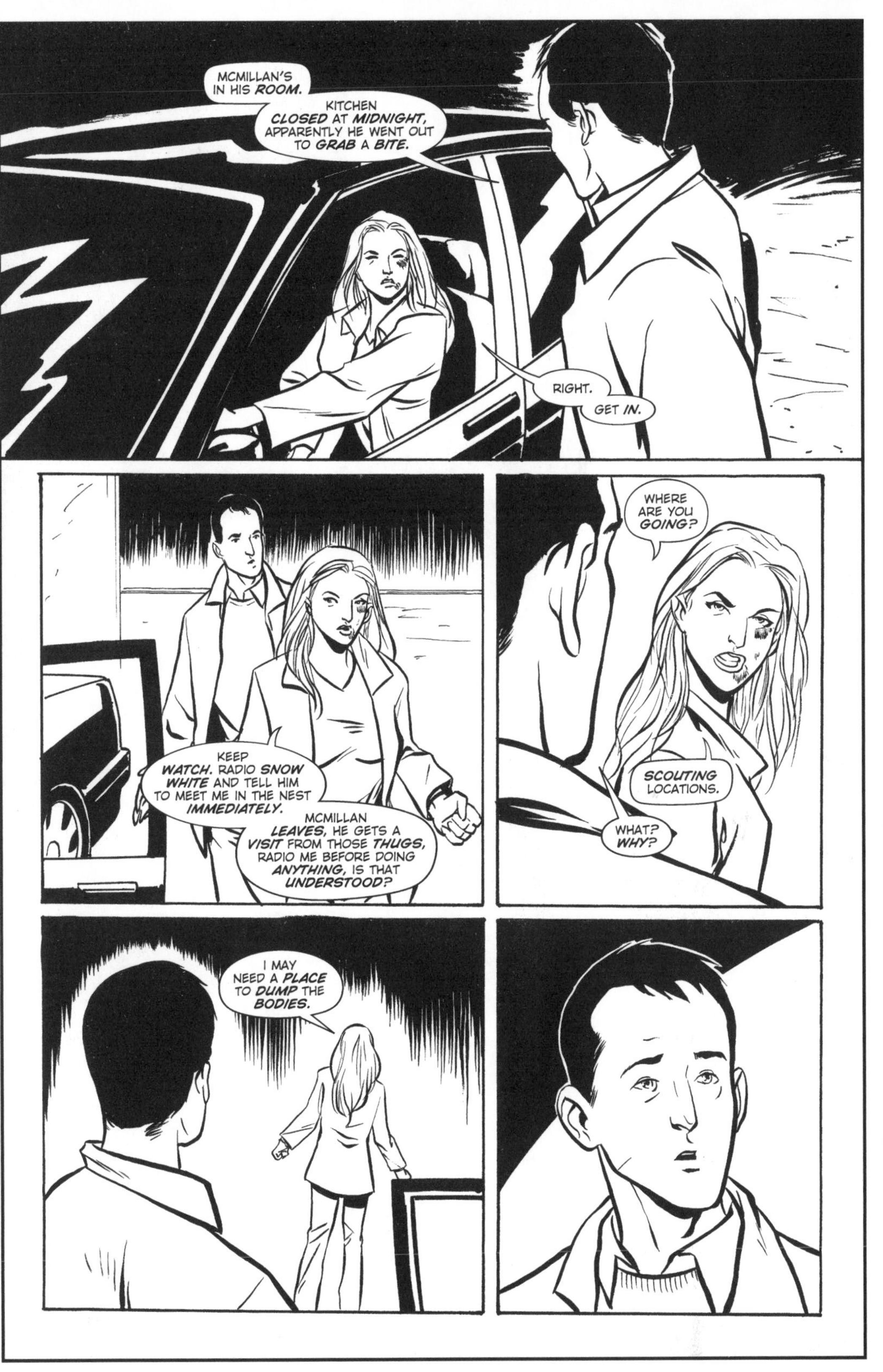

MCMILLAN'S IN HIS ROOM.
KITCHEN CLOSED AT MIDNIGHT, APPARENTLY HE WENT OUT TO GRAB A BITE.
RIGHT.
GET IN.
KEEP WATCH. RADIO SNOW WHITE AND TELL HIM TO MEET ME IN THE NEST IMMEDIATELY.
MCMILLAN LEAVES, HE GETS A VISIT FROM THOSE THUGS, RADIO ME BEFORE DOING ANYTHING, IS THAT UNDERSTOOD?
WHERE ARE YOU GOING?
SCOUTING LOCATIONS.
WHAT? WHY?
I MAY NEED A PLACE TO DUMP THE BODIES.

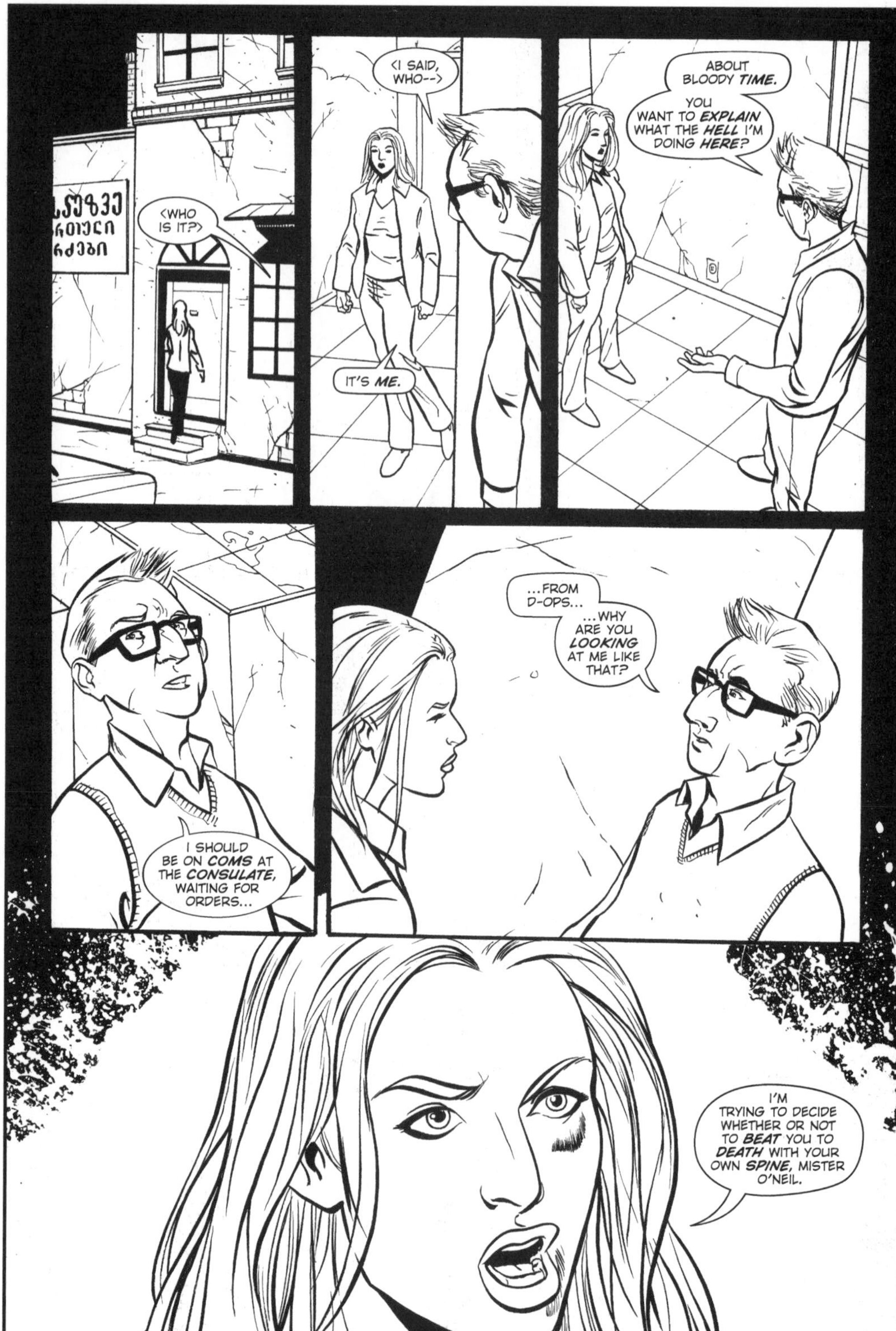
<WHO IS IT?>
<I SAID, WHO-->
IT'S **ME.**
ABOUT BLOODY **TIME.**
YOU WANT TO **EXPLAIN** WHAT THE **HELL** I'M DOING **HERE?**
I SHOULD BE ON **COMS** AT THE **CONSULATE,** WAITING FOR ORDERS...
...FROM D-OPS...
...WHY ARE YOU **LOOKING** AT ME LIKE THAT?
I'M TRYING TO DECIDE WHETHER OR NOT TO **BEAT** YOU TO **DEATH** WITH YOUR OWN **SPINE,** MISTER O'NEIL.

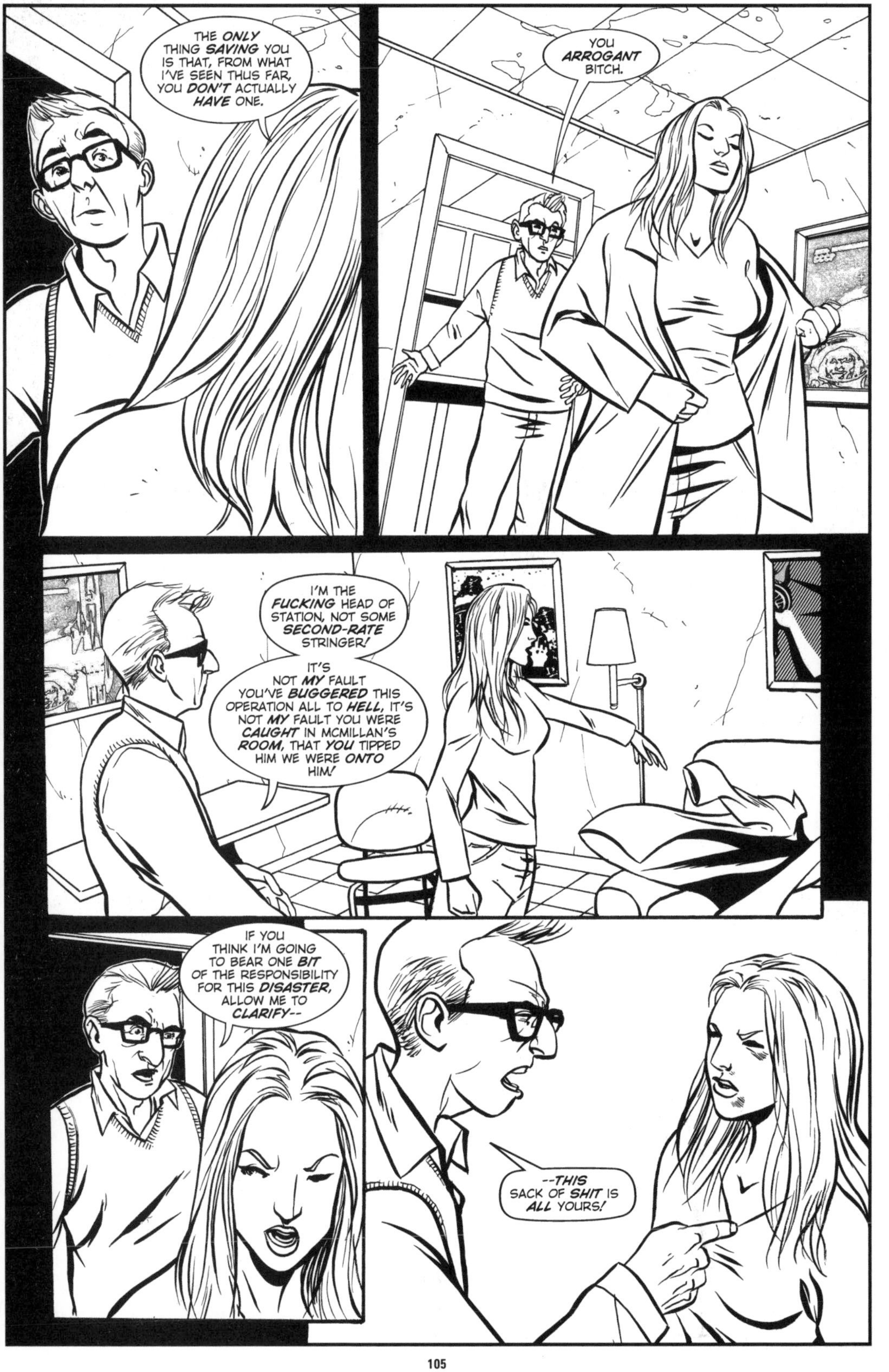
THE ONLY THING SAVING YOU IS THAT, FROM WHAT I'VE SEEN THUS FAR, YOU DON'T ACTUALLY HAVE ONE.
YOU ARROGANT BITCH.
I'M THE FUCKING HEAD OF STATION, NOT SOME SECOND-RATE STRINGER!
IT'S NOT MY FAULT YOU'VE BUGGERED THIS OPERATION ALL TO HELL, IT'S NOT MY FAULT YOU WERE CAUGHT IN MCMILLAN'S ROOM, THAT YOU TIPPED HIM WE WERE ONTO HIM!
IF YOU THINK I'M GOING TO BEAR ONE BIT OF THE RESPONSIBILITY FOR THIS DISASTER, ALLOW ME TO CLARIFY--
--THIS SACK OF SHIT IS ALL YOURS!

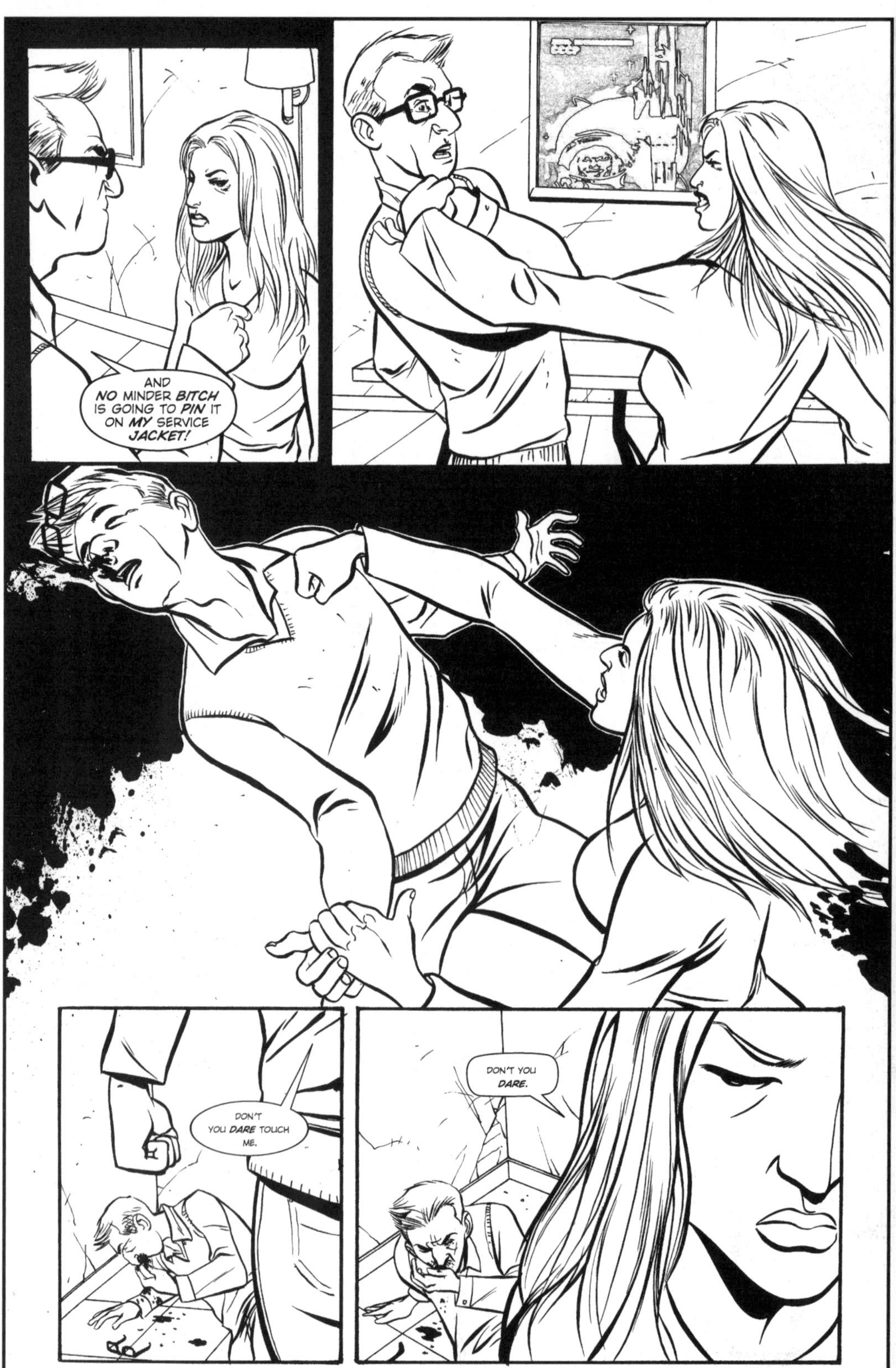
AND NO MINDER BITCH IS GOING TO PIN IT ON MY SERVICE JACKET!
DON'T YOU DARE TOUCH ME.
DON'T YOU DARE.

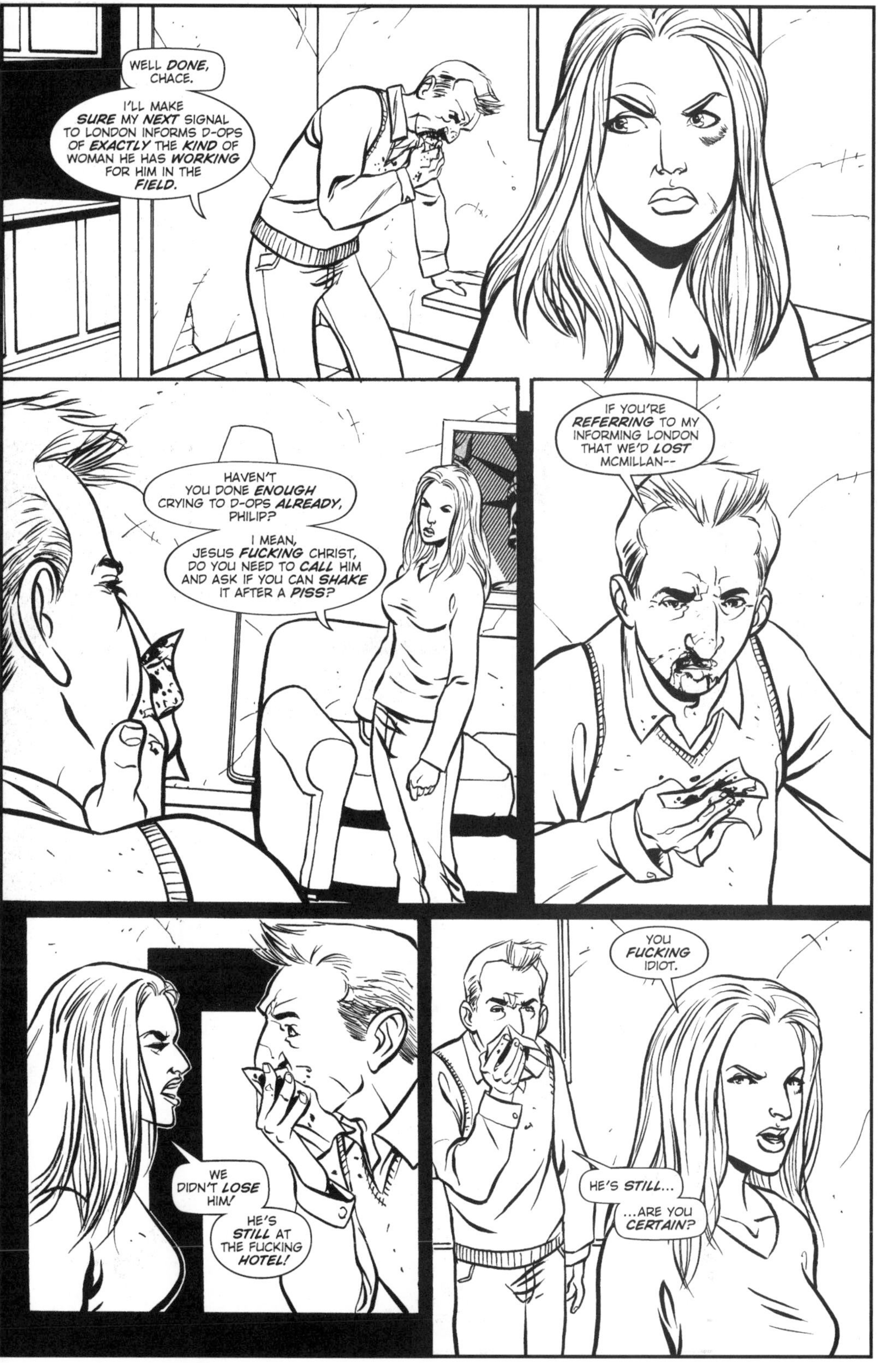
WELL DONE, CHACE.
I'LL MAKE SURE MY NEXT SIGNAL TO LONDON INFORMS D-OPS OF EXACTLY THE KIND OF WOMAN HE HAS WORKING FOR HIM IN THE FIELD.
HAVEN'T YOU DONE ENOUGH CRYING TO D-OPS ALREADY, PHILIP?
I MEAN, JESUS FUCKING CHRIST, DO YOU NEED TO CALL HIM AND ASK IF YOU CAN SHAKE IT AFTER A PISS?
IF YOU'RE REFERRING TO MY INFORMING LONDON THAT WE'D LOST MCMILLAN--
WE DIDN'T LOSE HIM!
HE'S STILL AT THE FUCKING HOTEL!
YOU FUCKING IDIOT.
HE'S STILL...
...ARE YOU CERTAIN?

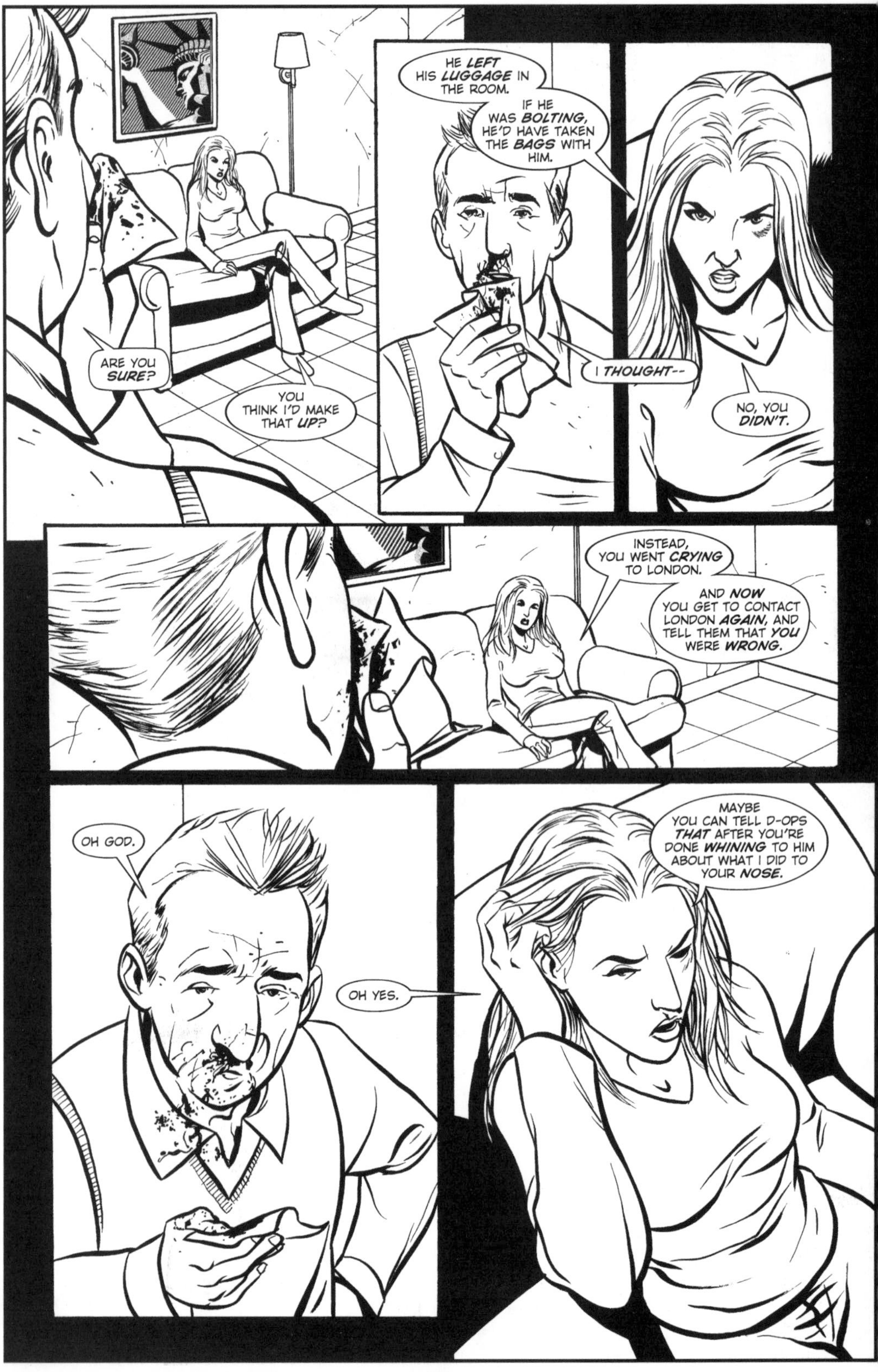
ARE YOU SURE?
YOU THINK I'D MAKE THAT UP?
HE LEFT HIS LUGGAGE IN THE ROOM.
IF HE WAS BOLTING, HE'D HAVE TAKEN THE BAGS WITH HIM.
I THOUGHT--
NO, YOU DIDN'T.
INSTEAD, YOU WENT CRYING TO LONDON.
AND NOW YOU GET TO CONTACT LONDON AGAIN, AND TELL THEM THAT YOU WERE WRONG.
OH GOD.
OH YES.
MAYBE YOU CAN TELL D-OPS THAT AFTER YOU'RE DONE WHINING TO HIM ABOUT WHAT I DID TO YOUR NOSE.

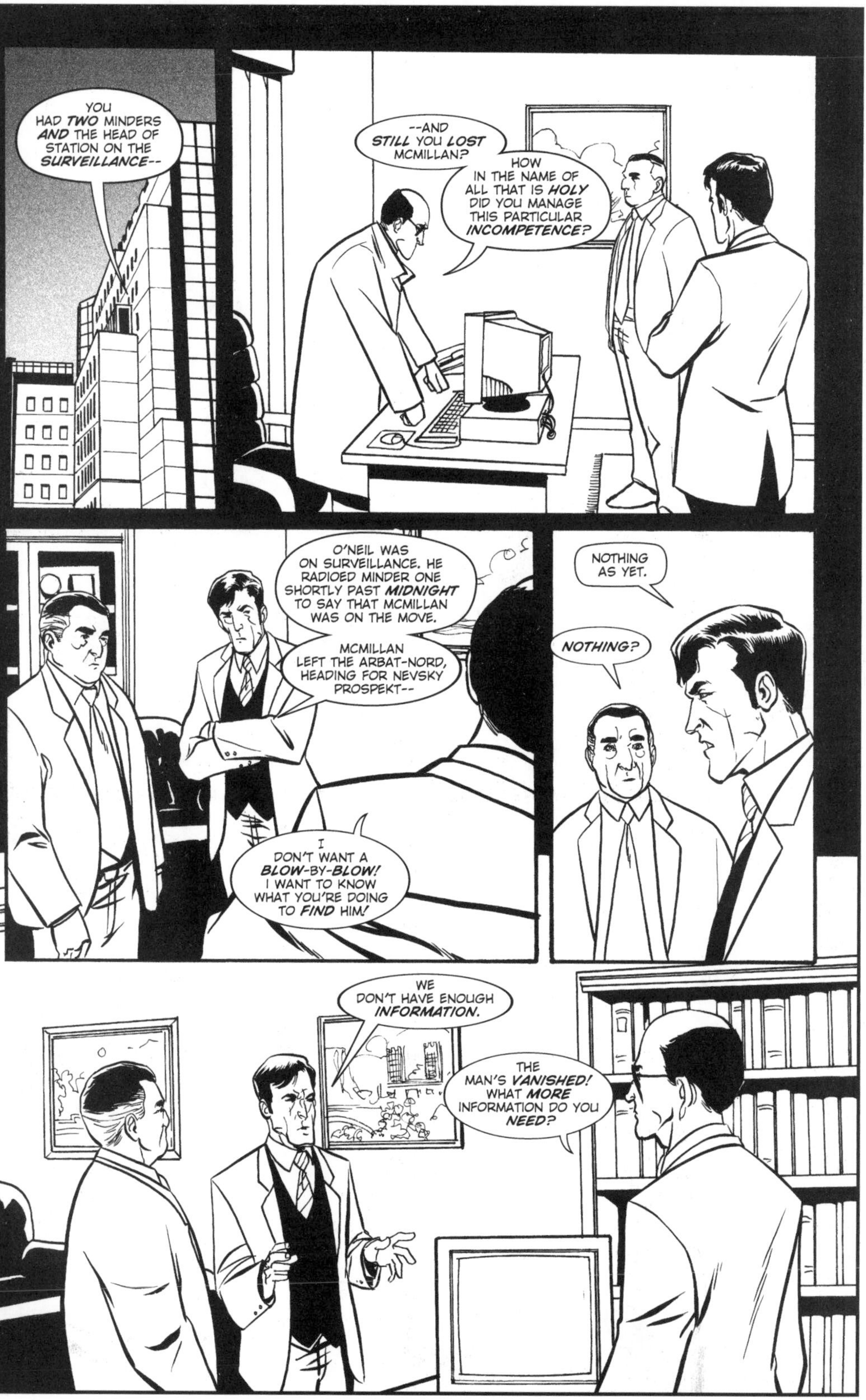
YOU HAD TWO MINDERS AND THE HEAD OF STATION ON THE SURVEILLANCE--
--AND STILL YOU LOST MCMILLAN?
HOW IN THE NAME OF ALL THAT IS HOLY DID YOU MANAGE THIS PARTICULAR INCOMPETENCE?
O'NEIL WAS ON SURVEILLANCE. HE RADIOED MINDER ONE SHORTLY PAST MIDNIGHT TO SAY THAT MCMILLAN WAS ON THE MOVE.
MCMILLAN LEFT THE ARBAT-NORD, HEADING FOR NEVSKY PROSPEKT--
I DON'T WANT A BLOW-BY-BLOW! I WANT TO KNOW WHAT YOU'RE DOING TO FIND HIM!
NOTHING AS YET.
NOTHING?
WE DON'T HAVE ENOUGH INFORMATION.
THE MAN'S VANISHED! WHAT MORE INFORMATION DO YOU NEED?

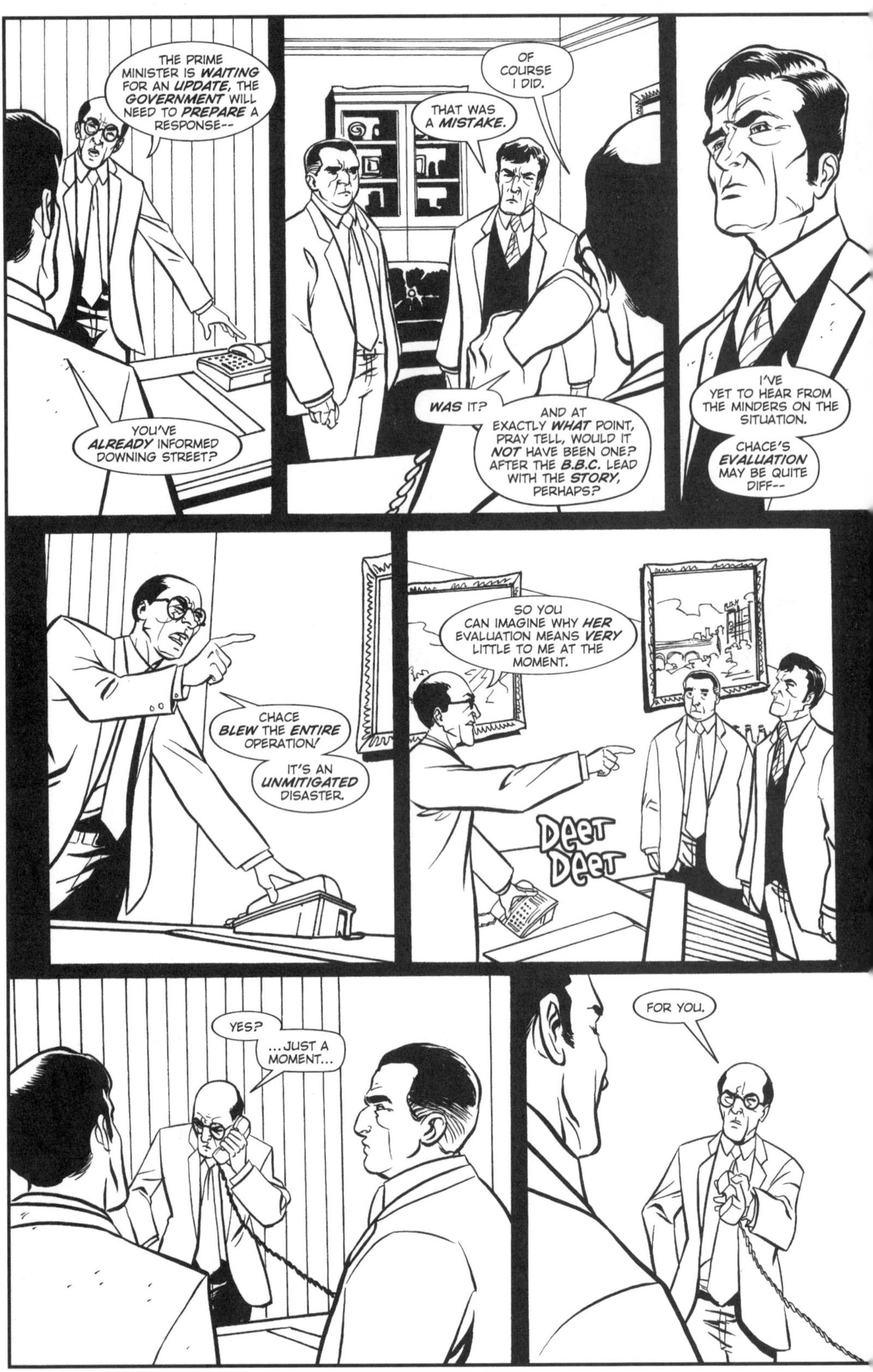
THE PRIME MINISTER IS WAITING FOR AN UPDATE, THE GOVERNMENT WILL NEED TO PREPARE A RESPONSE--
YOU'VE ALREADY INFORMED DOWNING STREET?
OF COURSE I DID.
THAT WAS A MISTAKE.
WAS IT?
AND AT EXACTLY WHAT POINT, PRAY TELL, WOULD IT NOT HAVE BEEN ONE? AFTER THE B.B.C. LEAD WITH THE STORY, PERHAPS?
I'VE YET TO HEAR FROM THE MINDERS ON THE SITUATION.
CHACE'S EVALUATION MAY BE QUITE DIFF--
CHACE BLEW THE ENTIRE OPERATION!
IT'S AN UNMITIGATED DISASTER.
SO YOU CAN IMAGINE WHY HER EVALUATION MEANS VERY LITTLE TO ME AT THE MOMENT.
DEET DEET
YES?
...JUST A MOMENT...
FOR YOU.

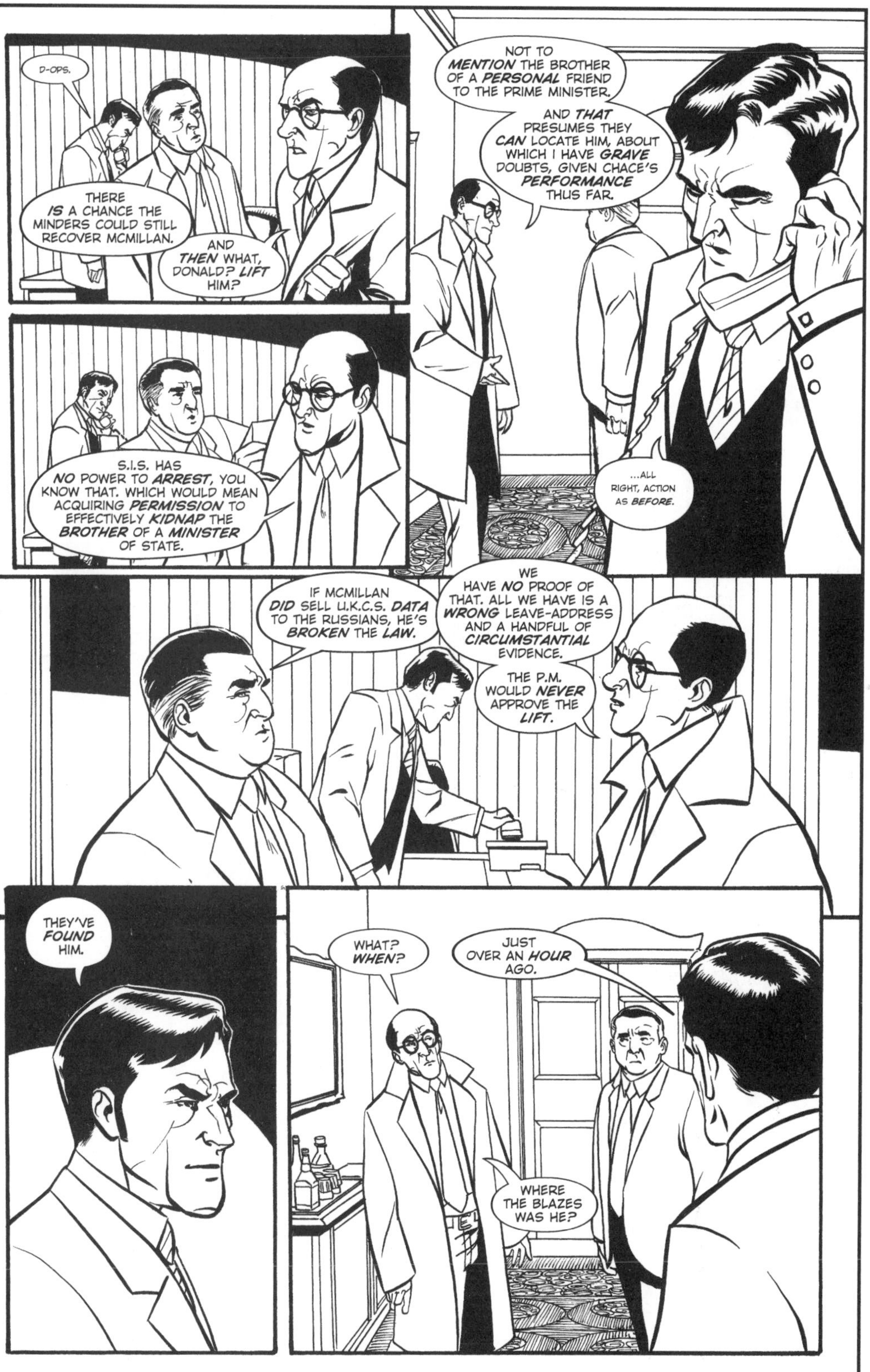
D-OPS.
THERE IS A CHANCE THE MINDERS COULD STILL RECOVER MCMILLAN.
AND THEN WHAT, DONALD? LIFT HIM?
S.I.S. HAS NO POWER TO ARREST, YOU KNOW THAT. WHICH WOULD MEAN ACQUIRING PERMISSION TO EFFECTIVELY KIDNAP THE BROTHER OF A MINISTER OF STATE.
NOT TO MENTION THE BROTHER OF A PERSONAL FRIEND TO THE PRIME MINISTER.
AND THAT PRESUMES THEY CAN LOCATE HIM, ABOUT WHICH I HAVE GRAVE DOUBTS, GIVEN CHACE'S PERFORMANCE THUS FAR.
...ALL RIGHT, ACTION AS BEFORE.
IF MCMILLAN DID SELL U.K.C.S. DATA TO THE RUSSIANS, HE'S BROKEN THE LAW.
WE HAVE NO PROOF OF THAT. ALL WE HAVE IS A WRONG LEAVE-ADDRESS AND A HANDFUL OF CIRCUMSTANTIAL EVIDENCE.
THE P.M. WOULD NEVER APPROVE THE LIFT.
THEY'VE FOUND HIM.
WHAT? WHEN?
JUST OVER AN HOUR AGO.
WHERE THE BLAZES WAS HE?

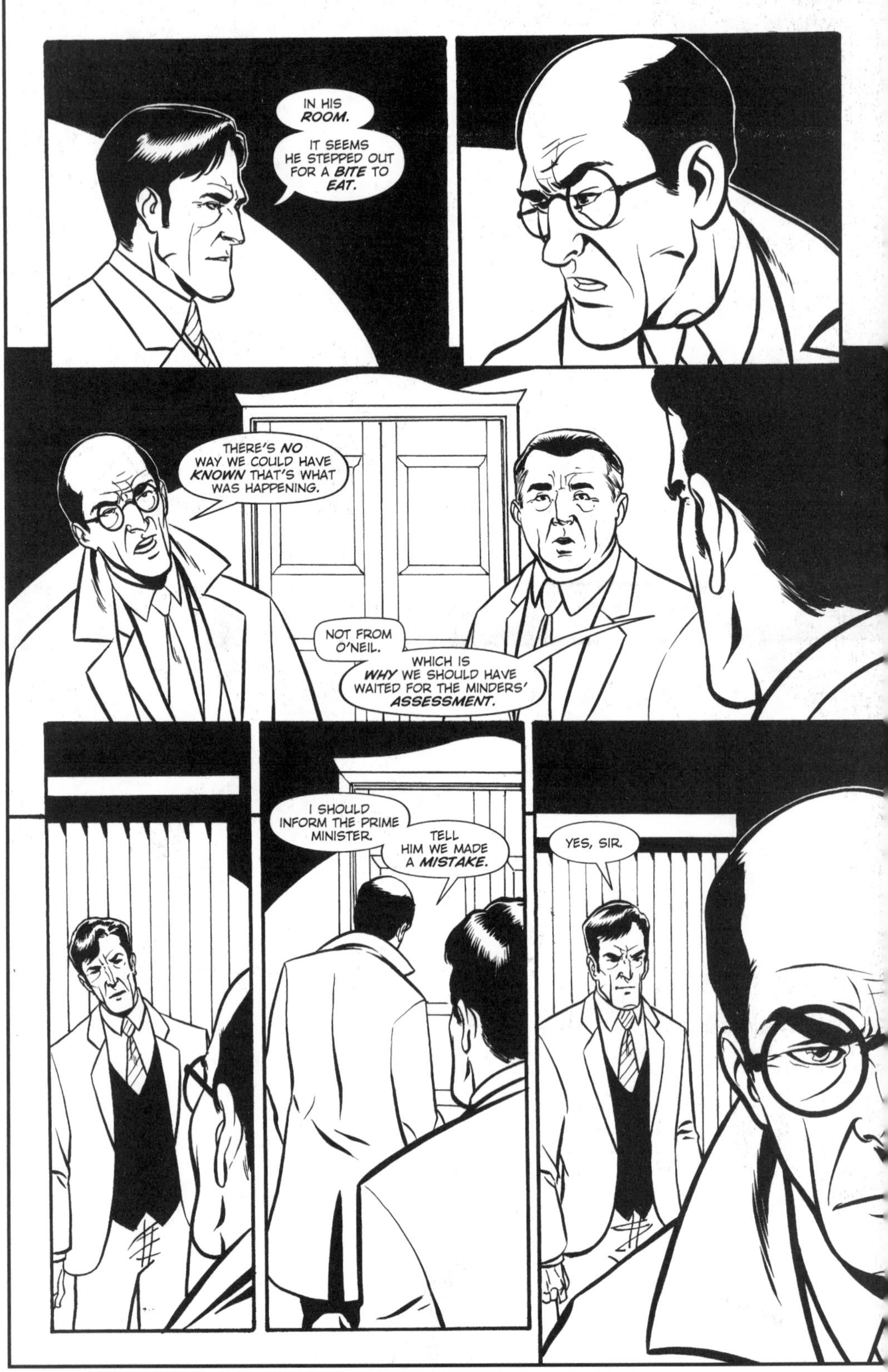
IN HIS ROOM.
IT SEEMS HE STEPPED OUT FOR A BITE TO EAT.
THERE'S NO WAY WE COULD HAVE KNOWN THAT'S WHAT WAS HAPPENING.
NOT FROM O'NEIL.
WHICH IS WHY WE SHOULD HAVE WAITED FOR THE MINDERS' ASSESSMENT.
I SHOULD INFORM THE PRIME MINISTER.
TELL HIM WE MADE A MISTAKE.
YES, SIR.

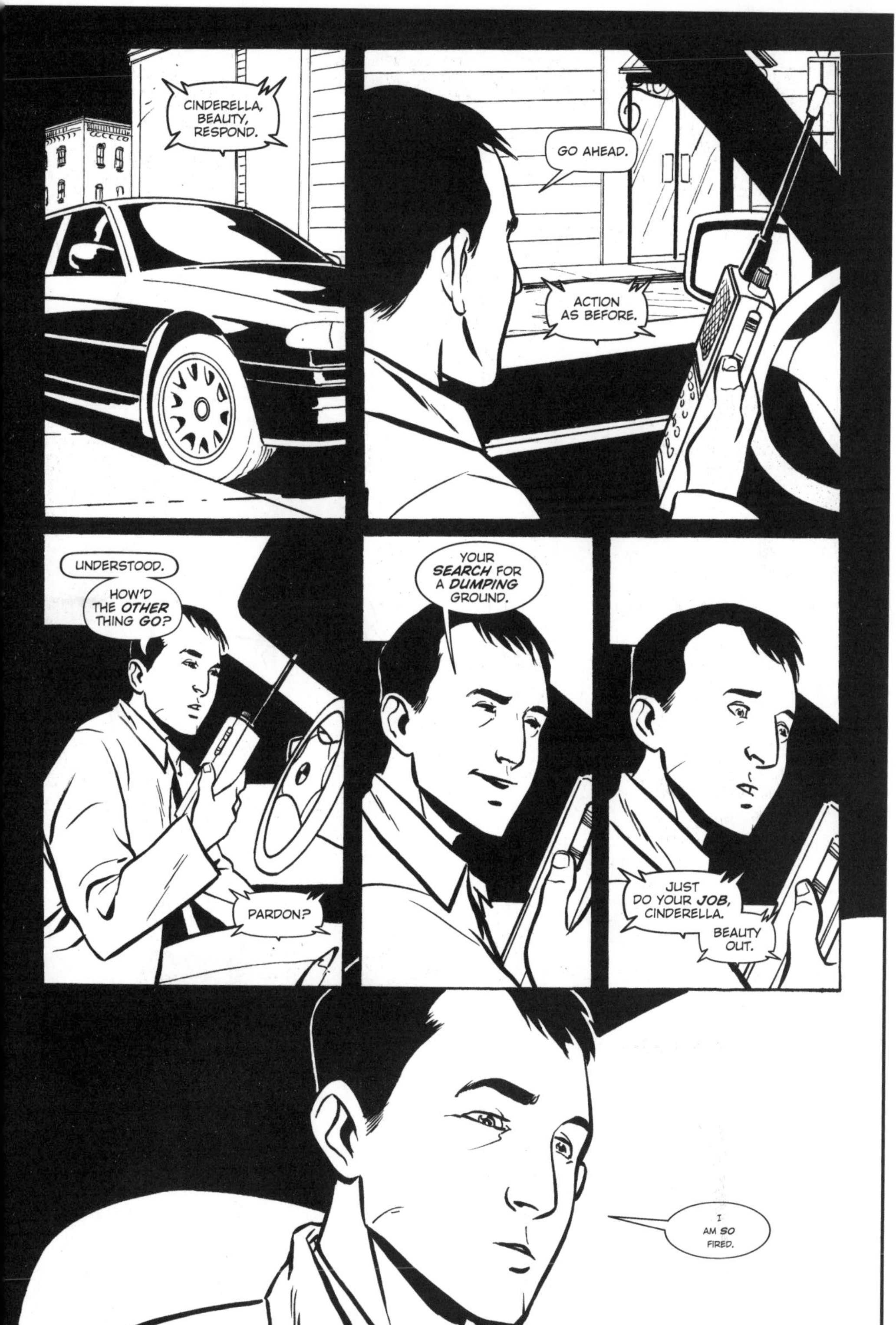
CINDERELLA, BEAUTY, RESPOND.
GO AHEAD.
ACTION AS BEFORE.
UNDERSTOOD.
HOW'D THE *OTHER* THING *GO?*
PARDON?
YOUR *SEARCH* FOR A *DUMPING* GROUND.
JUST DO YOUR *JOB,* CINDERELLA.
BEAUTY OUT.
I AM *SO* FIRED.

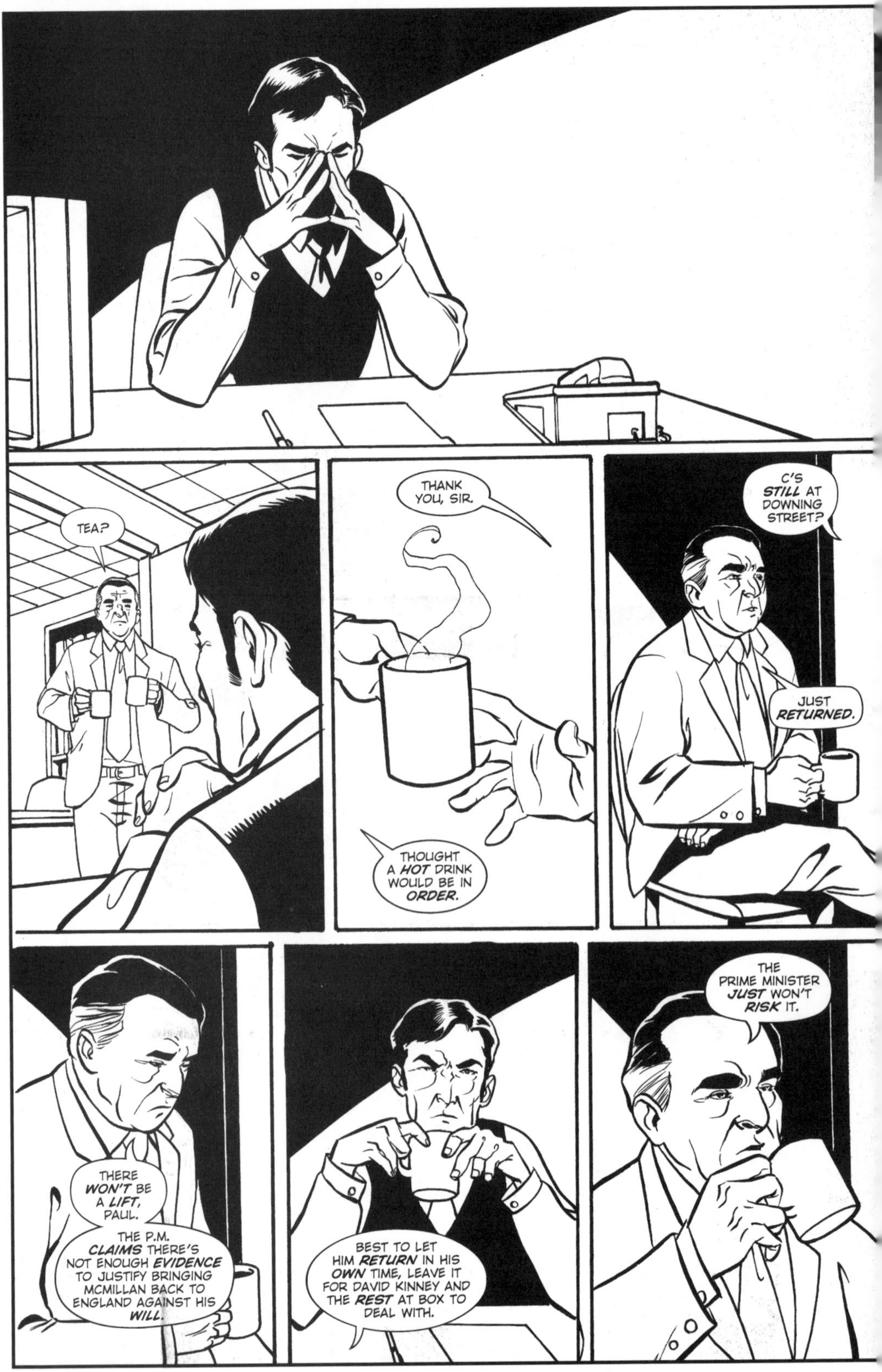
TEA?
THANK YOU, SIR.
THOUGHT A HOT DRINK WOULD BE IN ORDER.
C'S STILL AT DOWNING STREET?
JUST RETURNED.
THERE WON'T BE A LIFT, PAUL.
THE P.M. CLAIMS THERE'S NOT ENOUGH EVIDENCE TO JUSTIFY BRINGING MCMILLAN BACK TO ENGLAND AGAINST HIS WILL.
BEST TO LET HIM RETURN IN HIS OWN TIME, LEAVE IT FOR DAVID KINNEY AND THE REST AT BOX TO DEAL WITH.
THE PRIME MINISTER JUST WON'T RISK IT.

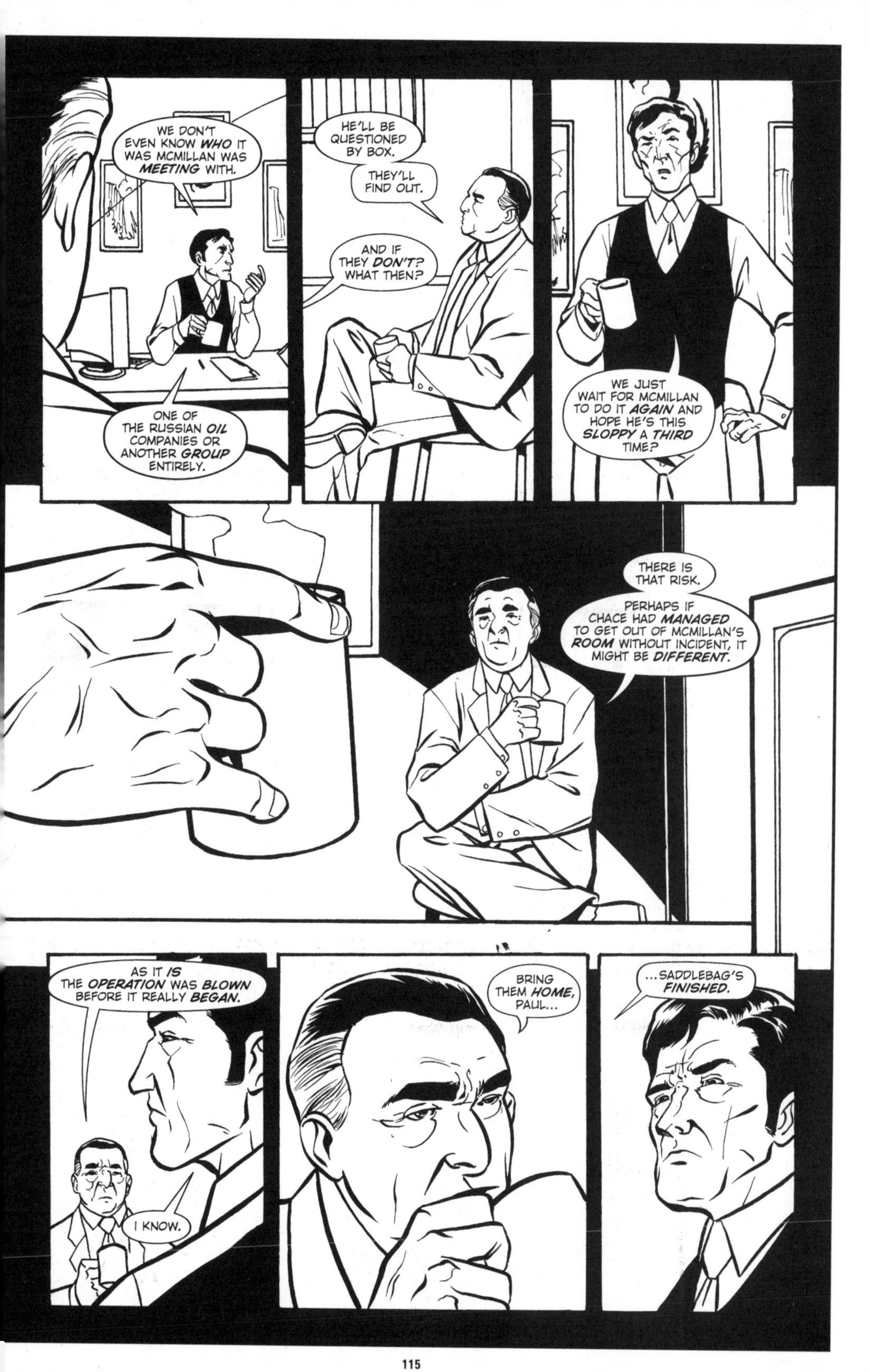
WE DON'T EVEN KNOW *WHO* IT WAS MCMILLAN WAS *MEETING* WITH.
ONE OF THE RUSSIAN *OIL* COMPANIES OR ANOTHER *GROUP* ENTIRELY.
HE'LL BE QUESTIONED BY BOX.
THEY'LL FIND OUT.
AND IF THEY *DON'T*? WHAT THEN?
WE JUST WAIT FOR MCMILLAN TO DO IT *AGAIN* AND HOPE HE'S THIS *SLOPPY* A *THIRD* TIME?
THERE IS THAT RISK.
PERHAPS IF CHACE HAD *MANAGED* TO GET OUT OF MCMILLAN'S *ROOM* WITHOUT INCIDENT, IT MIGHT BE *DIFFERENT*.
AS IT *IS* THE *OPERATION* WAS *BLOWN* BEFORE IT REALLY *BEGAN*.
I KNOW.
BRING THEM *HOME*, PAUL...
...SADDLEBAG'S *FINISHED*.

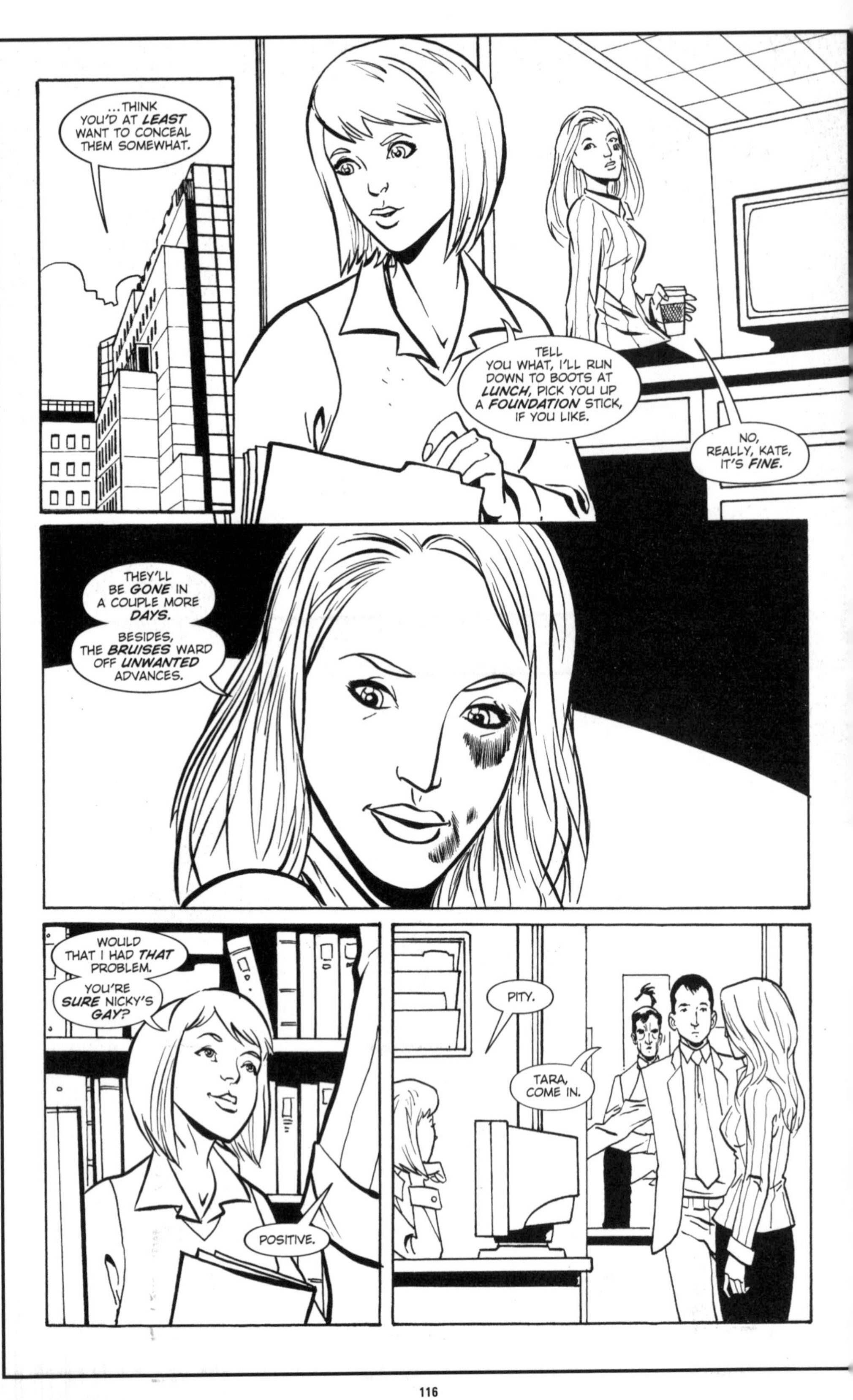
...THINK YOU'D AT LEAST WANT TO CONCEAL THEM SOMEWHAT.
TELL YOU WHAT, I'LL RUN DOWN TO BOOTS AT LUNCH, PICK YOU UP A FOUNDATION STICK, IF YOU LIKE.
NO, REALLY, KATE, IT'S FINE.
THEY'LL BE GONE IN A COUPLE MORE DAYS.
BESIDES, THE BRUISES WARD OFF UNWANTED ADVANCES.
WOULD THAT I HAD THAT PROBLEM.
YOU'RE SURE NICKY'S GAY?
POSITIVE.
PITY.
TARA, COME IN.

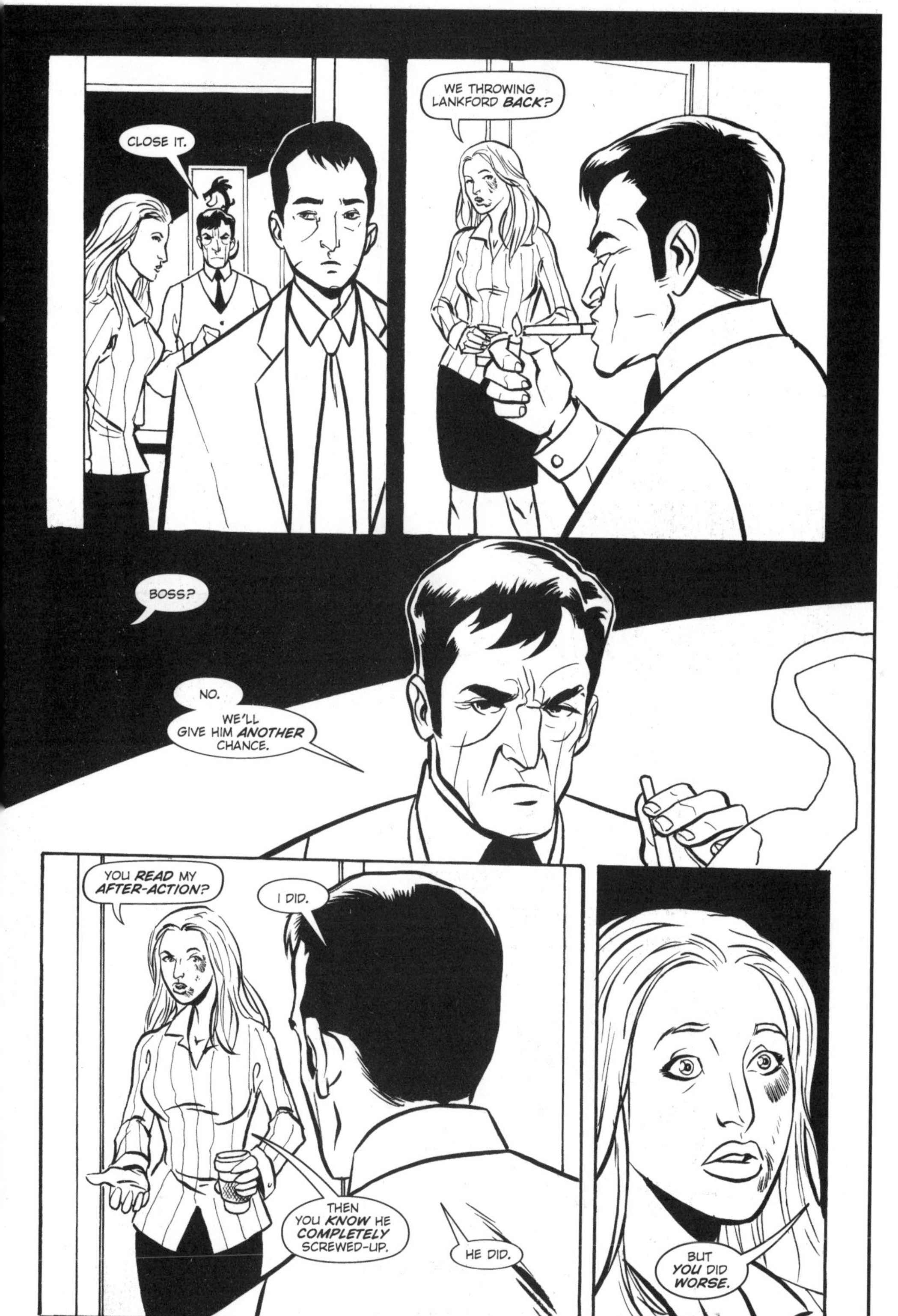
CLOSE IT.
WE THROWING LANKFORD BACK?
BOSS?
NO.
WE'LL GIVE HIM ANOTHER CHANCE.
YOU READ MY AFTER-ACTION?
I DID.
THEN YOU KNOW HE COMPLETELY SCREWED-UP.
HE DID.
BUT YOU DID WORSE.

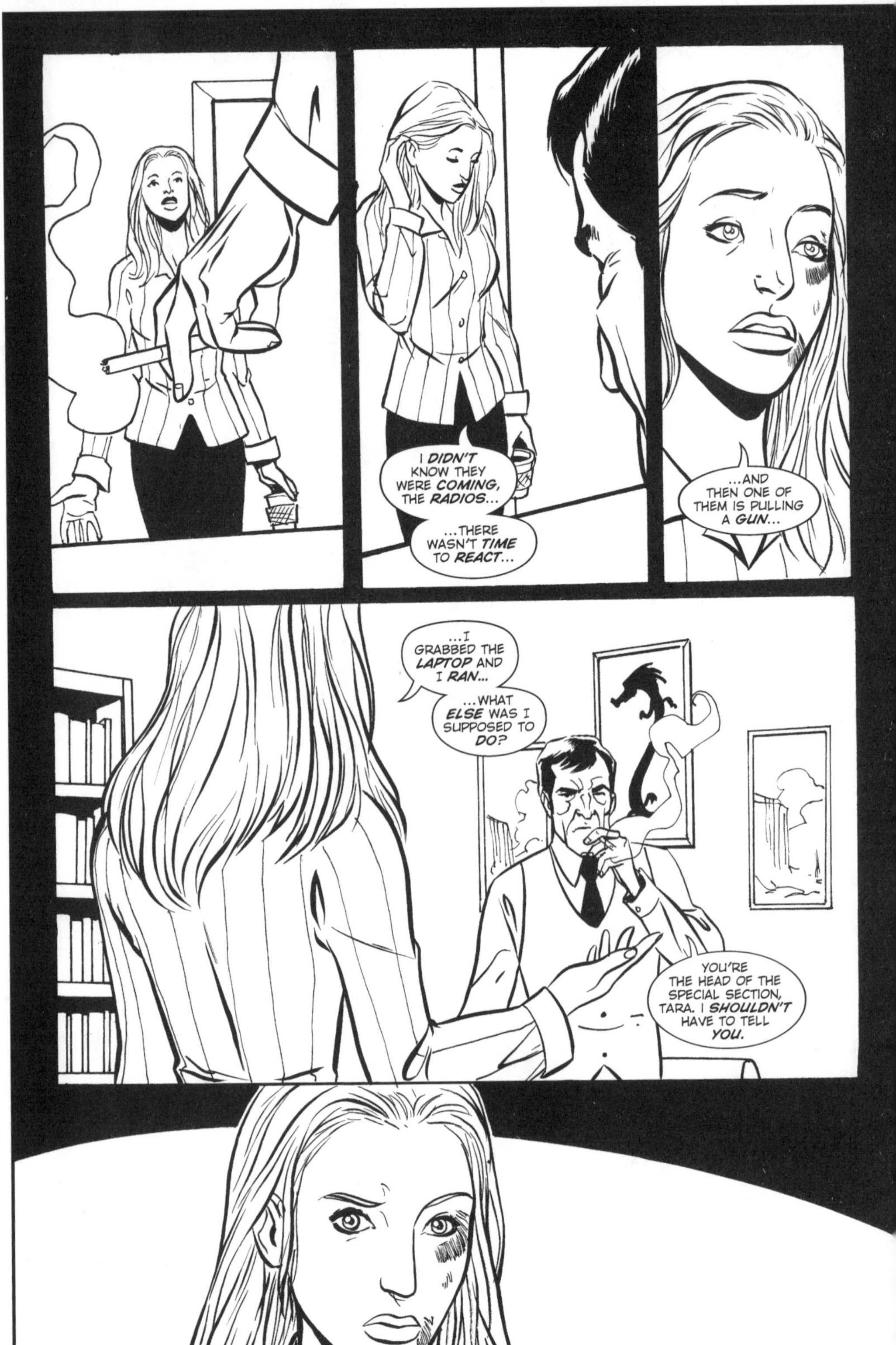
I *DIDN'T* KNOW THEY WERE *COMING*, THE *RADIOS*...
...THERE WASN'T *TIME* TO *REACT*...
...AND THEN ONE OF THEM IS PULLING A *GUN*...
...I GRABBED THE *LAPTOP* AND I *RAN*...
...WHAT *ELSE* WAS I SUPPOSED TO *DO?*
YOU'RE THE HEAD OF THE SPECIAL SECTION, TARA. I *SHOULDN'T* HAVE TO TELL *YOU.*

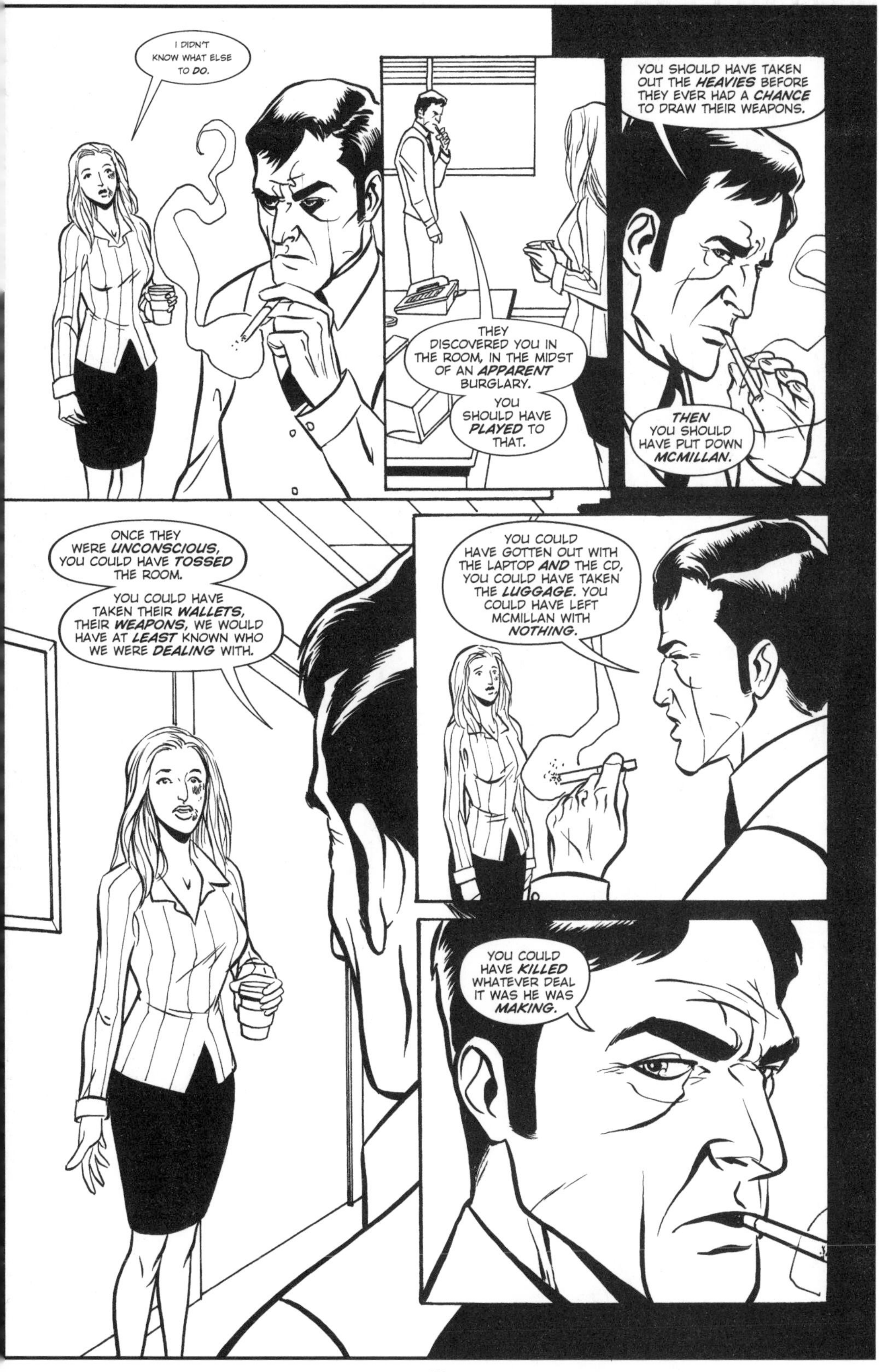
I DIDN'T KNOW WHAT ELSE TO DO.
THEY DISCOVERED YOU IN THE ROOM, IN THE MIDST OF AN APPARENT BURGLARY.
YOU SHOULD HAVE PLAYED TO THAT.
YOU SHOULD HAVE TAKEN OUT THE HEAVIES BEFORE THEY EVER HAD A CHANCE TO DRAW THEIR WEAPONS.
THEN YOU SHOULD HAVE PUT DOWN MCMILLAN.
ONCE THEY WERE UNCONSCIOUS, YOU COULD HAVE TOSSED THE ROOM.
YOU COULD HAVE TAKEN THEIR WALLETS, THEIR WEAPONS, WE WOULD HAVE AT LEAST KNOWN WHO WE WERE DEALING WITH.
YOU COULD HAVE GOTTEN OUT WITH THE LAPTOP AND THE CD, YOU COULD HAVE TAKEN THE LUGGAGE. YOU COULD HAVE LEFT MCMILLAN WITH NOTHING.
YOU COULD HAVE KILLED WHATEVER DEAL IT WAS HE WAS MAKING.

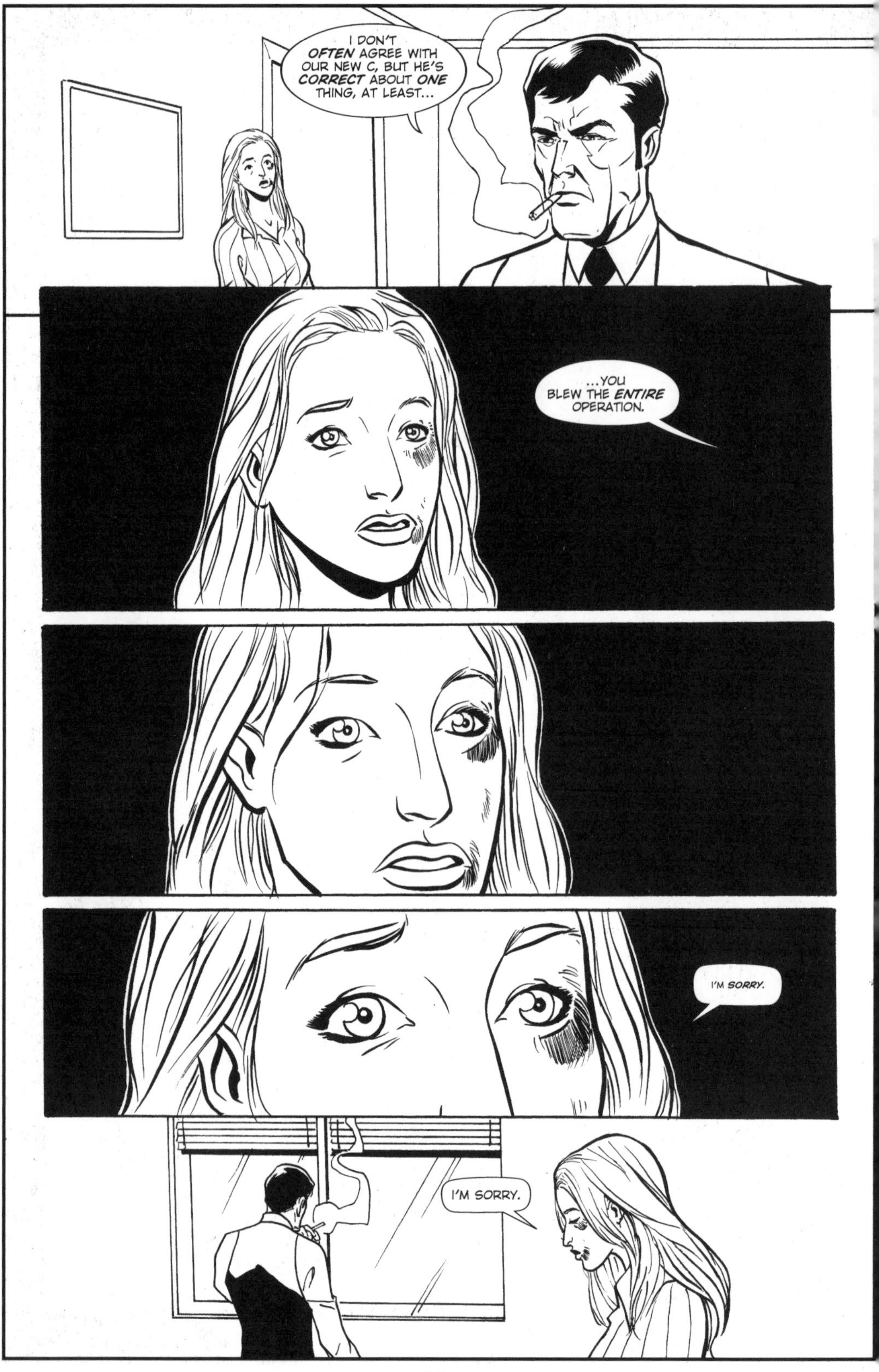
I DON'T OFTEN AGREE WITH OUR NEW C, BUT HE'S CORRECT ABOUT ONE THING, AT LEAST...
...YOU BLEW THE ENTIRE OPERATION.
I'M SORRY.
I'M SORRY.

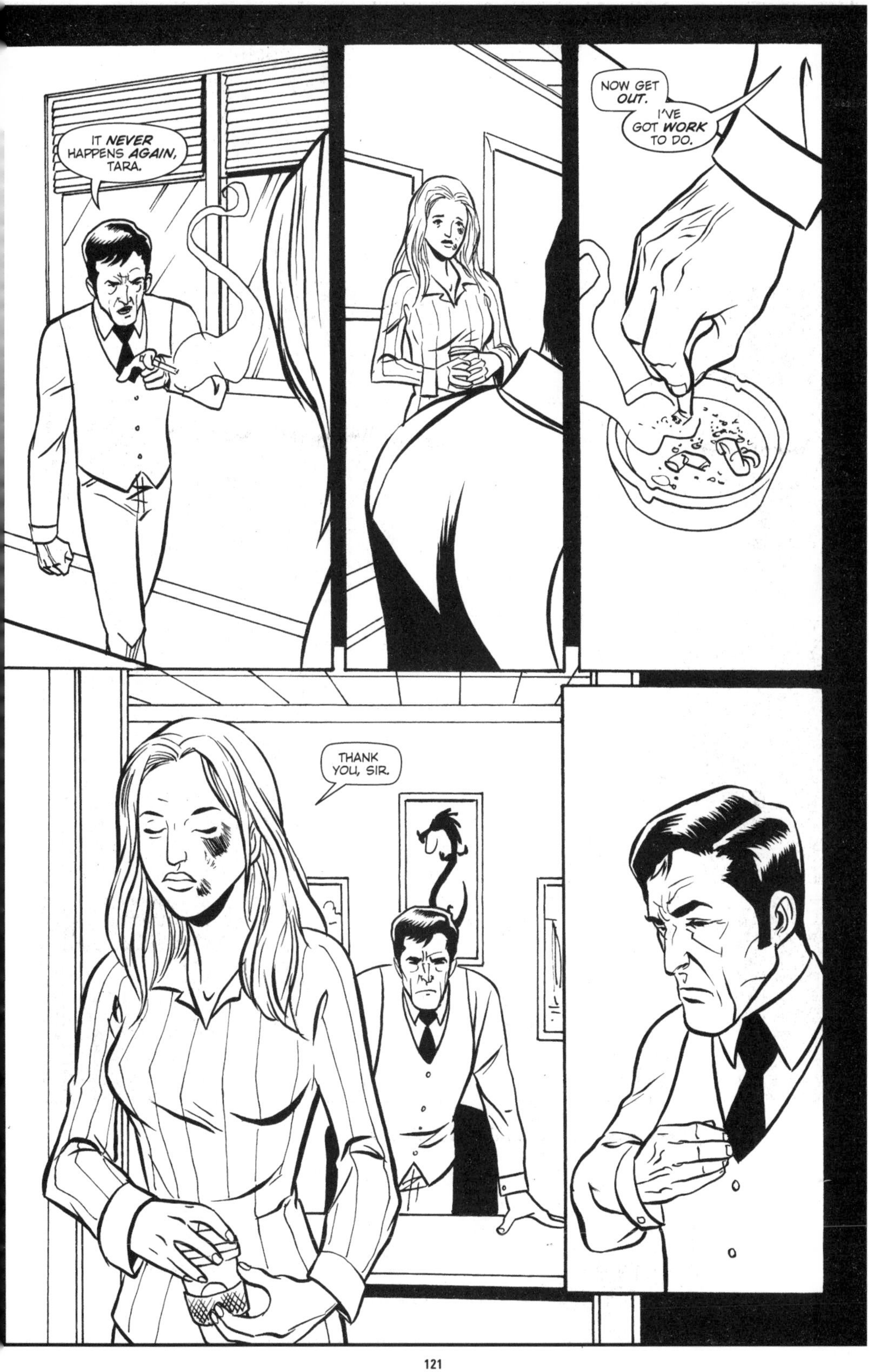
IT NEVER HAPPENS AGAIN, TARA.
NOW GET OUT.
I'VE GOT WORK TO DO.
THANK YOU, SIR.

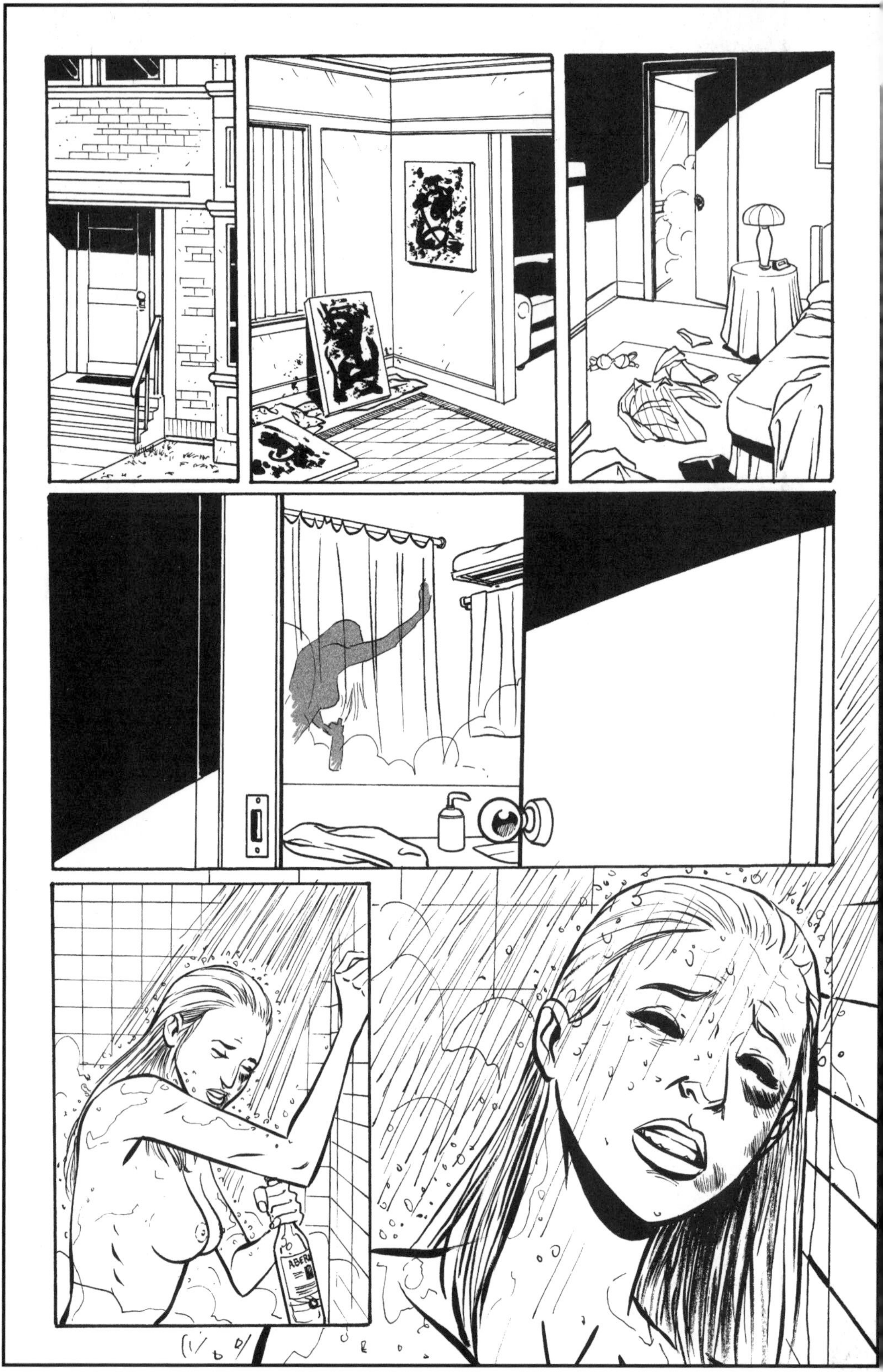

OPERATION: RED PANDA

WRITTEN BY
GREG RUCKA

ILLUSTRATED BY
CHRIS SAMNEE

LETTERED BY
JOHN DRANSKI & **DOUGLAS SHERWOOD**

ORIGINALLY EDITED BY
JAMES LUCAS JONES

AUTHOR'S NOTE:
The events in this story take place between the end of the
prose novel *A Gentleman's Game* and the start of the prose
novel *Private Wars*, both available from Bantam Books.

ROSTER

TARA CHACE—Head of Special Section, designated Minder One.

FRANCES BARCLAY—Chief of Service, also known as "C." Distinguished service as CIA-Liaison, Chairman of the Joint Intelligence Committee, and as Head of Station Prague (85-88), Saigon (89-91), and Paris (91-94).

CHRIS LANKFORD—The fourth man to hold the title of Minder Three in less than 18 months. Untested, Lankford's yet to spend significant time in the field.

PAUL CROCKER—Director of Operations, encompassing all field work in all theaters of operations. In addition to commanding individual stations, he has direct command of the Special Section—sometimes referred to as Minders—used for special operations.

NICK POOLE—Former S.A.S. and recently christened Minder Two.

DONALD WELDON—Deputy Chief of Service, has oversight of all aspects of Intelligence gathering and operations. Immediate superior to Crocker.

OPS ROOM STAFF   OTHERS

ALEXIS—Mission Control Officer (also called Main Communications Officer)– responsible for maintaining communications between the Operations Room and the agents in the field.

RON—Duty Operations Officer, responsible for monitoring the status and importance of all incoming intelligence, both from foreign stations and other sources.

KATE—Personal Assistant to Paul Crocker, termed PA to D.Ops. Possibly the hardest and most important job in the Service.

ELIZABETH CALLARD—Staff psychologist for the Intelligence Services. Her duties include regular evaluation of the agents' mental health and post-op counseling when appropriate.

DAVID KINNEY—Crocker's opposite number at M.I.5, also called the Security Services, with jurisdiction primarily confined to within the U.K.

TOM WALLACE—Former Head of Special Section and mentor of Tara Chace. Recently opted out of the Section in favor of a new career with a higher life expectancy.

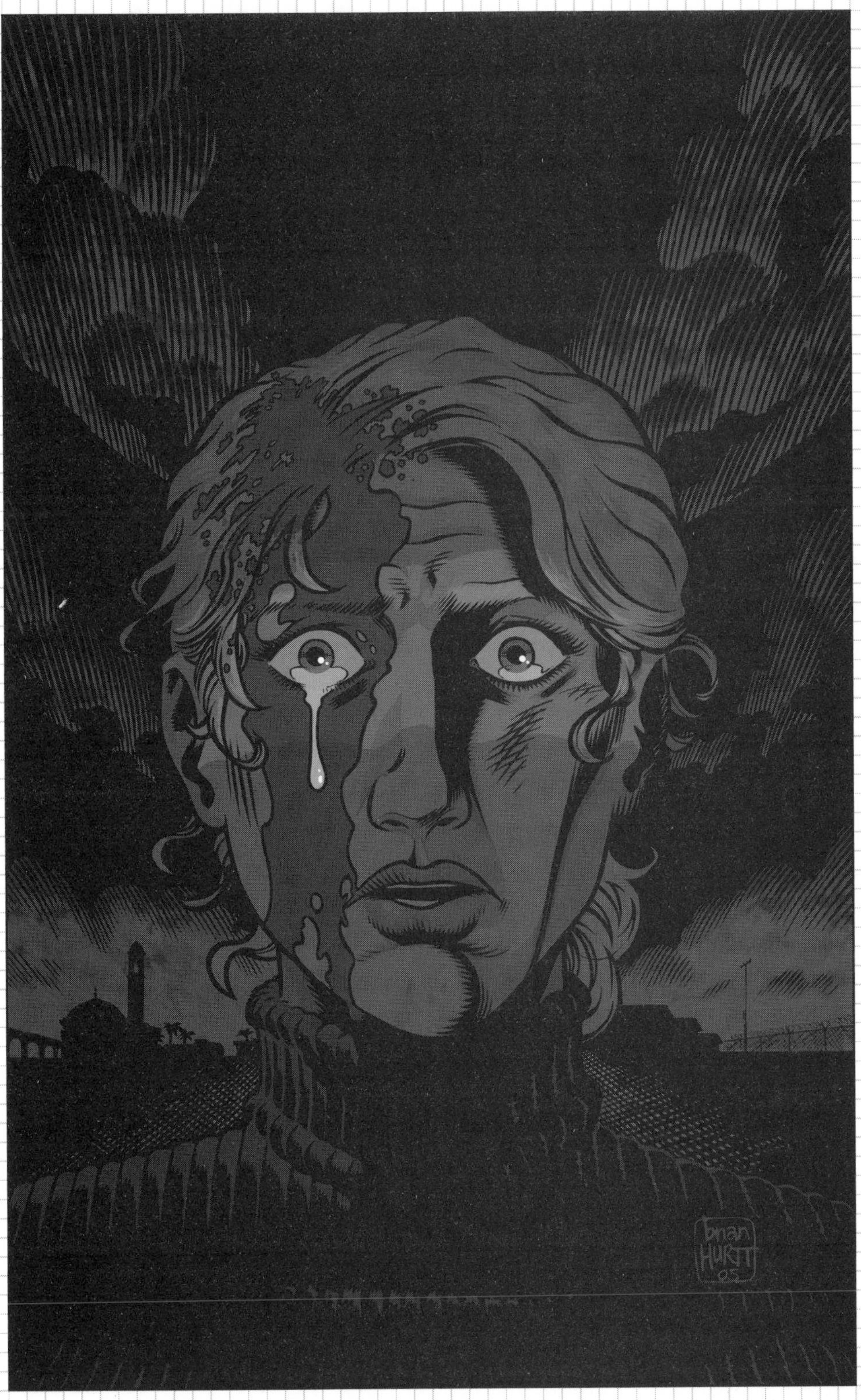
brian
HURTT
05

PROLOGUE

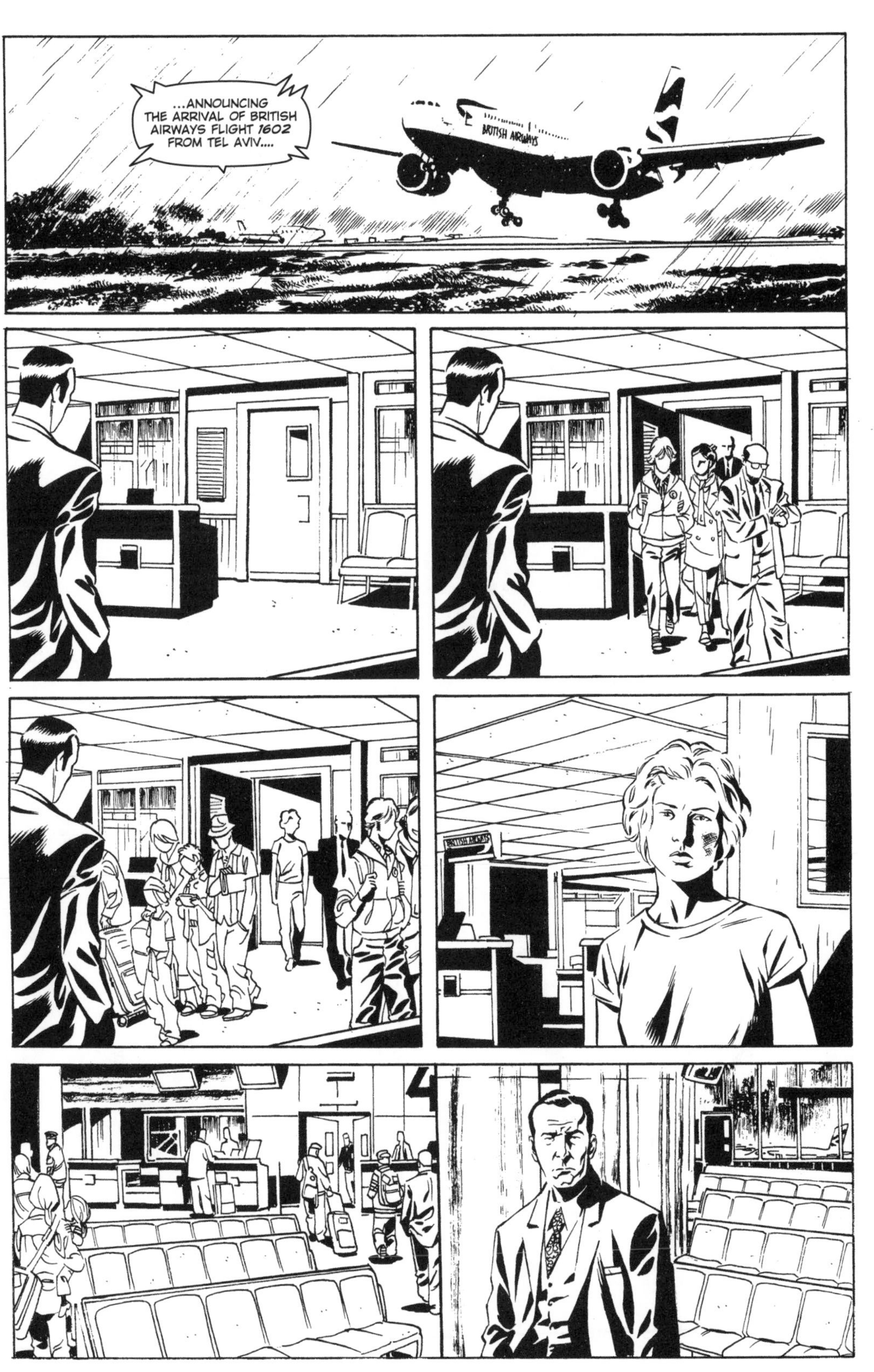
...ANNOUNCING THE ARRIVAL OF BRITISH AIRWAYS FLIGHT 1602 FROM TEL AVIV....
BRITISH AIRWAYS

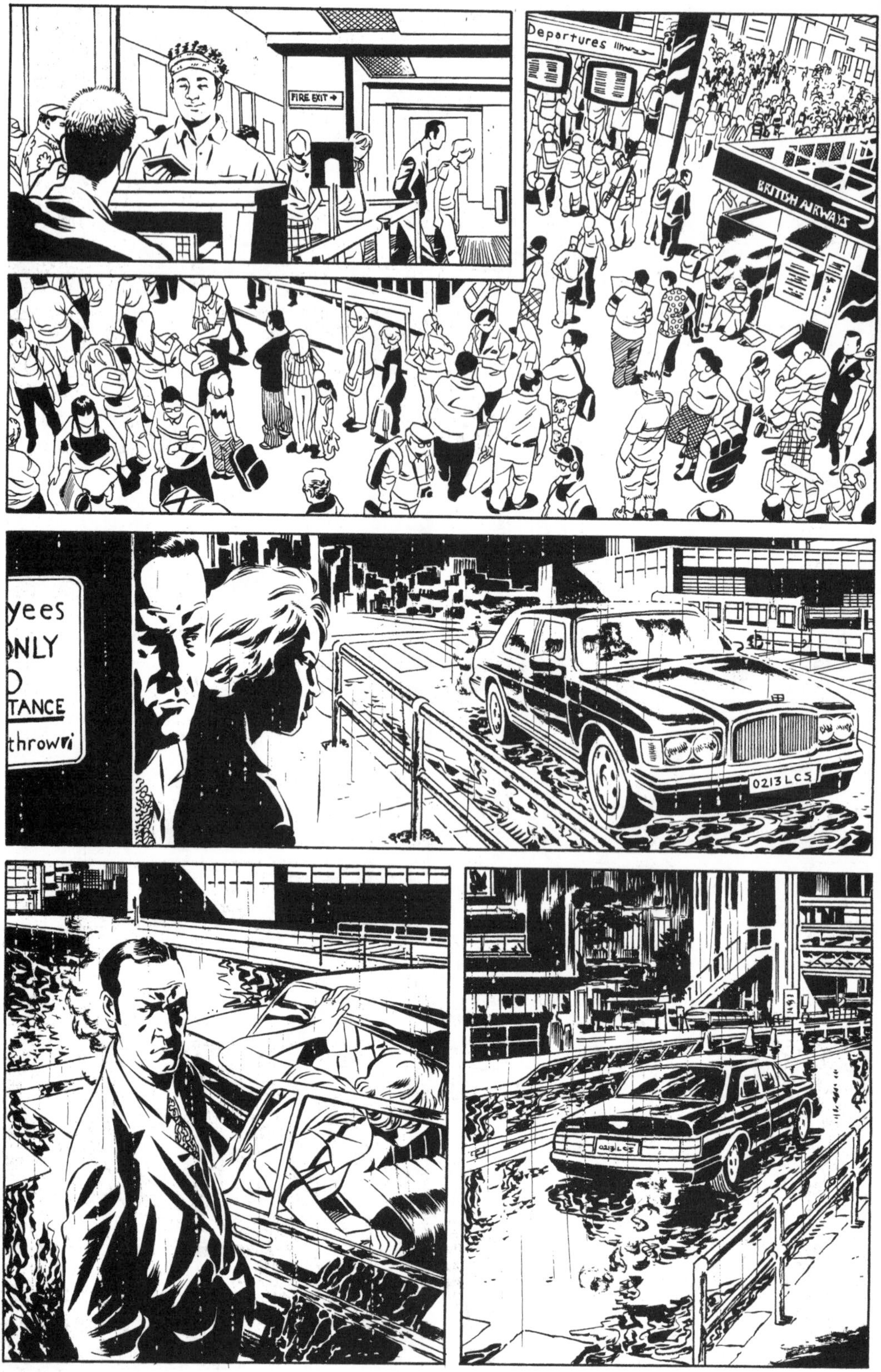
FIRE EXIT
Departures
BRITISH AIRWAYS
yees
ONLY
TANCE
throw
0213 LCS

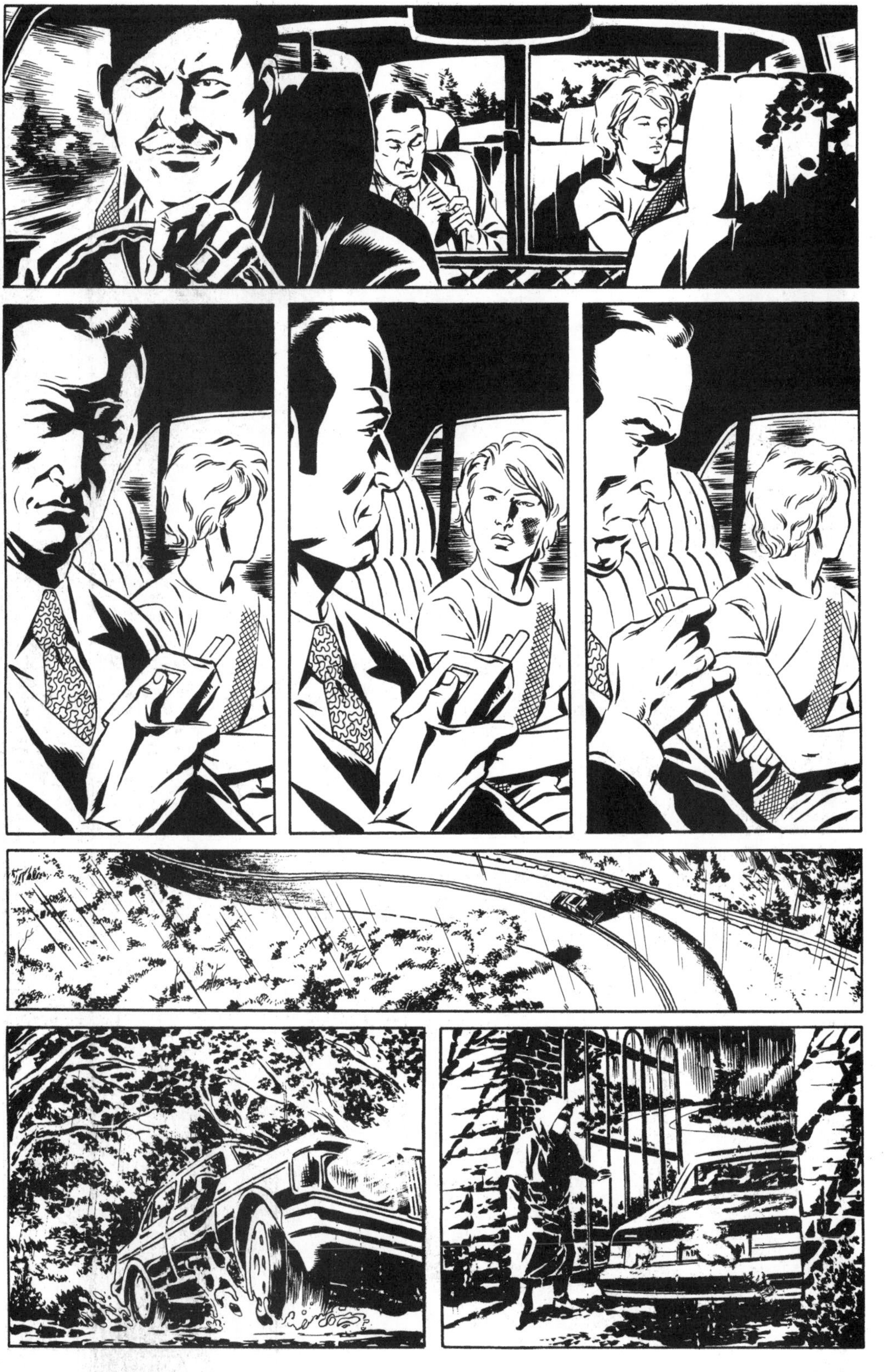

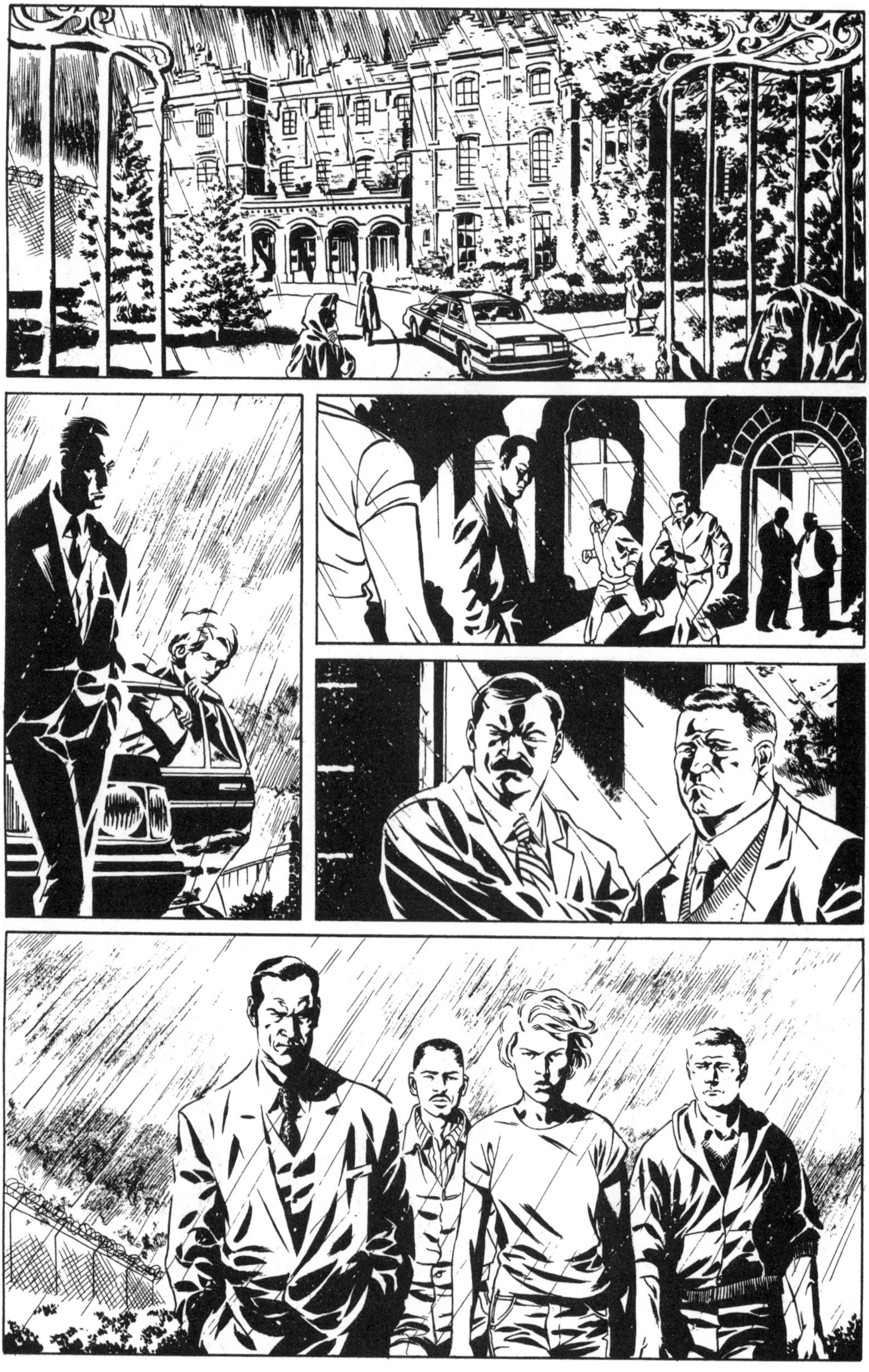

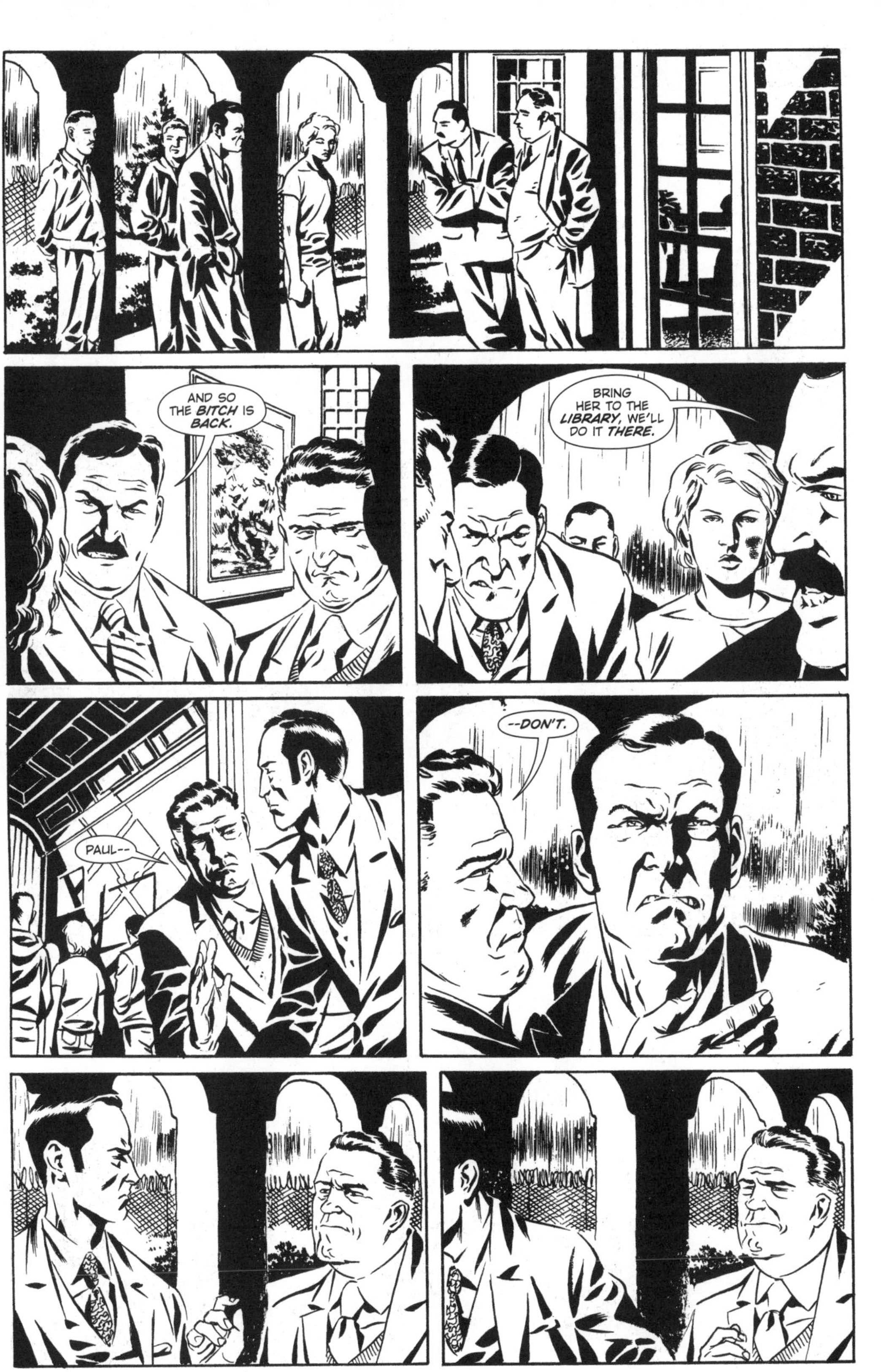
AND SO THE BITCH IS BACK.
BRING HER TO THE LIBRARY, WE'LL DO IT THERE.
PAUL--
--DON'T.

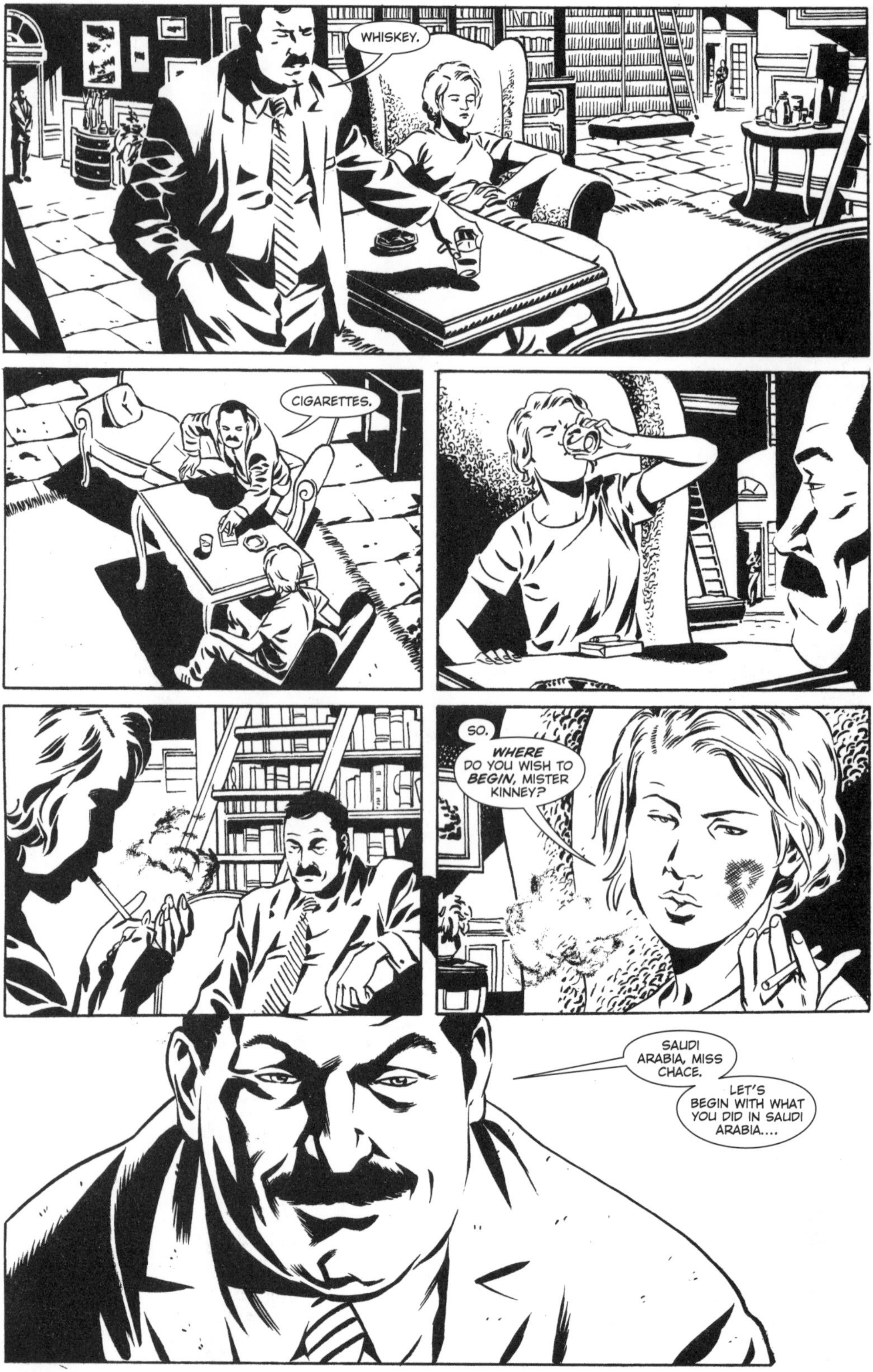
WHISKEY.
CIGARETTES.
SO.
WHERE DO YOU WISH TO BEGIN, MISTER KINNEY?
SAUDI ARABIA, MISS CHACE.
LET'S BEGIN WITH WHAT YOU DID IN SAUDI ARABIA....

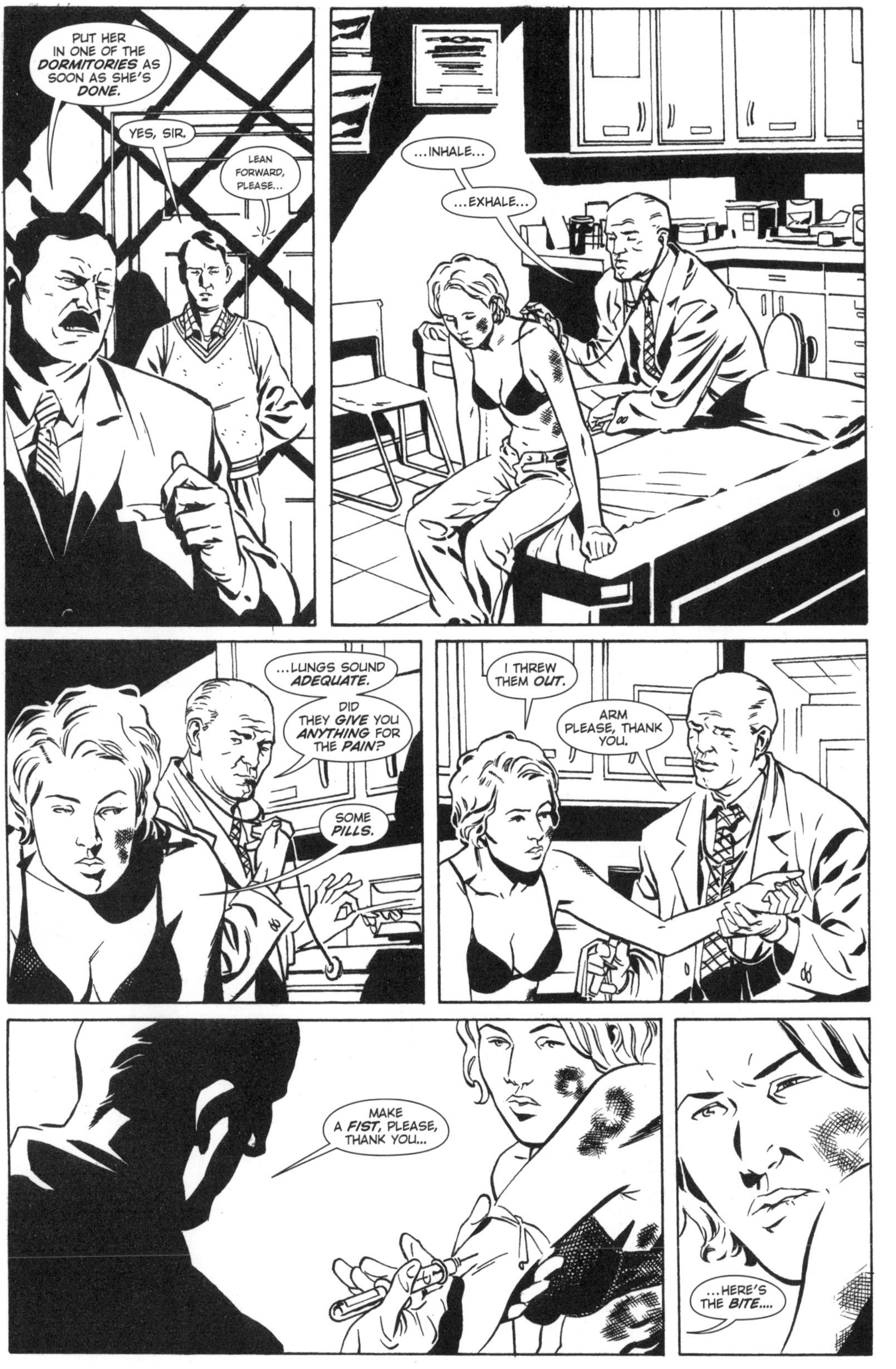
PUT HER IN ONE OF THE **DORMITORIES** AS SOON AS SHE'S **DONE.**
YES, SIR.
LEAN FORWARD, PLEASE...
...INHALE...
...EXHALE...
...LUNGS SOUND **ADEQUATE.**
DID THEY **GIVE** YOU **ANYTHING** FOR THE **PAIN?**
SOME **PILLS.**
I THREW THEM **OUT.**
ARM PLEASE, THANK YOU.
MAKE A **FIST,** PLEASE, THANK YOU...
...HERE'S THE **BITE....**

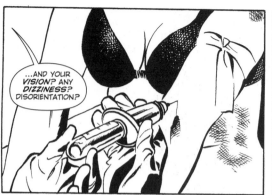

...AND YOUR *VISION?* ANY *DIZZINESS?* DISORIENTATION?

FINE.

REALLY? I'D HAVE *THOUGHT* YOU'D COMPLAIN OF A *HEADACHE,* AT LEAST...

...LOOKS LIKE IT WAS *QUITE* THE *CONCUSSION.*

RIFLE *BUTT,* I SHOULDN'T GUESS.

THE *STITCHES* CAN COME OUT IN ANOTHER *WEEK* OR SO.

I'D *URGE* YOU TO *REST,* TRY TO TAKE THINGS *EASY* FOR THE NEXT FEW DAYS...

...AND *LAY* OFF THE *FAGS* AND *WHISKEY* FOR A WHILE, AS WELL.

LET YOUR BODY *RECOVER,* ALL RIGHT?

CERTAINLY, DOCTOR.

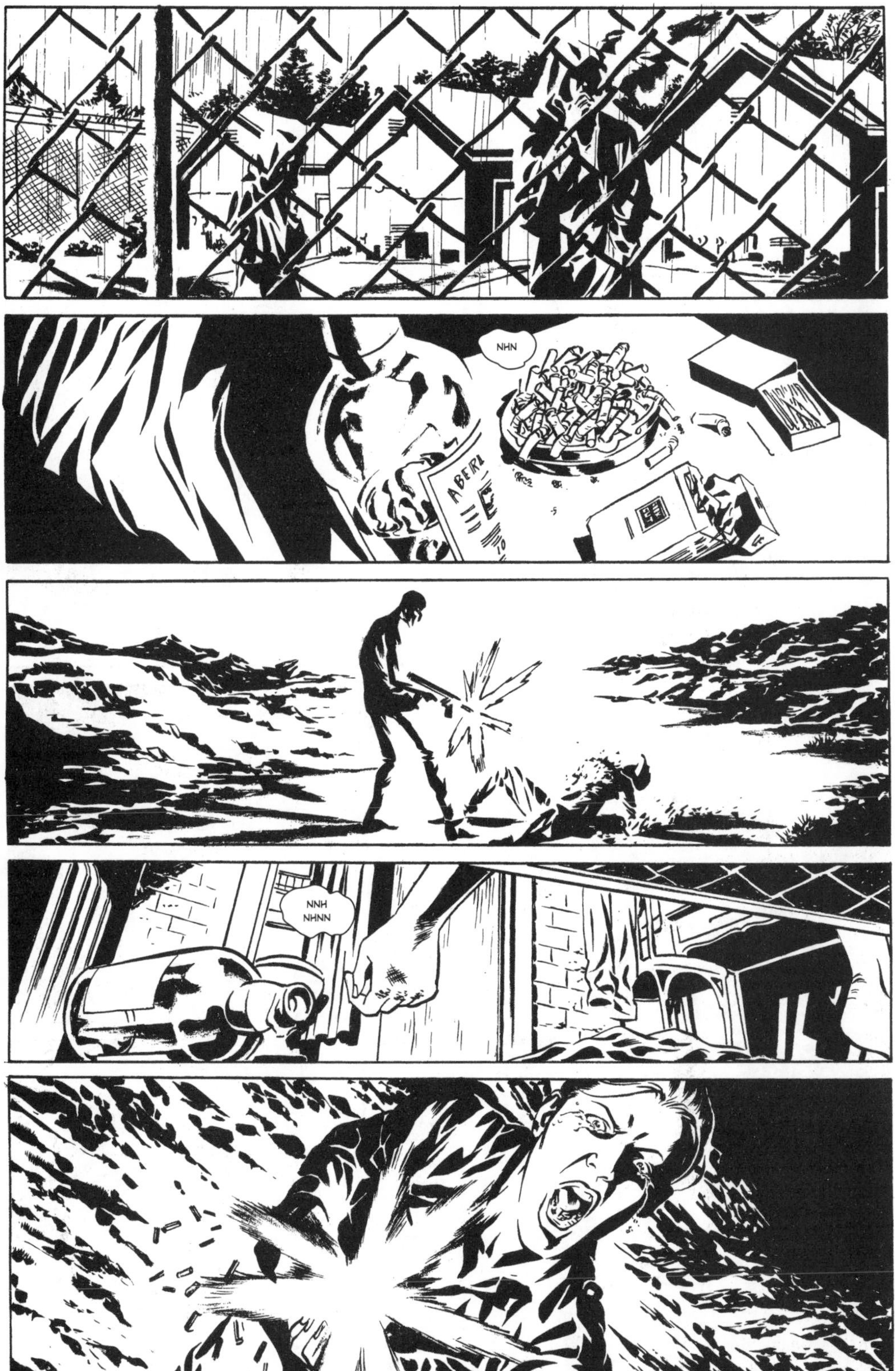
NHN
NNH NHNN

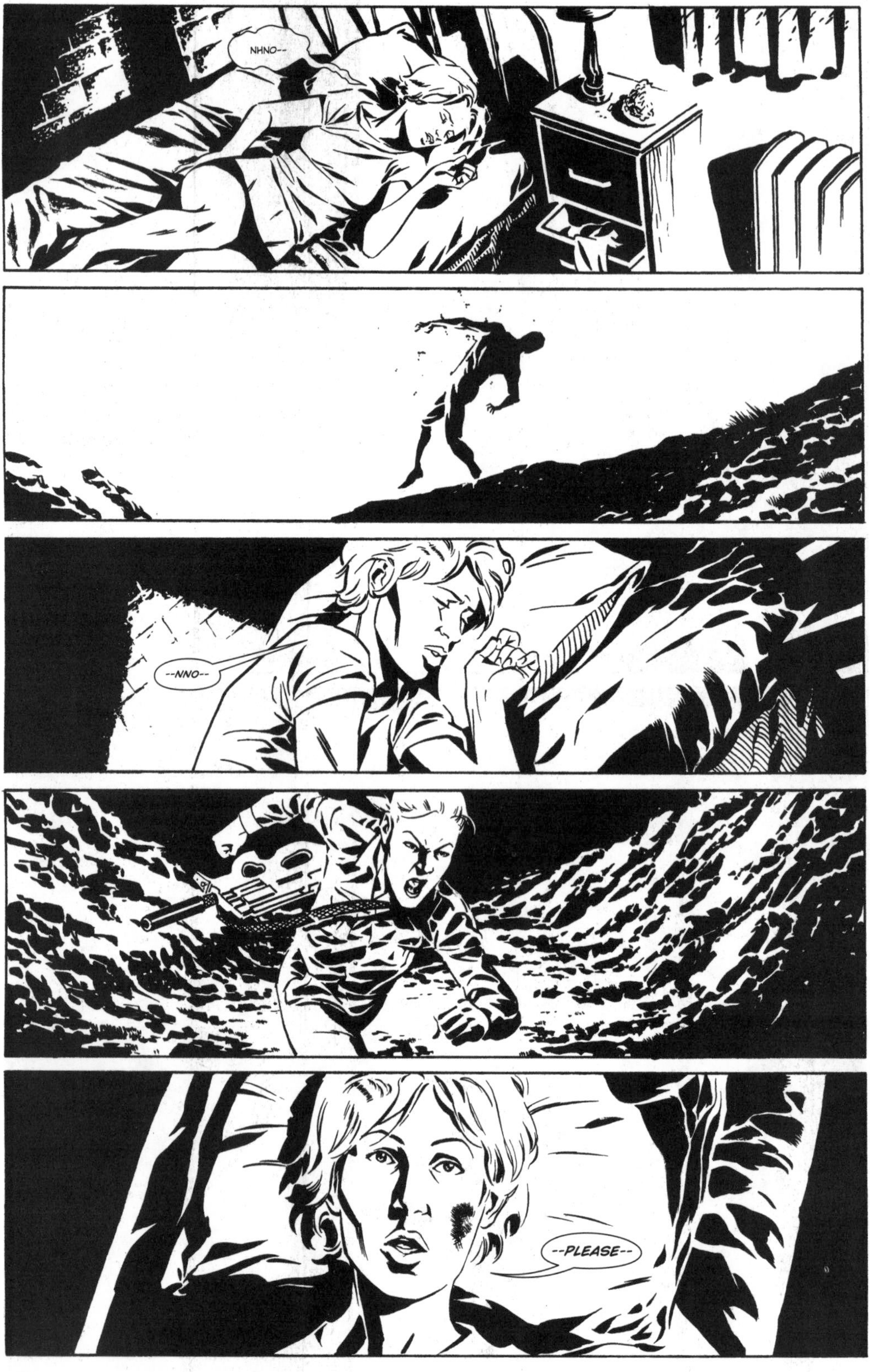
NHNO--
--NNO--
--PLEASE--

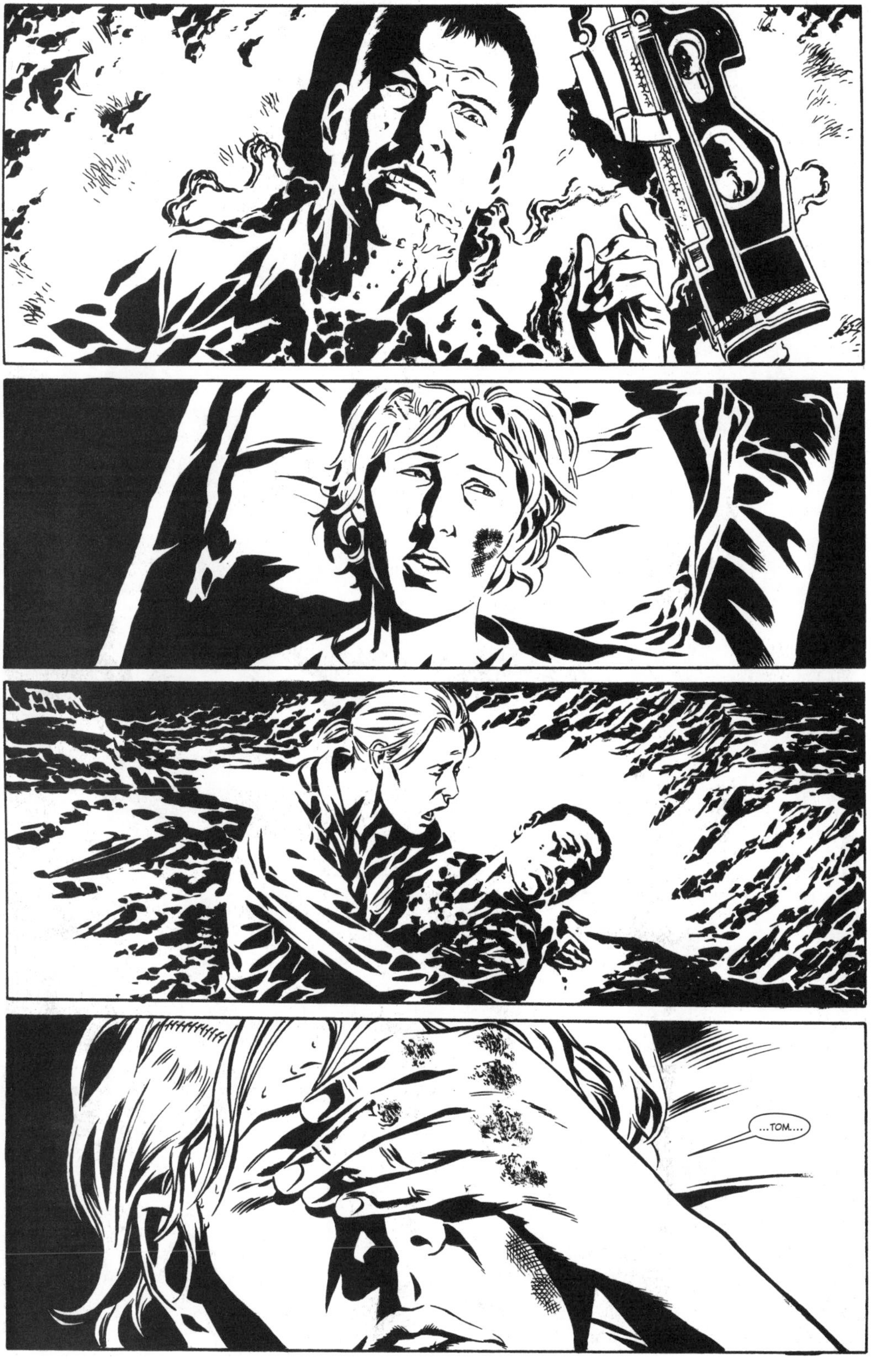
...TOM....

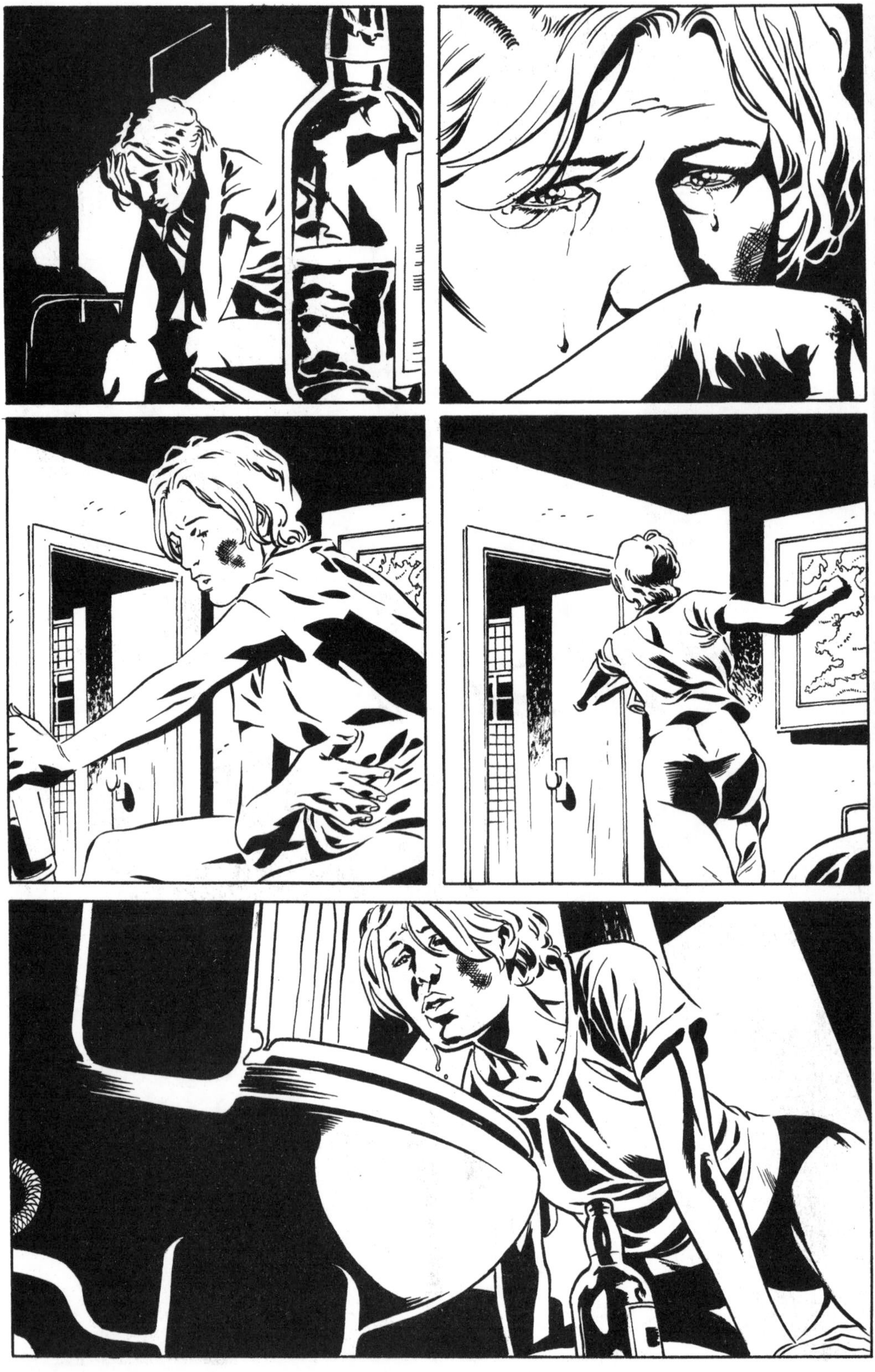

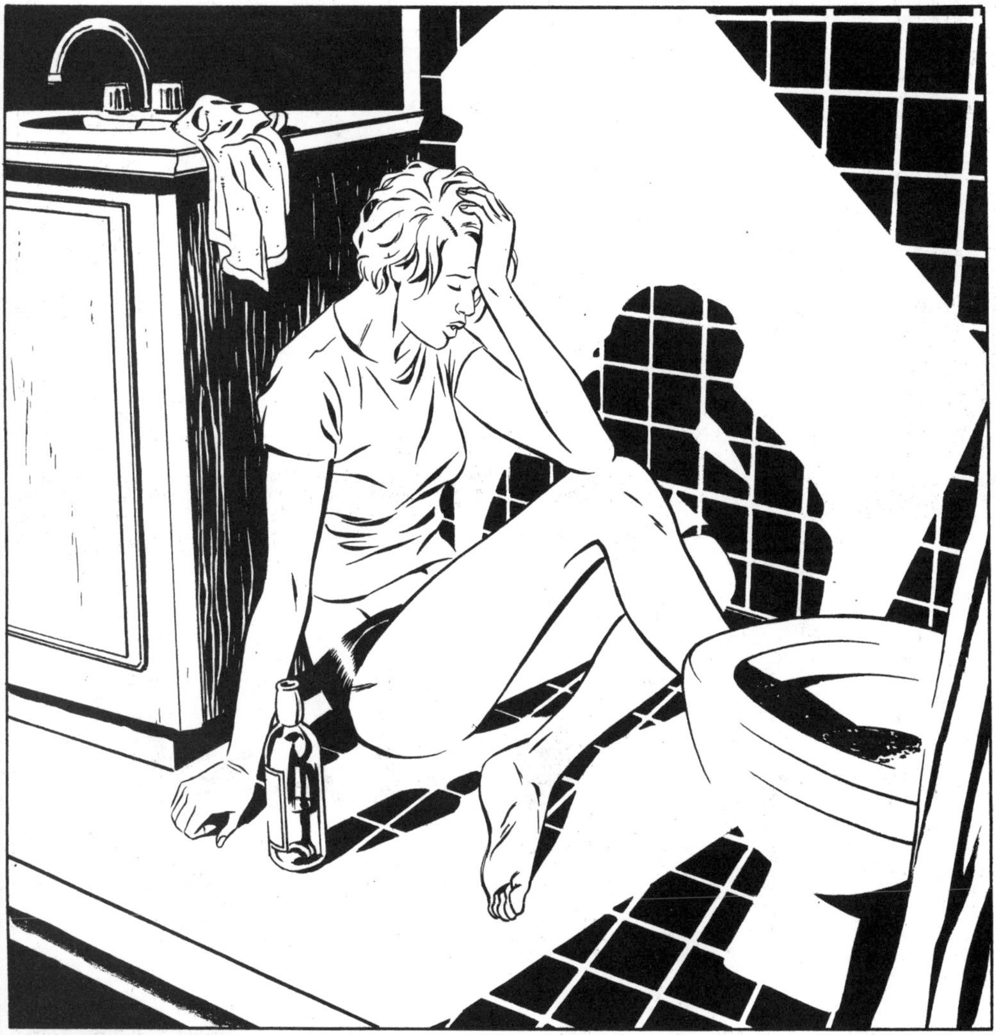

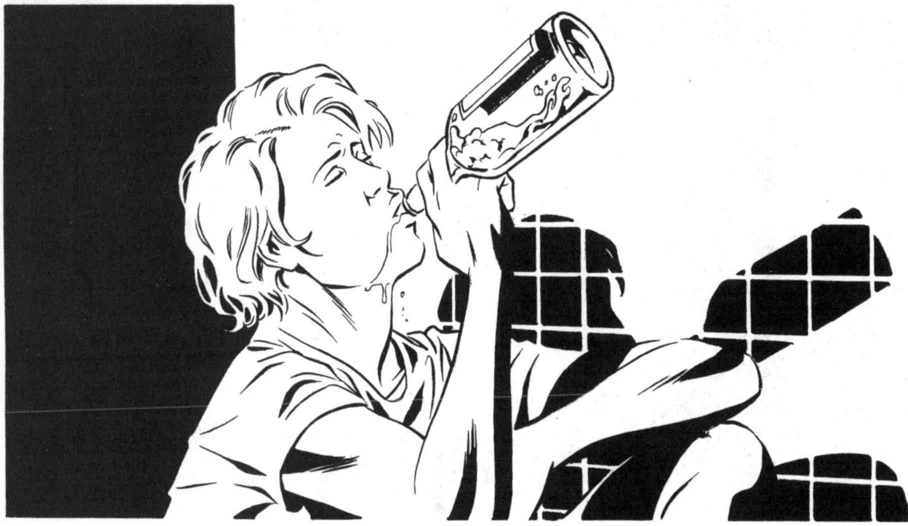

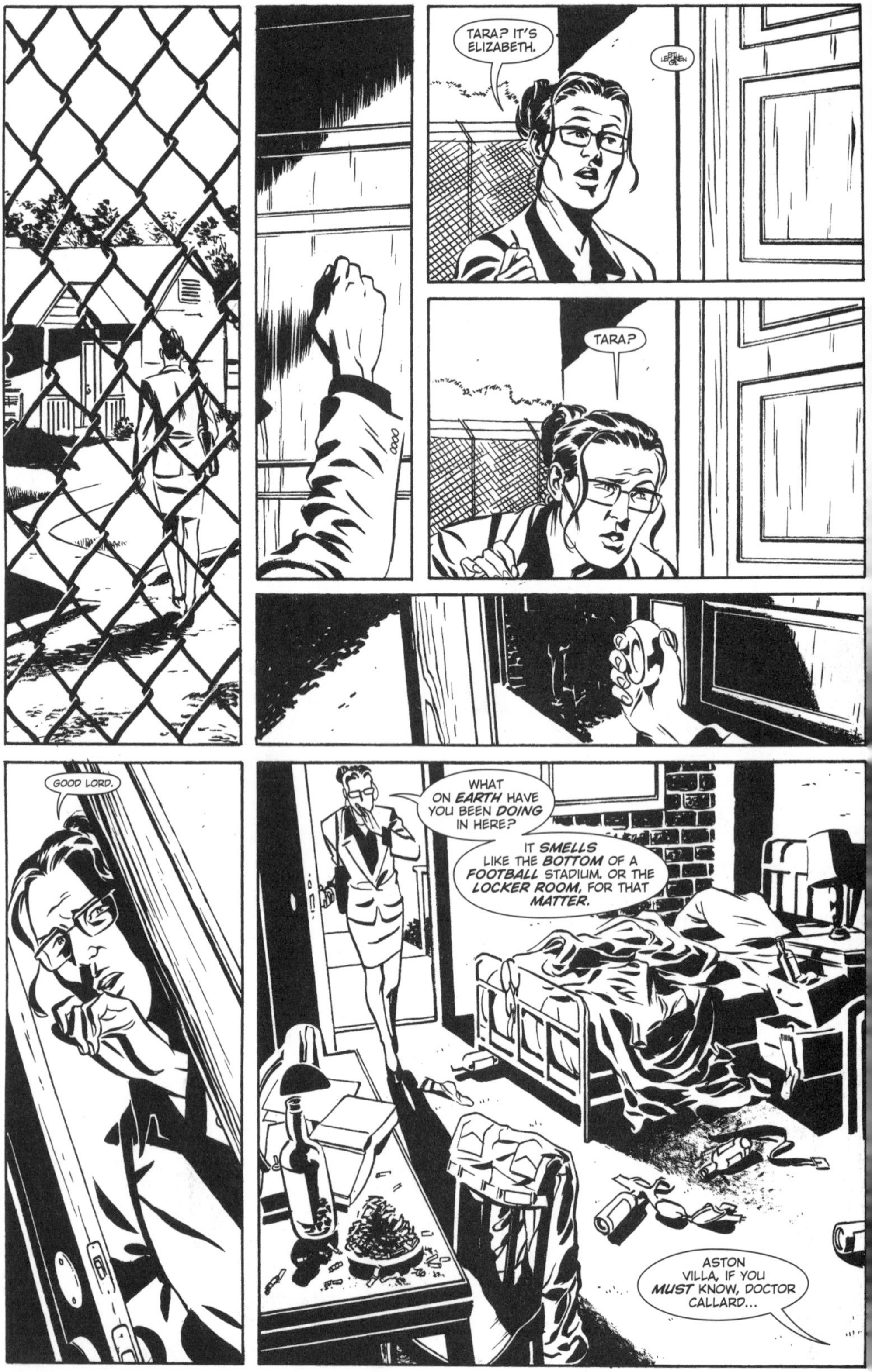
TARA? IT'S ELIZABETH.
TARA?
GOOD LORD.
WHAT ON EARTH HAVE YOU BEEN DOING IN HERE?
IT SMELLS LIKE THE BOTTOM OF A FOOTBALL STADIUM. OR THE LOCKER ROOM, FOR THAT MATTER.
ASTON VILLA, IF YOU MUST KNOW, DOCTOR CALLARD...

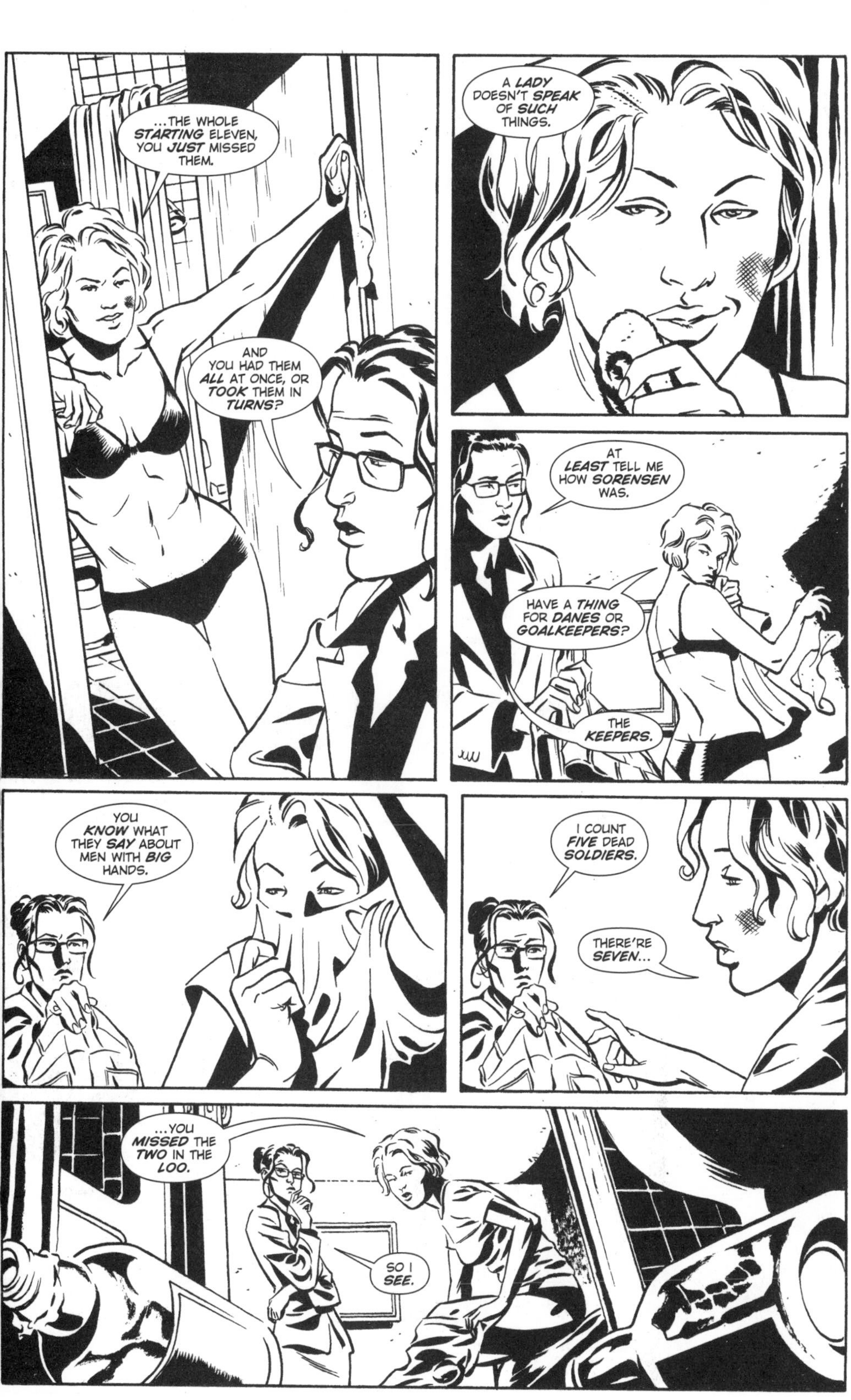
...THE WHOLE STARTING ELEVEN, YOU JUST MISSED THEM.
AND YOU HAD THEM ALL AT ONCE, OR TOOK THEM IN TURNS?
A LADY DOESN'T SPEAK OF SUCH THINGS.
AT LEAST TELL ME HOW SORENSEN WAS.
HAVE A THING FOR DANES OR GOALKEEPERS?
THE KEEPERS.
YOU KNOW WHAT THEY SAY ABOUT MEN WITH BIG HANDS.
I COUNT FIVE DEAD SOLDIERS.
THERE'RE SEVEN...
...YOU MISSED THE TWO IN THE LOO.
SO I SEE.

STILL HAVING *NIGHTMARES?*

NO.

DON'T *LIE* TO ME, TARA.

YES.

YOU'RE *SUFFERING* FROM PTSD.

DRINKING AND *DENIAL* ARE NOT CONSIDERED METHODS OF *TREATMENT.*

NO?

NO, ACTUALLY, THEY'RE *SYMPTOMS.*

SO IF YOU'RE *TRYING* TO *CONVINCE* ME THAT YOU'RE *READY* TO GO BACK TO *WORK*, YOU'RE DOING A DAMN *POOR* JOB OF IT.

I'M NOT TRYING TO CONVINCE YOU OF *ANYTHING*, DOCTOR CALLARD.

ARE YOU SAYING YOU *DON'T* WANT TO RETURN TO *WORK?*

I DON'T *KNOW.* DO I *STILL* HAVE A *JOB?*

MY UNDERSTANDING IS THAT D-OPS INTENDS TO *REINSTATE* YOU AS MINDER ONE.

FUCK D-OPS.

144

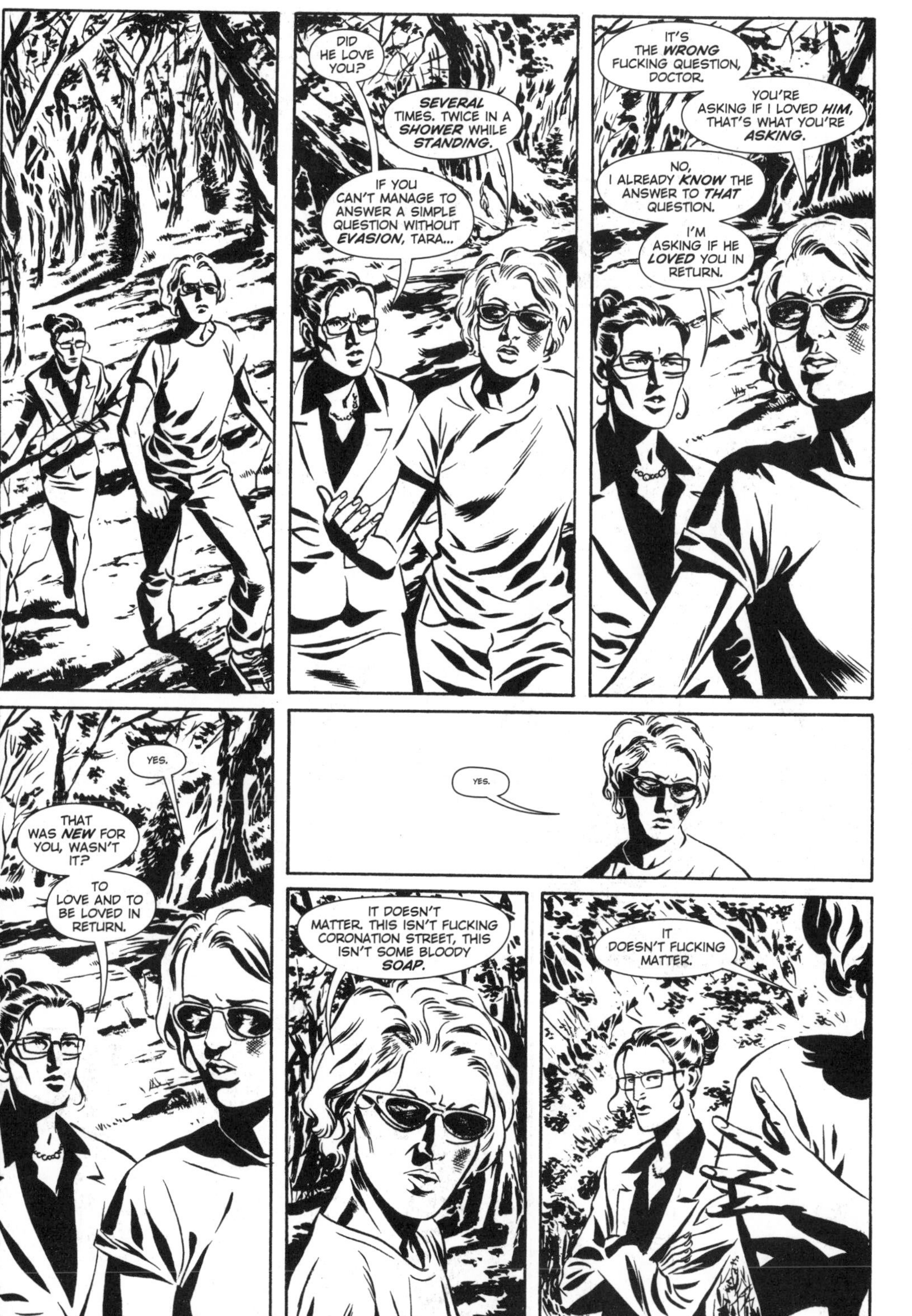
DID HE LOVE YOU?
SEVERAL TIMES. TWICE IN A SHOWER WHILE STANDING.
IF YOU CAN'T MANAGE TO ANSWER A SIMPLE QUESTION WITHOUT EVASION, TARA...
IT'S THE WRONG FUCKING QUESTION, DOCTOR.
YOU'RE ASKING IF I LOVED HIM, THAT'S WHAT YOU'RE ASKING.
NO, I ALREADY KNOW THE ANSWER TO THAT QUESTION.
I'M ASKING IF HE LOVED YOU IN RETURN.
YES.
THAT WAS NEW FOR YOU, WASN'T IT?
TO LOVE AND TO BE LOVED IN RETURN.
YES.
IT DOESN'T MATTER. THIS ISN'T FUCKING CORONATION STREET, THIS ISN'T SOME BLOODY SOAP.
IT DOESN'T FUCKING MATTER.

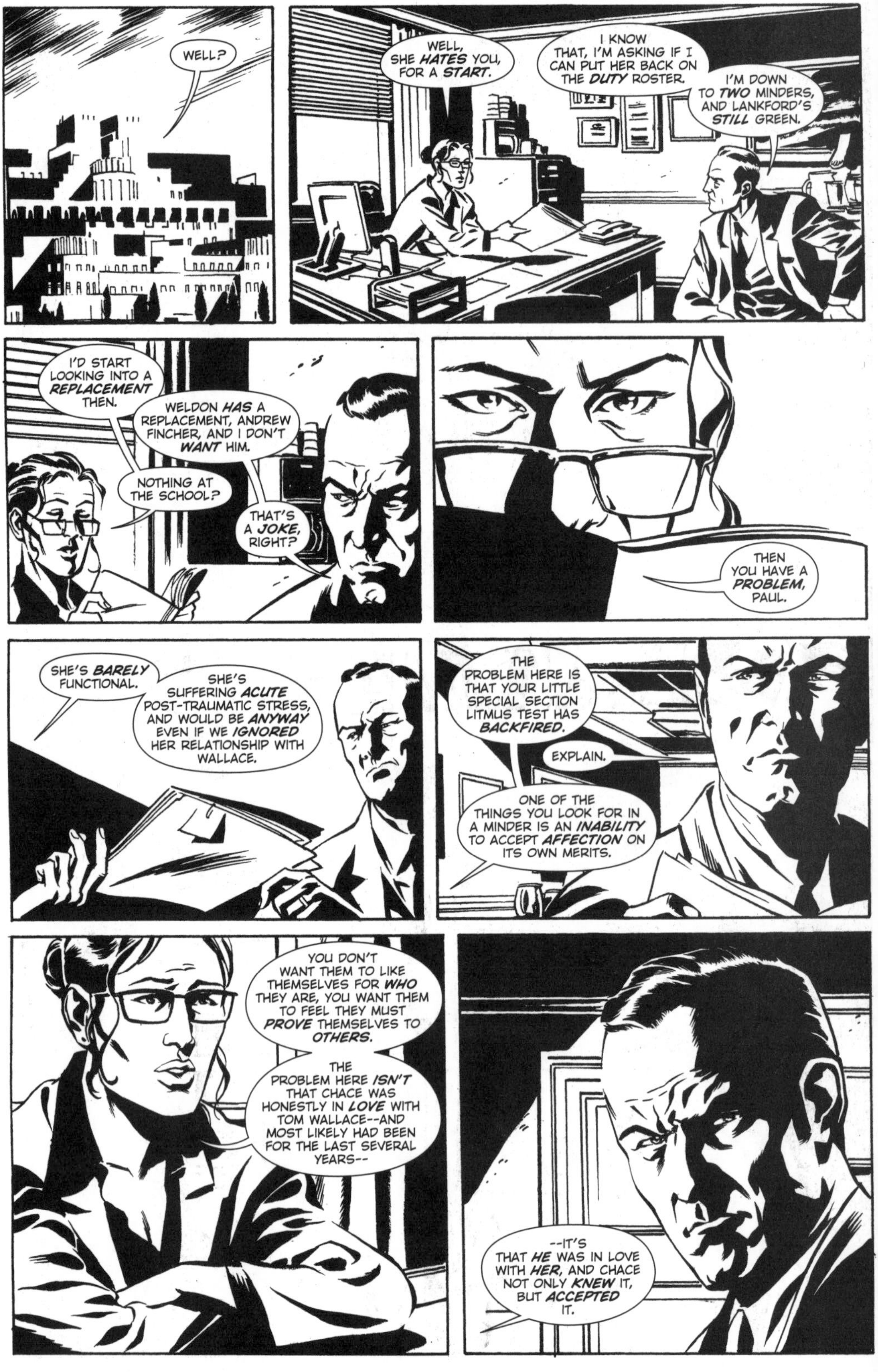
WELL?
WELL, SHE HATES YOU, FOR A START.
I KNOW THAT, I'M ASKING IF I CAN PUT HER BACK ON THE DUTY ROSTER.
I'M DOWN TO TWO MINDERS, AND LANKFORD'S STILL GREEN.
I'D START LOOKING INTO A REPLACEMENT THEN.
WELDON HAS A REPLACEMENT, ANDREW FINCHER, AND I DON'T WANT HIM.
NOTHING AT THE SCHOOL?
THAT'S A JOKE, RIGHT?
THEN YOU HAVE A PROBLEM, PAUL.
SHE'S BARELY FUNCTIONAL.
SHE'S SUFFERING ACUTE POST-TRAUMATIC STRESS, AND WOULD BE ANYWAY EVEN IF WE IGNORED HER RELATIONSHIP WITH WALLACE.
THE PROBLEM HERE IS THAT YOUR LITTLE SPECIAL SECTION LITMUS TEST HAS BACKFIRED.
EXPLAIN.
ONE OF THE THINGS YOU LOOK FOR IN A MINDER IS AN INABILITY TO ACCEPT AFFECTION ON ITS OWN MERITS.
YOU DON'T WANT THEM TO LIKE THEMSELVES FOR WHO THEY ARE, YOU WANT THEM TO FEEL THEY MUST PROVE THEMSELVES TO OTHERS.
THE PROBLEM HERE ISN'T THAT CHACE WAS HONESTLY IN LOVE WITH TOM WALLACE--AND MOST LIKELY HAD BEEN FOR THE LAST SEVERAL YEARS--
--IT'S THAT HE WAS IN LOVE WITH HER, AND CHACE NOT ONLY KNEW IT, BUT ACCEPTED IT.

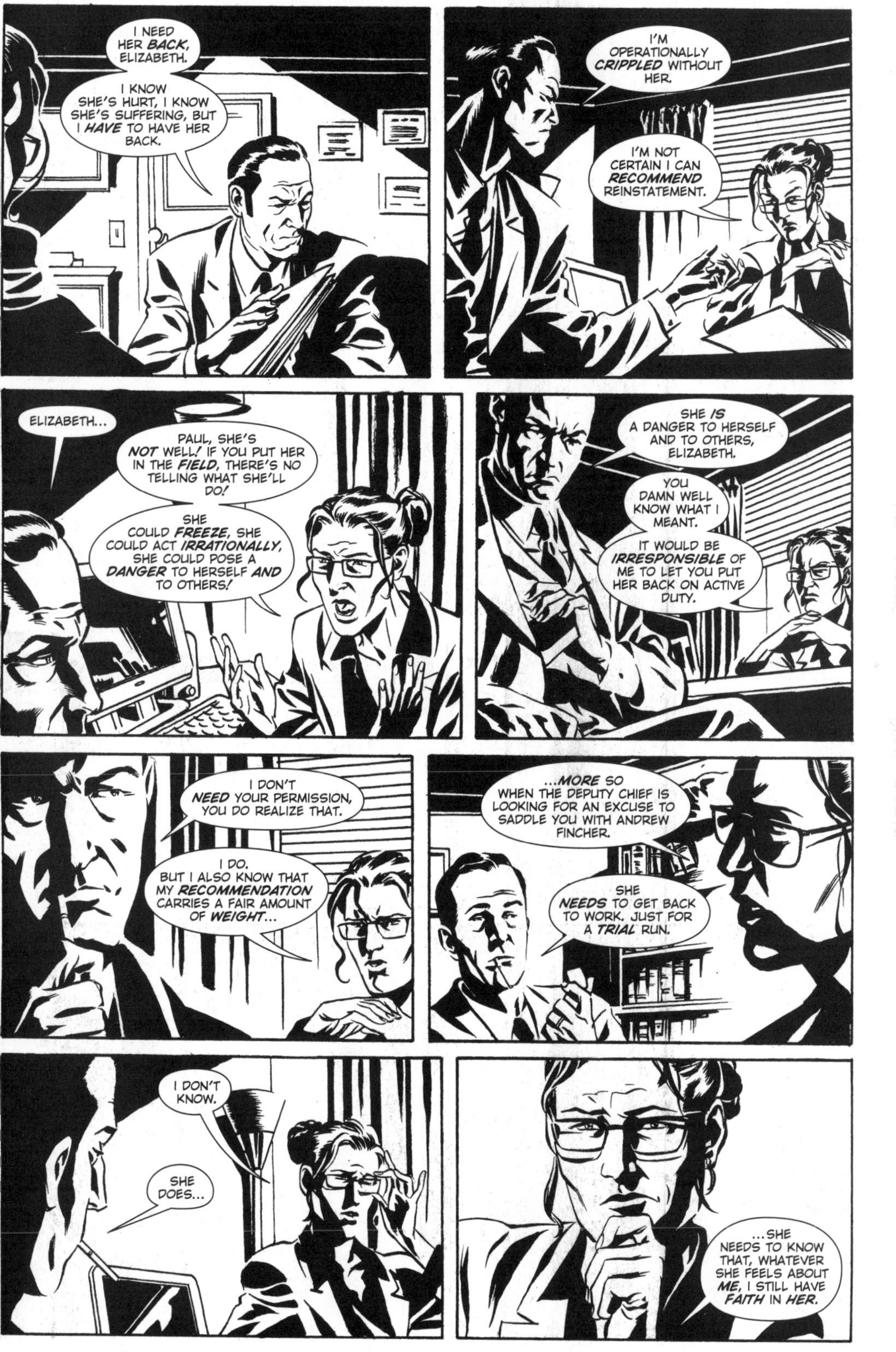
I NEED HER *BACK*, ELIZABETH.
I KNOW SHE'S HURT, I KNOW SHE'S SUFFERING, BUT I *HAVE* TO HAVE HER BACK.
I'M OPERATIONALLY *CRIPPLED* WITHOUT HER.
I'M NOT CERTAIN I CAN *RECOMMEND* REINSTATEMENT.
ELIZABETH...
PAUL, SHE'S *NOT* WELL! IF YOU PUT HER IN THE *FIELD*, THERE'S NO TELLING WHAT SHE'LL DO!
SHE COULD *FREEZE*, SHE COULD ACT *IRRATIONALLY*, SHE COULD POSE A *DANGER* TO HERSELF *AND* TO OTHERS!
SHE *IS* A DANGER TO HERSELF AND TO OTHERS, ELIZABETH.
YOU DAMN WELL KNOW WHAT I MEANT.
IT WOULD BE *IRRESPONSIBLE* OF ME TO LET YOU PUT HER BACK ON ACTIVE DUTY.
I DON'T *NEED* YOUR PERMISSION, YOU DO REALIZE THAT.
I DO. BUT I ALSO KNOW THAT MY *RECOMMENDATION* CARRIES A FAIR AMOUNT OF *WEIGHT*...
...*MORE* SO WHEN THE DEPUTY CHIEF IS LOOKING FOR AN EXCUSE TO SADDLE YOU WITH ANDREW FINCHER.
SHE *NEEDS* TO GET BACK TO WORK. JUST FOR A *TRIAL* RUN.
I DON'T KNOW.
SHE DOES...
...SHE NEEDS TO KNOW THAT, WHATEVER SHE FEELS ABOUT *ME*, I STILL HAVE *FAITH* IN *HER*.

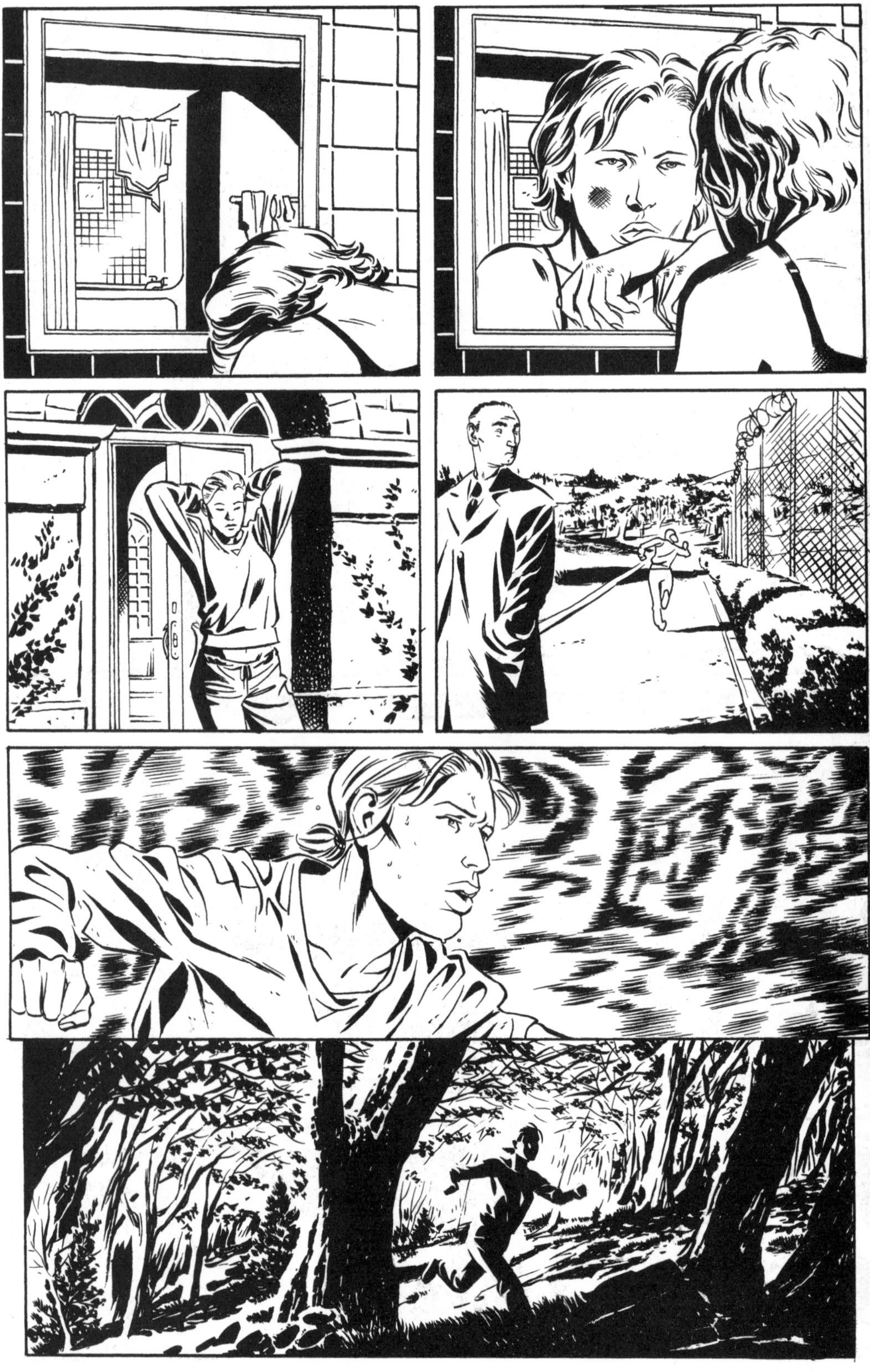

HELLO, SIR--

NEVER MIND THAT, IS HE IN?

YES, SIR.

DEPUTY CHIEF TO SEE YOU, SIR.

THANK YOU, KATE, I CAN SEE THAT.

WHAT IS THIS?

THE C-532 GENERAL MEMORANDUM I ASKED KATE TO DISTRIBUTE TO D-INT, YOU, AND C, DECLARING MY INTENTION TO *REINSTATE* CHACE AS MINDER ONE.

SHE WENT *ROGUE*, PAUL--

OH PLEASE, LET'S *NOT* START THAT *AGAIN*--

--SHE *DISOBEYED* DIRECT ORDERS, SHE *ABUSED* SIS RESOURCES, SHE *FLED* THE COUNTRY, SHE--

--WE WERE GOING TO *SELL* HER TO THE *SAUDIS*--

--RECKLESSNESS THAT CAUSED THE *DEATH* OF TOM WALLACE--

--TO *RISK* HER LIFE AND WE TURN AROUND AND *BETRAY* HER!

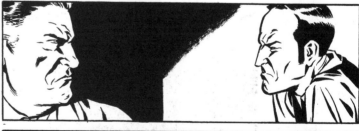

I *READ* CALLARD'S REPORT.

SHE SAYS CHACE ISN'T *FIT* FOR *DUTY*.

THAT'S *NOT* CALLARD'S *DECISION*.

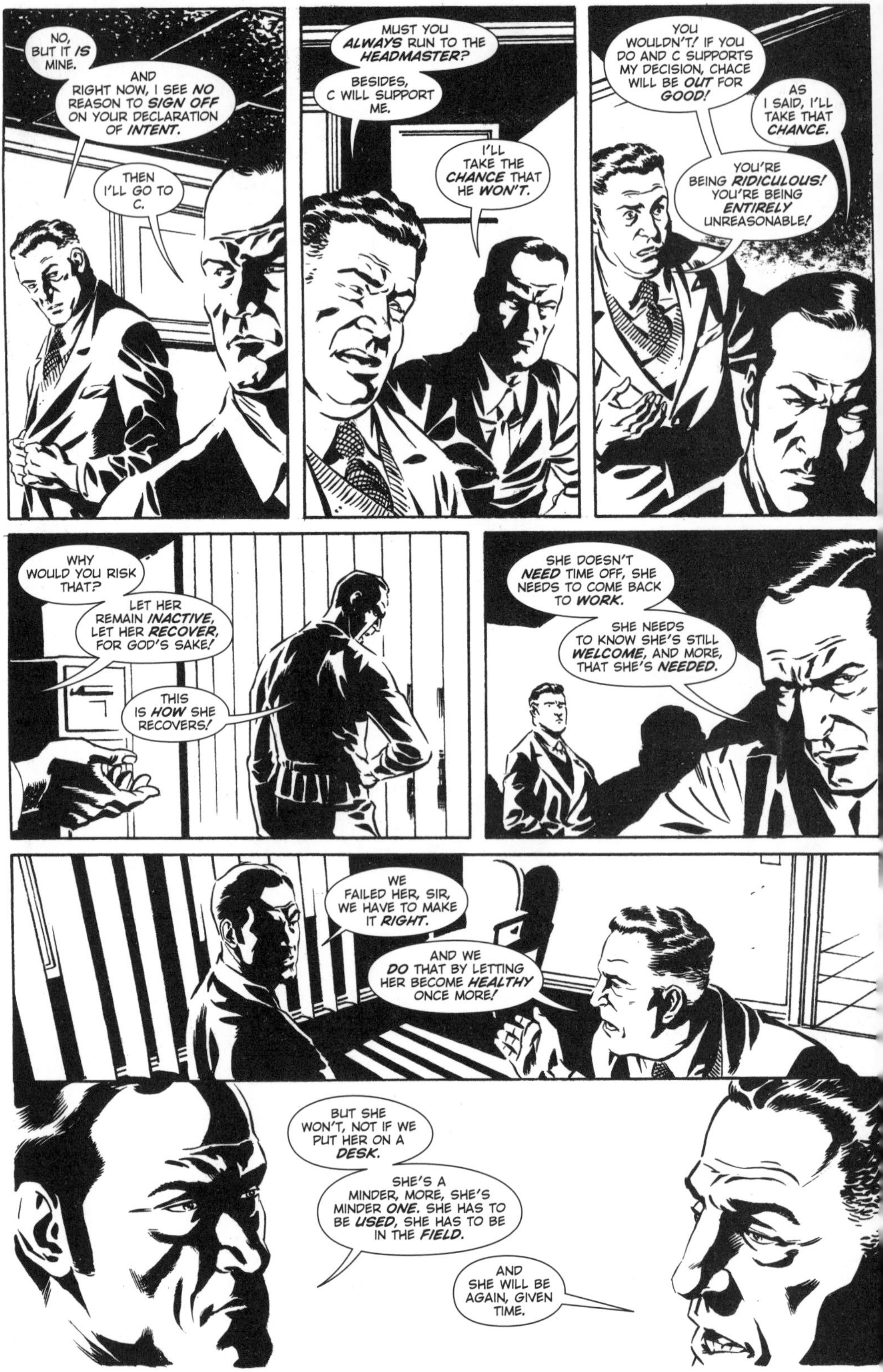
NO, BUT IT *IS* MINE.
AND RIGHT NOW, I SEE **NO** REASON TO **SIGN OFF** ON YOUR DECLARATION OF **INTENT.**
THEN I'LL GO TO C.
MUST YOU **ALWAYS** RUN TO THE **HEADMASTER?**
BESIDES, C WILL SUPPORT ME.
I'LL TAKE THE **CHANCE** THAT HE **WON'T.**
YOU WOULDN'T! IF YOU DO AND C SUPPORTS MY DECISION, CHACE WILL BE **OUT** FOR **GOOD!**
AS I SAID, I'LL TAKE THAT **CHANCE.**
YOU'RE BEING **RIDICULOUS!** YOU'RE BEING **ENTIRELY** UNREASONABLE!
WHY WOULD YOU RISK THAT?
LET HER REMAIN *INACTIVE*, LET HER *RECOVER*, FOR GOD'S SAKE!
THIS IS *HOW* SHE RECOVERS!
SHE DOESN'T **NEED** TIME OFF, SHE NEEDS TO COME BACK TO **WORK.**
SHE NEEDS TO KNOW SHE'S STILL **WELCOME,** AND MORE, THAT SHE'S **NEEDED.**
WE FAILED HER, SIR, WE HAVE TO MAKE IT **RIGHT.**
AND WE **DO** THAT BY LETTING HER BECOME **HEALTHY** ONCE MORE!
BUT SHE WON'T, NOT IF WE PUT HER ON A **DESK.**
SHE'S A MINDER, MORE, SHE'S MINDER **ONE.** SHE HAS TO BE **USED,** SHE HAS TO BE IN THE **FIELD.**
AND SHE WILL BE AGAIN, GIVEN TIME.

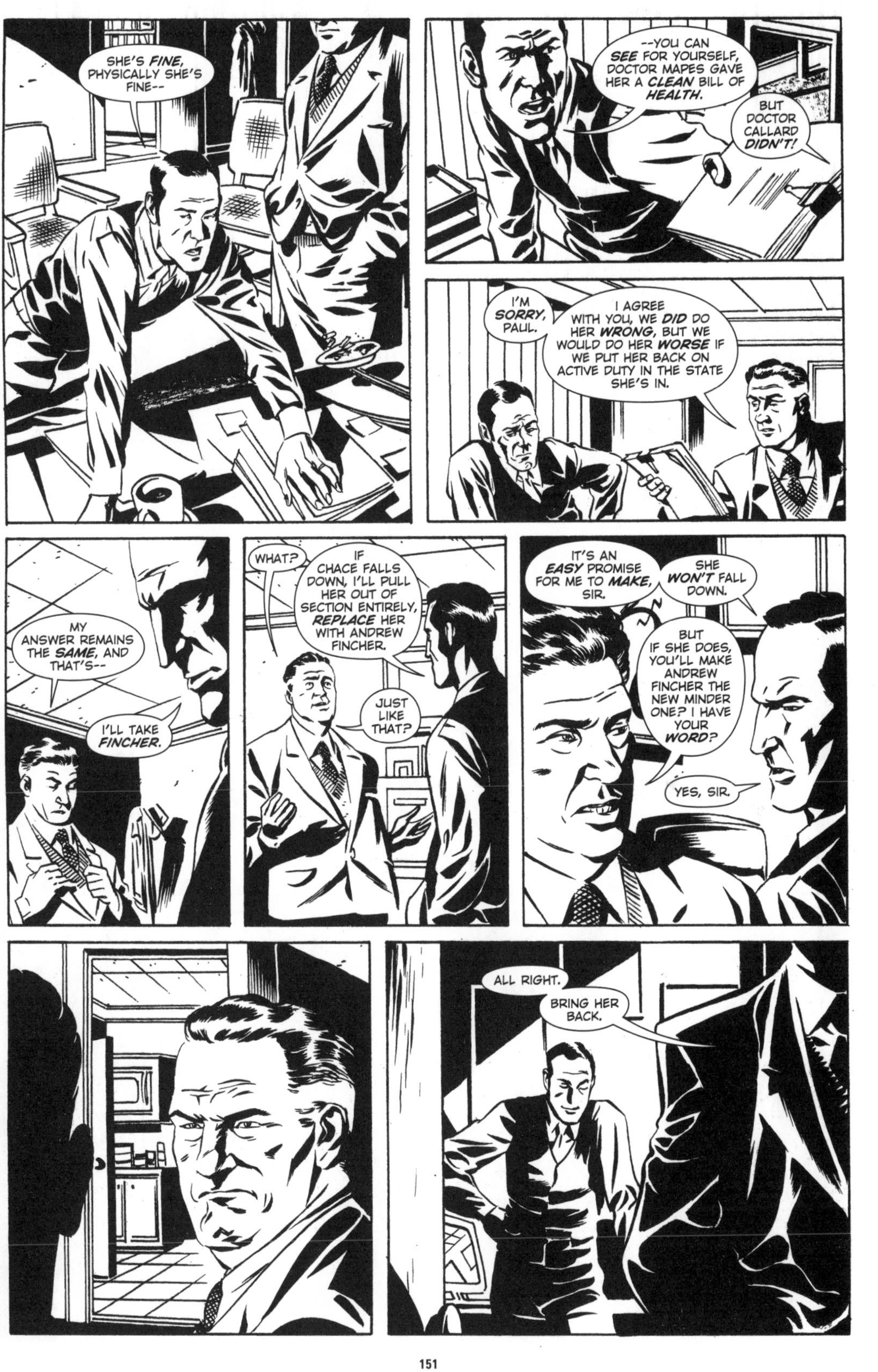
SHE'S *FINE,* PHYSICALLY SHE'S FINE--
--YOU CAN *SEE* FOR YOURSELF, DOCTOR MAPES GAVE HER A *CLEAN* BILL OF *HEALTH.*
BUT DOCTOR CALLARD *DIDN'T!*
I'M *SORRY,* PAUL.
I AGREE WITH YOU, WE *DID* DO HER *WRONG,* BUT WE WOULD DO HER *WORSE* IF WE PUT HER BACK ON ACTIVE DUTY IN THE STATE SHE'S IN.
MY ANSWER REMAINS THE *SAME,* AND THAT'S--
I'LL TAKE *FINCHER.*
WHAT?
IF CHACE FALLS DOWN, I'LL PULL HER OUT OF SECTION ENTIRELY, *REPLACE* HER WITH ANDREW FINCHER.
JUST LIKE THAT?
IT'S AN *EASY* PROMISE FOR ME TO *MAKE,* SIR.
SHE *WON'T* FALL DOWN.
BUT IF SHE DOES, YOU'LL MAKE ANDREW FINCHER THE NEW MINDER ONE? I HAVE YOUR *WORD?*
YES, SIR.
ALL RIGHT.
BRING HER BACK.

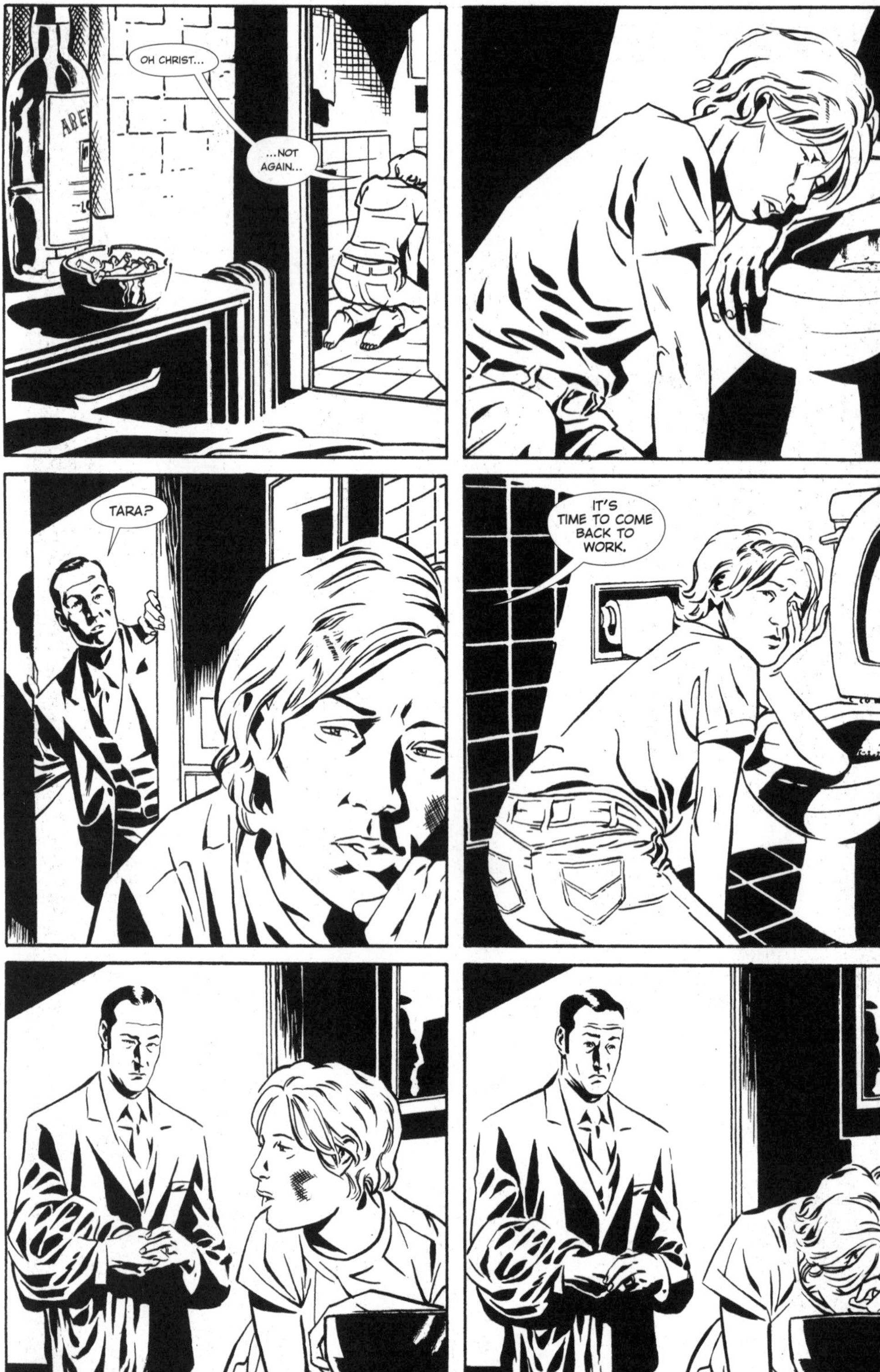
OH CHRIST...
...NOT AGAIN...
TARA?
IT'S TIME TO COME BACK TO WORK.

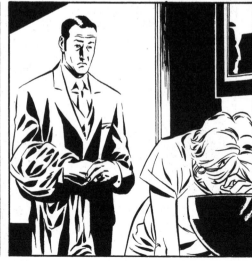

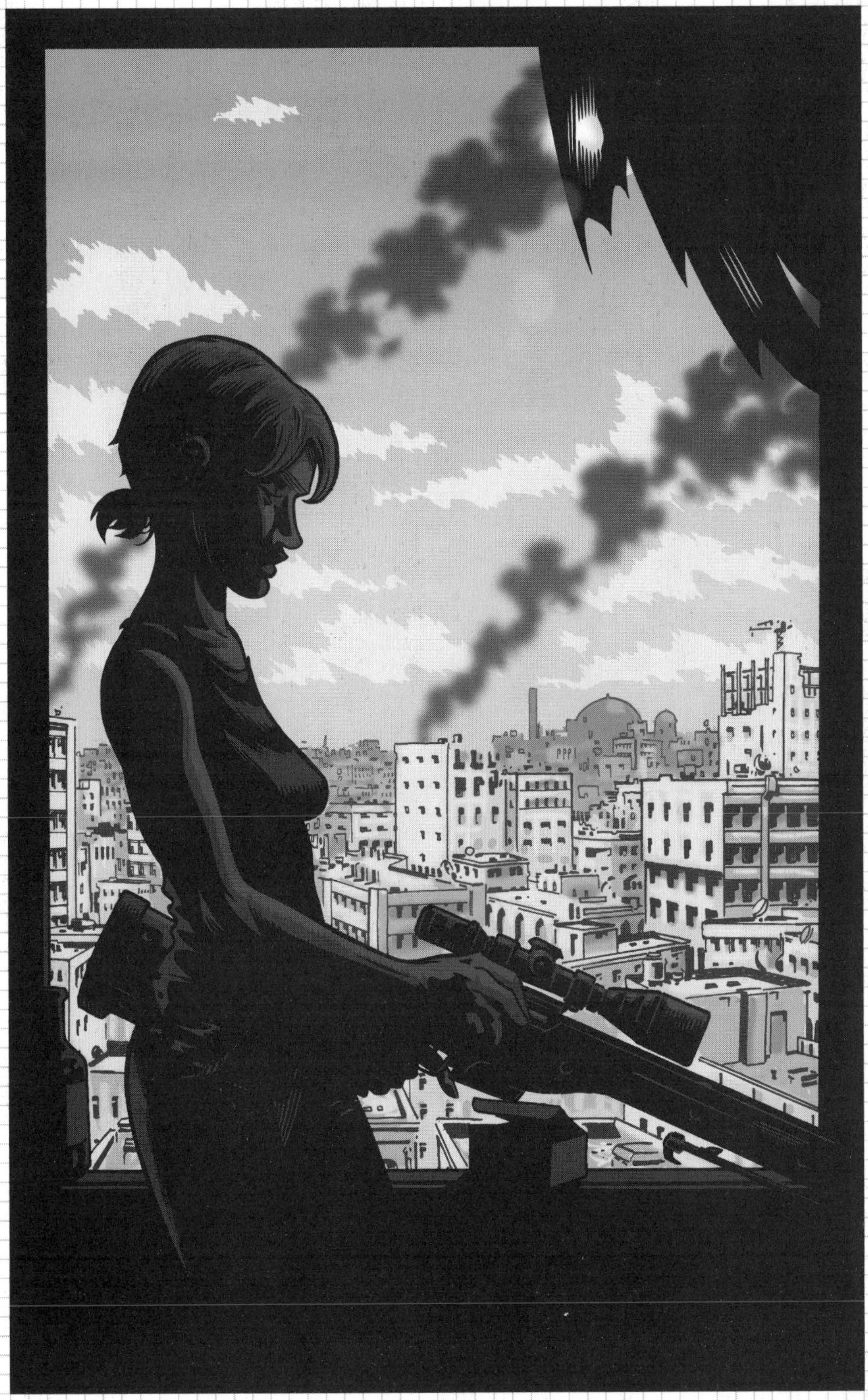

CHAPTER 1

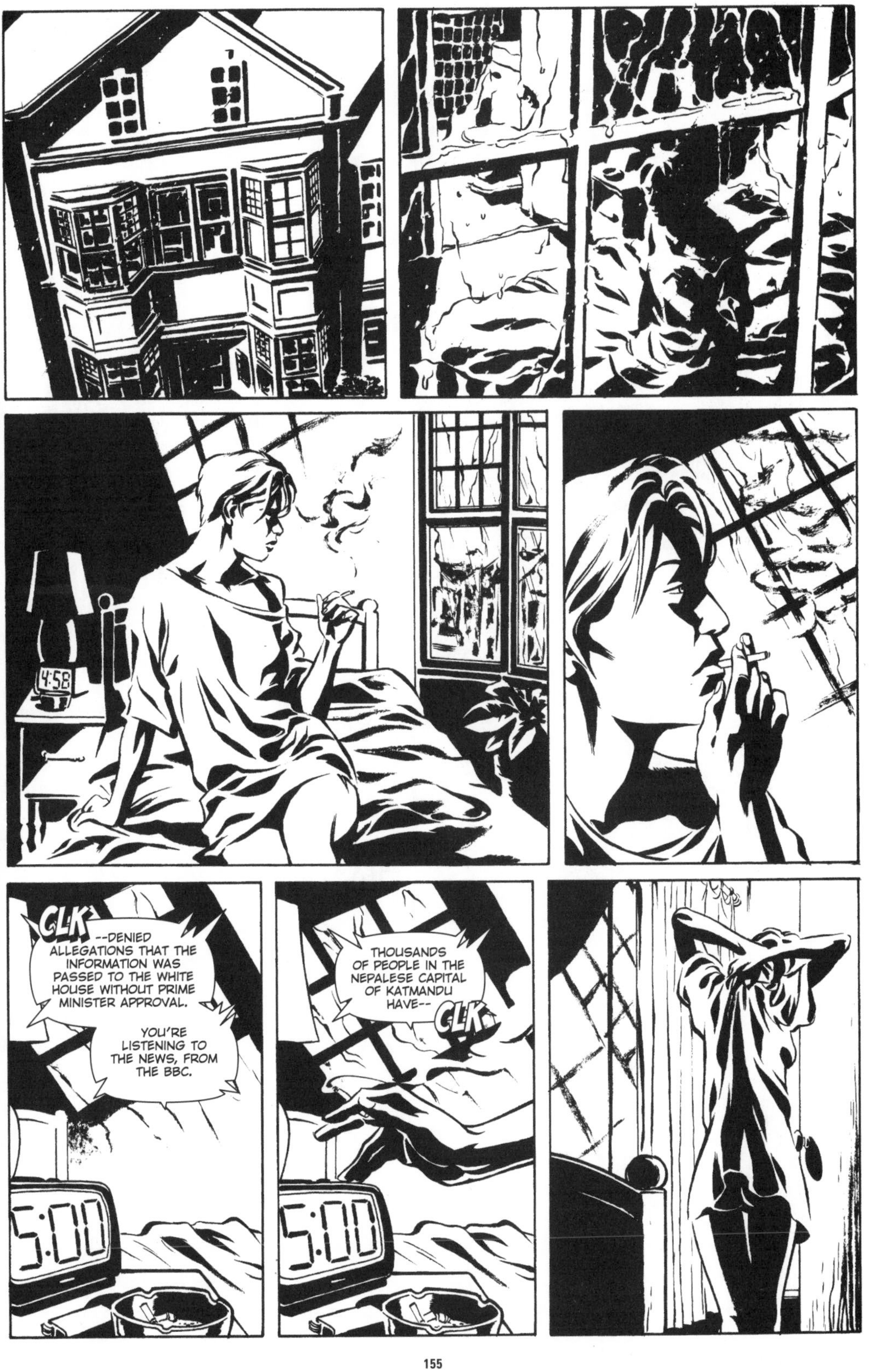
4:58
CLK
--DENIED ALLEGATIONS THAT THE INFORMATION WAS PASSED TO THE WHITE HOUSE WITHOUT PRIME MINISTER APPROVAL.
YOU'RE LISTENING TO THE NEWS, FROM THE BBC.
5:00
THOUSANDS OF PEOPLE IN THE NEPALESE CAPITAL OF KATMANDU HAVE--
CLK
5:00

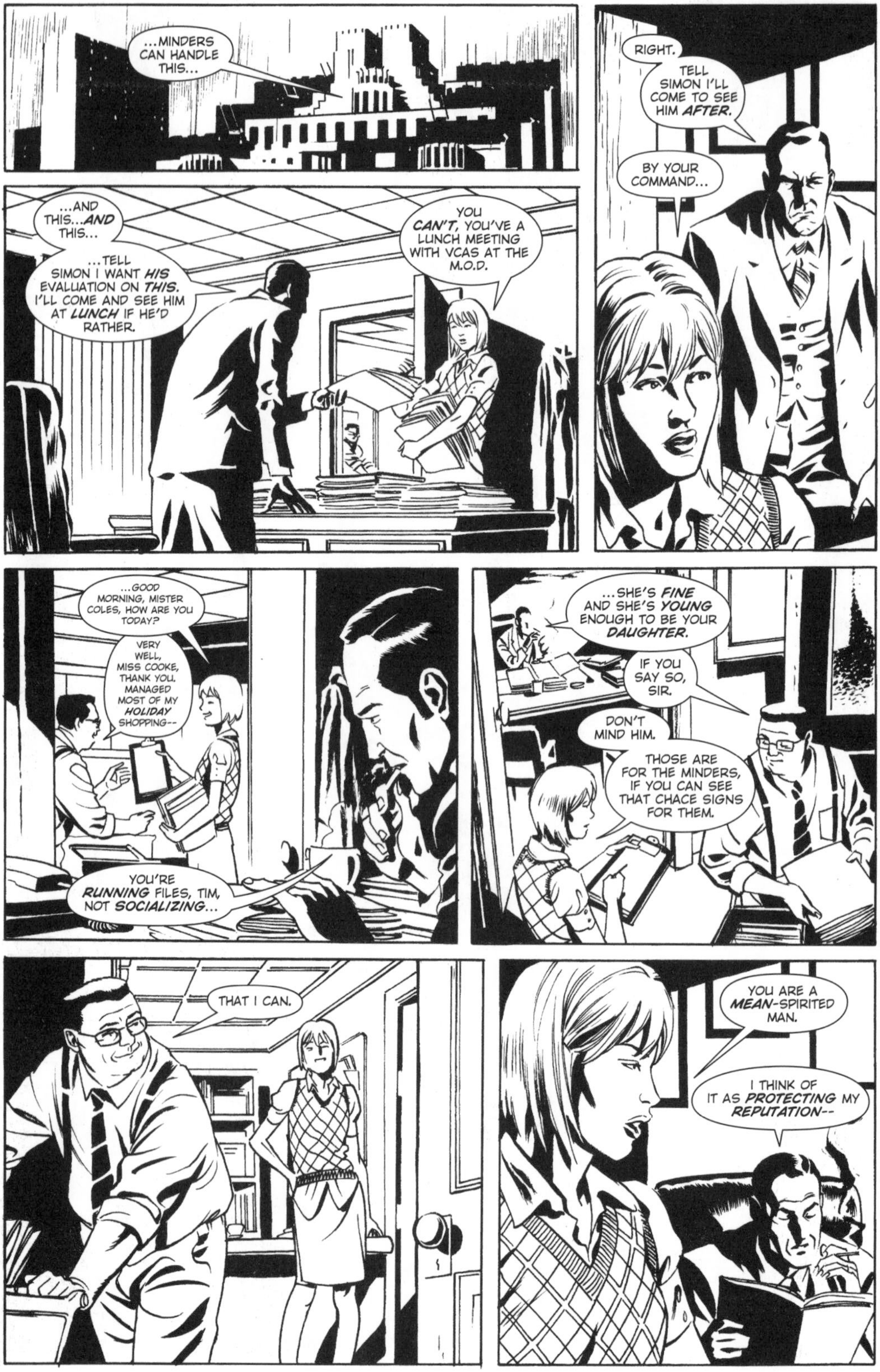
...MINDERS CAN HANDLE THIS...
RIGHT.
TELL SIMON I'LL COME TO SEE HIM *AFTER.*
BY YOUR COMMAND...
...AND THIS...*AND* THIS...
...TELL SIMON I WANT *HIS* EVALUATION ON *THIS.* I'LL COME AND SEE HIM AT *LUNCH* IF HE'D RATHER.
YOU *CAN'T,* YOU'VE A LUNCH MEETING WITH VCAS AT THE M.O.D.
...GOOD MORNING, MISTER COLES, HOW ARE YOU TODAY?
VERY WELL, MISS COOKE, THANK YOU. MANAGED MOST OF MY *HOLIDAY* SHOPPING--
YOU'RE *RUNNING* FILES, TIM, NOT *SOCIALIZING*...
...SHE'S *FINE* AND SHE'S *YOUNG* ENOUGH TO BE YOUR *DAUGHTER.*
IF YOU SAY SO, SIR.
DON'T MIND HIM.
THOSE ARE FOR THE MINDERS, IF YOU CAN SEE THAT CHACE SIGNS FOR THEM.
THAT I CAN.
YOU ARE A *MEAN*-SPIRITED MAN.
I THINK OF IT AS *PROTECTING* MY *REPUTATION*--

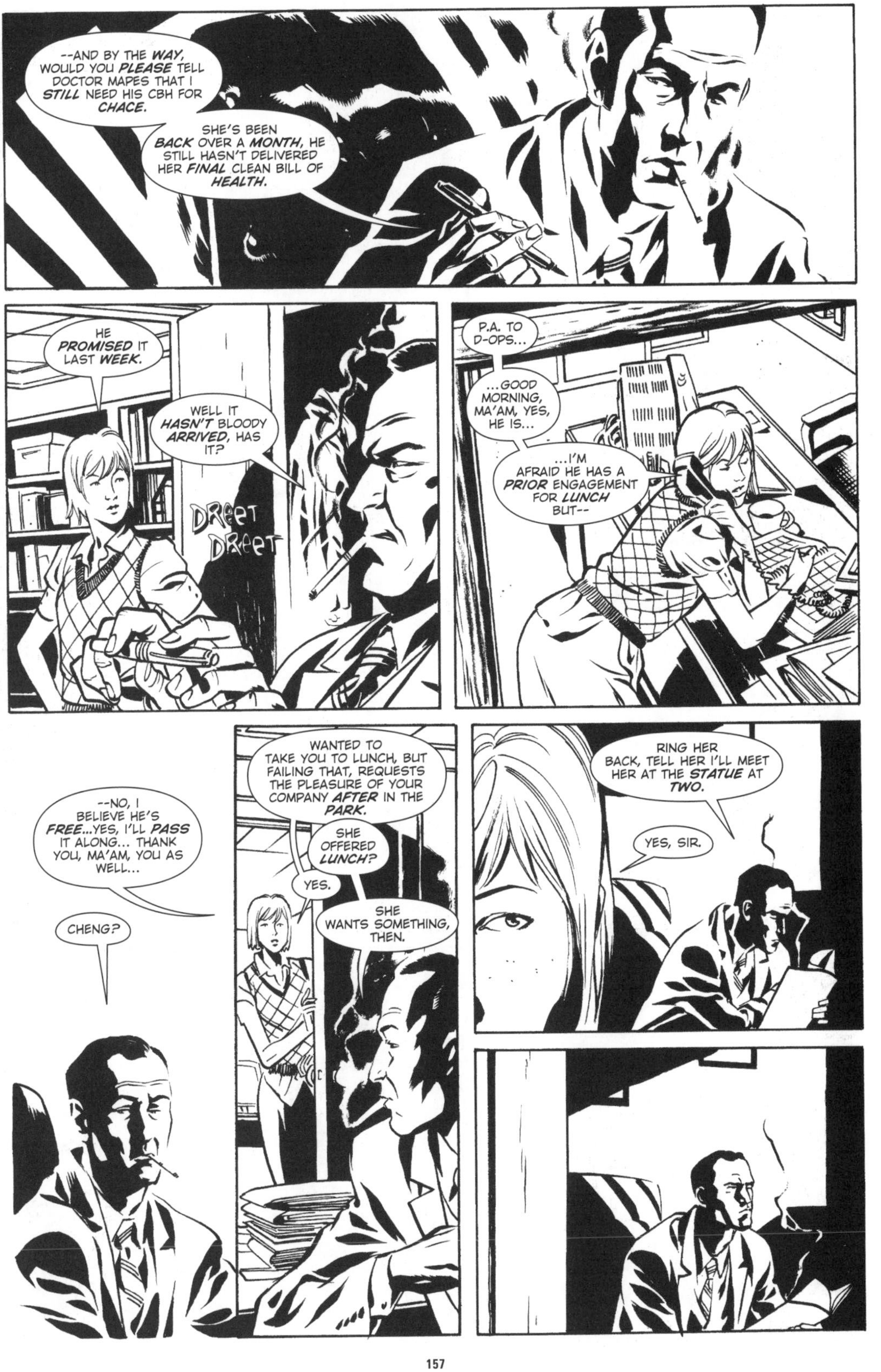
--AND BY THE WAY, WOULD YOU PLEASE TELL DOCTOR MAPES THAT I STILL NEED HIS CBH FOR CHACE.
SHE'S BEEN BACK OVER A MONTH, HE STILL HASN'T DELIVERED HER FINAL CLEAN BILL OF HEALTH.
HE PROMISED IT LAST WEEK.
WELL IT HASN'T BLOODY ARRIVED, HAS IT?
DREET DREET
P.A. TO D-OPS...
...GOOD MORNING, MA'AM, YES, HE IS...
...I'M AFRAID HE HAS A PRIOR ENGAGEMENT FOR LUNCH BUT--
--NO, I BELIEVE HE'S FREE...YES, I'LL PASS IT ALONG... THANK YOU, MA'AM, YOU AS WELL...
CHENG?
WANTED TO TAKE YOU TO LUNCH, BUT FAILING THAT, REQUESTS THE PLEASURE OF YOUR COMPANY AFTER IN THE PARK.
SHE OFFERED LUNCH?
YES.
SHE WANTS SOMETHING, THEN.
RING HER BACK, TELL HER I'LL MEET HER AT THE STATUE AT TWO.
YES, SIR.

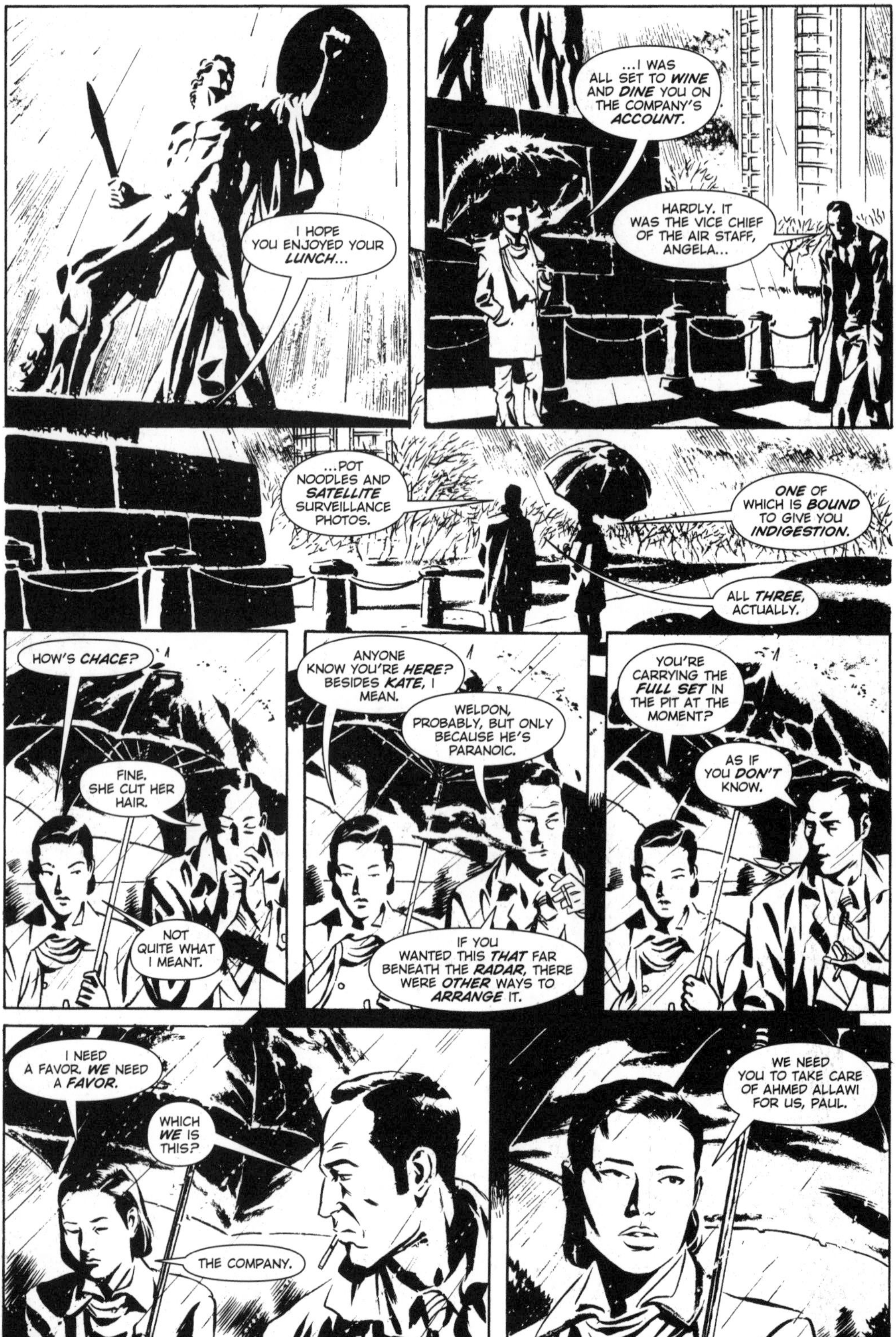
I HOPE YOU ENJOYED YOUR *LUNCH*...
...I WAS ALL SET TO *WINE* AND *DINE* YOU ON THE COMPANY'S *ACCOUNT*.
HARDLY. IT WAS THE VICE CHIEF OF THE AIR STAFF, ANGELA...
...POT NOODLES AND *SATELLITE* SURVEILLANCE PHOTOS.
ONE OF WHICH IS *BOUND* TO GIVE YOU *INDIGESTION*.
ALL *THREE*, ACTUALLY.
HOW'S *CHACE*?
FINE. SHE CUT HER HAIR.
NOT QUITE WHAT I MEANT.
ANYONE KNOW YOU'RE *HERE*? BESIDES *KATE*, I MEAN.
WELDON, PROBABLY, BUT ONLY BECAUSE HE'S PARANOIC.
IF YOU WANTED THIS *THAT* FAR BENEATH THE *RADAR*, THERE WERE *OTHER* WAYS TO *ARRANGE* IT.
YOU'RE CARRYING THE *FULL SET* IN THE PIT AT THE MOMENT?
AS IF YOU *DON'T* KNOW.
I NEED A FAVOR. *WE* NEED A *FAVOR*.
WHICH *WE* IS THIS?
THE COMPANY.
WE NEED YOU TO TAKE CARE OF AHMED ALLAWI FOR US, PAUL.

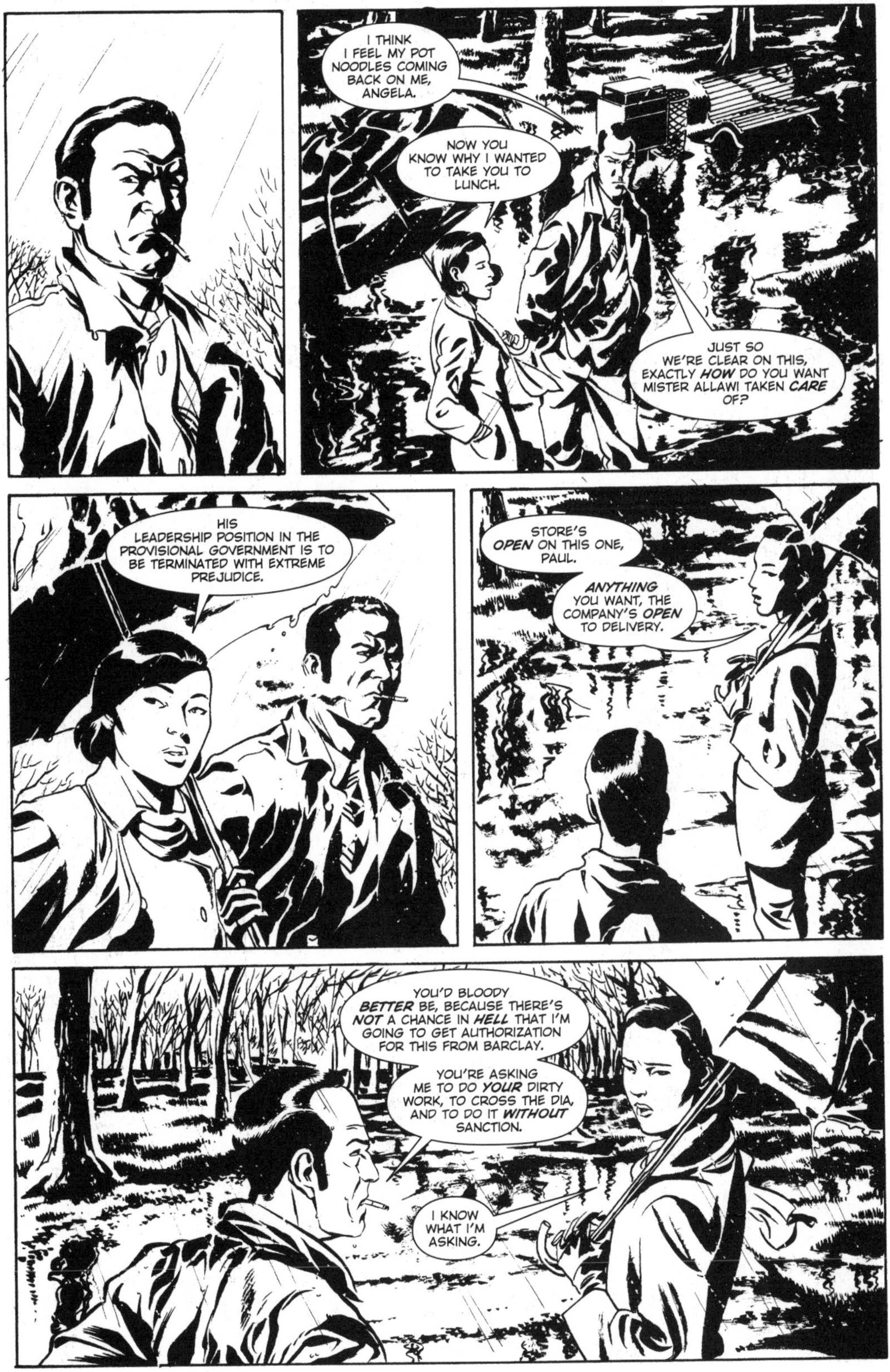
I THINK I FEEL MY POT NOODLES COMING BACK ON ME, ANGELA.
NOW YOU KNOW WHY I WANTED TO TAKE YOU TO LUNCH.
JUST SO WE'RE CLEAR ON THIS, EXACTLY HOW DO YOU WANT MISTER ALLAWI TAKEN CARE OF?
HIS LEADERSHIP POSITION IN THE PROVISIONAL GOVERNMENT IS TO BE TERMINATED WITH EXTREME PREJUDICE.
STORE'S OPEN ON THIS ONE, PAUL.
ANYTHING YOU WANT, THE COMPANY'S OPEN TO DELIVERY.
YOU'D BLOODY BETTER BE, BECAUSE THERE'S NOT A CHANCE IN HELL THAT I'M GOING TO GET AUTHORIZATION FOR THIS FROM BARCLAY.
YOU'RE ASKING ME TO DO YOUR DIRTY WORK, TO CROSS THE DIA, AND TO DO IT WITHOUT SANCTION.
I KNOW WHAT I'M ASKING.

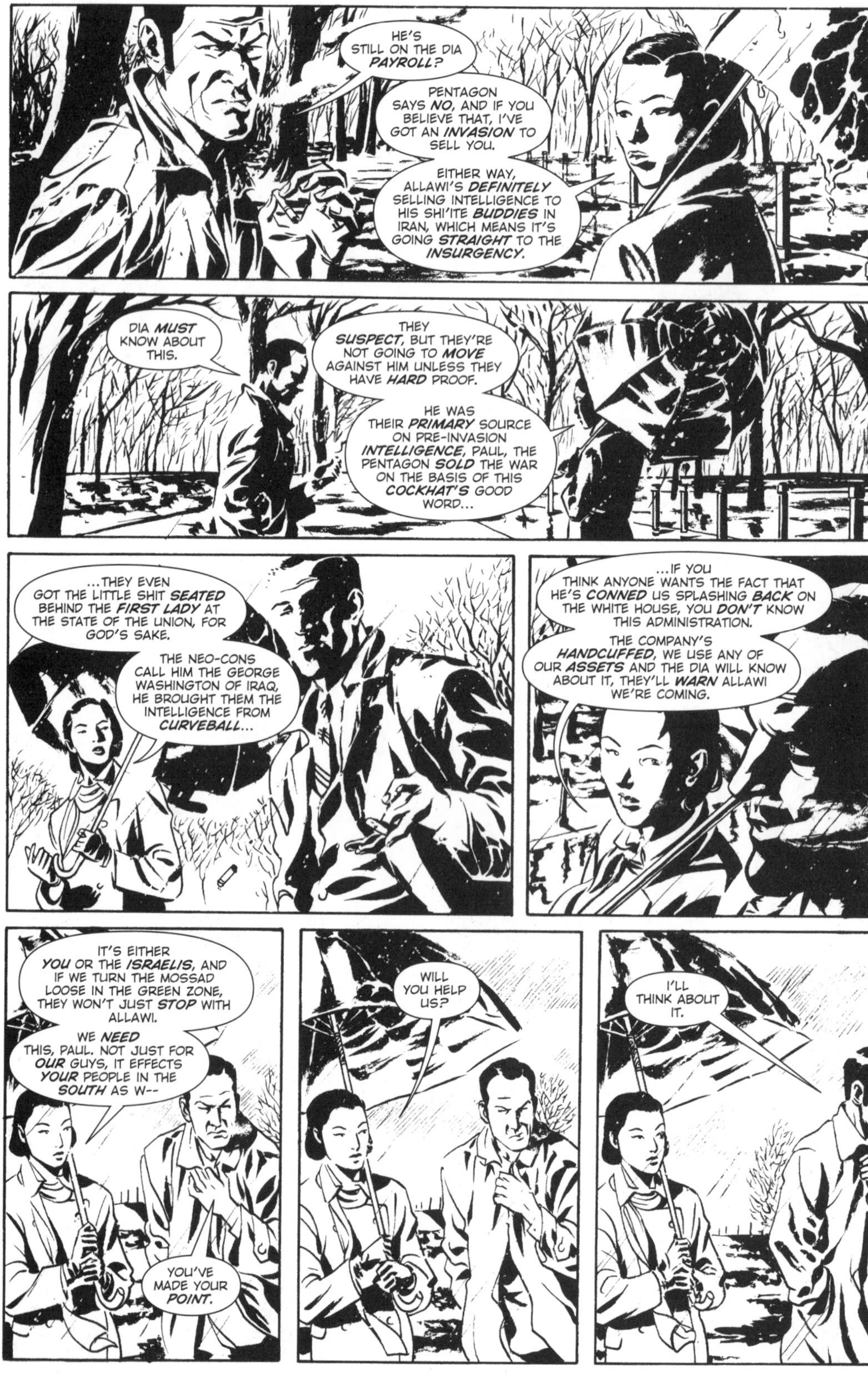
HE'S STILL ON THE DIA PAYROLL?
PENTAGON SAYS NO, AND IF YOU BELIEVE THAT, I'VE GOT AN INVASION TO SELL YOU.
EITHER WAY, ALLAWI'S DEFINITELY SELLING INTELLIGENCE TO HIS SHI'ITE BUDDIES IN IRAN, WHICH MEANS IT'S GOING STRAIGHT TO THE INSURGENCY.
DIA MUST KNOW ABOUT THIS.
THEY SUSPECT, BUT THEY'RE NOT GOING TO MOVE AGAINST HIM UNLESS THEY HAVE HARD PROOF.
HE WAS THEIR PRIMARY SOURCE ON PRE-INVASION INTELLIGENCE, PAUL, THE PENTAGON SOLD THE WAR ON THE BASIS OF THIS COCKHAT'S GOOD WORD...
...THEY EVEN GOT THE LITTLE SHIT SEATED BEHIND THE FIRST LADY AT THE STATE OF THE UNION, FOR GOD'S SAKE.
THE NEO-CONS CALL HIM THE GEORGE WASHINGTON OF IRAQ, HE BROUGHT THEM THE INTELLIGENCE FROM CURVEBALL...
...IF YOU THINK ANYONE WANTS THE FACT THAT HE'S CONNED US SPLASHING BACK ON THE WHITE HOUSE, YOU DON'T KNOW THIS ADMINISTRATION.
THE COMPANY'S HANDCUFFED, WE USE ANY OF OUR ASSETS AND THE DIA WILL KNOW ABOUT IT, THEY'LL WARN ALLAWI WE'RE COMING.
IT'S EITHER YOU OR THE ISRAELIS, AND IF WE TURN THE MOSSAD LOOSE IN THE GREEN ZONE, THEY WON'T JUST STOP WITH ALLAWI.
WE NEED THIS, PAUL. NOT JUST FOR OUR GUYS, IT EFFECTS YOUR PEOPLE IN THE SOUTH AS W--
YOU'VE MADE YOUR POINT.
WILL YOU HELP US?
I'LL THINK ABOUT IT.

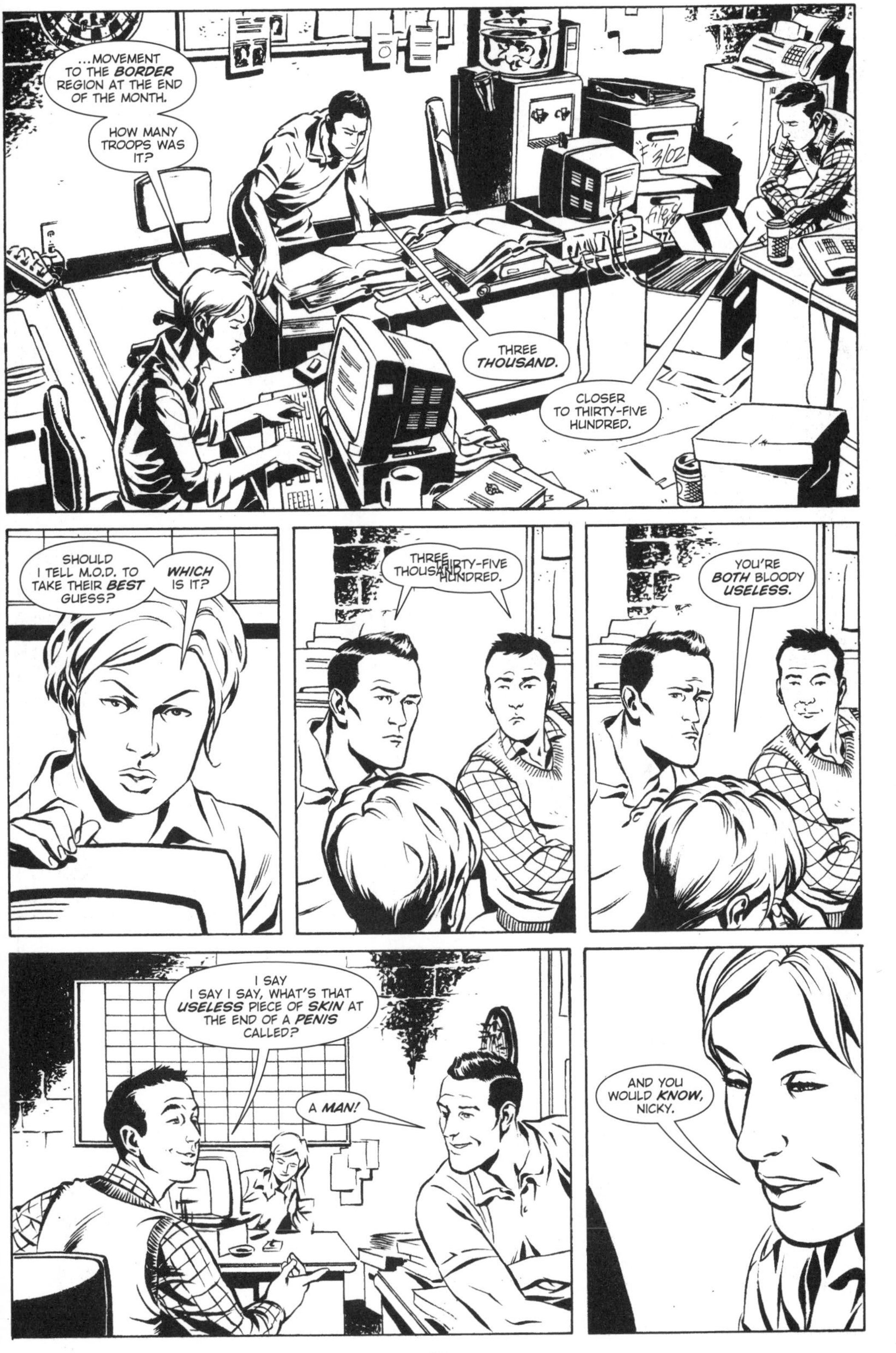
...MOVEMENT TO THE BORDER REGION AT THE END OF THE MONTH.
HOW MANY TROOPS WAS IT?
THREE THOUSAND.
CLOSER TO THIRTY-FIVE HUNDRED.
SHOULD I TELL M.O.D. TO TAKE THEIR BEST GUESS?
WHICH IS IT?
THREE THOUSAND.
THIRTY-FIVE HUNDRED.
YOU'RE BOTH BLOODY USELESS.
I SAY I SAY I SAY, WHAT'S THAT USELESS PIECE OF SKIN AT THE END OF A PENIS CALLED?
A MAN!
AND YOU WOULD KNOW, NICKY.

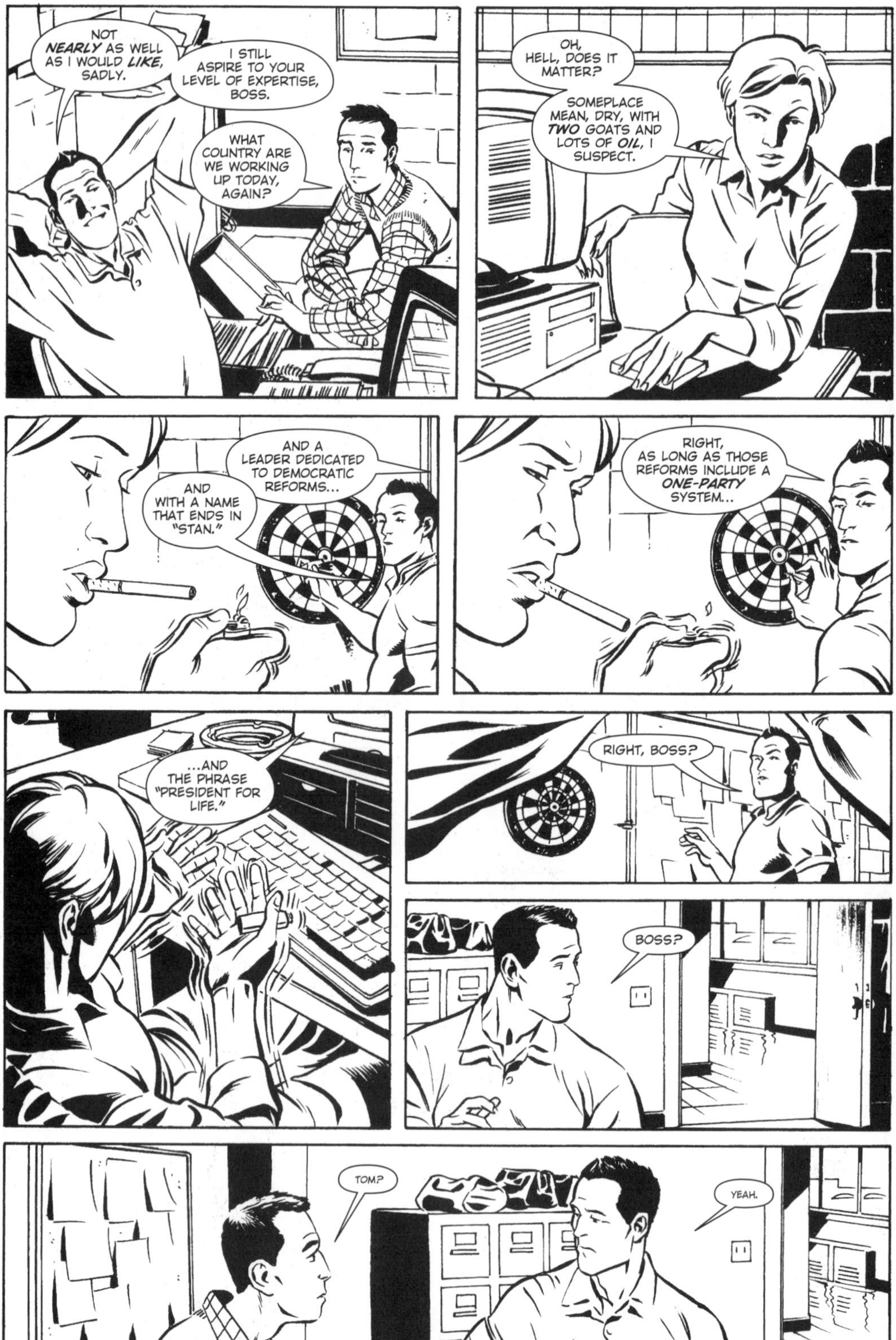
NOT NEARLY AS WELL AS I WOULD LIKE, SADLY.
I STILL ASPIRE TO YOUR LEVEL OF EXPERTISE, BOSS.
WHAT COUNTRY ARE WE WORKING UP TODAY, AGAIN?
OH, HELL, DOES IT MATTER?
SOMEPLACE MEAN, DRY, WITH TWO GOATS AND LOTS OF OIL, I SUSPECT.
AND A LEADER DEDICATED TO DEMOCRATIC REFORMS...
AND WITH A NAME THAT ENDS IN "STAN."
RIGHT, AS LONG AS THOSE REFORMS INCLUDE A ONE-PARTY SYSTEM...
...AND THE PHRASE "PRESIDENT FOR LIFE."
RIGHT, BOSS?
BOSS?
TOM?
YEAH.

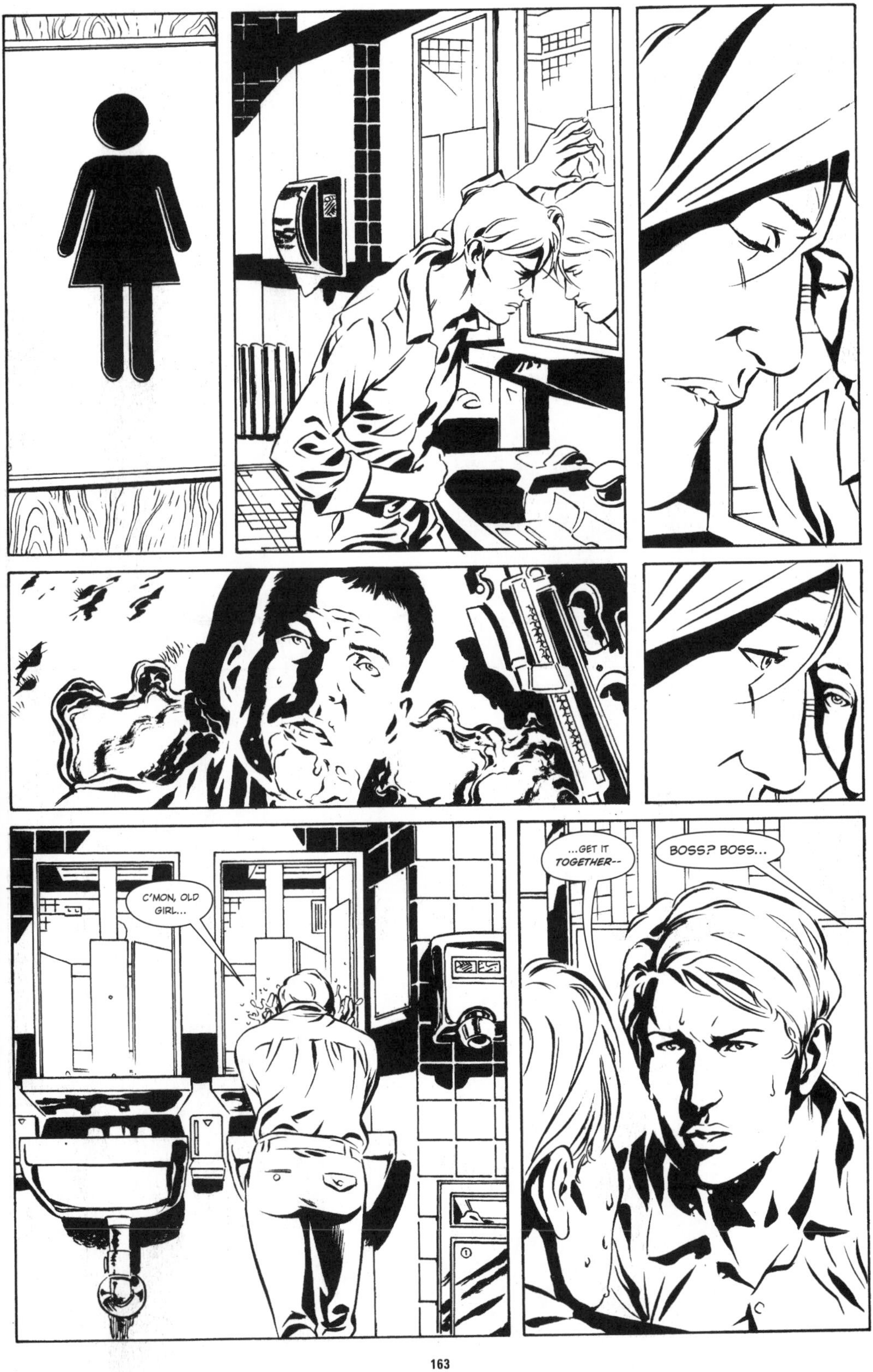
C'MON, OLD GIRL...
...GET IT TOGETHER--
BOSS? BOSS...

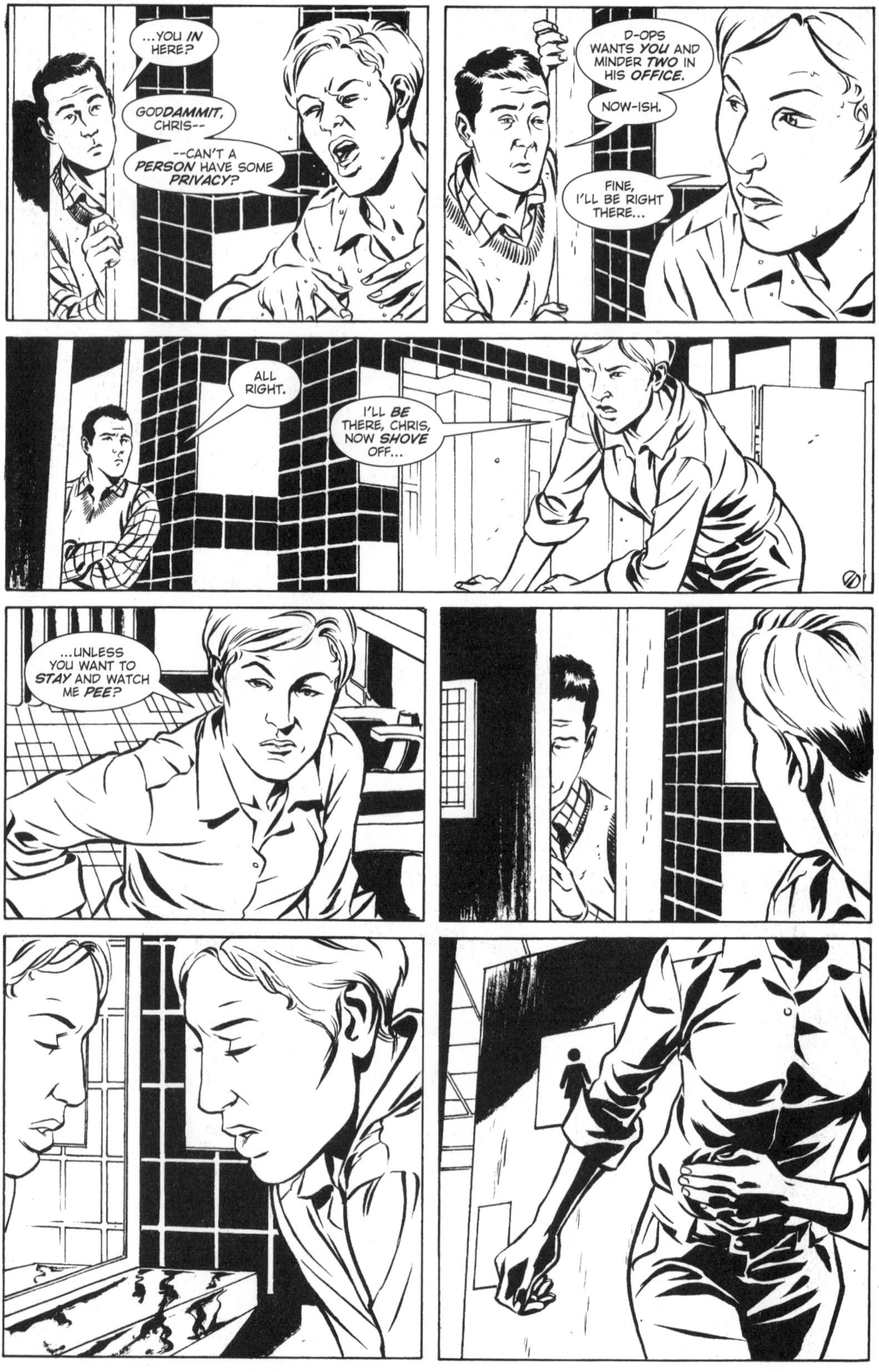
...YOU IN HERE?
GODDAMMIT, CHRIS--
--CAN'T A PERSON HAVE SOME PRIVACY?
D-OPS WANTS YOU AND MINDER TWO IN HIS OFFICE.
NOW-ISH.
FINE, I'LL BE RIGHT THERE...
ALL RIGHT.
I'LL BE THERE, CHRIS, NOW SHOVE OFF...
...UNLESS YOU WANT TO STAY AND WATCH ME PEE?

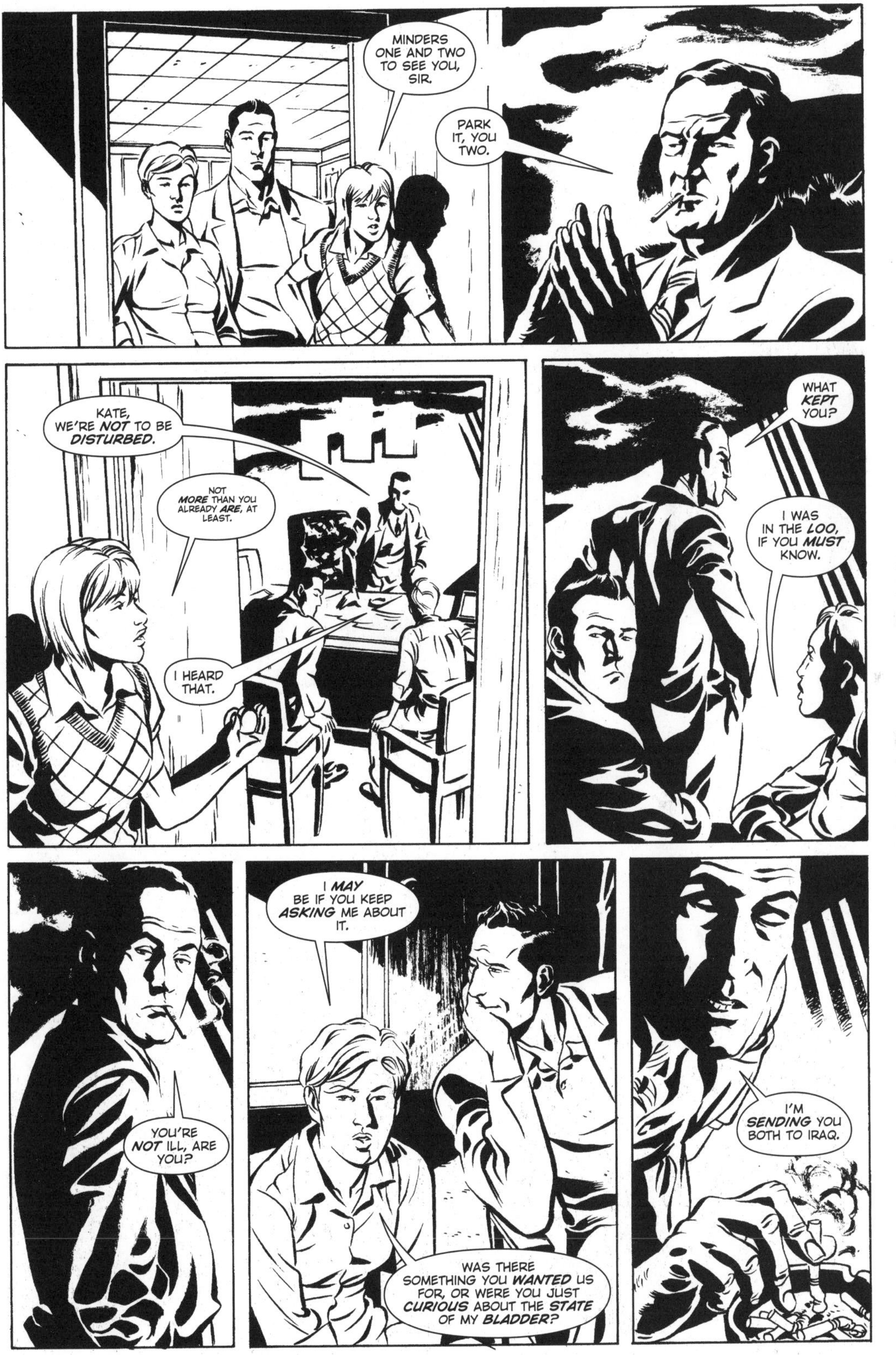
MINDERS ONE AND TWO TO SEE YOU, SIR.
PARK IT, YOU TWO.
KATE, WE'RE NOT TO BE DISTURBED.
NOT MORE THAN YOU ALREADY ARE, AT LEAST.
I HEARD THAT.
WHAT KEPT YOU?
I WAS IN THE LOO, IF YOU MUST KNOW.
YOU'RE NOT ILL, ARE YOU?
I MAY BE IF YOU KEEP ASKING ME ABOUT IT.
WAS THERE SOMETHING YOU WANTED US FOR, OR WERE YOU JUST CURIOUS ABOUT THE STATE OF MY BLADDER?
I'M SENDING YOU BOTH TO IRAQ.

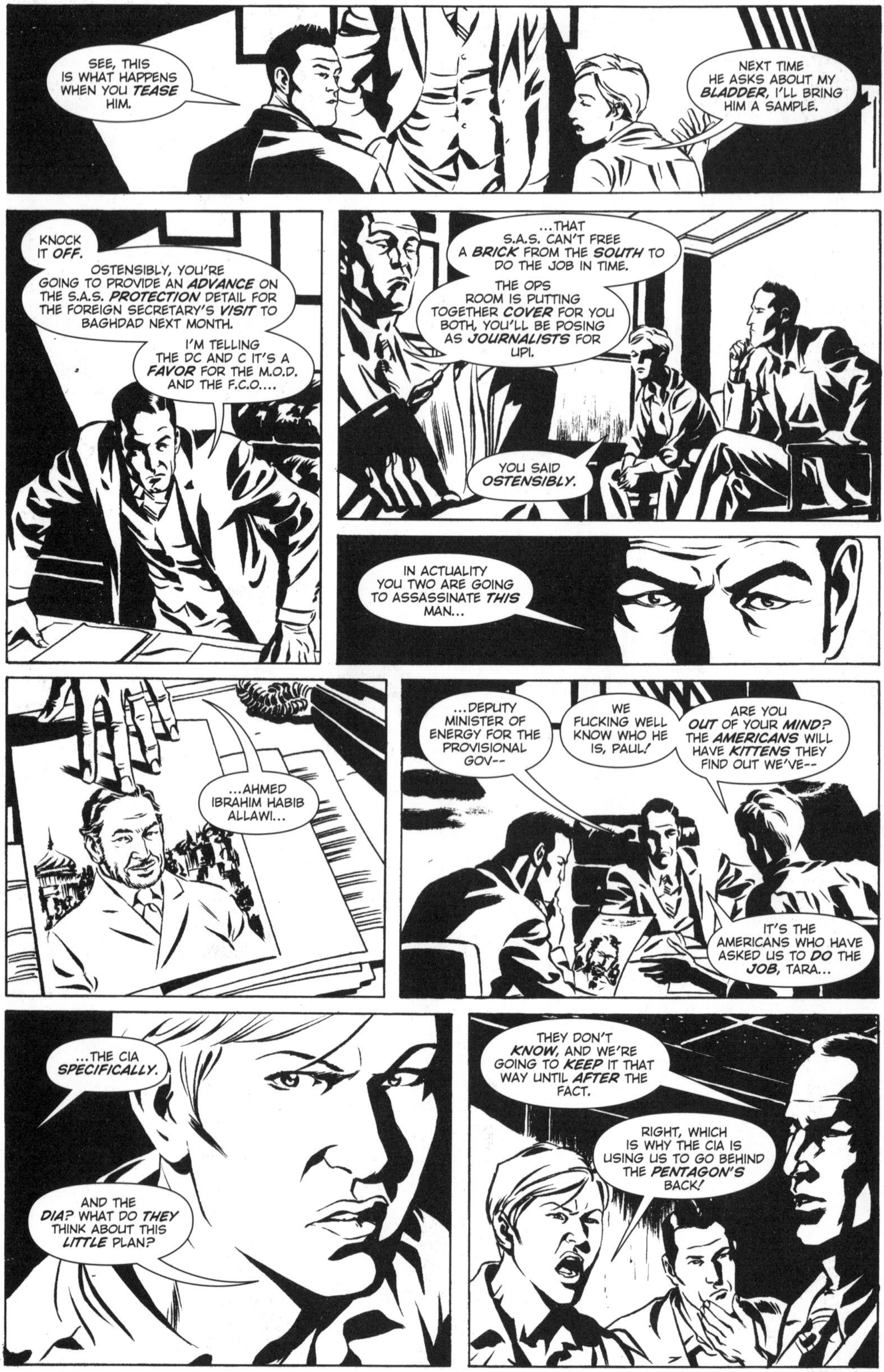
SEE, THIS IS WHAT HAPPENS WHEN YOU TEASE HIM.
NEXT TIME HE ASKS ABOUT MY BLADDER, I'LL BRING HIM A SAMPLE.
KNOCK IT OFF.
OSTENSIBLY, YOU'RE GOING TO PROVIDE AN ADVANCE ON THE S.A.S. PROTECTION DETAIL FOR THE FOREIGN SECRETARY'S VISIT TO BAGHDAD NEXT MONTH.
I'M TELLING THE DC AND C IT'S A FAVOR FOR THE M.O.D. AND THE F.C.O....
...THAT S.A.S. CAN'T FREE A BRICK FROM THE SOUTH TO DO THE JOB IN TIME.
THE OPS ROOM IS PUTTING TOGETHER COVER FOR YOU BOTH, YOU'LL BE POSING AS JOURNALISTS FOR UPI.
YOU SAID OSTENSIBLY.
IN ACTUALITY YOU TWO ARE GOING TO ASSASSINATE THIS MAN...
...AHMED IBRAHIM HABIB ALLAWI...
...DEPUTY MINISTER OF ENERGY FOR THE PROVISIONAL GOV--
WE FUCKING WELL KNOW WHO HE IS, PAUL!
ARE YOU OUT OF YOUR MIND? THE AMERICANS WILL HAVE KITTENS THEY FIND OUT WE'VE--
IT'S THE AMERICANS WHO HAVE ASKED US TO DO THE JOB, TARA...
...THE CIA SPECIFICALLY.
AND THE DIA? WHAT DO THEY THINK ABOUT THIS LITTLE PLAN?
THEY DON'T KNOW, AND WE'RE GOING TO KEEP IT THAT WAY UNTIL AFTER THE FACT.
RIGHT, WHICH IS WHY THE CIA IS USING US TO GO BEHIND THE PENTAGON'S BACK!

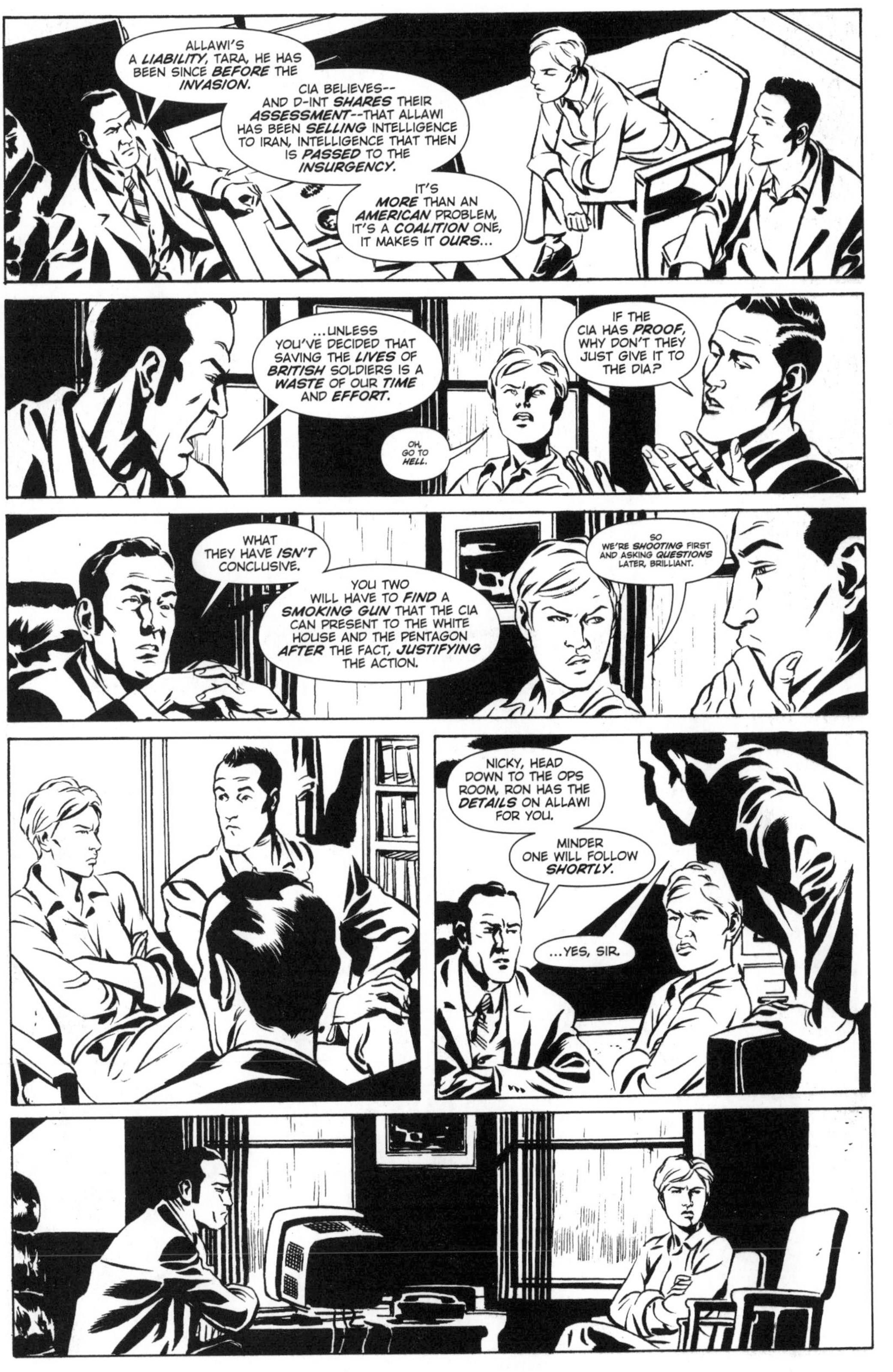
ALLAWI'S A LIABILITY, TARA, HE HAS BEEN SINCE BEFORE THE INVASION.
CIA BELIEVES-- AND D-INT SHARES THEIR ASSESSMENT--THAT ALLAWI HAS BEEN SELLING INTELLIGENCE TO IRAN, INTELLIGENCE THAT THEN IS PASSED TO THE INSURGENCY.
IT'S MORE THAN AN AMERICAN PROBLEM, IT'S A COALITION ONE, IT MAKES IT OURS...
...UNLESS YOU'VE DECIDED THAT SAVING THE LIVES OF BRITISH SOLDIERS IS A WASTE OF OUR TIME AND EFFORT.
OH, GO TO HELL.
IF THE CIA HAS PROOF, WHY DON'T THEY JUST GIVE IT TO THE DIA?
WHAT THEY HAVE ISN'T CONCLUSIVE.
YOU TWO WILL HAVE TO FIND A SMOKING GUN THAT THE CIA CAN PRESENT TO THE WHITE HOUSE AND THE PENTAGON AFTER THE FACT, JUSTIFYING THE ACTION.
SO WE'RE SHOOTING FIRST AND ASKING QUESTIONS LATER. BRILLIANT.
NICKY, HEAD DOWN TO THE OPS ROOM, RON HAS THE DETAILS ON ALLAWI FOR YOU.
MINDER ONE WILL FOLLOW SHORTLY.
...YES, SIR.

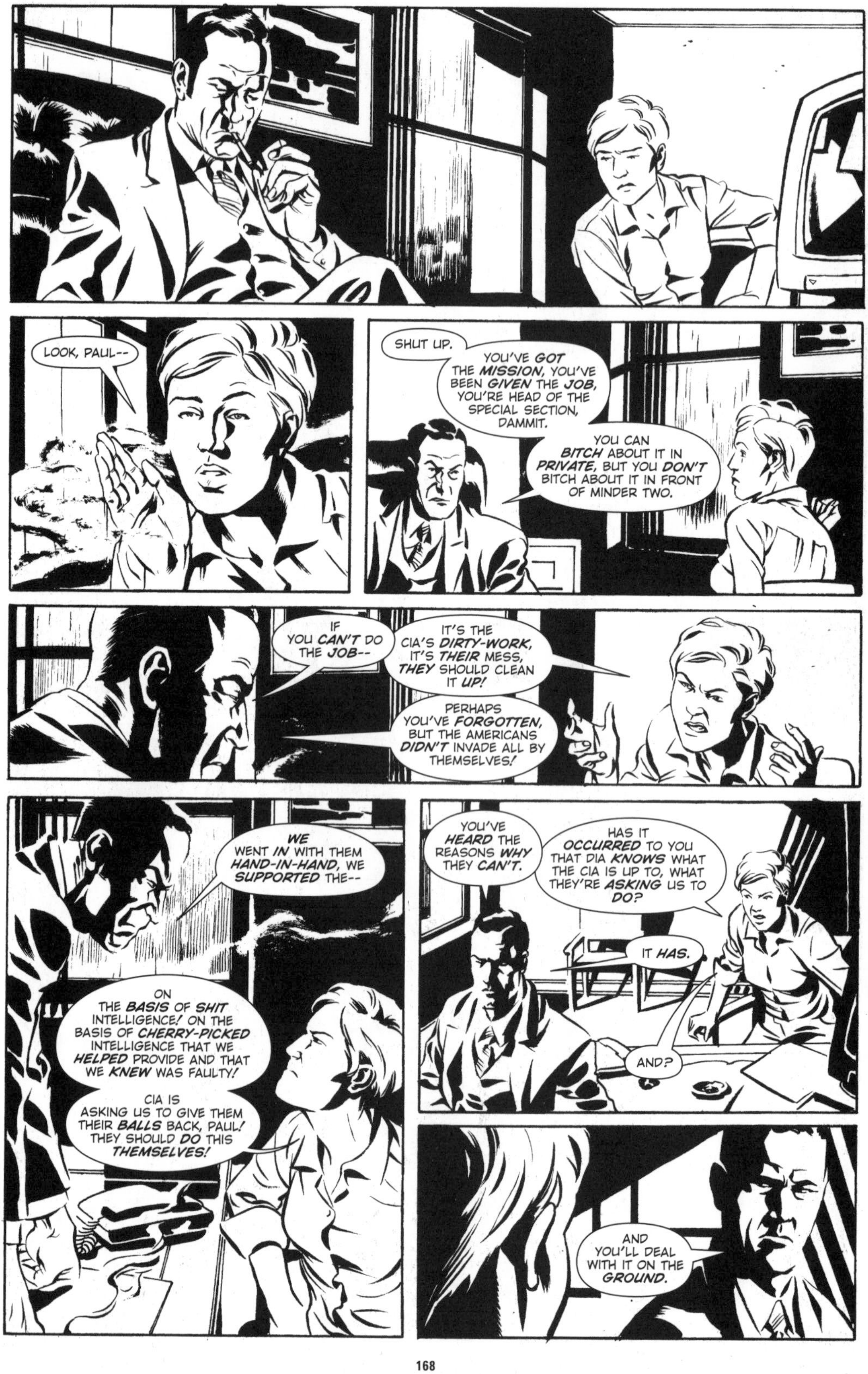
LOOK, PAUL--
SHUT UP.
YOU'VE GOT THE MISSION, YOU'VE BEEN GIVEN THE JOB, YOU'RE HEAD OF THE SPECIAL SECTION, DAMMIT.
YOU CAN BITCH ABOUT IT IN PRIVATE, BUT YOU DON'T BITCH ABOUT IT IN FRONT OF MINDER TWO.
IF YOU CAN'T DO THE JOB--
IT'S THE CIA'S DIRTY-WORK, IT'S THEIR MESS, THEY SHOULD CLEAN IT UP!
PERHAPS YOU'VE FORGOTTEN, BUT THE AMERICANS DIDN'T INVADE ALL BY THEMSELVES!
WE WENT IN WITH THEM HAND-IN-HAND, WE SUPPORTED THE--
ON THE BASIS OF SHIT INTELLIGENCE! ON THE BASIS OF CHERRY-PICKED INTELLIGENCE THAT WE HELPED PROVIDE AND THAT WE KNEW WAS FAULTY!
CIA IS ASKING US TO GIVE THEM THEIR BALLS BACK, PAUL! THEY SHOULD DO THIS THEMSELVES!
YOU'VE HEARD THE REASONS WHY THEY CAN'T.
HAS IT OCCURRED TO YOU THAT DIA KNOWS WHAT THE CIA IS UP TO, WHAT THEY'RE ASKING US TO DO?
IT HAS.
AND?
AND YOU'LL DEAL WITH IT ON THE GROUND.

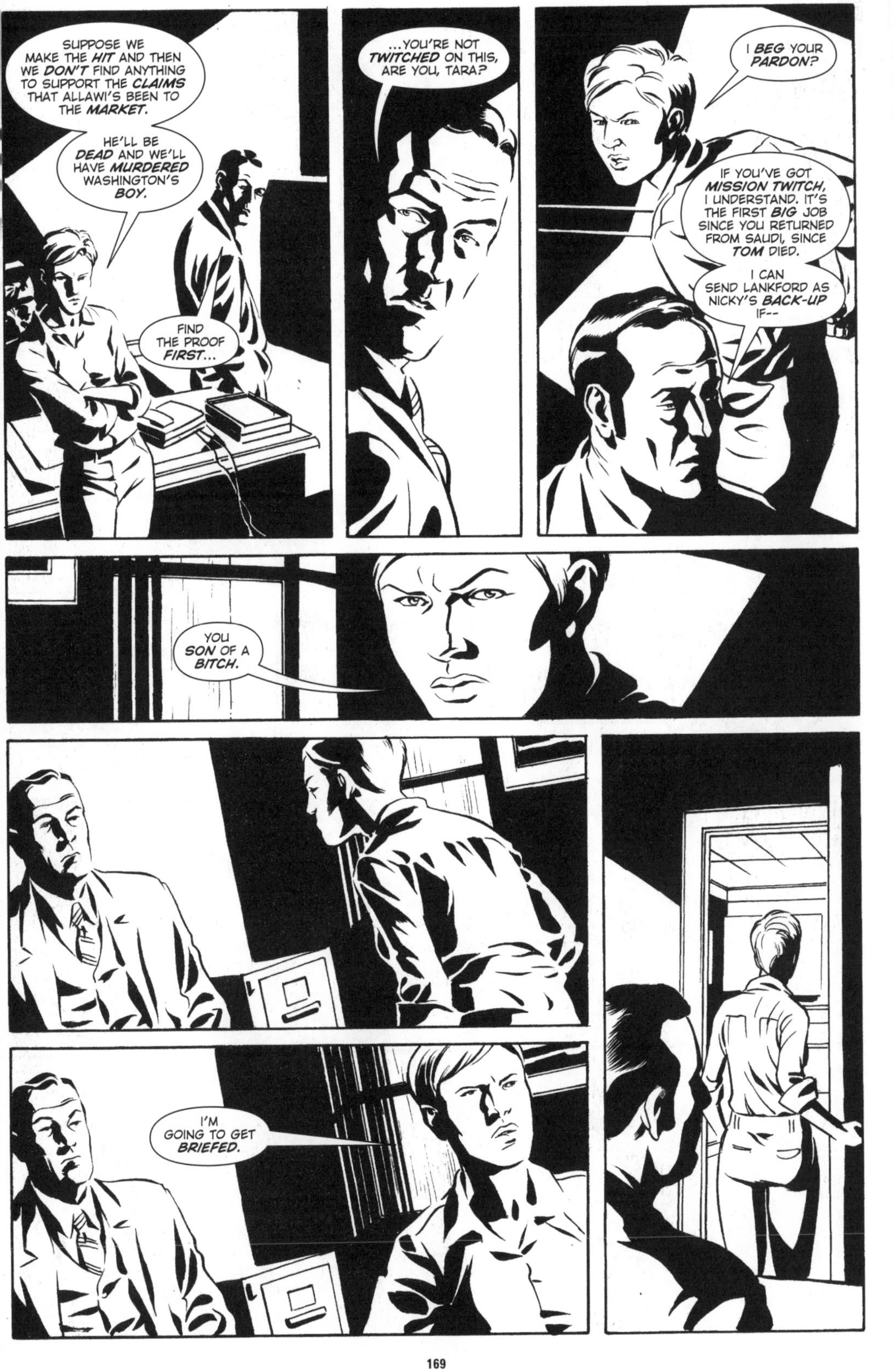
SUPPOSE WE MAKE THE HIT AND THEN WE DON'T FIND ANYTHING TO SUPPORT THE CLAIMS THAT ALLAWI'S BEEN TO THE MARKET.
HE'LL BE DEAD AND WE'LL HAVE MURDERED WASHINGTON'S BOY.
FIND THE PROOF FIRST...
...YOU'RE NOT TWITCHED ON THIS, ARE YOU, TARA?
I BEG YOUR PARDON?
IF YOU'VE GOT MISSION TWITCH, I UNDERSTAND. IT'S THE FIRST BIG JOB SINCE YOU RETURNED FROM SAUDI, SINCE TOM DIED.
I CAN SEND LANKFORD AS NICKY'S BACK-UP IF--
YOU SON OF A BITCH.
I'M GOING TO GET BRIEFED.

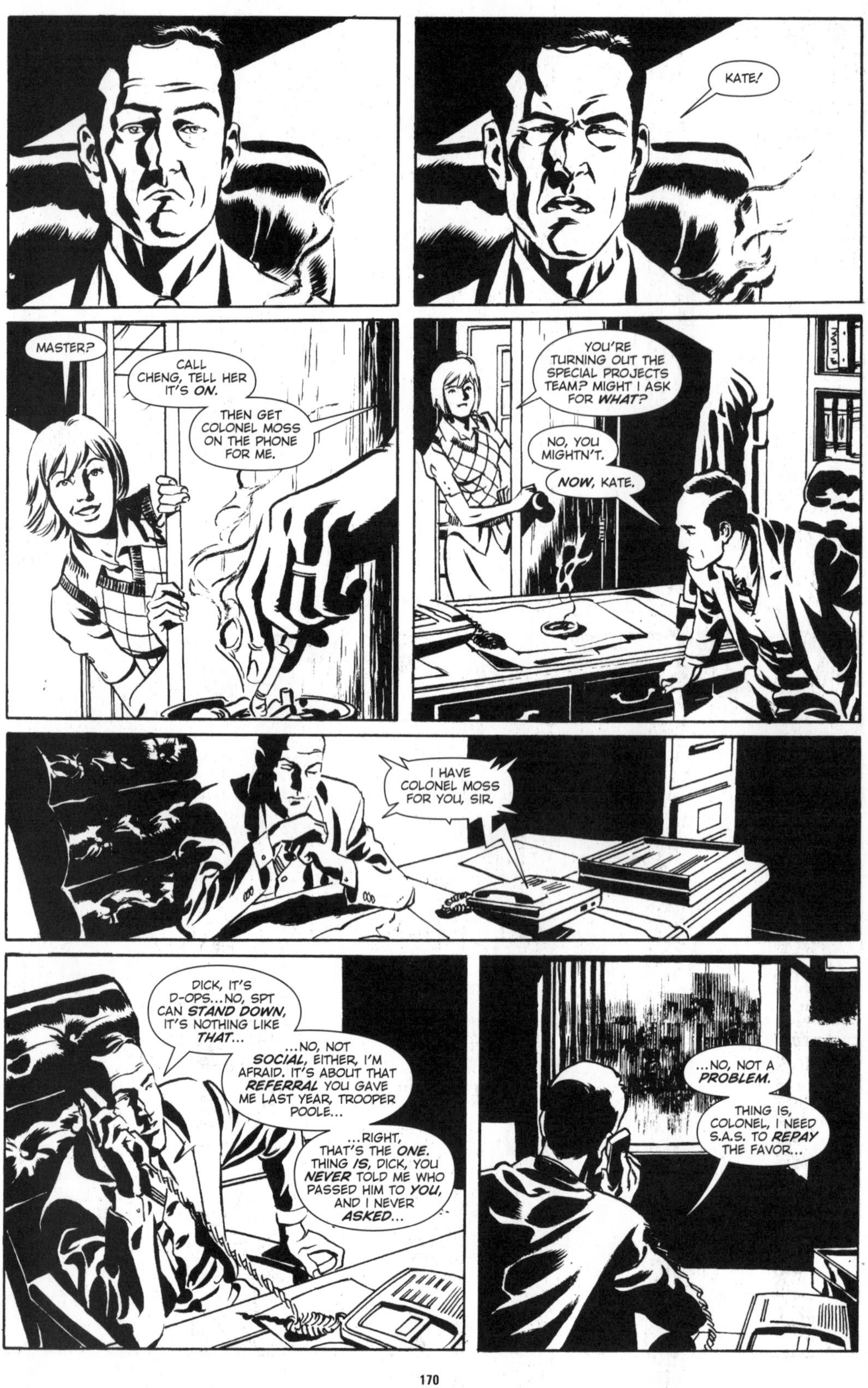
KATE!
MASTER?
CALL CHENG, TELL HER IT'S ON.
THEN GET COLONEL MOSS ON THE PHONE FOR ME.
YOU'RE TURNING OUT THE SPECIAL PROJECTS TEAM? MIGHT I ASK FOR WHAT?
NO, YOU MIGHTN'T.
NOW, KATE.
I HAVE COLONEL MOSS FOR YOU, SIR.
DICK, IT'S D-OPS...NO, SPT CAN STAND DOWN, IT'S NOTHING LIKE THAT...
...NO, NOT SOCIAL, EITHER, I'M AFRAID. IT'S ABOUT THAT REFERRAL YOU GAVE ME LAST YEAR, TROOPER POOLE...
...RIGHT, THAT'S THE ONE. THING IS, DICK, YOU NEVER TOLD ME WHO PASSED HIM TO YOU, AND I NEVER ASKED...
...NO, NOT A PROBLEM.
THING IS, COLONEL, I NEED S.A.S. TO REPAY THE FAVOR...

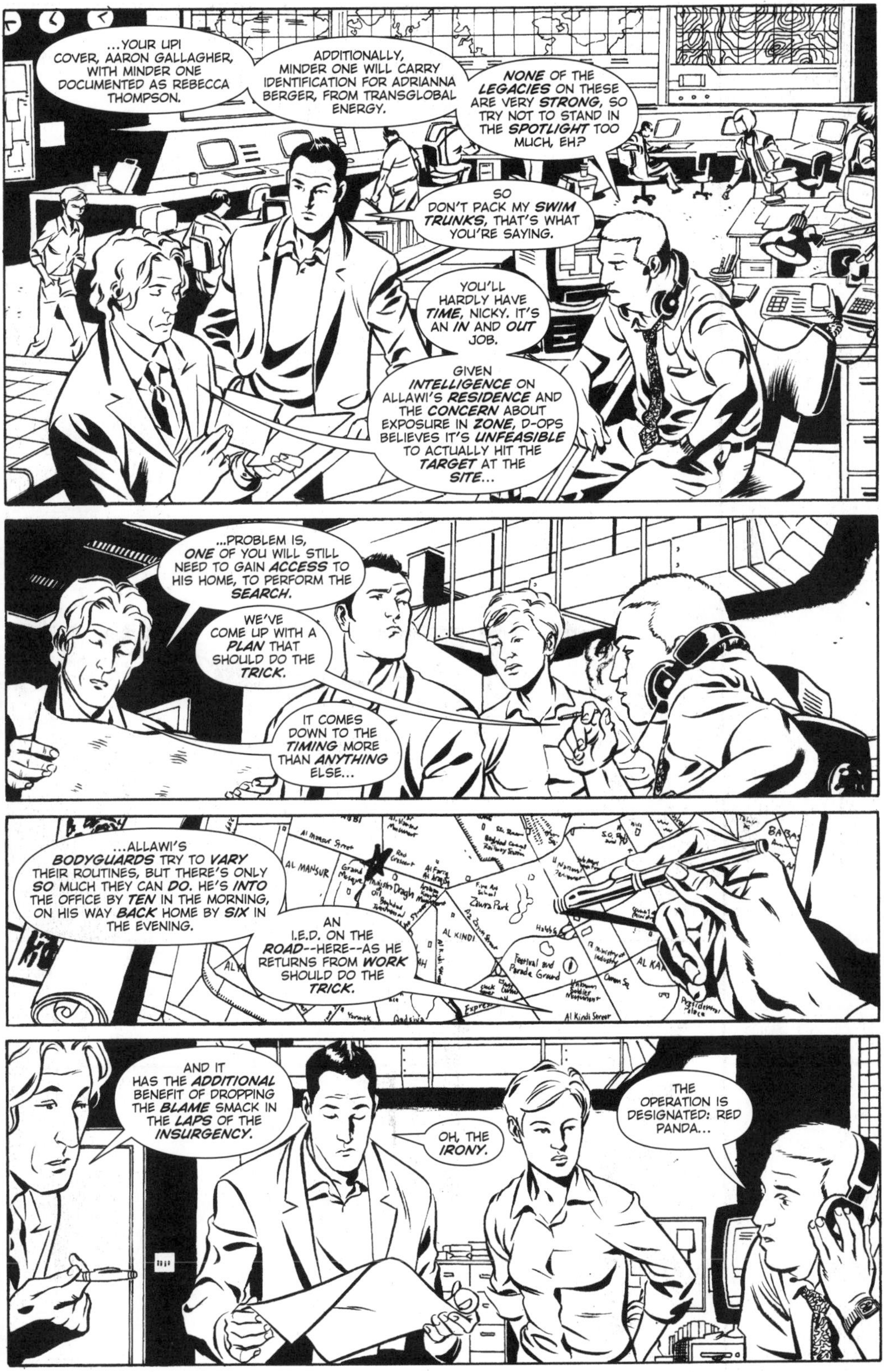
...YOUR UPI COVER, AARON GALLAGHER, WITH MINDER ONE DOCUMENTED AS REBECCA THOMPSON.
ADDITIONALLY, MINDER ONE WILL CARRY IDENTIFICATION FOR ADRIANNA BERGER, FROM TRANSGLOBAL ENERGY.
NONE OF THE LEGACIES ON THESE ARE VERY STRONG, SO TRY NOT TO STAND IN THE SPOTLIGHT TOO MUCH, EH?
SO DON'T PACK MY SWIM TRUNKS, THAT'S WHAT YOU'RE SAYING.
YOU'LL HARDLY HAVE TIME, NICKY. IT'S AN IN AND OUT JOB.
GIVEN INTELLIGENCE ON ALLAWI'S RESIDENCE AND THE CONCERN ABOUT EXPOSURE IN ZONE, D-OPS BELIEVES IT'S UNFEASIBLE TO ACTUALLY HIT THE TARGET AT THE SITE...
...PROBLEM IS, ONE OF YOU WILL STILL NEED TO GAIN ACCESS TO HIS HOME, TO PERFORM THE SEARCH.
WE'VE COME UP WITH A PLAN THAT SHOULD DO THE TRICK.
IT COMES DOWN TO THE TIMING MORE THAN ANYTHING ELSE...
...ALLAWI'S BODYGUARDS TRY TO VARY THEIR ROUTINES, BUT THERE'S ONLY SO MUCH THEY CAN DO. HE'S INTO THE OFFICE BY TEN IN THE MORNING, ON HIS WAY BACK HOME BY SIX IN THE EVENING.
AN I.E.D. ON THE ROAD--HERE--AS HE RETURNS FROM WORK SHOULD DO THE TRICK.
AL MANSUR
Zawra Park
AL KINDI
Al Kindi Street
AND IT HAS THE ADDITIONAL BENEFIT OF DROPPING THE BLAME SMACK IN THE LAPS OF THE INSURGENCY.
OH, THE IRONY.
THE OPERATION IS DESIGNATED: RED PANDA...

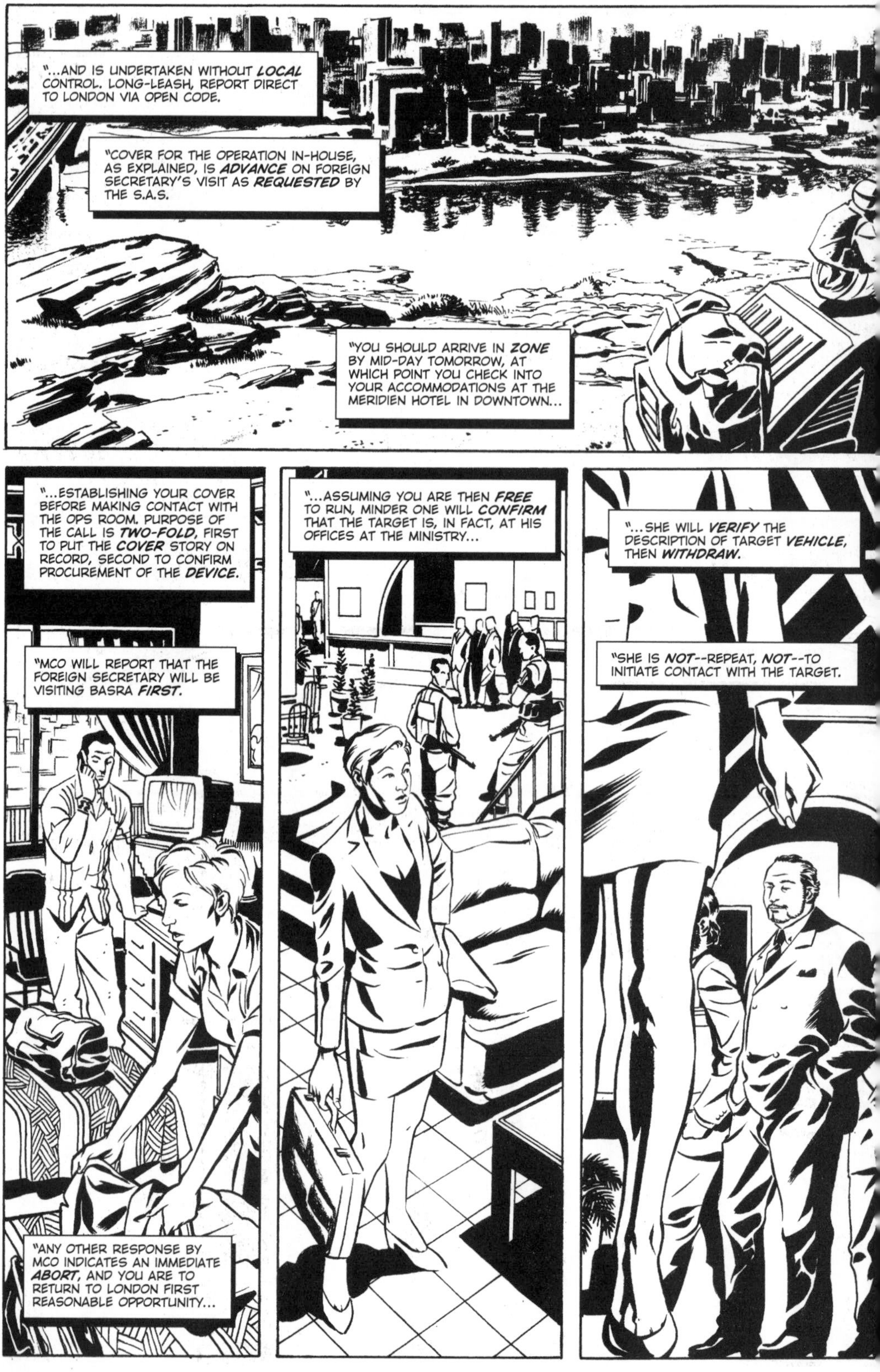
"...AND IS UNDERTAKEN WITHOUT *LOCAL* CONTROL. LONG-LEASH, REPORT DIRECT TO LONDON VIA OPEN CODE.
"COVER FOR THE OPERATION IN-HOUSE, AS EXPLAINED, IS *ADVANCE* ON FOREIGN SECRETARY'S VISIT AS *REQUESTED* BY THE S.A.S.
"YOU SHOULD ARRIVE IN *ZONE* BY MID-DAY TOMORROW, AT WHICH POINT YOU CHECK INTO YOUR ACCOMMODATIONS AT THE MERIDIEN HOTEL IN DOWNTOWN...
"...ESTABLISHING YOUR COVER BEFORE MAKING CONTACT WITH THE OPS ROOM. PURPOSE OF THE CALL IS *TWO-FOLD*, FIRST TO PUT THE *COVER* STORY ON RECORD, SECOND TO CONFIRM PROCUREMENT OF THE *DEVICE*.
"MCO WILL REPORT THAT THE FOREIGN SECRETARY WILL BE VISITING BASRA *FIRST*.
"ANY OTHER RESPONSE BY MCO INDICATES AN IMMEDIATE *ABORT*, AND YOU ARE TO RETURN TO LONDON FIRST REASONABLE OPPORTUNITY...
"...ASSUMING YOU ARE THEN *FREE* TO RUN, MINDER ONE WILL *CONFIRM* THAT THE TARGET IS, IN FACT, AT HIS OFFICES AT THE MINISTRY...
"...SHE WILL *VERIFY* THE DESCRIPTION OF TARGET *VEHICLE*, THEN *WITHDRAW*.
"SHE IS *NOT*--REPEAT, *NOT*--TO INITIATE CONTACT WITH THE TARGET.

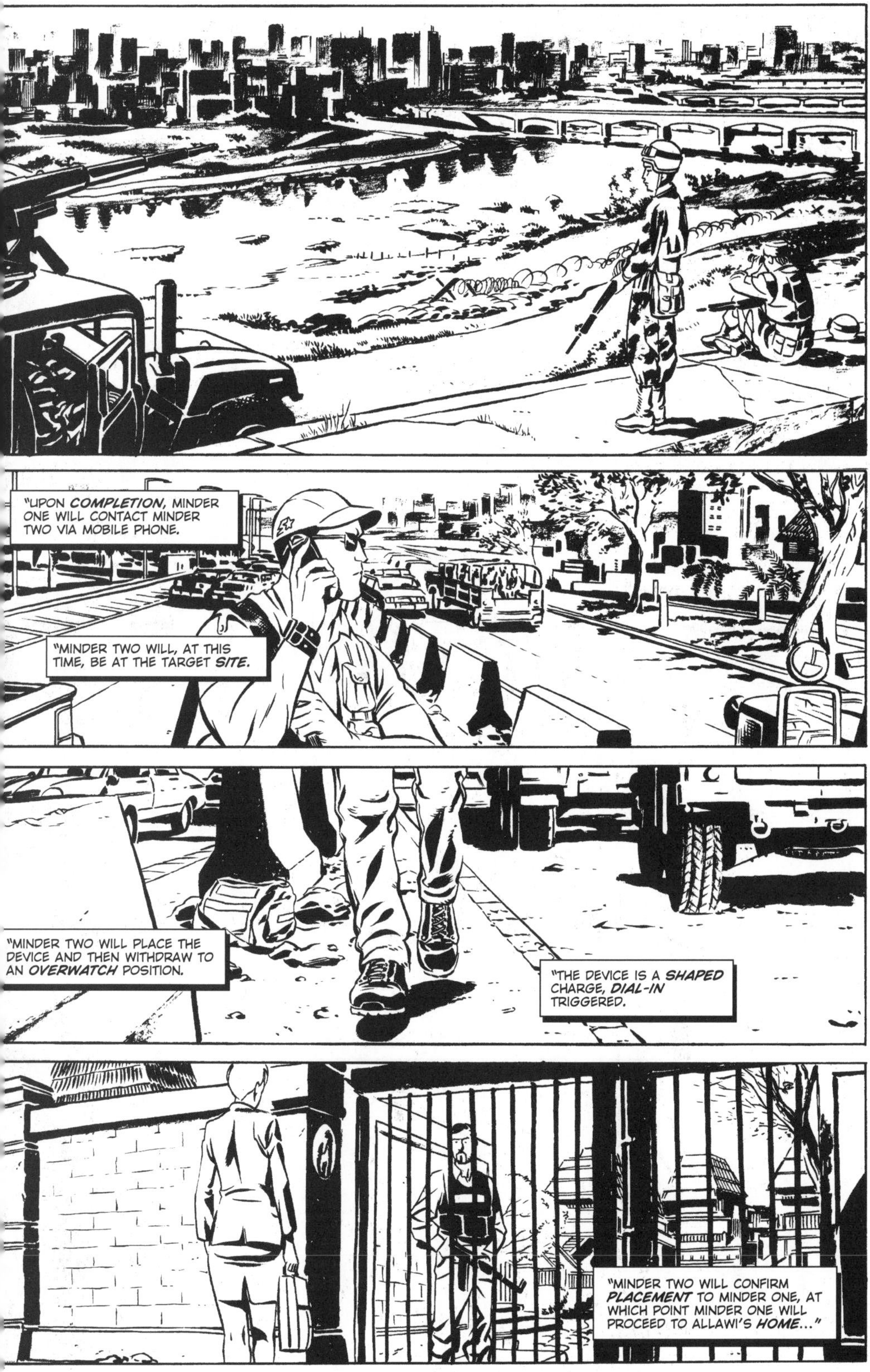
"UPON COMPLETION, MINDER ONE WILL CONTACT MINDER TWO VIA MOBILE PHONE.
"MINDER TWO WILL, AT THIS TIME, BE AT THE TARGET SITE.
"MINDER TWO WILL PLACE THE DEVICE AND THEN WITHDRAW TO AN OVERWATCH POSITION.
"THE DEVICE IS A SHAPED CHARGE, DIAL-IN TRIGGERED.
"MINDER TWO WILL CONFIRM PLACEMENT TO MINDER ONE, AT WHICH POINT MINDER ONE WILL PROCEED TO ALLAWI'S HOME..."

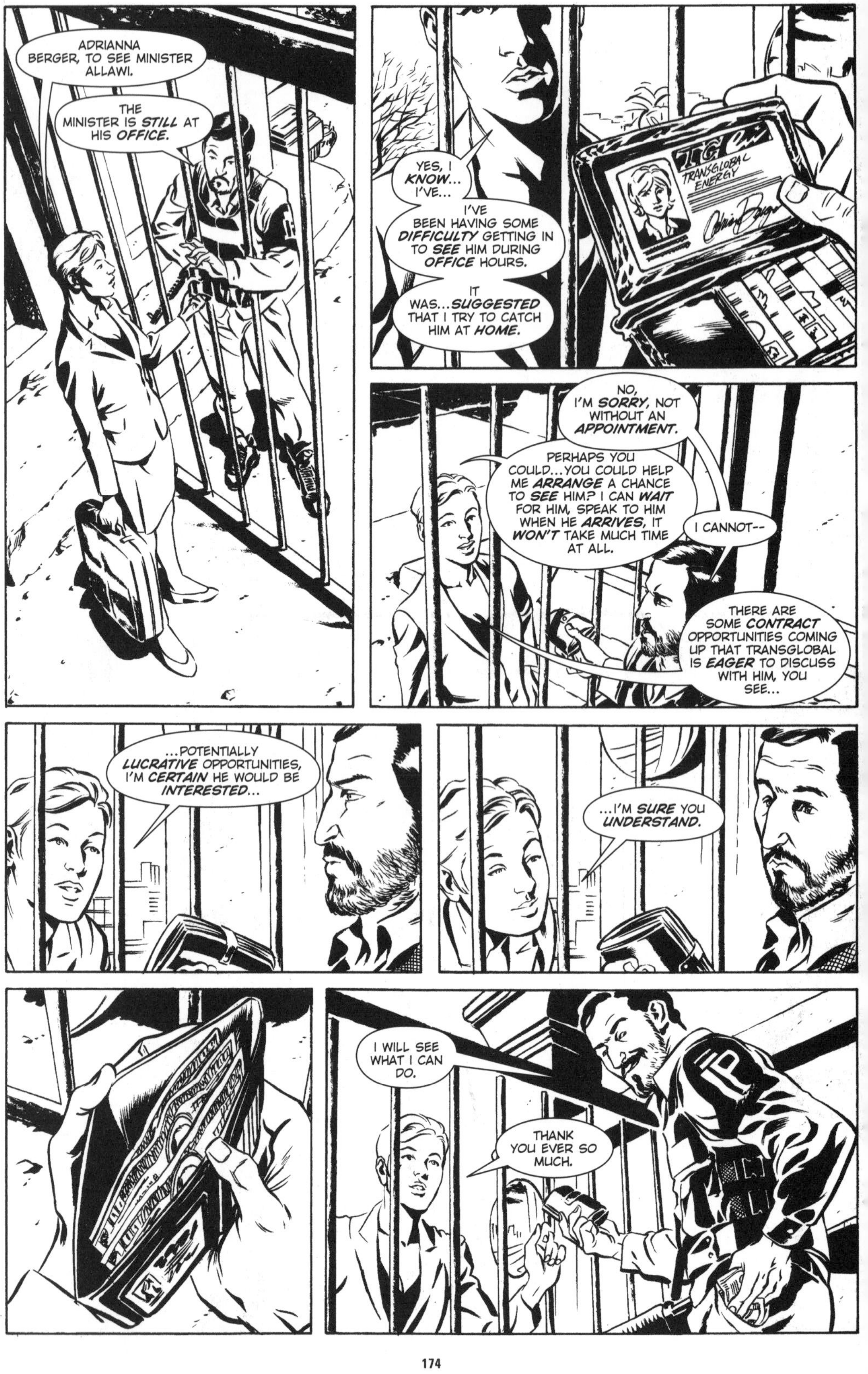
ADRIANNA BERGER, TO SEE MINISTER ALLAWI.
THE MINISTER IS *STILL* AT HIS *OFFICE.*
YES, I *KNOW*... I'VE...
I'VE BEEN HAVING SOME *DIFFICULTY* GETTING IN TO *SEE* HIM DURING *OFFICE* HOURS.
IT WAS...*SUGGESTED* THAT I TRY TO CATCH HIM AT *HOME.*
TRANSGLOBAL ENERGY
NO, I'M *SORRY,* NOT WITHOUT AN *APPOINTMENT.*
PERHAPS YOU COULD...YOU COULD HELP ME *ARRANGE* A CHANCE TO *SEE* HIM? I CAN *WAIT* FOR HIM, SPEAK TO HIM WHEN HE *ARRIVES,* IT *WON'T* TAKE MUCH TIME AT ALL.
I CANNOT--
THERE ARE SOME *CONTRACT* OPPORTUNITIES COMING UP THAT TRANSGLOBAL IS *EAGER* TO DISCUSS WITH HIM, YOU SEE...
...POTENTIALLY *LUCRATIVE* OPPORTUNITIES, I'M *CERTAIN* HE WOULD BE *INTERESTED*...
...I'M *SURE* YOU *UNDERSTAND.*
I WILL SEE WHAT I CAN DO.
THANK YOU EVER SO MUCH.

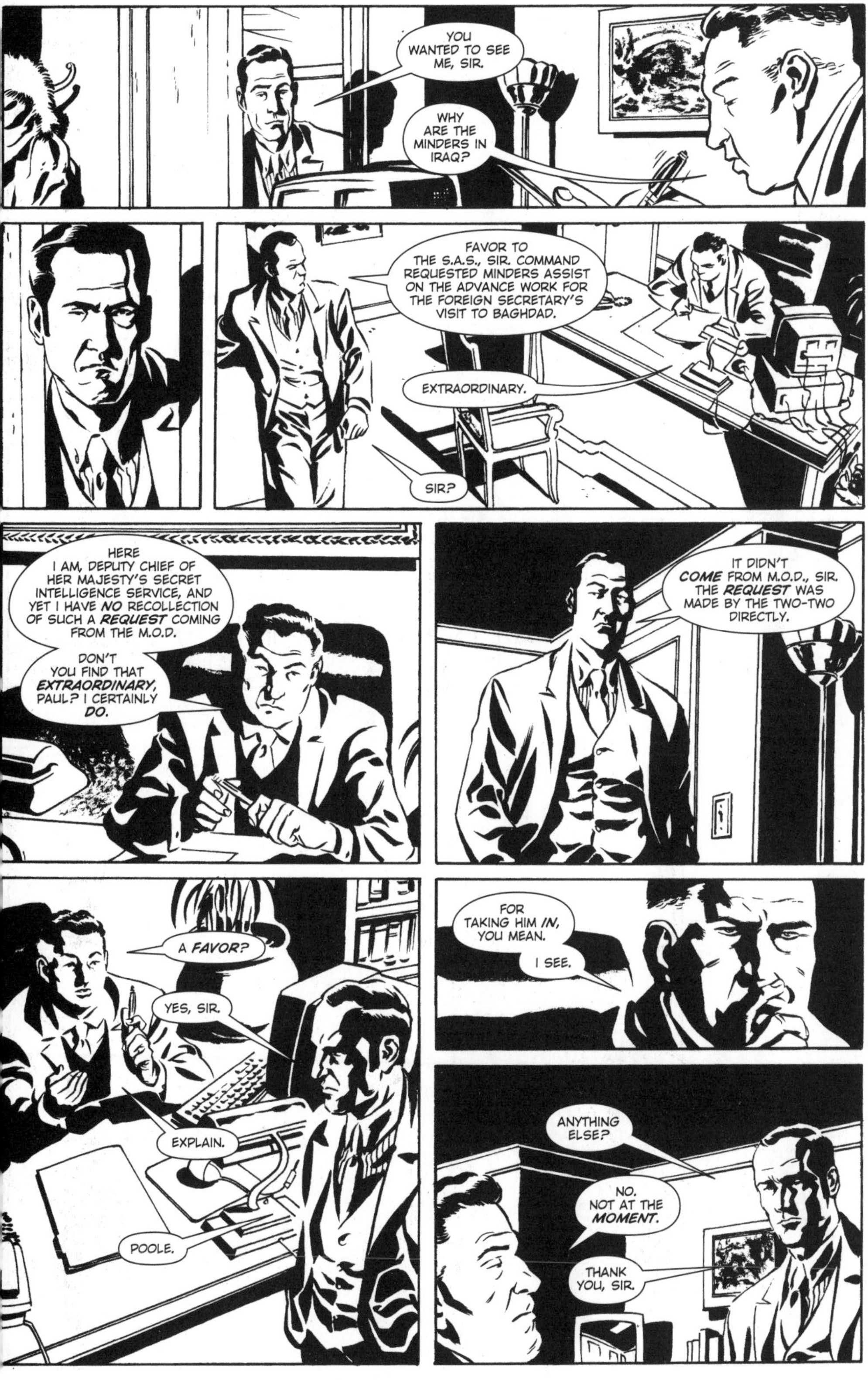
YOU WANTED TO SEE ME, SIR.
WHY ARE THE MINDERS IN IRAQ?
FAVOR TO THE S.A.S., SIR. COMMAND REQUESTED MINDERS ASSIST ON THE ADVANCE WORK FOR THE FOREIGN SECRETARY'S VISIT TO BAGHDAD.
EXTRAORDINARY.
SIR?
HERE I AM, DEPUTY CHIEF OF HER MAJESTY'S SECRET INTELLIGENCE SERVICE, AND YET I HAVE ***NO*** RECOLLECTION OF SUCH A ***REQUEST*** COMING FROM THE M.O.D.
DON'T YOU FIND THAT ***EXTRAORDINARY,*** PAUL? I CERTAINLY ***DO.***
IT DIDN'T ***COME*** FROM M.O.D., SIR. THE ***REQUEST*** WAS MADE BY THE TWO-TWO DIRECTLY.
A ***FAVOR?***
YES, SIR.
EXPLAIN.
POOLE.
FOR TAKING HIM ***IN,*** YOU MEAN.
I SEE.
ANYTHING ELSE?
NO. NOT AT THE ***MOMENT.***
THANK YOU, SIR.

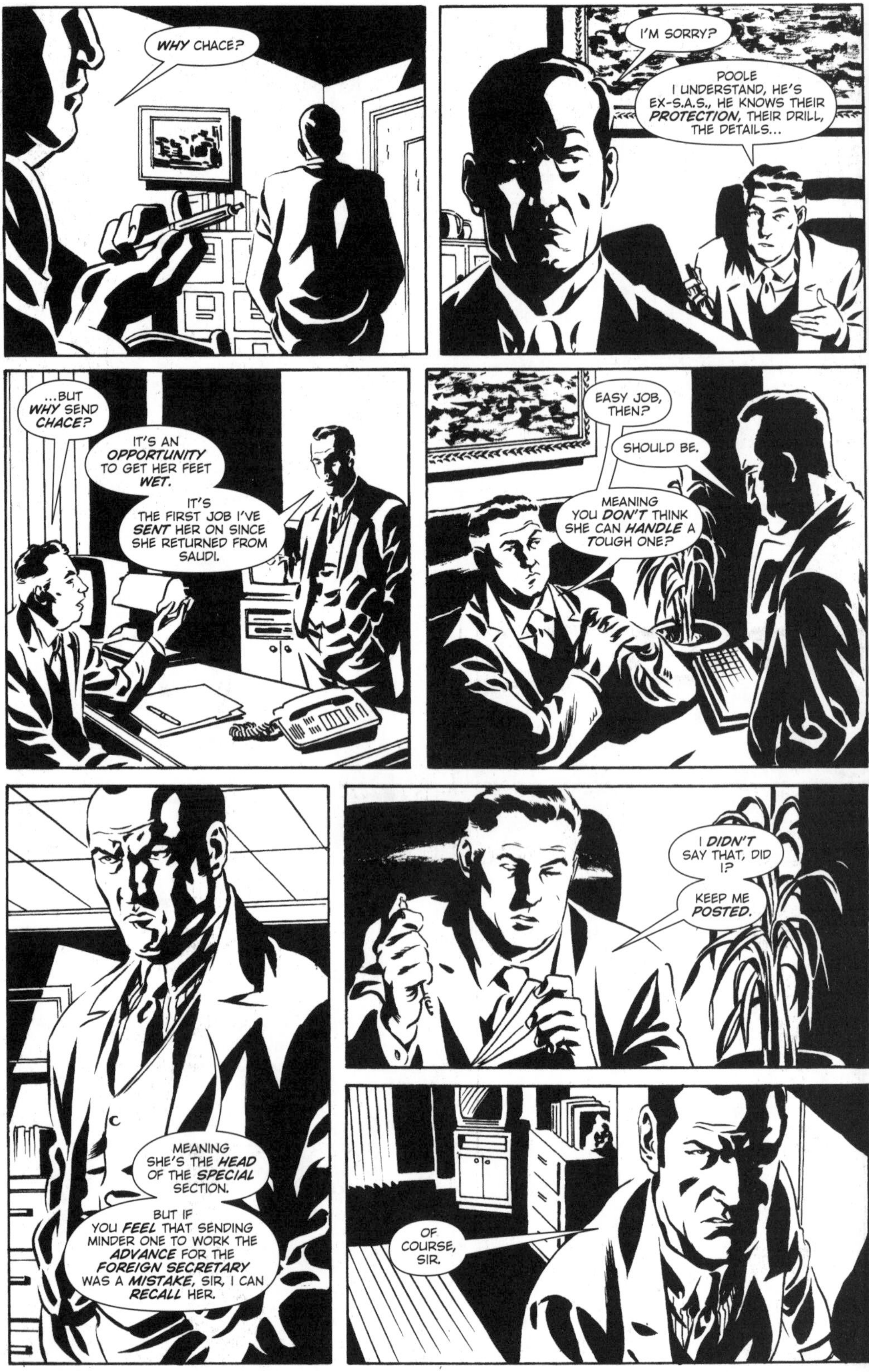
WHY CHACE?
I'M SORRY?
POOLE I UNDERSTAND, HE'S EX-S.A.S., HE KNOWS THEIR PROTECTION, THEIR DRILL, THE DETAILS...
...BUT WHY SEND CHACE?
IT'S AN OPPORTUNITY TO GET HER FEET WET.
IT'S THE FIRST JOB I'VE SENT HER ON SINCE SHE RETURNED FROM SAUDI.
EASY JOB, THEN?
SHOULD BE.
MEANING YOU DON'T THINK SHE CAN HANDLE A TOUGH ONE?
MEANING SHE'S THE HEAD OF THE SPECIAL SECTION.
BUT IF YOU FEEL THAT SENDING MINDER ONE TO WORK THE ADVANCE FOR THE FOREIGN SECRETARY WAS A MISTAKE, SIR, I CAN RECALL HER.
I DIDN'T SAY THAT, DID I?
KEEP ME POSTED.
OF COURSE, SIR.

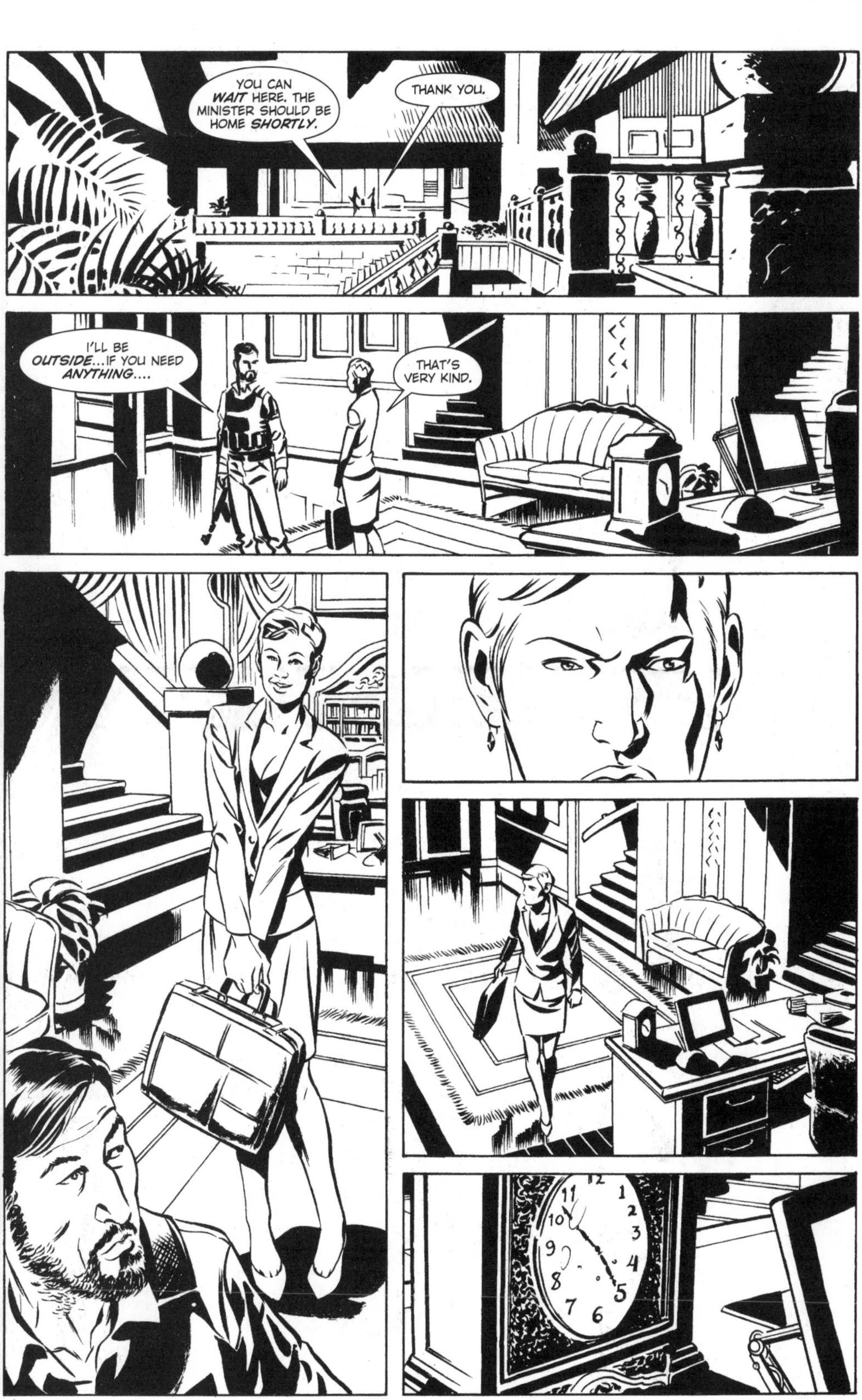
YOU CAN WAIT HERE. THE MINISTER SHOULD BE HOME SHORTLY.
THANK YOU.
I'LL BE OUTSIDE...IF YOU NEED ANYTHING....
THAT'S VERY KIND.

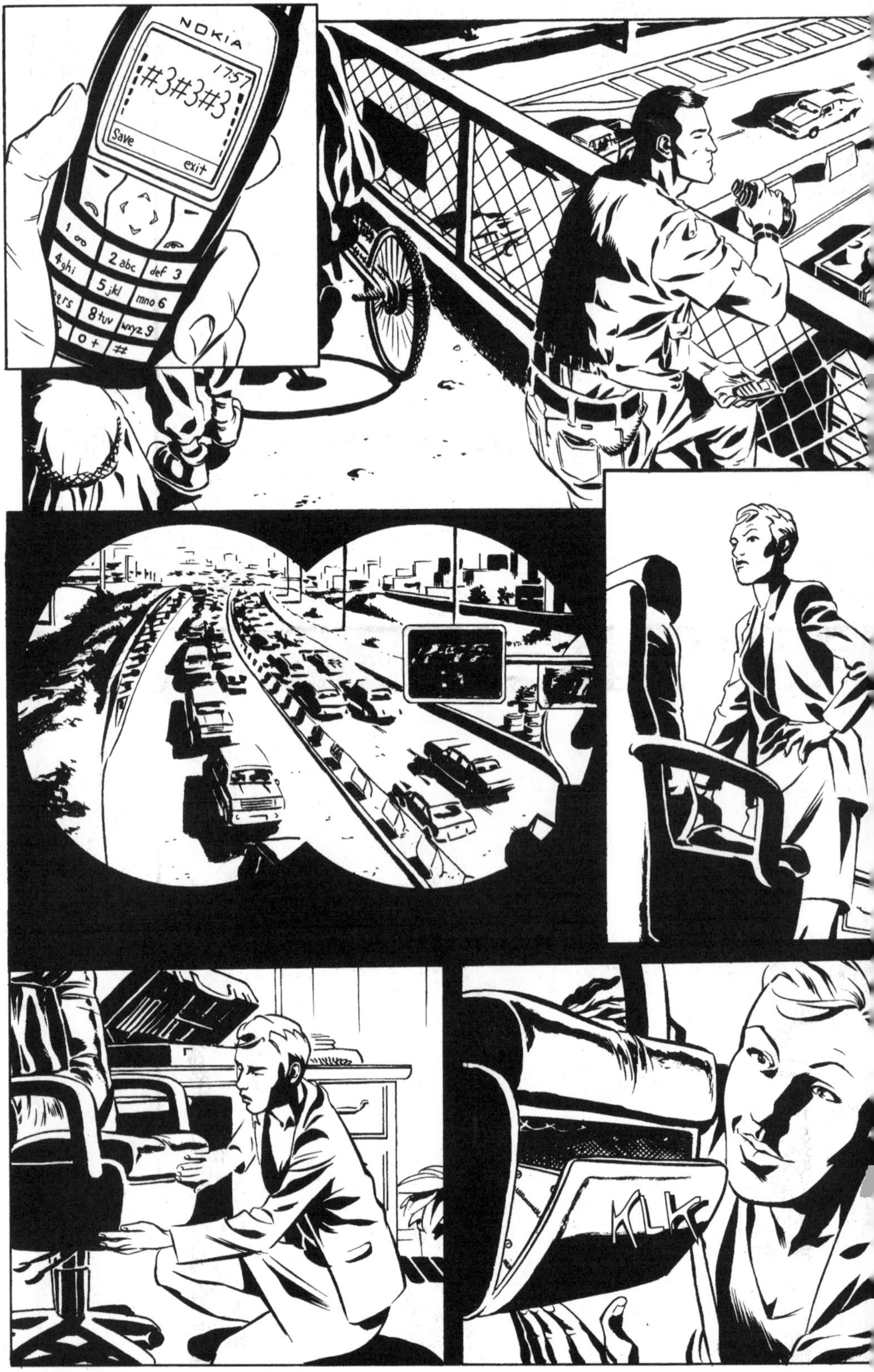
NOKIA
17:57
#3#3#3
Save
exit

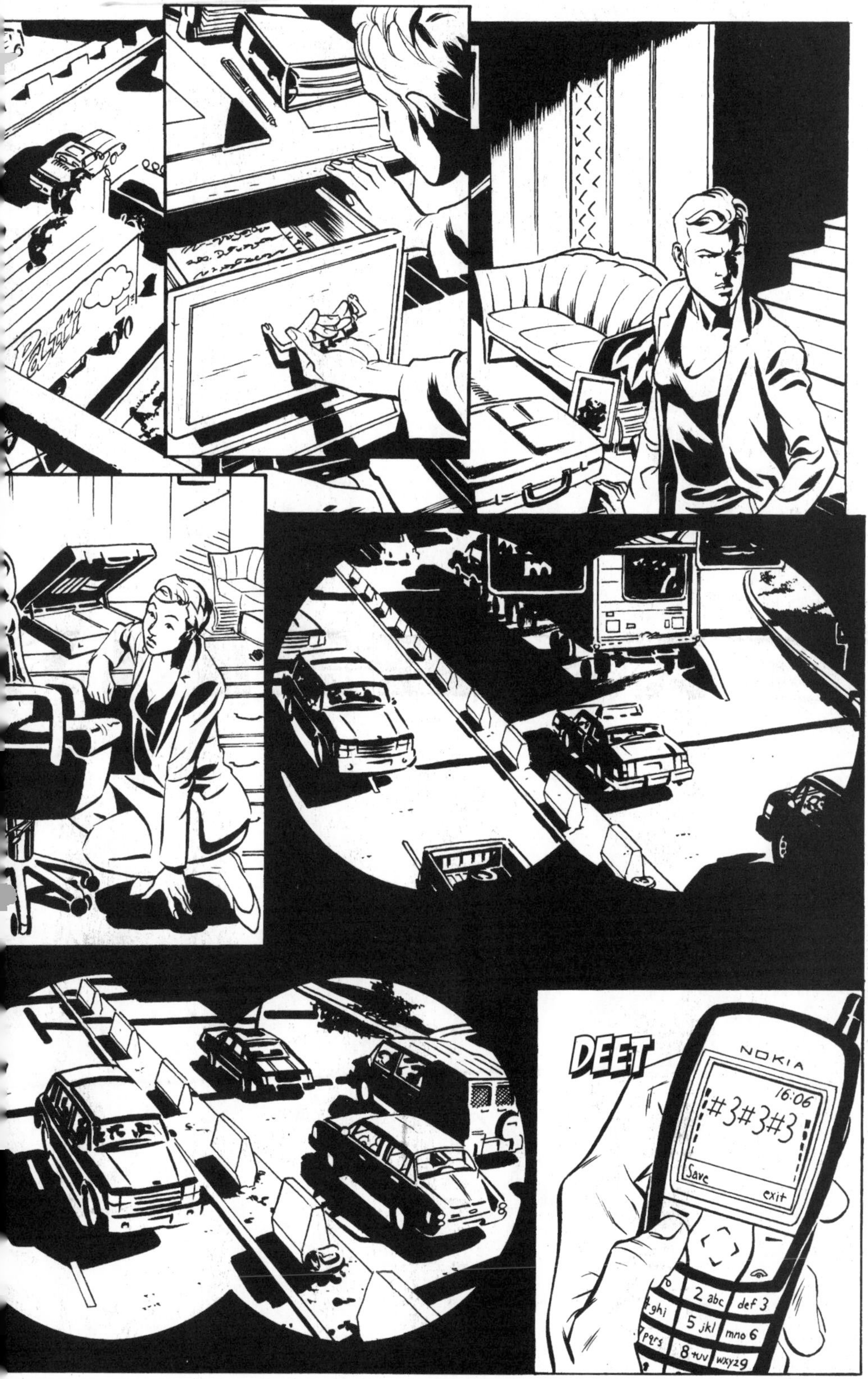
DEET
NOKIA
16:06
#3#3#3
Save
exit

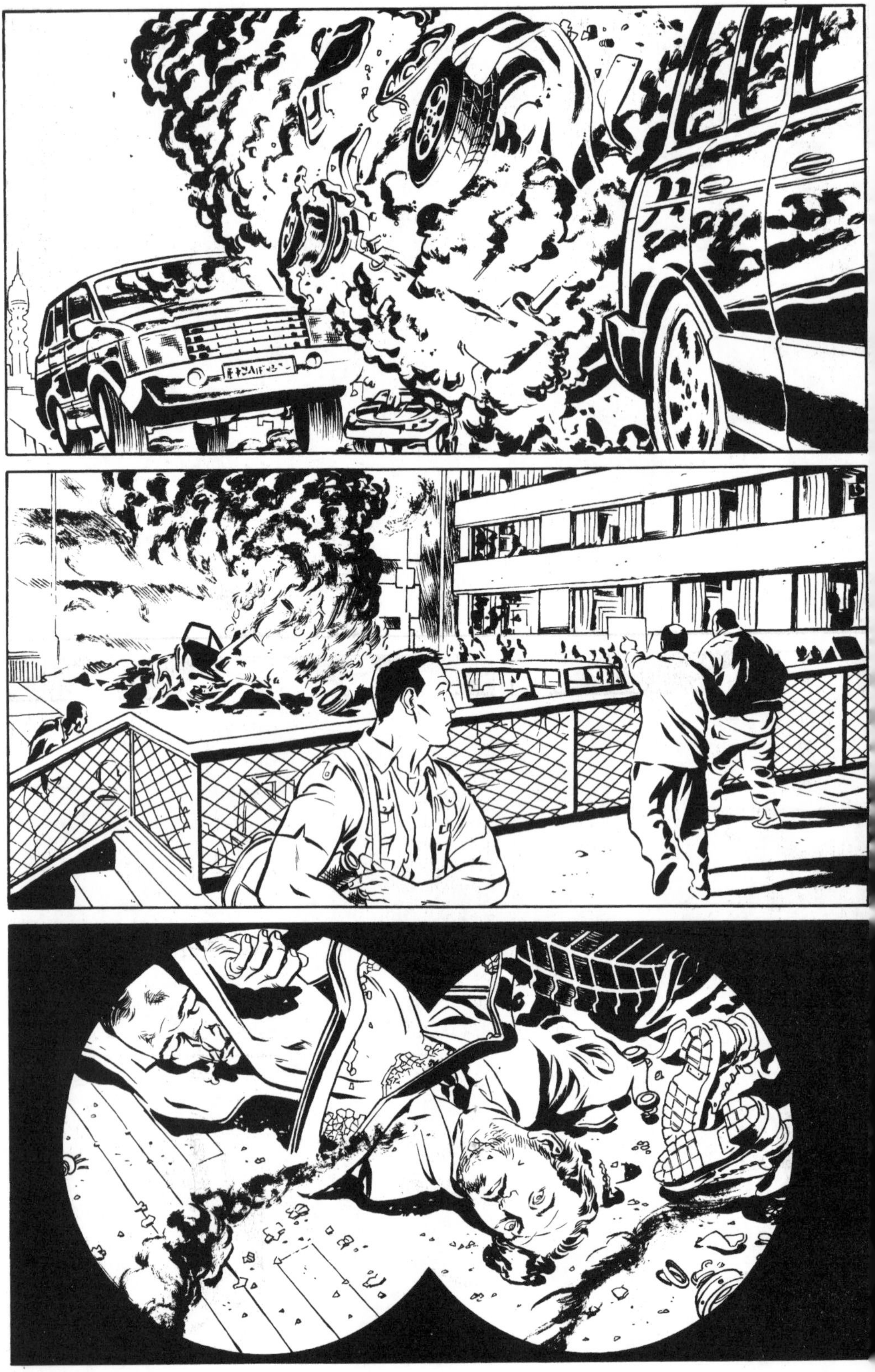

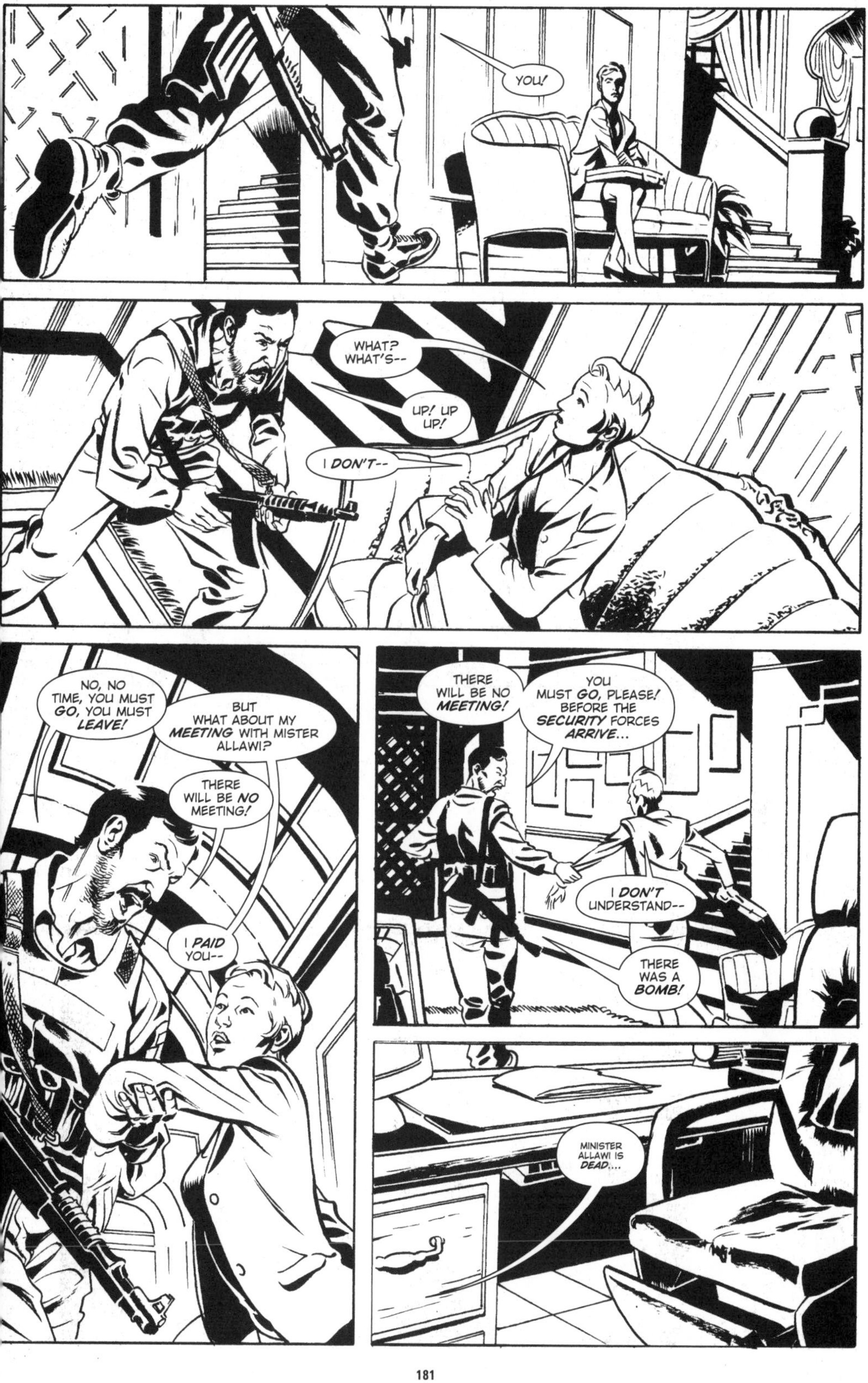
YOU!
WHAT? WHAT'S--
UP! UP UP!
I DON'T--
NO, NO TIME, YOU MUST GO, YOU MUST LEAVE!
BUT WHAT ABOUT MY MEETING WITH MISTER ALLAWI?
THERE WILL BE NO MEETING!
I PAID YOU--
THERE WILL BE NO MEETING!
YOU MUST GO, PLEASE! BEFORE THE SECURITY FORCES ARRIVE...
I DON'T UNDERSTAND--
THERE WAS A BOMB!
MINISTER ALLAWI IS DEAD...

CHAPTER 2

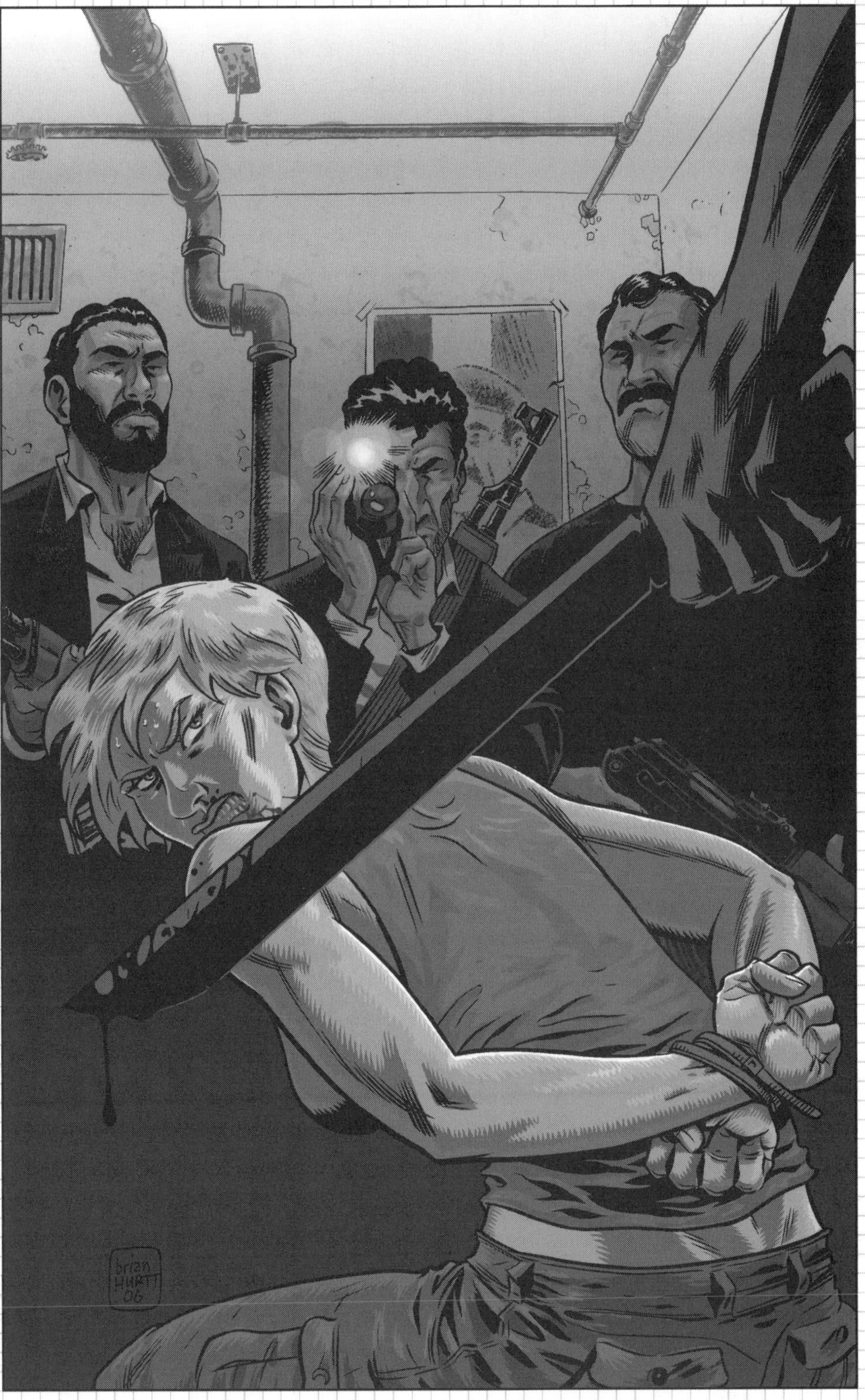
brian HURTT 06

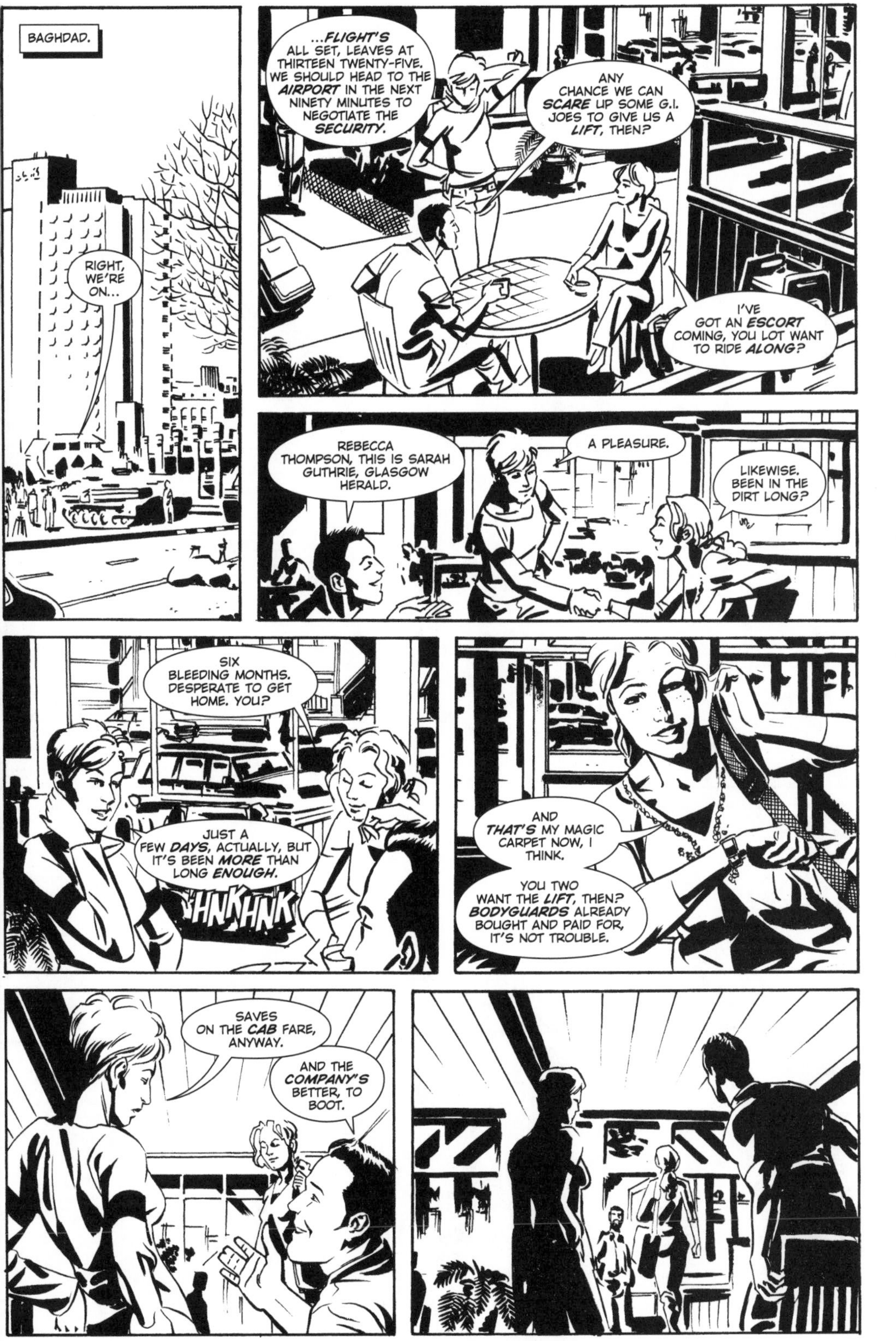
BAGHDAD.
RIGHT, WE'RE ON...
...FLIGHT'S ALL SET, LEAVES AT THIRTEEN TWENTY-FIVE. WE SHOULD HEAD TO THE AIRPORT IN THE NEXT NINETY MINUTES TO NEGOTIATE THE SECURITY.
ANY CHANCE WE CAN SCARE UP SOME G.I. JOES TO GIVE US A LIFT, THEN?
I'VE GOT AN ESCORT COMING, YOU LOT WANT TO RIDE ALONG?
REBECCA THOMPSON, THIS IS SARAH GUTHRIE, GLASGOW HERALD.
A PLEASURE.
LIKEWISE. BEEN IN THE DIRT LONG?
SIX BLEEDING MONTHS. DESPERATE TO GET HOME. YOU?
JUST A FEW DAYS, ACTUALLY, BUT IT'S BEEN MORE THAN LONG ENOUGH.
HNKHNK
AND THAT'S MY MAGIC CARPET NOW, I THINK.
YOU TWO WANT THE LIFT, THEN? BODYGUARDS ALREADY BOUGHT AND PAID FOR, IT'S NOT TROUBLE.
SAVES ON THE CAB FARE, ANYWAY.
AND THE COMPANY'S BETTER, TO BOOT.

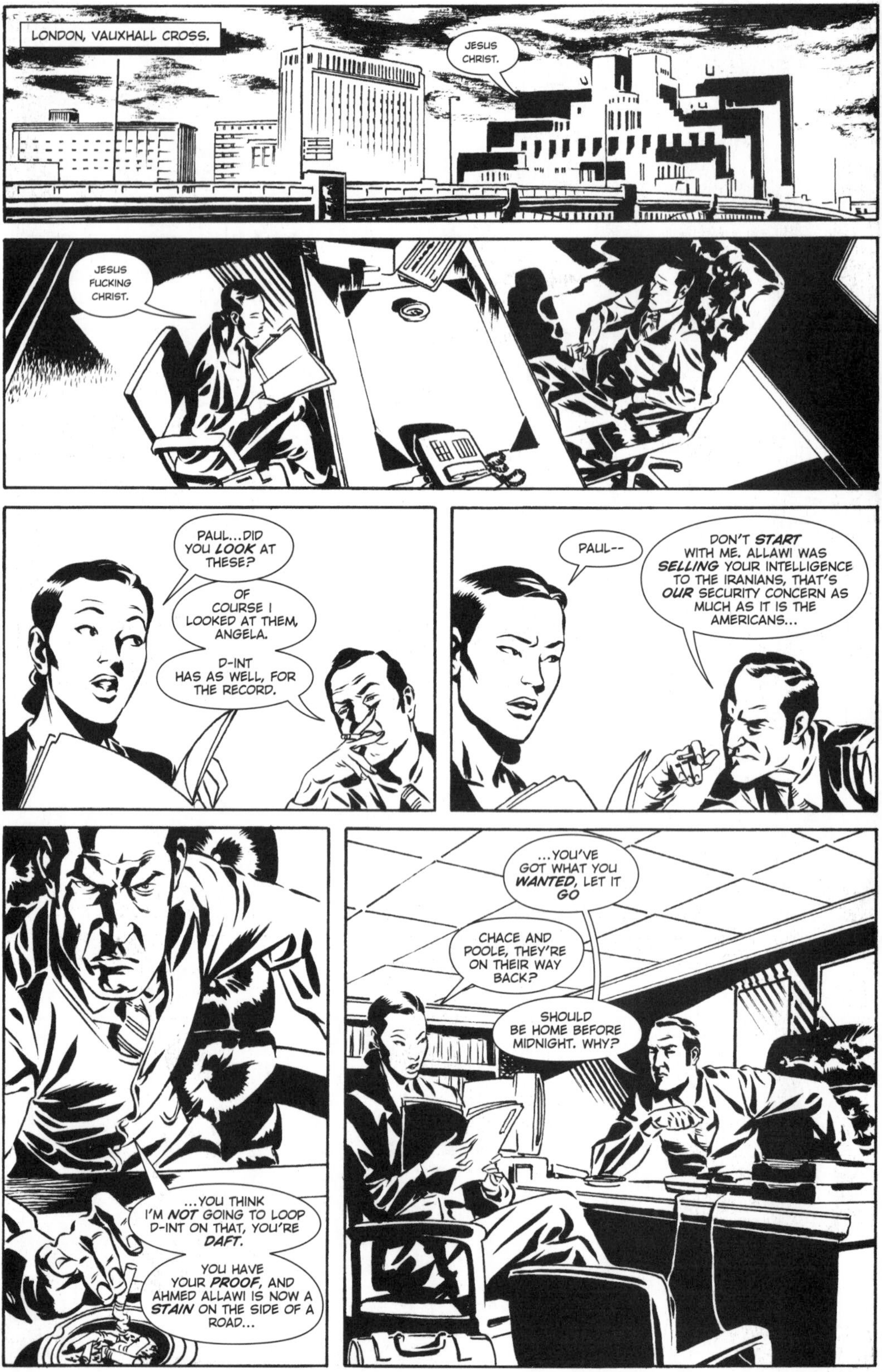

LONDON, VAUXHALL CROSS.
JESUS CHRIST.
JESUS FUCKING CHRIST.
PAUL...DID YOU *LOOK* AT THESE?
OF COURSE I LOOKED AT THEM, ANGELA.
D-INT HAS AS WELL, FOR THE RECORD.
PAUL--
DON'T *START* WITH ME. ALLAWI WAS *SELLING* YOUR INTELLIGENCE TO THE IRANIANS, THAT'S *OUR* SECURITY CONCERN AS MUCH AS IT IS THE AMERICANS...
...YOU THINK I'M *NOT* GOING TO LOOP D-INT ON THAT, YOU'RE *DAFT*.
YOU HAVE YOUR *PROOF*, AND AHMED ALLAWI IS NOW A *STAIN* ON THE SIDE OF A ROAD...
...YOU'VE GOT WHAT YOU *WANTED*, LET IT *GO*
CHACE AND POOLE, THEY'RE ON THEIR WAY BACK?
SHOULD BE HOME BEFORE MIDNIGHT. WHY?

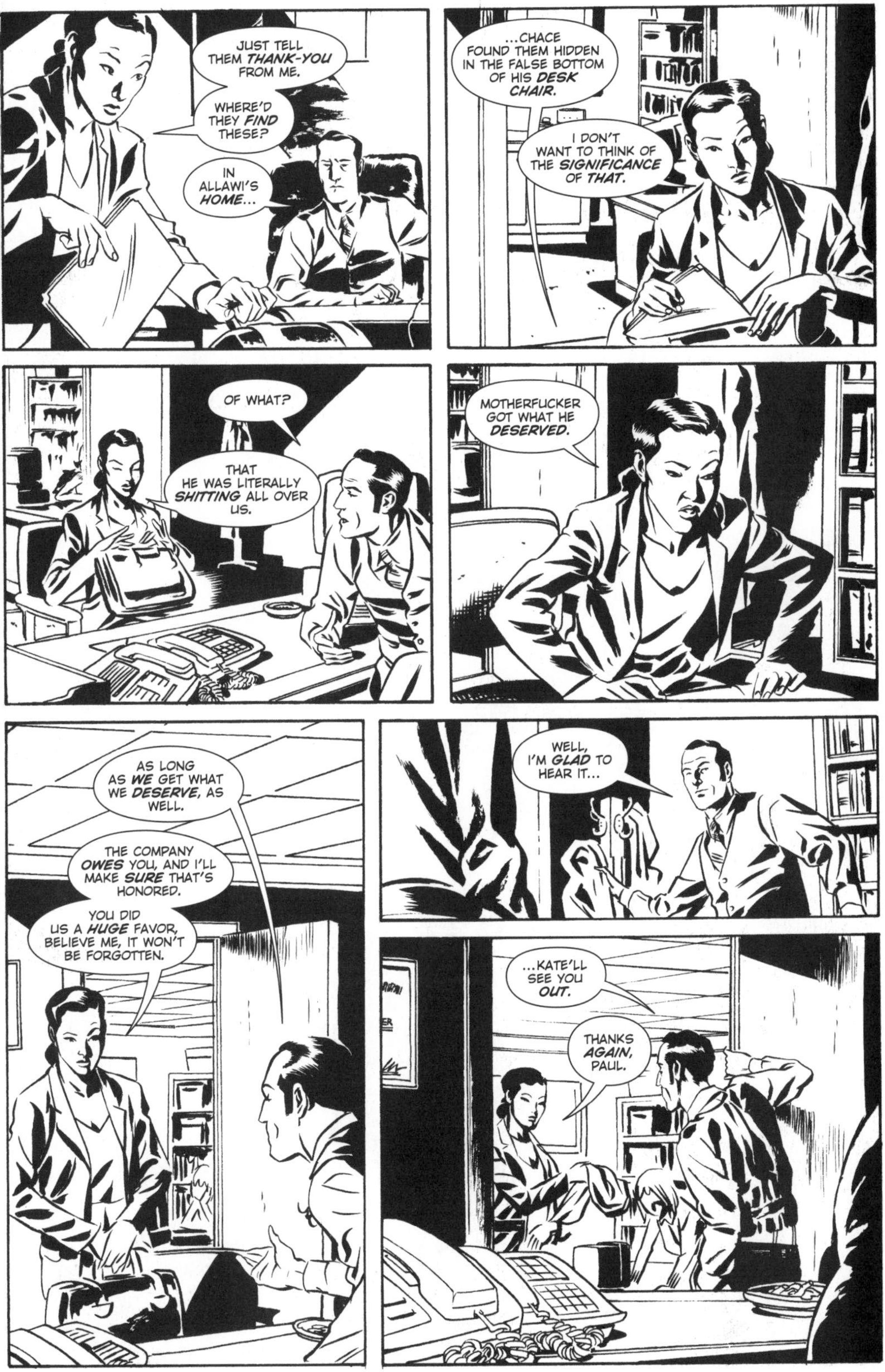
JUST TELL THEM THANK-YOU FROM ME.
WHERE'D THEY FIND THESE?
IN ALLAWI'S HOME...
...CHACE FOUND THEM HIDDEN IN THE FALSE BOTTOM OF HIS DESK CHAIR.
I DON'T WANT TO THINK OF THE SIGNIFICANCE OF THAT.
OF WHAT?
THAT HE WAS LITERALLY SHITTING ALL OVER US.
MOTHERFUCKER GOT WHAT HE DESERVED.
AS LONG AS WE GET WHAT WE DESERVE, AS WELL.
THE COMPANY OWES YOU, AND I'LL MAKE SURE THAT'S HONORED.
YOU DID US A HUGE FAVOR, BELIEVE ME, IT WON'T BE FORGOTTEN.
WELL, I'M GLAD TO HEAR IT...
...KATE'LL SEE YOU OUT.
THANKS AGAIN, PAUL.

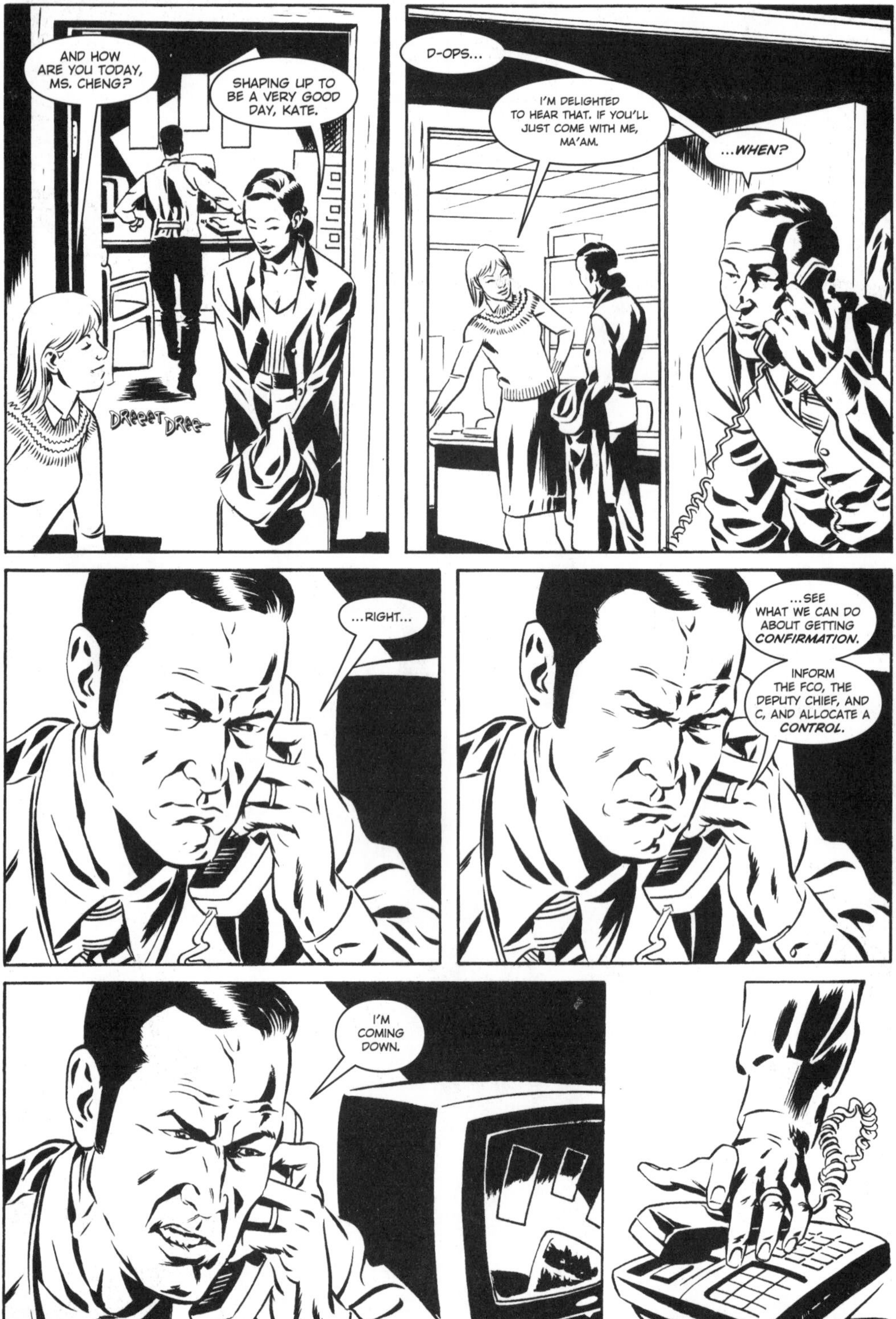
AND HOW ARE YOU TODAY, MS. CHENG?
SHAPING UP TO BE A VERY GOOD DAY, KATE.
DREEET DREE-
D-OPS...
I'M DELIGHTED TO HEAR THAT. IF YOU'LL JUST COME WITH ME, MA'AM.
...*WHEN?*
...RIGHT...
...SEE WHAT WE CAN DO ABOUT GETTING *CONFIRMATION.*
INFORM THE FCO, THE DEPUTY CHIEF, AND C, AND ALLOCATE A *CONTROL.*
I'M COMING DOWN.

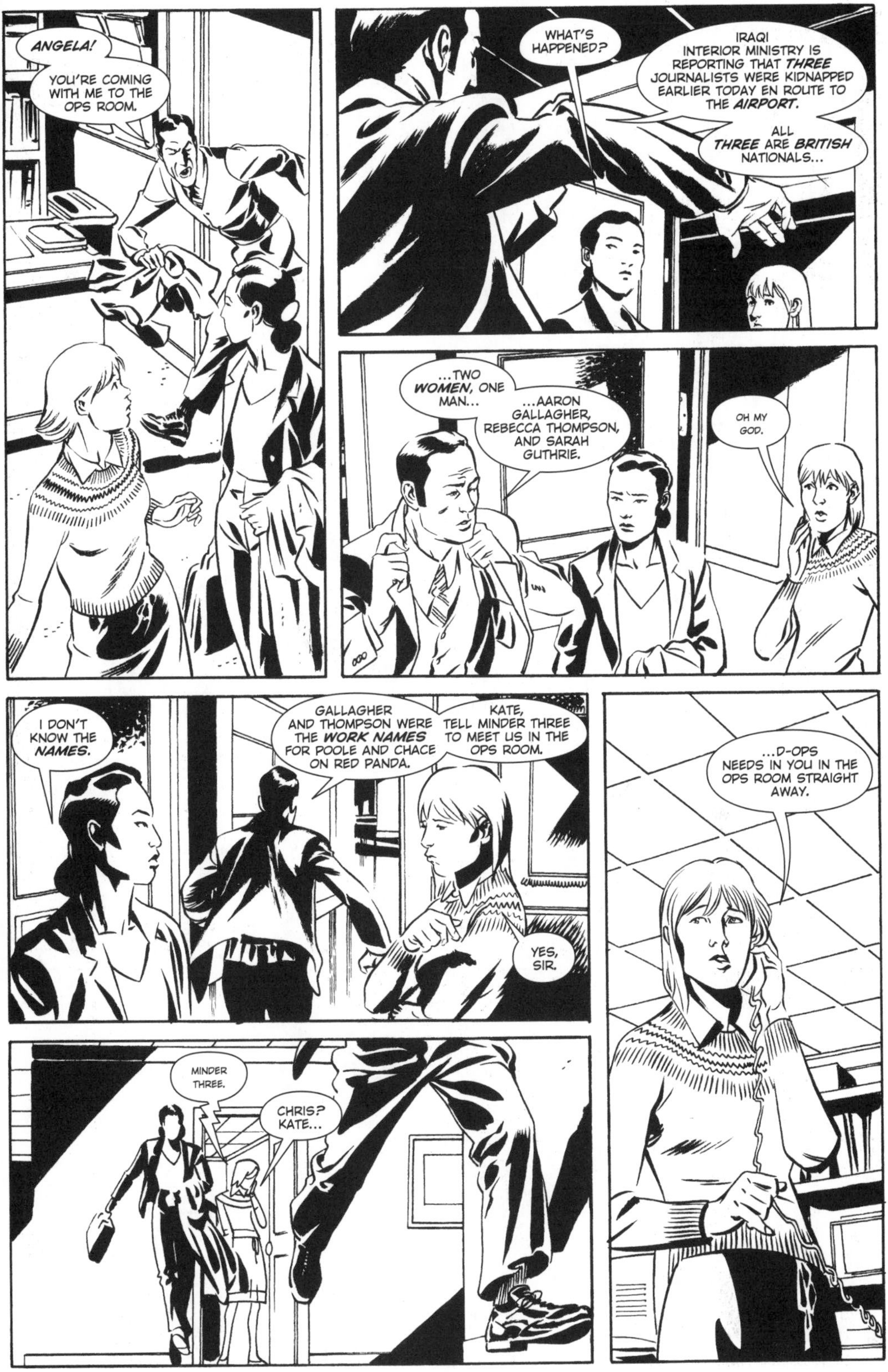
ANGELA!
YOU'RE COMING WITH ME TO THE OPS ROOM.
WHAT'S HAPPENED?
IRAQI INTERIOR MINISTRY IS REPORTING THAT THREE JOURNALISTS WERE KIDNAPPED EARLIER TODAY EN ROUTE TO THE AIRPORT.
ALL THREE ARE BRITISH NATIONALS...
...TWO WOMEN, ONE MAN...
...AARON GALLAGHER, REBECCA THOMPSON, AND SARAH GUTHRIE.
OH MY GOD.
I DON'T KNOW THE NAMES.
GALLAGHER AND THOMPSON WERE THE WORK NAMES FOR POOLE AND CHACE ON RED PANDA.
KATE, TELL MINDER THREE TO MEET US IN THE OPS ROOM.
YES, SIR.
...D-OPS NEEDS IN YOU IN THE OPS ROOM STRAIGHT AWAY.
MINDER THREE.
CHRIS? KATE...

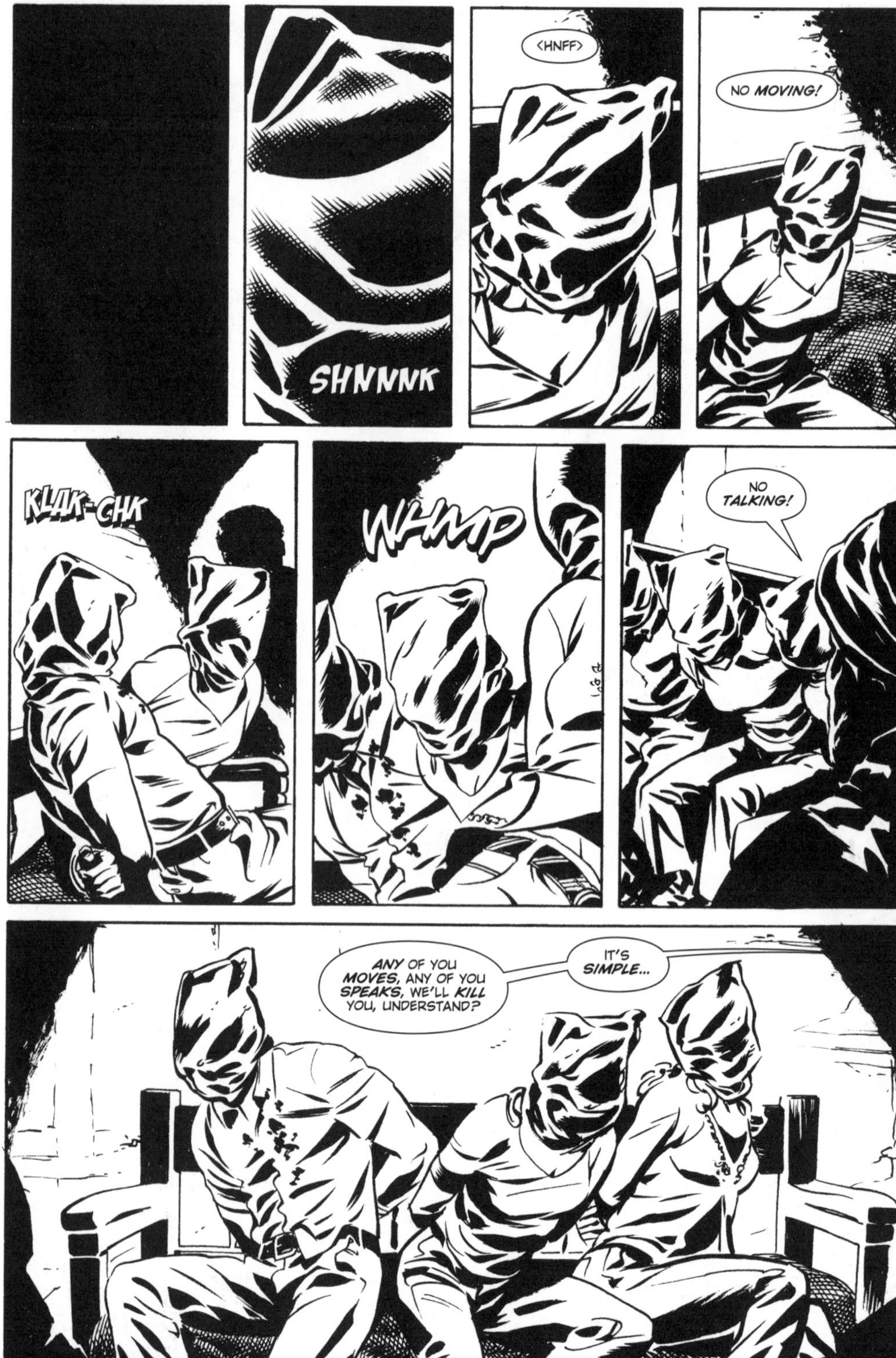
SHNNNK
<HNFF>
NO MOVING!
KLAK-CHK
WHMP
NO TALKING!
IT'S SIMPLE...
ANY OF YOU MOVES, ANY OF YOU SPEAKS, WE'LL KILL YOU, UNDERSTAND?

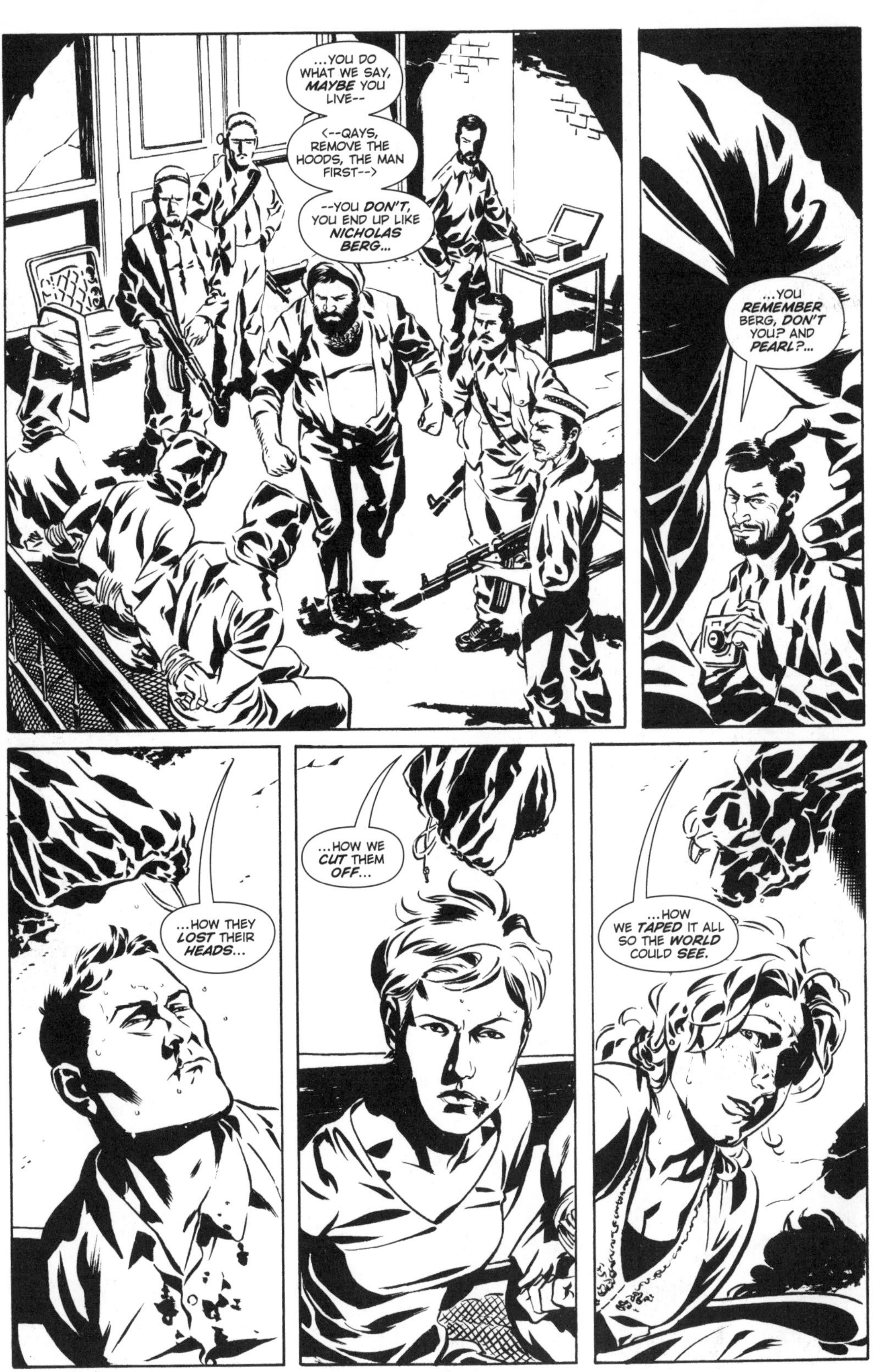

...YOU DO WHAT WE SAY, MAYBE YOU LIVE--
<--QAYS, REMOVE THE HOODS, THE MAN FIRST-->
--YOU DON'T, YOU END UP LIKE NICHOLAS BERG...
...YOU REMEMBER BERG, DON'T YOU? AND PEARL?...
...HOW THEY LOST THEIR HEADS...
...HOW WE CUT THEM OFF...
...HOW WE TAPED IT ALL SO THE WORLD COULD SEE.

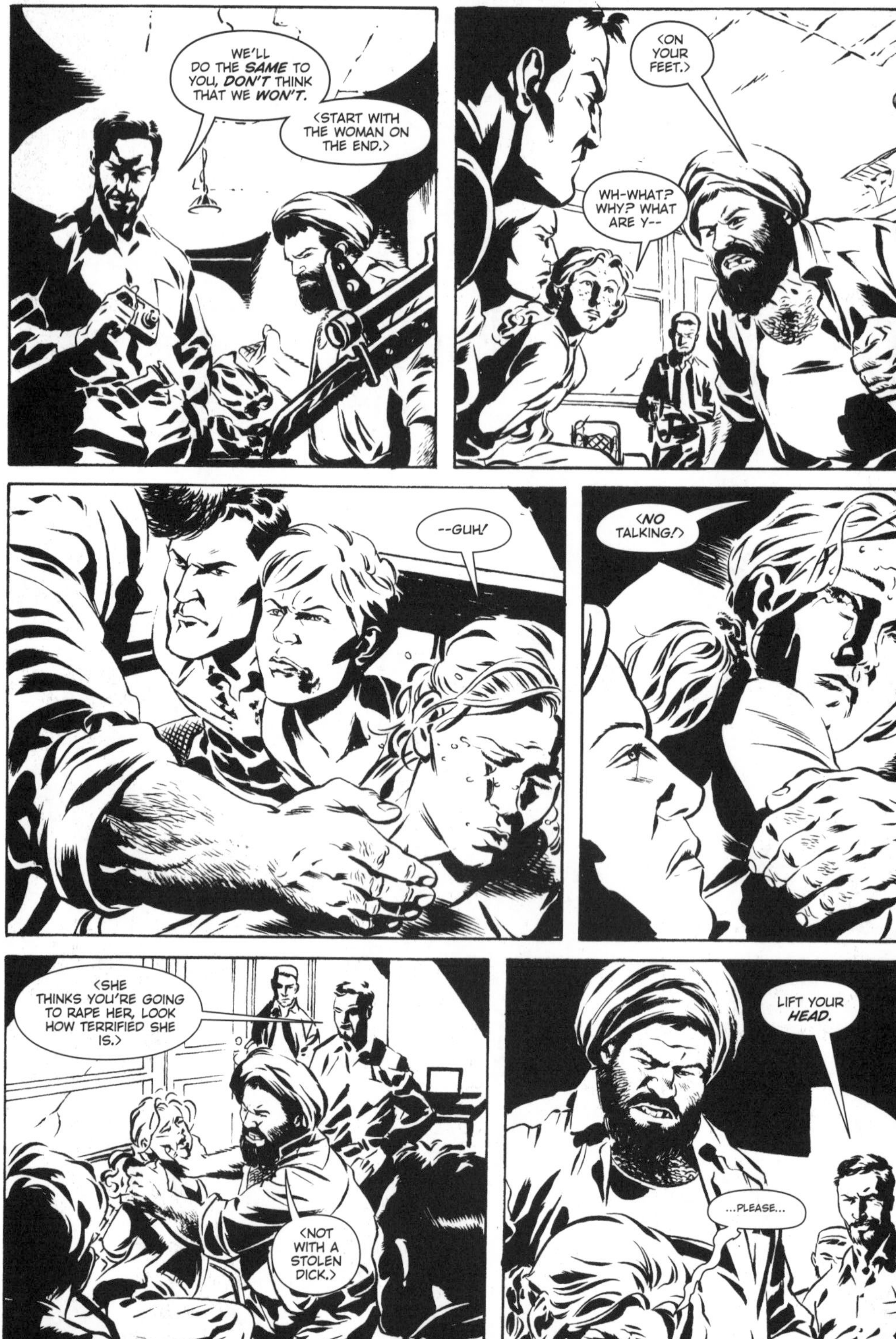
WE'LL DO THE **SAME** TO YOU, **DON'T** THINK THAT WE **WON'T.**
<START WITH THE WOMAN ON THE END.>
<ON YOUR FEET.>
WH-WHAT? WHY? WHAT ARE Y--
--GUH!
<**NO** TALKING!>
<SHE THINKS YOU'RE GOING TO RAPE HER, LOOK HOW TERRIFIED SHE IS.>
<NOT WITH A STOLEN DICK.>
LIFT YOUR **HEAD.**
...PLEASE...

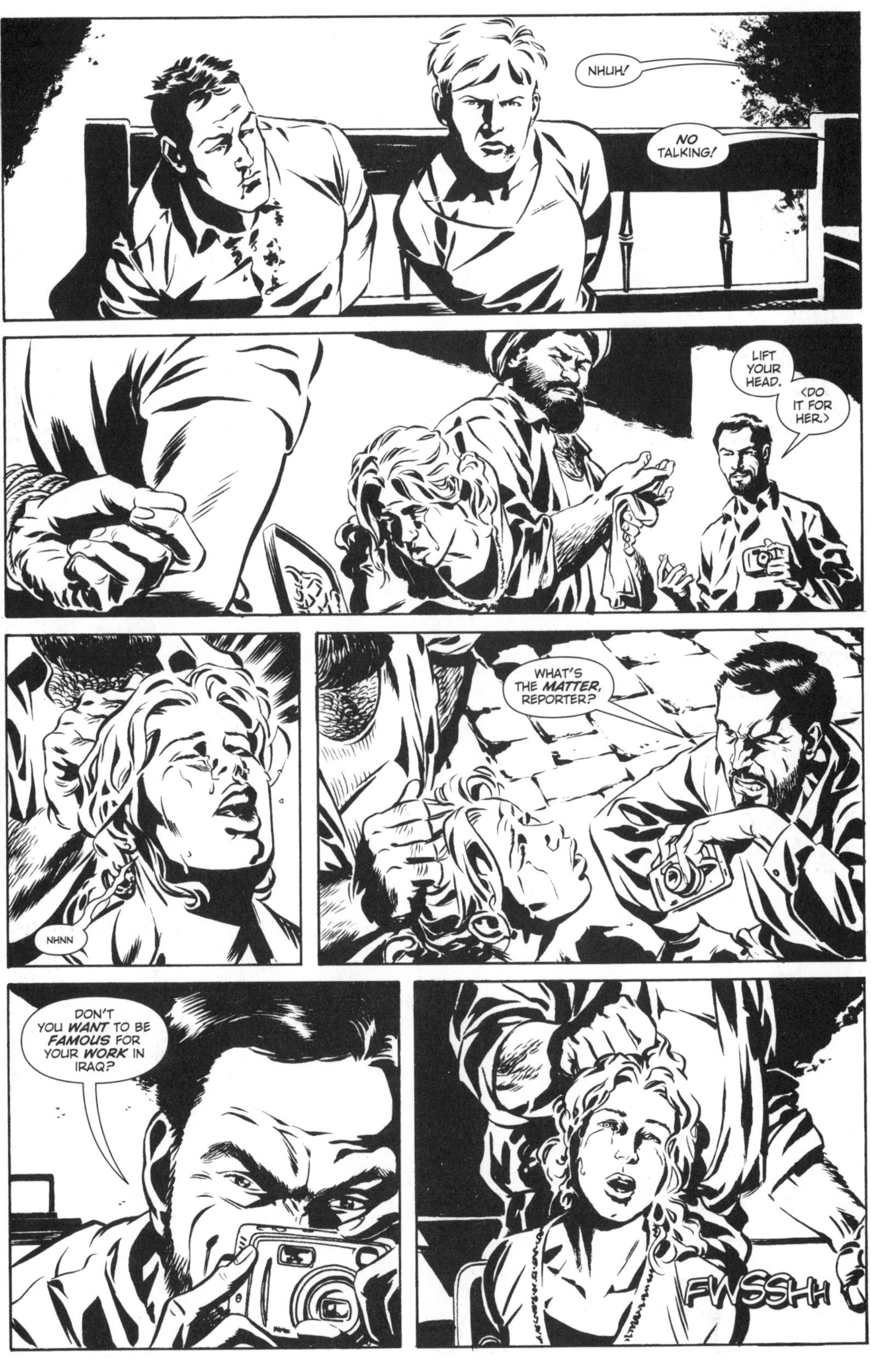
NHUH!
NO TALKING!
LIFT YOUR HEAD.
<DO IT FOR HER.>
NHNN
WHAT'S THE MATTER, REPORTER?
DON'T YOU WANT TO BE FAMOUS FOR YOUR WORK IN IRAQ?
FWSSHH

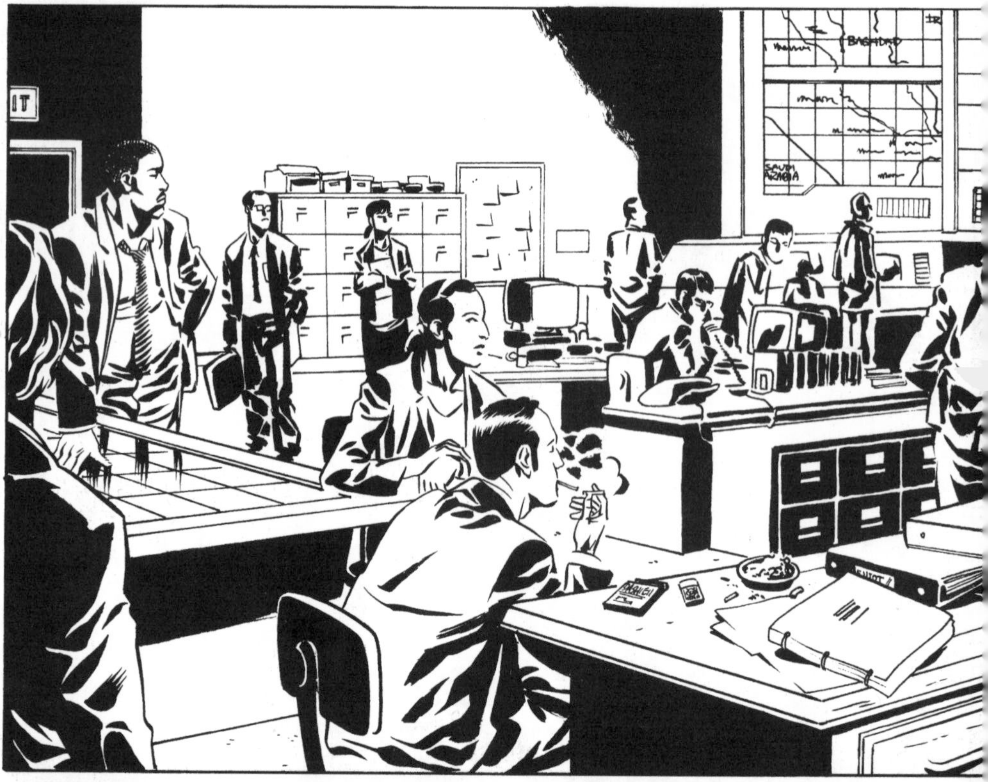
BAGHDAD
SOUTH ARABIA
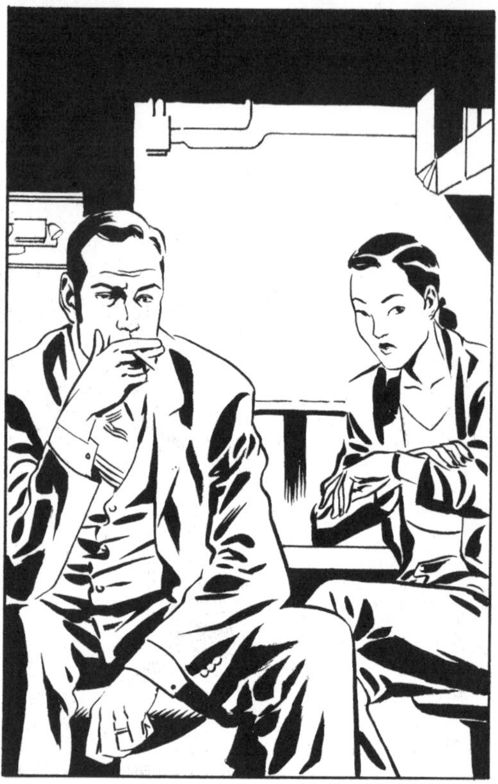
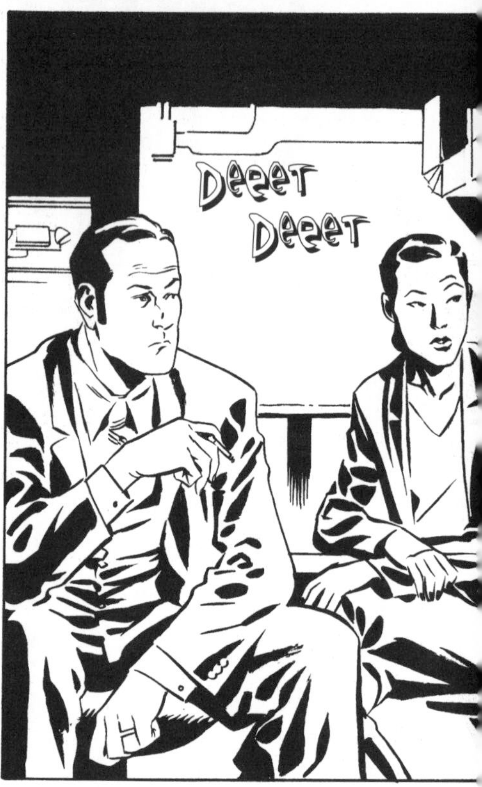
Deeet
Deeet

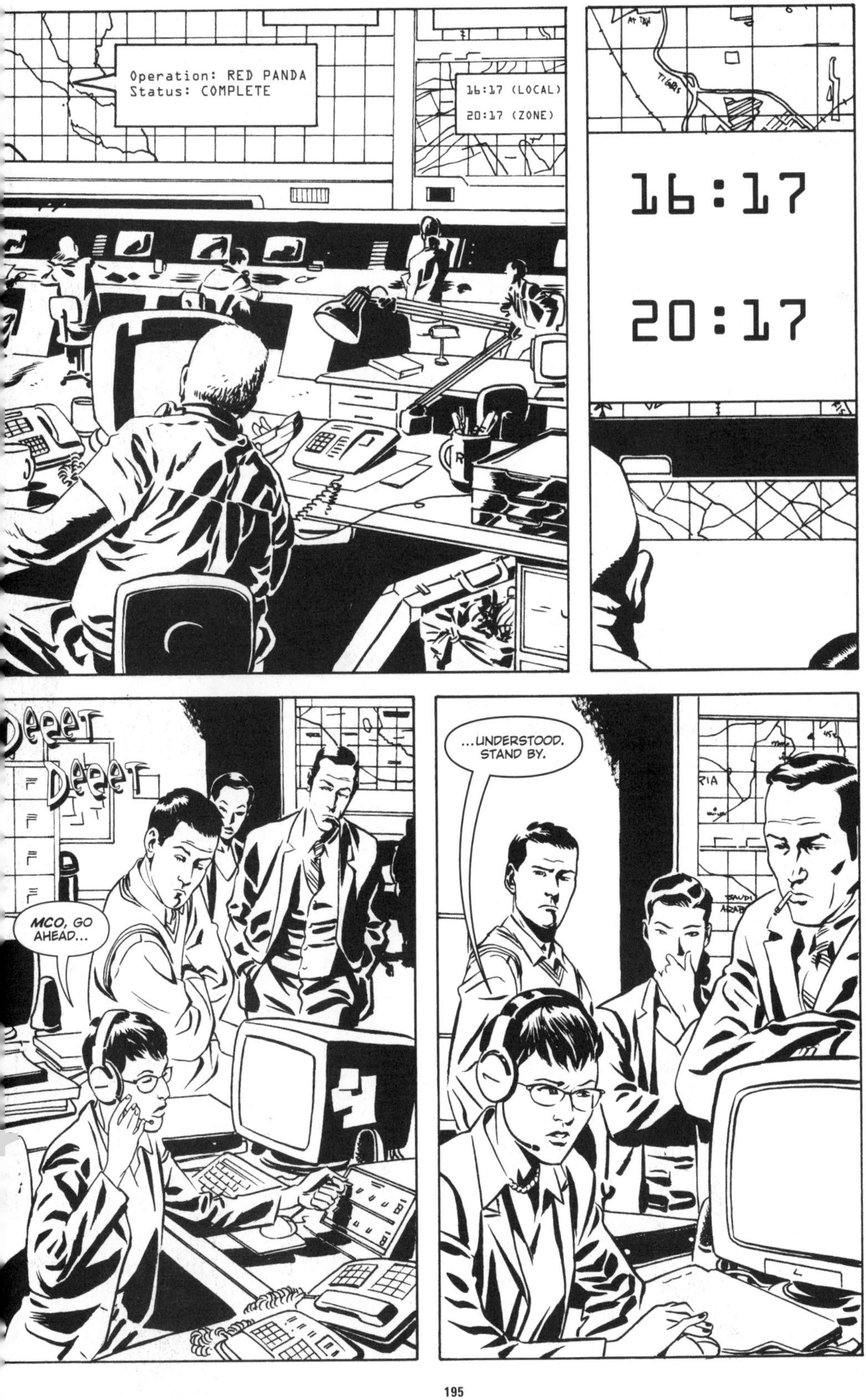
Operation: RED PANDA
Status: COMPLETE
16:17 (LOCAL)
20:17 (ZONE)
16:17
20:17
Deeet
Deeet
MCO, GO AHEAD...
...UNDERSTOOD. STAND BY.

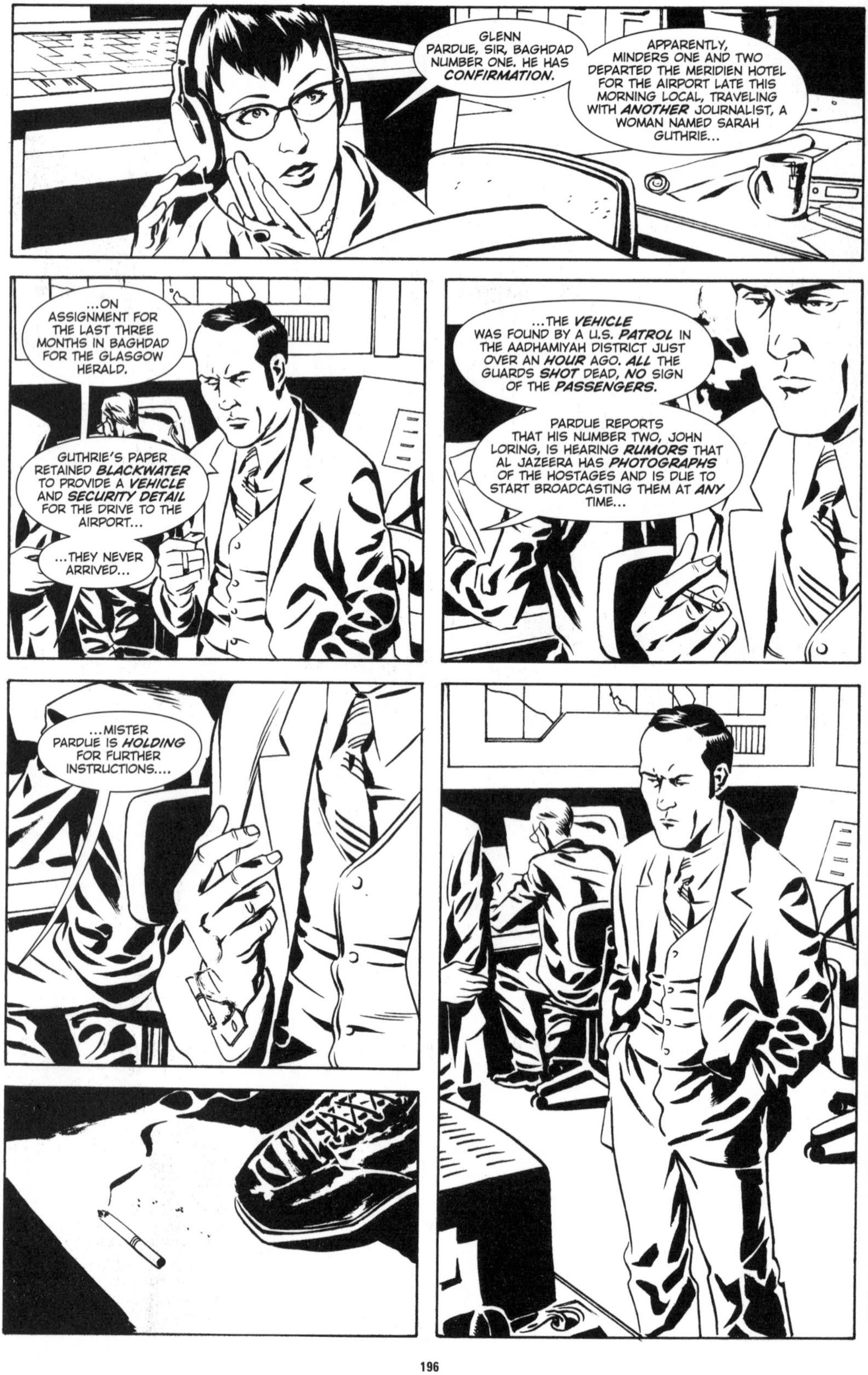
GLENN PARDUE, SIR, BAGHDAD NUMBER ONE. HE HAS *CONFIRMATION*.
APPARENTLY, MINDERS ONE AND TWO DEPARTED THE MERIDIEN HOTEL FOR THE AIRPORT LATE THIS MORNING LOCAL, TRAVELING WITH *ANOTHER* JOURNALIST, A WOMAN NAMED SARAH GUTHRIE...
...ON ASSIGNMENT FOR THE LAST THREE MONTHS IN BAGHDAD FOR THE GLASGOW HERALD.
GUTHRIE'S PAPER RETAINED *BLACKWATER* TO PROVIDE A *VEHICLE* AND *SECURITY DETAIL* FOR THE DRIVE TO THE AIRPORT...
...THEY NEVER ARRIVED...
...THE *VEHICLE* WAS FOUND BY A U.S. *PATROL* IN THE AADHAMIYAH DISTRICT JUST OVER AN *HOUR* AGO. *ALL* THE GUARDS *SHOT* DEAD, *NO* SIGN OF THE *PASSENGERS*.
PARDUE REPORTS THAT HIS NUMBER TWO, JOHN LORING, IS HEARING *RUMORS* THAT AL JAZEERA HAS *PHOTOGRAPHS* OF THE HOSTAGES AND IS DUE TO START BROADCASTING THEM AT *ANY* TIME...
...MISTER PARDUE IS *HOLDING* FOR FURTHER INSTRUCTIONS....

RIGHT.

RON, CONFIRMATIONS TO C, THE DC, AND THE FCO, AND STRESS TO ALL OF THEM THAT TWO OF THE HOSTAGES ARE OURS...

...LEX, TELL PARDUE TO GET LORING OUT BEATING THE BUSHES, I WANT A LINE ON WHO AND I WANT A LINE ON WHERE.

EVERY CONTACT, I DON'T CARE HOW SMALL. BRIBE THEM, THREATEN THEM, SEDUCE THEM, I DON'T CARE, GET US SOMETHING TO GO ON--

WILL! MAPS OF BAGHDAD, AADHAMIYAH DISTRICT!

--ANYTHING THEY PULL, THEY'RE TO REPORT IT HERE STRAIGHTAWAY. PARDUE IS TO KEEP THE LINE OPEN.

DUTY OPS OFFICER FOR C, MESSAGE FROM D-OPS...

I'LL HEAD BACK TO THE EMBASSY, SEE IF I CAN GET LANGLEY LOOPED IN...

YES, SIR.

...MINDERS ONE AND TWO ARE MIA IN BAGHDAD, BELIEVED KIDNAPPED...

...FROM D-OPS, REQUESTS YOUR STATION NUMBER TWO TO ACTIVATE ALL ASSETS, REGARDLESS OF PROFILE...

16:17 (LOCAL)
20:17 (ZONE)

--ESCORT FOR MS. CHENG, PLEASE...

Operation: RED PANDA
Status: COMPLETE

I WANT FLIGHTS.

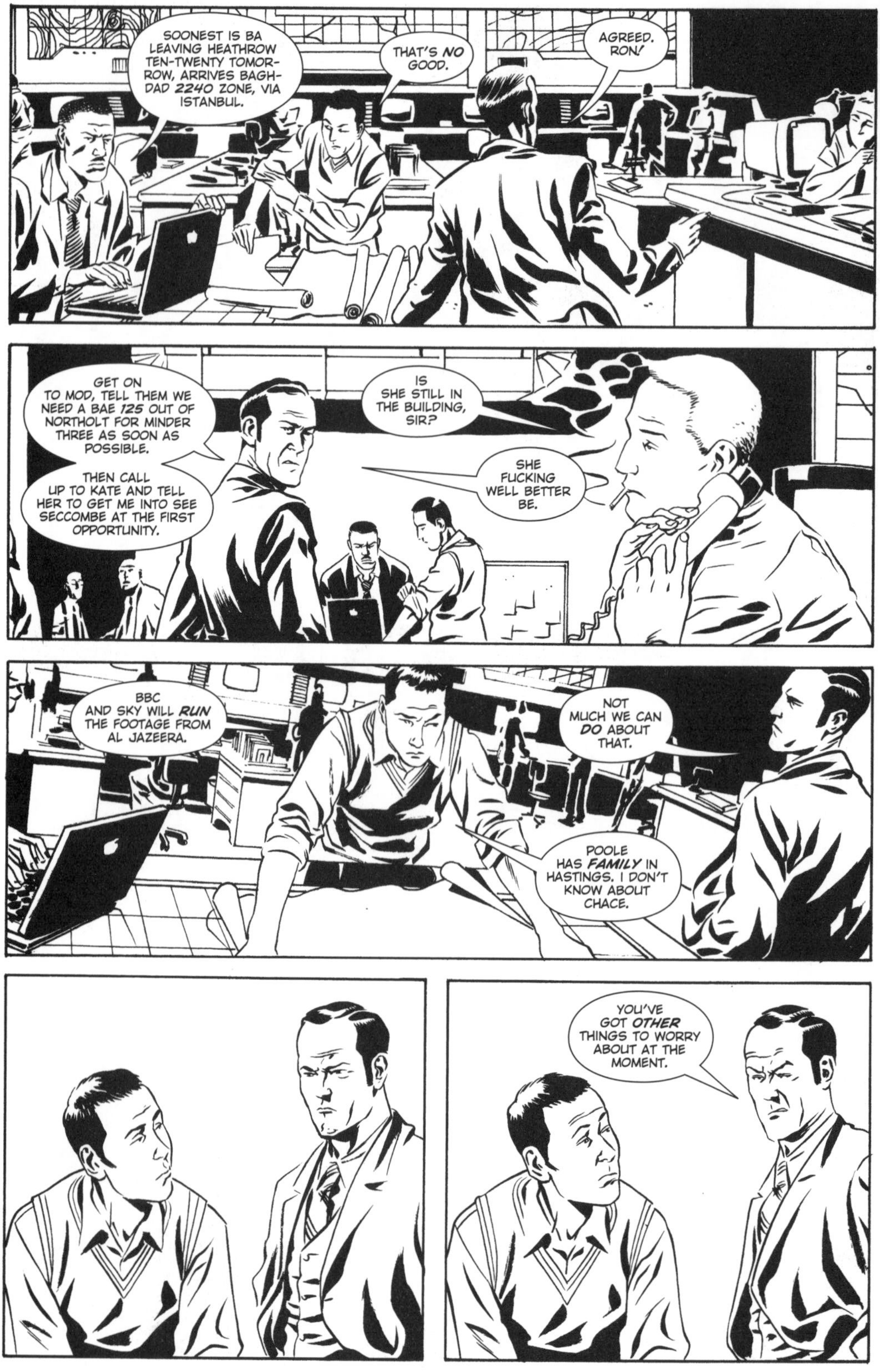
SOONEST IS BA LEAVING HEATHROW TEN-TWENTY TOMORROW, ARRIVES BAGHDAD 2240 ZONE, VIA ISTANBUL.
THAT'S *NO* GOOD.
AGREED. RON!
GET ON TO MOD, TELL THEM WE NEED A BAE 125 OUT OF NORTHOLT FOR MINDER THREE AS SOON AS POSSIBLE.
THEN CALL UP TO KATE AND TELL HER TO GET ME INTO SEE SECCOMBE AT THE FIRST OPPORTUNITY.
IS SHE STILL IN THE BUILDING, SIR?
SHE FUCKING WELL BETTER BE.
BBC AND SKY WILL *RUN* THE FOOTAGE FROM AL JAZEERA.
NOT MUCH WE CAN *DO* ABOUT THAT.
POOLE HAS *FAMILY* IN HASTINGS. I DON'T KNOW ABOUT CHACE.
YOU'VE GOT *OTHER* THINGS TO WORRY ABOUT AT THE MOMENT.

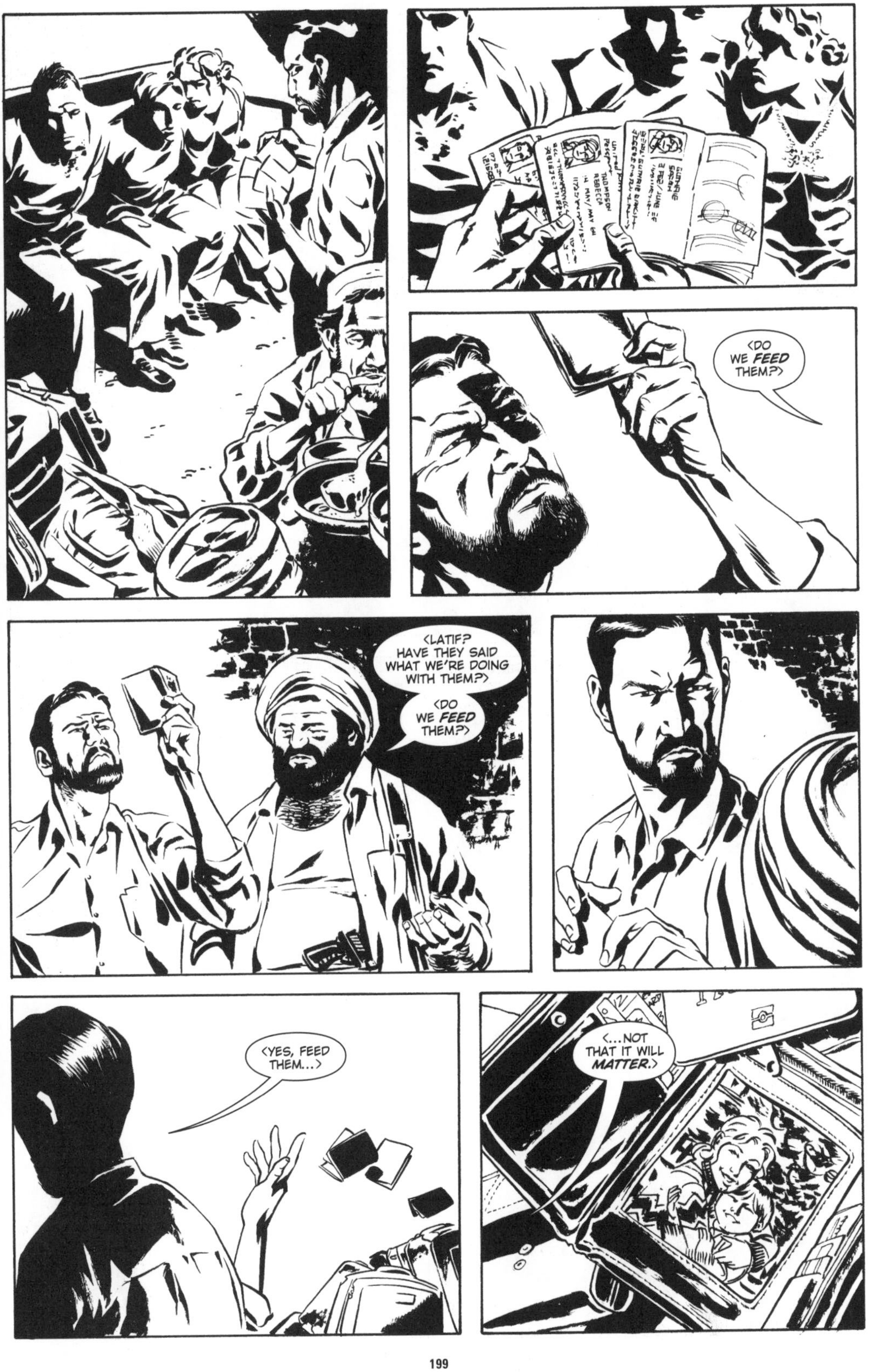
<DO WE FEED THEM?>
<LATIF? HAVE THEY SAID WHAT WE'RE DOING WITH THEM?>
<DO WE FEED THEM?>
<YES, FEED THEM...>
<...NOT THAT IT WILL MATTER.>

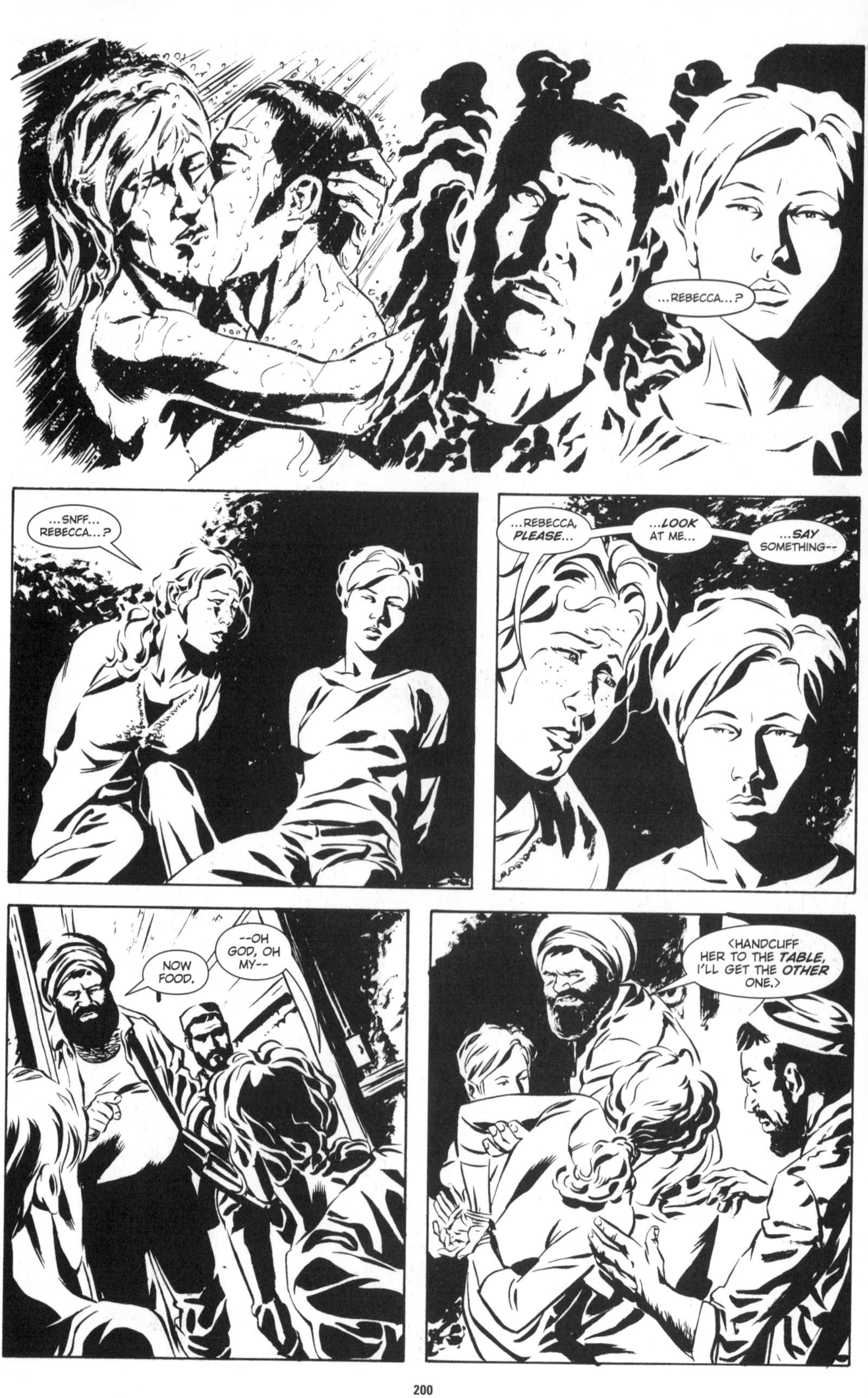
...REBECCA...?
...SNFF... REBECCA...?
...REBECCA, PLEASE...
...LOOK AT ME...
...SAY SOMETHING--
NOW FOOD.
--OH GOD, OH MY--
<HANDCUFF HER TO THE TABLE, I'LL GET THE OTHER ONE.>

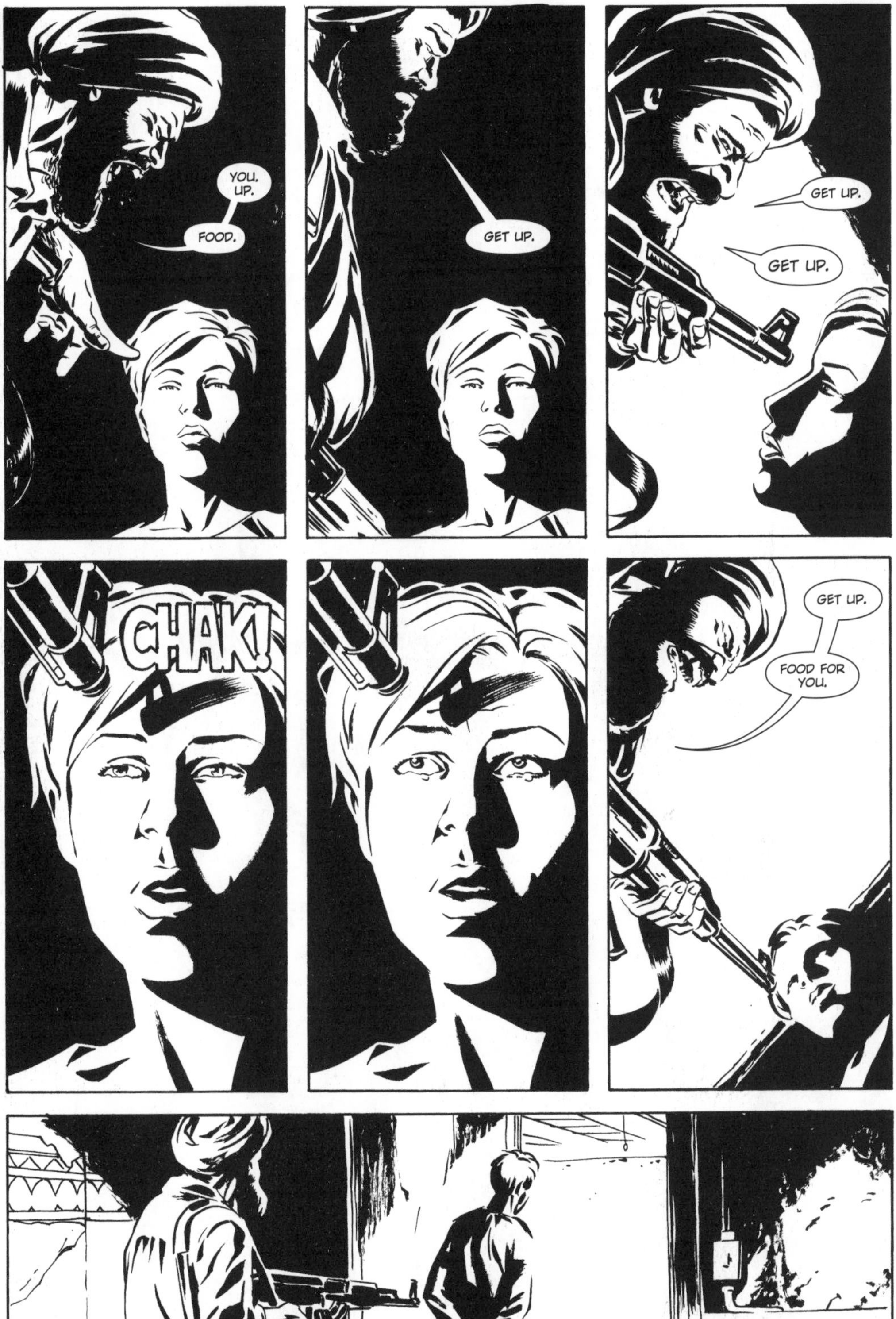
YOU. UP.
FOOD.
GET UP.
GET UP.
GET UP.
CHAK!
GET UP.
FOOD FOR YOU.

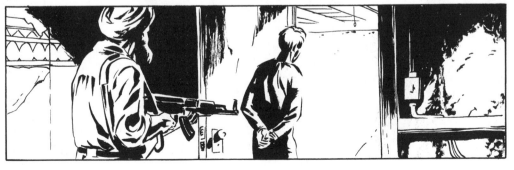

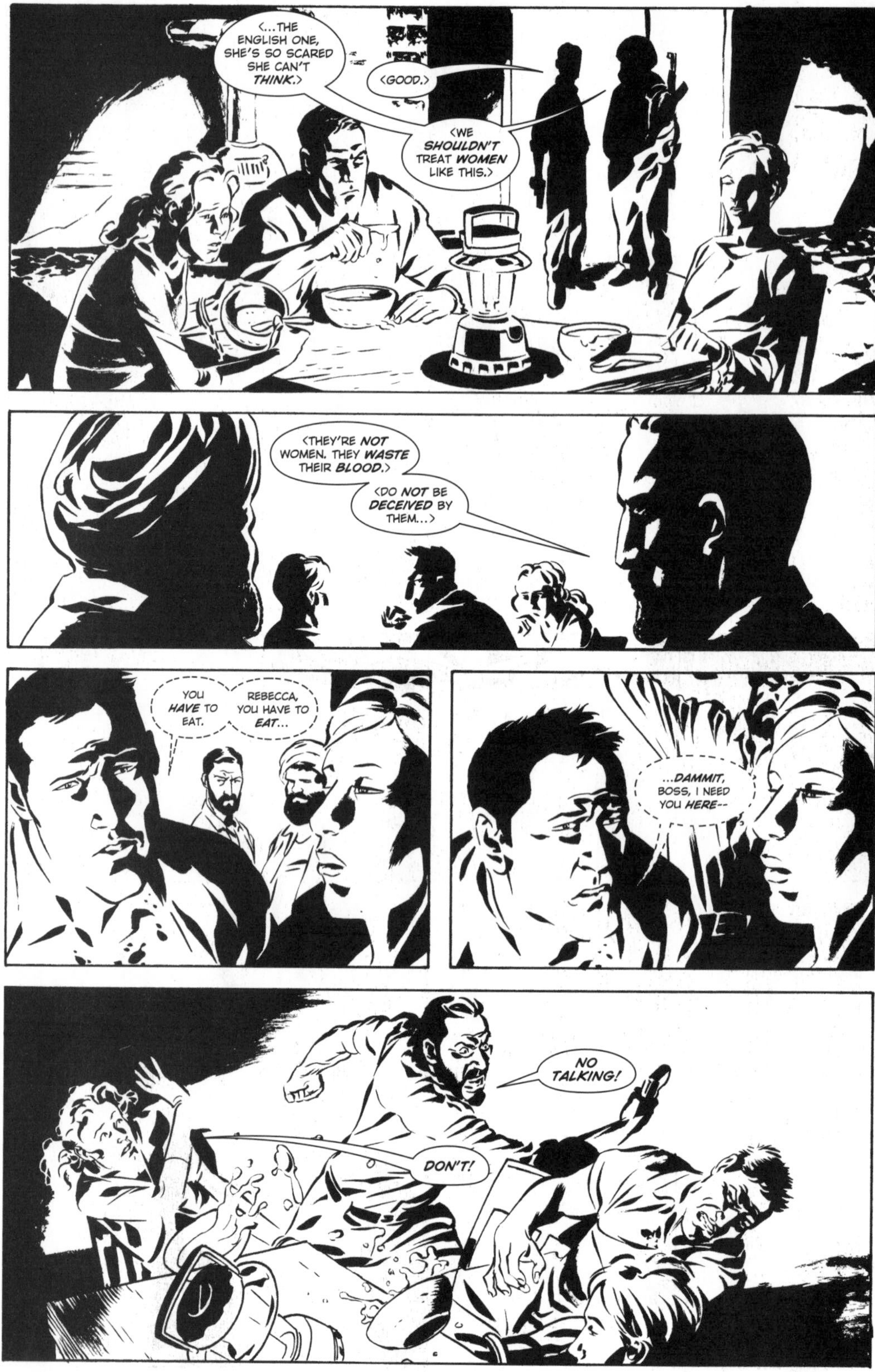
<...THE ENGLISH ONE, SHE'S SO SCARED SHE CAN'T THINK.>
<GOOD.>
<WE SHOULDN'T TREAT WOMEN LIKE THIS.>
<THEY'RE NOT WOMEN. THEY WASTE THEIR BLOOD.>
<DO NOT BE DECEIVED BY THEM...>
YOU HAVE TO EAT.
REBECCA, YOU HAVE TO EAT...
...DAMMIT, BOSS, I NEED YOU HERE--
NO TALKING!
DON'T!

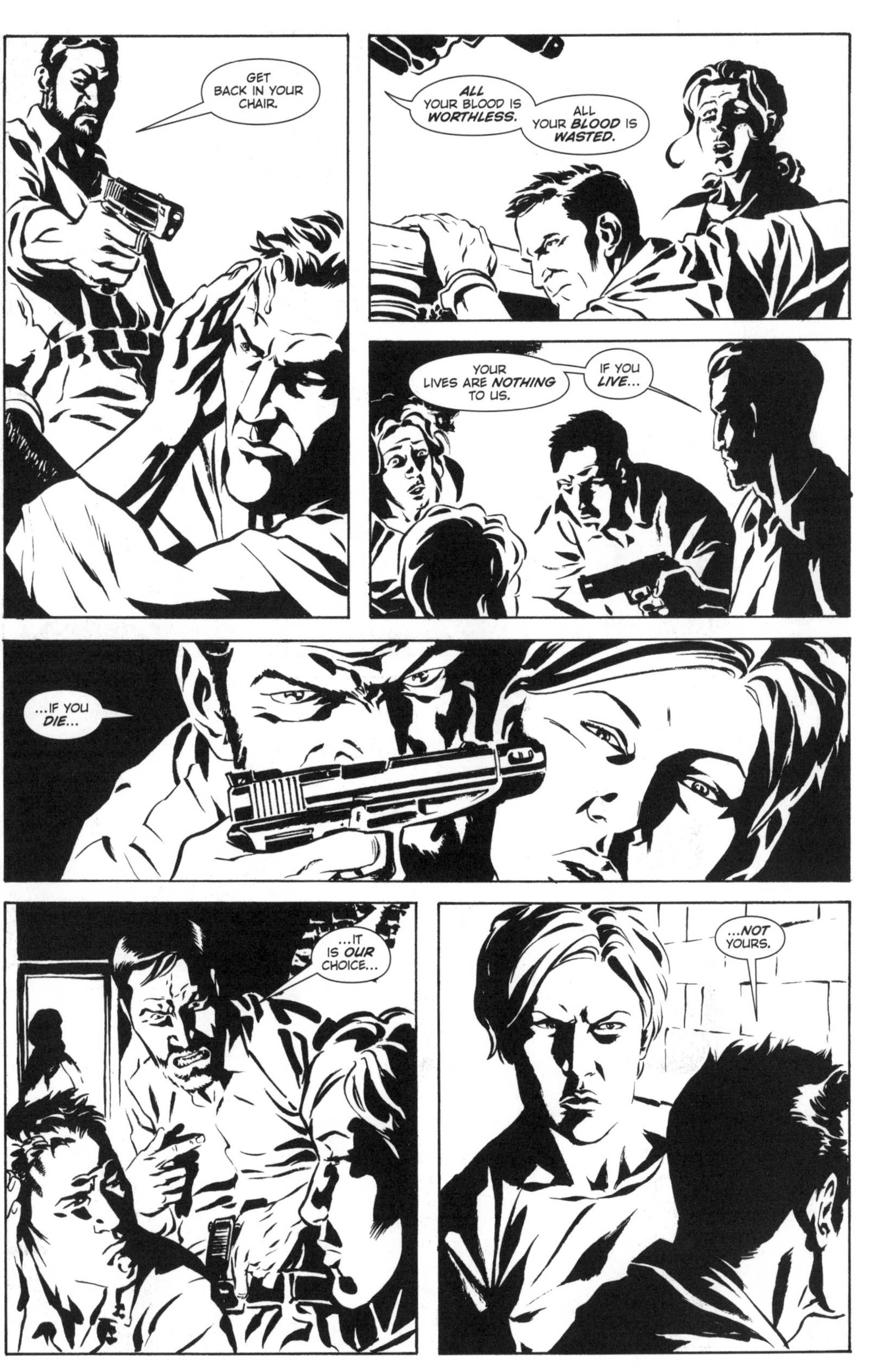
GET BACK IN YOUR CHAIR.
ALL YOUR BLOOD IS WORTHLESS.
ALL YOUR BLOOD IS WASTED.
YOUR LIVES ARE NOTHING TO US.
IF YOU LIVE...
...IF YOU DIE...
...IT IS OUR CHOICE...
...NOT YOURS.

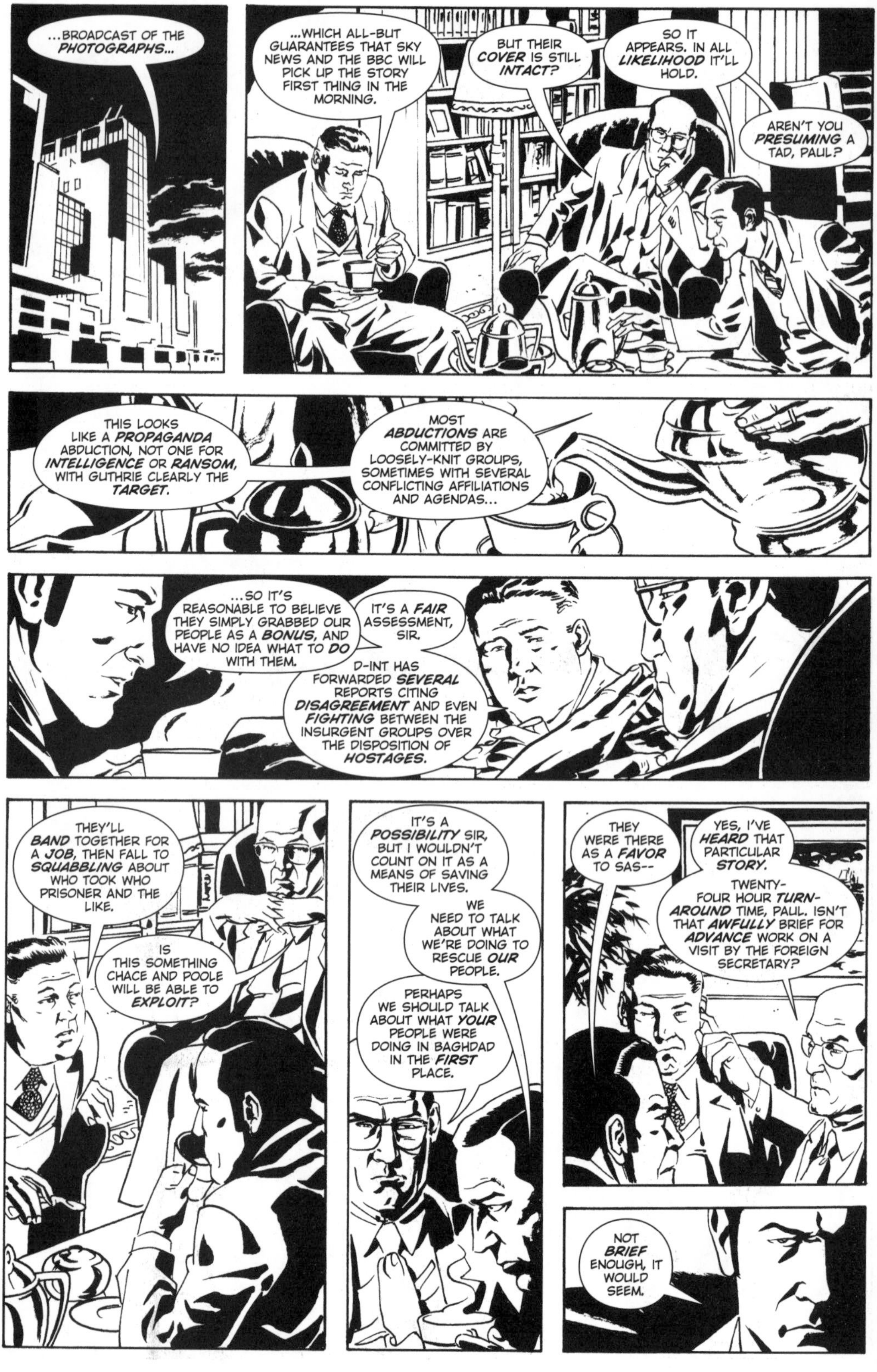
...BROADCAST OF THE PHOTOGRAPHS...
...WHICH ALL-BUT GUARANTEES THAT SKY NEWS AND THE BBC WILL PICK UP THE STORY FIRST THING IN THE MORNING.
BUT THEIR COVER IS STILL INTACT?
SO IT APPEARS. IN ALL LIKELIHOOD IT'LL HOLD.
AREN'T YOU PRESUMING A TAD, PAUL?
THIS LOOKS LIKE A PROPAGANDA ABDUCTION, NOT ONE FOR INTELLIGENCE OR RANSOM, WITH GUTHRIE CLEARLY THE TARGET.
MOST ABDUCTIONS ARE COMMITTED BY LOOSELY-KNIT GROUPS, SOMETIMES WITH SEVERAL CONFLICTING AFFILIATIONS AND AGENDAS...
...SO IT'S REASONABLE TO BELIEVE THEY SIMPLY GRABBED OUR PEOPLE AS A BONUS, AND HAVE NO IDEA WHAT TO DO WITH THEM.
IT'S A FAIR ASSESSMENT, SIR.
D-INT HAS FORWARDED SEVERAL REPORTS CITING DISAGREEMENT AND EVEN FIGHTING BETWEEN THE INSURGENT GROUPS OVER THE DISPOSITION OF HOSTAGES.
THEY'LL BAND TOGETHER FOR A JOB, THEN FALL TO SQUABBLING ABOUT WHO TOOK WHO PRISONER AND THE LIKE.
IS THIS SOMETHING CHACE AND POOLE WILL BE ABLE TO EXPLOIT?
IT'S A POSSIBILITY SIR, BUT I WOULDN'T COUNT ON IT AS A MEANS OF SAVING THEIR LIVES.
WE NEED TO TALK ABOUT WHAT WE'RE DOING TO RESCUE OUR PEOPLE.
PERHAPS WE SHOULD TALK ABOUT WHAT YOUR PEOPLE WERE DOING IN BAGHDAD IN THE FIRST PLACE.
THEY WERE THERE AS A FAVOR TO SAS--
YES, I'VE HEARD THAT PARTICULAR STORY.
TWENTY-FOUR HOUR TURN-AROUND TIME, PAUL. ISN'T THAT AWFULLY BRIEF FOR ADVANCE WORK ON A VISIT BY THE FOREIGN SECRETARY?
NOT BRIEF ENOUGH, IT WOULD SEEM.

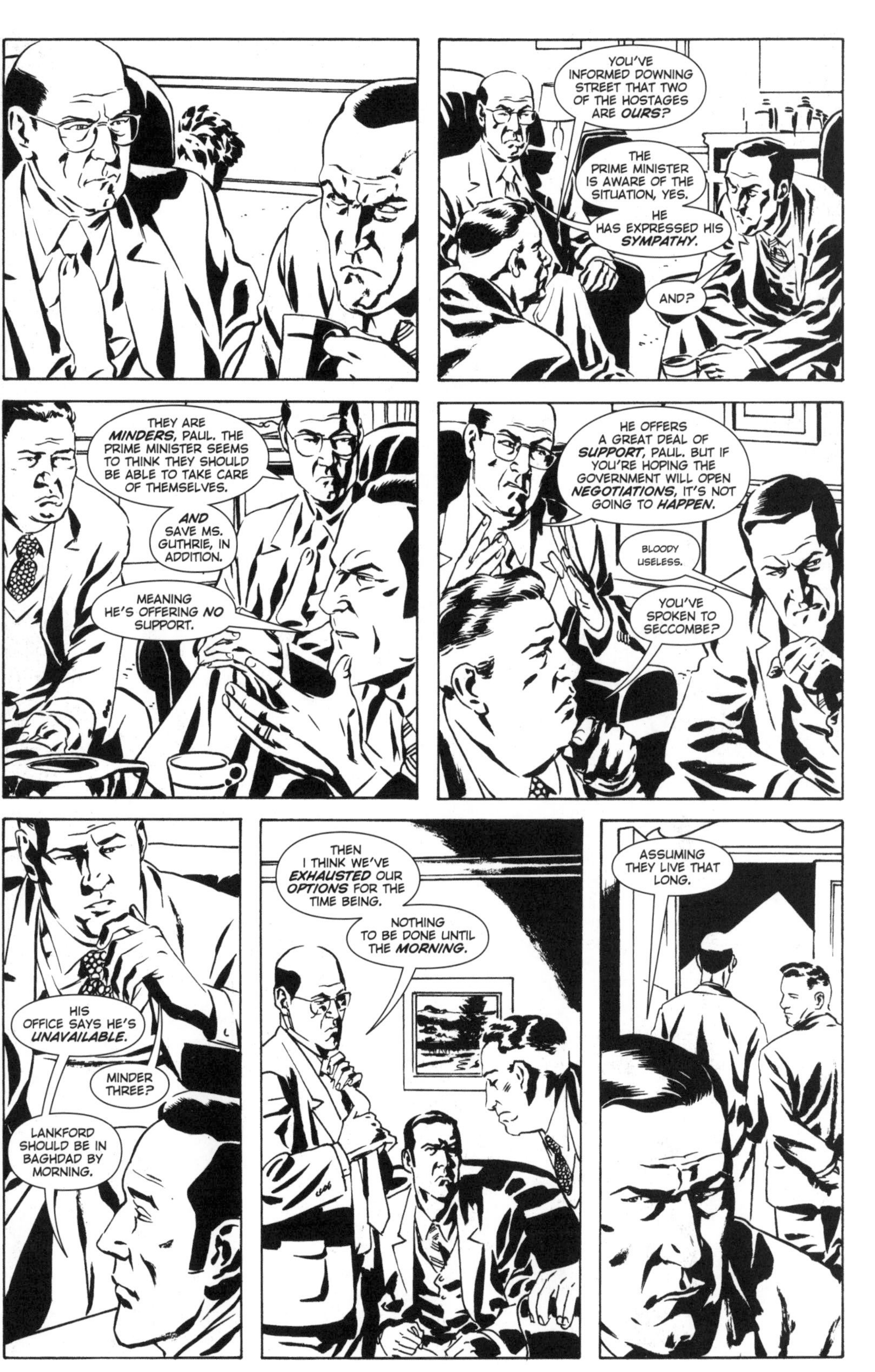
YOU'VE INFORMED DOWNING STREET THAT TWO OF THE HOSTAGES ARE *OURS?*
THE PRIME MINISTER IS AWARE OF THE SITUATION, YES.
HE HAS EXPRESSED HIS *SYMPATHY.*
AND?
THEY ARE *MINDERS*, PAUL. THE PRIME MINISTER SEEMS TO THINK THEY SHOULD BE ABLE TO TAKE CARE OF THEMSELVES.
AND SAVE MS. GUTHRIE, IN ADDITION.
MEANING HE'S OFFERING *NO* SUPPORT.
HE OFFERS A GREAT DEAL OF *SUPPORT*, PAUL. BUT IF YOU'RE HOPING THE GOVERNMENT WILL OPEN *NEGOTIATIONS*, IT'S NOT GOING TO *HAPPEN.*
BLOODY USELESS.
YOU'VE SPOKEN TO SECCOMBE?
HIS OFFICE SAYS HE'S *UNAVAILABLE.*
MINDER THREE?
LANKFORD SHOULD BE IN BAGHDAD BY MORNING.
THEN I THINK WE'VE *EXHAUSTED* OUR *OPTIONS* FOR THE TIME BEING.
NOTHING TO BE DONE UNTIL THE *MORNING.*
ASSUMING THEY LIVE THAT LONG.

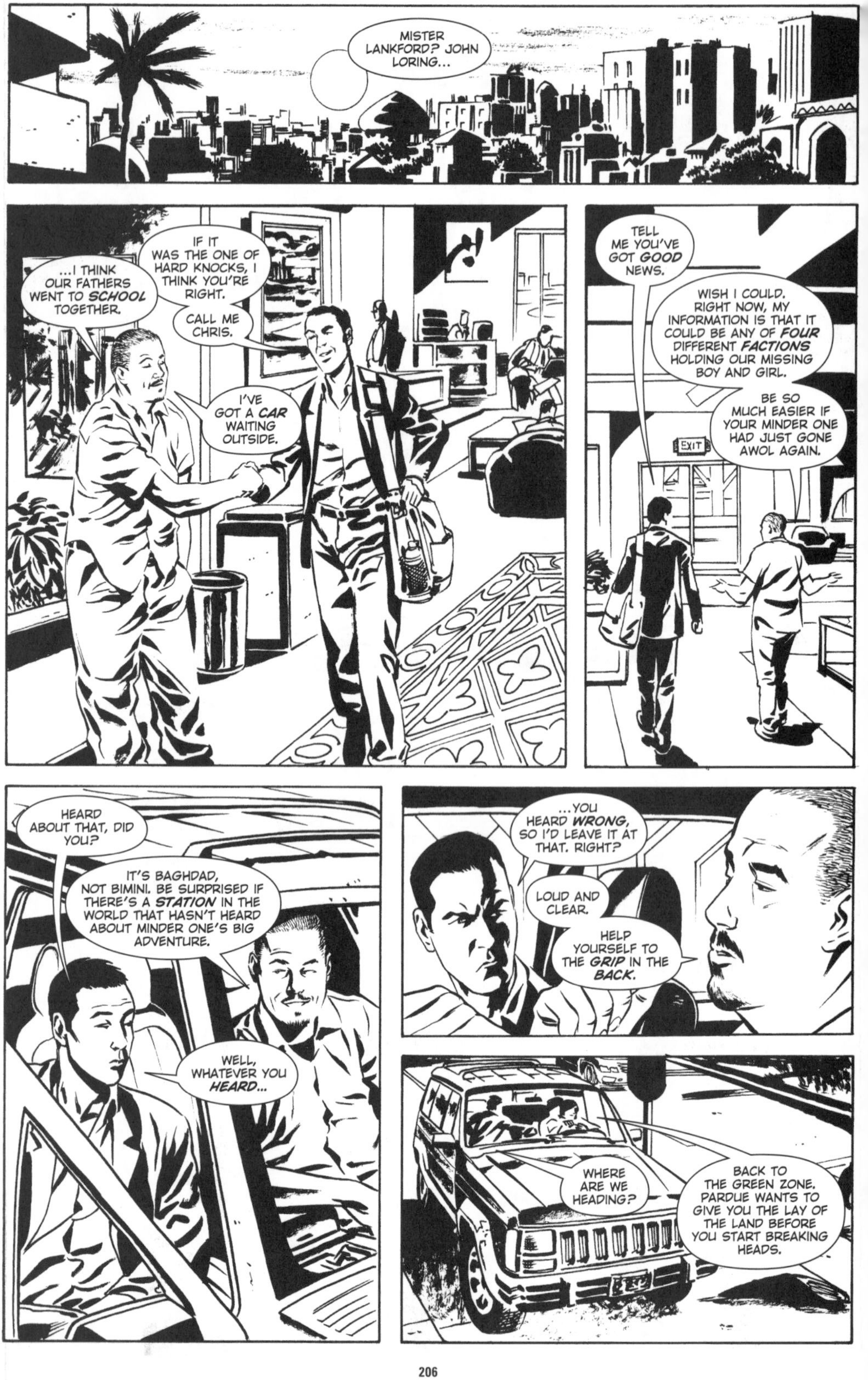
MISTER LANKFORD? JOHN LORING...
...I THINK OUR FATHERS WENT TO SCHOOL TOGETHER.
IF IT WAS THE ONE OF HARD KNOCKS, I THINK YOU'RE RIGHT.
CALL ME CHRIS.
I'VE GOT A CAR WAITING OUTSIDE.
TELL ME YOU'VE GOT GOOD NEWS.
WISH I COULD. RIGHT NOW, MY INFORMATION IS THAT IT COULD BE ANY OF FOUR DIFFERENT FACTIONS HOLDING OUR MISSING BOY AND GIRL.
BE SO MUCH EASIER IF YOUR MINDER ONE HAD JUST GONE AWOL AGAIN.
EXIT
HEARD ABOUT THAT, DID YOU?
IT'S BAGHDAD, NOT BIMINI. BE SURPRISED IF THERE'S A STATION IN THE WORLD THAT HASN'T HEARD ABOUT MINDER ONE'S BIG ADVENTURE.
WELL, WHATEVER YOU HEARD...
...YOU HEARD WRONG, SO I'D LEAVE IT AT THAT. RIGHT?
LOUD AND CLEAR.
HELP YOURSELF TO THE GRIP IN THE BACK.
WHERE ARE WE HEADING?
BACK TO THE GREEN ZONE. PARDUE WANTS TO GIVE YOU THE LAY OF THE LAND BEFORE YOU START BREAKING HEADS.

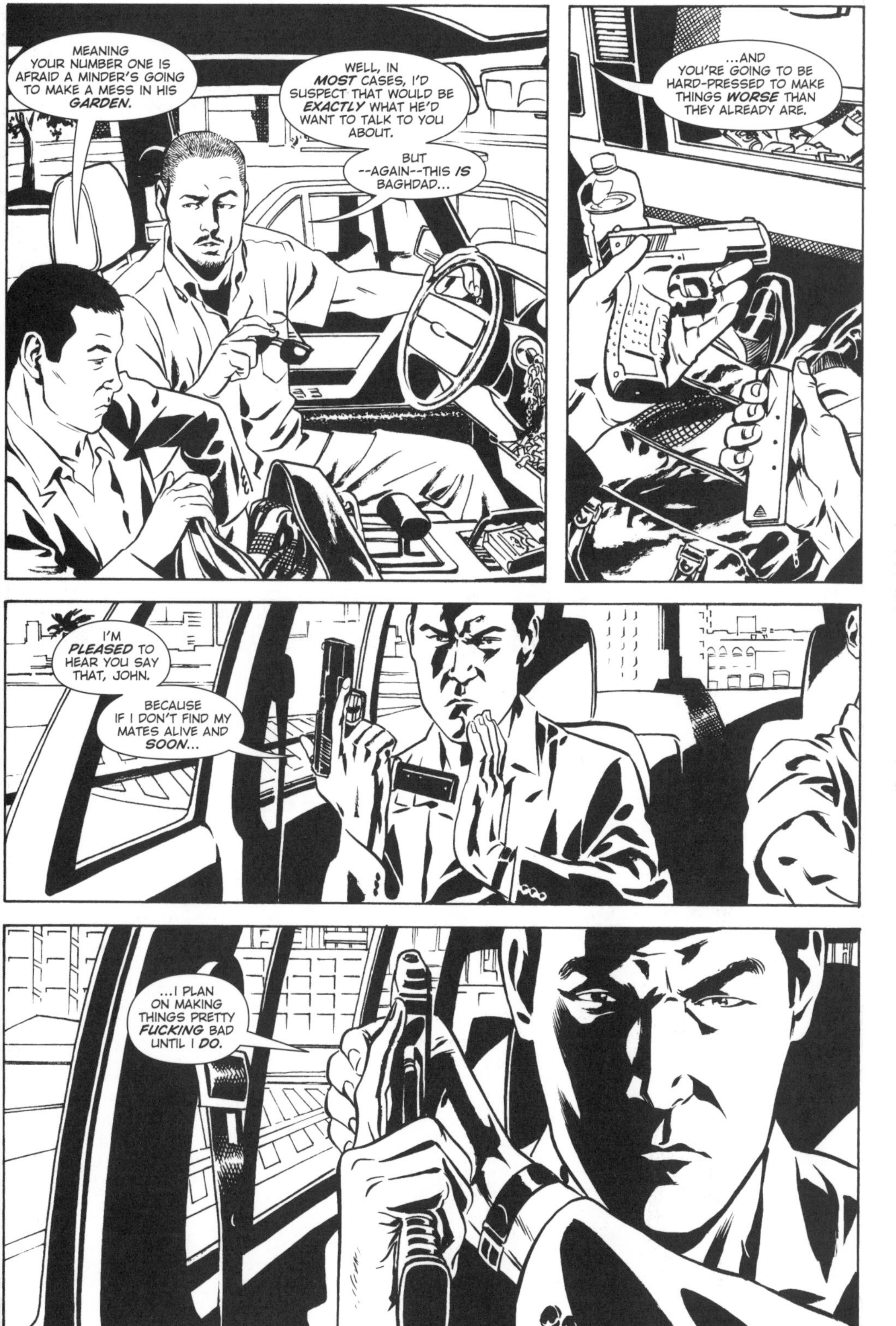
MEANING YOUR NUMBER ONE IS AFRAID A MINDER'S GOING TO MAKE A MESS IN HIS GARDEN.
WELL, IN MOST CASES, I'D SUSPECT THAT WOULD BE EXACTLY WHAT HE'D WANT TO TALK TO YOU ABOUT.
BUT --AGAIN--THIS IS BAGHDAD...
...AND YOU'RE GOING TO BE HARD-PRESSED TO MAKE THINGS WORSE THAN THEY ALREADY ARE.
I'M PLEASED TO HEAR YOU SAY THAT, JOHN.
BECAUSE IF I DON'T FIND MY MATES ALIVE AND SOON...
...I PLAN ON MAKING THINGS PRETTY FUCKING BAD UNTIL I DO.

CHAPTER 3

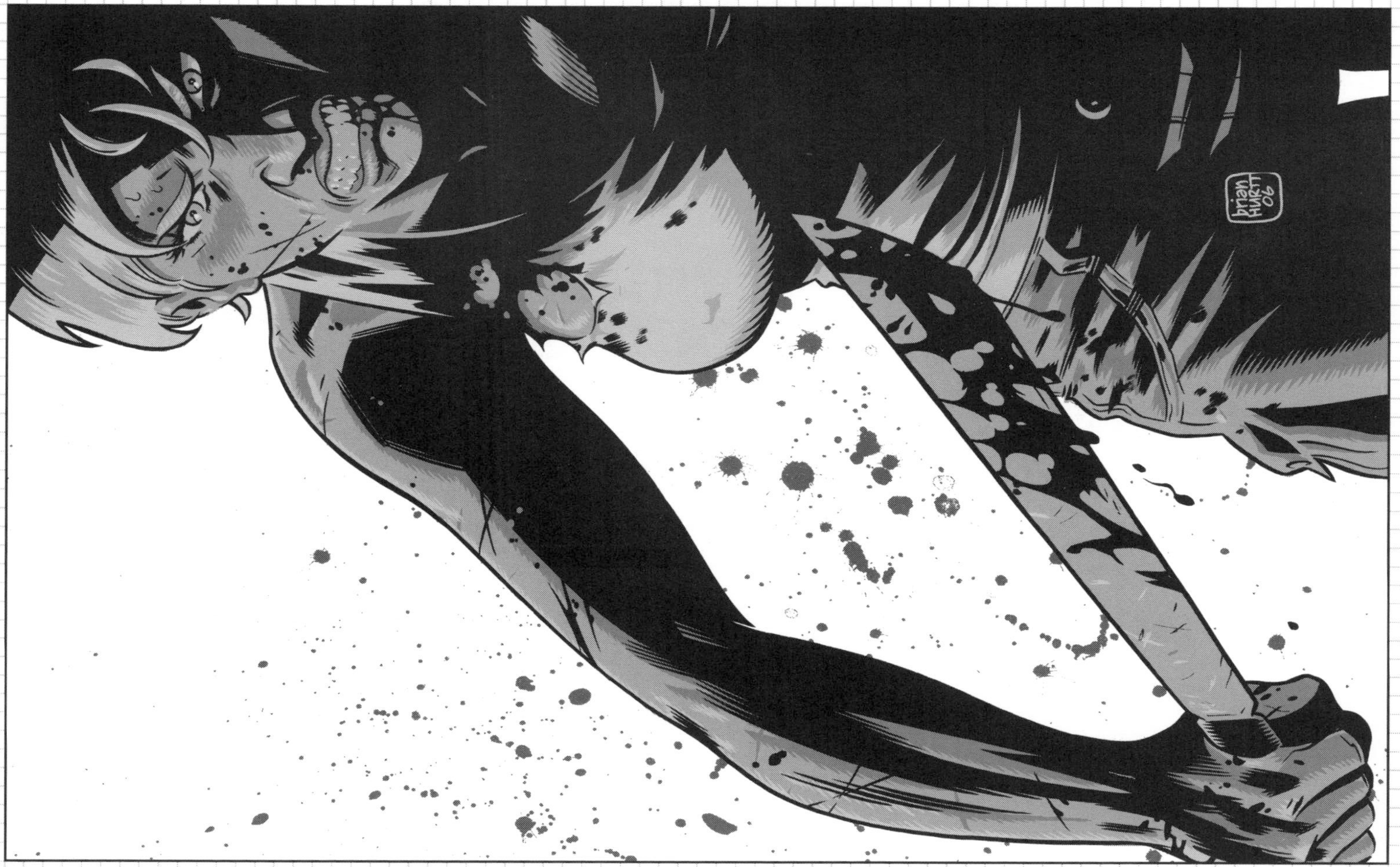
brian HURTT 06

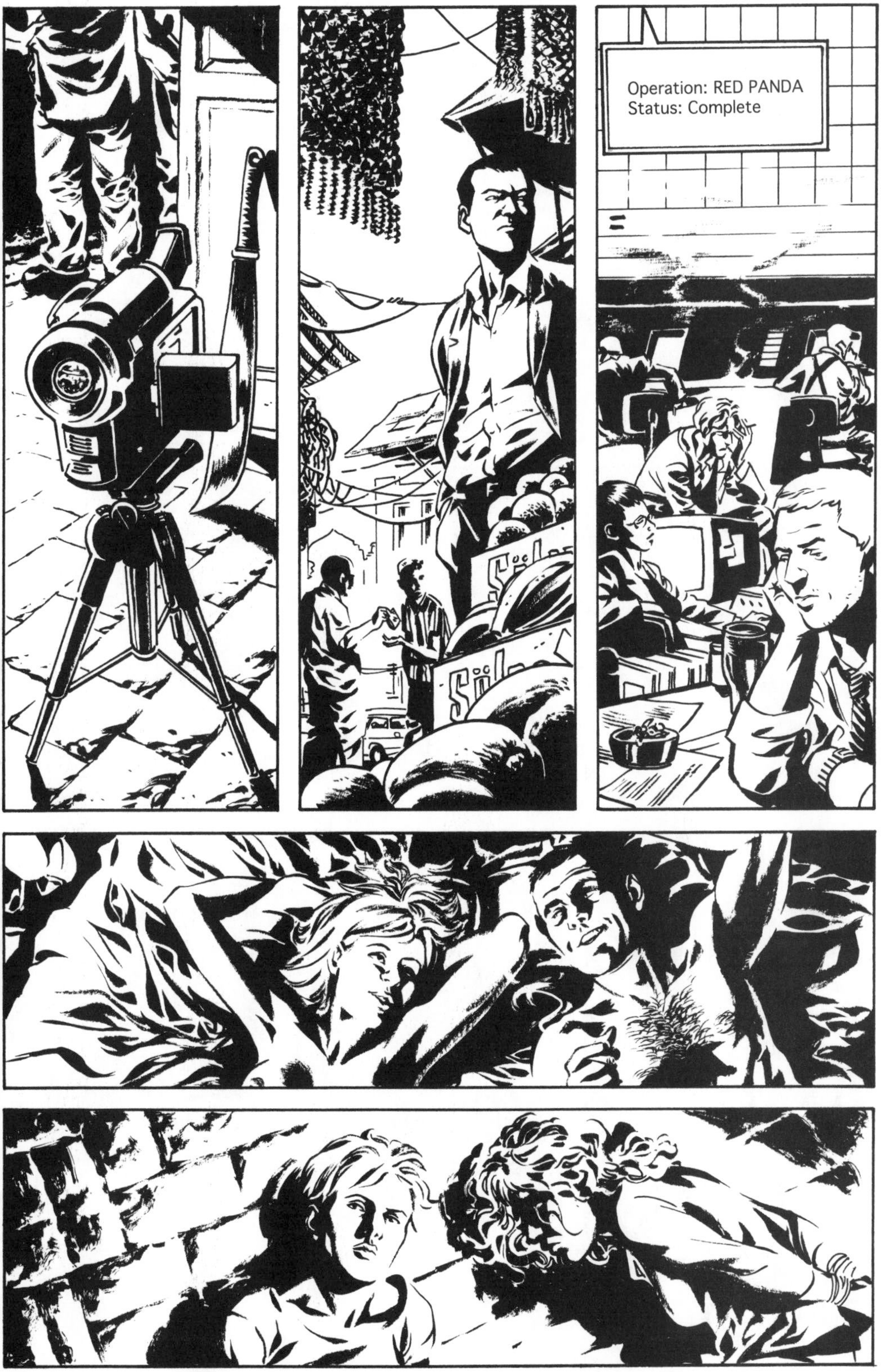
Operation: RED PANDA
Status: Complete

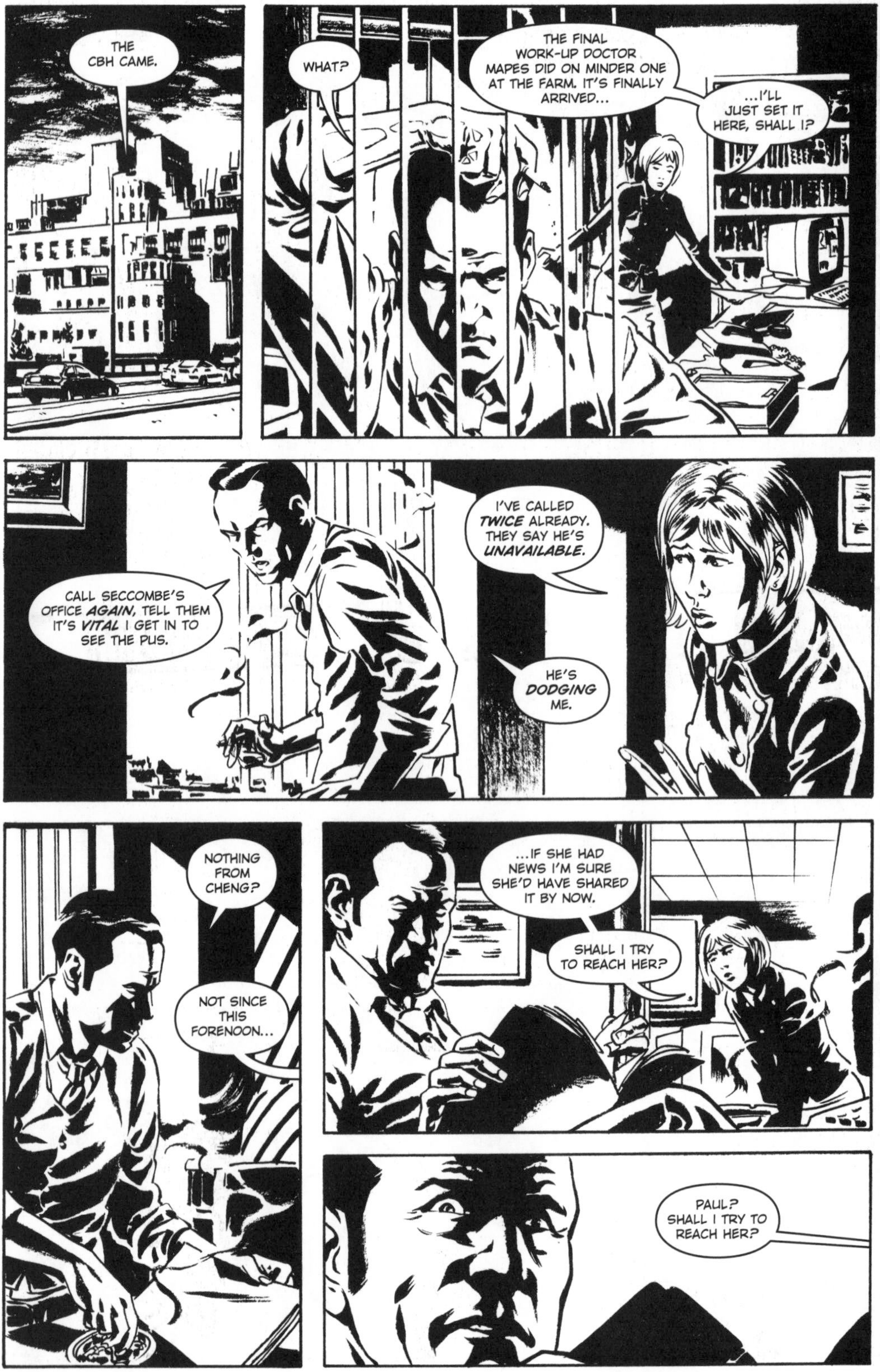
THE CBH CAME.
WHAT?
THE FINAL WORK-UP DOCTOR MAPES DID ON MINDER ONE AT THE FARM. IT'S FINALLY ARRIVED...
...I'LL JUST SET IT HERE, SHALL I?
CALL SECCOMBE'S OFFICE *AGAIN*, TELL THEM IT'S *VITAL* I GET IN TO SEE THE PUS.
I'VE CALLED *TWICE* ALREADY. THEY SAY HE'S *UNAVAILABLE*.
HE'S *DODGING* ME.
NOTHING FROM CHENG?
NOT SINCE THIS FORENOON...
...IF SHE HAD NEWS I'M SURE SHE'D HAVE SHARED IT BY NOW.
SHALL I TRY TO REACH HER?
PAUL? SHALL I TRY TO REACH HER?

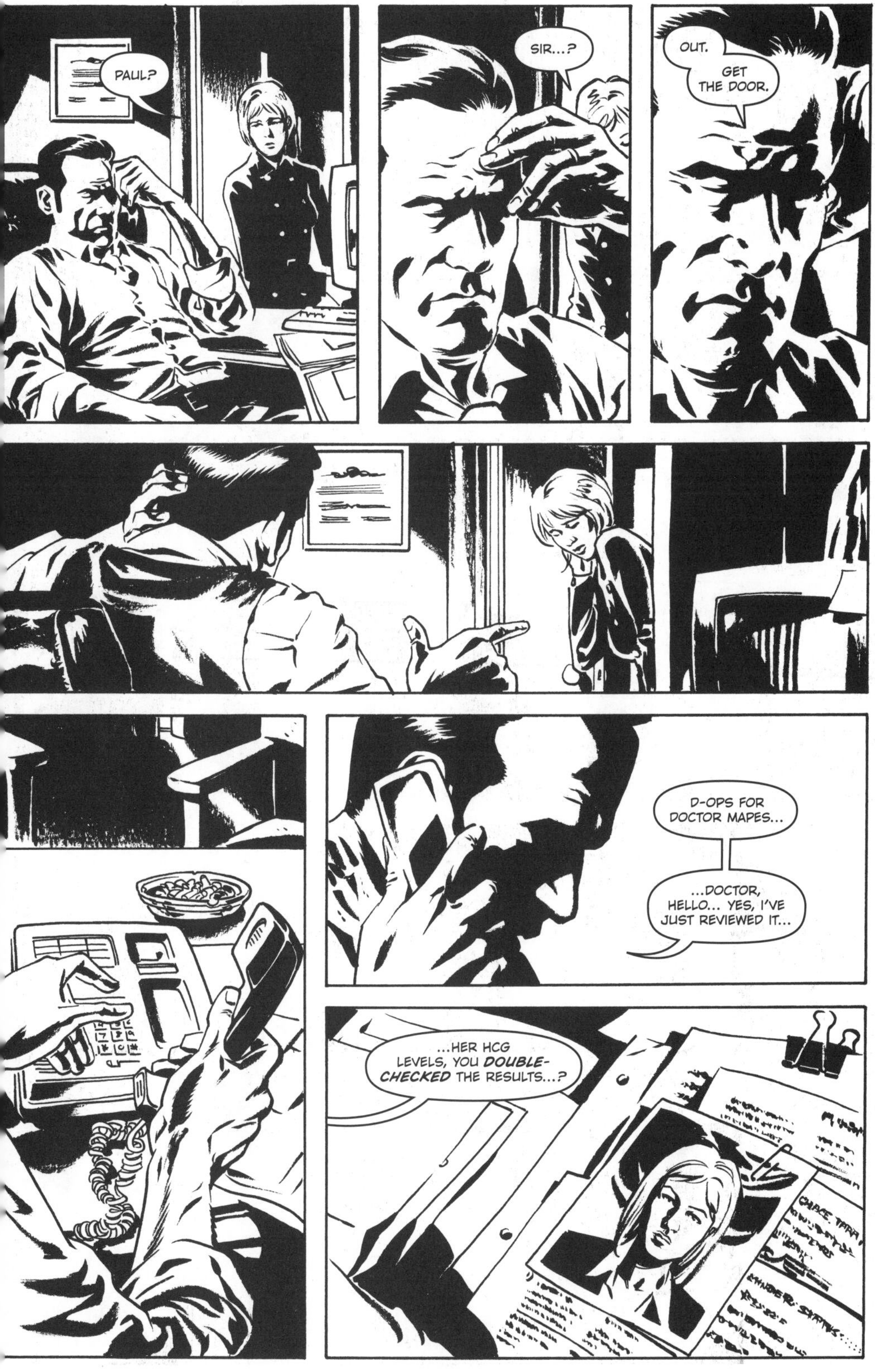
PAUL?
SIR...?
OUT.
GET THE DOOR.
D-OPS FOR DOCTOR MAPES...
...DOCTOR, HELLO... YES, I'VE JUST REVIEWED IT...
...HER HCG LEVELS, YOU ***DOUBLE-CHECKED*** THE RESULTS...?

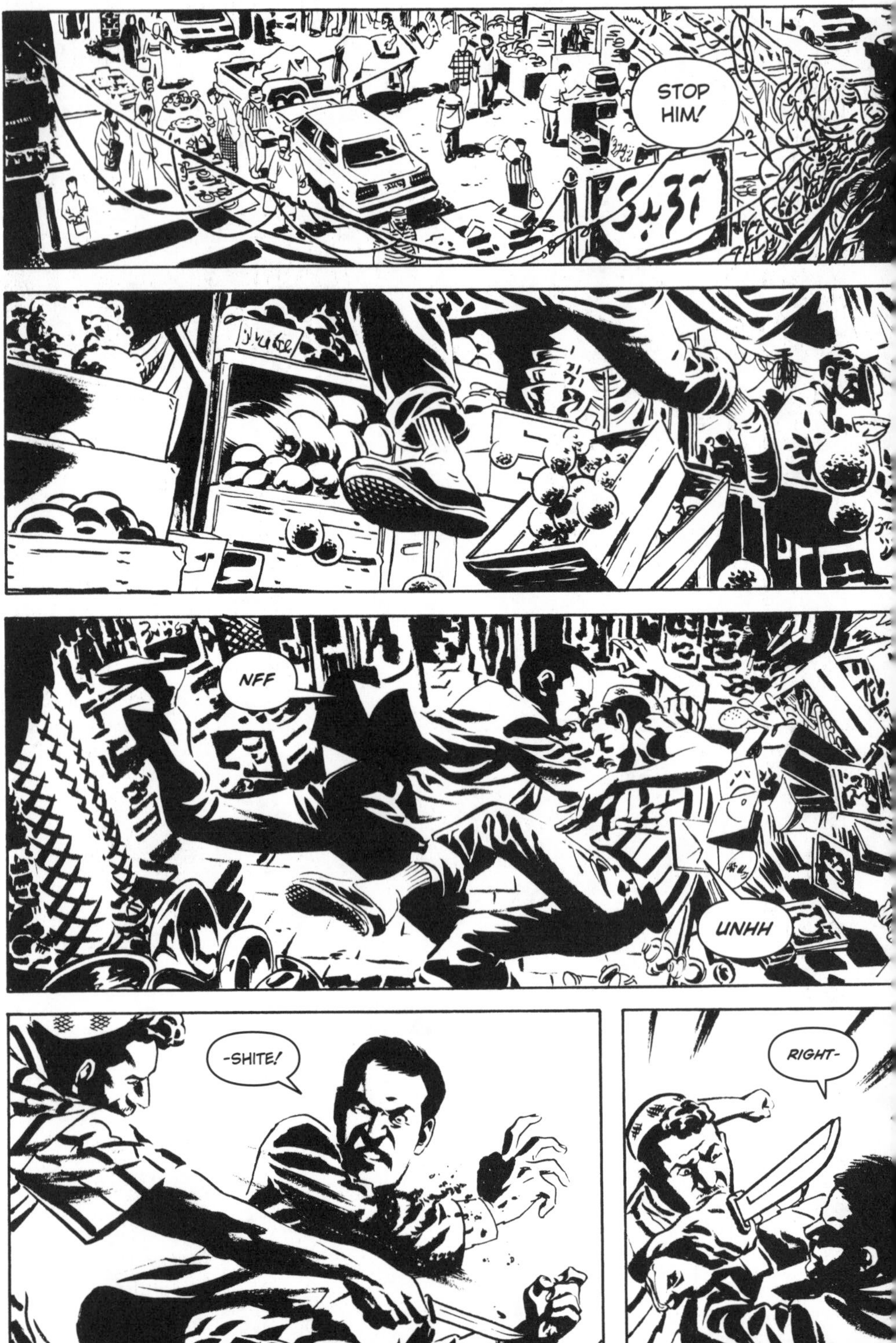
STOP HIM!
NFF
UNHH
-SHITE!
RIGHT-

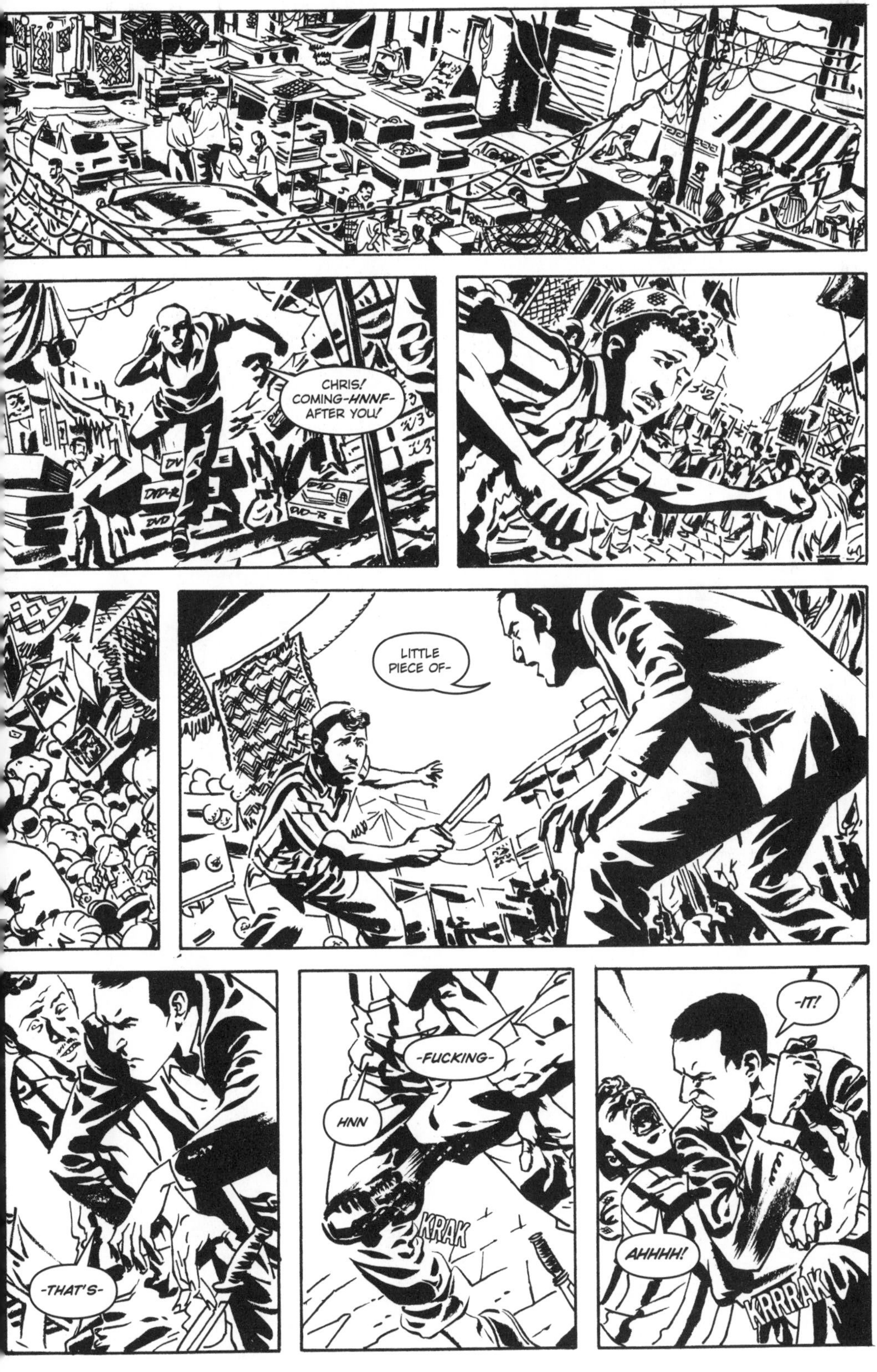
CHRIS! COMING-HNNF- AFTER YOU!
LITTLE PIECE OF-
-THAT'S-
-FUCKING-
HNN
KRAK
-IT!
AHHHH!
KRRRAK

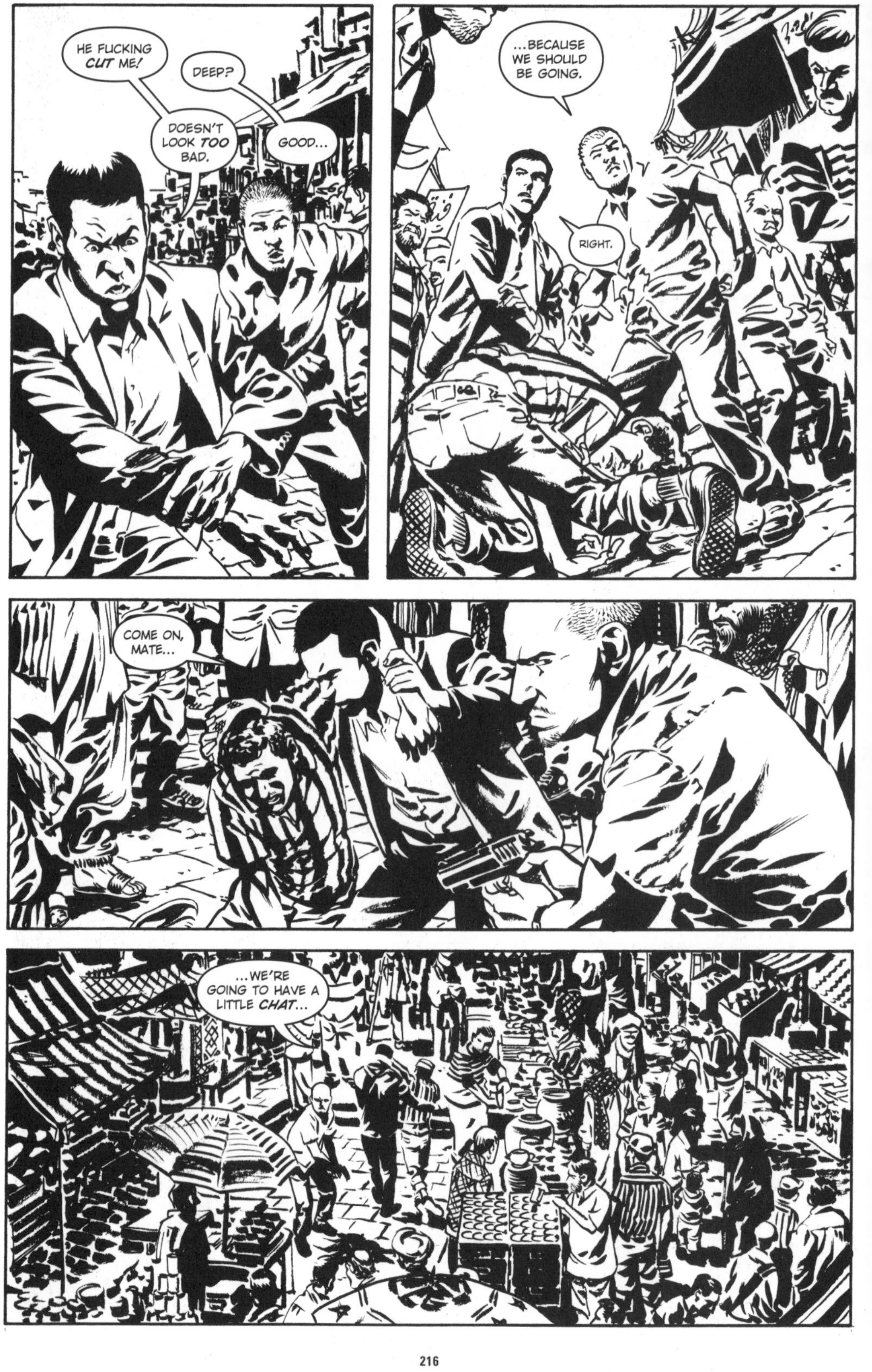
HE FUCKING *CUT* ME!
DEEP?
DOESN'T LOOK *TOO* BAD.
GOOD...
...BECAUSE WE SHOULD BE GOING.
RIGHT.
COME ON, MATE...
...WE'RE GOING TO HAVE A LITTLE *CHAT*...

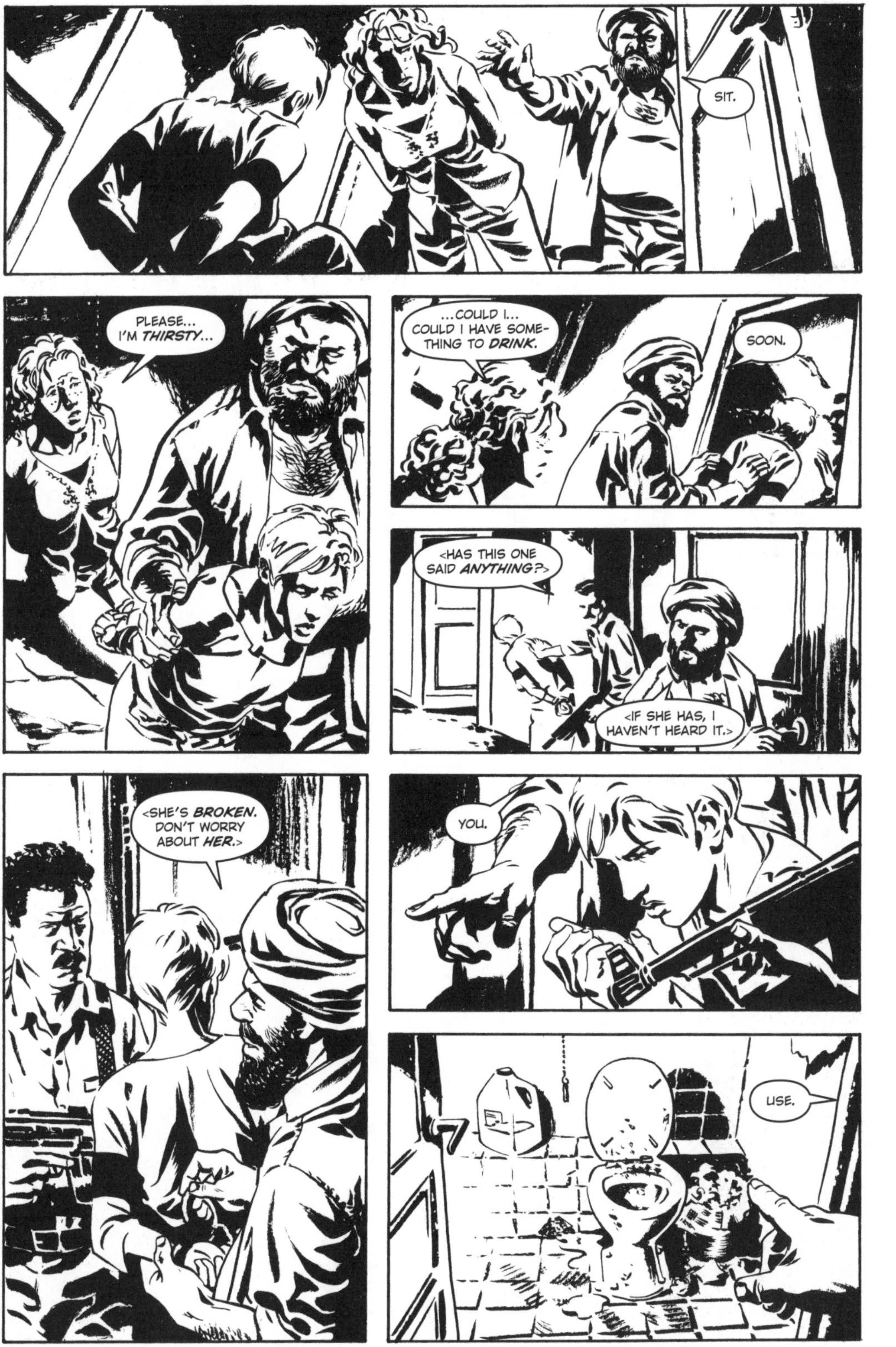
SIT.
PLEASE... I'M *THIRSTY*...
...COULD I... COULD I HAVE SOME-THING TO *DRINK*.
SOON.
<HAS THIS ONE SAID *ANYTHING*?>
<IF SHE HAS, I HAVEN'T HEARD IT.>
<SHE'S *BROKEN*. DON'T WORRY ABOUT *HER*.>
YOU.
USE.

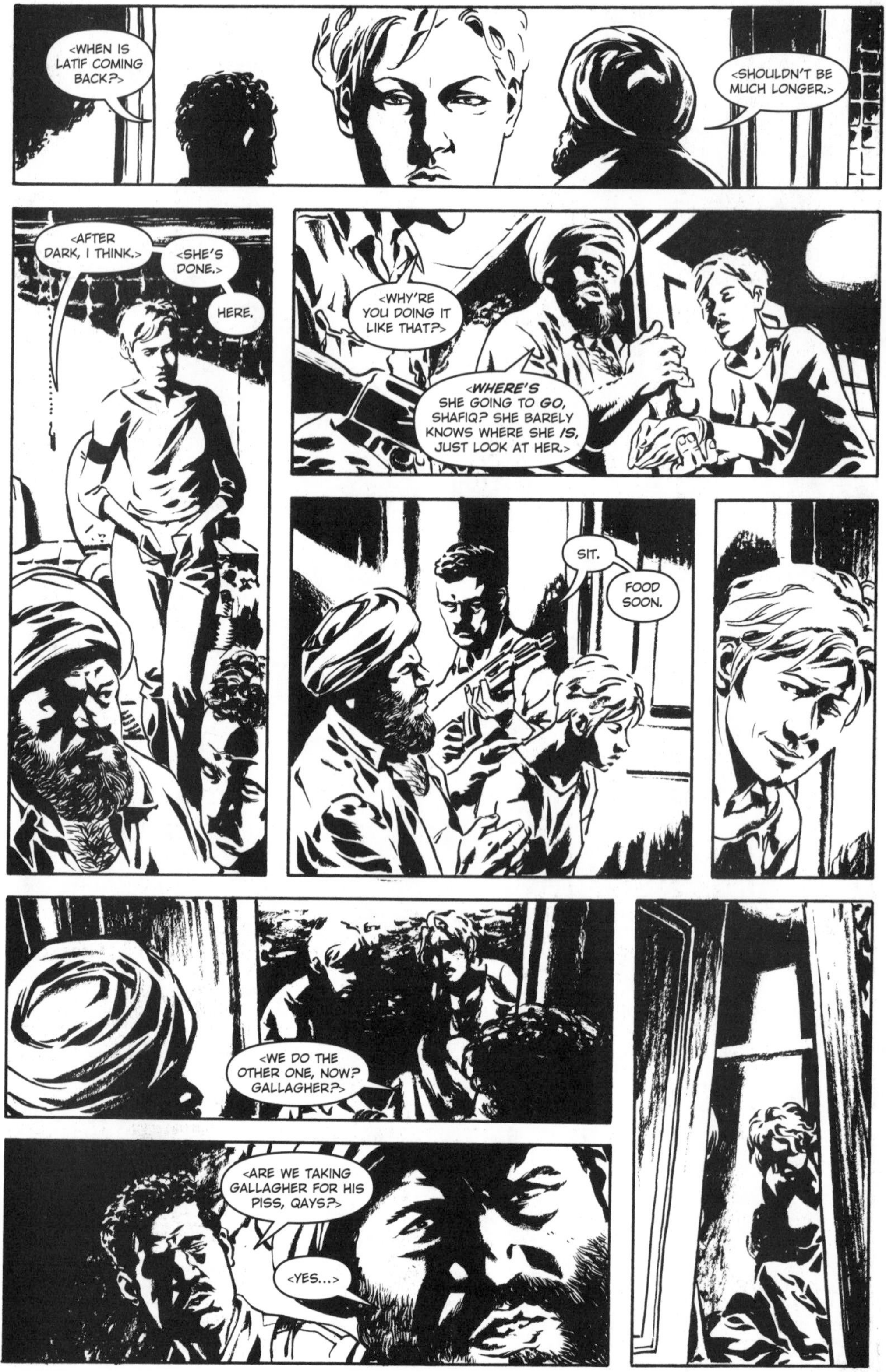
<WHEN IS LATIF COMING BACK?>
<SHOULDN'T BE MUCH LONGER.>
<AFTER DARK, I THINK.>
<SHE'S DONE.>
HERE.
<WHY'RE YOU DOING IT LIKE THAT?>
<*WHERE'S* SHE GOING TO *GO*, SHAFIQ? SHE BARELY KNOWS WHERE SHE *IS*, JUST LOOK AT HER.>
SIT.
FOOD SOON.
<WE DO THE OTHER ONE, NOW? GALLAGHER?>
<ARE WE TAKING GALLAGHER FOR HIS PISS, QAYS?>
<YES...>

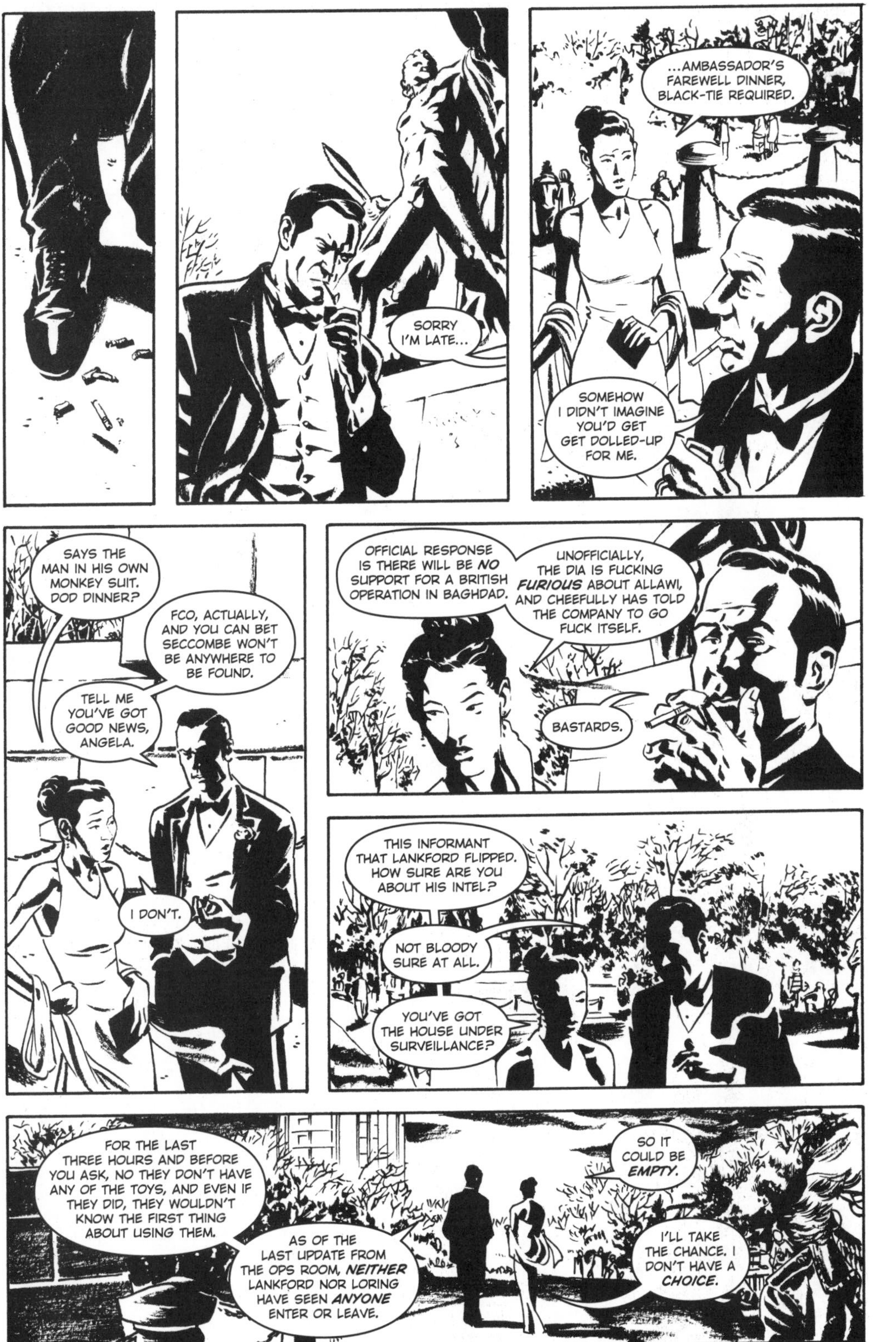
SORRY I'M LATE...
...AMBASSADOR'S FAREWELL DINNER, BLACK-TIE REQUIRED.
SOMEHOW I DIDN'T IMAGINE YOU'D GET GET DOLLED-UP FOR ME.
SAYS THE MAN IN HIS OWN MONKEY SUIT. DOD DINNER?
FCO, ACTUALLY, AND YOU CAN BET SECCOMBE WON'T BE ANYWHERE TO BE FOUND.
TELL ME YOU'VE GOT GOOD NEWS, ANGELA.
I DON'T.
OFFICIAL RESPONSE IS THERE WILL BE NO SUPPORT FOR A BRITISH OPERATION IN BAGHDAD.
UNOFFICIALLY, THE DIA IS FUCKING FURIOUS ABOUT ALLAWI, AND CHEEFULLY HAS TOLD THE COMPANY TO GO FUCK ITSELF.
BASTARDS.
THIS INFORMANT THAT LANKFORD FLIPPED. HOW SURE ARE YOU ABOUT HIS INTEL?
NOT BLOODY SURE AT ALL.
YOU'VE GOT THE HOUSE UNDER SURVEILLANCE?
FOR THE LAST THREE HOURS AND BEFORE YOU ASK, NO THEY DON'T HAVE ANY OF THE TOYS, AND EVEN IF THEY DID, THEY WOULDN'T KNOW THE FIRST THING ABOUT USING THEM.
AS OF THE LAST UPDATE FROM THE OPS ROOM, NEITHER LANKFORD NOR LORING HAVE SEEN ANYONE ENTER OR LEAVE.
SO IT COULD BE EMPTY.
I'LL TAKE THE CHANCE. I DON'T HAVE A CHOICE.

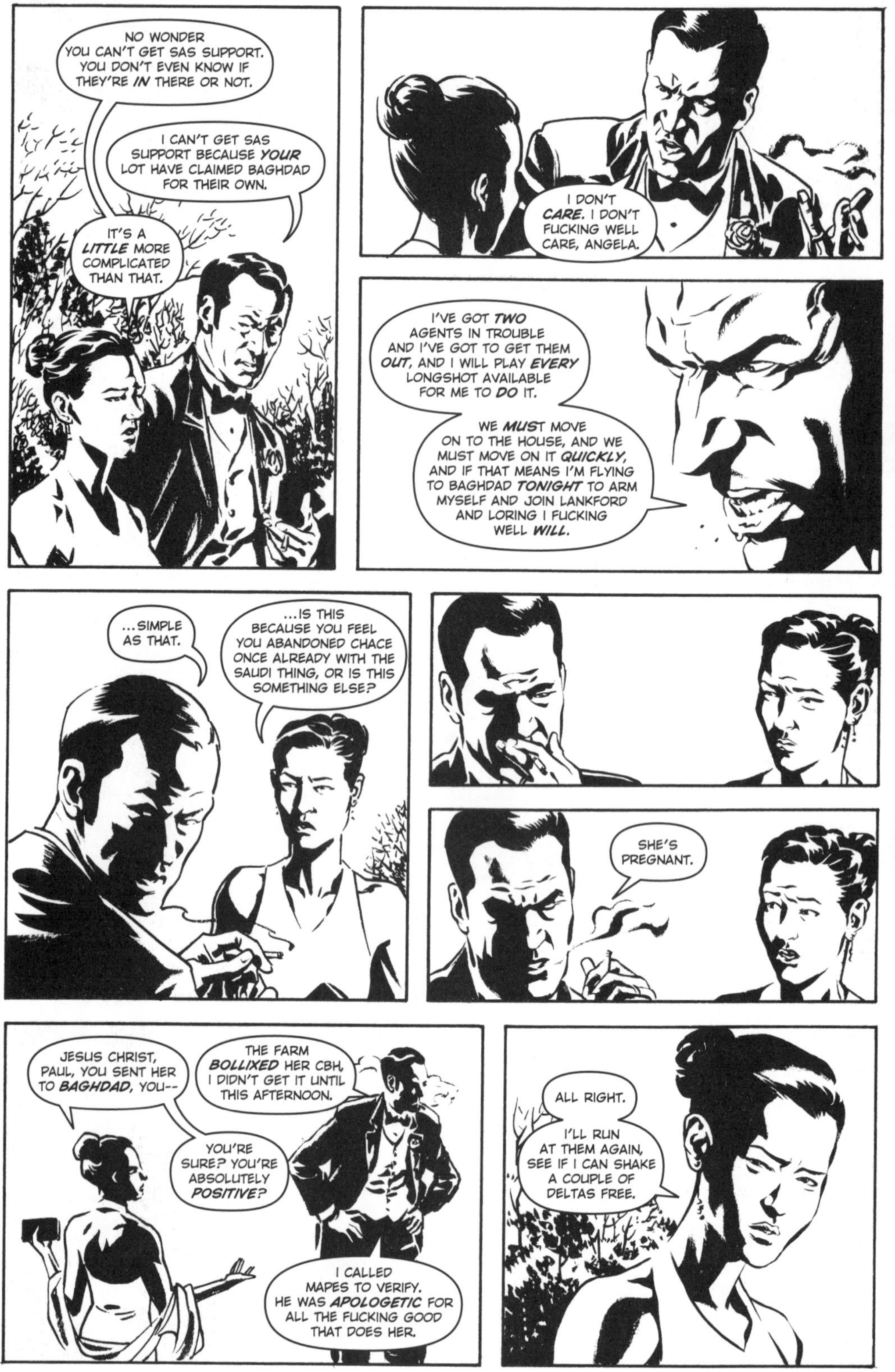
NO WONDER YOU CAN'T GET SAS SUPPORT. YOU DON'T EVEN KNOW IF THEY'RE *IN* THERE OR NOT.
I CAN'T GET SAS SUPPORT BECAUSE *YOUR* LOT HAVE CLAIMED BAGHDAD FOR THEIR OWN.
IT'S A *LITTLE* MORE COMPLICATED THAN THAT.
I DON'T *CARE.* I DON'T FUCKING WELL CARE, ANGELA.
I'VE GOT *TWO* AGENTS IN TROUBLE AND I'VE GOT TO GET THEM *OUT*, AND I WILL PLAY *EVERY* LONGSHOT AVAILABLE FOR ME TO *DO* IT.
WE *MUS*T MOVE ON TO THE HOUSE, AND WE MUST MOVE ON IT *QUICKLY,* AND IF THAT MEANS I'M FLYING TO BAGHDAD *TONIGHT* TO ARM MYSELF AND JOIN LANKFORD AND LORING I FUCKING WELL *WILL*.
...SIMPLE AS THAT.
...IS THIS BECAUSE YOU FEEL YOU ABANDONED CHACE ONCE ALREADY WITH THE SAUDI THING, OR IS THIS SOMETHING ELSE?
SHE'S PREGNANT.
JESUS CHRIST, PAUL, YOU SENT HER TO *BAGHDAD,* YOU--
THE FARM *BOLLIXED* HER CBH, I DIDN'T GET IT UNTIL THIS AFTERNOON.
YOU'RE SURE? YOU'RE ABSOLUTELY *POSITIVE?*
I CALLED MAPES TO VERIFY. HE WAS *APOLOGETIC* FOR ALL THE FUCKING GOOD THAT DOES HER.
ALL RIGHT.
I'LL RUN AT THEM AGAIN, SEE IF I CAN SHAKE A COUPLE OF DELTAS FREE.

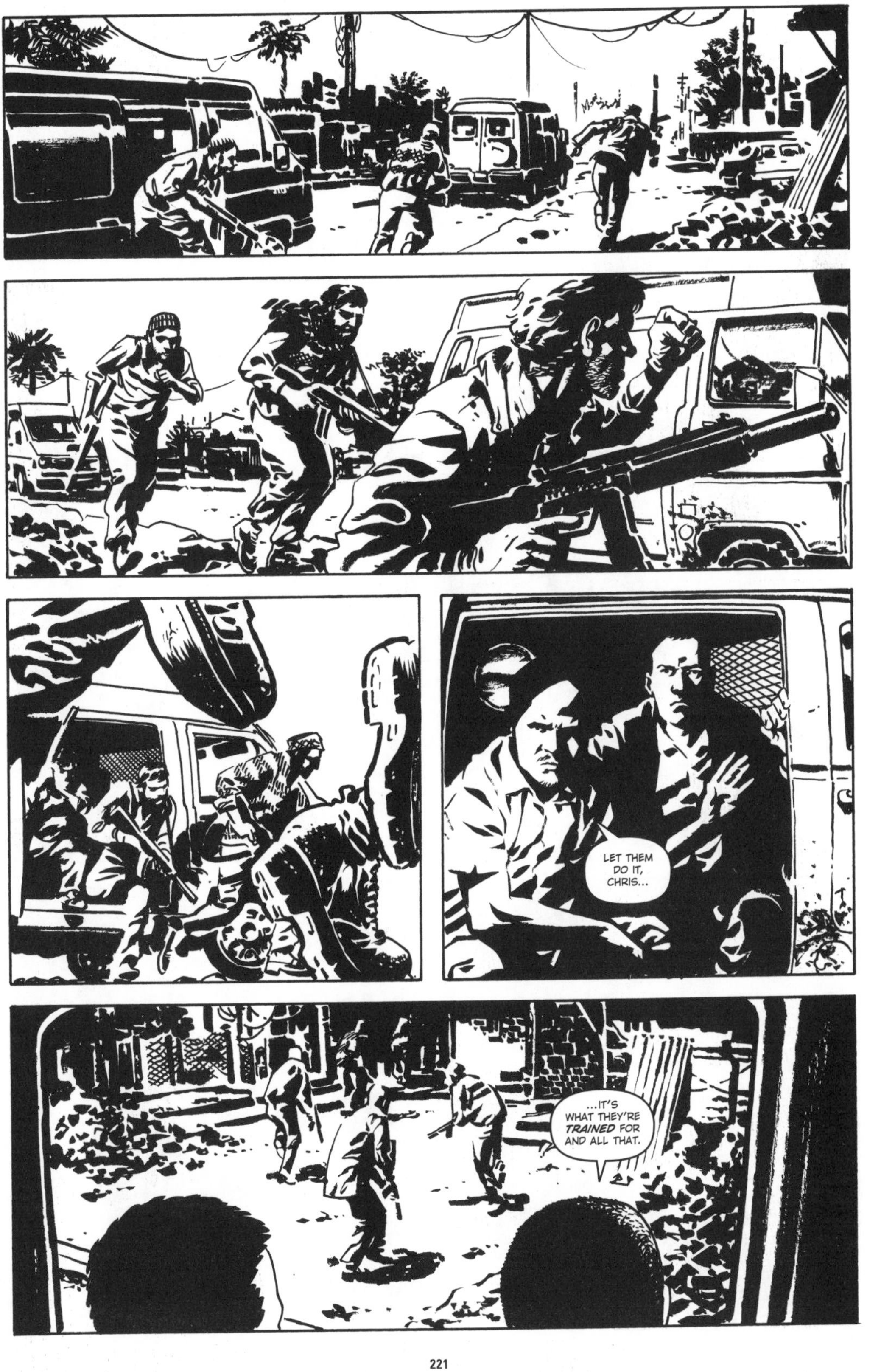
LET THEM DO IT, CHRIS...
...IT'S WHAT THEY'RE TRAINED FOR AND ALL THAT.

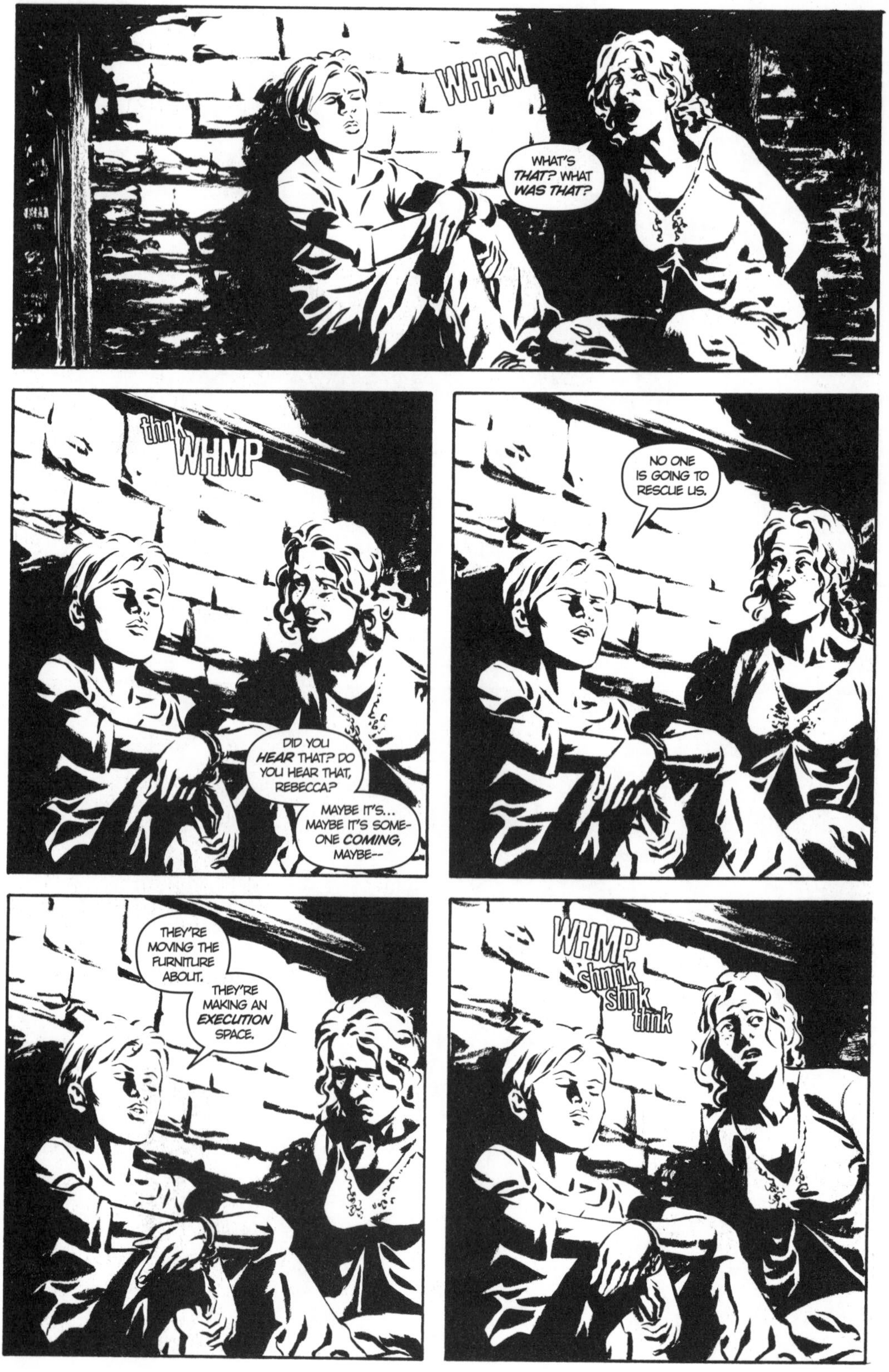
WHAM
WHAT'S *THAT?* WHAT *WAS THAT?*
think WHMP
DID YOU *HEAR* THAT? DO YOU HEAR THAT, REBECCA?
MAYBE IT'S... MAYBE IT'S SOME-ONE *COMING*, MAYBE--
NO ONE IS GOING TO RESCUE US.
THEY'RE MOVING THE FURNITURE ABOUT.
THEY'RE MAKING AN *EXECUTION* SPACE.
WHMP shnnk shnk think

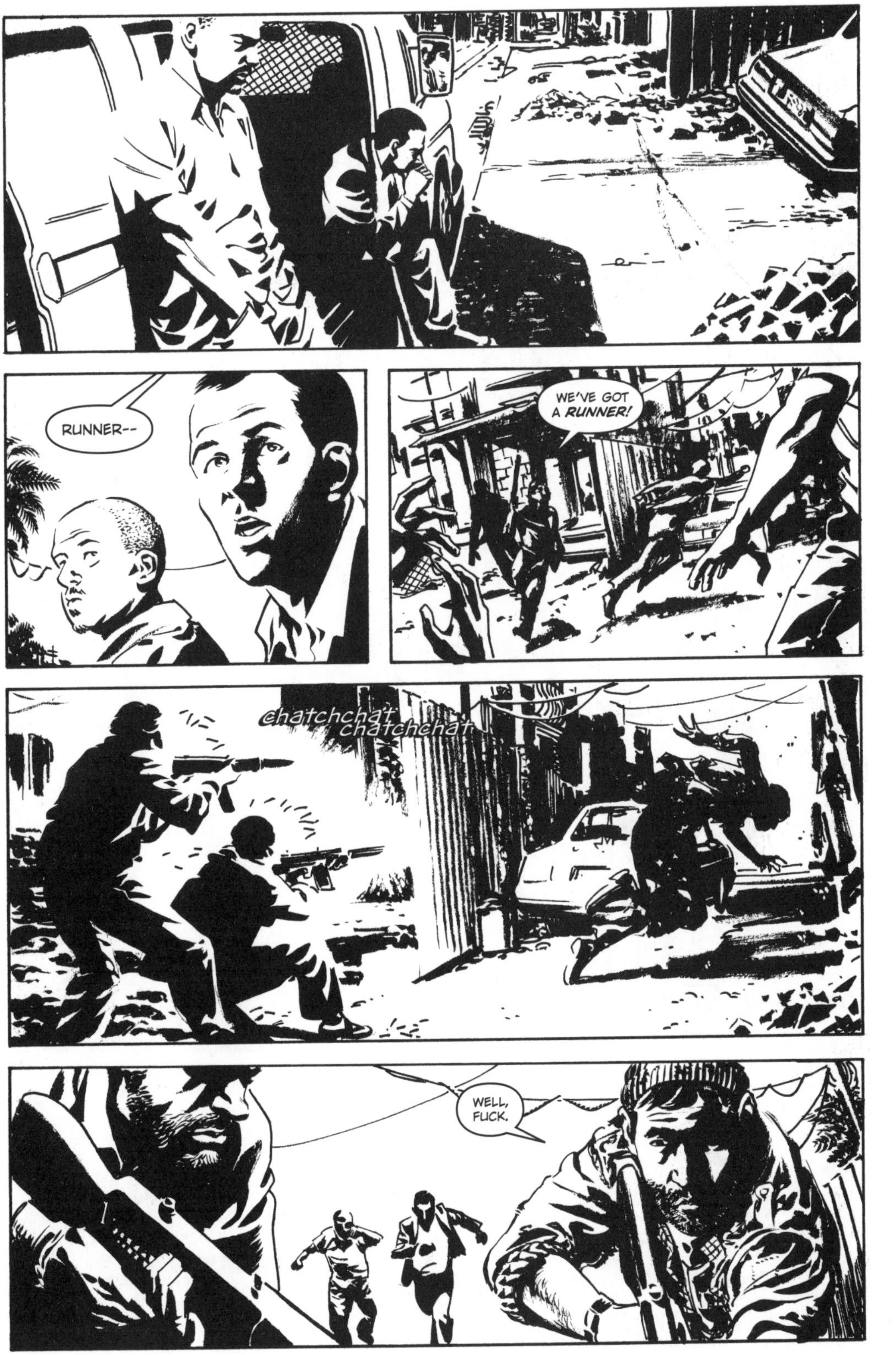
RUNNER--
WE'VE GOT A *RUNNER!*
chatchchat chatchchat
WELL, FUCK.

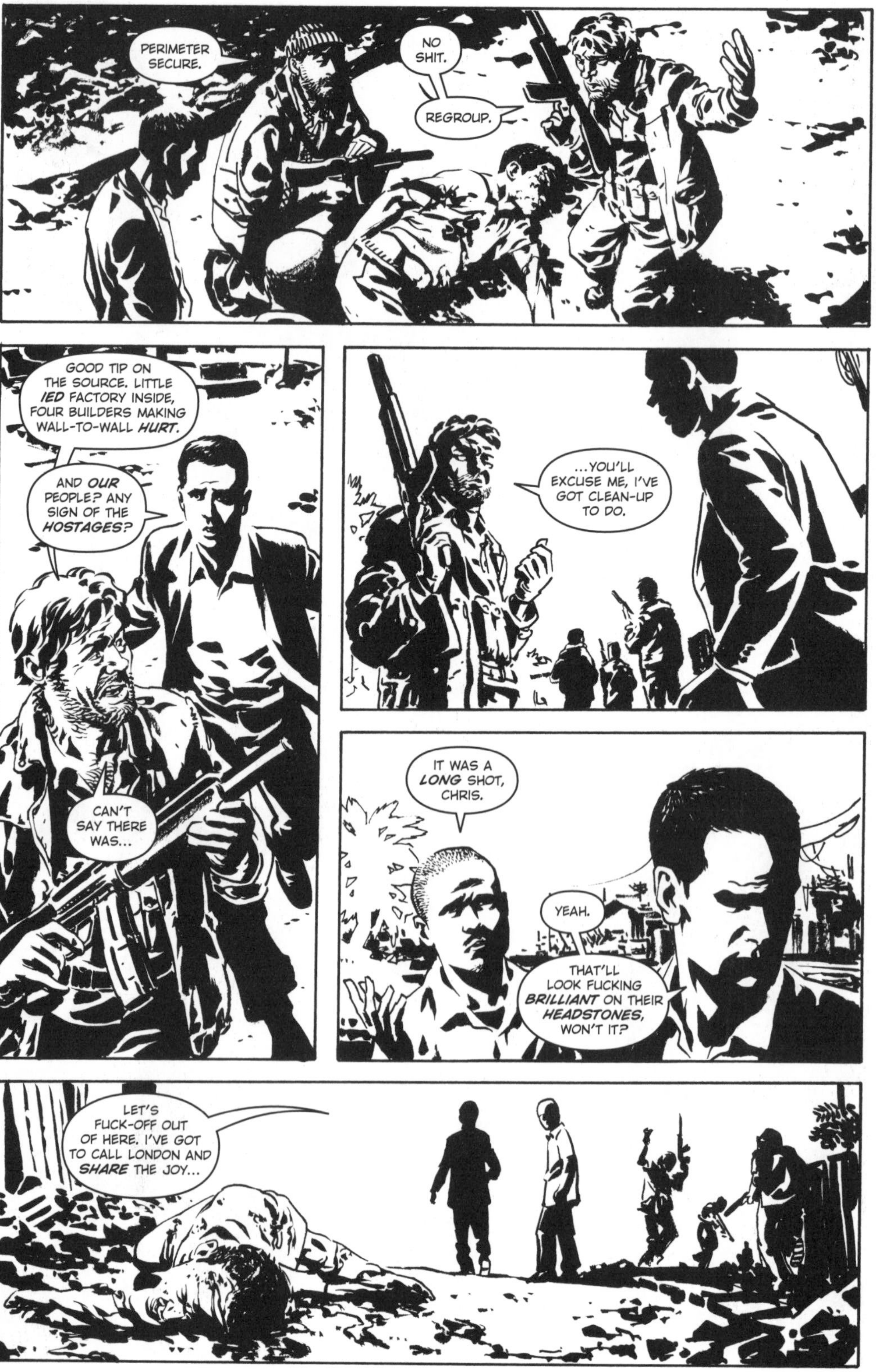
PERIMETER SECURE.
NO SHIT.
REGROUP.
GOOD TIP ON THE SOURCE. LITTLE IED FACTORY INSIDE, FOUR BUILDERS MAKING WALL-TO-WALL HURT.
AND OUR PEOPLE? ANY SIGN OF THE HOSTAGES?
CAN'T SAY THERE WAS...
...YOU'LL EXCUSE ME, I'VE GOT CLEAN-UP TO DO.
IT WAS A LONG SHOT, CHRIS.
YEAH.
THAT'LL LOOK FUCKING BRILLIANT ON THEIR HEADSTONES, WON'T IT?
LET'S FUCK-OFF OUT OF HERE. I'VE GOT TO CALL LONDON AND SHARE THE JOY...

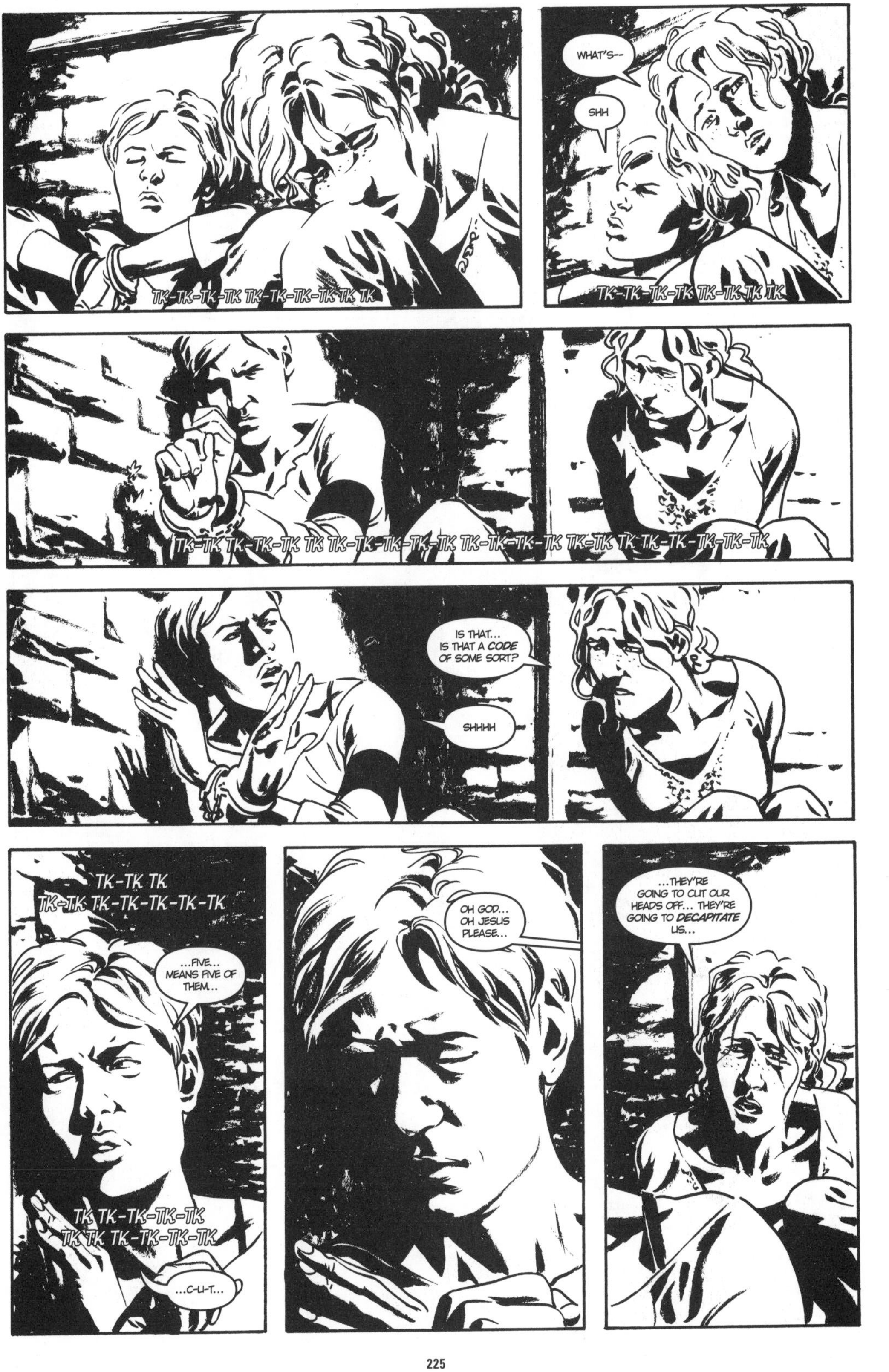
TK-TK-TK-TK TK-TK-TK-TK TK TK
WHAT'S--
SHH
TK-TK-TK-TK TK-TK TK TK
TK-TK TK-TK-TK TK TK-TK-TK-TK-TK TK-TK-TK-TK TK-TK TK TK-TK-TK-TK-TK
IS THAT... IS THAT A CODE OF SOME SORT?
SHHHH
TK-TK TK
TK-TK TK-TK-TK-TK-TK
...FIVE... MEANS FIVE OF THEM...
TK TK-TK-TK-TK
TK TK TK-TK-TK-TK
...C-U-T...
OH GOD... OH JESUS PLEASE...
...THEY'RE GOING TO CUT OUR HEADS OFF... THEY'RE GOING TO DECAPITATE US...

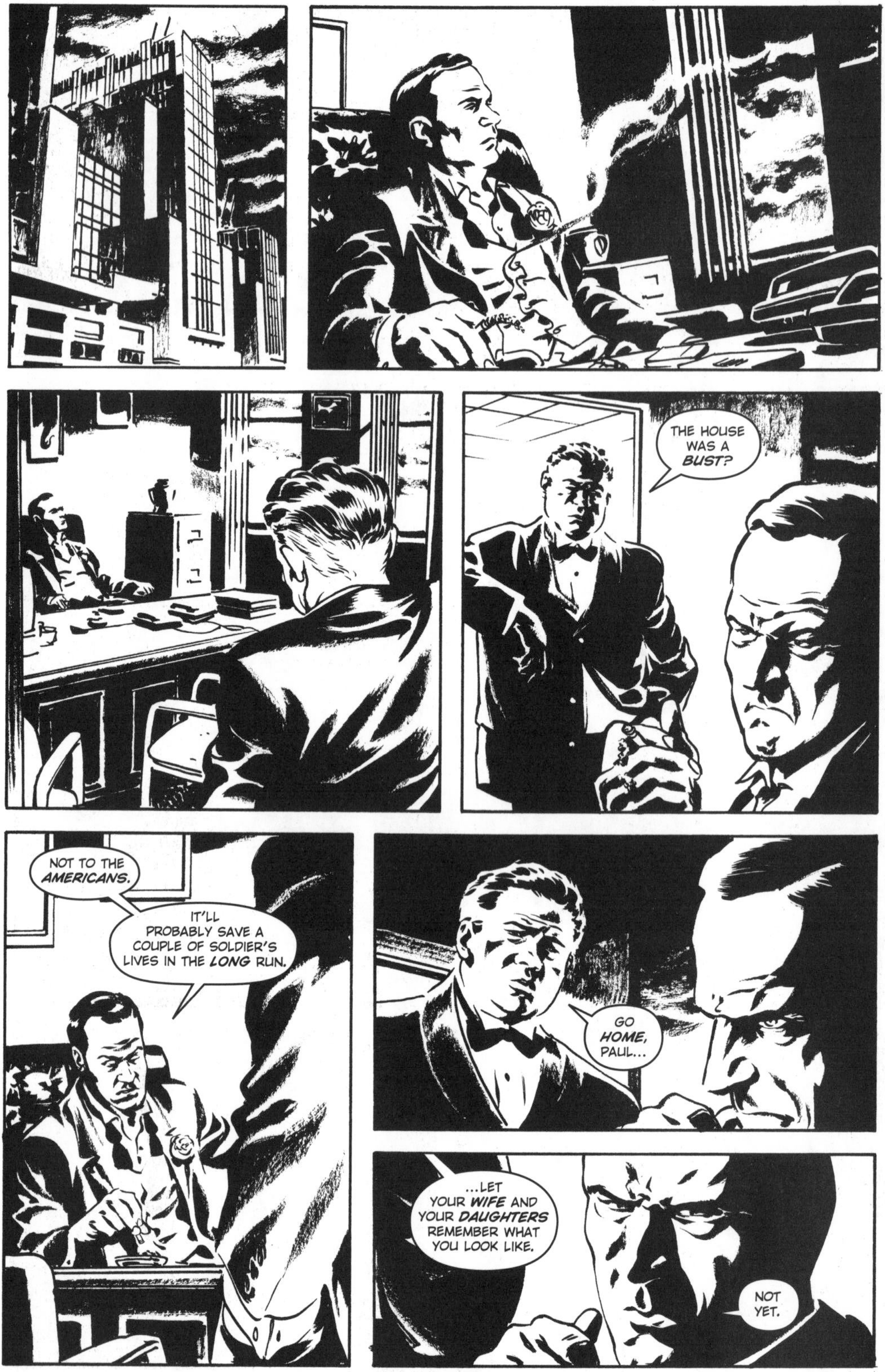

THE HOUSE WAS A *BUST?*
NOT TO THE *AMERICANS.*
IT'LL PROBABLY SAVE A COUPLE OF SOLDIER'S LIVES IN THE *LONG* RUN.
GO *HOME,* PAUL...
...LET YOUR *WIFE* AND YOUR *DAUGHTERS* REMEMBER WHAT YOU LOOK LIKE.
NOT YET.

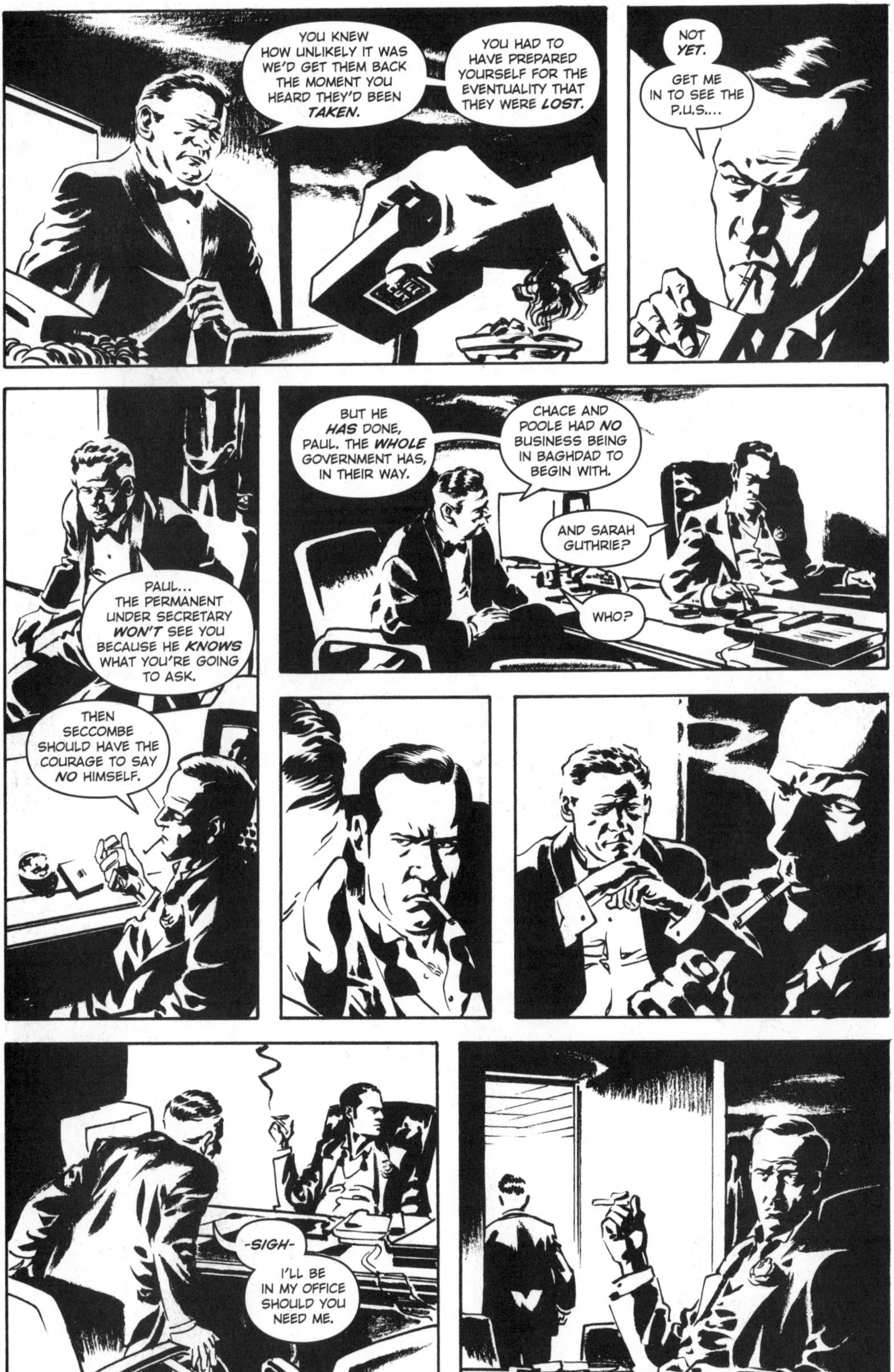
YOU KNEW HOW UNLIKELY IT WAS WE'D GET THEM BACK THE MOMENT YOU HEARD THEY'D BEEN *TAKEN*.
YOU HAD TO HAVE PREPARED YOURSELF FOR THE EVENTUALITY THAT THEY WERE *LOST*.
NOT *YET*.
GET ME IN TO SEE THE P.U.S....
PAUL... THE PERMANENT UNDER SECRETARY *WON'T* SEE YOU BECAUSE HE *KNOWS* WHAT YOU'RE GOING TO ASK.
THEN SECCOMBE SHOULD HAVE THE COURAGE TO SAY *NO* HIMSELF.
BUT HE *HAS* DONE, PAUL. THE *WHOLE* GOVERNMENT HAS, IN THEIR WAY.
CHACE AND POOLE HAD *NO* BUSINESS BEING IN BAGHDAD TO BEGIN WITH.
AND SARAH GUTHRIE?
WHO?
-SIGH-
I'LL BE IN MY OFFICE SHOULD YOU NEED ME.

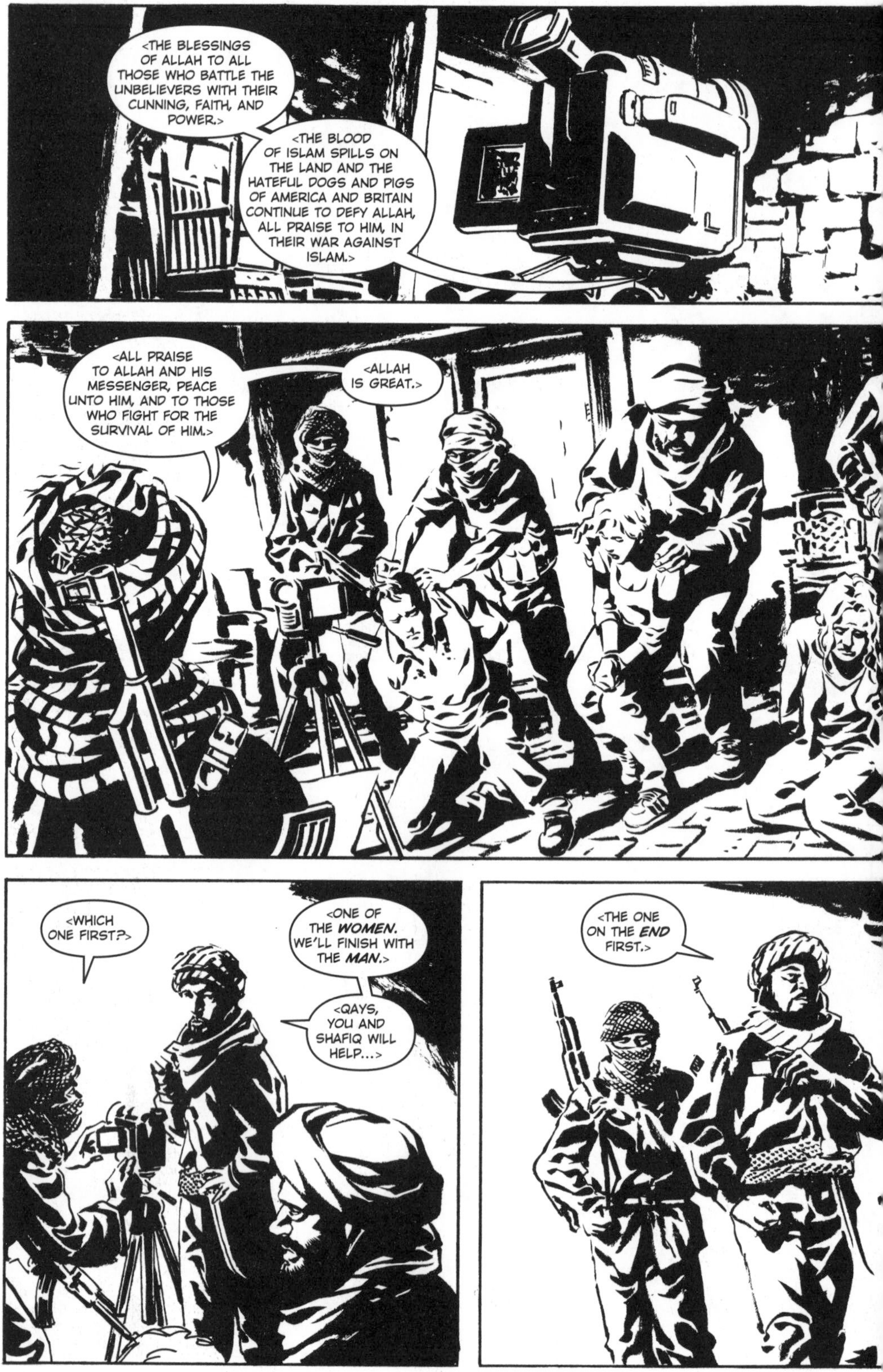
<THE BLESSINGS OF ALLAH TO ALL THOSE WHO BATTLE THE UNBELIEVERS WITH THEIR CUNNING, FAITH, AND POWER.>
<THE BLOOD OF ISLAM SPILLS ON THE LAND AND THE HATEFUL DOGS AND PIGS OF AMERICA AND BRITAIN CONTINUE TO DEFY ALLAH, ALL PRAISE TO HIM, IN THEIR WAR AGAINST ISLAM.>
<ALL PRAISE TO ALLAH AND HIS MESSENGER, PEACE UNTO HIM, AND TO THOSE WHO FIGHT FOR THE SURVIVAL OF HIM.>
<ALLAH IS GREAT.>
<WHICH ONE FIRST?>
<ONE OF THE ***WOMEN.*** WE'LL FINISH WITH THE ***MAN.***>
<QAYS, YOU AND SHAFIQ WILL HELP...>
<THE ONE ON THE ***END*** FIRST.>

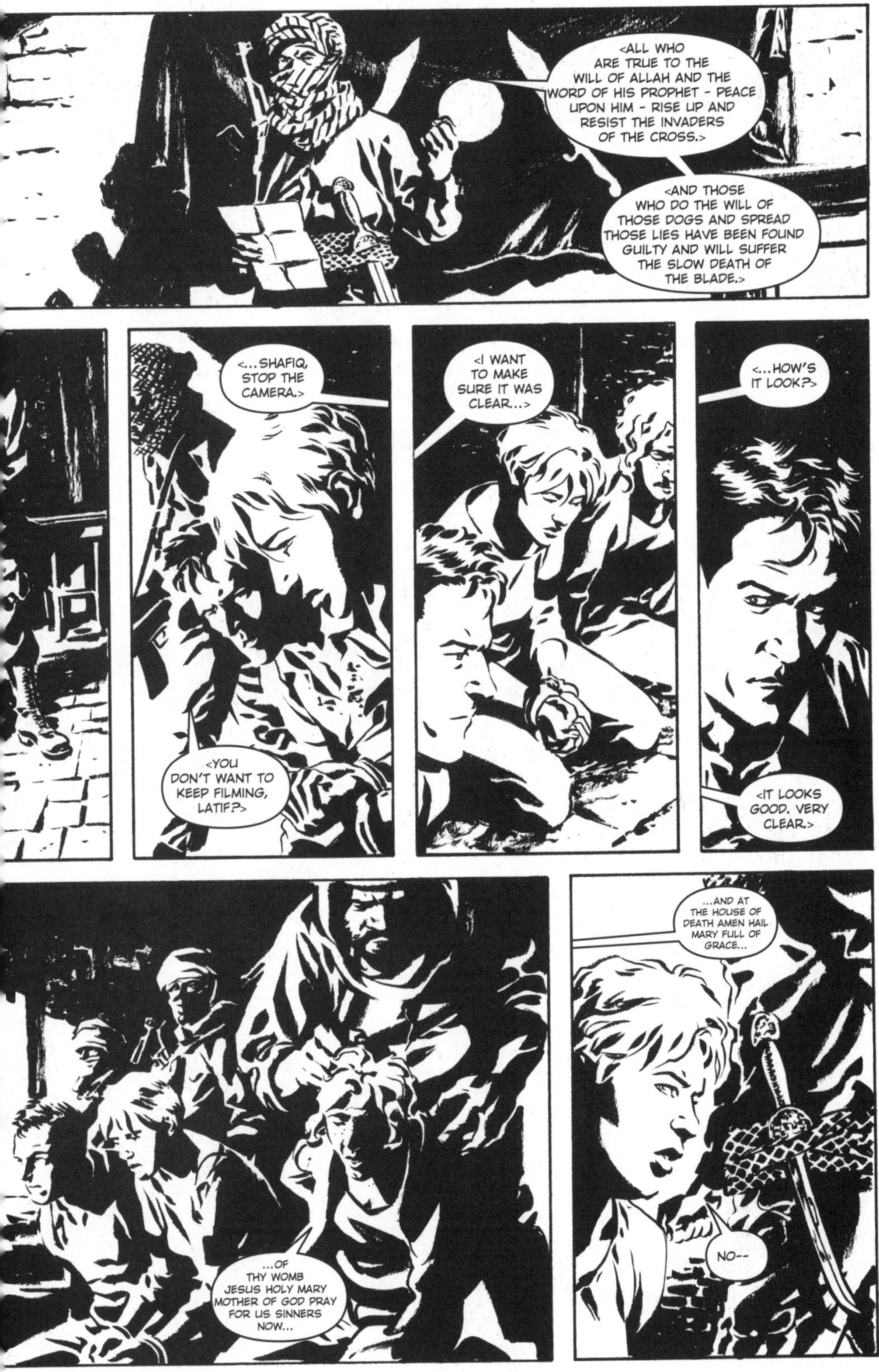
<ALL WHO ARE TRUE TO THE WILL OF ALLAH AND THE WORD OF HIS PROPHET - PEACE UPON HIM - RISE UP AND RESIST THE INVADERS OF THE CROSS.>
<AND THOSE WHO DO THE WILL OF THOSE DOGS AND SPREAD THOSE LIES HAVE BEEN FOUND GUILTY AND WILL SUFFER THE SLOW DEATH OF THE BLADE.>
<...SHAFIQ, STOP THE CAMERA.>
<YOU DON'T WANT TO KEEP FILMING, LATIF?>
<I WANT TO MAKE SURE IT WAS CLEAR...>
<...HOW'S IT LOOK?>
<IT LOOKS GOOD. VERY CLEAR.>
...OF THY WOMB JESUS HOLY MARY MOTHER OF GOD PRAY FOR US SINNERS NOW...
...AND AT THE HOUSE OF DEATH AMEN HAIL MARY FULL OF GRACE...
NO--

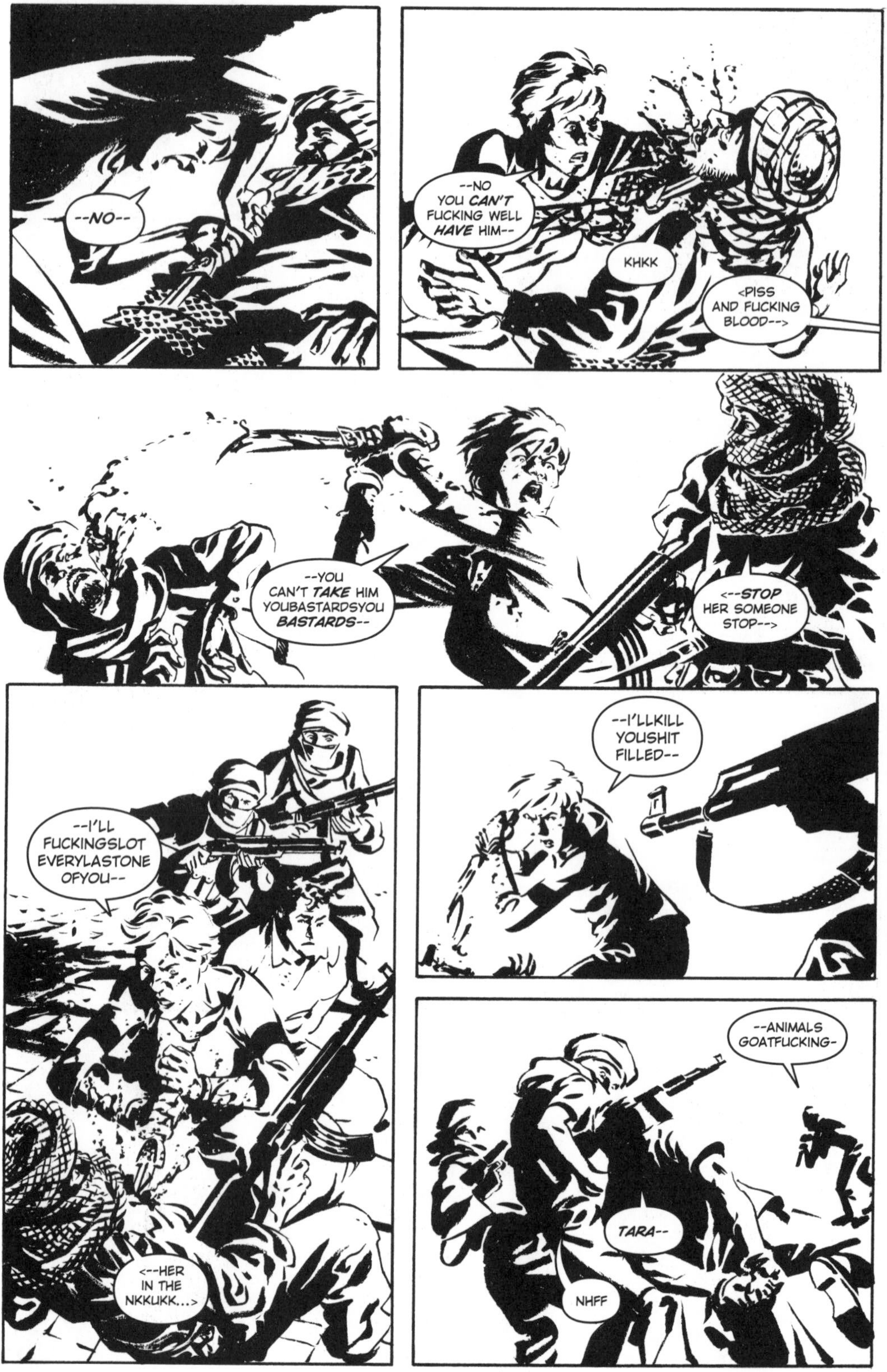
--NO--
--NO YOU CAN'T FUCKING WELL HAVE HIM--
KHKK
<PISS AND FUCKING BLOOD-->
--YOU CAN'T TAKE HIM YOUBASTARDSYOU BASTARDS--
<--STOP HER SOMEONE STOP-->
--I'LL FUCKINGSLOT EVERYLASTONE OFYOU--
<--HER IN THE NKKUKK...>
--I'LLKILL YOUSHIT FILLED--
--ANIMALS GOATFUCKING-
TARA--
NHFF

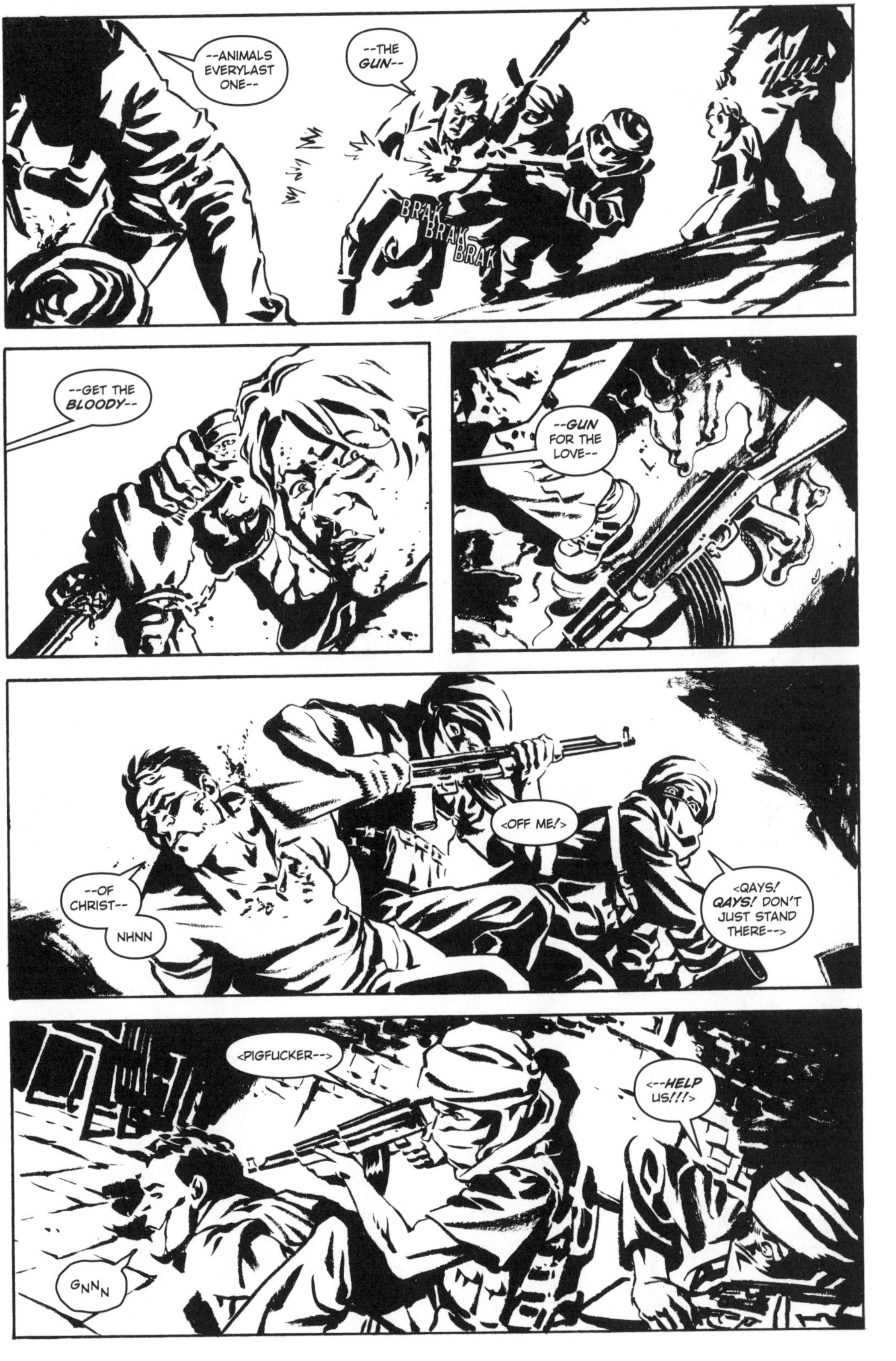
--ANIMALS EVERYLAST ONE--
--THE GUN--
BRAK-BRAK-BRAK
--GET THE BLOODY--
--GUN FOR THE LOVE--
--OF CHRIST--
NHNN
<OFF ME!>
<QAYS! QAYS! DON'T JUST STAND THERE-->
<PIGFUCKER-->
<--HELP US!!!>
GNNN

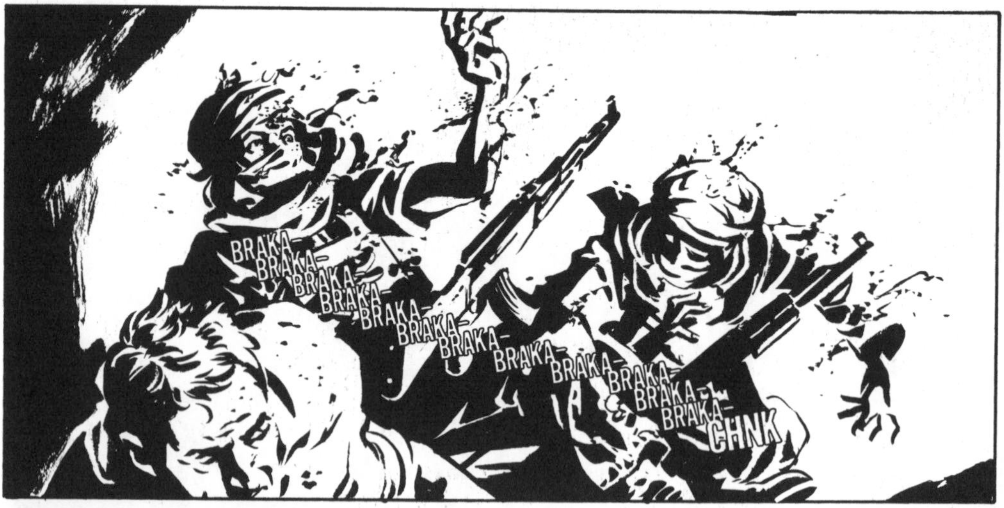
BRAKA-BRAKA-BRAKA-BRAKA-BRAKA-BRAKA-BRAKA-BRAKA-BRAKA-BRAKA-BRAKA-BRAKA-CHNK

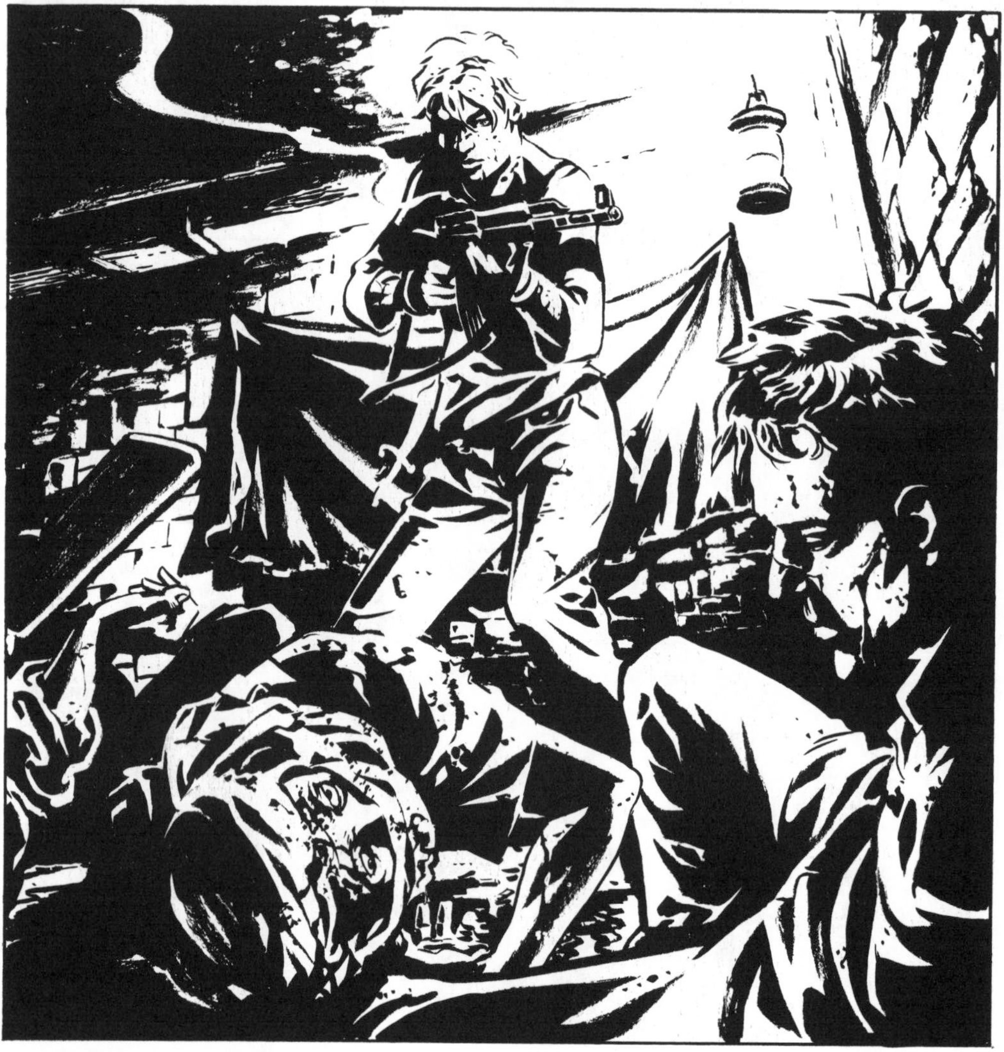

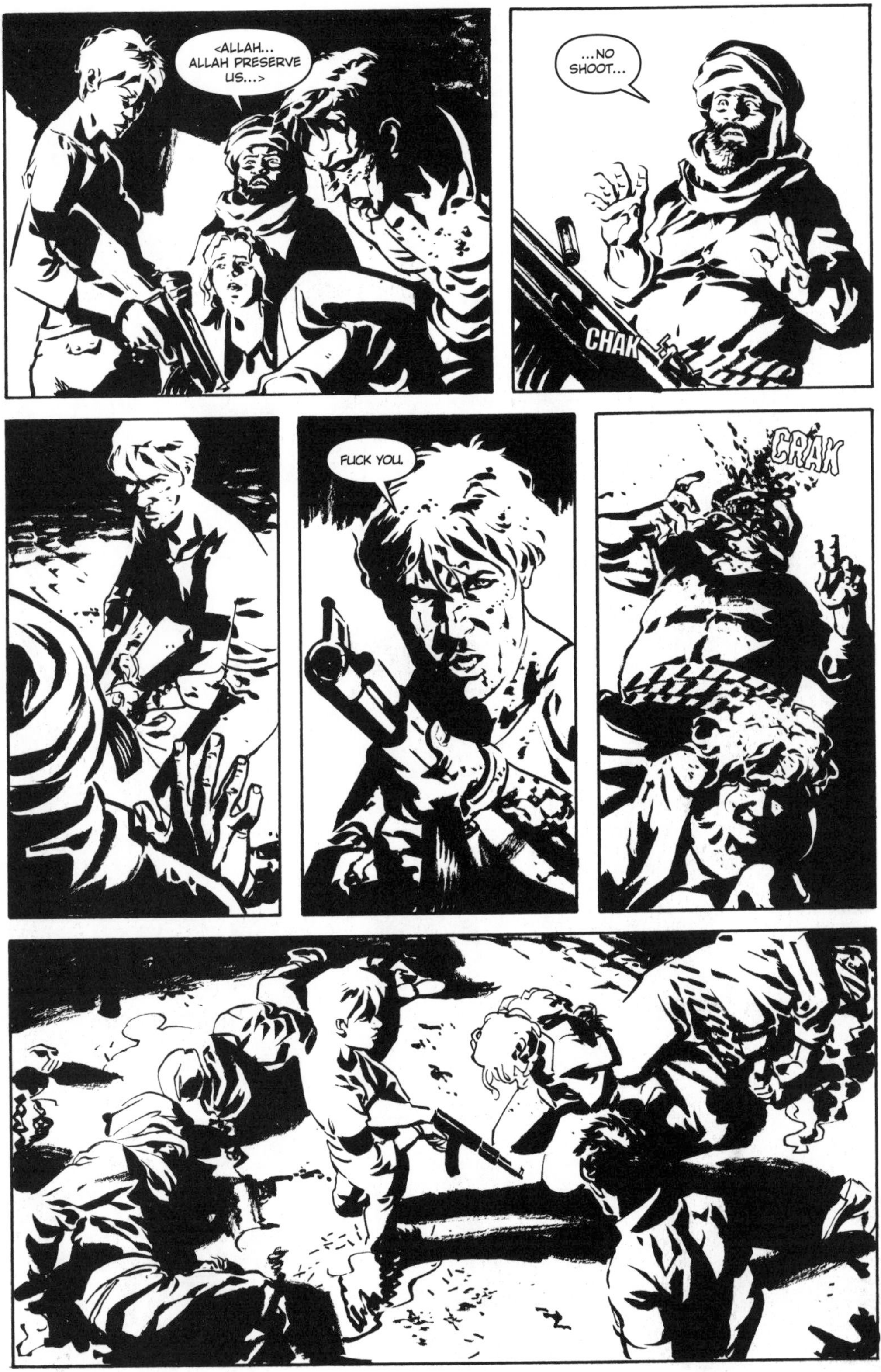
<ALLAH... ALLAH PRESERVE US...>
...NO SHOOT...
CHAK
FUCK YOU.
CRAK

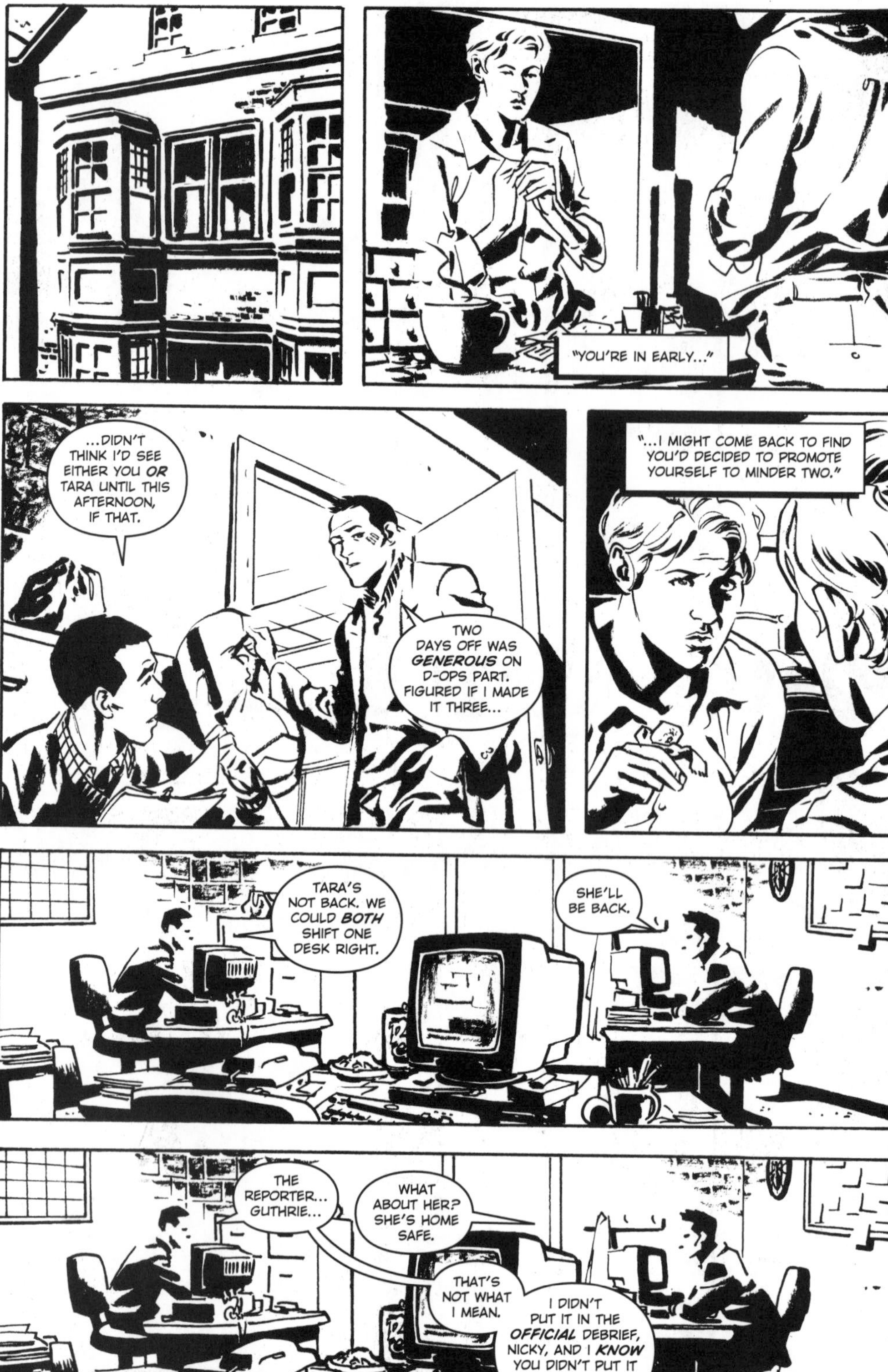
"YOU'RE IN EARLY..."
...DIDN'T THINK I'D SEE EITHER YOU OR TARA UNTIL THIS AFTERNOON, IF THAT.
TWO DAYS OFF WAS GENEROUS ON D-OPS PART. FIGURED IF I MADE IT THREE...
"...I MIGHT COME BACK TO FIND YOU'D DECIDED TO PROMOTE YOURSELF TO MINDER TWO."
TARA'S NOT BACK. WE COULD BOTH SHIFT ONE DESK RIGHT.
SHE'LL BE BACK.
THE REPORTER... GUTHRIE...
WHAT ABOUT HER? SHE'S HOME SAFE.
THAT'S NOT WHAT I MEAN.
I DIDN'T PUT IT IN THE OFFICIAL DEBRIEF, NICKY, AND I KNOW YOU DIDN'T PUT IT IN YOUR AFTER-ACTION...

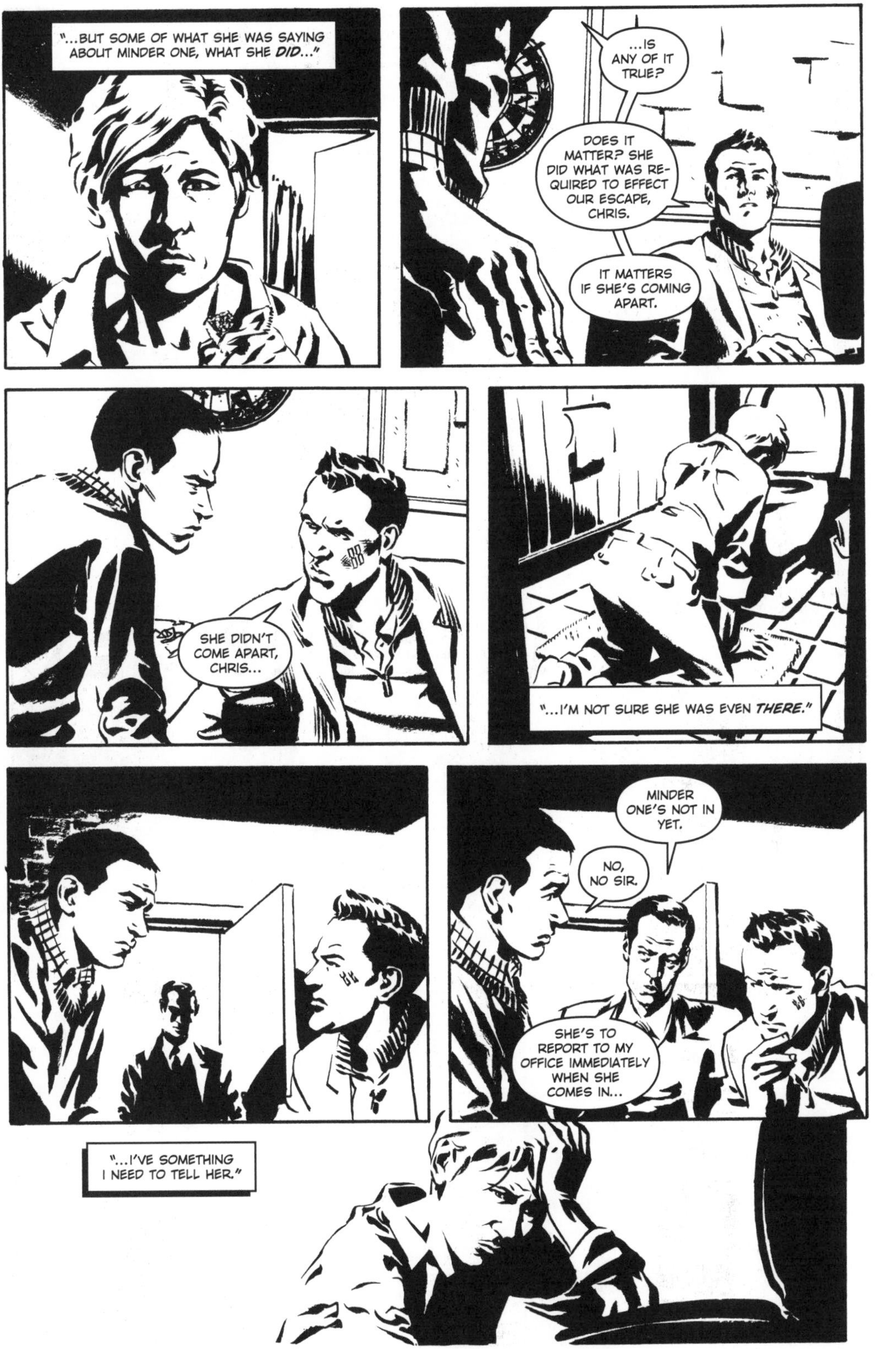
"...BUT SOME OF WHAT SHE WAS SAYING ABOUT MINDER ONE, WHAT SHE *DID*..."
...IS ANY OF IT TRUE?
DOES IT MATTER? SHE DID WHAT WAS REQUIRED TO EFFECT OUR ESCAPE, CHRIS.
IT MATTERS IF SHE'S COMING APART.
SHE DIDN'T COME APART, CHRIS...
"...I'M NOT SURE SHE WAS EVEN *THERE*."
MINDER ONE'S NOT IN YET.
NO, NO SIR.
SHE'S TO REPORT TO MY OFFICE IMMEDIATELY WHEN SHE COMES IN...
"...I'VE SOMETHING I NEED TO TELL HER."

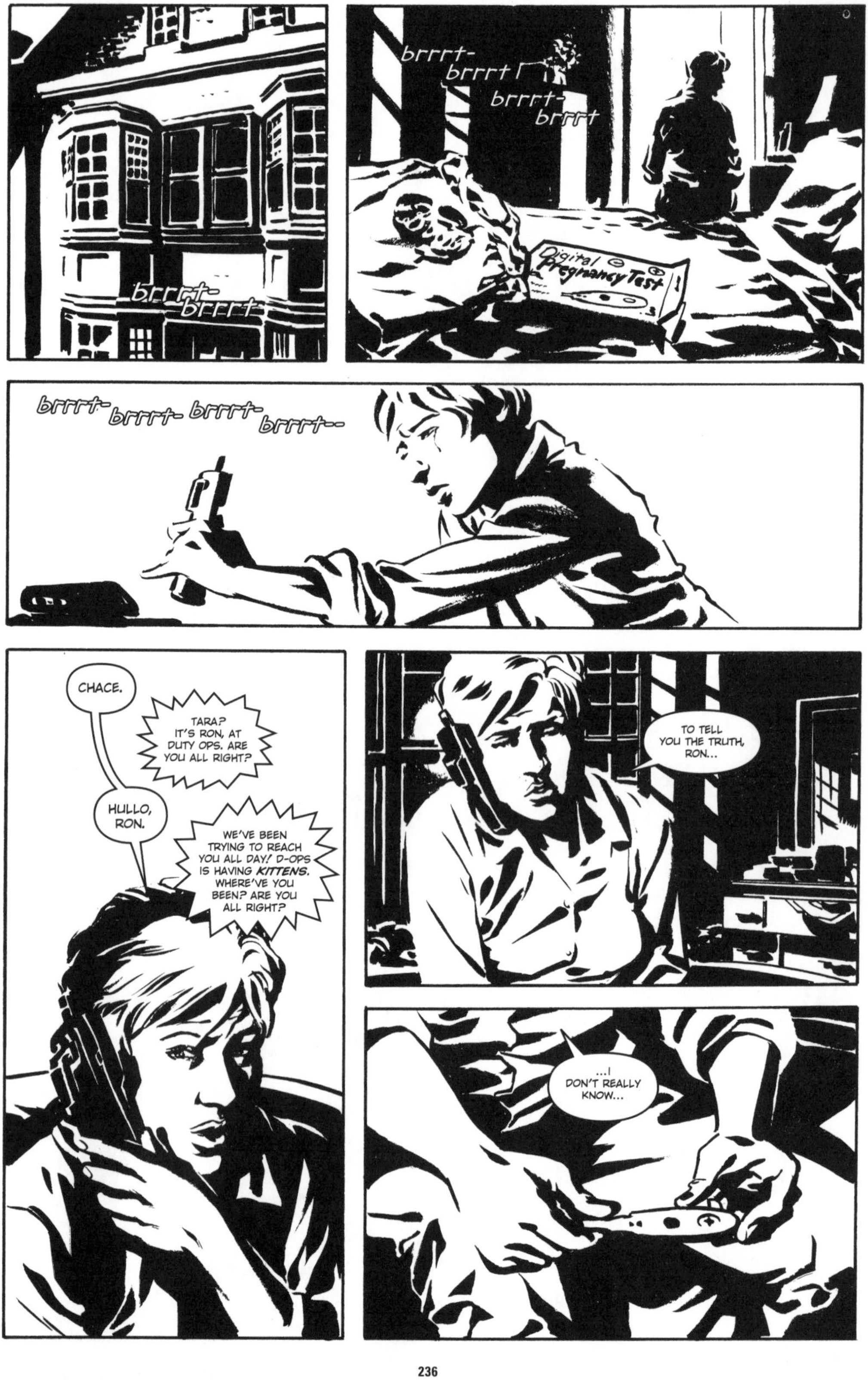
brrrt-
brrrt
brrrt-
brrrt!
brrrt-
brrrt
Digital Pregnancy Test
brrrt- brrrt- brrrt- brrrt--
CHACE.
TARA? IT'S RON, AT DUTY OPS. ARE YOU ALL RIGHT?
HULLO, RON.
WE'VE BEEN TRYING TO REACH YOU ALL DAY! D-OPS IS HAVING *KITTENS.* WHERE'VE YOU BEEN? ARE YOU ALL RIGHT?
TO TELL YOU THE TRUTH, RON...
...I DON'T REALLY KNOW...

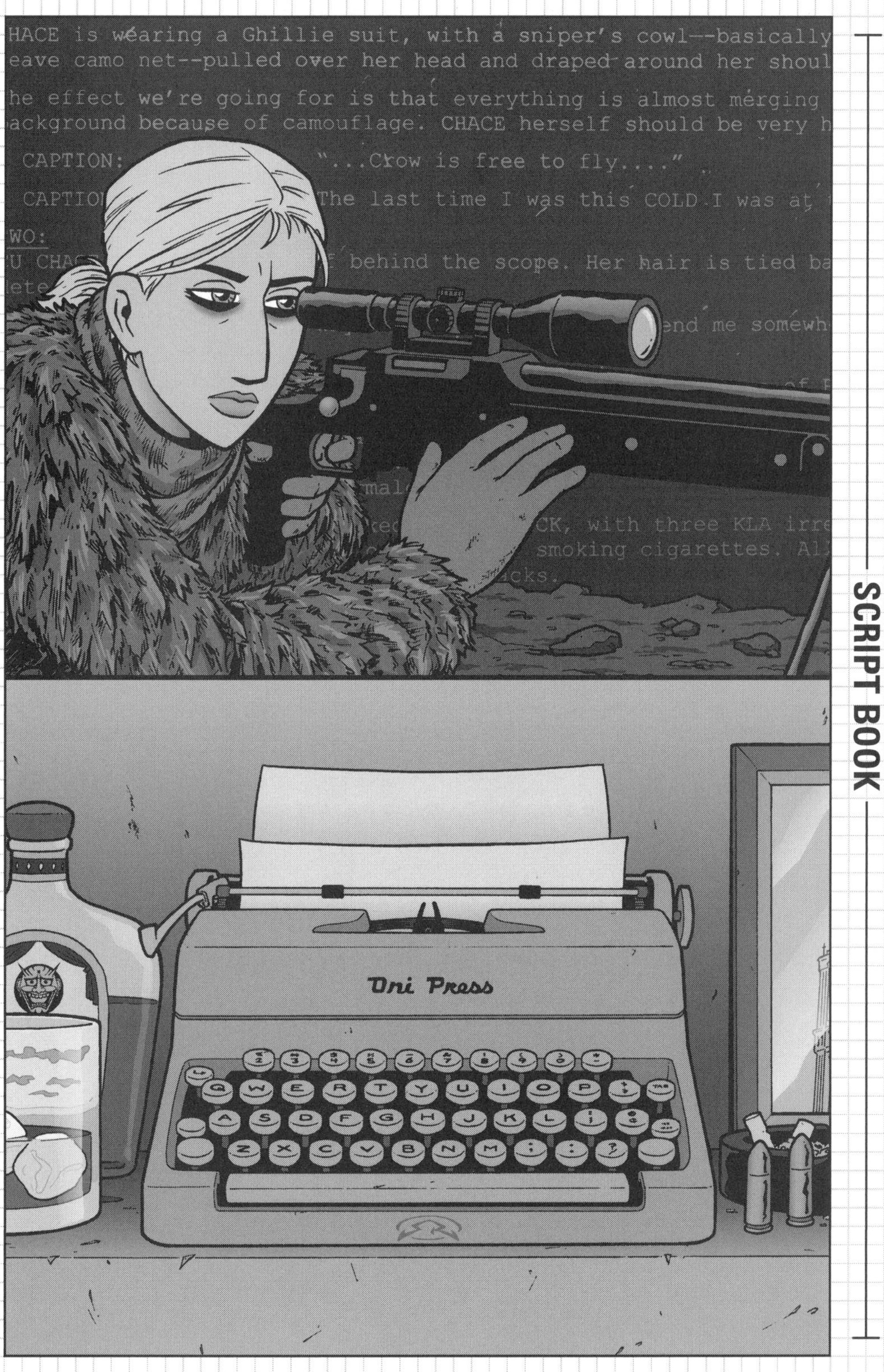
HACE is wearing a Ghillie suit, with a sniper's cowl--basically
eave camo net--pulled over her head and draped around her shoul
he effect we're going for is that everything is almost merging
ackground because of camouflage. CHACE herself should be very h
CAPTION: "...Crow is free to fly...."
The last time I was this COLD I was at
WO:
behind the scope. Her hair is tied ba
end me somewh
CK, with three KLA irre
smoking cigarettes. Al
Oni Press

QUEEN & COUNTRY SCRIPTBOOK

WRITTEN BY
GREG RUCKA

FEATURING ILLUSTRATIONS AND
DEVELOPMENTAL MATERIAL BY
STEVE ROLSTON

ADDITIONAL ILLUSTRATIONS BY
TIM SALE, BRIAN HURTT, & LEANDRO FERNANDEZ

ORIGINAL LAYOUT AND DESIGN BY
LAURENN MCCUBBIN

ORIGINAL SERIES EDITED BY
JAMIE S. RICH & JAMES LUCAS JONES

CHAPTER 1

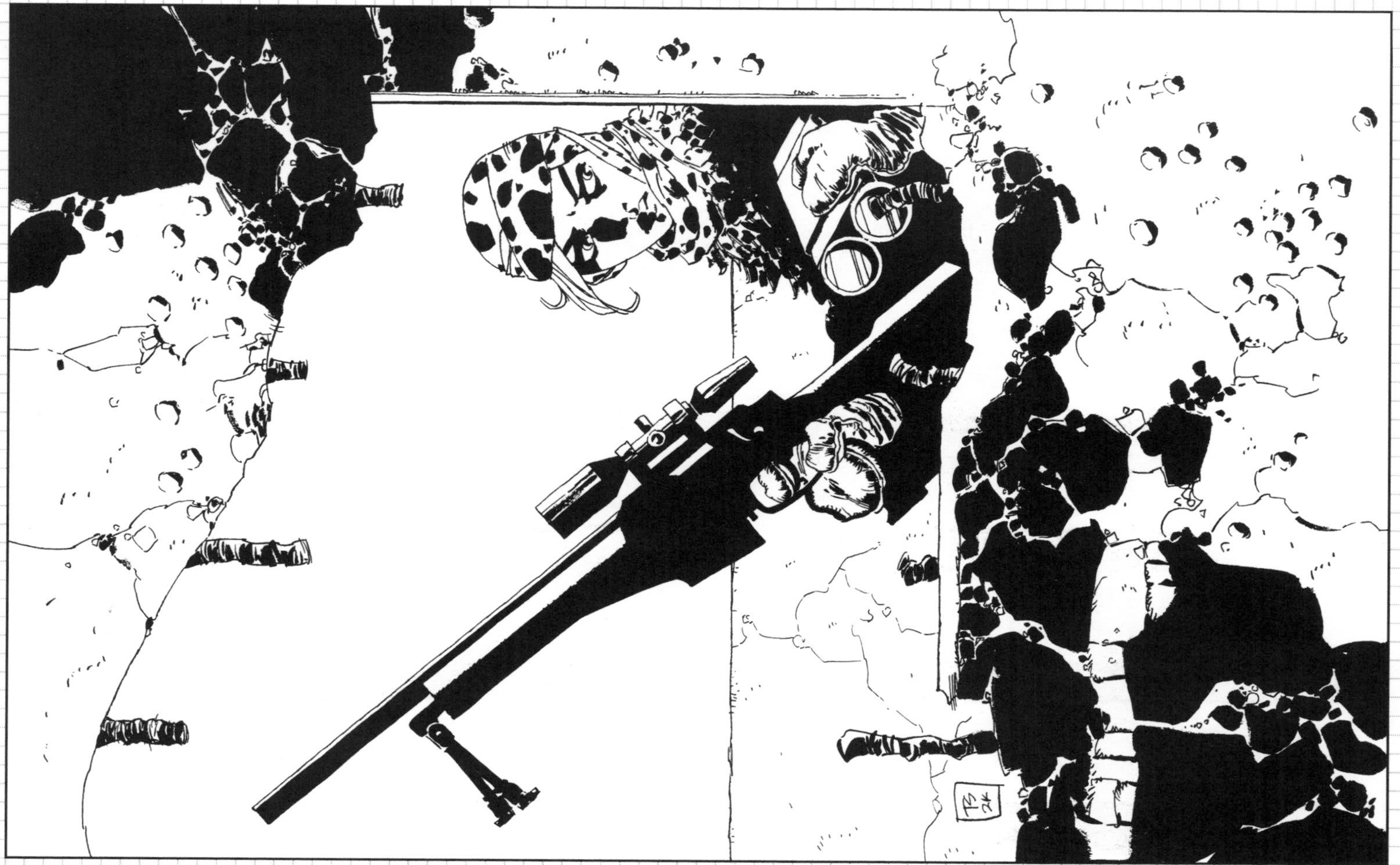

Page 1

ONE:
Wide, big shot, establishing the OPS ROOM at midnight.[1]

We're looking from the back wall at the front of the room, slight down angle. This should be something like a cross between the Ops. Room from *The Sandbaggers*[2] and the Ops. Room used in *Patriot Games*[3] during the SAS raid on the training compound in Libya. Well lit, a lot of cigarette smoke hanging in the air. Computers, communications equipment. A couple STAFF who never speak, but are constantly moving back and forth.

We can see TWO MAIN DESKS/POSTS set up, including one on a slightly raised platform for the DUTY OPERATIONS OFFICER, currently staffed by a SMALL WHITE GUY in his early thirties named RON. RON is dressed in a suit, the coat off, his sleeves rolled up, but still in his tie. He has a headset on, a cigarette going in one hand, is drinking from a cup of coffee in the other, all the while talking on the net.

Seated near RON, leaning back in his chair, cigarette in his mouth, is WALLACE—head of the Special Section, late thirties, white, fit, dressed in a cheap suit. Eyes are closed.

A WOMAN IN HER LATE 20's named ALEXIS is seated at the MISSION DESK, or more appropriately, practically surrounded by it, since the desk is a horseshoe shape around where she is seated. ALEXIS, too, wears a headset, and is professionally dressed—slacks, blazer, blouse. At the desk is a computer terminal on which she is typing. A couple maps are spread out on the surface of the desk at her elbow.

On the far wall is a giant computer/display screen, kinda like the one they have to monitor the Space Shuttle launches at Mission Control, except more high-tech. This is the centerpiece of the room, and should be an impressive piece of hardware—we'll be coming back to this screen time and again throughout the series. [*If you want reference, I'd suggest watching* Patriot Games—*specifically the sequence where the SAS takes out the IRA training camp in Libya; also the beginning*

1. This is a huge panel description, as far as I'm concerned. Normally, I try to keep my panel descriptions to a paragraph or two, mostly for clarity's sake—though I'm sure there are editors and artists out there who would disagree with that assertion. In this case, I was after something very specific, which was not just the physical set, but the atmosphere of the set, as well. The sense of tension, of professionalism, of secrecy and even intimacy, were all elements I wanted thrown at the reader as soon as they hit the page. Part of the job of a First Issue, after all, is to define the world, and to entice the reader into following you further inside. So the Ops Room, as that point of entry, was pretty damn critical. Steve nailed it; he nailed it to such an extent that every artist to follow him—including Brian Hurtt in the Declassified series, which technically takes place some 20 years prior to this story—used (and continued to use) his floorplan. The details change, but the essence of Steve's Ops Room remains.

2. I can never say this enough: without The Sandbaggers, there would be no Queen & Country. I was sixteen, bookish, shy, and spent far too much time watching PBS (KTEH Channel 54 out of San Jose, California, for the record), and somehow, someway, I saw this amazing piece of dramatic television. Most of the shows I was in love with when I was sixteen, they don't hold up. The Sandbaggers, dated though it now is, does. And it was brilliant. Created by the late Ian Mackintosh, the show ran initially on ITV from 1978 to 1980, and is now available on DVD. Everyone should watch it. For more information on the show, including some great trivia, insight, and analysis of "the best damn drama you never saw," go to www.opsroom.org.

3. Contrary to rumor, I can't stand the work of Tom Clancy. But some of those films, they sure are pretty.

OPS ROOM
—2 feet × 2 feet
8'-wide monitors
16'-wide monitor
8'-wide monitors
trashcan
illuminated glass for viewing map overlays
filing cabinets
Mission Desk
filing cabinets
Men's washroom
phones
Women's washroom
Duty Ops Desk
ashtray
bookcases
photo-copier
Horizontal map
slightly raised platform
hallway
coat rack
chairs
Kitchen
WINDOW
table
T.V. + VCR
water cooler

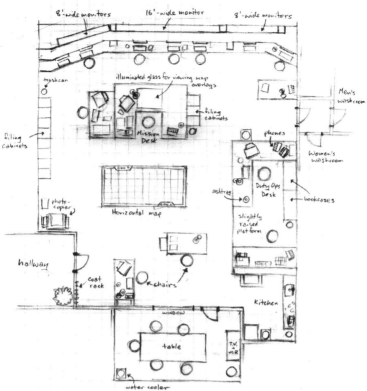

of <u>Tomorrow Never Dies</u>, when Bond is scoping the arms bazaar.][4]

Currently the display shows a MAP OF THE WORLD, with time zones appropriately noted. Only TWO ZONES are key—Over the UK, one reads "0403 LOCAL (GMT)"; and over KOSOVO, another reads "0503 (Z)".

Also over Kosovo, we can see a marker of some sort on the map, either an icon of a flag or a dot or something—this should be over the city of PRIZREN. PRISTINA should also be marked on the map, though not highlighted. There's a call-out on PRIZREN, with a notation that is too small for us to read at this point.

Finally, in the center of the room, back to us and staring at the map, is Director of Operations PAUL CROCKER. Crocker's in his early 40's, wears a three-piece suit, smokes like a chimney, and if we were casting parts, would look like Robert Carslyle.

<u>Everyone</u> looks like they need some sleep.

1 TAILLESS/elec/small:
…standing by…

4. I don't know why I started doing this, but somewhere in the course of writing for comics, I began adding these 'asides,' for lack of a better word, most often directed at the artist, but sometimes at the editor, or letter, or colorist.

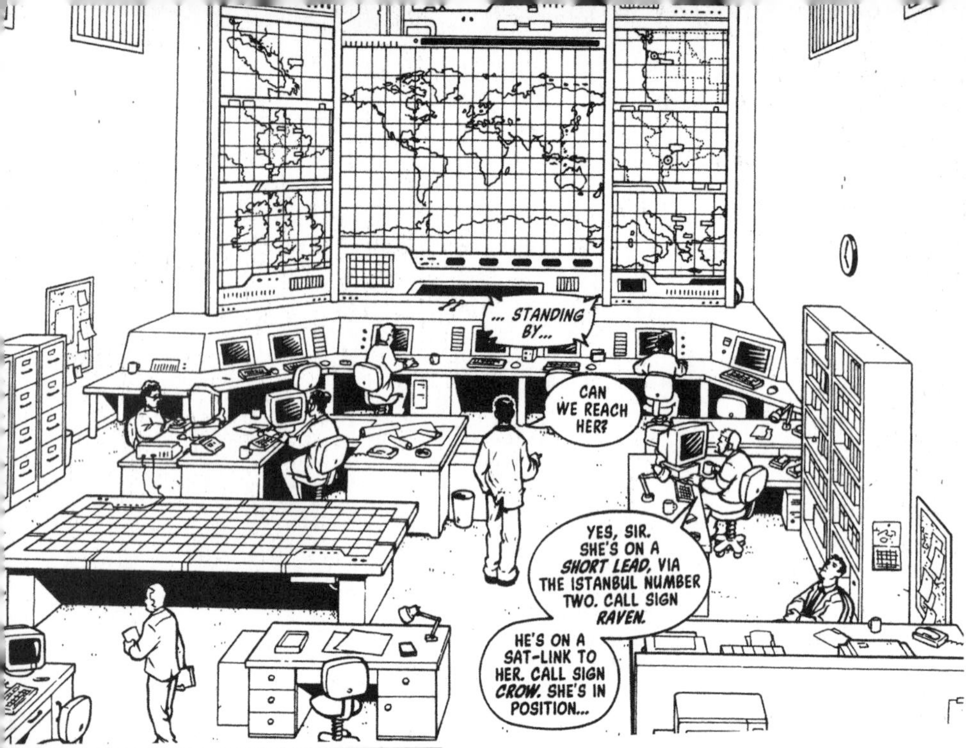
... STANDING BY...
CAN WE REACH HER?
YES, SIR. SHE'S ON A SHORT LEAD, VIA THE ISTANBUL NUMBER TWO. CALL SIGN RAVEN.
HE'S ON A SAT-LINK TO HER. CALL SIGN CROW. SHE'S IN POSITION...
OPS room by Steve Rolston, *Q&C* Issue 1

2 CROCKER:

Can we reach her?

3 RON:

Yes, sir, she's on SHORT lead, via the Istanbul Number Two, call sign RAVEN.

4 RON/linked:

He's on a sat-link to her, call sign CROW. She's in position…

TWO:

Zooming in on the map, now, OTS CROCKER, and we see the callout for KOSOVO and PRIZREN. The CLOCK now reads "0504 Z."

The callout reads:

OPERATION: BROKEN GROUND_

5 RON:

…been there ALL night.

6 CROCKER:

Must be bloody FREEZING.

7 RON:

Yes, sir.

8 TAILLESS/elec/small:

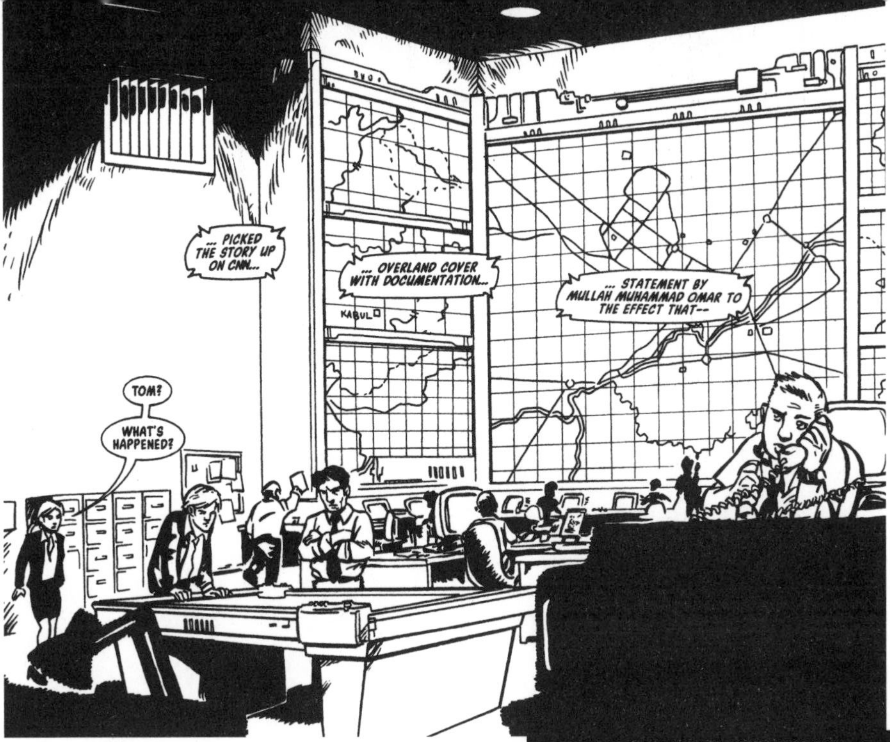
... PICKED THE STORY UP ON CNN...
... OVERLAND COVER WITH DOCUMENTATION...
... STATEMENT BY MULLAH MUHAMMAD OMAR TO THE EFFECT THAT--
KABUL
TOM?
WHAT'S HAPPENED?

OPS ROOM BY BRIAN HURTT & CHRISTINE NORRIE, *Q&C* ISSUE 6

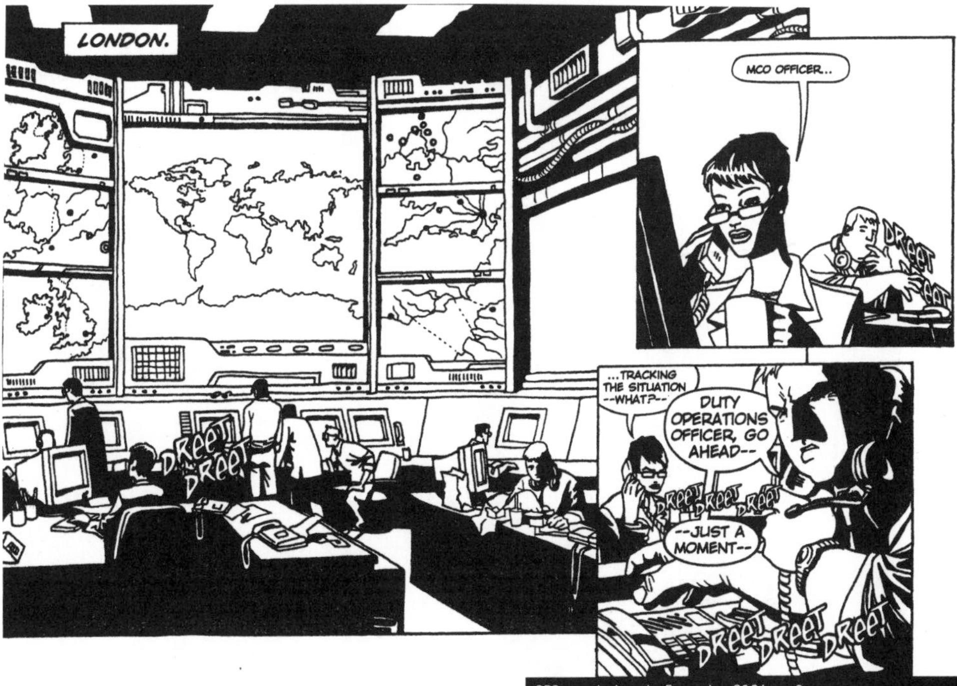
LONDON.
DREET DREET
MCO OFFICER...
DREET DREET
...TRACKING THE SITUATION --WHAT?--
DUTY OPERATIONS OFFICER, GO AHEAD--
DREET DREET DREET
--JUST A MOMENT--
DREET DREET DREET

OPS room by Leandro Fernandez, *Q&C* Issue 8

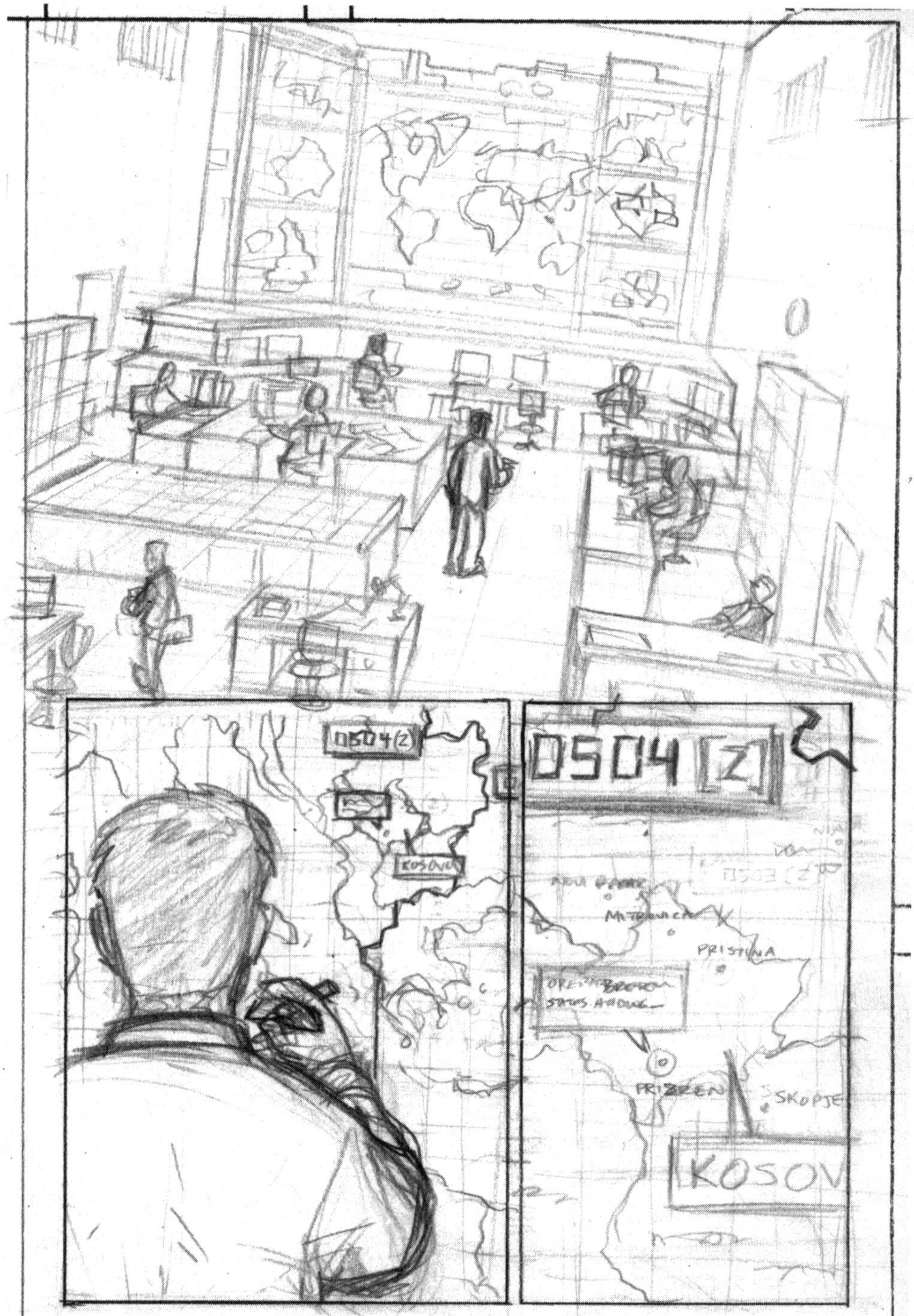
0504 [Z]
MITROVICA
PRISTINA
PRIZREN
SKOPJE
KOSOV

—entering Prizren now.

<u>THREE:</u>
This is the completion of the zoom on the map,
we're centered on KOSOVO, can see that the country
is appropriately marked on the map. We can see
that PRIZREN is also marked.

The callout now reads:

>OPERATION: BROKEN GROUND
>STATUS: HOLDING_

9 CROCKER/off:
>Lex, when's SUNRISE in ZONE?

Page 2

<u>ONE:</u>
Angle from the front, past ALEXIS at her desk,
looking at CROCKER. RON is partially in panel
at his desk. WALLACE has risen and is standing,
looking at CROCKER'S back. Everyone's expression
is very serious—they're talking life-or-death
shit, here.

1 ALEXIS:
>Oh-five-seventeen, sir.

2 WALLACE:
>Are we ABORTING?

<u>TWO:</u>
ECU CROCKER, scowling as he tips his head,
lighting a cigarette. WALLACE is coming closer in
background.

3 WALLACE:
>Paul?

<u>THREE:</u>
Angle looking past CROCKER in FG, WALLACE right
behind him, over his shoulder. Each of them is
wearing concern, but for different reasons—Wallace
is worried about his number two, and Crocker is
worried about the fallout of the operation and
everything that can go wrong.

4 CROCKER:
>SUNLIGHT hits her position, she'll
>be BLOWN.

5 WALLACE:
>She'll be BLOWN as soon as she
>pulls the TRIGGER.

6 WALLACE/linked:

                    The QUESTION is can she get out in
                    TIME?

FOUR:
CU CROCKER, having pivoted about halfway to face
WALLACE. CROCKER looks pissy, scowling. WALLACE
looks attentive, and still obviously tense.

7 CROCKER:
                    The question is CAN she HIT the
                    target?

8 WALLACE:
                    You KNOW she can, Boss...

FIVE:
Angle past WALLACE in FG, turning to look at
CROCKER, who is now leaning on the D.O.O.'s desk,
directing his speech to RON. RON has one hand to
his headset, checking.

9 WALLACE:
                    ...it's why you sent HER and not
                    me.

10 CROCKER:
                    What's Markovsky's ETA?

11 RON:
                    Checking, sir.

SIX:
Narrow panel, wide shot of the room from the back.
RON is checking for an answer, ALEXIS is busy at
her desk.

WALLACE and CROCKER are both looking at the map,
or more specifically, the clock over Kosovo.

12 CROCKER:
                    Well HURRY it up.

SEVEN:
ECU KOSOVO CLOCK.

Now reading:

0507 Z

NO COPY.

ONE:
Angle past ALEXIS in FG, one hand on her headset.
She's looking to CROCKER, who has turned, still
scowling, cigarette dangling from his lips.

RON is still busily doing his thing.

WALLACE is lighting himself another cigarette.

1 ALEXIS:
Sir?   RAVEN   is   asking   for
INSTRUCTIONS.

2 CROCKER: Tell him to bloody well wait. It's
not his ASS in the NEST, is it?

TWO:
OTS CROCKER, looking at WALLACE, whose expression is
something between incredulity and frustration.

3 CROCKER:
She   gets   CAUGHT,   the   Foreign
Office'll EAT me for DINNER.

4 WALLACE:
DON'T tell me you didn't CLEAR the
RUN?

THREE:
From the map, CROCKER looking at the clock, off.
RON is addressing his back.

5 CROCKER:
I couldn't risk Weldon saying NO.

6 RON:
It's CONFIRMED, sir. Markovsky
came in over the Macedonian border
twenty-three minutes ago, through
the German sector.

FOUR:
CROCKER looking at WALLACE. Both of them know
what this means, neither of them look particularly
happy.

7 WALLACE/small:
Well, that's THAT, then, isn't
it?

FIVE:
Angle past ALEXIS as CROCKER addresses her. The
scowl is gone. He's made his decision.

8 CROCKER:
Lex, order to RAVEN from D. Ops.
Tell him CROW is free to FLY.

9 ALEXIS:

                    Yes, sir.

SIX:
CU of the map, KOSOVO section again, the call-out.
Now reads:

                    OPERATION: BROKEN GROUND
                    STATUS: FREE RUN

10 ALEXIS/off:
                    M.C.O.   for   Raven,   orders   as
                    follow:
11 ALEXIS/linked/off:
                    From   Director   Operations   Paul
                    Crocker…

Page 4

ONE:
This is gonna be kinda tricky, so I apologize in
advance.

We're looking straight on at TARA CHACE[56]. She is
prone, in a sniper's nest, sheltered by rubble.
She's on the fifth floor of a bombed-out building,
sighting through a shattered wall. Broken concrete
and masonry, including exposed rebar, are providing
shelter.

It's dawn, and a light dusting of snow covers her
position.

She is settled behind an Accuracy International
AWP sniper's rifle with a pretty big scope on it
mounted on a bipod [*Steve—I've got reference for
this if you want it.*][7]. Beside her is a TWO-WAY
RADIO set, and a pair of HIGH-POWER BINOCULARS, on
a short tripod. All the equipment is camouflaged.

CHACE is wearing a Ghillie suit, with a sniper's
cowl—basically a very fine weave camo net—pulled
over her head and draped around her shoulders.

The effect we're going for is that everything
is almost merging with the background because of
camouflage. CHACE herself should be very hard to
spot.

1 CAPTION:
                    "…Crow is free to fly…."

2 CAPTION/Chace:
                    The last time I was this COLD I was
                    at the South Pole.[8]

TWO:
CU CHACE, settling herself behind the scope. Her
hair is tied back. She looks determined.

5. Tara Felicity Chace is a lovely young lady who now lives in Seattle and speaks something like forty-seven languages, and works as a professional translator. She and I went to high school together. She and I would stay up late and sit on the floor in the darkened living room of her parents' home in Monterey, and we would watch video tapes of spy stories—mostly Sir Alec Guinness as George Smiley in Smiley's People and Tinker, Tailor, Soldier, Spy, The Sandbaggers, and, if I remember correctly, The Prisoner. We were adolescents with bubbling hormones, and we'd sneak out in the middle of the night and watch spy stories together. Tell me that's not seriously fucked up. I mean, I don't think we even ever kissed. And we did this a lot. I look back on it, and I suspect we were probably madly in love with one another, and too dumb to realize it (well, at least I was), and I know that she was my best friend in the whole wide world then. But it was high school and there was adolescent bullshit, and I never told her that. So I'm telling her that now. And that's why Tara Chace is named Tara Chace.

6. Normally, when introducing a new character, I give a paragraph of description, as I did for Crocker back on script-page 1; here I didn't, simply because Steve had been faxing me sketches of Chace for months, and I'd been sending them back with notes like 'more like this' and 'no, no, icky,' and 'yes!!!'

7. He didn't.

3 CAPTION/Chace:
                Why doesn't Crocker EVER send me somewhere HOT?

THREE:
POV CHACE, through the scope, and we're seeing the wreckage of Prizren, a large open area of what was once an intersection on the main road. Buildings are in various stages of collapse and rubble—Prizren took it pretty bad during the war. At the same time, some obvious repair work has been done, and the city has signs of life and, even, normalcy.

At the intersection is a parked 3 TON TRUCK, with three KLA irregulars loafing nearby. They're joking with one another, smoking cigarettes. All have AK-47s slung over shoulders or across their backs.

Sunlight is starting to lance through gaps in the surrounding buildings.

Across the intersection, some crumpled NEWSPAPER is blowing from right to left.

4 CAPTION/Chace:
                Need to COMPENSATE for the WIND….

5 CAPTION/Chace:
                …maybe he won't SHOW….

FOUR:
Angle from the intersection, as another TRUCK, this one much older, rattles into the intersection opposite the 3 TON TRUCK.

KLA GUYS are moving to greet.

In EBG we can see CHACE'S BUILDING, where her sniper's nest is. Sunlight is creeping up the front of the building. We should not be able to actually see Chace.

NO COPY.

enters here
Markovsky
Tara
truck enters here
45° angle

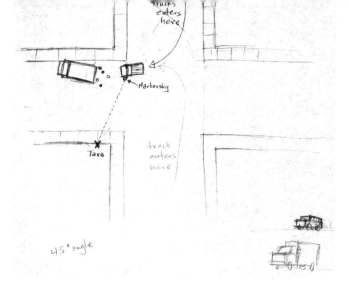

Page 5

ONE:
POV CHACE, through the scope. The OLD TRUCK has stopped about fifteen feet away from the back of the 3 TON TRUCK. TWO RUSSIAN MAFIA TYPES are coming out of the new truck, moving to greet the 3 KLA SOLDIERS.

1 CAPTION/Chace:
Dammit...

TWO:
OTS MARKOVSKY, still in the cab of the OLD TRUCK. Past him, over the hood, we can see the TWO RUSSIAN MAFIA TYPES walking to the back of the 3 TON TRUCK, escorted by ONE of the KLA SOLDIERS.

MARKOVSKY, for the record, is an entirely ordinary looking Russian in his late forties.

2 CAPTION/Chace:
...get OUT of the TRUCK, General.

THREE:
Angle past the TWO RUSSIAN MAFIA TYPES.

A KLA SOLDIER has pulled back the tarp covering the rear of the 3 TON TRUCK, revealing, inside, LOTS OF GUNS. We're talking rifles, pistols, heavy machine guns, some of it in crates, some of it loose. A small MORTAR rests in the middle of everything.[9]

3 CAPTION/Chace:
INSPECT the merchandise, do SOMETHING...

FOUR:
POV CHACE, angle on the cab of the OLD TRUCK. We can't see MARKOVSKY, only his slight shadow.

9. I do a lot of research. I try to use multiple sources. When I veer from reality, I tend to do so for one of two reasons—either because it's dramatically necessary, or because the reality is so convoluted and complicated that there's no hope of making it clear in a 24 page issue. The scenario being described above—with the exception of the CIA sanctioned assassination that Tara is about to commit—is entirely real.

Throughout the late '90s, the KLA was buying and selling arms like nobody's business on the black market, rather than surrendering them to NATO, as they were supposed to be doing. My interest in the subject came from reading an editorial in the British Medical Journal, from August 14, 1999, and then an article in the Hindustan Times, from Tuesday, August 17, 1999. Yes, I have strange reading habits. Incidentally, I've had it confirmed by someone who was actually in Kosovo at the time that the trade described above happened with alarming frequency.

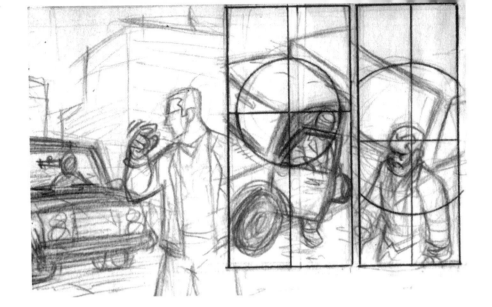

4 CAPTION/Chace:　　　...give me a SHOT.

FIVE:
Angle past ONE of the RUSSIAN MAFIA TYPES, who has
turned and is beckoning to MARKOVSKY in the cab
of the OLD TRUCK.

5 CAPTION/Chace:
　　　　　There you GO, they've brought the
　　　　　GUNS, now give the nice soldiers
　　　　　their MONEY...

SIX:
POV CHACE, through the scope, the cab of the OLD
TRUCK, as MARKOVSKY steps out. He's carrying a
DUFFEL BAG.

6 CAPTION/Chace:
　　　　　Good...good...

7 CAPTION/Chace:
　　　　　...inhale...

SEVEN:
POV CHACE, through the scope, as the crosshairs
come to rest on MARKOVSKY'S head.

8 CAPTION/Chace:　　　...exhale...

9 CAPTION/Chace:　　　...hold...

10 CAPTION/Chace:　　　...and...

Page 6

ONE:
Closer, angle as MARKOVSKY'S head is blown open by a .308 magnum round. The round has passed through Markovsky and has shattered the WINDOW on the OLD TRUCK.[10]

NO COPY.

TWO:
CU as MARKOVSKY slumps down the side of the trunk. The side of his head facing away from Chace's position is literally almost half gone—a .308 is a big round. The WINDOW has shattered, and blood, brain, and bone are misting the inside of the cab.

NO COPY.

THREE:
MARKOVSKY toppling to the ground, the KLA SOLDIERS and the RUSSIAN MAFIA TYPES all staring in shock, just now beginning to move.

MARKOVSKY has dropped the duffel.

NO COPY.

FOUR:
Smaller, narrow panel. CU CHACE, looking directly at her over the barrel of the rifle, as she comes off the sight. She's pulling the cowl down with one hand, revealing her features.

Her expression is grim. She's not proud of what she just did.

NO COPY.

10. Like the Ops Room on page 1, I wanted the violence here to be sharp, shocking, and realistic; in short, I wanted it to set the tone for the rest of the series—that bullets were very bad things and that people died, and they died quickly, and horribly, and rarely with the luxury of seeing it coming. This is one of those places where the panel descriptions really means nothing, it's all up to the artist. Steve did a brilliant job here, in my view, conveying not only the horror of the murder, but the shock of it, as well.

Page 7

ONE:
View of the intersection, and now the KLA SOLDIERS and the RUSSIAN MAFIA TYPES all diving for cover.

NO COPY.[11]

TWO:
Angle from behind the KLA SOLDIERS, behind cover, their weapons out. The LEAD KLA GUY speaking on a RADIO. Whatever it is he's saying, he's pretty damn upset.

The OTHER TWO are firing on Chase's position, off.

NO COPY.

THREE:

11. I use these silent panels a lot when I write comics. There are readers out there who think that makes me lazy. They're stupid and should go read books with lots of big sound effects, and leave me alone. I use NO COPY panels for a number of reasons, but primarily because what I write is only half—if that—of what a comic book is. The art is as crucial as any word, as any sound effect.

For this sequence, sound effects seemed to me to be entirely inappropriate; rather than filling the panels with word balloons of half-completed exclamations, it seemed far more elegant and powerful to drop into a complete silence, and let Steve's pencils provide the sound.

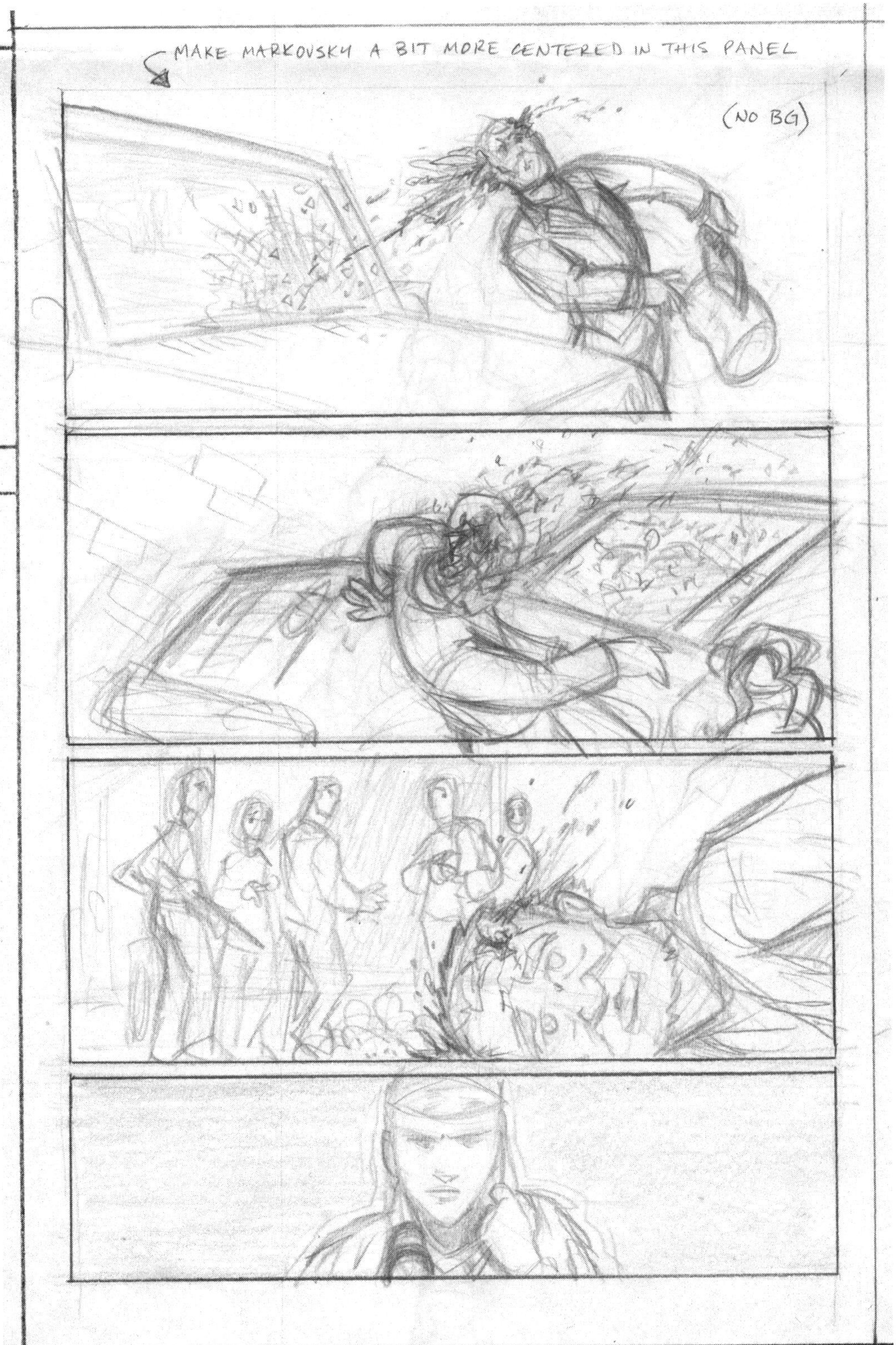
MAKE MARKOVSKY A BIT MORE CENTERED IN THIS PANEL
(NO BG)

Angle past the OLD TRUCK, as the KLA LEADER, still
yelling on his radio, is motioning the OTHER TWO
after him as he heads for the building.

NO COPY.

FOUR:
Angle from the exterior, but closer, on the nest.
No sign of Chace. BULLETS are tearing hell out of
the remaining masonry, ricocheting off brick.

The RIFLE, RADIO, and BINOCULARS are all still in
place. Chace herself is gone.

Lots of bullets hitting the position.

NO COPY.

FIVE:
Wide, extreme longshot of the intersection.
The KLA SOLDIERS are now advancing on CHACE'S
BUILDING, the RUSSIA MAFIA TYPES now crouched
around MARKOVSKY'S BODY.

This is pretty much a big tableau, still-life
almost.

NO COPY.

SIX:
CU of the SUN rising over the buildings in the
east. It is now officially daylight.

NO COPY.

Page 8

ONE:
Exterior of the building, this is the "back" of the
structure, the side away from the intersection.
Marginally more intact than the side that was
facing the intersection, previous.

CHACE is crouching in the broken doorway, swathed
in shadow, looking out. She's checking to see that
her route is clear across the street. She still
wears the Ghillie suit.

The SUN is still creeping higher, casting long
shadows up and down the block.

NO COPY.

TWO:
Shot along this new street, this can be about knee-
level or so, looking up slightly. The street is
peppered with broken rocks and bricks and glass.

CHACE is sprinting from the open doorway on our

left, where her sniper's nest was, towards another building on the opposite side of the street. She's running across the pockets of daylight. The Ghillie suit makes her hard to see.

NO COPY.

THREE:
OTS KLA SOLDIER, in FG, as he comes around the back corner of Chace's building, turning right. He is looking to his right, weapon ready. Looking nervous.

In EBG, we can see CHACE disappearing into the doorway of the building opposite the one she just left.

NO COPY.

FOUR:
Reverse of ONE.

CHACE is in her new doorway, pressing herself back into the shadows, looking back over her shoulder.

Past her, in BG, we can see TWO KLA SOLDIERS, one coming from either side of the building she just left. They're meeting in the doorway she just abandoned, looking around, preparing to go inside.

NO COPY.

FIVE:
POV CHACE, as the TWO KLA SOLDIERS enter the other building, covering one another as they disappear inside.

NO COPY.

SIX:
CU CHACE, her expression. Relief, but her eyes are still very wary. This is far from over.

NO COPY.

Page 9

ONE:
Interior of the new building. Lots of rubble, ruined furniture, more broken masonry.

CHACE is unzipping the Ghillie suit, pulling one arm free. She's wearing a flannel shirt over a turtleneck and heavy jeans beneath the suit.

NO COPY.

TWO:
Close on CHACE'S BOOTS as the Ghillie suit drops
to the ground. Past it, we can see a shadow-filled
gap behind some broken masonry.

NO COPY.

THREE:
Same angle as previous, but now CHACE is crouching,
reaching into the hole.

NO COPY.

FOUR:
Same as previous, but CHACE has now pulled a
BUNDLE from the hiding place.

NO COPY.

FIVE:
Same as previous, but now CHACE is stuffing the
Ghillie suit into the hiding place.

NO COPY.

SIX:
CHACE crouching in FG, unwrapping the bundle,
which we can now see is a JACKET.

NO COPY.

SEVEN:
CU CHACE'S BACK, pulling the jacket on. We can
see a stencil, the UNITED NATIONS LOGO. Above it
should be the words UNITED NATIONS or U.N. [*Steve-I
can't find an actual reference for this jacket, but
I'm reliably informed it exists in some form or
other—probably doesn't say "United Nations" on
it, but certainly would have the emblem.*][12]

NO COPY.

12. Doing this, of course, is entirely
illegal and honestly, pretty skanky;
but then again, the British bugged the
Secretary General's Office at the U.N.,
so I suppose this pales in comparison.

Page 10

ONE:
Wide, narrow shot, of the street. CHACE has emerged
from the building, in her U.N. JACKET, and is
walking briskly away, making for the corner in the
BG, right of panel.

In FG, turning the FG corner, left of panel, is
KLA LEADER, reacting.

1 CAPTION/Chace:
                And it was going so WELL...

TWO:
At the other corner, CHACE in FG, head down,
pretending she doesn't hear. Her expression is

scared, though.

In BG, coming from his corner, the KLA LEADER is running after her, raising his AK, shouting.

2 CAPTION/Chace:
...don't need to SPEAK Croatian[13] to know WHAT he's shouting.

13. I got this wrong. The KLA — the Kosovo Liberation Army — was/is comprised mostly of Kosovar Albanians; as such, they would either be shouting in Albanian, or, potentially, Serbian.

THREE:
OTS KLA LEADER, sighting with the AK at CHACE'S BACK, as she reaches the corner.

NO COPY.

FOUR:
Angle, as CHACE ducks around the corner in FG. In BG the KLA LEADER is opening fire.

NO COPY.

FIVE:
Along the street that CHACE has just turned down, as she sprints towards us, away from the corner.

In BG, opposite the corner she turned, at an angle, we can see where the ROUNDS from the LEADER'S SHOTS are RICOCHETING off the rubble, and then bouncing crazily around the street—into the air, into the street, and some of them are dangerously close to CHASE.

NO COPY.

Page 11

ONE:
High angle, looking down from the end of the street. At the top of the panel, KLA LEADER has turned the corner, still shooting. He is being joined by the TWO OTHER SOLDIERS.

At the bottom of the panel, CHACE is running for her life.

NO COPY.

TWO:
Lower angle, CHASE sliding over the hood of a PARKED CAR.

In EBG, the SOLDIERS are pursuing her.

The neighborhood is getting somewhat better, meaning less rubble, more repair.

1 CAPTION/Chace:
What is it Wallace always says?

THREE:
On the opposite side of the car, CHACE coming up
and running into an alley.

The KLA LEADER is reloading. The OTHER TWO are
still shooting, and doing a fair amount of damage
to the car.

RICOCHETS are bouncing around crazily, smashing
glass, burying themselves into brick and the
like.

2 CAPTION/Chace:
              It's not the BULLET that has your
              NAME on it you have to worry
              about…

FOUR:
Shot of the entrance of the alley, at an angle.
CHACE'S head is moving out of panel, ducking.

BULLETS are ripping into the brick where her head
would have been, RICOCHETING.

3 CAPTION/Chace:
              …it's all those OTHER ones…

FIVE:
CU CHACE'S left calf, as one of the RICOCHETS[14]
punches through her pants leg.

4 CAPTION/Chace:
              …marked to WHOM it may CONCERN—[15]

SIX:
Angle on the street as CHACE tumbles from the hit,
going down, hard.

5 CAPTION/Chace:
              …bloody HELL...

SEVEN:
CU CHACE'S FACE, grimacing in pain as she rolls
onto her back on the ground.

6 CAPTION/Chace:
              …I DON'T want to DIE in Kosovo.

Page 12[16]

ONE:
ECU of an overflowing ashtray on the D.O.O.'s desk,
as WALLACE'S hand crushes out yet another smoke. We
can see just a fraction of RON past the ashtray.

1 RON:
              Sir? Just in from PRIZREN…

TWO:

14. This was important to me—though I suspect I was the only who cared; if the bullet had struck Chace's leg dead on, there was a good chance she could have lost the leg. I wanted the wounds to be as realistic as the violence in this series, and thus, I had to burn off a lot of the round's velocity before I could let the bullet strike her. Hence the ricochet.

15. This line was stolen from my very good friend Jerry Hennelly, who has served as one of my main research sources for several years, now. Jerry currently works as a cop. He has served in the Army, and worked as a Personal Security Agent for several years. He knows all sorts of things that fascinate and frighten me. He's also a hell of a guy, and a dear, dear friend. It was he who told me this line over lunch in a restaurant in New York several years ago, and I'd been looking for a place to use it ever since then.

16. There's a line by the late Douglas Adams that was used in the second series of the Hitchhiker's Guide to the Galaxy radio series: "And since this is of course an immensely frustrating and nervewracking moment for the narrative to suddenly switch tracks again, that is precisely what the narrative will now do." Which is another way to say, hey, look, dramatic pacing.

In the OPS ROOM, angle past CROCKER as he turns to exchange looks with WALLACE. Not very happy.

RON is visible past WALLACE'S ELBOW, speaking to CROCKER.

2 RON: …reports of GUNFIRE and a PURSUIT.

3 CROCKER: Anything ELSE?

4 RON: Yes, sir. One FATALITY, male.

THREE:
CROCKER and WALLACE, heads together.

5 CROCKER: So she got him before she was blown.

6 WALLACE: Is that going to help you SLEEP better when she doesn't come back?[17]

FOUR:
CROCKER crossing to the MONITOR WALL, focused on it. ALEXIS is snapping into action.

WALLACE stands still in BG, very concerned.

7 CROCKER: Lex, what's the EGRESS?

8 ALEXIS: Istanbul Number Two recruited DRIVER picks her up north of Prizren. Travel via U.N. vehicle, U.N. cover north to PRISTINA...

FIVE:
OTS CROCKER, looking at the MONITOR as it changes to a zoom of KOSOVO, showing the roadways from PRIZREN to PRISTINA. The map also marks the various sectors—PRISTINA is U.K., PRIZREN is GERMAN. Also shows the ITALIAN, FRENCH, and AMERICAN sectors.

9 ALEXIS/off: …to the British Sector, where she meets our CONTACT and is FLOWN out of country.

10 CROCKER: If she misses the rendezvous? Is there a fall-back?

SIX:
OTS CROCKER, looking at ALEXIS. ALEXIS is sober.

11 ALEXIS: No, sir. She's on her own.

SEVEN:

17. Wallace is Crocker's conscience. He's not saying anything that Crocker doesn't know, of course.

OTS CROCKER, now taking in WALLACE and ALEXIS.

12 WALLACE:

And UNARMED?

13 ALEXIS:

Yes. She was to go WEAPONLESS[18] after the HIT, in case she was STOPPED at any of the CHECKPOINTS….

18. This was another point I wanted to make clear in this issue, especially in light of the events in Issue Three; guns are a big deal. They create as many, if not more, problems than they solve; Tara trying to cross a border with a gun is a quick way to get arrested, for instance. Unlike James Bond, the Minders do not go armed unless absolutely necessary.

There's an additional dramatic dividend, here; when the Minders are ordered to take up arms, it adds that much more tension to their situation. By establishing the respect and reluctance to use firearms, I was trying to give them the weight they deserve.

Page 13

ONE:
Wide of the OPS ROOM, everyone still, and in their same positions.

NO COPY.

TWO:
CROCKER turning back to WALLACE once more, putting a cigarette to his lips. RON, in BG, is answering one of the phones on his desk.

3 RON/small:

Duty Ops. Officer…

4 CROCKER:

Eighty-seven kilometers from PRIZREN to PRISTINA…

6 WALLACE:

With KLA, NATO, and U.N. troops all along the way.

THREE:
Angle past RON, still on the phone. WALLACE is lighting CROCKER'S cigarette.

7 WALLACE:

You going to notify the Foreign Office?

8 CROCKER:

Not YET. She COULD still make it.

9 RON/small:

Yes, sir, I'll tell him.

FOUR:
OTS RON, CROCKER reacting to the statement. CROCKER is angry as ever.

10 RON:

Deputy Chief, sir. Wants you in his office right away.

FIVE:
Angle from the entrance of the OPS ROOM, CROCKER

storming towards us, not happy at all. RON, WALLACE, and ALEXIS all looking after him.

11 CROCKER:
Call me if there are any developments.

12 WALLACE:
What're you going to tell Weldon?

SIX:
CROCKER, snarling.

13 CROCKER: Depends on how much he already KNOWS.

Page 14

ONE:
Back in Prizren, the alley.

CHACE is pulling herself upright using the side of a building. A DOORWAY is further along the alley.

1 CAPTION/Chace:
First rule...

TWO:
Angle from the opposite end of the alley, as CHACE limps her way towards us, trailing blood from her wounded calve.

2 CAPTION/Chace:
...keep MOVING.[19]

19. Again, I didn't make this up, though I can't remember the source for them off the top of my head. Probably some declassified Army manual on Escape & Evasion tactics.

THREE:
CU CHACE'S expression, she's sweating, in pain, but her eyes are lighting up.

3 CAPTION/Chace:
Second rule...

FOUR:
Slight down angle, overlooking a SQUARE filled with Albanian and Croatian WOMEN and children, all of them gathered around a WELL in its center. They are filling buckets with water, doing laundry, etc. These women are predominantly Muslim, and as such are dressed accordingly, heavy black cloaks, faces covered.

In BG, from the alley, CHACE is emerging, pulling off her jacket.

In low FG, a TRUCK is parked, just inside panel.

4 CAPTION/Chace:
...find a CROWD.[19]

FIVE:
CHACE pushes through the crowd, trying to disappear
into it. The jacket is off and in her hands.

NO COPY.

SIX:
Angle from inside the alley, past the THREE KLA
SOLDIERS as they reach the end, looking out to see
the crowd of WOMEN around the WELL.

NO COPY.

Page 15

ONE:
Angle as the KLA LEADER gestures for his men
to disperse the crowd. The TWO KLA SOLDIERS are
trying to follow the orders, but the WOMEN aren't
moving.

NO COPY.

TWO:
KLA LEADER, with his AK in the air, opening fire.

NO COPY.

THREE:
OTS LEADER, as the WOMEN all scatter for cover,
grabbing their CHILDREN, abandoning their
buckets, terrified. LAUNDRY is left in piles on
the ground.

NO COPY.

FOUR:
POV KLA LEADER, looking at the pile of laundry,
the U.N. JACKET atop it, and a trail of blood
leading around the well.

NO COPY.

FIVE:
Angle, as the KLA LEADER follows the trail of
blood to the CAB OF THE PARKED TRUCK, motioning
the TWO SOLDIERS to cover him.

NO COPY.

SIX:
Close angle, KLA LEADER against the truck, AK
wedged to his hip, reaching for the door to the
cab of the truck. The TWO SOLDIERS are sighting
on the cab.

NO COPY.

SEVEN:
KLA LEADER yanks the door open.

NO COPY.

EIGHT:
OTS KLA LEADER, looking at the empty cab.

NO COPY.

Page 16

ONE:
Back in London, interior of WELDON'S OFFICE, which
is a nicely appointed room, a little cramped, with
a large desk and several filing cabinets. A couple
paintings on the walls. A computer on the desk.

WELDON, in his late forties, kind of a Bob Hoskins
type, is in a suit, sipping a cup of tea behind
his desk.

CROCKER has just entered the office, one hand still
on the door.

Sunlight is edging through the windows.

1 WELDON:
                    Paul. Hope I didn't DISTURB you.

2 CROCKER:
                    I was in the Ops. Room.

3 WELDON:
                    Yes, I KNOW...

TWO:
OTS CROCKER as he moves to the desk, opposite
WELDON. WELDON is leaning back in his chair,
holding his cup of tea in both hands. He's looking
like he doesn't take shit from anyone, least of
all Crocker.

4 WELDON:
                    ...what I DON'T know is why Tara
                    Chace is in Kosovo.

5 CROCKER:
                    Is she?

6 WELDON:
                    You DAMN well KNOW she IS!

THREE:
Angle as WELDON leans forward, snarling. CROCKER
doesn't move.

7 WELDON:
                    You're running a SPECIAL operation
                    in KOSOVO and I want to know WHY!

8 WELDON/linked:
                    What the hell is Broken Ground?

FOUR:
OTS WELDON, CROCKER'S expression, mouth shut, almost contemptuous.

9 WELDON:
                    I want an ANSWER, Paul!

FIVE:
OTS WELDON, CROCKER'S expression, considering what to say.

NO COPY.

SIX:
CROCKER, relenting.

10 CROCKER:
                    It's a FAVOR to the CIA. Former
                    Russian General, Igor Grigorivich
                    Markovsky.

SEVEN:
WELDON, still suspicious, again sipping his tea.
CROCKER is still standing, not relaxed, but not
as confrontational.

11 WELDON:
                    He's retired, Markovsky.

12 CROCKER:
                    He's Russian MOB, buying GUNS from
                    the KLA and then selling them to
                    the CHECHENS.
Page 17

ONE:
OTS WELDON, at CROCKER.

1 CROCKER:
                    CIA asked if we could put a STOP to
                    it.

TWO:
WELDON, setting his cup of tea down very carefully
on his desk. He's furious. He's not looking at
Crocker.

2 WELDON:
                    You used one of Her Majesty's
                    agents to commit MURDER at the
                    American's behest?

THREE:
CROCKER, unrepentant.

3 CROCKER:
                    Not for FREE.

4 CROCKER/linked:
                    In exchange we get KEYHOLE[20] support
                    and analysis for OUR operations in
                    North Africa and Asia.

20. Referring to the satellite system, of course, but you all probably already knew that. The Keyhole is a pretty amazing device, and it's the one we know about; the thing's got a camera resolution down to something like 18 inches—that's good enough so that Keyhole satellite images have been introduced into evidence at various war crimes trial in the Hague and the like.

FOUR:
WELDON, rising, both hands on the desk, still just
livid with CROCKER. CROCKER is, paradoxically, the
most relaxed we've seen him—he's almost smiling.

5 CROCKER:
That's INTELLIGENCE we couldn't
get otherwise—

6 WELDON:
That HARDLY justifies you mounting
an UNAUTHORIZED assassination!

FIVE:
OTS WELDON, CROCKER, sincere.

7 CROCKER:
I think it DOES. The CIA does
favors for US all the time.

8 CROCKER/linked:
Now they owe me—

9 WELDON: YOU?

SIX:
CU CROCKER, bare smile.

10 CROCKER: Us.
11 CROCKER/linked:
Now they owe US. It's GOOD for the
Service, sir.

SEVEN:
WELDON, fuming.

NO COPY.

EIGHT:
WELDON, picking up his tea once more, the kind
of fury that makes you whisper instead of shout.
CROCKER is turning to go.

12 WELDON: I HOPE that'll be CONSOLATION for
Chace's FAMILY.

13 CROCKER: I doubt it, Sir.

NINE:
CU CROCKER.

14 CROCKER: She doesn't HAVE any.[21]

21. Crocker is lying, but it's mostly
because he knows Chace, rather than
because he's trying to deceive Weldon,
here. Current readers of Queen &
Country will have noted that in Issue 25,
Tara goes to visit her mother, Annika
Bodmer-Chace. Mother and daughter
have...difficulty communicating, shall
we say.

Page 18

ONE:
OTS CHACE, looking out a cracked window at a
street in Prizren. A HUMVEE is rolling down the
street, U.N. Peacekeepers atop it. It's passing a
parked car.

CHACE is wearing the black robe the Muslim women
were wearing.

1 CAPTION/Chace:
                    Blown the rendezvous to HELL.

TWO:
Reveal that CHACE is in an empty bedroom, a little
bed in a corner. The place looks like it was
abandoned in a hurry. She's sitting on the bed,
her left knee up, her foot on the bed with her.
She's rolled the pant's leg up. There's a lot of
blood.

2 CAPTION/Chace:
                    Crocker must be APOPLECTIC.

THREE:
CHACE, taking a corner of the black cloak between
her teeth and tearing a strip free.

3 CAPTION/Chace:
                    Weldon's got to know by now, too.

FOUR:
CHACE tying the strip of fabric tightly around the
wound in her calf. For the record, it's a flesh
wound. Most of the bullet was spent when it hit
her.

4 CAPTION/Chace: Wonder who won THAT fight.

FIVE:
CHACE rolling her pant leg back down.

5 CAPTION/Chace:
                    Lucky it was only a RICOCHET that
                    hit me.
6 CAPTION/Chace:
                    Hurts like HELL all the SAME.

SIX:
OTS CHACE, again looking out the window.

The HUMVEE is gone, but the parked car remains on
the street. SOLDIERS are patrolling nearby.

7 CAPTION/Chace: Time to GO.

Page 19

ONE:
Exterior street, the SOLDIERS are on patrol.
Civilians in various garb are out and about, too.
Some are being questioned by the PEACEKEEPERS.

CHACE is crossing the street, wrapped in the black
cloak, making for the car.

It's about 10:30 local time, now, the SUN is high.
Puddles on the street from melted snow.

NO COPY.

TWO:
Angle past a PEACEKEEPER in FG, who has turned
from the MAN he is questioning to watch CHACE as
she reaches the car.

1 CAPTION/Chace:
               Too much to HOPE that the KEYS are
               in.

THREE:
POV CHACE as she tries the door and discovers it
is unlocked, swinging slightly open.

2 CAPTION/Chace:
               At least the DOOR'S unlocked.

FOUR:
OTS PEACEKEEPER from panel Two, as CHACE gets into
the car.

As she does, the cloak rides, up and exposes her
BLOODIED PANT-LEG.

3 CAPTION/Chace:
               Old-fashion IGNITION, good…

FIVE:
POV PEACEKEEPER, CU of the BLOODIED PANT-LEG.

4 CAPTION/Chace:
               …just need a few seconds…

SIX:
Angle in the car, as CHACE, wrapped in the black
cloak, hotwires the ignition.

5 CAPTION/Chace:
               C'mon give a GIRL a BREAK…

SEVEN:
POV CHACE, looking in the rearview mirror, seeing
the PEACEKEEPER approaching the vehicle, one hand
out.

6 CAPTION/Chace: …C'MON start…

EIGHT:
CU of the exhaust pipe, as a nice burst of black
exhaust comes out.

7 CAPTION/Chace: …THANK YOU.

Page 20

ONE:
Angle as the CAR pulls away down the street,
leaving the PEACEKEEPER to wave his arms.

NO COPY.

TWO:
Another POV CHACE, checking the mirror, this one
on the side. PEACEKEEPER is visible getting on
his radio.

NO COPY.

THREE:
CHACE behind the wheel, pulling the cloak off
with her free hand as she drives. Looks pretty
determined.

NO COPY.

FOUR:
Angle on the CAR as it speeds along the broken
road out of Prizren. Passing some PEDESTRIANS as
they walk along the side of the road.

FIVE:
CHACE rolling down the window as she drives, now
out of the cloak.

NO COPY.

SIX:
Angle behind the car as CHACE sticks out an arm,
holding the cloak, which is snapping in the
wind.

NO COPY.

SEVEN:
The cloak, fluttering in the air as it falls, the
CAR already in the distance as she really floors
it.

NO COPY.

Page 21

ONE:
Large panel, bird's eye shot, as the CAR makes it's way along the narrow road. Broken countryside, still recovering from the war.

NO COPY.

TWO:
Another angle on the CAR as it passes an EXCAVATION at the side of the road, U.N. PEACEKEEPERS working backhoes, wearing surgical masks.

Basically, she's passing a mass grave, but we're being subtle about it.

The SUN is strong overhead.

NO COPY.

THREE:
Angle past the CAR as it slows. In BG, ahead of the vehicle, we can see the GERMAN SECTOR CHECKPOINT.

A SIGN on the side of the road, bent and bullet-marked, says:

PRISTINA 62 KM

[*And if we can get that in the proper language, even better, but I don't know what it would be...*][22]

NO COPY.

22. This is the first instance of what would become a very real problem for me in the later story arcs; that of language. The comic book convention of using carets (</>) to denote speaking a foreign tongue seemed to me very coy and ill-suited to a spy story; especially when there would be times when not understanding what was being said would be as important and being able to follow it. In this instance, it's simply a detail for added verisimilitude; in later issues (especially around 13-15), it became much more important.

ONE:
OTS CHACE, behind the wheel. Through the windshield
we can see a GERMAN STAFFED CHECKPOINT. A GERMAN
FLAG is visible flying from the side of a tent.

1 CAPTION/Chace:
                    Now we LEARN if that bloke got the
                    LICENSE on this thing or NOT.

TWO:
Angle from seat, looking at CHACE as she smiles
brilliantly at the young SOLDIER who has stopped
her.

2 YOUNG SOLDIER:
                    <Where are you heading?>

3 CHACE: <Pristina.>

THREE:
From outside of the car, ANOTHER GUARD at the
checkpoint, reaching for a satellite phone. YOUNG
SOLDIER at CHACE'S WINDOW.

CHACE is handing him a billfold.

4 YOUNG SOLDIER:
                    <You have your PASS?>

5 CHACE: <Here.>

FOUR:
OTS YOUNG SOLDIER as he flips open the billfold and
removes a FOLDED PIECE OF PAPER.

NO COPY.

FIVE:
POV YOUNG SOLDIER as he unfolds the PAPER. A
WALLET-SIZE PHOTO has been folded in with it, and
falls free.

The PAPER, such as we can see, has the U.N. LOGO
on it.

6 YOUNG SOLDIER: <What's this?>

SIX:
OTS CHACE, a very slight smile, as the YOUNG
SOLDIER bends to pick up the photograph.

The OTHER SOLDIER is still on the satellite phone
in BG.

7 CHACE:
                    <Oh… uh, nothing, it's NOTHING…>

SEVEN:
CU SOLDIER, as he rises holding the PHOTOGRAPH,
the PAPER now forgotten in his other hand. His

eyes are wide with surprise and the beginning of
some amusement.

8 CHACE/off: <…can I just have that BACK?>

9 YOUNG SOLDIER:
                    <One moment, please.>

Page 23

ONE:
Angle past CHACE as YOUNG SOLDIER approaches
the OTHER SOLDIER, beckoning him to get off the
phone.

1 CAPTION/Chace:
                    That's right, that's it, ignore
                    the PASS…

TWO:
POV CHACE, watching as YOUNG SOLDIER shows the
PHOTOGRAPH to OTHER SOLDIER, gesturing back at
Chace/us.

YOUNG SOLDIER appears amused. OTHER SOLDIER looks
vaguely bewildered.

2 CAPTION/Chace:
                    …it's a FORGERY after ALL…

THREE:
Stet previous, but closer, and now YOUNG SOLDIER,
still holding the PHOTOGRAPH for OTHER SOLDIER,
is smiling at Chace/us. The OTHER SOLDIER is
grinning, very amused.

3 CAPTION/Chace:
                    …and DON'T pay any ATTENTION to
                    the BLOOD on my TROUSER LEG…

FOUR:
Stet previous, OTHER SOLDIER is still grinning
our way. YOUNG SOLDIER is smiling, coming back,
folding the paper with one hand, still holding the
PHOTOGRAPH.

4 CAPTION/Chace:
                    …just look at the PICTURE, that's
                    FINE.

FIVE:
Angle outside the car, past YOUNG SOLDIER as he
hands the PAPER back to CHACE.

CHACE looks embarrassed.

5 YOUNG SOLDIER:
                    <Everything appears FINE. Have a
                    SAFE trip.>

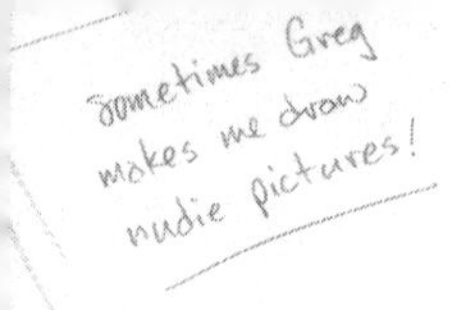
Sometimes Greg
makes me draw
nudie pictures!

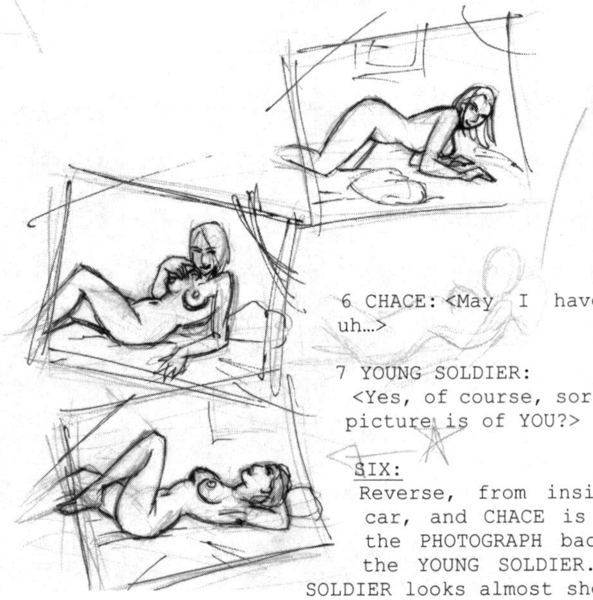

6 CHACE: <May I have, my… uh…>

7 YOUNG SOLDIER:
<Yes, of course, sorry. The picture is of YOU?>

SIX:
Reverse, from inside the car, and CHACE is taking the PHOTOGRAPH back from the YOUNG SOLDIER. YOUNG SOLDIER looks almost sheepish. CHACE still looks embarrassed.

8 CHACE: <It's for my BOYFRIEND.>

10 YOUNG SOLDIER:
<Of course, of course…>

SEVEN:
POV CHACE, putting the PHOTOGRAPH[23] back in the PAPER, and now, of course, we get to see it.

It's a picture of her, nude, posing on a bed. *Playboy* quality, not *Penthouse*![24]

11 YOUNG SOLDIER:
<…drive CAREFULLY.>

12 CHACE: <Thank you.>

23. This is a complete and total steal from The Sandbaggers, though used here with a new wrinkle. In The Sandbaggers, one of the agents gets past a roadblock in Russia by "accidentally" handing over a stack of "novelty postcards." It seemed to me that, if the agent in question were female, and the picture was of herself, you might potentially get an even better reaction, since the instinctive response to another's embarrassment is to let them off the hook—and thus, send Tara on her way as quickly as possible.

24. As you can see from the collection of Steve's sketches, we spent a lot of time on this, and not for the prurient reasons, no matter what you may be thinking. The picture had to be the right one; innocent enough to be forgiven, but compromising enough to be adequately embarrassing. I think I sent Steve back on the sketches three or four times, and I'm sure, at the end, he thought I was just trying to get a stack of naked Tara's for some perverse purpose. All I can say to that is Steve's the one who held onto the sketches, not me. Very important moment, in my opinion.

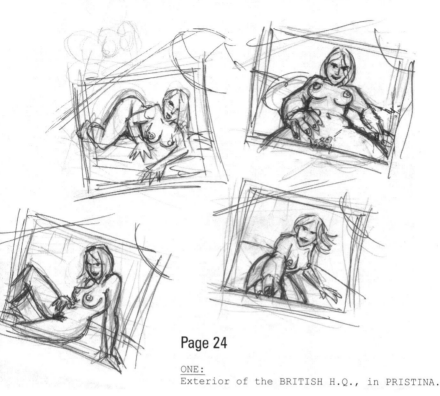

more "come hither" + amateurish

Page 24

<u>ONE</u>:
Exterior of the BRITISH H.Q., in PRISTINA.

The CAR is parked beside a couple of JEEPS, a TANK, the appropriate Peacekeeping force vehicles.

BRITISH SOLDIERS mill about, doing their thing.

A HUT is to one side.

1 CHACE/hut: Sergeant Ramsey?…

<u>TWO</u>:
Interior of the hut, CHACE is standing in front of a field-desk. RAMSEY, a staff sergeant in his late-twenties, is rising and offering her a handshake. She's accepting it. The hut is filled with maps and papers and radio equipment.

2 CHACE: …my name's Chace, Tara Chace.

3 RAMSEY:

                I was getting WORRIED about you,
                Miss Chace. You were supposed to
                be here HOURS ago.

CU CHACE, slight smile. She looks exhausted. Still in pain. But genuinely relieved to have made it this far.

4 CHACE: There was TRAFFIC on the ROAD.

FOUR:
Angle from the side, as RAMSEY sees CHACE'S wounded leg, reacting.

CHACE looking down, as if she'd forgotten about her injury.

5 RAMSEY:
              Good Lord, are you all right? You
              want a MEDIC to take a look at
              that?

6 CHACE: If it's not too much BOTHER.

FIVE:
Angle past CHACE, as she lowers herself into a chair. RAMSEY is passing her, heading out of the hut.

7 RAMSEY: Not at ALL. I'll be RIGHT BACK.

8 CHACE: Take your TIME…

SIX:
CU CHACE, now seated, eyes closing. Exhausted, safe. Smile.

9 CHACE: …take your time.

Page 25

ONE:
Interior of Crocker's Office, and it's about half the size of Weldon's, very Spartan. He's working at his desk, scribbling in a folder with a pen.

WALLACE is coming through the door. Past WALLACE, at the desk, we can see CROCKER'S PERSONAL ASSISTANT, KATE. Kate's in her mid-twenties, very pretty.

1 WALLACE: Boss?

2 CROCKER: What do you WANT, Tom?

TWO:
OTS CROCKER, looking up from his work, at WALLACE, who is leaning against the doorframe.

3 WALLACE: Signal from Istanbul Station.

4 WALLACE/linked:
              Crow is on her way home.

THREE:
OTS WALLACE, CROCKER looking at him. No smile.
Considering. Seems vaguely satisfied with this
turn of events.

5 CROCKER: Is she all right?

6 WALLACE: She got CLIPPED in the leg, but it
                wasn't SERIOUS.

FOUR:
POV WALLACE, as CROCKER goes back to work.

7 CROCKER: Good.

8 CROCKER/linked:
                I'll want her REPORT on my DESK
                tomorrow.

FIVE:
WALLACE looking at CROCKER. Not quite incredulous.
CROCKER is ignoring him.

9 CROCKER: Was there something ELSE?

10 WALLACE: No, sir.

11 CROCKER: Then SHOVE OFF, Tom. I've got WORK
                to do.

SIX:
OTS CROCKER as WALLACE exits, shutting the door
behind him.

NO COPY.

SEVEN:
CROCKER, slight smile, putting pen back to
paper.

12 CROCKER/small: That's my girl.[25]

25. That no matter how much of a
bastard Crocker is—to his superiors,
his friends, his colleagues—we can see
in this moment how much he honestly
cares for his agents.

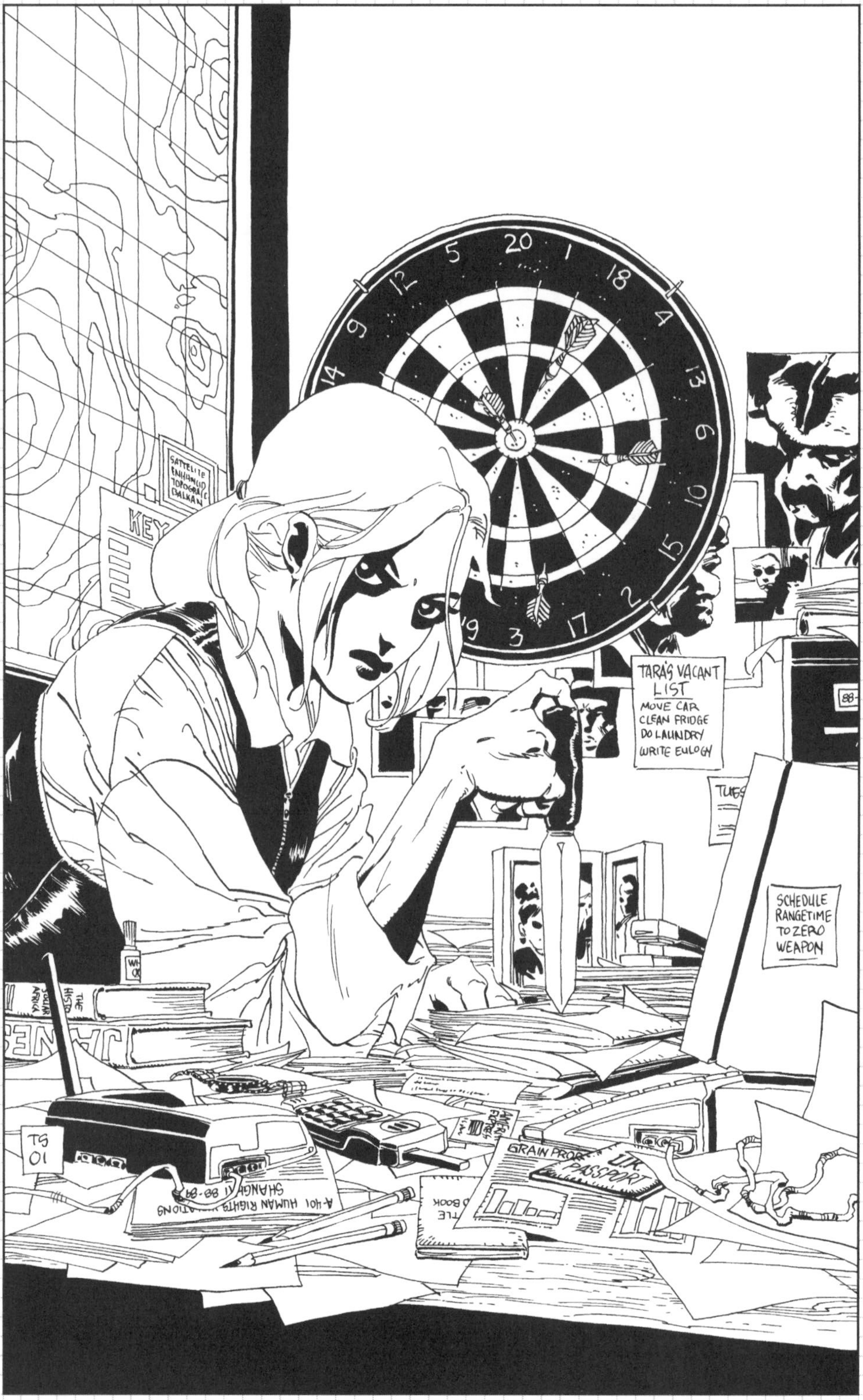
SATTELITE ENHANCED TOPOGRAPHIC BALKAN
KEY
TARA'S VACANT LIST
MOVE CAR
CLEAN FRIDGE
DO LAUNDRY
WRITE EULOGY
SCHEDULE RANGETIME TO ZERO WEAPON
GRAIN PROD
U.K. PASSPORT
TS 01

Page 1

ONE:
Establishing shot, London skyline—Big Ben, the Houses of Parliament, and, if possible, the MI6 Building across the Thames. [*Steve—there's actual reference for the building all over the Web and such, and there are some good shots of it at the start of the Bond film, The World is Not Enough*][1].

It is night, and it is raining rather heavily.

1 CAPTION: London.

TWO:
Angle on a lane on the top of a slight, bare, slope.[2] A VAN is parked to the side of the street, back to us.

Past the VAN, down the hillside and in the distance, we can see the MI6 Building in BG.

It's roughly three in the morning, and the streets are pretty darn bare. The rain is coming down hard enough to bounce off the street and VAN.

NO COPY.

THREE:
Angle as the driver's side door opens—remember we're in England—and a MAN steps out. The dome light in the van has been disabled, so there's not really any ambient light. MAN is perhaps in his mid-thirties, dressed like a casual laborer. Clean shaven. His pulling the hood up on his parka.

NO COPY.

FOUR:
Interior of the VAN, in the back, looking out as the MAN opens the DOORS. In FG, laying just inside the VAN, is a CRATE.

NO COPY.

FIVE:
Close angle, CU MAN'S HANDS, as he twists the

---

1. And no illustration can do this place justice. One of its nicknames is "Legoland." Seriously. Looks like some very obsessive-compulsive kids built this giant pyramid-esque structure along the Thames. "What's that wild looking building?" "Oh, that? That's the headquarters of British Secret Intelligence." Truth is so much stranger than fiction.

2. Utter fiction. No such slope. This we call "dramatic license."

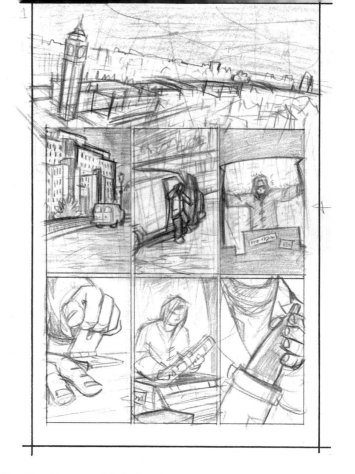

latches on the CRATE. We can see that he has TATTOOS on his FINGERS [*Steve—these are Russian Mob flags, and they each mean something different… I'll see if I can find a source for you*].[3]

The CRATE is labeled in CYRILLIC, with phrases such as CAUTION and EXPLOSIVE.

NO COPY.

<u>SIX:</u>
Close angle, from behind the open trunk, looking just over the lid as MAN lifts out a ROCKET LAUNCHER.[4]

NO COPY.

<u>SEVEN:</u>
Close angle, CU as MAN drops a ROCKET down the TUBE.

NO COPY.

3. I've found several references to this kind of tattooing in various places, but I've rarely encountered anything definitive. My understanding is that, for the most part, the tattoos act as credentials of a sort—symbol X means the subject is a stone-cold killer, etc.

In 2002, the Russian Interior Ministry estimated that somewhere between 70 to 80 percent of private businesses and banks in the country were paying out to some sort of protection or extortion racket of one form or another (MSNBC, August 31, 2002). In 1997, the Center for Strategice and International Studies (a non-partisan organization) estimated that Russian Organized Crime had 200 separate groups operating in some 58 countries around the world.

4. Not sure what the weapon system I was thinking of here. Not that it much matters—right now, there are so many shoulder-launched missile systems available on the black market around the world, it's giving intelligence agencies nightmares. Here, the rocket is being used to attack a building; it could just as easily have been directed at an aircraft. Note, I say just as easily; not just as successfully.

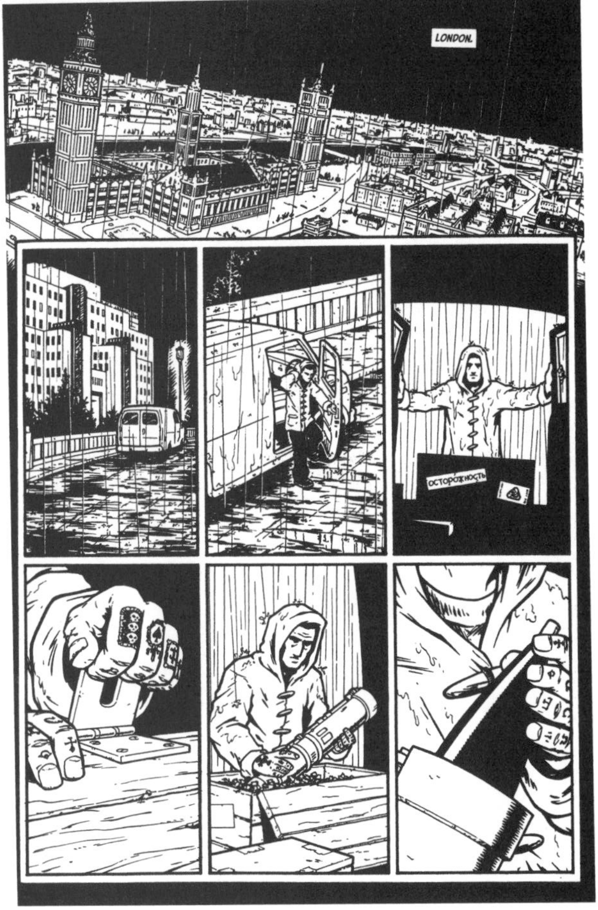
LONDON.
ОСТОРОЖНОСТЬ

Pages 2 and 3

Lay this out in two tiers across each page. Upper tier is our interiors of MI6, lower tier is the rocket man. Perhaps if the panels of the upper tier slightly overlap the top of the panels in the lower tier we'll get the chronological, this-is-happening-at-the-same-time effect I'm after here.. Panels 1 through 6 are upper, 7 through 12 are lower.

<u>ONE:</u>
First tier.

Interior MI6 Building. This is a pretty drab and dull looking industrial corridor, with offices along both sides of the hall. In FG, A JANITOR, probably not white, is mopping the hallway. A PASS dangles from a chain around his neck.

TWO JUNIOR SIS OFFICERS are walking down the hallway, coming at us from BG. One of them carries a FILE of some sort. ALBERT is white, in his late twenties, wearing glasses. Looks like he's been up all night.

JILL is also white, female, also late twenties.

1 ALBERT:
> …then shouting at the RUSSIAN
> desk.

2 JILL:
> And what did his EMINENCE D. Ops
> want?

TWO:
First tier.

Angle off ALBERT, as he opens an office door,
allowing JILL to enter. It's a small office, in
the Intelligence division, and there's a wall of
file cabinets, as well as a desk with a computer.
WINDOWS are behind the desk. The desk itself is
cluttered with papers.

3 ALBERT:
> Trying to track transfers from St.
> Petersburg to London Maritime Bank
> or some such.

4 ALBERT/linked:
> Though why this has CROCKER'S
> knickers in a TWIST I've no CLUE.

THREE:
First tier.

OTS ALBERT as he drops his FILE onto his desk.

JILL has stopped inside the doorway, now leaning
back against the wall, looking at ALBERT.

5 JILL:
> Well, he's planning a SPECIAL OP
> most like, isn't he?

6 ALBERT:
> Undoubtedly. Who knows? Maybe he'll
> even get PERMISSION first[5].

5. The second reference to Crocker's habit of "shooting first, asking questions later," in two issues.

FOUR:
First tier.

OTS JILL, as ALBERT straightens up behind his
desk.

Behind ALBERT, through the window, we can only see
the London skyline, no hint of the rocket.

7 JILL:
> You mean the way he cleared Chace's
> run in Kosovo?

8 ALBERT:
> Could do. I hear they're forecasting
> SNOW in HELL later today, as
> well.

FIVE:
First tier.

Angle as JILL turns to leave the office. ALBERT, behind his desk, is frowning at the papers arrayed before him.

9 ALBERT/small:
                    We're going to be at this ALL night.

10 JILL:
                    With that in mind, you want a coffee?

SIX:
First tier.

JILL holding in the doorway, as ALBERT looking up to give her a grateful smile.

11 ALBERT:
                    You'd be saving my LIFE, Jill—

SEVEN:
Second tier.

From the side of the VAN as the MAN steps back.

Past him we can see the MI-6 BUILDING, a gleaming and somewhat inviting target. A couple lights on in the building.

NO COPY.

EIGHT:
Second tier.

From behind the MAN as he hoists the LAUNCHER onto his shoulder, sighting the building.

12 MAN/small:
                    <Fuck with US...>

NINE:
Second tier.

ECU MAN'S hand on the grip, finger pulling the trigger.

13 MAN:
                    <...we fuck you BACK.>[6]

TEN:
Second tier.

From behind the MAN, a TRAIL of FLAME and SMOKE from the launch blast, as the ROCKET speeds towards the MI-6 BUILDING in BG.

NO COPY.

6. For the novel Critical Space, I had a major character who was Russian, and I wanted to pepper her speech with appropriate words and phrases. I picked up a couple of books, including one on colloquial Russian...and discovered that, apparently, profanity in Russian is something glorious to behold. Insults are graded into different tiers, and some of them are incredibly inventive. This has lead to my habit of giving Russian characters very foul mouths, indeed, most recently seen in Q&C 26-29, and the Q&C novel, A Gentleman's Game.

<u>ELEVEN:</u>
Second tier.

Stet previous, but the ROCKET is receding rapidly, towards the building.

NO COPY.

<u>TWELVE:</u>
Second tier.

Stet previous, still behind the MAN, who is still holding the launcher on his shoulder.

There's no sign of the rocket, no trail, no light, no smoke. It's basically disappeared against the face of the building.

NO COPY.

Page 4

<u>ONE:</u>
Same angle as Twelve, previous, but MAN is now turning away from the building in BG, dropping the LAUNCHER off his shoulder.

In BG, we can see the EXPLOSION as the ROCKET detonates against the building. A flash of violent light, perhaps even some debris illuminated by the flame.[7]

NO COPY.

<u>TWO:</u>
Profile of the MAN, as he replaces the LAUNCHER in the back of the VAN. He's white, Russian, and thuggish, though only two of those facts are really going to be apparent. He's got a self-satisfied sneer going.

Rain drops drip from his hood and nose.

NO COPY.

<u>THREE:</u>
High angle, looking down at the VAN, as MAN gets behind the wheel once more.

NO COPY.

<u>FOUR:</u>
High angle, looking down, as we see the VAN driving away on the lane to one side of the panel as EMERGENCY VEHICLES come streaming in on a separate road, heading for the SMOKING MI6 BUILDING.

NO COPY.

7. On Wednesday, 20 September, 2000, the SIS building was attacked in similar manner. The weapon used was a Russian-built MK 22 anti-tank rocket—a very small and compact weapon system, so I've been given to believe. The attack was believed to have been carried out by the Real IRA, an IRA splinter group. The attack hit the eighth floor of the building, though SIS was, as you might expect, circumspect about the damage the blast caused. I've done occasional looking since this incident, and have utterly failed to find any more information about who was responsible, or whether or not the attacker(s) were apprehended.

Page 5

ONE:

Small establishing shot, exterior, South Kensington[8], same night, still raining. We're looking at a row of townhouses.

The street is empty, cars parked all along.

8. I chose this location for Chace's first flat—she's since moved in the series to Camden—for the simple reason that, when I first visited London as a wide-eyed innocent of 12 years old, traveling with my father, we stayed at a B & B in South Kensington, and I had a vague recollection of what some of the streets around there looked like.

TWO:

Interior of CHACE'S BEDROOM. We're looking down on her from an angle above and beyond the foot of her bed, so we can take in the whole room.

The room is something of a mess. Clothes and papers are strewn about. A couple empty liquor bottles are scattered on the floor. The nightstand has a LAMP, CLOCK, PHONE, PAGER, and ANOTHER BOTTLE of scotch, half-empty.

CHACE herself is asleep on the bed, sprawled out in a torment of bedclothes. She's sleeping in a t-shirt and underwear, and while she's mostly covered, her wounded leg is free of the sheets, and we can see the BANDAGE on her leg.

1 SFX: brrt brrt

THREE:

Angle from the nightstand, looking past the CLOCK, PHONE, and BOTTLE, at CHACE, now painfully awake, pulling the phone to her ear.

The CLOCK reads 3:57 A.M..

2 SFX: brrt br—

3 CHACE:

Chace.

FOUR:

Angle, CHACE on her back, hand over her eyes, as she puts the RECEIVER to her ear.

4 TAILLESS/elec:

Duty Ops Officer. From D. Ops, MINDERS to the Ops Room.

5 CHACE:

Ten minutes.

FIVE:

Stet previous, CHACE on her back. She's dropped the RECEIVER beside her head, and uncovered her eyes.

She looks exhausted, and mildly alarmed.

6 CHACE/small:

Oh damn.

Angle from the nightstand side of the bed. In BG
we can see the open door to the bathroom, the
toilet visible, and perhaps the sink.

CHACE is tumbling out of the bed, lurching for the
bathroom door.

7 CHACE: Oh damn…

SEVEN:
From the bedroom, looking into the bathroom, where
CHACE is kneeling at the toilet, throwing up in
BG.[9]

9. Something you never see in James
Bond, tell you that much.

NO COPY.

Page 6

ONE:
Exterior of the MI6 BUILDING, still dark, still
raining, but now there are TWO FIRE ENGINES parked
outside the building, and EMERGENCY PERSONNEL are
running back and forth.

CONSTABLES are on the scene, in their slickers,
trying to control the area.

Angle up from street level, and we can see the
blast damage, roughly five stories above. The
ground is scattered with broken glass and chunks
of the building.

NO COPY.

TWO:
Angle on the street, and we see a CONSTABLE leaning
in at the driver's window of a just-parked car.

Emergency work continuing in BG.

1 CONSTABLE:
                Move the vehicle, please…

THREE:
OTS CONSTABLE, as he steps back from the opening
door.

CHACE is getting out, extending her pass towards
the CONSTABLE'S FACE with one hand. She's not
looking at him; rather, she's looking at the
building.

She looks better, her hair pulled back. Wearing a
shirt and jeans and jacket.

2 CONSTABLE:
                …you can't park here.

3 CHACE:

                  Yes, I can.

FOUR:
CU CHACE, her reaction to the damaged building.
She looks shocked.

4 CHACE/small:

                  Jesus.

FIVE:
Angle past the CONSTABLE, back to us in FG, as
CHACE, in BG, enters the building. CHACE is again
presenting her pass to the WARDEN on duty at the
door. The WARDEN is middle-aged, in an overcoat.

NO COPY.

Page 7

ONE:
Interior of the building, CHACE is being let
through a set of doors by another WARDEN. In BG,
we can see the first WARDEN at the front door, and,
jogging past him to catch CHACE, is WALLACE. CHACE
is turning her head in response to his call.

1 WALLACE: Tara!

TWO:
Through the second set of doors, CHACE is through
and waiting for WALLACE, who is addressing her as
he shows his pass to the WARDEN there.

2 WALLACE: What the hell happened?

3 CHACE: You're Head of Section, YOU tell
               ME.

THREE:
From the end of a hallway, CHACE and WALLACE
coming towards us. WARDEN in the EBG.

4 CHACE: I'm supposed to still be on
               DISABILITY.

5 WALLACE: There is no disability when Crocker
               SCRAMBLES the section.

FOUR:
Behind CHACE and WALLACE as they wait for the
elevator.

6 WALLACE: How ARE you feeling?

7 CHACE: Leg's fine, Tom.

FIVE:
Inside the elevator, CHACE leading, looking down

slightly. WALLACE is entering behind her, looking at her with some care.

8 WALLACE:

They're both FINE, you ask me, but that's NOT what I meant.

9 CHACE:

I know what you MEANT[10].

SIX:
In the elevator, WALLACE at one side, looking at CHACE. CHACE at the other, not returning the gaze.

NO COPY.

SEVEN:
Exterior of the elevator, doors open, CHACE coming forward. WALLACE still in the car.

NO COPY.

Page 8

ONE:
Interior of the Operations Room, and it's buzzing with activity. RON and ALEXIS are each on their posts, and there are THREE ADDITIONAL RUNNERS moving back and forth through the space, carrying papers or talking on telephones.

Behind RON'S POST, on the raised dais, are a couple of chairs. CROCKER is standing in the midst of them, smoking, and looking pretty damn pissed off. He's in the same three-piece suit he wore last time we saw him, though if you want to get tricky, maybe the tie is different.

In one of the chairs is the third member of the Special Section, EDWARD KITTERING. KITTERING is white, with unruly hair that's bordering on being just a little too long. He's wearing jeans and a sweatshirt. He's the youngest member of the Special Section, perhaps 24.

WALLACE and CHACE have just entered.

1 TAILLESS:

...rotating the surveillance...

2 TAILLESS:

...the M.O.D.[11] about short-range rockets...

3 TAILLESS:

...at the Home Office, sending someone from FIVE[12]...

10. A note on the use of caps, here. At this point in my ever-evolving script style, I used CAPS to indicate words I wanted emphasized. I don't know why it is, because I believe I have a good ear for dialogue. But try as I might, I can't seem to place the emphasis in the right place most of the time. These days, I use bold to indicate emphasis, rather than caps—something that came about as a result for writing for Marvel during the Jemas-Quesada days, when they decided that dialogue needed to be in both upper and lower-case.

My understanding is that someone somewhere at Marvel read something by someone that argued it was easier for kids to read if the words were in both upper and lower case. I personally think this is utter bullshit, but it was the editorial directive, and thus, my writing changed to reflect that. These days, I still use bold, because old habits die hard.

11. The Ministry of Defense.

12. Another example of how things change; if I knew then what I knew now, the line would have read, "...sending someone from BOX..." as I have since learned that nobody refers to the Security Services as "Five" except for wannabes and authors of espionage comics.

4 CROCKER:
> Where the HELL have you two BEEN?

TWO:
OTS CROCKER, as WALLACE mounts the dais reaching for a chair. KITTERING is raising a hand in greeting.

CHACE is following.

5 WALLACE:
> The HONEYMOON was short but SWEET.

6 WALLACE/linked:
> Morning, Ed.

7 KITTERING:
> Hey, Tom.

8 KITTERING/linked:
> Tara. How's your leg?

THREE:
From behind KITTERING, WALLACE now seated, as CHACE takes the remaining chair. CROCKER stands over them, positively glowering.

9 CHACE:
> It works.

10 CHACE/linked:
> Sir.

11 CROCKER:
> Sit down, Tara.

Page 9

ONE:
Angle past RON at his desk, on his headset, rapidly shuffling through papers. A RUNNER is handing him a FOLDER.

In BG, we can see CROCKER standing, talking to CHACE, WALLACE, and KITTERING.

1 CROCKER:
> At SIX minutes before FOUR this morning, the FIFTH FLOOR was hit by a ROCKET ATTACK.

2 CROCKER/linked:
> Right now we don't know WHO, WHAT, or WHY.

TWO:
Angle behind WALLACE, with KITTERING partially in panel on the left, CHACE on the right. CROCKER is

this section has good
examples of me
figuring out how to
fit lots of characters
into each panel and
still make the dialogue
+ composition flow
decently.

TWCK

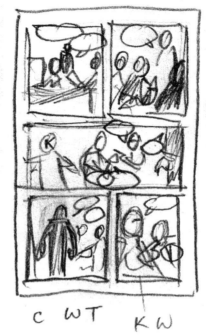

C WT KW

addressing the three of them. WALLACE is pulling
a cigarette from his pack with his teeth.

3 CROCKER:

        Intel is on with the M.O.D.,
        trying to determine the nature of
        the weapon, and the POLICE have
        started a canvass.

THREE:
Kind of a three-shot, chair level, with KITTERING
closest to us, then WALLACE, then CHACE.

CROCKER stands just inside the panel, and we can
perhaps see his trousers, or his hand as he flicks
ash.

KITTERING is leaning back. WALLACE is offering
CHACE a cigarette from his pack, and she's taking
it, speaking to CROCKER. All look very attentive
and concerned.

4 CHACE:

        How bad was it?

5 CROCKER:

        Two dead, one wounded.

6 WALLACE:

        We got off LIGHT.

FOUR:
CROCKER scowling. Past him, we can see WALLACE and
CHACE passing a lighter between them.

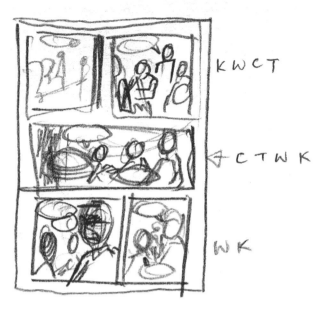

KWCT

← CTWK

WK

7 CROCKER:

    That's NOT our problem.

8 CROCKER/linked:

    Our problem is we've been ATTACKED in our HOME, and that CANNOT stand.

FIVE:
KITTERING waving a gust of smoke away with one hand. CROCKER still glowering. Past KITTERING, we can see WALLACE, agreeing.

9 KITTERING:

    Not much we can do about that.

10 WALLACE:

    He's right, Boss. It's DOMESTIC.

Page 10

ONE:
CROCKER, not scowling so much as grimly adamant.

1 CROCKER:

    I don't CARE.

TWO:
CHACE, looking sideways at the Ops Room, as CROCKER and WALLACE argue.

2 WALLACE:

    We're not CHARTERED for domestic work, Boss, you know that. It's the PURVIEW of MI5.

3 CROCKER:

> Five wasn't ATTACKED, Tom. WE were.

THREE:
OTS CROCKER, WALLACE still arguing with him.

KITTERING and CHACE are exchanging glances.

4 CROCKER:

> The FOREIGN OFFICE will give us backing.

5 WALLACE:

> And the HOME OFFICE[13] will OPPOSE.

6 WALLACE/linked:

> I can SEE where you're HEADING, Boss...

FOUR:
Angle on RON, answering a PHONE. CROCKER, WALLACE, KITTERING, and CHACE as before in BG, but CROCKER and WALLACE are on the verge of each pissing the other seriously off.

7 WALLACE:

> ...but if SIS goes mucking about in a FIVE investigation—

8 CROCKER:

> They can INVESTIGATE to their HEART'S CONTENT, Tom!

9 CROCKER/linked:
> That's NOT what I want!

FIVE:
Angle on CHACE, looking at the cigarette burning between her fingers. Eyes are kind of distant.

10 CHACE:
> What do you want, sir?

SIX:
CROCKER, calm, and perhaps dangerously serious.

11 CROCKER:

> Retaliation.

SEVEN:
CROCKER standing in front of CHACE, WALLACE, and KITTERING, all of them silent.

In BG, we can see still RON on the phone.

NO COPY.

13. Traditionally, the Foreign and Commonwealth Office has purview over SIS, since SIS technically operates only on foreign soil; the Security Services fall under the domain of the Home Office. Things get confused and rather tricky when talking about dominion, however; the Home Office tends to view those colonies/former colonies as their own territories.

Page 11

ONE:
Past RON, RECEIVER to his chest, turning to CROCKER, behind him. CROCKER turning to acknowledge RON.

WALLACE, CHACE, and KITTERING are still, silent. WALLACE is exhaling smoke.

1 RON:
Sir? The Deputy Chief wants you in C's office.

2 CROCKER:
Tell them I'm coming up.

TWO:
CROCKER turning back to address the three.

3 CROCKER:
I want you three in the PIT, wait there 'til I NEED you…

THREE:
CU CROCKER using the toe of his shoe to kill his cigarette.

4 CROCKER/above:
…I'll call when I'm done with C and Weldon.

FOUR:
OTS CROCKER as he starts to turn, WALLACE looking kinda pissy at him.

5 WALLACE:
And while we WAIT, what? SHARPEN our KNIVES?

FIVE:
CROCKER snarling, heading for the door, without looking back. CHACE, WALLACE, and KITTERING watching his departure.

6 CROCKER:
You can get digging, Tom.

7 CROCKER/linked:
And ANOTHER crack like THAT, I'll find myself a NEW head of section.

SIX:
From behind KITTERING, CHACE, and WALLACE, as CROCKER exits in BG.

NO COPY.

SEVEN:
CHACE looking at WALLACE, slight eyebrow arch.

WALLACE looks pissed.

8 CHACE:
Does that mean I get YOUR job?[14]

14. We call this "foreshadowing," though it took us some 25 issues to execute it. What can I say, I like to take my time.

9 WALLACE:

Sod off,[15] Tara.

15. An example of a line I really wish I hadn't used. It reads as "forced British" to me, now.

Page 12

ONE:
Interior of C's Office. This is the nicest office in the building, obviously, and unlike Weldon's and Crocker's, it's got class. Large space, broken into two sections—one is the work area, marked by bookshelves, a desk with a computer, various appropriate desk items.

The other section is almost a small sitting room, with two small leather couches and a leather armchair, with a small coffee table and a couple end-tables. A tea and coffee service has been laid out on a tray on the table.

Wide establishing, from the sitting room portion, WELDON seated on one of the couches, back to us, with C seated in the easy chair.

C is in his late sixties, face clean shaven but lined, bushy eyebrow, dark and tiny eyes. He wears a hastily put on and ill-fitting suit. Looks like a wacky little old man, kind of.

1 WELDON:

...should be here in half an hour.

2 C:

He'll meet with Crocker.

TWO:
Angle past the coffee table, as C leans forward, using a POT to fill his CUP.

3 WELDON/off:

I'm not certain that's WISE, sir—

4 C:

Whatever HISTORY exists between them, they'll be PROFESSIONAL.

THREE:
Angle past WELDON, frowning. C is sitting back in his chair with his cup and saucer.

In BG, we can see the door to the office has opened and CROCKER is entering.

5 WELDON:

Professional isn't the WORD I use to describe—

6 CROCKER:

Sorry to keep you WAITING.

New angle, WELDON on the couch to the left, C in his
chair to the right, as CROCKER steps forward.

7 C:

You were in the Ops Room?

8 CROCKER:

Yes, sir.

9 C:

Anything?

FIVE:
OTS C as CROCKER, still standing, bends to fix
himself a cup of coffee.

10 CROCKER:

We're still waiting to hear from
the M.O.D. about the

weapon.
11 CROCKER:

Hopefully that will give us a
LEAD.

SIX:
OTS CROCKER, straightening. WELDON on the couch—
and it's important here to note that while WELDON
and CROCKER don't often agree and can often barely
stand one another, they really are professionals,
so when Weldon disagrees, he's not just being
contrary—leaning slightly forward.

C is now looking at WELDON.

12 WELDON:

Unlikely, don't you think, Paul?
13 WELDON/linked:

These days one can buy a ROCKET
LAUNCHER at any corner STORE.

14 CROCKER:

I am AWARE, sir…

Page 13

ONE:
Side angle, CROCKER turning to address the rest
to C, who appears engrossed in the contents of
his cup.

1 CROCKER:

…but right now that's all we
have.

2 C:

You'll give whatever you LEARN to
FIVE, of course.

TWO:
CROCKER still standing, C now looking up, as
WELDON growls.

3 CROCKER:
                    I'll SHARE it with them, yes sir.

4 WELDON:
                    It's an ACADEMIC distinction.

5 CROCKER:
                    I don't think it is.

THREE:
OTS CROCKER, C again musing at his cup, WELDON
getting testy.

6 WELDON:
                    It'll be THEIR investigation.

7 CROCKER:
                    It was OUR people who were MURDERED.
                    I'm not about to let those PRATS in
                    FIVE speak for them.

FOUR:
OTS C, as WELDON and CROCKER stare at one
another.

NO COPY.

FIVE:
Reverse, now looking at C in his chair, CROCKER
and WELDON on each side, as before.

8 C:
                    Those PRATS, as you put it, Paul, are
                    our COLLEAGUES in INTELLIGENCE.

9 C/linked:
                    Implying that departmental RIVALRY
                    will influence the QUALITY of their
                    investigation is CHILDISH.

SIX:
OTS C, looking at CROCKER, who looks somewhat
chastised.

10 C:
                    Don't you think?

11 CROCKER:
                    It's not the QUALITY I'm worried
                    about, sir, but the RESULT.

SEVEN:
WELDON, settling back in his seat, somewhat
mollified.

12 WELDON:
                    They'll see the responsible parties
                    IDENTIFIED and IMPRISONED.

13 CROCKER/off:
                    I don't WANT them imprisoned…

EIGHT:
OTS CROCKER, C and WELDON'S reactions. C is mildly
aback at Crocker's statement, but WELDON looks
like he might burst a vessel.

14 CROCKER:
                    …I want them DEAD.

Page 14

ONE:
Interior of The Pit, which is slang for the
Special Operations Officer's offices. [How's that
for a confusing sentence?]

This is a room with THREE DESKS arrayed around the
space, one facing away from each wall, with the
exception of the entry wall, which is bare but for
a couple of filing cabinets.

Nearest the door is WALLACE'S DESK, which is a
pretty clean, with TWO PHONES—one red—some files,
and a PC.

CHACE'S DESK is opposite the door, and is a mess,
covered with papers which have pretty much buried
the computer.

KITTERING'S DESK is opposite Wallace's, and is a
mixture of the two.

A MAP OF THE WORLD is on one wall, and a DART BOARD
is positioned on the wall above CHACE'S DESK.

Only other detail of importance is that by the
door, perhaps on the filing cabinets, are THREE
DUFFEL BAGS, each of them different from one
another. These are the agent's go-bags, the ones
they grab when they have to hustle.

WALLACE is throwing darts at the BOARD while CHACE
leans back in her chair, legs up on the desk,
apparently unconcerned with the sharp pointed
objects flying about two feet over her head. A
couple DARTS are already imbedded in the BOARD.

KITTERING is seated, and actually looks like he's
working.

1 WALLACE:
                    Sure you don't want to run to the
                    COMMISSARY and grab yourself an
                    APPLE?

2 WALLACE/linked:
I do a MEAN William Tell.

3 CHACE:
You're a RIOT, Tom.

4 CHACE/linked:
He's a riot, isn't he?

5 KITTERING:
If you mean the kind with PROPERTY DAMAGE and LOSS of LIFE, then yes.[16]

16. This was Jamie S. Rich's favorite line this issue. For a while, every time I'd turn in a script, he'd either call or email me with his notes, and then deliver a verdict on "favorite line." In issue 1, it was the bit about the bullets marked "to whom it may concern."

TWO:
Past KITTERING, looking up at WALLACE. WALLACE, last dart in hand, ready to throw, is glancing at KITTERING.

CHACE looking at WALLACE, amused.

6 WALLACE:
I'll remember you said that when I'm preparing your ANNUAL review.

7 KITTERING:
You don't SCARE me...

THREE:
From the DART BOARD as WALLACE'S throw nails the BULL'S EYE. Below, CHACE is looking at KITTERING, grinning.

8 KITTERING:
...she'll have YOUR job by the end of the DAY.

9 KITTERING:
You'll be NICE to me, won't you Tara?

10 CHACE:
Do you SWEAR ever-lasting LOYALTY, to live and die at my COMMAND?

FOUR:
OTS CHACE, KITTERING holding up his hands in mild protest.

10 KITTERING:
I fear I have CONFUSED you with someone ELSE.

11 KITTERING/linked:
I thought you were Tara Chace, NOT Paul Crocker.

FIVE:
Wide, the THREE AGENTS, momentarily silent, in thought.

NO COPY.

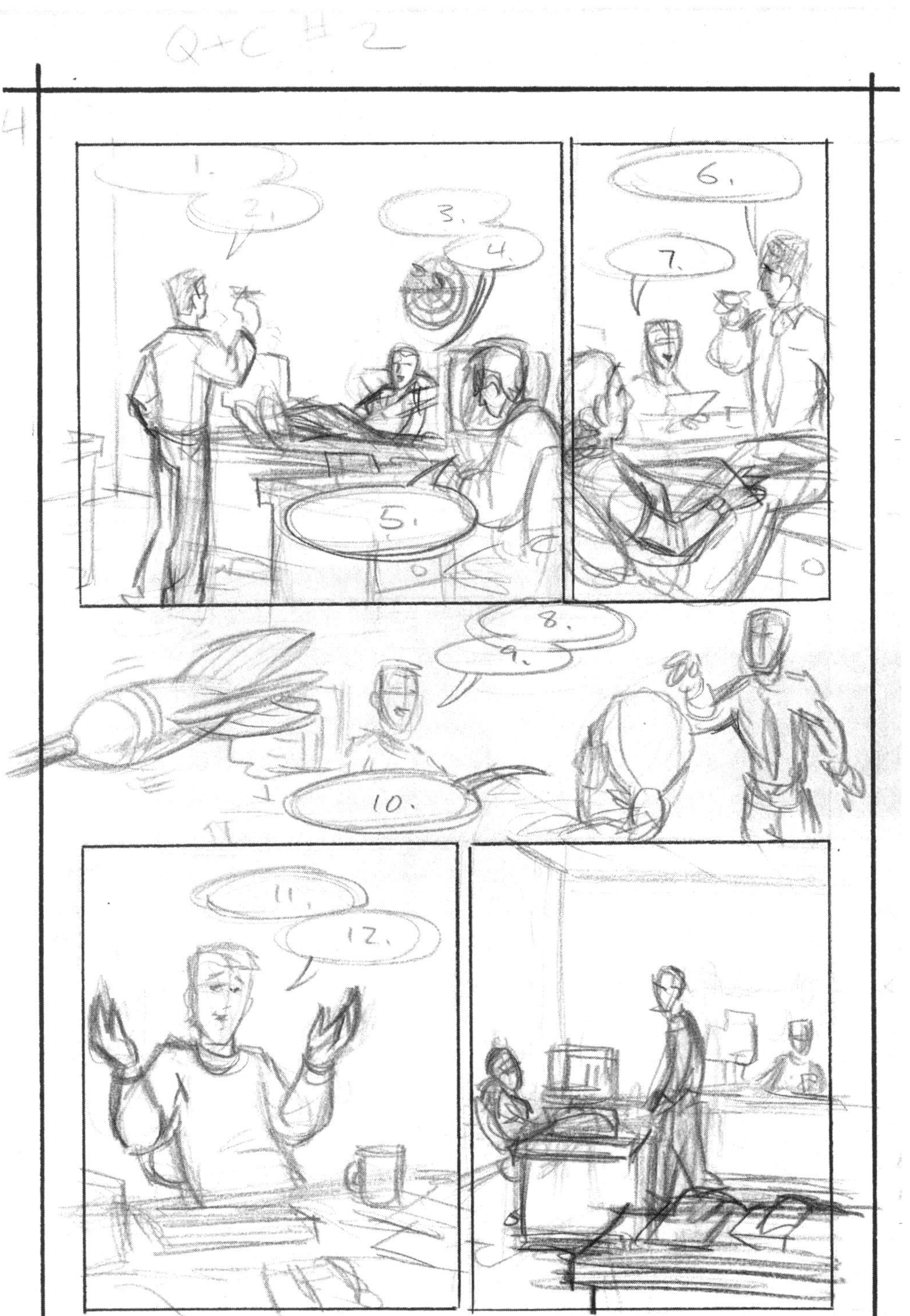
Q+C #2
14
1.
2.
3.
4.
5.
6.
7.
8.
9.
10.
11.
12.

Page 15

ONE:
Angle past WALLACE, as he pulls the DARTS from the
board. CHACE, beneath him, looking up to address
him.

1 CHACE:
>   Rocket hit the Fifth Floor?

2 WALLACE:
>   Yes.

3 CHACE:
>   Who was working up there?

TWO:
Past KITTERING, as WALLACE turns to head back to
his throwing position. CHACE'S attention still on
WALLACE.

4 KITTERING:
>   Jill Baron, Albert Cooper, and
>   a fellow from MAINTENANCE named
>   Ravi.

5 CHACE:
>   Baron and Cooper were on the
>   Russian Desk.

6 WALLACE:
>   It's COINCIDENCE…

THREE:
OTS CHACE, as WALLACE turns, preparing to throw
again.

7 WALLACE:
>   …they weren't the TARGET.

8 CHACE:
>   Not SPECIFICALLY, no…

FOUR:
CU CHACE, thinking. Gosh, she's purty.[17]

9 CHACE/below:
>   …we were.

FIVE:
Past CHACE, looking at KITTERING, who now has his
chin resting in his hand. WALLACE appears deeply
engrossed in his dart game.

10 KITTERING:
>   You mean ALL of us, the SERVICE.

11 CHACE:
>   Very deft, Ed. You should be a
>   SPY.

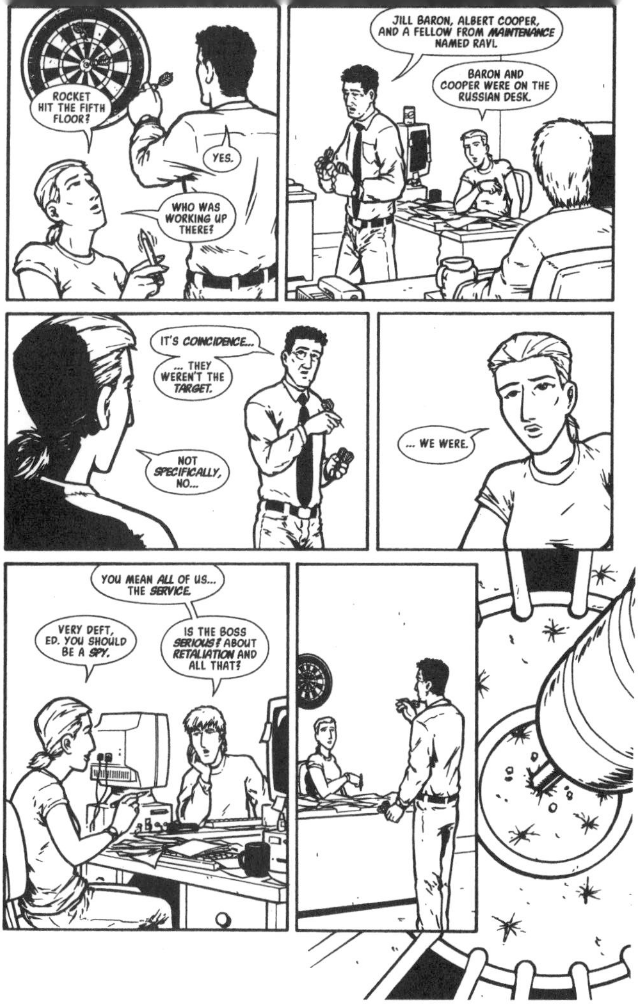
ROCKET HIT THE FIFTH FLOOR?
YES.
WHO WAS WORKING UP THERE?
JILL BARON, ALBERT COOPER, AND A FELLOW FROM MAINTENANCE NAMED RAVI.
BARON AND COOPER WERE ON THE RUSSIAN DESK.
IT'S COINCIDENCE...
... THEY WEREN'T THE TARGET.
NOT SPECIFICALLY, NO...
... WE WERE.
YOU MEAN ALL OF US... THE SERVICE.
VERY DEFT, ED. YOU SHOULD BE A SPY.
IS THE BOSS SERIOUS? ABOUT RETALIATION AND ALL THAT?

12 KITTERING:

Is the Boss SERIOUS? About RETALIATION and all that?

SIX:
WALLACE and CHACE exchanging looks. WALLACE is poised for another throw.

NO COPY.

SEVEN:
ECU of the DART burying itself into the BOARD, dead on.[18]

NO COPY.

Page 16

ONE:
Interior of C's Office, and CROCKER and WELDON are arguing. C is rising from his chair.

17. I'm often at odds with myself about Chace's appearance, her looks. I have always imagined her as attractive, certainly sexy, and often beautiful... but of that kind of beauty that ebbs and flows, depending on situation and circumstance. To my mind, she's never more attractive than when she's being smart, when she's doing her job, and doing it well. For that reason, every so often in a script I'll have a note like this, where I feel almost embarrassed in pointing out the fact.

18. Note the rather terse description of this panel, and then compare it to what Steve did, and how Steve constructed the whole page to lead to this panel. This is why Steve Rolston kicks ass.

1 WELDON:

...turn EVERYTHING into your own PERSONAL crusade?[19]

2 CROCKER:

It's not MY crusade, it's for the good of the Service!

TWO:
C, who is rather small, comparatively, is heading for his desk, as CROCKER and WELDON continue.

3 CROCKER:

If we're not seen to take EVERY measure to PROTECT and AVENGE our people, how can we expect them to TRUST us![20]

4 WELDON:

There is a LITTLE thing called PATRIOTISM, Paul, perhaps you've HEARD of it?

THREE:
View across C's DESK, as C takes a PIPE from a small rack with one hand, opening a TIN of TOBACCO with the other.

In BG, CROCKER is railing at WELDON. WELDON is on his feet, giving as good as he gets.

5 CROCKER:

Patriotism doesn't GUARANTEE loyalty, it only INITIATES it!

6 WELDON:

And the UNSPOKEN corollary to your code of VENGEANCE is what, exactly?

7 WELDON/linked:

Betray us at the COST of your LIFE?

FOUR:
OTS WELDON, on CROCKER, and he's deadly serious.

8 CROCKER:

If it prevents another PHILBY or MACLEAN or BURGESS, yes, sir.[21]

FIVE:
CU on C, who is lighting his pipe. An eyebrow is arching. He's listening, all right.

In BG, WELDON is still facing CROCKER, calmer now. CROCKER is just as defiant and arrogant.

9 WELDON:

I see.

19. This is another mistake, and a minor one, I admit, but worth pointing out for those of you who are interested in the choices I make. I started this line with an ellipsis—"..."—but I should have started it with an em-dash—"—"—to indicate that we were joining the scene late, and that the dialogue had already been flying.

20. This establishes another recurring theme for the series, and one that plays a huge part in the first Q&C novel, A Gentleman's Game.

21. The so-called "Cambridge Spies." Guy Burgess, Donald MacLean, and Kim Philby all served as double-agents within the British Government, working for the Soviets. There's been much speculation as to how they were able to penetrate so successfully and so deeply without rousing suspicion, something that, in turn, has been attributed to the "old-boys network"—the idea that these men were Englishmen, dammit, who had come from the "best schools" and were therefore beyond reproach or suspicion! Philby, in particular, has held a particular fascination for spy writers and espionage aficionados; John LeCarre's fabulous Tinker, Tailor, Soldier, Spy, is just one of many works inspired by this betrayal.

Peter Wright's Spycatcher—which was banned in the UK for violating the Official Secrets Act—was one of the first books to speculate that the Cambridge Three were actually Four... or potentially even more.

Theories continue to this day, some of them going so far as to suggest, or even outright declare, that the Security Services, and even SIS, had moles working at the highest levels.

Crocker's vehemence here was meant to illustrate two things—first, his absolute commitment to his job; second, his absolute commitment to his people (something the series touches on again and again in later stories).

SIX:
ECU C'S hand, as he puts the extinguished MATCH
into his ashtray.

10 WELDON/off:

>   And if the WHOLE of S.I.S. serves
>   in FEAR, that's just a HAPPY by-
>   product?

SEVEN:
Angle on C, puffing on his pipe, raising his right
hand to indicate that he wants the argument to
stop. WELDON and CROCKER in BG. C's not looking at
them at all, but rather past us.

11 CROCKER:

>   Of course not! But RELYING on the
>   OLD BOY—

12 C:

>   That's ENOUGH.

EIGHT:
Angle past CROCKER and WELDON, looking at C'S
back. C has lowered his hand.

Past C, we can see, through the window, that dawn
is breaking.

13 C:

>   Why don't you leave us ALONE,
>   Donald?

NINE:
Angle from C'S door as WELDON exits, scowling.
In BG, CROCKER is approaching C's DESK, while C
continues to look out the window.

NO COPY.

Page 17

ONE:
Looking at C, puffing on his pipe, looking out the
window. CROCKER just at his shoulder, frowning,
looking out the window, as well.

1 C:

>   Donald   Weldon   is   the   Deputy
>   Chief.

2 C/linked:

>   He demands—rightly—the RESPECT due
>   him.

TWO:
Stet previous, but C has turned to look up at
CROCKER. CROCKER is frowning and now looking down,
not wanting to meet his gaze.

3 CROCKER:
                    I do RESPECT him.

4 C:

                    You respect the POSITION, not the
                    MAN. An ATTITUDE that will get your
                    into TROUBLE, Paul.

THREE:
Angle past CROCKER, still standing as before, as
C takes his seat behind the desk.

5 C:
                    You're MARGINALLY easier to REPLACE
                    than he is.

6 C/linked:
                    Don't FORCE me to CHOOSE.

FOUR:
Past C, now seated, adjusting his pipe, as CROCKER
continues looking out the window, no longer
frowning, but now just looking like a chastised
teenager.

7 CROCKER:
                    Understood, sir.

8 C:

                    It so happens that I agree with
                    you. An ATTACK like this MUST be
                    answered. And we must be SEEN to
                    answer it.

FIVE:
OTS CROCKER, looking at C, now, who is gazing up
at him. C holds the PIPE in position with one
hand.

9 CROCKER:
                    Then let me use the MINDERS to—

10 C:
                    Answering   it   does   not   mean
                    MURDER.

SIX:
C opening one of the files on his desk, dismissing
CROCKER.

11 C:
                    David Kinney will be in your office
                    in ten minutes.

12 C/linked:
                    I expect you to COOPERATE with
                    him.

SEVEN:
CROCKER looking at C, who is now pretty much
ignoring him.

NO COPY.

EIGHT:
From the door, as CROCKER opens it. He's cranky, but trying to hide it.

C is working at his desk in BG.

13 C:
>   I mean it, Paul.

14 CROCKER:
>   Yes, sir.

Page 18

ONE:
ANTE-ROOM TO CROCKER'S OFFICE, as he blows through the door. KATE, working at her desk, is looking up.

1 CROCKER:
>   Kate, call the U.S. Embassy, find out if Franks[22] is free for lunch.

2 KATE:
>   Can I tell him what it's about?

3 CROCKER:
>   He'll KNOW.

TWO:
Interior CROCKER'S OFFICE, as CROCKER continues in, jamming a cigarette into his mouth.

KATE, at her desk in the ante-room, is rising, looking after him.

4 KATE:
>   David Kinney is being ESCORTED up from RECEPTION.

5 CROCKER:
>   Any chance he'll get LOST on the WAY?

6 KATE:
>   The Wardens are OLD, but not THAT old.

THREE:
CROCKER falling into his chair, lighting his cigarette, as KATE steps out again, shutting the door after her.

7 CROCKER:
>   Send him in when he gets here.

8 KATE:
>   Yes, sir.

22. Franks? Who the hell is "Franks?" I hear you cry.

I do this a lot, too. I change names. I change names two or three times during the course of a story, sometimes, and I don't always manage to catch them all before I send out the script/story/whatever. For those of you who know the series, this line should read, "Cheng," and the pronouns that follow should all be feminine, rather than masculine. At this time, though, I had thought that the CIA Station Chief in London would be a man named, yes, Franks. No idea what his first name was going to be. Not even sure why I ultimately changed it, but I suspect it was because I didn't want Tara to be the only woman in a position of authority—all the other female characters presented thus far (here Kate, Crocker's Personal Assistant, and earlier Alexis, the Main Communications Officer) had been in subordinate staff positions, and it mattered to me that there be at least one other female character in a position of power.

FOUR:
Angle from corner, CROCKER glaring at the closed
door.

NO COPY.

FIVE:
Past the ASHTRAY on the DESK, CROCKER has turned
his chair and is staring at a wall, deep in thought,
cigarette dangling from his lower lip.

NO COPY.

SIX:
From the back of the office, above CROCKER, as the
DOOR OPENS, and KATE leans in.

9 KATE:
                    David Kinney, sir.

10 CROCKER:
                    Thanks, Kate.

Page 19

ONE:
Two-shot, as CROCKER rises and offers a hand to
KINNEY. Kinney is, essentially, Crocker's opposite
number at MI5, which is part of the reason they hate
one another. KINNEY is Crocker's age, stockier,
mustached, in a suit.

They're both acting like they're pleased to see
each other.

1 CROCKER:
                    David.

2 KINNEY:
                    Paul.

3 CROCKER:
                    Take a PEW.

TWO:
OTS CROCKER, still on his feet, as KINNEY sits in
one of the chairs in front of the desk.

4 KINNEY:
                    Bad business. Sorry about YOUR
                    people.

5 CROCKER:
                    Yes. Thanks.

6 CROCKER/linked:
                    What have you got?

THREE:
KINNEY, seated, smoothing his tie.

7 KINNEY:

We're less than SIX HOURS into our investigation.

8 KINNEY/linked:

What makes you think we have ANYTHING?

FOUR:

OTS KINNEY, as CROCKER, who has come around to front of the desk, leans back, arms folded. Cigarette still burns between fingers.

9 CROCKER:

The fact that you'd sooner eat BROKEN GLASS than ask for my HELP.

FIVE:

Reverse, OTS CROCKER as he takes a drag on his smoke. KINNEY grinning. Barely friendly.

10 KINNEY:

And the fact that YOU'D rather FELLATE a PONY than give it to ME.[23]

23. This was the "second favorite line" of the issue.

SIX:

POV CROCKER, on KINNEY, who is now seriously smiling in a very smug way.

11 KINNEY:

But yes, we DO have something.

12 KINNEY/linked:

And you're going to HATE it.

SEVEN:

CROCKER, waiting, annoyed, over-tired, under-fed, with a nicotine headache.

13 CROCKER:

Well?

EIGHT:

Across the DESK, with the RED PHONE in FG, KINNEY indicating it. From his position at the side of the desk, CROCKER looking at the phone, to see what is being indicated.

14 KINNEY:

Your MINDERS in their PIT?

Page 20

ONE:
In the PIT, KITTERING, WALLACE, and CHACE working
at their desks, reading either off their monitors
or out of files.

WALLACE and CHACE are both smoking.

NO COPY.

TWO:
Shot across WALLACE'S DESK, ECU of the RED PHONE
as he reaches for it.

1 SFX: dreet dreet

THREE:
Angle past CHACE as she looks over at WALLACE,
serious and somewhat expectant. WALLACE holding
the phone to his ear.

2 WALLACE:
                Minder One.

FOUR:
Angle between KITTERING and CHACE, exchanging
looks, while WALLACE listens to the phone.

NO COPY.

FIVE:
OTS CHACE on WALLACE, hanging up the phone, brow
furrowed.

3 CHACE:
                You on your bike?

4 WALLACE:
                No…

SIX:
POV CHACE, WALLACE looking at her, slightly
confused.

5 WALLACE:
                …D. Ops wants you in his OFFICE.

SEVEN:
From behind CHACE'S DESK, she's exiting in BG,
WALLACE and KITTERING looking at one another,
wondering what the hell is going on.

NO COPY.

Page 21

ONE:
Exterior of the MI6 BUILDING, and we can see the damaged from the blast better now that it's daylight.

1 KATE/inside:
>   Minder Two to see you, sir.

TWO:
Interior Crocker's Office, he's behind his desk, looking at the open door. KATE is stepping back as CHACE enters.

KINNEY is still in the same chair as before.

2 CROCKER:
>   Roll her IN.

3 CHACE:
>   Sir?

THREE:
OTS CHACE, KINNEY seated to her right, giving her a look-over.

CROCKER, behind his desk, is lighting a new cigarette.

4 CROCKER:
>   Don't think you've met David Kinney. He's my OPPOSITE NUMBER at Five.

FOUR:
CROCKER tossing his lighter down as CHACE shakes KINNEY'S HAND, though KINNEY still hasn't risen.

5 CHACE:
>   It's a pleasure, sir.

6 KINNEY:
>   Well, we'll SEE about that.

7 CROCKER:
>   You can SIT, Tara.

FIVE:
POV CHACE, looking at CROCKER, who has taken the lighter up again, and is worrying it in his hands, cigarette dangling.

NO COPY.

SIX:
STET Previous, but CROCKER is now looking up, at CHACE. Dead serious.

8 CROCKER:
>   Our BROTHERS at Five know who
>   gave us the EARLY wake-up this
>   morning.

SEVEN:
CHACE turning to look at KINNEY, who is very
pleased with himself.

9 KINNEY:
>   Group of RUSSIANS, used to work
>   for a man named MARKOVSKY.

10 KINNEY/linked:
>   Ring any BELLS?

Page 22

ONE:
OTS CHACE, looking to CROCKER for confirmation.

1 CROCKER:
>   He knows ALL about it, Tara, don't
>   worry.

TWO:
OTS KINNEY, CHACE, looking at him, stony-faced.

2 CHACE:
>   I killed him.

THREE:
OTS CROCKER, KINNEY, pleased with himself, looking
at CROCKER. CHACE still looking at KINNEY.

3 KINNEY:
>   Yes, you did.

4 KINNEY/linked:
>   Quite DEFTLY, too, from what we've
>   heard.

5 KINNEY:
>   Problem is, Markovsky had MATES…

FOUR:
Past CHACE, as KINNEY and CROCKER continue.

6 KINNEY:
>   …a LOT of them.

7 CROCKER:
>   Five says the Russians KNOW who
>   PULLED the TRIGGER.

8 CROCKER/linked:
>   They're after US in general, and
>   YOU specifically.[24]

24. Back when Oni Press did their Summer Color Specials, I had the honor of working with Stan Sakai, the amazingly talented creator of Usagi Yojimbo, on a story for the anthology. The story was, I believe, six pages, and told how Markovsky's people discovered that it was Chace who had pulled the trigger on their man.

FIVE:
Angle past KINNEY, grinning, at CHACE, who is
looking at CROCKER. CROCKER is returning her
gaze.
9 KINNEY:

> You're leaving out the BEST part,
> Paul.

SIX:
CU CHACE, expressionless, eyes slightly down.
There's some reasonable fear.

10 KINNEY/off:

> There's a BOUNTY on YOUR head, Ms.
> Chace…

SEVEN:
KINNEY, looking smug.

11 KINNEY:

> …ONE MILLION U.S. for the head of
> MINDER TWO.

Page 23

ONE:
CROCKER is up and crossing to KINNEY, who is still
seated.CHACE is motionless.

1 CROCKER:

> Get out!

2 KINNEY:

> We're NOT fini—

TWO:
CROCKER yanking KINNEY from the chair by the back
of his collar.

3 CROCKER:

> I ALWAYS knew you were BASTARD,
> David—

THREE:
CROCKER, opening the door to his office with one
hand, propelling KINNEY through with the other.
KATE is looking up in surprise.

5 CROCKER:

> —I just didn't know you were a
> SADIST, as well.

FOUR:
CHACE, still as before, in chair, in FG, as CROCKER
shuts the door and turns back.

NO COPY.

<u>FIVE:</u>
Stet previous, CROCKER coming around CHACE'S seat.
She's bringing her eyes back up level, now.

6 CHACE:
                 They want me to be BAIT.

7 CROCKER:
                 If they make a TRY at you they'll
                 EXPOSE themselves.

<u>SIX:</u>
OTS CHACE, CROCKER standing at his window, looking
out as he fishes another cigarette.

8 CROCKER:
                 Once they're in the OPEN, we can
                 TAKE them.

9 CROCKER:
                 Make   them   ANSWER   for   THIS
                 MORNING.

<u>SEVEN:</u>
CU CHACE, thinking.

10 CHACE:
                 Assuming I SURVIVE the TRY.

<u>EIGHT:</u>
ECU CROCKER, he won't look at her.

11 CROCKER:
                 Assuming.

Page 24

<u>ONE:</u>
Past CROCKER, still looking out the window.

CHACE in the chair.

NO COPY.

<u>TWO:</u>
OTS CROCKER, looking at CHACE. CHACE is honestly
curious.

1 CHACE:
                 Did you know Jill Baron or Albert
                 Cooper?

<u>THREE:</u>
POV CHACE, CROCKER, looking unhappy.

2 CROCKER:
                 Yes.   Couldn't   STAND   either   of
                 them.

3 CROCKER:

                    But the JANITOR[25]… Ravi Diop…

25. "Janitor" is an Americanism. I should have used "Custodian," instead.

FOUR:
CU CHACE, serious, listening. If she's surprised, it's not registering.

4 CROCKER:

                    …he was a NICE man.

FIVE:
OTS CROCKER, as CHACE rises.

NO COPY.

SIX:
CHACE in the doorway, looking back at us/ Crocker.

6 CHACE:

                    Tell KINNEY I'll start whenever
                    he's READY.

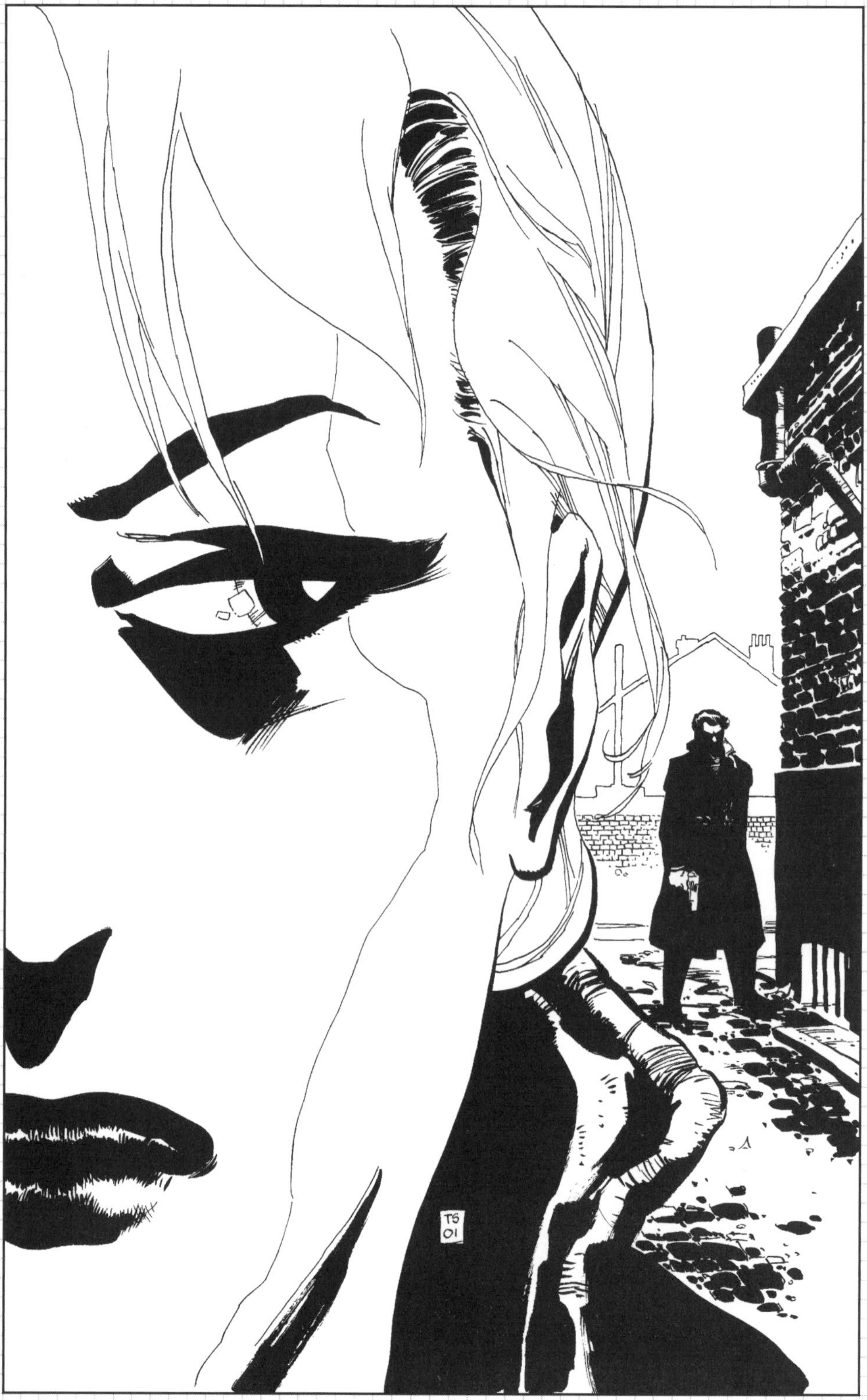
TS
01

Page 1

ONE:
Exterior, view of TARA'S HOME in South Kensington. It's night and raining. A couple CARS are parked on the street. Other townhouses flank Tara's, running the length of the block. Uniform brick structures mostly. An OLD MAN walks a DOG down the block, in BG. Other than that, it's pretty much silent and still, as this is an establishing shot.

CHACE is barely visible as a silhouette through one of her windows, moving in her kitchen.

1 TAILLESS/elec:
Still there, Rose[1]?

1. I used "Crow" and "Raven" as call-signs in issue 1, following a bird theme. Here I went with flowers. I was intentionally trying to make the call-signs as bland and, frankly, unimaginative, as possible. It seemed more realistic to me than using, say, "Cobra" and "Sexy Mommma" and others along those lines.

TWO:
Interior of TARA'S HOME in South Kensington. We're in the kitchen/dining area. This is a small townhouse, remember, so the space is somewhat cramped. Angle across the kitchen table, where Tara has finished eating her dinner-for-one. A HALF-EMPTY glass of JUICE is on the table, some crumbs, a small hand-held RADIO, and a PISTOL.

CHACE is moving away from the table, putting her dish in the sink, in BG.

2 TAILLESS/elec:
Still here, Tulip. See anything worth reporting?

3 TAILLESS/elec:
Not much...

THREE:
Angle on the RADIO and PISTOL. CHACE has returned to the table, picking up the GLASS, so we're basically looking at her mid-section.

4 TAILLESS/elec:
...though the BIRD in three-ten might be worth watching if she CHANGES for BED...

FOUR:
CHACE taking the radio in one hand, the PISTOL now

tucked in her waist band, carrying her glass in the other, heading for the sink.

5 TAILLESS/elec:
> …but I have to REPORT that, sadly, DAISY'S NEIGHBORS are all DAMN UGLY.

FIVE:
At the sink, CHACE has set the RADIO on the sideboard, the glass in the sink, and is pulling a cigarette from a pack with her teeth. It's unclear if she's actually listening.
6 TAILLESS/elec:
> Well, you know what you DO, Rose.

7 TAILLESS/elec:
> You SPY on DAISY. Sure to get an EYEFUL that way.

SIX:
CU CHACE, as she lights her cigarette. An eyebrow is arching. She's clearly listening.

8 TAILLESS/elec:
> Brilliant, Tulip.

9 TAILLESS/elec:
> Then DAISY kills ME, the RUSSIANS kill her…

SEVEN:
From the sink, CHACE, carrying the RADIO in one hand, her cigarette still burning in the other, her back to us, as she heads out of the kitchen.

10 TAILLESS/elec:
> …and you're suddenly HEAD of the SPECIAL SECTION.

11 TAILLESS/elec:
> Ah, you've seen through my CUNNING PLAN…

Page 2

ONE:
Living room of Tara's home, wide shot. Again, it's a somewhat cramped space, papers and books and CD jewel cases scattered about. A couple pictures on the walls—though they are pretty much devoid of sentiment. Maybe an old concert poster or two (Elvis Costello or Joe Jackson, I'm thinking, but I'm biased as hell[2]).

2. Meaning these are my music tastes, rather than Tara's.

CHACE is making for the couch, RADIO and cigarette still with her.

1 TAILLESS/elec:
> …you REALIZE what that MEANS, of

2 TAILLESS/elec:
>I DO, indeed…

TWO:
CHACE on the couch, on her back, the cigarette in her mouth, the RADIO on her stomach, the PISTOL still in her waist band. Her expression is kind of tense.

3 TAILLESS/elec:
>…it means it's TIME for a new PLAN.

4 CHACE/small:
>…it means it's time for a new plan.

THREE:
Stet previous, but now CHACE is holding her smoke up and away from her face, and has brought the RADIO up to speak to it.

5 CHACE:
>Tulip, Rose, it's Daisy.

6 CHACE/linked:
>Shut the BLOODY HELL up.

FOUR:
Stet previous, but CHACE has moved the RADIO away from her mouth, and is taking a drag off the cigarette.

NO COPY.

FIVE:
Stet previous, but CHACE has the RADIO back to her mouth, the cigarette again out of the way.

7 CHACE:
>Thank you.
8 CHACE/linked:
>Daisy out.

Page 3

ONE:
Exterior of the townhouse, and now it's late at night. The rain is still coming down.

The lights inside are out.

We're looking past a parked CAR in FG. KITTERING is slouched behind the wheel.

1 CAPTION/Chace:
                    I feel JUSTIFIED in a certain
                    TARTNESS of TONE.³

TWO:
Interior of Tara's bathroom, OTS/behind CHACE as
she splashes water on her face at the sink. She's
in a tank-top/undershirt and her panties—oops,
pardon me, I meant knickers—basically ready for
bed.

The RADIO and PISTOL are balanced on the side of
the sink.

2 CAPTION/Chace:
                    I am, after all, worth one MILLION
                    dollars.

THREE:
Stet previous, Chace looking at her reflection. She
looks a little haggard, a little tired. A little
ill, as if she's been puking up her guts off an on
for a while now.

3 CAPTION/Chace:
                    Or at least, that's what the RED
                    MAFIYA is willing to PAY for my
                    head.

FOUR:
Close, as CHACE comes past us out of the bathroom,
switching off the light. The RADIO and PISTOL are
now on the nightstand.

4 CAPTION/Chace:
                    Not REALLY the same thing, is it?

FIVE:
Angle from above, as CHACE collapses onto her
bed.

5 CAPTION/Chace:
                    One wonders how they go about
                    making THAT particular request.

6 CAPTION/Chace:
                    Wanted: SIS Officer Tara Chace's
                    HEAD, preferably on PLATTER...

SIX:
Past the nightstand, RADIO, PISTOL visible, to
a CU of CHACE, looking at us, her head on her
pillow. She looks tense and tired.

7 CAPTION/Chace:
                    ...BODY optional....

SEVEN:
Stet previous, but she's closed her eyes.

NO COPY.

3. We made it through the second issue
without resorting to Tara's narrative,
but I fell back upon it here, for a couple
of reasons, none of them very good.
Mostly, I was afraid I'd lost the reader,
and that someone picking up the book
wouldn't have the first clue what was
going on. For that reason, Tara's narrative here is entirely expository, and
that's just Bad Writing, in my book. It
doesn't really forward the action, and
what it reveals about her personality
is just as evident in the visuals, in the
"acting."

This was the moment, honestly, when
I realized that the first-person narrative
was inappropriate for the series, and
that it needed to go. I kept it through
issue 4, to maintain a manner of con-
sistency, but if I could do it again, I
wouldn't bother to even pretend.
Steve's art was more eloquent than any
of my narrative, and while I was able
to turn a couple of cute phrases here
and there, that's pretty much all I got
out of it. I look at it now, and I cringe,
the same way I cringe when I hear Har-
rison Ford's narration in Blade Runner.
It's unnecessary, and it insults the audience by presuming that the audience
isn't smart enough to figure out what's
going on in the story.

I firmly believe that's insulting, and I
just as firmly believe in not insulting my
audience.

Pages 4 and 5

[*This is all MI6 office stuff, and should be laid out as functionally as possible, without becoming a boring grid. Maybe we can take a page from some of Bendis'[4] layouts when he gets dialogue heavy...*]

4. I'm not as much a fan of Brian Bendis' dialogue, per se, as how brilliantly he uses dialogue visually, and makes it part of the art. It's something I tried to aspire to for a while, but never managed to capture, and thus decided to stick with what I know. Bendis writes a very specific kind of dialogue, inspired heavily by David Mamet, who is also one of my influences. But Mamet dialogue is a peculiar beast, and one that I've learned the hard way to let alone.

ONE:
Daylight, establishing of the MI6 building, with the BLAST DAMAGE visible from the previous issue. WORKMEN are repairing like nuts.

1 WALLACE/inside:
                    ...sat on her ALL NIGHT and there was
                    NO SIGN of anything...

TWO:
Interior of Crocker's Office, from behind Crocker's desk. CROCKER is standing, back to us, shrugging out of his overcoat. His focus is on the PAPERS on his desk.

WALLACE, looking rumpled, is in the doorway.

KATE is trying to edge past with two cups of coffee.

2 WALLACE:
                    ...Ed's watching her place NOW.

3 CROCKER:
                    You get any sleep?

4 WALLACE:
                    As you know, I am a MASTER of the
                    art of WANG-O-WANG which allows
                    one to SLEEP with his eyes OPEN.

5 WALLACE/linked:
                    I even DREAMED. Some of them were
                    DIRTY. Want to hear one, boss?

THREE:
New angle, KATE setting the first cup on the desk, as CROCKER, still staring at his papers, flips through a couple. WALLACE is watching KATE with a slight grin.

6 CROCKER:
                    You're about HALF the wit you think
                    you are, Tom.[5]

5. And this was Jamie's favorite line for this issue. Take that as you will.

7 CROCKER/linked:
                    What about Minder Two?

8 WALLACE:
                    Lights went off at TWENTY-THREE
                    HUNDRED, about—

FOUR:
OTS WALLACE, taking the cup of coffee from KATE as

This is the only thumbnail I could find from #3. As you can see, this was drawn before I realized it was two pages worth + Greg had just left the page break up to me. It sure felt like too many panels. I guess it pays to read the script more closely!

Steve

she heads towards us, out of the office. CROCKER in BG is looking up with a scowl, having seen the exchange of smiles.

9 WALLACE:
—thanks Kate—

10 WALLACE/linked:
—what Tara did AFTER that, I've no clue.

11 CROCKER:
Not much bloody USE, are you?

12 CROCKER/linked:
KATE!

FIVE:
OTS CROCKER, as WALLACE jerks back in the doorway, trying to keep coffee from spilling on himself. KATE has turned around to look at Crocker, attentive.

13 KATE:
Paul?

14 CROCKER:
Did you call CHENG?[6]

6. And miraculously, Franks is Angela Cheng. For those who are interested in Easter Eggs and that kind of thing, Angela Cheng-Caplan is one of the two agents who represents my work (she handles the film rights and the like; my other agent, David Hale Smith, handles my literary work, and about a thousand other things). The character of Angela Cheng, CIA Station Chief, London, is based entirely on Angela Cheng, the Agent. This should give you a good sense of what she's like as an agent, and why I am devoted to her.

... SAT ON HER ALL NIGHT AND THERE WAS NO SIGN OF ANYTHING...
... ED'S WATCHING HER PLACE NOW.
YOU GET ANY SLEEP?
AS YOU KNOW, I AM A MASTER OF THE ART OF WANG-O-WANG, WHICH ALLOWS ONE TO SLEEP WITH HIS EYES OPEN.
I EVEN DREAMED. SOME OF THEM WERE DIRTY. WANT TO HEAR ONE, BOSS?
YOU'RE ABOUT HALF THE WIT YOU THINK YOU ARE, TOM.
WHAT ABOUT MINDER TWO?
LIGHTS WENT OFF AT TWENTY-THREE HUNDRED, ABOUT...
--THANKS, KATE--
-- WHAT TARA DID AFTER THAT, I'VE NO CLUE.
NOT MUCH BLOODY USE, ARE YOU?
KATE!
PAUL?
DID YOU CALL CHENG?
OF COURSE I DID.
AND?
AND SHE'LL BE FREE AFTER ONE THIS AFTERNOON.
NOT BEFORE?
NO. NOT BEFORE.

I SHOULD FIRE HER.
DESTROY US ALL.
DESPITE WHAT KATE WOULD HAVE YOU BELIEVE, TOM, SHE DOES NOT RUN THE SERVICE.
YOU'RE JUST CRANKY BECAUSE RUSSIANS ARE TRYING TO KILL YOUR GIRL.
I SHOULD HAVE SENT YOU TO KOSOVO, TOM.
YEAH, PROBABLY. BUT I WOULD'VE MISSED THE SHOT ON MARKOVSKY, AND THEN WHERE WOULD WE BE?
GO GET SOME SLEEP, THEN RELIEVE ED.
YOU COMMAND, AND I OBEY.

15 KATE:

Of course I did.

16 CROCKER:

And?

17 KATE:

And she'll be FREE after ONE this afternoon.

18 CROCKER:

Not BEFORE?

SIX:
From the ante-room, Kate's office, as KATE comes towards us. WALLACE in BG, looking after her with a grin, and CROCKER fuming at the desk in EBG.

19 KATE:

No. Not before.

SEVEN:
CROCKER glaring after Kate, who is out of sight. WALLACE is now grinning at CROCKER.

20 CROCKER:

I should FIRE her.

21 WALLACE:

Do that and you'll DESTROY us all.

EIGHT:
Past WALLACE, sipping his coffee, as CROCKER drops
into his chair.

22 CROCKER:
Despite what KATE would have you
believe, TOM, she does NOT run the
Service.

23 WALLACE:
You're just cranky because Russians
are trying to kill your GIRL.

NINE:
Two-shot, CROCKER just shooting pure venom at
WALLACE.

WALLACE grinning.

NO COPY.

TEN:
Stet previous.

24 CROCKER:
I should have sent YOU to Kosovo.

25 WALLACE:
Yeah, probably. But I would've
MISSED the shot on Markovsky, and
then where would we be?

ELEVEN:
CROCKER has his head down, going through the
files in front of him. WALLACE is heading out the
door.

26 CROCKER:
Go get some sleep, then relieve
Ed.

27 WALLACE:
You COMMAND and I OBEY.

Page 6

ONE:
View of the CLOCK on the wall above Kate's
Desk. It's reading three minutes to one in the
afternoon.

1 KATE/below:
Paul! You're going to be LATE.

TWO:
Pull back, and we see that KATE is leaning on her
desk, head turned to CROCKER'S open office door.

CROCKER is emerging, pulling on his overcoat.

2 CROCKER:
                    Call the Embassy, tell her I'll be
                    in the PARK.

3 KATE:
                    She's probably already LEFT—

4 CROCKER:
                    She hasn't LEFT, she's running
                    LATE, too.

THREE:
OTS KATE, as CROCKER heads out the door to the
ante-room, just as WELDON is coming in.

5 CROCKER:
                    And when Minder Three gets in, tell
                    him I'll see him when I get BACK—

6 WELDON:
                    Paul.

FOUR:
CROCKER and WELDON. WELDON is trying to be
pleasant. CROCKER looks seriously annoyed.

7 CROCKER:
                    Sir.

8 WELDON:
                    Heading out?

9 CROCKER:
                    Meeting with Cheng.

FIVE:
From the ante-room doorway, as WELDON moves past
KATE'S DESK, into CROCKER'S OFFICE.

CROCKER has turned in absolute frustration to
follow him.

KATE, at the desk, is looking sympathetic, and
reaching for the phone.

10 WELDON: A minute in your OFFICE, please.

SIX:
Tight, as WELDON enters the office. CROCKER
glowering at him.

NO COPY.

SEVEN:
Past CROCKER, as he goes back to his office. KATE
is already on the phone.

11 CROCKER:
>   Kate?

12 KATE:
>   I'll let her know.

Page 7

ONE:
From Crocker's desk, WELDON standing in the middle
of the office, CROCKER shutting the door behind him
as he enters.

NO COPY.

TWO:
Pretty much stet on the angle, WELDON hasn't moved,
CROCKER coming past him, not looking at Weldon.

1 WELDON:
>   I saw a MEMO from MATERIEL this
>   morning about THREE Walther P99s.[7]

2 WELDON/linked:
>   Did you ARM the Minders?

3 CROCKER:
>   Chace is being hunted by THUGS in
>   the middle of LONDON, sir...

THREE:
CROCKER has stopped at his desk, not yet traveling
behind it. WELDON is looking at his back. WELDON
is on the verge of losing patience, but isn't
there yet. CROCKER looks frustrated, pulling a
cigarette from a pack on the desk.

4 CROCKER:
>   ...of COURSE I armed the MINDERS.

5 WELDON:
>   I can't have S.I.S. running about
>   LONDON like extras from some
>   American ACTION film, Paul.

FOUR:
OTS WELDON, CROCKER with a cigarette dangling,
just about to light it. His eyes are very dark—
he's not fucking about.

6 WELDON:
>   You get away with THAT behavior on
>   STATION, not at HOME.

7 WELDON/linked:
>   And certainly NOT when KINNEY and
>   the rest of FIVE breathing down
>   our necks.

FIVE:
WELDON, making a pinched face. He understands why

7. I chose this weapon for no other
reason than that I like the gun.
Apparently I'm not the only one; it's
the gun James Bond is now using in
the films.

Paul did it, but he can't let it stand.

8 WELDON:
>You have to DISARM them.

SIX:
WELDON and CROCKER. CROCKER is frustrated. WELDON
is calm, almost matter-of-fact.

9 CROCKER:
>And when the Russians make their
>TRY, what is Chace supposed to
>DO?

10 CROCKER/linked:
>Bat her EYES and ask them SWEETLY
>to not MURDER her TOO MUCH?

SEVEN:
OTS CROCKER, WELDON starting to turn for the door.
He really does understand the problem.

11 WELDON:
>I'm NOT saying it'll be EASY.

12 WELDON/linked:
>But Wallace, Chace, and Kittering
>comprise your SPECIAL SECTION...

EIGHT:
CU on CROCKER, just shy of snarling. Really
unhappy, angry, frustrated. Just generally a guy
who rarely ever smiles. Right now, he'd like to
kill someone, but he doesn't know who to blame—
Weldon's right, and he hates him for that.

13 WELDON/off:
>...perhaps it's TIME they PROVE how
>SPECIAL they ARE.[8]

8. This line is one of the many I've stolen from Ian Mackintosh over the course of the series. It works so well, I used it in the first Q&C novel, as well.

Page 8

ONE:
Interior of Chace's home, we're looking at the
floor in the doorway to her bedroom. The RADIO and
GUN are on the floor.

CHACE'S KNEES and FEET are hanging in panel—she's
doing pull-ups, but we'll see that in a couple of
panels. Right now we're going to be artsy-fartsy.
She's got her knees bent so her feet are crossed
at 90 degrees, parallel to the floor, behind her.

NO COPY.

TWO:
Stet previous, but now there's no sign of Tara.

NO COPY.

THREE:
Stet panel one.

NO COPY.

FOUR:
Stet panel two.

1 TAILLESS/elec:
            Daisy? It's TULIP…

FIVE:
Pull-back, still framed by the doorway. CHACE has
dropped from the pull-up bar in the doorway. She's
in jeans and a t-shirt, perspiring. She's been
doing a lot of these. She is reaching for the
RADIO.

2 TAILLESS/elec:
            …your PHONE is about to RING.

3 SFX: brrt brrt

SIX:
Stet angle, but now CHACE has taken the GUN and
RADIO from the floor, and is moving into BG, back
to us, heading for the phone on the nightstand.
CHACE is speaking into the radio.

4 CHACE:
            That was very CLEVER, Tulip.

5 CHACE/linked:
            Can you tell me what happens next
            week on *Holby City*?[9]

6 TAILLESS/elec:
            Sorry.

7 SFX: brrt brrt

9. Holby City is a spin-off of Casualty,
which in turn was the BBC's take on ER.

SEVEN:
Stet angle, but now CHACE is answering the phone
in the BG.

8 CHACE:
                    Chace.

9 CROCKER/phone:
                    Tara? It's Paul.

10 CHACE:
                    Yes, sir?

EIGHT:
Stet previous, but CHACE'S posture has changed,
head now down.

11 CROCKER/phone:
                    I just had a meeting with the
                    Deputy Chief.

12 CROCKER/phone/linked:
                    He's ORDERED the Minders to turn
                    in their WEAPONS.

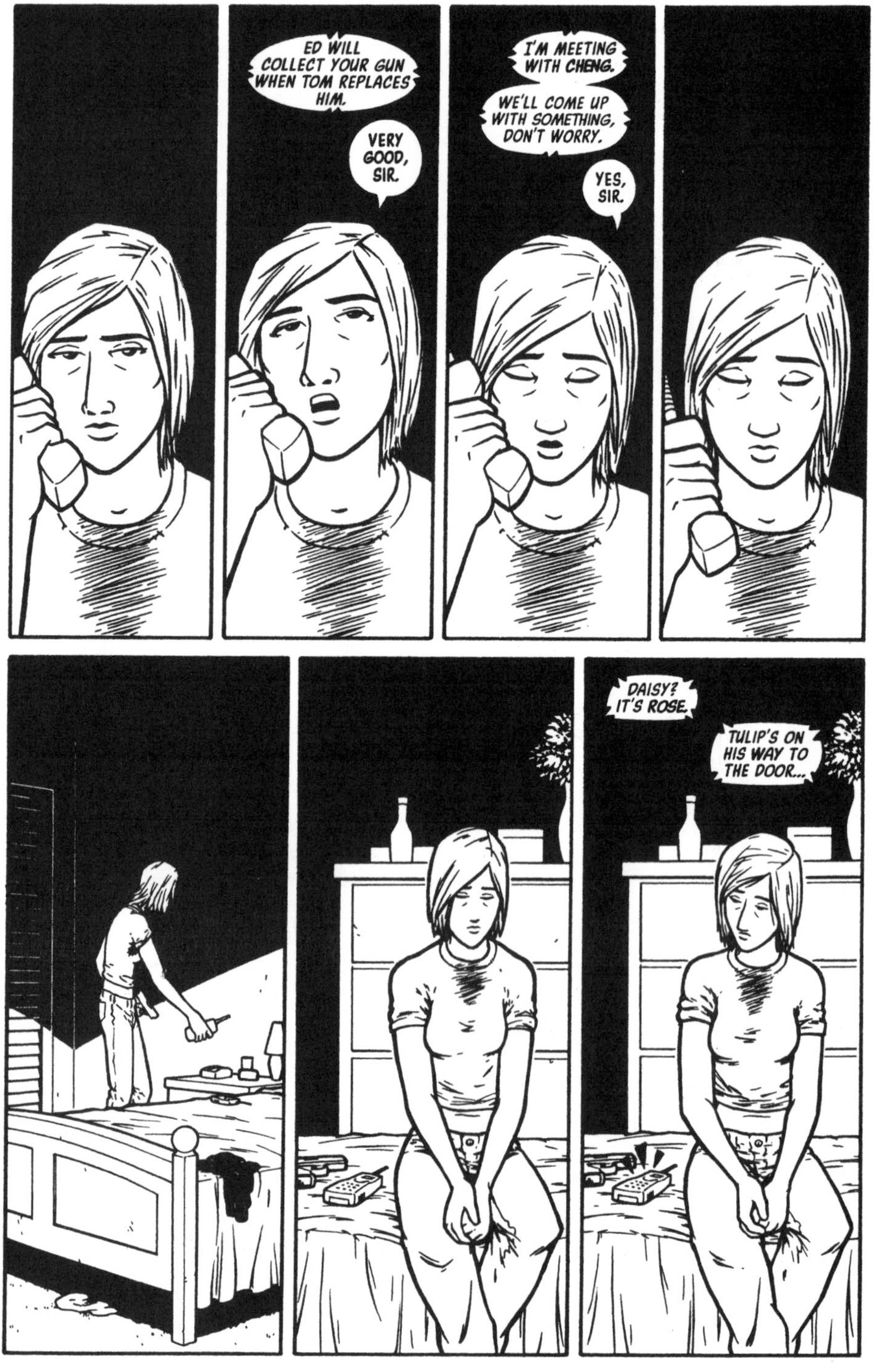
ED WILL COLLECT YOUR GUN WHEN TOM REPLACES HIM.
VERY GOOD, SIR.
I'M MEETING WITH CHENG.
WE'LL COME UP WITH SOMETHING, DON'T WORRY.
YES, SIR.
DAISY? IT'S ROSE.
TULIP'S ON HIS WAY TO THE DOOR...

10. Steve, it turned out, was brilliant at these kinds of pages. I can't put my finger on exactly what it is he does, but he managed—time and again over these four issues—to bring an incredible emotional weight to the moments of stillness. Given that Steve got a lot of critical heat at the start of the series for his art style—he was called "too cartoony" by several different "critics" in several different forums, I think this gives proof to their lies.

Of interest, perhaps, is the fact that Steve was only the first to get this treatment. Throughout the series, each artist has had the pleasure of being unfavorably compared to the one who preceded him/her. This lasts until a new artist comes on the book, and then the last guy or gal is suddenly the Best Q&C Artist Ever.

Page 9[10]

ONE:
CU on CHACE, on the phone. Serious expression. She's thinking that the Deputy Chief has probably just guaranteed she'll be dead soon.

NO COPY.

TWO:
Stet.

1 CROCKER/phone:
        Ed will collect your gun when Tom
        replaces him.

2 CHACE:
        Very good, sir.

THREE:
Stet. CHACE has closed her eyes.

3 CROCKER/phone:
        I'm meeting with CHENG.

4 CROCKER/phone/linked:
        We'll come up with SOMETHING, don't
        worry.

5 CHACE:
        Yes, sir.

FOUR:
Stet, eyes still closed.

6 SFX/phone: klik

FIVE:
Across the bed, as CHACE hangs up the phone.

NO COPY.

SIX:
CHACE, sitting on the bed, RADIO and GUN next to her. Her posture is tense and somewhat depressed.

NO COPY.

SEVEN:
Stet, but CHACE is looking down at the RADIO.

7 TAILLESS/elec:
        Daisy? It's ROSE.

8 TAILLESS/elec/linked:
        Tulip's on his WAY to the door...

Pages 10 and 11

ONE:
This is the big image, spanning two pages.
Across the top and bottom run panels Two through
Thirteen.

Exterior of Hyde Park, day. Gray and overcast.
People walk with umbrellas. Nannies push prams.
Just what you'd expect. Some people are jogging.
But it is a beautiful park in the middle of
London.

CHENG and CROCKER, small, are walking side by side.
Each walks with their hands in their pockets.

ANGELA CHENG, for the record, is the CIA Station
Chief in London, based out of the Embassy in
Grosvenor Square. She's about a foot shorter than
Crocker, better dressed and better paid, and still
looks over-worked and over-tired. Her hair is
shoulder length. She's Chinese-American.

NO COPY.

TWO:
This is a side shot, upper bodies, of CROCKER
and CHENG, walking side by side, talking. CROCKER
should be in FG, closer to the camera. They rarely
look at one another as they talk, mostly watching
what's happening around them.

1 CHENG:
                    You're the ONLY man I let keep me
                    WAITING.

2 CROCKER:
                    You let your AMBASSADOR keep you
                    waiting.

3 CHENG:
                    Actually, I DON'T.

THREE:
Stet previous, minor changes in posture. Perhaps
a breeze blows some of Cheng's hair.

4 CHENG:
                    What happened?

5 CROCKER:
                    Weldon wanted a PIECE of me.

6 CROCKER/linked:
                    Doesn't like the Minders going
                    ARMED in London.

FOUR:
Stet, again, minor changes.

7 CHENG:

> Can't say I BLAME him. They start SHOOTING, everyone on your FLOOR will need to update a resume.

8 CROCKER:

> Oh, I know he's CORRECT, Angela.

9 CROCKER/linked:

> I just wish he wasn't so damn SMUG about it.

FIVE:
Stet, again, minor changes.

10 CHENG:

> Is that what you wanted to meet about?

11 CROCKER:

> No, but it makes this more PRESSING.

12 CROCKER/linked:

> You know the situation?

SIX:
Stet previous, but CROCKER is actually looking at CHENG.

13 CHENG:

> Red Mafiya wants Chace's HEAD because of what she did to Markovsky.

SEVEN:
Now on the bottom row, and here we reverse, so that CHENG is in FG, CROCKER in BG, but postures and layout as above.

14 CROCKER:

> Should I even ASK how you KNOW?

15 CHENG:

> I'm CIA. We know EVERYTHING.[11]

EIGHT:
Stet previous, slight changes. CHENG is grinning. CROCKER is not.

16 CROCKER:

> Like you knew about AMES.[12]

17 CHENG:

> No fair! You didn't know about Philby, Maclean, Burgess—

18 CROCKER:

> Point taken.

11. They don't, actually, as George Tenent recently explained to the 9-11 Commission.

12. Aldrich "Rick" Ames was a CIA Intelligence Officer arrested in 1994 along with his wife for spying for the Soviets. Ames' arrest lead, in turn, to the revelation that, like the British, the KGB had succeeded in recruiting several double-agents in the US. This came as quite a shock to a great many, who had thought the CIA untouched by such deceptions. It's thought that Ames betrayal cost the lives of at least 10 agents who were executed by the Soviets, as well as the compromise of some 100 separate intelligence operations. Ames worked in the Counterintelligence Division at the CIA, where he was responsible for—wait for it—directing analysis of Soviet intelligence operations.

NINE:
Stet previous, slight changes, both now serious, though.

19 CROCKER:

Can you help?

20 CHENG:

Help how?

21 CROCKER:

Give me some back-up.

TEN:
Stet, again with the slight changes. CHENG is frowning, brow furrowed.

22 CHENG:

Don't you have Five backing you? What's his name? Kinney?

23 CROCKER:

David Kinney, yes, and that's NOT the HELP I'm looking for.

24 CROCKER/linked:
Kinney wants an ARREST.

ELEVEN:
Stet, again, still walking. CHENG is now looking at CROCKER, vaguely alarmed. CROCKER is ignoring the look.

25 CROCKER:

I want them DEAD.

26 CHENG:

Jesus Christ, Paul!

TWELVE:
Stet, both now walking without looking at each other, thinking.

NO COPY.

THIRTEEN:
Stet, but now CHENG has stopped, and CROCKER is moving out of panel.

27 CROCKER:

They ATTACKED us in our HOME, Angela.

Page 12

ONE:
Still in the park. We're OTS CHENG, now looking at CROCKER who has taken a bench and is pulling out a cigarette.

NO COPY.

TWO:
CHENG sitting next to CROCKER. CROCKER is lighting
his cigarette. CHENG is thoughtful, watching the
pedestrians.

1 CROCKER:
                    Can you help?

2 CHENG:
                    What   do   I   look   like,   Lady
                    Macbeth?

THREE:
From behind the bench, both seated. CHENG is
leaning back. CROCKER is now leaning forward,
elbows on thighs.

3 CROCKER:
                    One of MY people is being HUNTED
                    because of a FAVOR I did the CIA.

4 CROCKER/linked:
                    Chace took Markovsky at Langley's
                    request.

FOUR:
Side shot, past CHENG in FG, CROCKER still leaning
forward, now glancing at her, vaguely hopeful.
CHENG is almost stern.

5 CHENG:
                    For which Langley is GRATEFUL.

6 CHENG/linked:
                    But they're not grateful enough
                    to allow me to authorize a COVERT
                    action in downtown London.

7 CROCKER:
                    You could ASK.

FIVE:
CHENG looking at CROCKER with some frustration.
He's looking kinda depressed now.

8 CHENG:
                    I KNOW what they'll say. They'll
                    say NO.

9 CHENG/linked:
                    And with GOOD reason. Can you
                    imagine the political SHITSTORM
                    we'd be in if anything LEAKED?

SIX:
Past CROCKER, who is now looking off into the
middle-distance, drawing on his cigarette.

CHENG is adjusting her hair, frowning.

335

10 CHENG:

Forget the MIRROR, it'd be in the Washington Fucking POST.

11 CHENG/linked:

No way the NEW President will let THAT happen. His position is TOO SHAKY right now.[13]

13. Truth, baby, is far stranger than any fiction of which I can conceive.

I believe this line was written before the results of the 2000 "election," hence the vagueness of the 'new President' line.

SEVEN:
Narrow horizontal band, CHENG and CROCKER on the bench.

NO COPY.

Page 13

ONE:
Looking past a ROMANTIC COUPLE in FG, as they walk with their arms around each other.

In BG, CROCKER and CHENG seated at the bench. CROCKER is leaning back.

1 CROCKER:

All right, if you can't give me PERSONNEL, can you give EQUIPMENT?

2 CHENG:

If you're going to say what I THINK you're going to say…

TWO:
CROCKER watching the ROMANTIC COUPLE pass by in the BG. CHENG is glaring at him, though she is, perhaps, amused at his lunacy.

3 CROCKER:

Three PISTOLS, doesn't matter the MAKE, as long as they WORK.

4 CHENG:

Hell no. Company GUN or Company GUNMAN, it's the SAME problem, Paul!

5 CROCKER:

You have UNTRACEABLE weapons.

THREE:
CHENG, almost flopping back, exasperated. CROCKER is examining his burning cigarette.

6 CHENG:

For use by OUR people, not YOURS.

7 CROCKER:

So you've got NOTHING for me?

FOUR:
CHENG looking at CROCKER, annoyed. CROCKER is flicking his butt away.

8 CHENG:

Only more verbal DARTS.[14]

9 CROCKER:

Sadly, Chace isn't in a position to PLAY games.

FIVE:
On the bench, as CHENG rises, adjusting her overcoat. CROCKER is frowning off in the distance, barely listening, now.

10 CHENG:

Well, it might get her out of her FLAT. And KIDS always have the best toys.

11 CHENG/linked:

I've got to get back to the Embassy.

12 CROCKER:

Yes.

SIX:
Longshot, as CHENG walks away, leaving CROCKER on the bench.

13 CHENG:

Good luck with it.

14. Not sure how many—if any—people picked up on this, but Cheng's line here, and the one that follows, were very deliberate. She's suggesting to Crocker that, if he can't get real guns, use fake ones. A suggestion he follows.

Page 14

ONE:
CROCKER walking out of the park, distance shot. He's in a foul mood.

NO COPY.

TWO:
CROCKER on a London street, passing shops. Head down, deep in thought, scowling.

NO COPY.

THREE:
Side shot, as CROCKER passes a COMIC STORE, where there are displays. Appropriate SUPER HERO garbage in the windows, some ACTION FIGURES and DOLLS, and a couple of discreetly placed PELLET GUNS.

He's not paying any attention.

NO COPY.

<u>FOUR:</u>
Stet previous, of the COMIC STORE WINDOW, with the DISPLAY, Crocker is out of shot.

NO COPY.

<u>FIVE:</u>
Stet previous, but CROCKER is back, his back to us, looking into the window.

NO COPY.

<u>SIX:</u>
From the street, CROCKER stepping into the store.

NO COPY.

Page 15

<u>ONE:</u>
Exterior of the MI6 building. Afternoon. Repair work continues on the blast damage.

  1 CROCKER/inside:
            Kate!

<u>TWO:</u>
CROCKER entering the ante-room to his office, carrying a SHOPPING BAG. KATE is springing up behind her desk, alarmed.

  2 KATE:
            Paul?

  3 CROCKER:
            Where's Minder Three?

<u>THREE:</u>
Angle from the doorway to Crocker's office, as CROCKER drops the SHOPPING BAG on Kate's DESK, already heading our way, pulling off his overcoat.

KATE is uncertain whether she should look in the bag or follow him.

  4 KATE:
            He's in the PIT, has been for over
            an HOUR now. PAUL—

  5 CROCKER:
            Good, make sure he doesn't LEAVE.

  6 CROCKER/linked:
            Actually, don't, I'll CALL him.

<u>FOUR:</u>
Angle on KATE, looking into the bag with some trepidation, arching an eyebrow.

7 KATE:
>Paul, David Kinney—

8 CROCKER:
>RUN that down to DESIGN...

9 CROCKER/linked:
>...tell them I want it by TONIGHT, and to make them look PROPER.

FIVE:
Inside Crocker's office, as CROCKER blows through the door.

DAVID KINNEY is standing in front of the desk, turning around to face him.

CROCKER is surprised—which translates to angry.

In BG, we can see that KATE has already taken up the bag, and is looking at us through the doorway, waiting for the rest of her instructions.

10 KATE:
>David Kinney is here to see you.

11 KINNEY:
>Paul.

SIX:
CU CROCKER, just scowling.

NO COPY.

SEVEN:
Past KINNEY, looking at CROCKER, who in turn is glancing at KATE in BG.

12 CROCKER:
>Get it done.

13 KATE:
>Tonight, and proper.

Page 16

ONE:
In the office, CROCKER moving to his desk. KINNEY is standing, watching him.

1 CROCKER:
>Hope you WERE waiting long.

2 KINNEY:
>Not VERY.

3 KINNEY/linked:
>What's the hold-up?

TWO:
Past the DESK, CROCKER'S HAND dropping his pack
of cigarettes. KINNEY looking at CROCKER, being
a hard-ass.

4 CROCKER/above:
                    Hold-up?

5 KINNEY:
                    Chace hasn't moved in TWO DAYS.
                    What are you WAITING for?

THREE:
CROCKER in his chair, looking at KINNEY with barely
hidden contempt. KINNEY is returning it.

6 CROCKER:
                    I want my people in place before
                    she goes under FIRE, if that's all
                    RIGHT.

7 KINNEY:
                    MY people are ALREADY in place.

FOUR:
Past KINNEY, CROCKER leaning forward and taking
a cigarette from his pack. He's not looking at
Kinney, and is perhaps mildly amused.

8 CROCKER:
                    Then you UNDERSTAND my FEARS.

FIVE:
CU KINNEY, getting ticked.

9 KINNEY:
                    I understand you're CODDLING her.
                    She stays INDOORS, the RUSSIANS
                    won't MOVE on her.

10 KINNEY/linked:
                    She's supposed to be DRAWING them
                    OUT.

SIX:
CROCKER, holding his lighter, but his eyes are on
KINNEY.

11 CROCKER:
                    And in TIME she will.

12 KINNEY:
                    Time we don't HAVE.

SEVEN:
Angle past CROCKER'S ELBOW, as he sets the lighter
back down. KINNEY is leaning forward, hands on
the desk.

13 KINNEY:
                    I want this DONE tonight.

14 KINNEY/linked:
>Order her into MOTION and quit STALLING.

Page 17

ONE:
Two-shot. CROCKER and KINNEY glaring at each other.

NO COPY.

TWO:
Stet, but KINNEY has straightened up, is adjusting his suit-coat.

1 KINNEY:
>Do I need to speak to WELDON?

2 CROCKER:
>Your NOSE does seem REMARKABLY free of SHITE.

3 CROCKER/linked:
>A quick VISIT couldn't HURT.

THREE:
OTS CROCKER, KINNEY almost livid.

4 KINNEY/small:
>right.

FOUR:
Angle as KINNEY leaves Crocker's office, nearly smashing into KATE as she comes around the corner to look in on Paul.

NO COPY.

FIVE:
In the doorway, KATE now looking after Kinney, off. CROCKER has joined her, eyebrow arched.

5 KATE:
>You're still MATES, I see.

6 CROCKER:
>Shut up.

7 CROCKER/linked:
>He's going to WELDON.

SIX:
On KATE, now looking after Crocker as he goes back into his office.

8 KATE:
>Why?

9 CROCKER/off:
>   He's accusing me of CODDLING
>   Chace...

SEVEN:
OTS KATE, CROCKER at the desk, standing, picking
up the RED PHONE.

10 CROCKER:
>   ...wants the DC to order me to order
>   her to give the RUSSIANS their
>   SHOT.

11 CROCKER/linked:
>   What about the OTHER thing?

12 KATE:
>   Ready by sixteen hundred.

EIGHT:
CU CROCKER on the phone.

13 CROCKER:
>   Good.

14 CROCKER/linked:
>   Ed? It's D. Ops. My OFFICE,
>   please...

Page 18

ONE:
On the street outside Chace's home. It's night.

WALLACE is kneeling in FG, tying his shoe. He's
stopped in front of one of the houses on the
street. The house has a small alcove and the
front door is within that. On the second floor of
the building we can see that the curtains in the
window have been slightly parted, and we can see
a HAND adjusting them.

In WALLACE'S LEFT EAR, we can see the little
RECEIVER for his radio, and a CABLE running down
to his collar, disappearing inside his shirt.[15]

1 CHACE/elec/tailless:
>   ...how many?

2 WALLACE/small:
>   At least TWO, so DOUBLE that
>   number.

3 WALLACE/small/linked
>   Tulip there?

TWO:
Interior of Chace's place, with CHACE in BG,
peering out her blinds discreetly. It's pretty

15. This is a fine example of Greg asking for too many things in a single panel, something I do with alarming frequency, I'm afraid. My philosophy when scripting for a comic essentially comes down to this—my panel descriptions are about 80% optional; I'm far more concerned with conveying to the artist the movement of the story: what is happening, why it matters, what the characters feel about it, what the theme, tone, and emotional intent is. Ideally, after reading one of my scripts, the artist knows what it is I'm trying to accomplish, and then can tailor his or her choices to that best effect. I'm not an artist; I've tried, God knows, but it's a sad sight to see me with a pencil and a sketchpad. I leave the visuals to the professionals, and I handle the words and the story, so to speak.

If you compare the script with the actual comic, the work that Steve did, he followed me very closely, perhaps to the story's detriment, because sometimes I make very bad choices. I'm not saying that this is one; I'm just saying that my visual sense is for shit for the most part. Steve's, thank God, isn't.

dark inside. She's on her RADIO.
In FG, back to us, is KITTERING, holding the
SHOPPING BAG.

4 CHACE:
                    Just arrived.

5 WALLACE/elec/tailless:
                    I'll be right in, then.

THREE:
Two-shot, wide, as CHACE turns away from the
window to face KITTERING. KITTERING is trying to
be cheerful, but CHACE looks exhausted.

6 CHACE:
                    He's coming.

7 KITTERING:
                    Good.

8 CHACE:
                    You want a DRINK?

FOUR:
Past KITTERING, watching CHACE as she pours herself
a Scotch from the bottle at the sideboard. She
still holds the RADIO in one hand.

9 KITTERING:
                    Doesn't strike me as the TIME.

10 CHACE:
                    Me, either.

FIVE:
CHACE draining the glass.

KITTERING watching.

NO COPY.

SIX:
OTS CHACE, looking at the back door. KITTERING has
turned to look, as well.

WALLACE is entering.

11 WALLACE:
                    Sorry about that.

12 KITTERING:
                    We're SURE it's them?

13 WALLACE:
                    Them or FIVE.

SEVEN:
CHACE putting her glass back down.

14 CHACE:
                    It's them.

Page 19

ONE:
Angle on WALLACE, KITTERING, and CHACE in the living room. KITTERING has set the BAG on the coffee table, and is reaching inside.

1 WALLACE:
So what is the GOOD WORD from Master Crocker?

2 KITTERING:
He offers TOYS and INSTRUCTIONS.

3 KITTERING/linked:
We're each to take one of THESE…

TWO:
Looking into the BAG as KITTERING lifts out a PELLET GUN, black, and a passable fake for a real gun is you don't look <u>too</u> hard at it.[16]

4 KITTERING/above:
…and then watch Tara go for a WALK by the WATER.

THREE:
KITTERING handing PELLET GUNS to CHACE and WALLACE.

Both CHACE and WALLACE look almost expressionless, taking the weapons, looking at them.

5 WALLACE:
Are these PELLET GUNS?

6 KITTERING:
Yes. We're to BLUFF with them.

7 WALLACE:
Bluff.

8 KITTERING:
Yes.

9 KITTERING/linked:
Gets WORSE. Kinney got the DC to ORDER Tara into the OPEN…

FOUR:
On CHACE, as she holds up the PELLET GUN, examining it. Again, almost no expression whatsoever.

10 KITTERING/off:
…assured him that FIVE would provide ADEQUATE back-up.

16. This isn't as ludicrous as it may first appear; at the San Diego Comic Con for the last several years, there have been at least three dealers selling "fake" guns that fire hard plastic BBs. Apparently, you can use these things for paintball—a recreation I have never tried, myself—and target shooting. The guns are available in almost every common make and model available, and they look incredibly realistic. So realistic, in fact, that were you to wander around with one outdoors, there's a very good chance you'd get shot by a cop. The few that have safety orange pieces around the end of the barrel don't really do much to convince one that these are not the real thing.

The idea here was that, of course, Crocker had procured exactly these kinds of pistols.

FIVE:
KITTERING and WALLACE watching CHACE, as she looks at the gun in her hand. It's pretty clear that all of them are thinking that she's going to die shortly, including her.

11 WALLACE:
      Five wants ARRESTS. They'll try to
      take the RUSSIANS alive.

12 KITTERING:
      Which means they'll WAIT until
      AFTER the try.

SIX:
Stet previous, but CHACE has lowered the PELLET GUN, now looking off, to the window. Her expression is still blank, resigned.

NO COPY

SEVEN:
Past WALLACE, as he and KITTERING watch CHACE head into her bedroom.

13 CHACE:
      I'll get my COAT.

Page 20

ONE:
Exterior of the house, night. We're OTS KITTERING, watching from shadow.

CHACE is emerging from inside, well-illuminated from above by her porch/door light. She's in her coat, hands deep in pockets.

NO COPY.

TWO:
OTS WALLACE, opposite end of the block.

CHACE is small in BG, coming towards us slowly.

NO COPY.

THREE:
Almost a bird's-eye, from above the street. CHACE walking alone on her side of the street.

KITTERING in SHADOW at the top of the street.

NO COPY.

FOUR:
From the doorway of the HOUSE WITH THE CURTAINS, TWO MEN are emerging slowly, looking after CHACE.

CHACE is at the end of the block, turning the corner. No sign of Kittering or Wallace.

NO COPY.

SIX:
FIVE:
Angle along the street, as the TWO MEN move to catch up with Chace, now out of sight.

1 TAILLESS/elec:
You've got TWO, Daisy.

2 TAILLESS/elec:
Understood.

SIX:
Past WALLACE, watching the TWO MEN turn the corner. CHACE is in EBG. WALLACE is speaking into his radio.

Down the street where Tara's home is, we can see KITTERING approaching the doorway the two men emerged from.

3 WALLACE/small:
Tulip, go.

SEVEN:
Tight past KITTERING, as he edges up to the doorway where the TWO MEN emerged.

In EBG, we see WALLACE is moving to follow the Two Men, who are now off.

4 KITTERING/very small:
In motion.

Page 21

[*Greg's general note on violence: make this as savage and fast as possible, please. It should be nasty, it should be painful, it should be ugly. Thanks and have a nice day!*]

ONE:
Looking straight on at the doorway where the two men emerged. KITTERING is pressed against the wall beside the doorway, listening, waiting. Very tense. He has the PELLET GUN in his hand.

Another TWO MEN—these are all of the Russian Thug variety—are coming out the door.

NO COPY.

TWO:
OTS KITTERING, as the TWO RUSSIANS emerge. The FIRST is looking in the direction Chace and the others headed. The SECOND is turning to look in

Kittering's direction. Both of them look confident and wary and willing to do violence.

NO COPY.

THREE:
KITTERING hits the SECOND RUSSIAN in the throat with the knuckles of his free hand. This is almost a karate style attack, though not a hi-ya thing.[17]

FIRST RUSSIAN, now slightly ahead, is reacting to this sudden noise and movement, trying to turn and pull a PISTOL at the same time.

NO COPY.

17. Very deliberate. Kittering's strike to the throat is done to keep the man silent, as well as to put him down. He crushes the windpipe so no alarm can be raised.

FOUR:
SECOND RUSSIAN has dropped to his knees, eyes wide, clutching at his throat. He's choking to death, because Kinney just cracked his trachea. If we can really see his expression, it's the look of a man who is suffocating.

KITTERING is striking the FIRST RUSSIAN alongside the head with the PELLET GUN.[18] The FIRST RUSSIAN has his hands tangled in his jacket, trying to free his gun.

NO COPY.

FIVE:
FIRST RUSSIAN going down on his knees in FG, blood streaming down the side of his face, as KITTERING bashes him again with the PELLET GUN.

In BG, SECOND RUSSIAN has collapsed, dying.

NO COPY.

18. You've probably seen pistol-whipping in far too many films to count. I try to avoid using that particular tactic, because nobody who actually relies on a firearm to keep themselves alive would ever use their weapon as a club; it's just not done. In this instance, of course, Kittering is using the gun as a hammer, because that's essentially all that it is.

Page 22

ONE:
KITTERING, sweating, breathless, on his radio. His eyes are dark. Ideally, this should be a somewhat disturbing panel, since KITTERING is the youngest and most innocent looking of the bunch. He's looking down at the bodies in front of him.

1 KITTERING:
Rose, Daisy. Two DOWN…

TWO:
Wide shot, KITTERING in front of the house, with the TWO RUSSIANS down.

2 KITTERING:
…I'll call HOME and have them COLLECTED…

<u>THREE</u>:
CU CHACE, walking towards us, hands still in her pockets.

In BG, we can see the TWO MEN are following her, about 100 feet back. We're walking down towards the Thames, now, and the architecture should reflect that.

The streets are empty and quiet.

3 KITTERING/elec/tailless:
        ...the rest are yours.

4 CAPTION/Chace:
        Two of them.

<u>FOUR</u>:
Wide shot, CHACE at one end of the panel, turning to walk along the water.

The TWO MEN are in mid-panel, walking side-by-side, heads canted together.

No sign of Wallace.

5 CAPTION/Chace:
        Wallace and I can TAKE two of them.

<u>FIVE</u>:
Close on the TWO MEN. One of them is looking in Chace's direction, plotting murder.

The OTHER MAN is looking over his shoulder, suspicious.

6 CAPTION/Chace:
        Just pick the MOMENT.

Page 23

<u>ONE</u>:
OTS OTHER MAN, and there's no sign of Wallace. His PARTNER is tapping him on the shoulder, gesturing to a point off panel.

1 CAPTION/Chace:
        Just don't PANIC.

<u>TWO</u>:
Down-angle, CHACE in FG, walking along the water. In EBG, we see the TWO MEN splitting up, ONE moving in closer on CHACE, the OTHER sprinting into an alley.

2 CAPTION/Chace:
        That's all it's about.

THREE:
CU CHACE, and we can see the tension on her face.

Over her shoulder, we can see the MAN still on her trying to nonchalantly close the distance.

3 CAPTION/Chace:
It's not about THEM. Croatia or Colombia…

4 CAPTION/Chace:
…it's NEVER about them….

FOUR:
From above, and we see that CHACE is moving towards an alley that dumps into her path. CRATES or some other obstruction hides the opening from her view. It's all very secluded. The MAN following her is perhaps only twenty-five feet back, now.

6 CAPTION/Chace:
It's about the FEAR.[19]

FIVE:
Angle, past the opening of the alley. CHACE is coming towards us. Very tense. The MAN behind her is closing.

In FG, coming into the opening that CHACE is heading for, is the OTHER MAN. OTHER MAN has a GUN in his hand.

7 CAPTION/Chace:
Wait.

8 CAPTION/Chace:
Wait.

19. I like that Tara feels fear. It humanizes her immensely, in my opinion, and it's one of the things that grounds the series in reality.

Page 24

ONE:
Tight CU CHACE, painfully aware of the MAN closing
behind her.

Over her shoulder, we see the MAN moving in,
looking grim, ready to produce a gun of his own.

1 CAPTION/Chace:
          Wait...

2 CAPTION/Chace:
          ...closer...

3 CAPTION/Chace:
          ...closer...

TWO:
From behind the MAN who has been following CHACE,
as he stops, startled, drawing his gun.

CHACE has spun around, drawing the PELLET GUN and
bringing it up in both hands.

There's at least 20 feet between them.

4 CAPTION/Chace:
          ...oh damn oh dammit too FAR...[20]

5 CHACE/big:
          DROP IT! DROP IT—

THREE:
CHACE charging the MAN who has been following her,
both hands holding the PELLET GUN, her face full
of fury and adrenaline-fear.

The MAN is raising his GUN, refusing to be
cowed.

In BG, the OTHER MAN is emerging, ready to shoot
her.

6 CAPTION/Chace:
          ...not going to going to shoot close
          the distance run close the distance
          run RUN—

FOUR/FIVE/SIX:
POV CHACE, as the MAN fires at her three times.
Set these up however you like—the same image with
three gutters or the same image stet three times
or whatever works.

7 SFX:
          BLAMM BLAMM BLAMM

20. From this range, the pellet/BB would
have expended pretty much all of its
energy reaching its target. This, tied to
the fact that 20 feet is a fair distance to
cover when someone is pointing a gun at
you, are why Tara reacts as she does.

I'm not particularly happy with the
ending of this issue, as far as it goes. As
with the narrative captions earlier this
issue, I look back at this and think I'm
crutching, that I was afraid I'd lose the
reader if I didn't go out on something
Very Big and Very Dramatic. Hence the
firing sequence, which really is far more
"tune in next week!" than I normally like
for Queen & Country.

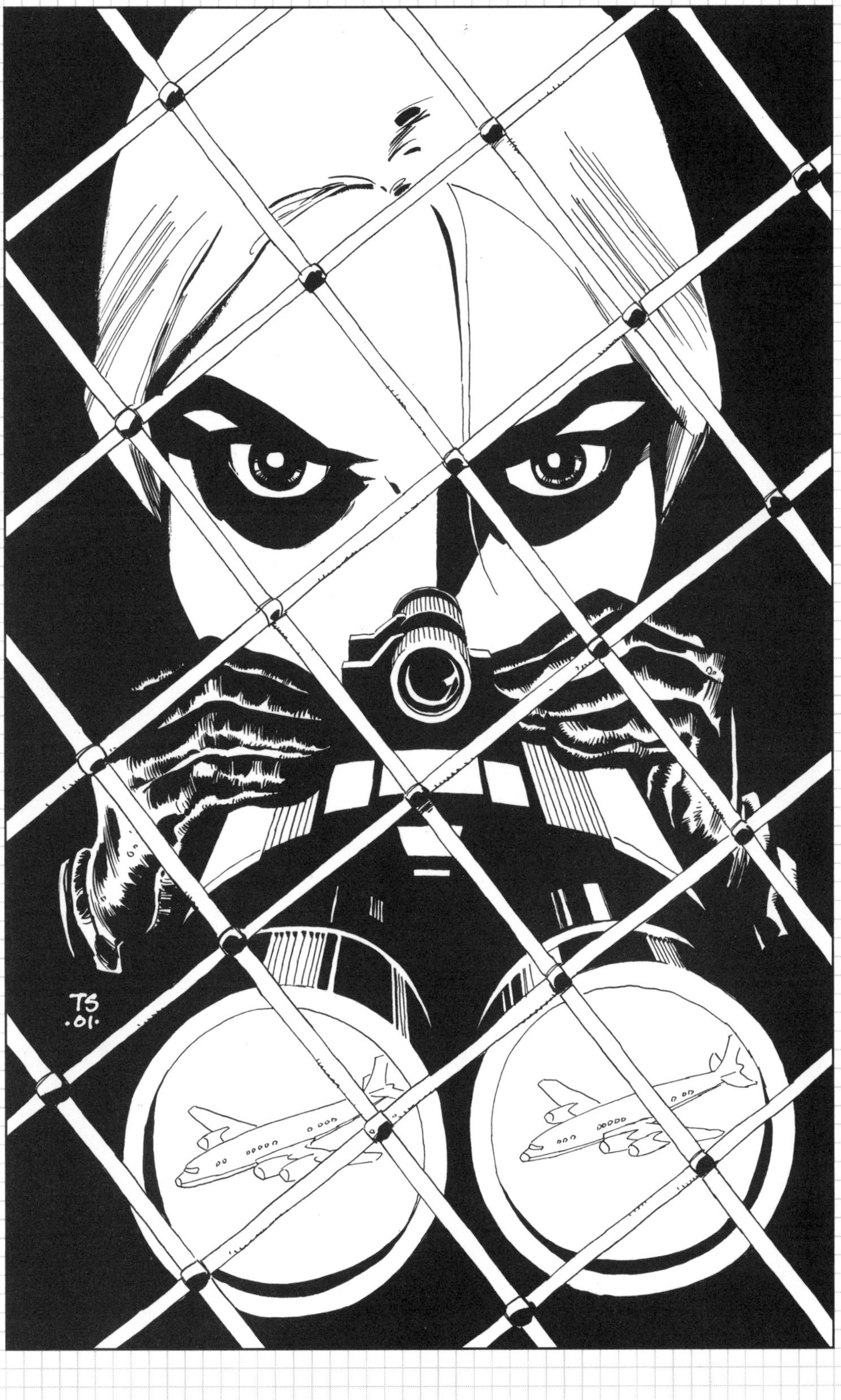

CHAPTER 4

Page 1

ONE:
Overhead shot, horizontal, of the location from the end of last issue, the MAN at the far left, arm extended with gun in hand, firing at CHACE who is charging him from the right. She's about 15 feet from the MAN.

From the far right, behind CHACE, the OTHER MAN has emerged, raising his gun.

1 CAPTION/Chace:
>   There's a trick, they teach it to
>   you at the School.

2 CAPTION/Chace:
>   When someone pulls a GUN on you,
>   they say…

TWO:
POV CHACE, of the MAN, firing at her. He holds his PISTOL in one hand, and he's squeezing off rounds as fast as he can, an expression of determined hate on his face.

3 CAPTION/Chace:
>   …CHARGE   at   him   like   a   bloody
>   LUNATIC…

THREE:
POV MAN, still firing with CHACE just about on him. CHACE still holds her PELLET GUN. A BULLET has just torn through the shoulder of her jacket.

In EBG, past CHACE, we can see the OTHER MAN falling.

4 CAPTION/Chace:
>   …it's the LAST thing they EXPECT
>   and most of them can't hit WATER
>   from a SUBMARINE anyway…

FOUR:
CHACE leaping.

5 CAPTION/Chace:
>   …and repeat to yourself OVER and
>   OVER that you're doing this for
>   QUEEN and COUNTRY.[1]

1. I actually have no idea if they teach this technique anywhere at all, but there are at least a couple of facts that support the theory that charging the shooter in this instance may be the best option. First, she has the element of surprise. Second, most of the folks—read, Bad Guys—don't know how to shoot; they've learned all their firearms technique from movies and television, and let me tell you, you fire a pistol "gangsta style," all you're doing is spraying lead. Third, most shooting instances are "uncontrolled," meaning that the weapon isn't fired in a moderated fashion; it's not squeeze, bang, squeeze, bang, but rather Ohmygod bangbangbangbangbangclickclickclick.

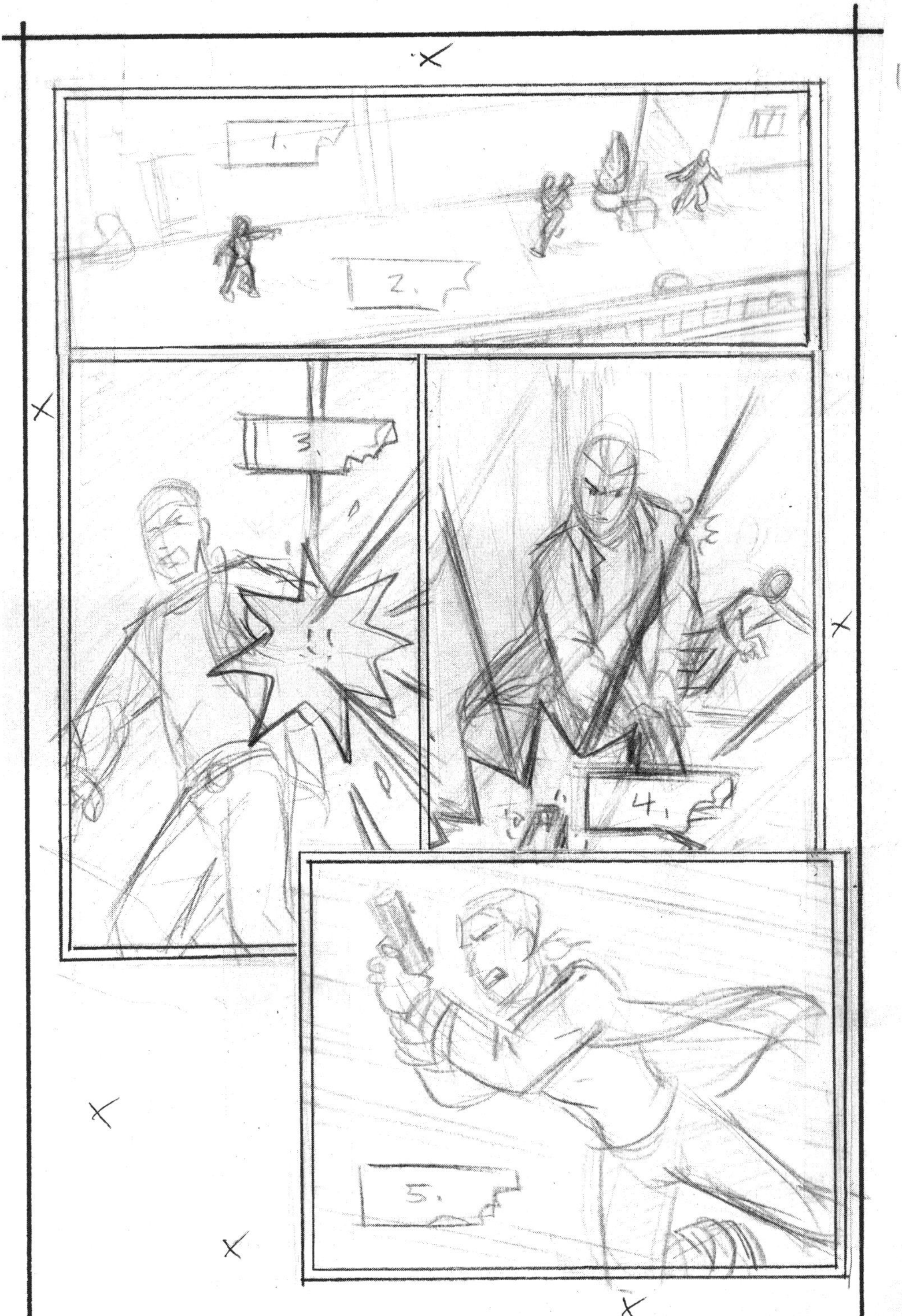
1.
2.
3.
4.
5.

Page 2

ONE:
CHACE smashing into the MAN, forcing his gun arm
out and away, a final shot going wild.

NO COPY.

TWO:
CHACE and the MAN hitting the ground, with her
basically riding him down, in full flight-or-fight
mode with the switch taped to the 'fight' position.
One hand is on the MAN'S gun, twisting it out of
his grip, and with her other she is beating him
with the PELLET GUN.

NO COPY.

THREE:
CU CHACE grabbing the MAN'S GUN with one hand,
CLUBBING HIM with the PELLET GUN in the other.
There's blood.

NO COPY.

FOUR:
Angle, along the ground, looking at the top of
the MAN'S HEAD, CHACE basically astride him, now
pressing the PELLET GUN to the man's left eye.

WALLACE is approaching in BG, visible.

NO COPY.

FIVE:
Tight shot from the side, CHACE holding the PELLET
GUN to the MAN'S HEAD. The MAN, bloodied and
dazed, staring up at her. CHACE is breathless, her
hair wild, and she's ready to kill him.

WALLACE'S LEGS are in the panel, now, and he's
putting a hand on CHACE'S SHOULDER.

1 WALLACE/above:
              Tara.

SIX:
Stet previous.

NO COPY.

SEVEN:
Stet previous, CHACE now looking up at WALLACE.
She looks almost stunned.

4 WALLACE/above:
              It's DONE.

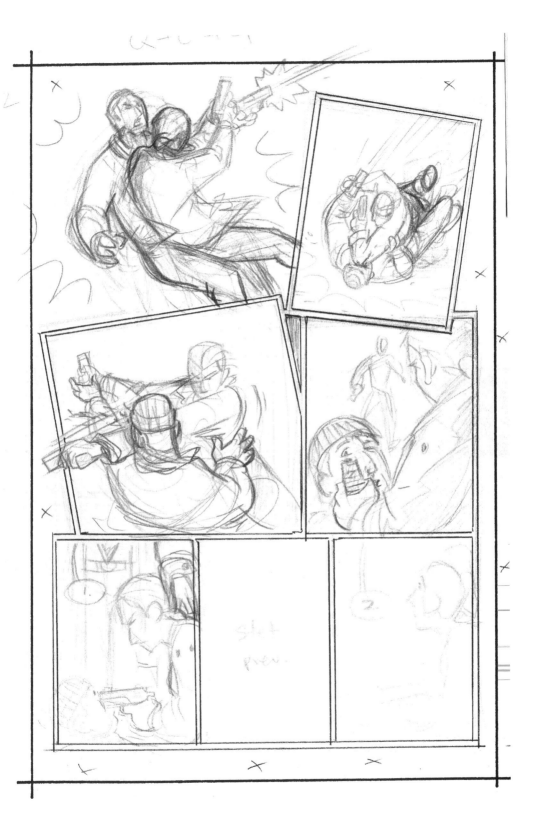

Page 3

ONE:
Wider, as WALLACE helps CHACE to her feet. She's unsteady.

1 CHACE:
There was ONE more.

2 WALLACE:
Yeah, he's NOT going to be TROUBLE.

TWO:
Past the OTHER MAN, who on the ground by the mouth of the alley, on his back, dead. A pool of blood is spreading beneath him.

In BG, CHACE and WALLACE are looking at him.

3 WALLACE:
One of the ROUNDS that missed you FOUND him.

4 CHACE/small:
Christ.

5 WALLACE:
It's HOLLYWOOD what does it, you ask me.

6 WALLACE/linked:
These blokes see a MOVIE where everyone's prancing about, firing CANNONS with one HAND…

THREE:
Tight on WALLACE and CHACE. CHACE is still semi-dazed, staring at the corpse, off.

WALLACE is crouching down over the MAN, searching him.

7 WALLACE/off:
…they're more concerned with looking GOOD during a gunfight than with LIVING through the damn thing.

FOUR:
CHACE fumbling out her cigarettes. Still the same expression.

8 WALLACE/off:
What they don't REALIZE, you see, is that EVERY bullet has to go SOMEWHERE.[2]

FIVE:
CU CHACE, noticing the BULLET HOLE, almost a curious expression.

2. A personal pet peeve, but I hate it in film or television when I see a gunfight where the bullets that miss just disappear into the ether. They don't. They hit something, sooner or later, and sometimes, it's something that has a pulse.

NO COPY.

<u>SIX:</u>
CHACE poking her finger through the hole, and it
comes out the other side.

9 CHACE:
                Hey… Tom?

10 WALLACE:
                Yes, love?

<u>SEVEN:</u>
WALLACE looking up from where he's pulling the MAN
to his feet, but not at CHACE, rather past her and
off panel.

CHACE is just looking at him kind of
thoughtfully.

11 CHACE:
                …nothing.

12 CHACE/linked:
                Never mind.[3]

13 WALLACE:
                Ah, good Master Kinney and Etcetera
                have ARRIVED.

3. Violence is random by nature, yet another theme of the series. It doesn't care where it falls, and you can do everything right, and still die, and do everything wrong, and still live. Nothing, in my experience, more typifies this fact than a bullet. They're terribly unpredictable creatures, even before they enter a human body; the second the hit something—anything—a million factors come into play upon them. And when a bullet entires a body, all bets are off. They bounce and twist and ricochet and rebound. They make little holes the size of a pen cap, and big holes the size of a cantelope. They tear and rip and puncture and slice. They are vicious little creatures.

The fact that this mystery bullet hole appears goes to that point—clearly, Tara was closer to dying than even she realized. Where'd it come from? How'd it miss her? When did it happen? None of it matters.

She almost died there, and she knows it. And there's really nothing anyone can say to that.

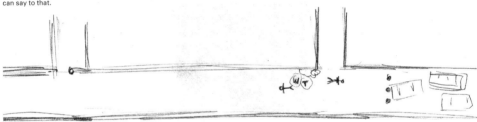

Page 4

<u>ONE:</u>
CHACE is lighting her cigarette, while WALLACE,
now with the MAN on his feet, is looking past her
into the BG, where we can see the flashing lights
of a couple POLICE CARS have stopped, their doors
open. An UNMARKED CAR is also present.

KINNEY and a couple of CONSTABLES run towards her
from the BG.

1 KINNEY:
                What the HELL happened here?

<u>TWO:</u>
Angle on CHACE as KINNEY storms up behind her.
KINNEY is furious. CHACE is closing her lighter,
trying to keep her mouth shut.

CONSTABLES are moving past the two of them like they're a rock in the middle of a stream of police.

2 KINNEY:
> You! CHACE!

3 KINNEY/linked:
> I want an ANSWER, by GOD!

THREE:
Angle past WALLACE in FG, handing over the MAN to a pair of CONSTABLES.

KINNEY, past them, is now behind CHACE, who is stowing her lighter, and looking at WALLACE with an expression that says she'd happily kill Kinney if only she thought she could get away with it.

4 KINNEY:
> You stupid BITCH!

5 KINNEY/linked:
> Your ORDERS were to draw them OUT, NOT to ENGAGE!

FOUR:
Tighter, with KINNEY fuming beyond CHACE'S shoulder—and of course it is the shoulder with the bullet hole.

6 KINNEY:
> I KNEW Crocker would try something like THIS—

Page 5

ONE:
CHACE has rounded on KINNEY, and her look is pure savage venom, barely contained. It's taking Kinney by surprise.

1 KINNEY:
> —turning his THUGS loose to pursue a VENDETTA—

2 CHACE:
> MISTER Kinney!

TWO:
KINNEY taking a step back, as CHACE gets in his face. She's taller than him, she's got some blood spattered on her face, she's had a rotten fucking week, and she knows eleven different ways to kill him.

KINNEY seems to be realizing all of these things, too.

NO COPY.

THREE:
Stet, but CHACE is pushing him out of her way, preparing to go past.

3 CHACE:
SOD fucking OFF.

THREE:
Past KINNEY, turning to see CHACE already moving away. WALLACE is moving to follow her, just passing KINNEY with a small smile and nod.

4 CHACE:
You have a PROBLEM with my PERFORMANCE, you're free to take it up with my D. OPS…

FOUR:
Behind KINNEY in FG, watching as WALLACE catches up to CHACE.

In BG, COPS are moving around the corpse of the OTHER MAN. Lights continue to flash.

5 CHACE:
…at which point I'll be DELIGHTED to tell the HOME OFFICE about how you arrived just AFTER the nick of TIME.

FIVE:
Stet, but KINNEY is turning to face us, expression dark, very angry. In BG, CHACE and WALLACE are passing through the cops.

6 KINNEY/small:
Damn bitch.

Page 6

ONE:
Exterior of MI-6, day. The repair work on the blast damage outside is nearly complete, now.

1 CROCKER/inside:
—to the FARM[4] for interrogation.

TWO:
Interior of Weldon's office. WELDON seated behind his desk, a cup of tea steaming in front of him. Morning light is streaming through the windows.

WELDON is king of his domain, very pleased with himself.

CROCKER stands in front of the desk, in his suit, giving his report. He's not quite so happy, but

4. Terms like "The Farm" and "The School" are stolen straight from LeCarré. "The School," as such, actually exists; it's Fort Monkton, in Gosport, near Portsmouth, and has been used as the SIS training facility for ages. I've heard rumors—and may have encountered a legitimate reference or two at some point, though I can't recall where—of an SIS debriefing facility somewhere in the Midlands, presumably "The Farm," though where it is, I don't know. Certainly, it's known that SIS maintains facilities throughout England for operational use.

In his book, MI-6: Inside the Covert World of Her Majesty's Secret Intelligence Service, author Stephen Dorril references "cooler" facilities in Chelsea, as well as a sound-proofed "rubber room" which is, inexplicably, located in the basement of one of London's finer hotels. Both locations are apparently used for the interrogation and debriefing of "recalcitrant officers and agents under suspicion."

for once he doesn't look like he wants to staple
anyone to anything.

He has a FOLDER beneath one arm, tucked.

2 CROCKER:

> They're under guard now, and Kinney
> has his QUESTIONERS en route.

3 WELDON:

> And the Minders?

THREE:
OTS WELDON, CROCKER continuing.

4 CROCKER:

> I sent them home after they filed
> their reports.

5 CROCKER/linked:

> Wallace and Chace will be back in
> the PIT on STAND-BY before NOON.

FOUR:
CU of the cup of tea, as WELDON squeezes a lemon
wedge into the cup.

Perhaps a portion of CROCKER is visible.

6 WELDON/above:

> Not KITTERING?

7 CROCKER/off:

> Edward's with Doctor Callard[5], then
> OFF for the rest of the DAY.

FIVE:
WELDON, looking at Crocker/us with some surprise
and some genuine concern.

8 WELDON:

> The report said NOTHING about
> Kittering taking an INJURY.

SIX:
CROCKER, respectful as he can be, thinking that
Weldon's an idiot.

9 CROCKER:

> That's CORRECT, sir.

10 CROCKER/linked:

> He did, however, KILL one of the
> RUSSIANS with his BARE HANDS.

SEVEN:
WELDON taking his tea, more interested in its
contents than in thinking about the hypocrisy of
what he's saying. CROCKER watching.

11 WELDON:

> Ah, right.

5. Doctor Elizabeth Callard appears in
the second arc, Operation: Morningstar.
Again, this is an example of the 'logical
extrapolation' game I play while writing.
I have no direct sources indicating that
SIS maintains a staff psychiatrist whose
duties include the mental health and well-
being of SIS Officers. But it seems to me,
in a day and age where the NSA actually maintains a Gay/Lesbian/Bi Support
Group for its personnel, that such a thing
would not exist.

Whether or not an evaluation would be
required as a matter of course after an
agent kills in the line of duty is pure speculation, and probably unreasonable.

12 WELDON/linked:

          Well, he didn't have any CHOICE,
          did he, Paul?

13 CROCKER:

          No, sir.

Page 7

ONE:
OTS CROCKER, as WELDON sips his tea.

NO COPY.

TWO:
Stet, WELDON looking up at CROCKER in some
surprise.

1 WELDON:

          Was there something ELSE, Paul?

2 CROCKER:

          What will happen to the Russians
          AFTER Five finishes their
          INTERROGATION?

THREE:
WELDON setting down his tea, still relatively
happy, if minutely annoyed. CROCKER is as before,
calm and somewhat complacent.

3 WELDON:

          Don't KNOW, to be honest, and don't
          much CARE.

4 WELDON/linked:

          EXTRADITION back to MOSCOW most
          likely.

5 WELDON:

          Why?

FOUR:
CROCKER offering WELDON the folder he's been
carrying.

6 CROCKER:

          I'm looking for your APPROVAL on
          this.

7 WELDON:

          Is this IMMEDIATE?

FIVE:
WELDON taking the FOLDER, looking at CROCKER with
curiosity.

8 CROCKER:

          Close of PLAY will be FINE, sir.

9 WELDON:
                    Very well.

10 WELDON/linked:
                    That'll be ALL for now.

SIX:
CROCKER almost out the door, stopping.

11 WELDON/off:
                    Paul!

12 CROCKER:
                    Sir?

SEVEN:
OTS CROCKER as he leans back into the office. WELDON
at the desk, offering a very smarmy smile.

13 WELDON:
                    Congratulate the Minders for me.

14 WELDON/linked:
                    Job well done.

15 CROCKER:
                    Yes, sir.

EIGHT:
CU CROCKER, in the hall, closing the door. His
expression is pure contempt.

NO COPY.

Page 8

ONE:
Interior of the Pit, angle on CHACE at her desk.
Her hands are steepled, and she's holding a
CIGARETTE between her fingers, watching it burn
down. Smoke is wafting.

She looks tired and a little haunted.

NO COPY.

TWO:
POV CHACE, past the smoke from her cigarette, over
to KITTERING'S EMPTY DESK.

NO COPY.

THREE:
Angle on CHACE, either staring at the smoke or
nothing.

1 CHACE:
                    Tom?

2 WALLACE/off:
>   Hmm?

FOUR:
Angle past WALLACE, who is at his desk, legs up, a folder against his thighs, reading. He's got a pen in one hand.

CHACE hasn't moved.

3 CHACE:
>   You ever seen Callard?

4 WALLACE:
>   The Madwoman of the Second Floor?

5 WALLACE/linked:
>   Not for a while, no.

Page 9

ONE:
CU CHACE, profile, as she takes a drag on the cigarette. Still focused on Kittering's desk, off.

NO COPY.

TWO:
From KITTERING'S DESK, CHACE still staring.

WALLACE has noticed that she's acting kind of off, and is straightening at his desk, feet back on the floor.

1 WALLACE:
>   Coming up on FOUR years, in fact.

THREE:
WALLACE, brow creasing as he leans forward. Concern.

2 WALLACE:
>   You didn't see her after KOSOVO?

FOUR:
CHACE looking at WALLACE as if she's just remembered they're in the same office. WALLACE still has the same gentle concern on his face.

3 CHACE:
>   Wasn't TIME.

4 CHACE/linked:
>   Sick LEAVE from the INJURY. Then this THING with the RUSSIANS.

FIVE:

OTS WALLACE, CHACE looking at him. Expression is
much the same. The burning cigarette between her
fingers. It's like she's looking at him, but not
seeing him. A Thousand Yard Stare.

5 WALLACE:
                    You should make an APPOINTMENT.

SIX:
ECU CHACE'S fingers as she crushes out the
cigarette in the empty, stained, glass ashtray on
her desk.

6 CHACE/above:
                    I'm fine, Tom.[6]

6. For a secret agent, she's not a terribly
convincing liar, here.

Page 10

ONE:
Interior, the ante-room to Crocker's office. KATE is
refilling the coffeemaker. The door into Crocker's
office is open, and CROCKER is visible at his desk,
suit jacket off, examining some eight-by-tens.

The door from the hall has just been slammed open,
and WELDON is barreling into the space.

1 KATE:
                    ...make this and then I'm OFF.

2 CROCKER:
                    Who said you could GO?

3 KATE:
                    It's twenty past SIX on a FRIDAY,
                    Paul—

4 WELDON:
                    WHERE IS HE?

TWO:
OTS CROCKER, looking up as WELDON fills his
doorway.

KATE is just past WELDON'S shoulder.

5 KATE:
                    Deputy Chief to see you, Sir.

6 CROCKER:
                    Hullo, sir.

THREE:
WELDON at CROCKER'S DESK, slamming the FOLDER
from that morning onto the arrayed eight-by-tens.
The eight-by-tens are all satellite surveillance
shots.

7 WELDON:
                    Will you NEVER learn?

8 CROCKER:
>> Can I assume the proposal will go
>> to 'C' WITHOUT your endorsement?

FOUR:
WELDON is frustrated beyond words. CROCKER is
still seated, and he's almost amused.

9 WELDON:
>> It won't go to 'C' at ALL, Paul!

10 WELDON/linked:
>> You will not MOUNT, I will not
>> ENDORSE, and 'C' will not AUTHORIZE
>> an assassination of this KIND.

FIVE:
CROCKER leaning forward slightly, perhaps one
elbow on the desk.

11 CROCKER:
>> What sort of ASSASSINATION will
>> you ENDORSE?

12 CROCKER/linked:
>> Perhaps we can work something
>> out....

Page 11

ONE:
WELDON fuming at the desk, staring at CROCKER, who
is returning it evenly.

NO COPY.

TWO:
Stet.

1 WELDON:
>> The RUSSIANS are in CUSTODY.

2 WELDON/linked:
>> It's OVER. It's FINISHED.

THREE:
WELDON'S HAND as it takes the FOLDER from Crocker's
DESK.

3 WELDON/off:
>> So you had BEST forget about your
>> VENDETTA...

FOUR:
OTS CROCKER as WELDON goes through the doorway,
back to us. He has the FOLDER in his HAND.

KATE is at her desk in BG, pulling on her coat.

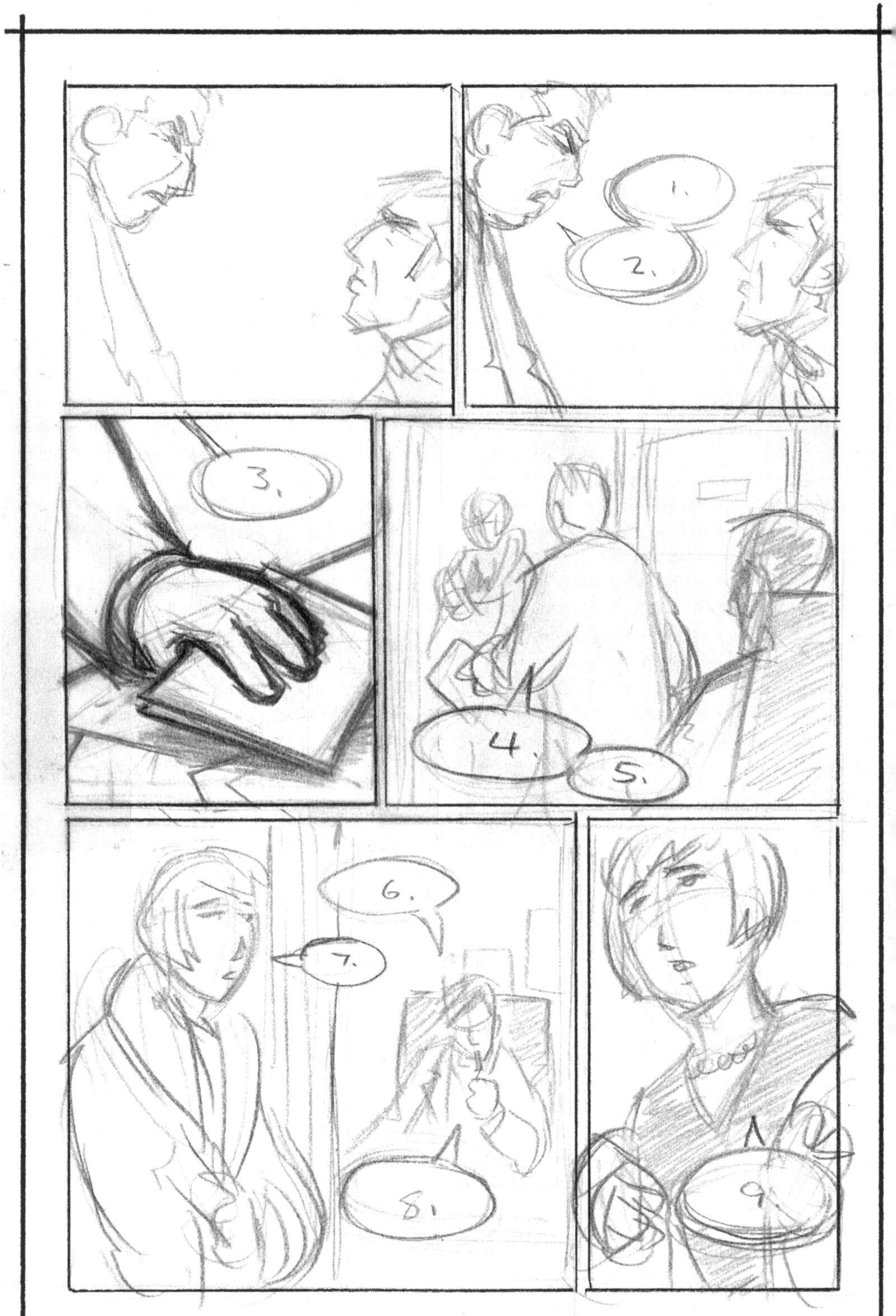
1.
2.
3.
4.
5.
6.
7.
8.
9.

4 WELDON:

      …and turn your ATTENTION to operations ELSEWHERE.

5 WELDON:

      Good evening.

FIVE:

Past KATE, looking at where WELDON has exited the office, the door slamming behind him.

In CROCKER'S office, we can see CROCKER lighting a cigarette.

6 CROCKER:

      He GONE?

7 KATE:

      Yes.

8 CROCKER:

      Then call CHENG. Tell her I need to TALK to her TONIGHT.

SIX:

CU of KATE, almost rolling her eyes, and removing her overcoat.

10 KATE:

      She's dining with a TRADE GROUP at eight….

Page 12

ONE:

Exterior South Kensington street, night. Outside CHACE'S home, as CHACE gets out of her car.

The street is mostly bare, lit by a couple street-lamps. A COUPLE is walking hand-in-hand on the opposite side of the street.

NO COPY.

TWO:

Angle on CHACE as she closes her door, watching the COUPLE. Her expression is tired, almost in blank.

NO COPY.

THREE:

ECU of CHACE'S hand, her keys as she fits them in the lock of her door.

NO COPY.

FOUR:

Interior of the house, the front hall, as CHACE closes the door behind her. With one hand she's pulling the curtains back that cover the window on the side of her front door.

NO COPY.

FIVE:
Very tight, past CHACE, peering through the
gap. The COUPLE is going on their way, utterly
innocent.

NO COPY.

Page 13

ONE:
Tight CU of CHACE'S, maybe upper body, same blank
expression, cigarette burning at her lips.

NO COPY.

TWO:
Interior of the Kitchen, and we're behind CHACE,
and we see that she's standing in front of
her REFRIGERATOR, staring at the almost empty
shelves.

NO COPY.

THREE:
Stet.

NO COPY.

FOUR:
Stet angle, but now the REFRIGERATOR is closed,
and CHACE has turned, reaching to a cabinet where
she is pulling down a BOTTLE OF SCOTCH and a
GLASS.

NO COPY.

FIVE:
From behind, framed in an interior doorway, CHACE
walking away from us, BOTTLE in one hand, GLASS in
the other, cigarette still burning.

NO COPY.

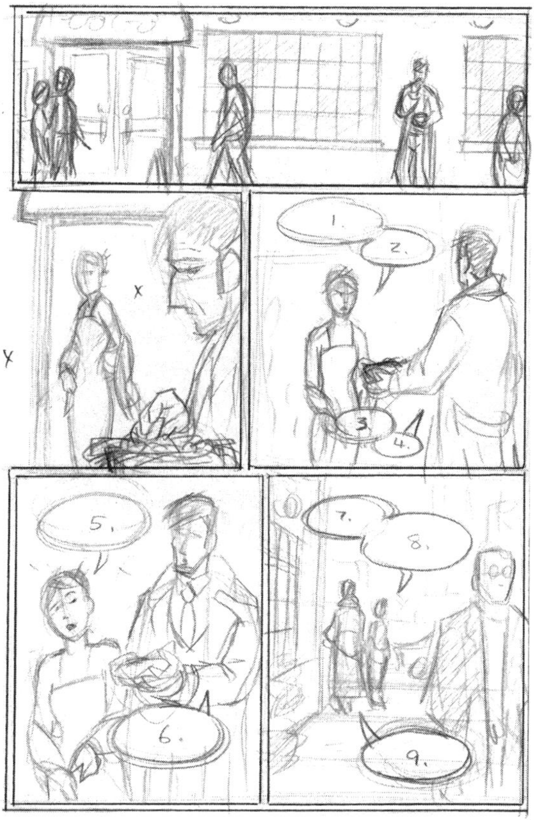
1.
2.
3
4.
5.
6.
7.
8.
9.

Page 14

<u>ONE:</u>
Exterior London Street, night, outside of a Very Nice Restaurant.

PEDESTRIANS move back and forth, some well-dressed, some quite casual.

CROCKER is leaning against a wall, still in his three-piece suit, eating FISH and CHIPS from a wrapper.

NO COPY.

<u>TWO:</u>
Angle past CROCKER, who is apparently quite interested in his FISH AND CHIPS, as CHENG comes out of a restaurant behind him. CHENG is looking quite elegant, wearing a very nice dress with a wrap.

NO COPY.

<u>THREE:</u>
CROCKER turning to see her as she approaches. CHENG is scowling.

1 CHENG:
Kate made it sound like the WORLD was ENDING.

2 CHENG/linked:
Is the world ENDING?

3 CROCKER:
I need a FAVOR.

4 CROCKER/linked:
Chip?

<u>FOUR:</u>
CHENG and CROCKER walking down the street. CHENG is making a face and pulling her head back as if the FISH AND CHIPS smell revolting.

5 CHENG:
I was in the middle of a veal escalope and YOU offer me a piece of FRIED potato.

6 CROCKER:
Wish I could do BETTER. On my WAGE, I can hardly AFFORD to SAY 'veal escalope.'

FIVE:
Wide angle as CHENG and CROCKER turn a corner,
basically planning on walking around the block.

7 CHENG:
> My CUP of PITY is OVERFLOWING.

8 CHENG/linked:
> What do you need that can't WAIT
> until tomorrow?

9 CROCKER:
> I think FIVE is going to LOSE the
> RUSSIANS.

Page 15

ONE:
CHENG adjusting her wrap, CROCKER walking
alongside, eating.

1 CHENG/small:
> Dammit it's COLD.

2 CHENG/linked:
> Lose them HOW?

3 CROCKER:
> Not sure. But Weldon was talking
> about EXTRADITION to MOSCOW.

TWO:
From the side, CHENG almost shrugging. CROCKER is
looking off to a side.

4 CROCKER:
> I spoke with Rayburn[7], and he's
> heard rumors that there's a DEAL
> already in PLACE.

5 CROCKER/linked:
> Doesn't know with WHOM.

6 CHENG:
> D. Int hears a rumor and therefore
> you ruin my dinner.

7 CHENG/linked:
> Let it GO, Paul, let it be someone
> else's PROBLEM for

ONCE.

THREE:
CROCKER dropping his FISH AND CHIPS into a
trashcan.

CHENG is alongside, watching the street.

7. I believe this is the first reference
to Crocker's opposite number within
SIS, Simon Rayburn, the Director of
Intelligence (D-Int). Simon's one of those
characters who has yet to really break out
of the background of series, which is a
pity, since he's a neat guy and I'd like to
show more of him. One of the drawbacks
in writing a 24 page comic book.

8 CROCKER:
        It's not what I WANT.

9 CROCKER/linked:
        I tried to get OFFICIAL sanction, but WELDON stopped me before I even had my BOOTS on.

<u>FOUR:</u>
CROCKER moving forward, towards us, CHENG still past him, not moving, watching. Not happy.

10 CROCKER:
        They're at the FARM now, but it won't be for much longer. No idea where they'll be moved next. No idea when.

11 CHENG:
        Paul, why are you telling me this? What do you WANT?

<u>FIVE:</u>
OTS CHENG, CROCKER giving her a look that pretty much says, if you have to ask, you're dumb, and you're not dumb, so why are you even asking.

NO COPY.

<u>SIX:</u>
CU CHENG, sighing.

13 CHENG:
        Fine.

14 CHENG/linked:
        But remember, YOU asked ME.

Page 16

ONE:
Exterior of MI-6, morning, bright and shiny.

1 'C'/inside:
          …to address Donald's CONCERNS.

TWO:
Interior of C's office, with CROCKER standing by
C's desk as 'C' comes around the side, holding up
the FOLDER from page 11.

2 'C':
                    This   is   an   ALARMING   proposal,
                    Paul.

3 CROCKER:
                    It SHOULD be, sir.

4 CROCKER/linked:
                    The purpose of that operation is
                    to put the FEAR of GOD into ANY
                    group that would HUNT and KILL our
                    agents.

THREE:
Angle on the desk, as 'C' slaps the FOLDER back
down.

5 'C':
          It goes TOO far.

FOUR:
CROCKER, evenly, and verging on disrespectful.
'C' is turning from the desk to face him again,
and is mildly alarmed by Crocker's tone.

6 CROCKER:
          I   DISAGREE,   sir.   It   doesn't   go   far
ENOUGH.

7 'C':
          I BEG your pardon?

8 CROCKER:
          We were ATTACKED in our HOME.

9 CROCKER/linked:
          They put a BOUNTY on the HEAD of Minder
Two.

FIVE:
OTS 'C', CROCKER is passionate. He's not yelling,
but he absolutely believes in his job, and to him,
the situation is intolerable. This, incidentally,
is why Crocker downs about three gallons of Maalox
a week.

10 CROCKER:
                    We   are   HMG's   SECRET   INTELLIGENCE

SERVICE, yetthese HOODS attempted
to TERRORIZE us.

11 CROCKER/linked:
We MUST strike BACK, sir.

SIX:
CU CROCKER, emphatic.

12 CROCKER:
We owe it to CHACE, and to ALL of
our agents.

13 CROCKER/linked:
Not just for what we've asked of
them, but for what we MAY ask of
them.

SEVEN:
CROCKER,   turning   away   slightly,   almost
embarrassed.

14 CROCKER:
    Unless our agents KNOW we will fight for
them, how can we ask them to give their lives for
US?
15 CROCKER:
We MUST strike back.

Page 17

ONE:
Past CROCKER, still looking away from 'C.' For his
part, 'C' has his hands deep in his pockets, his
chin on his chest, deep in thought.

NO COPY.

TWO:
Angle, 'C' looking at CROCKER.

1 'C':
Even   KNOWING   this   government's
policy   on   ASSASSINATION,   you
proposed this operation ANYWAY.

THREE:
Past CROCKER, watching as 'C' comes back around
the desk, returning to his seat.

2 'C':
I don't know if that SPEAKS of you
WELL, or as a FOOL.

3 CROCKER:
We HAVE to PUNISH—

3 'C':
They ARE being PUNISHED, Paul.

<u>FOUR</u>:
Two-shot, 'C' leaning forward at his desk, CROCKER
stiff as a rod.

4 CROCKER:
>   The FARM isn't really HARD TIME,
>   though, is it?

5 'C':
>   The FARM is not the end of their
>   JOURNEY.

<u>FIVE</u>:
CROCKER reacting, trying to cover his alarm.

6 CROCKER:
>   Then they ARE going back to
>   Russia?

<u>SIX</u>:
OTS CROCKER, 'C' looking at him levelly.

7 'C':
>   Don't EVEN consider it, Paul.

8 'C'/linked:
>   There are OTHER things at stake
>   here besides your OVER-DEVELOPED
>   sense of DOMINION.

<u>SEVEN</u>:
CROCKER turning to go.

'C' returning to his work on the desk.

9 'C':
>   And I told you ALREADY, you're
>   REPLACEABLE.

Page 18

<u>ONE</u>:
Exterior of Hyde Park, day. Sunny and bright and
lovely, and people are wandering around, doing
their things.

In the center of our shot sits ANGELA CHENG at a
bench, sunglasses on, looking at the world as it
goes by.

She has a NEWSPAPER on her lap.

NO COPY.

<u>TWO</u>:
Stet. Pedestrians continue to move to and fro.

CROCKER is approaching the bench.

1 TAILLESS/elec:
>   P.A to D. Ops.

2 TAILLESS/elec:
>   Kate, it's D. Ops. How many Minders
>   are in the Pit?

THREE:
Stet. CROCKER is now seated at the bench with
CHENG, the paper between them.

3 TAILLESS/elec:
>   You've got the complete set.

4 TAILLESS/elec:
>   Get them into the Ops Room QUIETLY.
>   I'll BRIEF them when I get back.

FOUR:
Stet. CHENG is gone.

5 TAILLESS/elec:
>   By quietly you mean 'without Weldon
>   finding out'?

6 TAILLESS/elec:
>   Just do it, Kate.

FIVE:
Stet, and the bench is empty. The NEWSPAPER is
gone.

7 TAILLESS/elec:
>   Of course, sir.

Page 19

ONE:
Interior of the OPS ROOM. RON is at his desk
eating a sandwich.

KITTERING is flirting with ALEXIS.

CHACE is seated at the briefing desk, with WALLACE.
Both are smoking.

CROCKER is entering, carrying a rolled up map.

1 CROCKER:
>   Ed, if you can stop MOLESTING Lex
>   for a few minutes, I'd APPRECIATE
>   your ATTENTION.

TWO:
At the Briefing Desk, WALLACE and CHACE are watching
KITTERING, as KITTERING hurries to take a seat.
CROCKER stands over them, impatient.

2 KITTERING:

>   It was NOTHING, boss. Totally
>   INNOCENT.

3 CROCKER:

>   If Lex is INNOCENT, I'm your
>   mother.

4 CROCKER:

>   They're moving the Russians off
>   the Farm TONIGHT.

5 CROCKER/linked:

>   If it's going to be DONE, it's got
>   to be done THEN.

THREE:
Around the table, CHACE, WALLACE, and KITTERING
listening closely as CROCKER explains.

6 CROCKER:

>   If any of you has TROUBLE with
>   this, say it NOW.

7 KITTERING:

>   No, sir.

8 WALLACE:

>   You didn't get CLEARANCE, did
>   you?

FOUR:
Past CROCKER, not glaring, but honestly not wanting
the debate with WALLACE. WALLACE isn't looking for
a fight either, but he's genuinely not happy to
know this is unauthorized.

9 CROCKER:

>   No, I didn't. You're free to go if
>   you'd rather, Tom.

10 WALLACE:

>   I'm not going anywhere.

11 CROCKER:

>   Glad to hear it.

FIVE:
OTS CROCKER, unrolling a roadmap onto the table.

12 CROCKER:

>   It needs to look like an
>   ACCIDENT…

Page 20

[*Steve—We're going for a sense of serious time passage here, and I'm not sure the best way to highlight that. Perhaps with an underlying image, or simply by having some of the panels bleed off the page. Whatever works best—GR*]

ONE:
Exterior, the 158 in the Cotswolds, night. An utterly average and mundane looking CAR is parked just off the road, beneath the trees, it's lights off. CHACE is behind the wheel, fighting to stay awake. She wears the jacket from the beginning of the issue.

NO COPY.

TWO:
Outside CHACE'S car, and in EBG on the other side of the road, we can see ANOTHER CAR, also parked and partially hidden.

NO COPY.

THREE:
Interior of the OTHER CAR, and we can see KITTERING behind the wheel. Past him, in the EBG, we can see the back of TARA'S PARKED CAR.

NO COPY.

FOUR:
Angle on the TWO CARS. Dark, quiet night.

Nothing is happening.

A leaf blows by.

NO COPY.

Page 21

ONE:
Interior of Crocker's home, the front hallway. This is a fairly nice house outside of London.

CROCKER is coming down the hall in a bathrobe, switching on the light. He's clearly just woken up.

NO COPY.

TWO:
OTS CROCKER, opening the front door to see CHACE, with KITTERING right behind her. Their CARS are visible, parked in the BG.

Again, establish that CHACE is wearing the jacket from the beginning of the issue, with the same bullet-hole in its shoulder.

It's just before dawn, now.

1 CHACE:
              We've been HAD.

THREE:
Reverse, OTS CHACE of CROCKER in the doorway, leaning against the doorframe and rubbing at his eyes.

2 CROCKER:
              They didn't SHOW?

FOUR:
View of CHACE and KITTERING, CROCKER in the doorway. CROCKER is practically scowling, his mind racing.

3 KITTERING:
              NO one SHOWED.

4 CHACE:
              Wallace RADIOED from outside the FARM, says the WHOLE place is shut TIGHT.

FIVE:
Angle in the hallway, CROCKER turning. CHACE and KITTERING visible through the doorway.

5 CROCKER:
              Let me get DRESSED.

6 CROCKER/linked:
              Ed, head back to the OFFICE. Tara, you STAY.

7 CHACE:
              Do I get to COME inside, then?

SIX:
Angle past CHACE, watching as CROCKER ascends the stairs.

8 CROCKER:
              My WIFE wouldn't APPROVE.[8]

8. Many people read this as a throwaway, but Crocker's wife, Jenny, actually does make an appearance in the first Declassified series, as well as the novel. I wanted a contrast; where we've seen Chace alone and isolated, returning to an empty flat with a bottle of scotch for company, here we have Crocker, still cranky, still generally unpleasant, but at least somehow maintaining a home life. I also wanted to humanize Crocker's zealotry. For all he says and does, he's happily married, and at the end of the day, he has a home and a family waiting for him.

Page 22

ONE:
Exterior of an AIRFIELD outside of London. Dawn is
starting to break.

We're looking through the gate at CHACE'S car,
which has pulled to a stop on the side of the
road. CROCKER is emerging from one side, CHACE
from behind the wheel.

1 CROCKER:
> You have OPTICS?

2 CHACE:
> Binoculars in the boot.

3 CROCKER:
> Bring them.

TWO:
CHACE and CROCKER, almost side-by-side, at the
fence. This is pretty tight on them. CROCKER is
raising the BINOCULARS.

NO COPY.

THREE:
CROCKER'S POV, view of the TWO RUSSIANS being
escorted onto the parked JET on the airfield.

NO COPY.

FOUR:
CROCKER'S POV, and the view has slid along the
fuselage of the plane, to the tail, where a small
AMERICAN FLAG has been painted.

NO COPY.

FIVE:
CU CROCKER, lowering the binoculars.

Angry.

3 CROCKER:
> Bastards.

Page 23

ONE:
Angle past CHACE, of CROCKER, now by the gate as a
string of CARS passes. ONE has pulled to a side,
stopping.

NO COPY.

TWO:
CHACE by the passenger door, CROCKER in front of
it. The door has opened, and CHENG is getting
out.

We can see that there is ANOTHER PASSENGER in the
car.

1 CHENG:
                    Paul.

2 CHENG/linked:
                    They'd ALREADY arranged the DEAL
                    with FIVE—

3 CROCKER:
                    You're BLOODY CIA in LONDON,
                    Angela!

4 CROCKER/linked:
                    You should have told Langley to
                    FUCK OFF.

THREE:
Angle past CHACE, looking into the back of the
car. CHENG and CROCKER moving into BG, arguing.

5 CHENG:
                    I'm trying to TELL you it WASN'T
                    the Company that DID this!

FOUR:
OTS CHACE looking into the car, where we see
KINNEY seated, looking at her. He looks pretty
smug.

6 CHENG/off:
                    Kinney went to the FBI before the
                    Russians were even in CUSTODY.

FIVE:
POV KINNEY, of CHACE, just looking at him. It's
that same almost blank look she's been cultivating
all throughout the book so far. It's a look that
says she knows eleven different ways to kill him
right now, and if she's bored enough, she might
try them all.

The BULLET HOLE is still evident in the shoulder
of her jacket.

In EBG, we can see CHENG and CROCKER still going
at it.

7 CHENG:
                    I didn't find OUT until I went to do
                    you a FAVOR yesterday.

8 CROCKER:
                    You should have warned me OFF.

<u>SIX</u>:
Stet, a little tighter. CHACE is removing her jacket, but she's not looking away from Kinney, off.

9 TAILLESS/small:
> …a BREAK…NOT going to SCREW the FBI—

10 TAILLESS/small:
> —screw US instead…

<u>SEVEN</u>:
Stet, even tighter, and CHACE has just the tiniest hint of a smile. Jacket is off.

11 TAILLESS/small:
> …BASTARD tried to get my agent KILLED….

12 CHACE/small:
> WORD of advice for you, Mister Kinney…

Page 24

<u>ONE</u>:
OTS CHACE, leaning in, jacket bunched in one hand.

KINNEY in the backseat is fairly intimidated, but trying to hide it.

1 CHACE:
> …next time you find someone SHOOTING at YOU…

<u>TWO</u>:
Angle on the seat and perhaps KINNEY'S thigh, as Chace's JACKET lands. BULLET HOLE visible.

2 CHACE/off:
> …and you're UNARMED…

<u>THREE</u>:
POV KINNEY, of CHACE crouched just outside the car, as before. Her expression has changed, is almost innocently sweet. She's cocked her head slightly to a side, as if trying to imagine the scenario.

3 CHACE:
> …run AT the shooter.

4 CHACE/linked:
> It throws off their AIM, you see.

<u>FOUR</u>:
Almost stet, but this is now a CU of CHACE, and

her smile is anything but sweet, and her eyes are
very angry.

5 CHACE:

                    If you're very lucky.

<u>FIVE</u>:
From above the car, angle, CHACE walking away.

In BG CROCKER and CHENG are still arguing
silently.

NO COPY.

<u>SIX</u>:
On CHACE, coming towards us. She looks emotionally
wrecked, just drained—a far cry from the act she
was giving Kinney.

CROCKER and CHENG still arguing in the BG.

NO COPY.

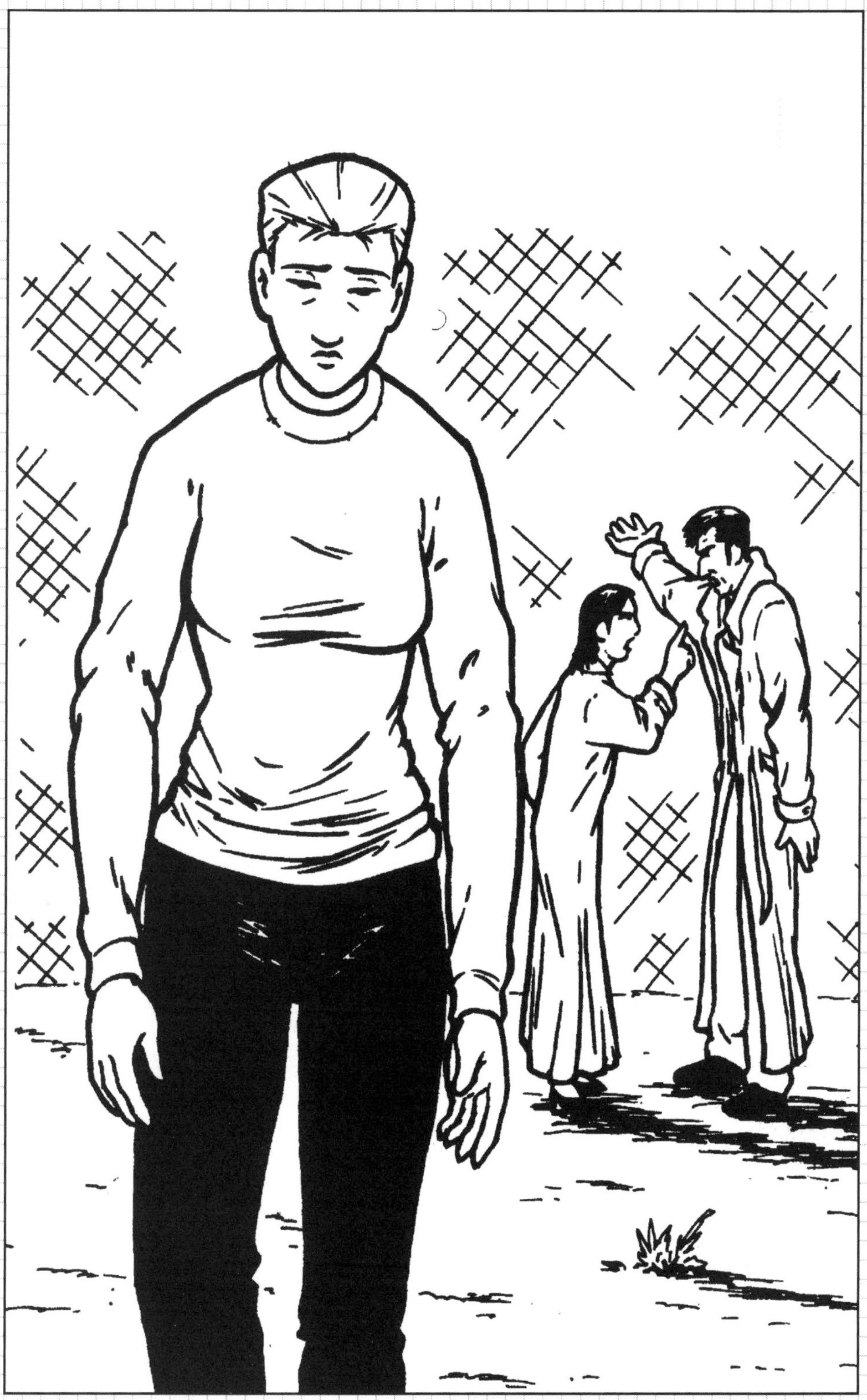

QUEEN & COUNTRY™

BEHIND THE SCENES

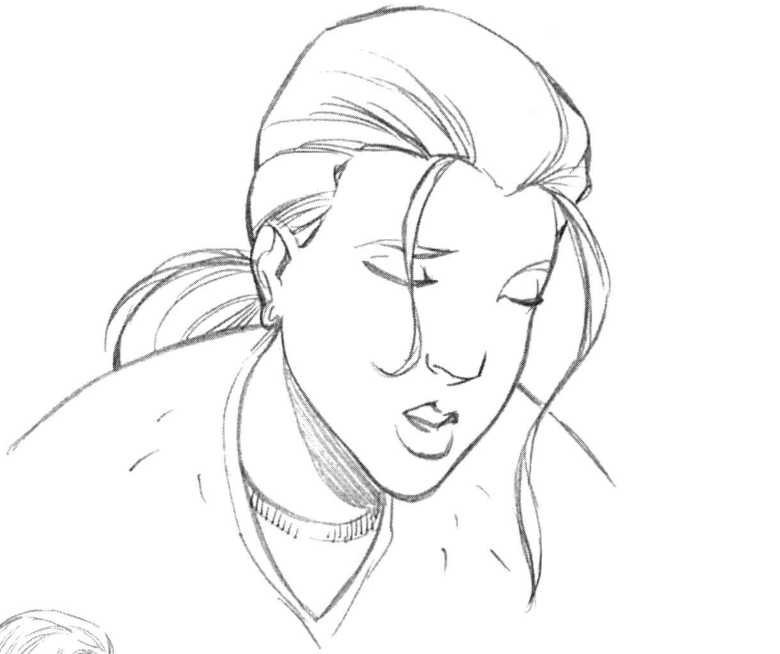

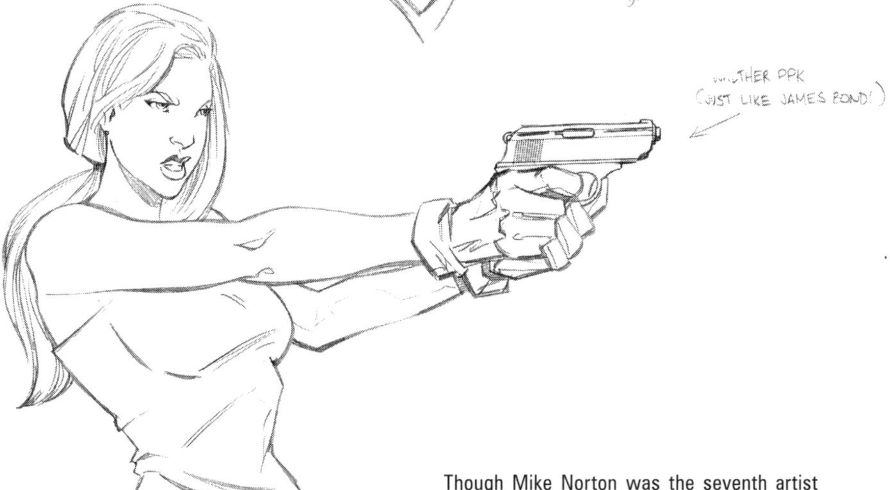
(JUST LIKE JAMES BOND!)

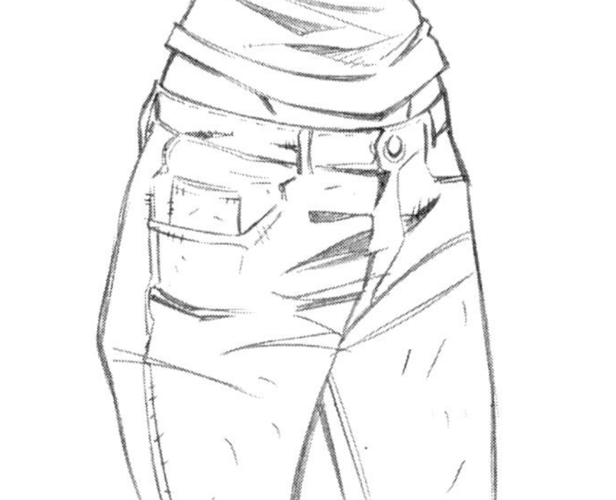

Though Mike Norton was the seventh artist to collaborate with Mr. Rucka on *Q&C*, he was actually the first artist to submit samples after the book premiered. We immediately knew Mike was going to have to draw an arc for us, but scheduling conflicts prevented him joining the team until *Operation: Saddlebag*. Presented over the next four pages are Mike's original sketches for the cast of the Special Section—cooked up almost three years before he would actually draw them in the comics.

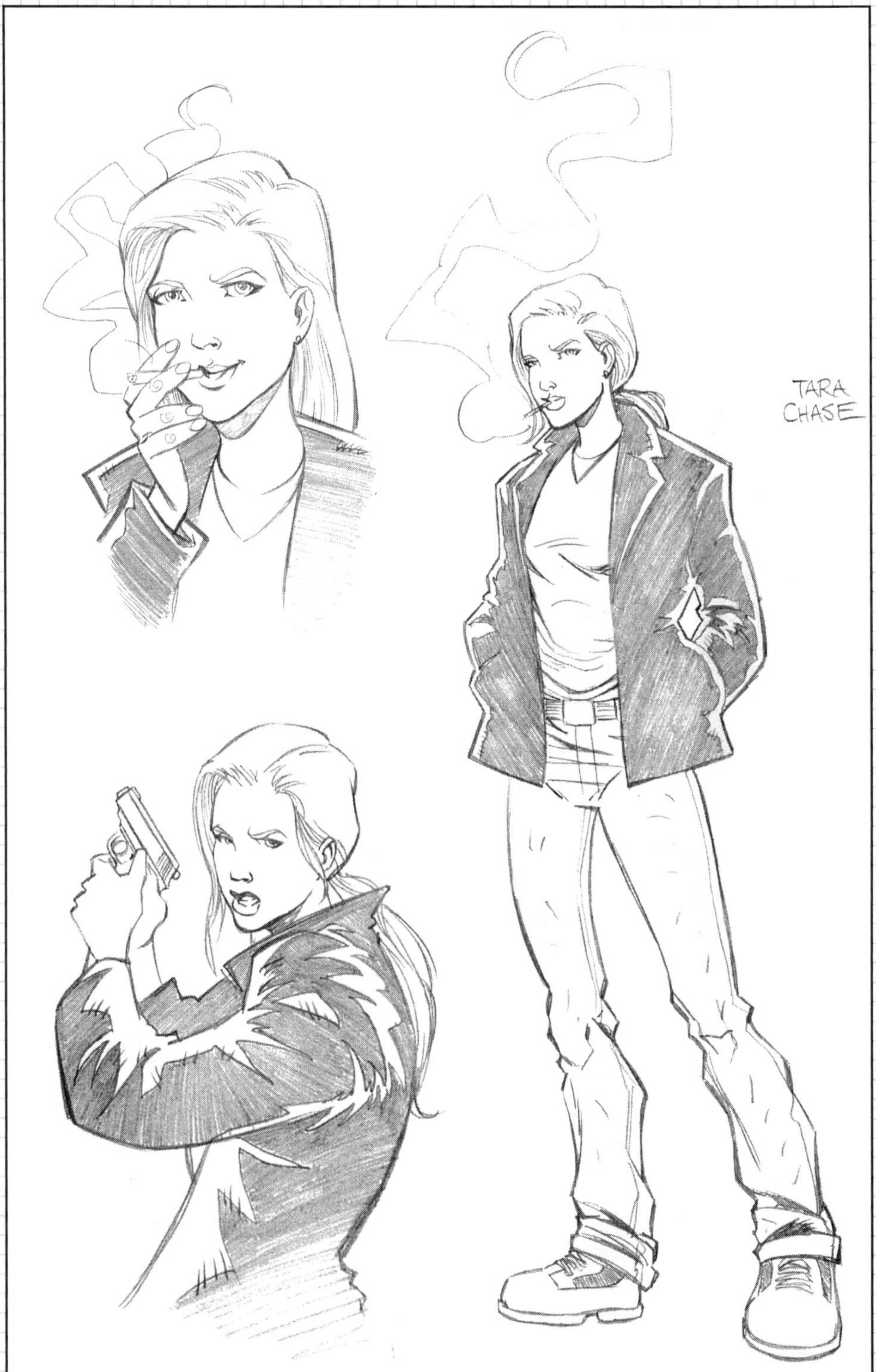
TARA
CHASE

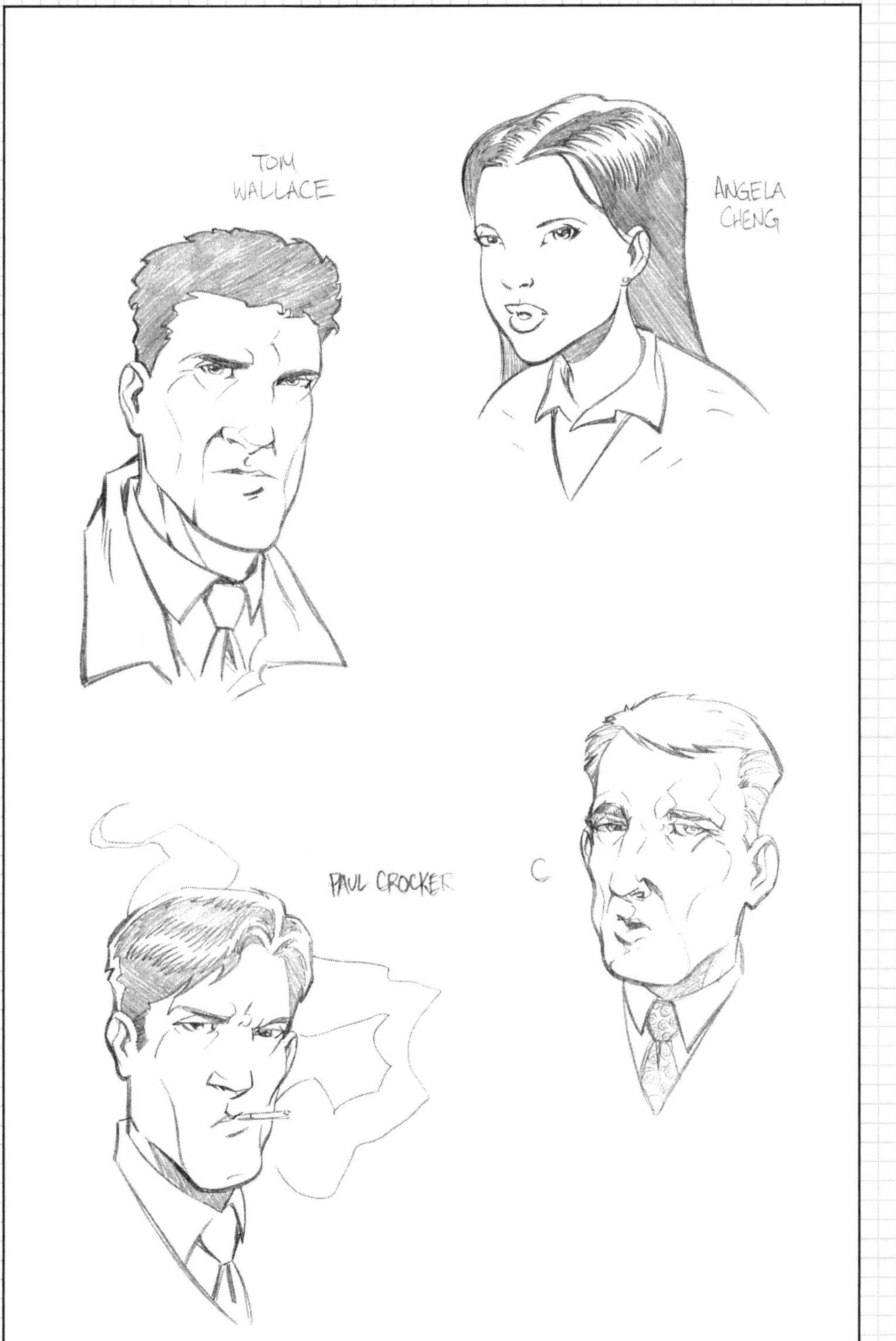
TOM
WALLACE
ANGELA
CHENG
PAUL CROCKER

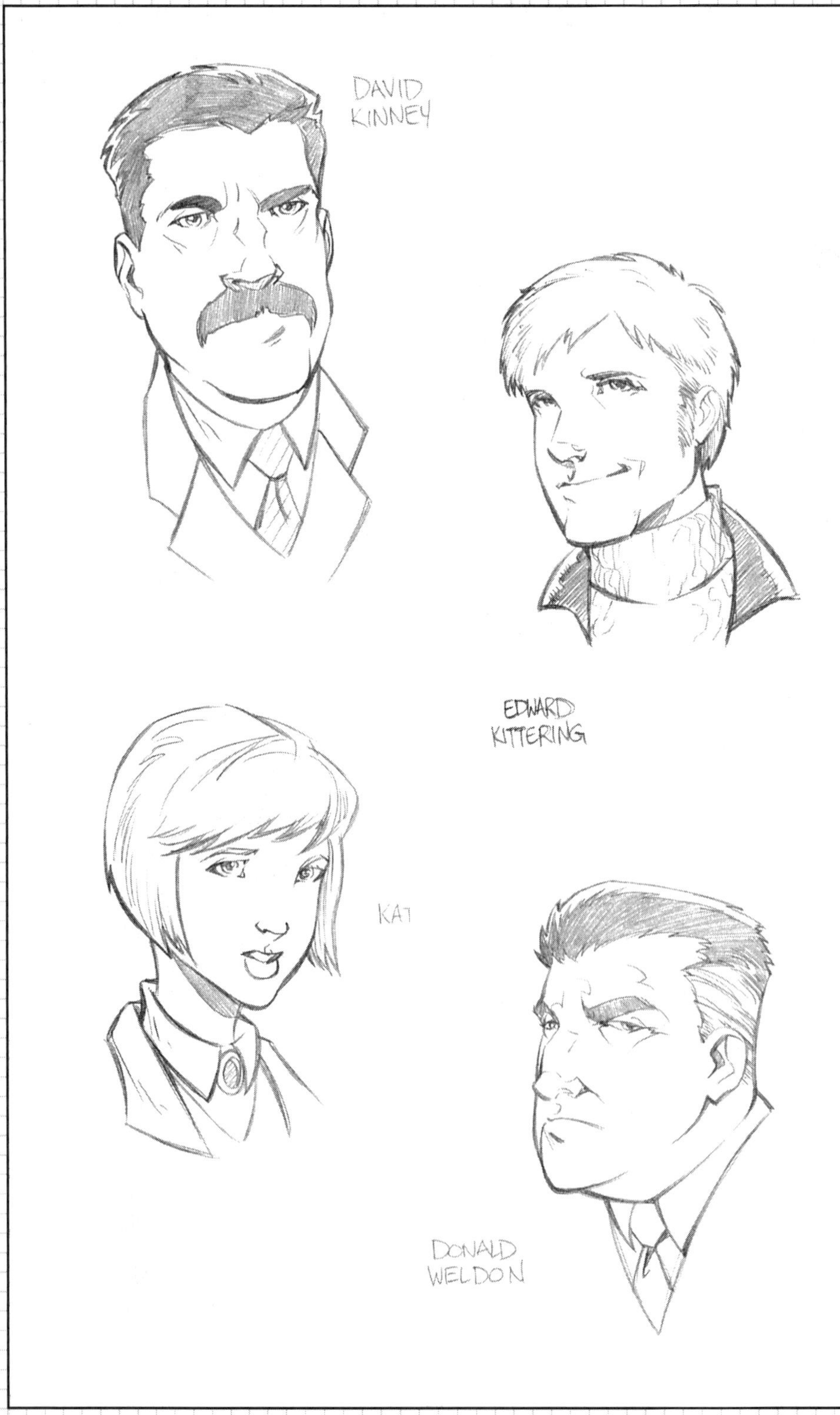
DAVID
KINNEY
EDWARD
KITTERING
KAT
DONALD
WELDON

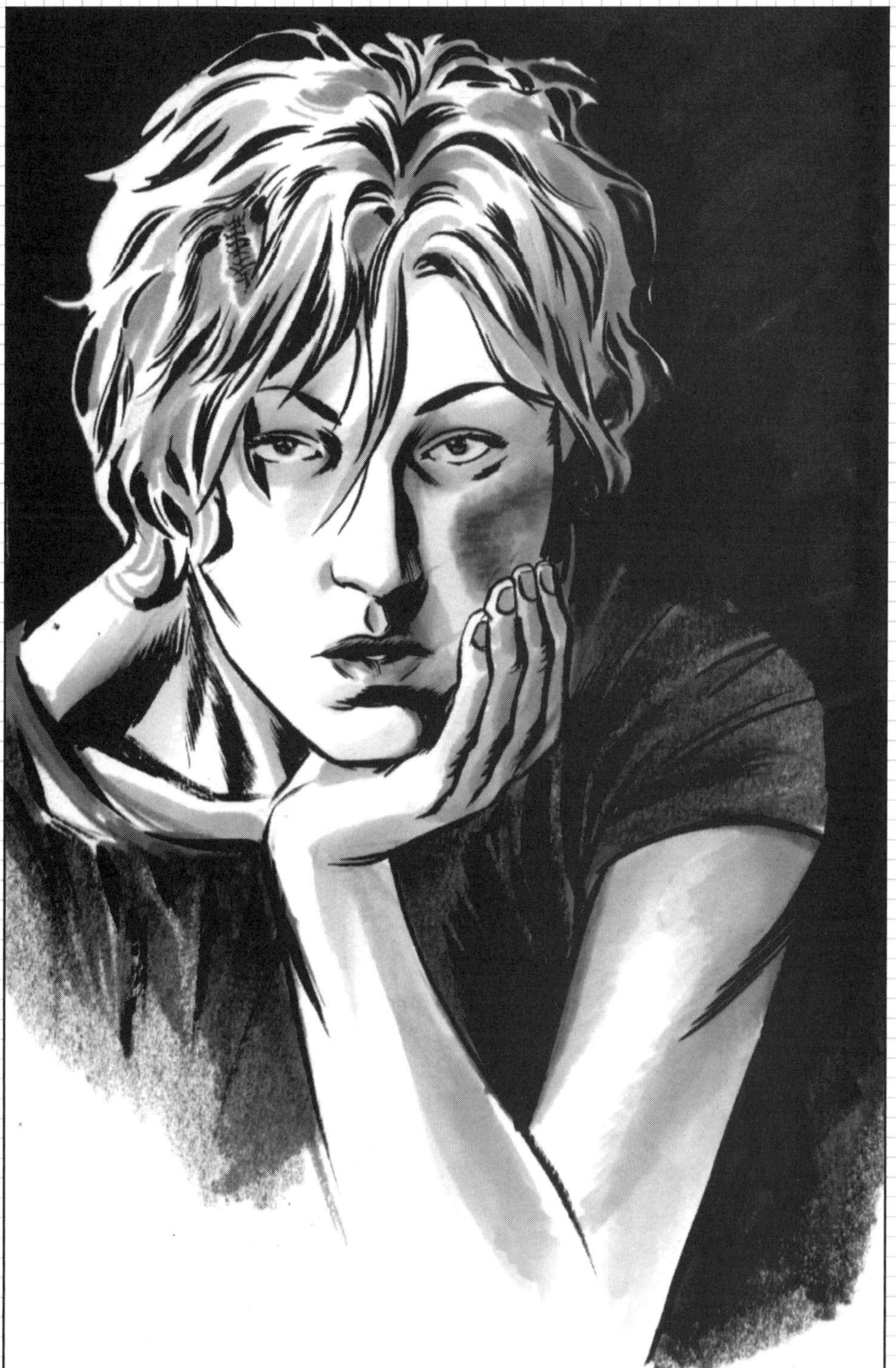

A character study of Tara Chace by *Operation: Red Panda* artist Chris Samnee.

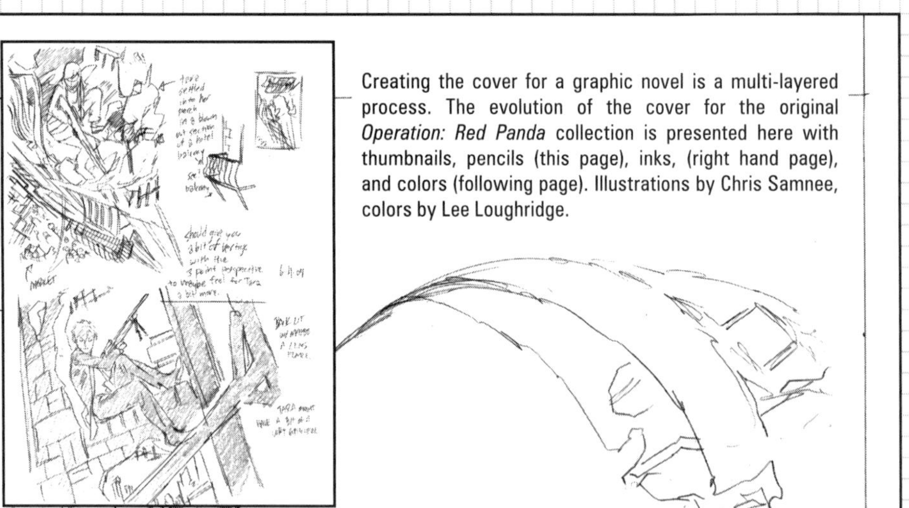

Creating the cover for a graphic novel is a multi-layered process. The evolution of the cover for the original *Operation: Red Panda* collection is presented here with thumbnails, pencils (this page), inks, (right hand page), and colors (following page). Illustrations by Chris Samnee, colors by Lee Loughridge.

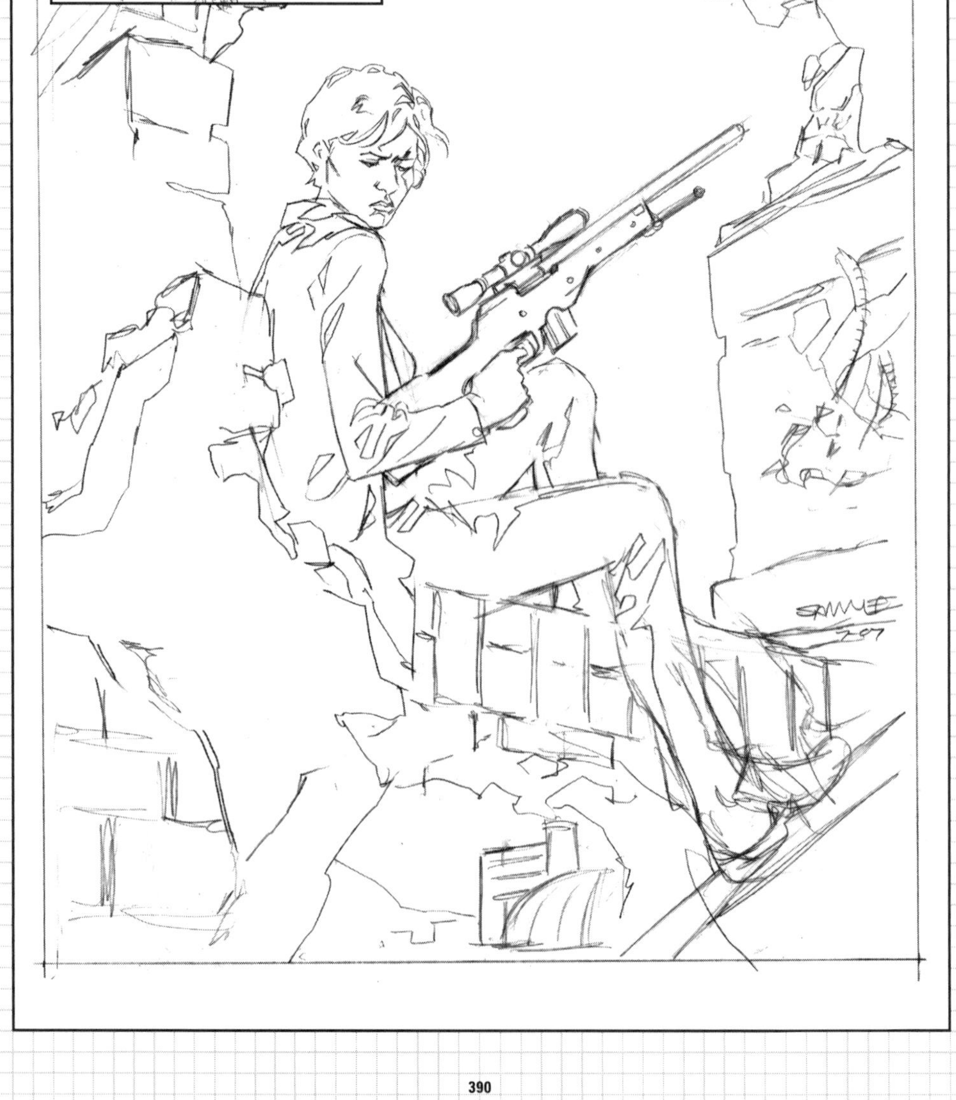
SAMNEE

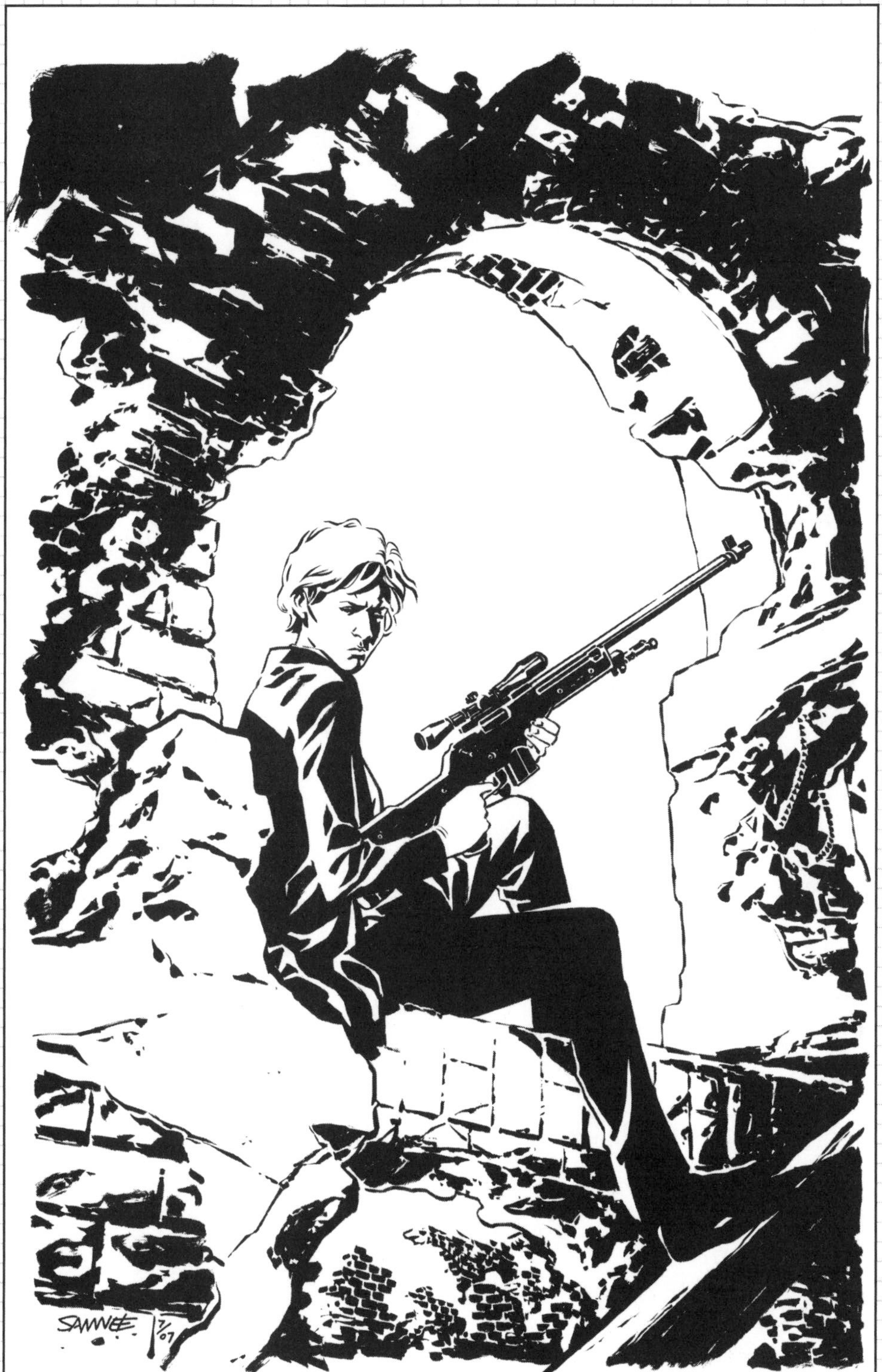
SAMNEE
7/07

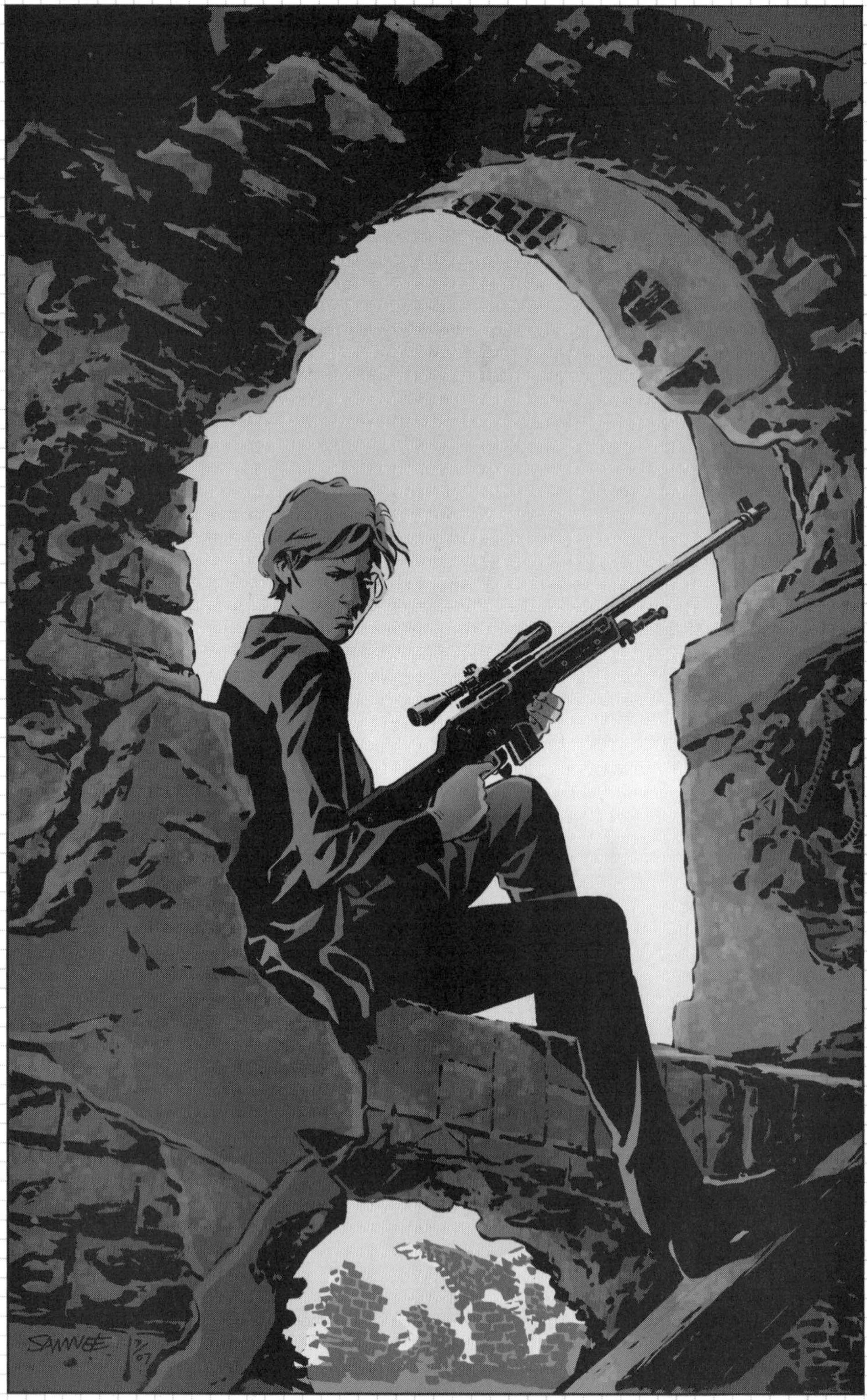
SAMNEE 3/07

QUEEN & COUNTRY™

ABOUT THE AUTHORS . . .

GREG RUCKA was born in San Francisco and raised on the Central Coast of California, in what is commonly referred to as "Steinbeck Country." He began his writing career in earnest at the age of 10 by winning a county-wide short-story contest, and hasn't let up since. He graduated from Vassar College with an AB in English, and from the University of Southern California's Master of Professional Writing program with an MFA.

He is the author of nearly a dozen novels: six featuring bodyguard Atticus Kodiak, and two featuring Tara Chace, the protagonist of his *Queen & Country* series. Additionally, he has penned several short-stories, countless comics, and the occasional non-fiction essay. In comics, he has had the opportunity to write stories featuring some of the world's best-known characters—Superman, Batman, and Wonder Woman—as well as penning several creator-owned properties himself, such as *Whiteout* and *Queen & Country*, both published by Oni Press. His work has been optioned several time over, with *Whiteout*—starring Kate Beckinsale—being the first to actually be made. His services are also in high demand in a variety of creative fields as a story-doctor and creative consultant.

Greg resides in Portland, Oregon, with his wife, author Jennifer Van Meter, and his two children. He thinks the biggest problem with the world is that people aren't paying enough attention.

MIKE NORTON has been working in comics for 10 years now, gaining recognition for projects such as *The Waiting Place* and *Jason and the Argobots*. Eventually, he became Art Director for Devil's Due Publishing where he drew the first *Voltron* mini-series. He has since made a name for himself working on books like *Gravity*, *Runaways*, *All-New Atom*, *Green Arrow/Black Canary*, and (of course) *Queen & Country*.

He is also very, very tall.

STEVE ROLSTON is best known as the premiere artist on Greg Rucka's Eisner Award winning spy series *Queen & Country*. Since then he has illustrated *Pounded*, *Jingle Belle*, *Mek*, *Tales of the TMNT*, *The Escapists*, *Degrassi: Extra Credit* and *Emiko Superstar*. With both his artist and writer hats on, he created the cartoony *Jack Spade & Tony Two-Fist* and the "slacker noir" graphic novel *One Bad Day*.

Steve lives in Vancouver, Canada.

CHRIS SAMNEE has done work for Oni Press, Vertigo, DC and Marvel. He lives in St. Louis with the loveliest of wives, Laura and the happiest of cats, Scout. Chris can usually be found working until the wee hours and trying to keep eraser shavings from sticking to his toes. Visit Chris at www.chrissamnee.com.

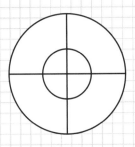